'O'Shaughnessy has developed a unique way of looking at consumers and consumer research that is informed by the philosophy of science. Here, he lets us share in his panoramic view of the subject. Climbing up the mountain might not be easy but the view is certainly rewarding. You will never look at consumer research the same again.'

– Dr Robert Clueley, Lecturer in Marketing, University of Nottingham, UK

'*Consumer Behavior* provides a fantastic "view from manywheres" approach to consumer behavior. The book is a welcome change from more mainstream approaches, highlighting a range of fascinating new, established and developed areas, many of which are often overlooked. The text will provide advanced undergraduates, masters and PhD students with an invaluable source of information on this complex and multifaceted area.'

– Dr Victoria Wells, Senior Lecturer in Marketing and Director of Full-Time Postgraduate Marketing Programmes, Durham University, UK

Consumer Behavior

Perspectives, Findings and Explanations

By John O'Shaughnessy
Professor Emeritus of Business, Columbia Business School, USA

First published 2013 by
PALGRAVE MACMILLAN

Palgrave Macmillan in the UK is an imprint of Macmillan Publishers Limited, registered in England, company number 785998, of Houndmills, Basingstoke, Hampshire RG21 6XS.

Palgrave Macmillan in the US is a division of St Martin's Press LLC, 175 Fifth Avenue, New York, NY 10010.

Palgrave Macmillan is the global academic imprint of the above companies and has companies and representatives throughout the world.

Palgrave® and Macmillan® are registered trademarks in the United States, the United Kingdom, Europe and other countries.

ISBN 978–1–137–00376–8

This book is printed on paper suitable for recycling and made from fully managed and sustained forest sources. Logging, pulping and manufacturing processes are expected to conform to the environmental regulations of the country of origin.

A catalogue record for this book is available from the British Library.

Library of Congress Cataloging-in-Publication Data
O'Shaughnessy, John, 1927–
    Consumer behavior : perspectives, findings and explanations / by
    John O'Shaughnessy.
        p.   cm.
    ISBN 978–1–137–00376–8
    1. Consumer behavior.   I. Title.
    HF5415.32.O737 2013
    658.8′342—dc23   2012036866

10   9   8   7   6   5   4   3   2   1
22   21   20   19   18   17   16   15   14   13

Printed in China

Contents

List of Figures

List of Tables

Preface

How can we justify publishing another text on consumer behavior? There are many such books on the market, so lack of choice cannot be the justification. Just as a company enters a market because it believes it has something unique to offer that is of central importance to a target audience, this book has uniqueness and centrality for the student of consumer behavior. The following are some of these key features:

- Instead of a series of chapters on topics such as consumer decision-making, consumer perceptions, consumer motivation and so on, each chapter is devoted to one or other of the social sciences, demonstrating its contribution to understanding consumer behavior. In this way the reader can appreciate the standpoint of each perspective and the claims it makes about consumer behavior, together with the perspective's strengths and weaknesses, biases and limitations. As we move from one social science perspective or paradigm to another, there is no suggestion of this being a movement from error to truth but as providing either additional windows into the human condition or answering questions ignored by other perspectives. As the blurb on Richard A. Shweder's *Why Do Men Barbecue?* (2003) states: 'The world, Shweder observes, is incomplete if seen from any one point of view, incoherent if seen from all points of view at once, and empty if seen from nowhere in particular. He urges readers to strike for "the view from manywheres" in a diverse but interdependent world.'
- Every inquiry operates from a given perspective in order to conceptualize and talk about what is going on. Simply focusing on the activities of the consumer will not lead to any depth of understanding unless the student of behavior has a set of concepts that give the activities meaning. Concepts organize our thoughts into categories. Unfortunately, strict adherence to one's own perspective can lead to people not talking to each other, talking past each other or being indifferent to other perspectives. Yet it is often essential for understanding social science findings to know where the social scientist is coming from, and it is a real weakness at present that the focus on findings is not supplemented by any corresponding knowledge of the relevant paradigms or perspectives that have directed the research and interpretation of findings.
- The emphasis is on conceptual clarity. Conceptual clarity comes before quantification and this is a prerequisite to any discussion about methods of inquiry, validity of findings and conflicts over interpretations

and inferences. The whole of social science, not just marketing, is riddled with conceptual confusion, which is often hidden by technical jargon and mathematical symbols. The author's intention is to help the reader to think critically with behavioral concepts. Critical thinking with behavioral concepts involves having a healthy skepticism about their meaningfulness and claims to truth resulting from their use. It means reflecting upon, reasoning about and questioning what the Greeks called *nomos* (*nomoi* in the plural) or the ruling orthodoxy of the day. It means evaluating what we read: evaluation is always the major part of all critical thinking. Reason can often tell us what is not valid even if it cannot show us where truth lies. The aim in this book is not to tell the reader *what* to think but *how* to think about consumer behavior. Social science concepts are typically social constructions that have sense-meaning without necessarily being (nor on occasion needing to be) firmly anchored in corresponding observables. Even if the sense-meaning of a concept has a counterpart in something observable in reality, there is still the problem of determining how far the sense-meaning and the corresponding referential-meaning of a concept overlap so they are in alignment.

- The book neither explicitly nor implicitly suggests there are universal laws in social science from which valid predictions can be made about consumer behavior in various contexts. There are no *universal* laws in social science that are not just truisms such as saying people desire to avoid pain and seek happiness. As a consequence, there is a need to judge whether a social science finding has applicability to the context of interest. This is not to suggest that the domain of application of a certain finding be necessarily restricted to the context in which the study or experiment took place, but that care needs to be exercised in judging whether the application is valid.

- The common error of conflating logic with psychology is exposed. To use logic is a purely rational exercise in applying reason in looking for inconsistencies and determining what is the logical thing to do given the situation. But what is logical or rational may not reflect what actually happens. A logical course of action or a logical mental process may not be descriptive of what happens empirically. Logic is concerned with the rational, while psychology is an empirical science that is tested against nature and not just logic.

- There is a chapter on folk psychology, or ethnopsychology, which is the systematic study of folk psychology. Consumers use their own folk psychology to predict and guide behavior in daily life that does not rely on the psychologist's psychology. So do most marketing managers. It was not scientific psychology that told Colgate that consumers would not follow the loudly stated advice from dentists to brush their teeth three times a day. They responded to the recommendation with an advertising slogan for Colgate toothpaste that cashed in on folk psychology: 'The toothpaste for people who can only brush twice a day.' Folk psychology tends to be ignored by mainstream psychology on the grounds that it is not a scientific pursuit even when studied under the heading of ethnopsychology. But we all depend to some extent on our own psychology. Even if someone had absorbed the whole of scientific psychology and its findings, it would not be enough for dealing with others. Folk psychology is needed to fill the gaps and to check on whether findings make sense in real-life situations.

- The book draws on concepts from philosophy of science and the philosophy of action whenever such concepts add insight or depth to understanding the nature and limitations of social science. In fact the claim is made that the philosophical debates in the philosophy of science have direct relevance to many controversies in the social sciences.
- Consumer psychology is viewed here as a distinct field of application, not a distinct discipline that has developed in a vacuum divorced from the various other psychological disciplines. It draws on the paradigms of the established disciplines, giving them coherence by their relevance to consumer behavior. It is not surprising to discover that the findings on consumer behavior have relevance and application for other aspects of life and this book occasionally but not extensively shows this. It might be argued that consumer behavior is simply used as an exemplar for the employment of the social sciences and that this book is equally suitable as a review of the social sciences.

Finally, I would like to thank my friend and former colleague Morris Holbrook for his comments on an earlier draft of the book. It was his encouragement that motivated me in writing the book.

Chapter 1

Introduction: Perspectivism and Other Basic Notions for Understanding the Nature of the Social Sciences

UNDERSTANDING CONSUMER BEHAVIOR

Marketing makes myriad assumptions about human behavior, whether that behavior is consumer behavior, the behavior of channel intermediaries or the behavior of competitors. The focus in this book is on the consumer, whether called client, patient or just customer, who goes about reflecting on what to buy and how to use the product. Most of the assumptions that marketers make regarding their customers are based on experience, for example that their customers are sensitive to price or that certain consumer habits (such as watching television) will continue. But there are other assumptions that rely on a deeper understanding of consumer behavior to even appreciate what is being assumed or to help settle disputes about the validity of claims made. This book helps in gaining that understanding of consumer behavior. This is not to downplay the role of the marketing manager's experience. Experience is like history in providing lessons or analogies to justify entertaining certain hypotheses or understanding a set of events but experience supplemented by social science perspectives, concepts and findings is likely to lead to greater consumer understanding.

BEHAVIORAL SCIENCE CONCEPTS

The book describes the perspectives social scientists espouse to study people's behavior as well as reporting findings on consumer behavior. Social science concepts draw attention to categories of behavior that might otherwise be overlooked. They also provide a vocabulary for expressing our thoughts on what is going on – a new vocabulary that helps us understand consumers better. Without knowledge of such concepts, discussion of buyer behavior is impoverished.

1

In reading about consumer behavior or studying research reports that include sections on consumer behavior, managers should understand where the author is coming from by being able to identify the author's basic stance or perspective on behavior. This is because different social science perspectives represent different windows into problems or answer different questions about behavior, and are not necessarily in competition. This is not to suggest that social science perspectives are set in stone, since each generation of social scientists is apt to give a retrospective reading of their own perspective to judge progress in tracking truth and identifying progressive changes that might be made. But when the adoption of a perspective blinds us to other perspectives, that perspective can take on the mantle of an ideology. Thus Hilary Rose, a sociologist of science, and Steven Rose, a neuroscientist (2011), have this to say in reviewing a book on the science of sex differences:

> But what shouts loudest in all these studies is the ways in which the researchers' preconceptions of what counts as appropriate male or female behavior shapes their research. Girls (and apparently even infant female vervet monkeys) are *supposed* to prefer pots and pans and dolls to trucks and Meccano. When girls turned out to be as interested as boys in playing with a construction kit called Lincoln Logs, a Lego airplane was substituted instead. It is hard to avoid the conclusion that these studies tell one more about the prevailing ideology of the researchers than about their subjects.
>
> (Rose and Rose 2011)

GENERAL QUESTIONS RAISED ABOUT CONSUMER BEHAVIOR

Every marketing manager has an interest in questions such as the following and the social sciences offer at least partial answers:

1. How can we best view the consumer?
2. What types of influence affect behavior?
3. What characteristics or dispositional states of the buyer affect the impact of those influences?
4. What mental processes are involved in intentional actions like buying?
5. How rational is the buyer?

How we answer such questions, or whether we are even willing to ask them, depends somewhat on the particular perspective adopted.

PERSPECTIVISM AND PERSPECTIVES

Fay (1996) describes *perspectivism* as the claim that there can be no intellectual activity without an organizing conceptual scheme that reflects a perspective. A perspective provides a lens through which to interpret what is going on and what action might be taken. Every deliberated decision is tied to a perspective. Alan Greenspan, former chairman of the Federal Reserve, in describing the free market ideology as a well-developed and all-encompassing way of thinking about the world, was in fact describing the particular economic perspective he endorsed. The notion of arguing from a perspective is reflected in remarks like: 'It all depends on your viewpoint' or 'That's a different way of looking at it'. The notion of being guided in our thinking by the perspective adopted rejects the claim of there being just one true picture of social reality.

Perspective can determine what facts to collect and how things are to be interpreted. Take an example from history, namely the 1857–8 uprising in India against the British. Rosie Llewellyn-Jones (2007) points to the many 'causes' that are quoted to explain the uprising: a peasant revolt (based on a Marxist perspective); unfair treatment of the sepoy (the soldier-historian's perspective); the changing role of the East India Company (the political historian's perspective); the changing balance of trade (the economic historian's perspective); the Evangelical movement originating in Britain (the social historian's perspective). These different perspectives give rise to the selection of different 'facts', while coloring interpretations of the facts selected.

If a perspective embodies theoretical presumptions, then that perspective constitutes a scientific paradigm. The term 'scientific paradigm' in the philosophy of science equates with a science's theoretical orientation or theoretical perspective, such as when we speak of the Freudian perspective. A paradigm in social science: (a) guides the study of behavior by providing a way of viewing that behavior; and (b) is used to impute the paradigm to behavioral data or findings so we can judge how far the paradigm or theory explains the findings. Where mathematical or statistical models are inferred from a paradigm, they constitute scientific hypotheses. The mathematics helps bring out the implications of data and expose assumptions; it does not create knowledge out of nothing. Although we sometimes speak of a given study of consumer behavior as being *method-driven* in the sense that the appropriateness of the tools (usually a statistical package) at our disposal determines what is studied, it is still the researcher's basic perspective that is in the driver's seat, providing a framework for decision-making.

No social scientist comes to the study of human behavior with a completely open mind; each is guided by his or her perspective on what facts to collect, while perspectives color interpretations of the 'facts' and impact on decisions. In fact, even the interpretation of DNA evidence, at least in complex cases, is subject to bias in interpretation (*The Economist,* 21 January 2012: 90). Interpretations are tied to one's perspective and – less clearly – to values, with Dworkin (2011) arguing in law that interpretations are value-laden 'all the way down'. John Locke's notion of a social contract constitutes the perspective that influenced the Founding Fathers of the United States (US), embodying the ideas of the people being sovereign; government originating from the consent of the governed; government legislating only for the common good; citizens having inalienable rights, and justifying resistance to tyranny. This constellation of ideas supplied the foundational perspective for the US Declaration of Independence and Constitution.

Consumers also have a point of view and it helps the marketer in persuading them if that point of view is reinforced or at least not challenged. Defining an issue, for example, in a certain way ('putting a spin on it') is often used in advertising to try to change current perspectives, just as Philip Morris tried to define cigarette advertising as defending the right to freedom of choice: a right that coheres with American values. Values reflect higher level concerns and the end-states in life that we support. What we *are* depends on what we *are for*, and our values reflect these adherences. This notion of values focuses on terminal concerns, rejecting the distinction between terminal and instrumental values, a view popularized by Rokeach (1973). To accept the notion of instrumental values is to contradict the very notion of values being superordinate – it is better to speak of 'instrumental means' rather than instrumental values. And there is something to be said about marketers considering instrumental *means* since this promotes *laddering*, whereby we start with products bought, used and consumed to trace the link to the likely values of the consumer. (Consumer values are distinguished from 'value' as used in economics which is defined as the sum of the net benefits occurring as the result of an exchange.)

Perspectives incorporate both values and beliefs. In politics it is often argued that it is more important that a politician claims to share a voter's values or convictions than that he or she fully endorses the party's expressed policies. But the feasibility of such sharing is not unproblematic because values are multiple and conflicting, for example between individual freedom and social responsibility. Consumers, like everyone else, are always involved in trade-offs – not just at the pedestrian level of trading off a lower price for lower quality but also at the highest level of human values like trading off more income for more equality in society. There is no single human value that tops all others, though some people talk as if 'tolerance' should be the absolute virtue and all other values, like integrity and honesty, should be subordinated to it. Honesty and integrity go together in that they presuppose truthfulness whereby people do not assert what they do not believe. We view a person of integrity as being trustworthy so perceptions of integrity enter into perceptions of credibility.

PERSPECTIVES, PARADIGMS, THEORIES AND MODELS

Science and the word 'theory' are closely associated because the word 'theory' is concerned with explicating explanatory frameworks: the 'why' of things, which is what science is about. Without theory, findings can amount to no more than interesting curiosities and there are lots of such interesting curiosities in the consumer behavior literature. Without 'theory' in social science you just have fashion, as is often the case in the literature on management. Even the findings from an experiment need to be interpreted in the light of background theory. However, the word 'paradigm' is coming to replace the word 'theory' in social science as 'theory' has come to have too diffuse a meaning. Thus Zaltman et al. (1982) in marketing define theory as 'a system for ordering concepts in a way that produces understanding or insights'. This does not distinguish theory from model or indeed from the manufacture of any intelligible statement.

A social science paradigm is simply a scientific perspective. Models give structural form to aspects of theories or paradigms. If the structure of system X helps us in understanding the structure of system Y, then system X is a model of system Y. The social scientist constructs a model that, within a domain or range of phenomena, can be shown to agree more or less with observation of actual behavior.

It is not uncommon in a debate to move from using theory in the sense of an explanatory set of coherent and corroborated hypotheses to just meaning any speculative hypotheses ('it is, after all, only a theory'). Whenever a word in common usage receives a technical ('stipulated') definition, there is always this danger of slipping from the technical definition to how the word is employed in common usage. This is something to guard against in reading the literature.

It was Thomas Kuhn (1962), in *The Structure of Scientific Revolutions*, who used the term scientific paradigm in the sense in which we use it today. Since the notion of a scientific paradigm is now so much part of any reading on social science, it is part of any education in the social sciences to know what the term means. A scientific paradigm implicitly takes into account beliefs, values, concepts, theories, models and applications. Understanding a paradigm, argues Kuhn, does not come about from memorizing laws or theories or models but by mastering applications; being able to solve a certain class of problem and being able to recognize further applications in different situations. All this talk about understanding through doing resembles what Michael Polanyi (1958/1962) said about acquiring knowledge through working under a master, so in order to be trained as a medical diagnostician there is a need to undertake a long apprenticeship under the guidance of an expert. But surely students need to absorb the relevant theoretical concepts as well as undertaking the practice? Kuhn himself denied that Polanyi influenced him very much, although many disagree. Polanyi was a polymath, having a background as a medical doctor as well as being a top scientist in chemistry, a social scientist and a philosopher. The anti-rationalism in his philosophy of science was off-putting to philosophers who were more interested in justifying science than describing it, but the originality of his thinking is now being recognized (Nye 2011).

Kuhn's initial (1962) definition of a paradigm was criticized for its vagueness and for having many variants of the concept. Kuhn (1974) later defined 'paradigm', as applied to the *natural* sciences, in two related senses:

> *First*, as a disciplinary matrix: 'disciplinary' because the paradigm is the common possession of a scientific community and a 'matrix' because every paradigm embodies sets of orderly elements such as:
>
> - Symbolic generalizations or expressions
> - Beliefs and values sought, such as predictive accuracy, simplicity and consistency
> - Models
> - Exemplars: the shared set of crucial, striking, successful examples of problem solving applications.
>
> *Second*, as a set of exemplars: while exemplars are part of the disciplinary matrix, they also characterize the field. Exemplars represent the paradigm-as-achievement and serve as models for future generations of scientists. They represent in the most fundamental sense the paradigm concept since they are the concrete successes attributable to the disciplinary matrix's power. Their acceptance equates with the sharing of a common ideology, which makes for solidarity and mutual understanding.

Through his or her familiarity with the field's exemplars, the scientist absorbs the rules to be followed for extending the application of the disciplinary matrix. Rules refer to types, not particulars. Working with the exemplars a scientist learns to interpret such and such as a 'fact' of a certain sort, while exemplars also provide implicit criteria as to what solutions are acceptable. The existence of a disciplinary matrix within a scientific community or specialist area of a science explains the ease of communication and wide agreement obtained.

The concept of a disciplinary matrix comes closer to defining the type of explanatory systems we have in social science than does the view of a science as being composed of theories along the lines traditionally proposed. On this basis, the various explanatory systems discussed in this book can be viewed as 'paradigms', although Kuhn would not agree since he seemed to believe that, in any discipline, one scientific paradigm should dominate. There is a lack of recognition here that different paradigms in social science address different questions or provide different windows into the same problem. In general when we move from one paradigm to another, for example from behaviorism to cognitive psychology, we are not progressing from error to truth but to an additional source of knowledge (defined as *justified* belief). Nonetheless, different paradigms may on occasion conflict or provide contradictory advice, just as a psychotherapist may insist it is necessary to know a patient's early history, while the cognitive therapist may claim it is not necessary. On the other hand, recommendations stemming from various paradigms can be compatible or consistent in the sense that there is no contradiction among them. Although paradigms can be incommensurable, in that they cannot be ranked or ordered on a single measure or common scale, this does not mean they cannot be compared in that there are always bases for comparison even if simply on the basis of predicted effects.

There are different paradigms or perspectives in social science and it is easy to get locked into a perspective which becomes a mindset that rules out as heresy alternative viewpoints. A social science paradigm should not be an ideological credo but regarded as a conceptual lens through which to view human behavior. Because different paradigms may use different methods for tracking truth, perspectivism goes hand in hand with *methodological pluralism*, a doctrine which rejects any claim that there is just one set of methods that gives privileged access to understanding and explaining human behavior.

What perspectivism implies is that there is no absolute truth other than truth relative to one's perspective, with the likelihood of each perspective having its own domain of suitability. Perspectives are not entirely substitutes for each other, with their suitability varying with purpose. But it is a compliment to business schools researching consumer behavior that they have not confined themselves to just one paradigm, in that we find most of the background paradigms being manifest in journal articles on consumer behavior. On the other hand, it is not true that academics in consumer behavior have invented new paradigms that lie beyond those discussed in this book. It is simply the field of application that is more or less new.

As we have said, social science models are imputed to data or findings to see if the data coheres with the paradigm. When they apply, they enrich understanding by providing a way to interpret behavior that may otherwise be puzzling and incoherent. They do not entirely displace commonsensical understanding. This is because, whichever social science models are imputed to data, there will always be gaps to be filled as there are no universal laws of a non-trivial nature that give a complete picture.

Many marketing academics view marketing as a technology rather than a science. Whereas the natural sciences seek explanations, technology is a rule-governed activity where the search is for rules that are neither true nor false but effective or ineffective in bringing about the result of interest. In economics, technology comes under technical rationality since it is geared to goal achievement. There is an attraction in viewing marketing as a technology, but understanding the consumer is related more to explanation. Those who advocate viewing marketing as a technology are often those who reject the notion of seeking 'theory' because there are no universal laws to be found. There is also the problem of external validity in the extent to which the findings of experiments can be generalized to other populations or to other contexts when what is significant about the experimental context is not necessarily known. Even an experiment cannot distinguish cause from a co-existing factor at work.

Many research findings on consumer behavior are like proverbs or principles of marketing in that they have *objective relativism*. The word principle is simply a more 'upmarket' term for the word 'rule', and suggests greater legitimacy. Proverbs and marketing principles are often ridiculed as there is usually an opposite contradictory proverb or marketing principle. Thus, the proverb 'too many cooks spoil the broth' can be contradicted by the principle 'many hands make light work'. This simply demonstrates that proverbs are *relative* to the situation; but, since we all know the situations in which each of these two proverbs are *objectively* applicable, the application of a proverb can be relatively objective. Hence we have the concept of *objective relativism*. Although research findings or marketing principles might not apply universally but are relative to the situation, we commonly have no problem in identifying situations where they are objectively applicable. In any case, the very sharp distinction between the objective and the subjective is perhaps overblown in that the 'objective' is dependent on the cognitive and other capacities of people and in this sense the objective is linked to the subjective.

The choice of paradigm depends on our concerns. It makes no sense to ask which is best without first answering the question: 'best for what?' when each approach is addressing different concerns. This is not to deny that different perspectives can on occasion be in conflict, where both perspectives cannot be true – though both can be false. But the fact that there can be conflict does not mean there are no truths or any need to examine what the social sciences have to say – that would be to dismiss the experiments, reflections, insights and investigations of many bright social scientists.

Conflict is always likely to arise over fundamental questions about human nature since the evidence does not give an unequivocal answer. What is consciousness? This is a question that is still debated with no satisfactory answer beyond perhaps saying it is a qualitative, subjective feeling of awareness. We can view the consumer as a highly rational animal but also as a seeing, feeling animal with flawed rationality. All we can do in a dispute is disagree about which way the balance of evidence tilts in any particular case. As Jonathan Cohen (1986) says:

> But it is in the nature of fundamental issues that they do not admit of universally acceptable solutions. Such solutions are possible only within an adequate framework of agreed premises or principles of inference, and controversy about fundamental issues arises where it does arise just because this kind of framework does not exist there.
>
> (Cohen 1986: 3)

Paradigms, theories and models are perspectives that tell us what to look for in studying behavior since we see what we are taught to see and change what we see as our attention is redirected. There is a danger of seeing *only* what we are directed to see, particularly when adherents of one particular paradigm limit themselves to the questions the paradigm addresses and its corresponding methodology. Thus if our paradigm teaches us to look for unconscious motives in dreams, we are more likely to find them.

Theory can be self-validating and this has been a constant criticism of psychoanalytic psychology. Even in mainstream psychology, there is a danger of defining the predicted consequences of the hypotheses implied by a paradigm in such a way that it actually implies the hypothesis. Thus I may 'hypothesize' that 'the better the consumer's attitude towards the brand, the more likely is the intention to buy' while at the same time defining 'intention to buy' in a way that is conceptually embraced by the definition of a highly favorable attitude. When research in marketing commits this error the only thing established is a link between meanings of terms, not the discovery of behavioral relationships.

INTERPRETATION IN SCIENCE GUIDED BY A PERSPECTIVE

Interpretation in science is guided by a certain perspective. No final, absolutely true interpretation can ever be proven. This is because some conjecture in interpretation is inevitable as facts are selected, connected and put into a plausible pattern. Unlike inference, interpretation always involves an element of conjecture. This is sometimes forgotten when we speak of 'making inferences' when the consumer substitutes guesses for missing information in making a decision. This confuses inference with interpretation. Interpretation can be defined as a conclusion reached from examining the data when the data do not provide explicit evidence for the conclusion. On the other hand, inference in logic is the process of deriving conclusions from actual premises. If the conclusion follows logically from a single premise, this in logic is called 'immediate inference', while a logical conclusion derived from two or more premises jointly is known as 'mediate inference'.

If paradigms or perspectives affect the interpretation of facts, for some commentators this casts doubt on whether observation can be free from theoretical orientation. This has given rise to the claim that observation is 'theory-driven'. But the interpretation is not completely dictated by a person's theoretical orientation, since interpretation is constrained by relevant, unambiguous facts on the ground. In debates on the matter, the claim that interpretation always depends on theories held is disputed by Hacking (1983), the philosopher of science, who denies that all scientific observations are interpretations in the light of theories held. For example, he points out that the early development of optics depended solely on noticing surprising phenomena that preceded any formulation of theory.

While not all observation will result in an interpretation in line with a person's theoretical orientation or perspective, all perspectives create a framework of expectations that is apt to put blinders on what to look for. These blinders push interpretations to fit a paradigm, theory or model, on occasion ignoring inconvenient facts. Thus the effectiveness of lemon juice as a prophylactic against scurvy was accepted by seamen from the time of Columbus but medical men up to the mid-nineteenth century rejected this claim because their theoretical orientation convinced them that this disease, like all diseases, was caused by either bad air or an imbalance of the humors: a case of bad knowledge driving out good (Wootton 2006).

If an explanation of consumer behavior, in line with the researcher's paradigm, appears to be final it may only be because not all questions about the problematic situation were considered. One of the reasons for encouraging interdisciplinary research is that it helps in looking for rival explanatory hypotheses or novel questions that might be suggested by perspectives from other disciplines. But drawing on rival perspectives is typically resisted because rival paradigms are believed to be deviant and wrong.

Researchers seek solutions by utilizing paradigms drawn from their own discipline or subdiscipline because, at the problem definition stage, there is nothing but a perceived difficulty – until the problem is diagnosed. Diagnosing a problem implies pointing to where a solution might lie. Solutions are naturally sought within a researcher's own discipline and corresponding perspective. An organizational behavior consultant is likely to diagnose the difficulty of poor sales performance as a problem of salesperson motivation, and this points to where the solution lies. On the other hand, other disciplines may diagnose the problem as lying elsewhere, such as in poor salesmanship or poor call-cycle planning.

A PARADIGM AS A CONCEPTUAL LENS

The scientist's paradigm constitutes a conceptual lens for selecting facts and interpreting results. The key here is the concepts making up the paradigm. Galileo (1564–1642) claimed he viewed nature as a 'text' written in symbols that could be interpreted correctly only by those with a grasp of mathematics. Being able to see mathematical patterns in the data was the core of his perspective. But without relevant concepts there will be no corresponding perception. Thus two scientists, one an eighteenth-century biologist and one living today, with their different conceptual frameworks, would perceive a slide with bacteria on it in different ways, since the eighteenth-century biologist would have no concept of bacteria. One way of making progress in social science is simply to explicate its concepts and make inferences about relationships between these concepts. Thus the content of the concept of 'credibility', if explicated into notions of technical expertise and trustworthiness, has implications for criticizing and evaluating the credibility of a communication source and building credibility in communications. In any case, defective concepts in any science can distort inquiries, just as the notion of the *ether* once did in physics. Social science is more prone to defective concepts than physical science since so many of its concepts are *social constructs*, not kinds of physical things like electric currents or types of rocks. Every judgment we make as language users involves the application of concepts. To grasp a concept is to understand what attributes or properties the things to which it applies will have, with the structure of complex concepts having statistical rather than fixed relationships (Murphy 2002).

Observation is not always theory-driven but is concept-loaded. Thus the interpretations of a psychoanalyst make sense only in terms of the Freudian concepts embodied in the Freudian psychoanalytic paradigm, particularly the view of the unconscious as the repository of all those pleasures a person would desire if he or she were free from the realities of life. All this means that the development of concepts is vital to the development of a discipline, since concepts divide the world into categories and missing relevant categories impoverish any investigation. What limits the prediction of future innovations is that the concepts on which future innovations will be built may not yet be known.

A constant problem in specifying and applying a scientific paradigm is the shifting or unstable meaning of concepts. When 'value' concepts, for example freedom, democracy and justice, are involved, there are constant disputes over interpreting their meaning since getting agreement on meaning is basic to solving many disputes. Take the word 'democracy' as an example: a term of great interest to those in political marketing. Is democracy simply the sovereignty of the majority, regardless of how it treats minorities, or does it imply a normative ideal about the government showing equal concern for each of its citizens? If democracy is believed to be a system for ensuring that political decisions reflect the will of the voters ('what voters want'), there are reasons for doubting this happens. Ringen (2003) reaches the conclusion, after exhaustive research on Norwegian democracy (considered an exemplar of democracy), that the democratic idea of governance under the control of the voters is so at variance with what actually happens that the very quintessence of rule by popular consent is disintegrating before our eyes. This is a depressing conclusion that cannot be entirely dismissed.

QUANTIFICATION AND CONCEPTUAL DEVELOPMENT

Conceptual development occurs prior to quantification, whereas conceptual confusion impedes the development of knowledge since people are not sure of what is being addressed. This is often forgotten in research into consumer behavior as experiments proceed as if the basic concepts are unproblematic, which is seldom true. Yet it seems that conceptual papers in marketing journals are declining even though, as MacInnis (2004) says, they are crucial to the development of a discipline. Lehmann (1999) claims that technical jargon is what limits interdisciplinary conversation and in the process diminishes the richness of marketing. This is very much the view of a quantitative model builder who sees the problem of communication mainly as a matter of learning each other's technical vocabulary, rather than the more basic task of achieving conceptual clarity and avoiding conceptual confusion. Jargon, as technical terminology, can be an essential tool for communication while also facilitating measurement. But much jargon in the world of business and business consultancy is there for image management as it often adds nothing to conceptual clarity over the ordinary language for which it substitutes.

If a paradigm is wedded to a certain type of explanation, such as a causal explanation or a technology or methodology like statistical analysis, it can lead to bias, for example a researcher may persevere in testing procedures until supportive results are obtained (Greenwald et al. 1986). This happens when researchers keep applying various statistical tests until they obtain a significant result – and then only publish that result. There is often an implicit assumption that quantitative methods can produce knowledge out of nothing. They cannot, but quantitative methods may be essential for structuring a problem and bringing out the implications of the data. If we set up a mathematical model, the assumptions tend to be clearer and this makes it easier to judge how effective it is likely to be. The model can be used to make predictions which, if not corroborated, lead to its being rebuilt or discarded. The distinction between a mathematical model and a statistical model, however, is not clear-cut since typically the properties of statistical tools are established mathematically. With respect to the claim that mathematical models ignore the rich texture of social life, this is true but should not necessarily be dismissed since the rules governing human behavior may not be complex in all cases.

There is pressure for mathematical model building in all the social sciences, sometimes because the need is there, or because there is a desire to appear more scientific, or simply to imitate mathematical economics and achieve its prestige or because some academics want to carve out a segment of expertise that suits their particular talents. There is a danger at present of mathematical model builders simply exchanging ignorance with each other, with no one else – certainly not marketing managers – bothering to listen. This happens when models are constructed purely for personal satisfaction (expressive behavior) and changes when models are built that demonstrate practical significance. The focus of the quantitative journals at present is in danger of selecting articles for their statistical methodology rather than their utility to marketing.

Each disciplinary paradigm discussed in the chapters that follow reflects a perspective that is likely to be better for answering some questions than for answering others. If we focus on just one paradigm or methodology, we restrict the questions we might ask or others will want to ask. Each system of psychology or sociology seeks out questions that can be addressed by its paradigm and seeks a solution that coheres with its basic stance. This suggests the need for methodological pluralism and multiperspectivism. As Shweder (2003), a professor of human development at the University of Chicago, says:

> The knowable world is incomplete if seen from any one point of view, incoherent if seen from all points of view at once and empty if seen from nowhere in particular.
>
> (Shweder 2003: 45)

Shweder is arguing for a multiperspective approach in social science. Different perspectives give rise to debates over which is best without asking: 'best for what?' This is the most basic question. Battles are fought, not just over competing answers to the same set of questions, but also between competing questions.

Can the various paradigms be integrated in some way to provide more explanatory power? Some social scientists are trying. Foxall (2007) has sought in his writings to integrate radical behaviorism, behavioral economics and cognitive psychology (or at least cognitive psychology that focuses on intentional behavior) and neuroscience. One of his recent books is a persuasive defense of behaviorism and his own particular modifications of it (Foxall 2009).

Paradigm or theoretical biases can become entrenched. Not long ago, the child psychology paradigm viewed infant feelings and habits as dominating later in life: a form of infant determinism. All the social sciences implicitly make assumptions that go unseen because they are just embedded in the perspective. Even today some anthropologists talk as if they believe in cultural determinism which was once part of the notion of seeking universal laws. Kuper (1999) accuses Sahlins, a well-known anthropologist, of writing this way. McCracken (1988), in his book *Culture and Consumption* (see Chapter 13), seems disposed to accept cultural determinism – that it is culture that determines behavior – which is rather a limiting view when it comes to the consumer.

How much of our behavior is in fact influenced by nature, rather than nurture? Nature and nurture are not the only factors. Nature does not cover all the biological factors that may be at work during conception that are generally considered to constitute our make-up. Are all our predispositions accounted for by nurture and nature? Do not free will and contextual factors play a contributory role in determining action? While culture inevitably influences behavior, individual 'deviant' decision-makers over time affect culture. In any case, nature versus nurture is one of those fundamental questions that do not yield easy answers. As to the contentious issue of *free will*, free will is something most of us endorse because we have the conscious experience of deciding what we will do given the circumstances. It might be added that this conscious experience is in no way negated by knowing that environmental factors make it more than likely that we decide in the way we do.

Steven Pinker's (2002) perspective on human behavior, as an evolutionary psychologist, cognitive scientist and linguist, leads him to argue that many of our biases and mental aptitudes are hardwired. Steven Pinker's book *The Blank Slate: The Modern Denial of Human Nature* is in line with the most recent trend of assigning more weight to inherited biological factors than was formerly the case when everyone seemingly wanted to believe that success in life depended purely on individual effort; that we are all born equal even if we become unequal in the sequel. While genes, he argues, do not determine all of what we are, together with environment and chance, genes do have great influence on behavior. But genes alone cannot determine all, hence the re-emergence of 'epigenetics': the study of how genes are activated and influenced by environmental experiences. While genes are important, analyzing strings of DNA is never likely to tell us the whole story about who we are. Yet Pinker's claim cannot be ignored but needs to be challenged, both by those who currently endorse cultural determinism and those stressing the role of free will. In any case, his metaphor of our behavior being 'hardwired' can mislead in that, as the genes evolve into a human body, they depend on and are influenced by the environment.

IMPUTATIONAL INTERPRETATION

In *imputational* interpretation, we take our paradigm and assess how far it explains the behavior of interest or predicts outcomes of interest. Thus if *behaviorism* is the paradigm, we impute to behavior the notion of behavior being conditioned and check whether this claim can be sustained in the examples we have before us. A behaviorist seeks explanations in terms of conditioning in contrast to a cognitive psychologist who seeks explanations that involve mental goings-on.

Imputational interpretation need not necessitate a scientific paradigm for application since imputation can be guided by any set of interconnected concepts that can act collectively as a model. Thus in interpreting the performance of salespersons, we might be guided by the belief that sales performance is a function of:

(a) Ability to do the job
(b) Motivation to do the job
(c) The opportunity to do the job
(d) Resources to do the job
(e) The right beliefs for giving direction about the relation of action to reward.

These five factors would typically be regarded as a sort of checklist but in constituting a performance system they could be viewed as a model explaining performance. The five factors provide more realism and comprehensiveness than the usual restriction to just the first three factors, beloved of those in organizational behavior but more recently appearing in marketing as the MAO (motivation, ability and opportunity) model of action (MacInnis et al. 1991).

All intentional activity is motivated as all activity involves striving. But ability and motivation will come to nothing unless opportunity is present. This has been the reason behind the push for equal opportunity. It is sad when a minority is denied opportunity yet that minority's relative overall performance is judged as if it were an equal opportunity society.

Intentional action is strictly purposive behavior, while psychoanalytic theory claims that unconscious motivation causes purposeful behavior that is not intentional (Robinson 1985).

Scientific theories or paradigms are important to give direction to science. *The Economist*, talking on the subject of cancer research, words it well:

> the discovery of cancer stem cells illustrates how the most fruitful scientific findings are often not those of individual experiments, however intriguing, but those that organize knowledge into theory. The chemical industry took off within a decade or so of Dmitri Mendeleev's arrangement of the chemical elements into the periodic table, just as radio communications followed James Clerk Maxwell's mathematical unification of electricity and magnetism, and antibiotics came after Pasteur and Koch.
>
> (The Economist, 13–20 September 2008: 15)

We would like to be able to advise marketing management on whether its strategies and tactics will bring about the desired behavior on the part of a particular target audience. This would not be difficult if we had empirically backed theories on how people have responded to similar actions in similar circumstances in the past. But what is it that is taken to be 'similar' action and 'similar' circumstances? There are always innumerable similarities in actions and structures.

THE ROLE OF METAPHORS AND ANALOGIES

Steven Pinker (2007) quotes Lakoff (1996) who views day-to-day political debates as contests between metaphors (metaphors being mini-perspectives). This is commonly the case in debates about consumer behavior over, say, the rationality of the individual consumer's behavior. Lakoff argues that citizens do not in fact act rationally as they pay no attention to the facts, except as they fit into the *frames* already fixed in their brains. The word 'frames' here equates with perspectives. In George W. Bush's first term as President of the US, for example, Bush promised tax relief, which framed taxes as an affliction, the reliever as a hero and anyone obstructing this as a villain. This was a perspective that many voters were predisposed to support and they did. Democratic presidents act similarly. A more striking metaphor is the description of the increased patting down at airports in the interests of security as 'gate-rape'. But Steven Pinker attacks the corresponding notion that 'frames trump facts', with dominant frames (perspectives) imposed by those with the power to enforce their will, on the grounds that this is too cynical a theory of politics, implying as it does that people are universally gullible. He agrees that people (including consumers) are influenced by framing (putting claims into a preferred perspective) but this does not imply that people are enslaved by their metaphors or the framing that accompanies them. Metaphors *defamiliarize* the familiar to bring about a change in perspective. People are influenced by an appealing perspective but it need not blind them to alternatives. A perspective, like models in general, is a way of seeing and also a way of not-seeing but not-seeing is not the same as being permanently blind to other perspectives.

The English language is steeped in metaphors; these are essential for expressing abstract ideas to provide concreteness. One joke that has spread across the Internet exploits the pervasiveness of metaphor by telling us there is no need for any fitness program because we are forever jumping to conclusions, flying off the handle, running down the company, knifing friends in the back, dodging responsibility, pushing our luck. Metaphors can encourage people to appreciate something emotionally, as when a pain reliever is promoted as *rubbing* out the pain. But while metaphors can direct thinking, they are not like full-blown perspectives since they can be questioned and rejected as inappropriate. Perspectives capture the way we look at things and are not easily displaced. But just as metaphors help in visualizing, the sensitizing concepts developed by social scientists provide a vocabulary for clearing our thoughts, and in doing this help to guide us into taking appropriate actions.

Analogies focus on relationships. If a model is viewed as an analogy, the focus is on structural relationships. The more powerful the metaphor, the more it resembles an analogy or model that stresses relational structures. Turning a metaphor into a simile is the difference between saying the consumer is like a hunter in her search for bargains versus saying the consumer is a hunter after bargains. Using a simile instead of a metaphor weakens the impact.

THE ANTI-IMPUTATIONAL STANCE

We have talked about how social scientists are guided by their research paradigms or perspectives which they impute to guide research and interpretation of findings to judge applicability. Imputational interpretation to some, however, smacks of the Rorschach inkblot, a projective technique whereby the respondent reads into a vague stimulus of an inkblot the interpretation that comes most easily to mind. For the anti-imputationalist, a methodology should be chosen without any guiding paradigm. Novitz (1987), while rightly claiming that interpretation, unlike deductive inference, involves conjecture, regards imputational interpretations as fanciful and gratuitous. If the imputation is tied to a validated social science paradigm, this is just not so. Cunningham (2002), while granting that any text will be read in the shadow of a theoretical framework or perspective, argues that such theories should be replaced by honest-to-goodness hands-on reading. This assumes theories can, if there is sufficient will, be discarded in interpretation. This is doubtful since our paradigm's stock of concepts directs attention as to how something is viewed.

Viewing everything to be interpreted as a 'text', all texts are interpreted in the shadow of a conceptual or paradigm 'bias'. Even Montaigne (1533–92) in the sixteenth century was aware of the problem, as he regarded all physicians as interpreting symptoms to fit their universal remedies. Is it so surprising to find that the interpretation of the US Constitution mirrors the political preferences of Supreme Court justices?

The anti-imputationalists seem to believe that the researcher accepts any interpretation resulting from an imputational interpretation, particularly since the research or investigation itself has been guided by the adopted paradigm. This is not so. No one is claiming that whatever is imputed is necessarily valid since imputations may not cohere sufficiently with the facts. Any interpretation, for example, of another culture involves one's own culture as a backdrop perspective and this offers scope for misleading analogies. Even imputational interpretation based on a disciplinary paradigm must fit the indisputable facts and provide a satisfactory answer to the question asked – preferably one that is better than answers provided by rival paradigms.

The fear of social science biasing historical research in its imputations drove Elton (1969), a Cambridge University historian, to write his own approach to history, *The Practice of History*, promising to ignore all social science findings and theories. Elton could be described as an 'archival positivist' whose dogmatism, if adopted, would close out useful concepts and findings that might have applicability to understanding history. Whatever we think of the theories produced, social science has provided us with concepts that *sensitize* us to what to look for in social investigations. Like all scientific concepts, these concepts are refined as researchers get a better grasp of the phenomenon in question. Concepts, like mathematical concepts, can lead us to see patterns in data that are not otherwise discernible. Krausz (1993) quotes Margolis (1980) in arguing that aesthetic designs can be rigorously imputed to particular works of art when they cannot be determinately found in them.

NARRATIVE REALISM, NARRATIVE CONSTRUCTIVISM AND NARRATIVISM

The imputational versus anti-imputational debate echoes the debate over whether or not, in the process of interpretation, we discover or construct a pattern, structure or framework and then impose it on otherwise formless material. Do we discover or simply creatively construct?

Narrative realism claims that structures or patterns of consumer behavior are out there, waiting to be discovered, just as the nervous system was there to be discovered. In history, those who subscribe to narrative realism argue that the narratives of historians, if history is done properly, will always have beginnings, middles and endings that capture actual beginnings, middles and endings of events that do actually occur: the narrative structure is already there waiting to be discovered and explicated.

There is something right about this claim. But it cannot be the whole story since the causal consequences of many actions in history only work themselves out over the long term, while the meaning or significance of past events varies in different periods of history. If perspectives differ as history moves on, concerns in later time periods will differ and the significance of events will accordingly differ. And there are always new findings to consider and unanticipated consequences to record. Even where there is agreement on the 'facts', these facts can be rearranged in innumerable ways depending on the historian's perspective. The limitation of narrative realism is not that there are no narratives embodied in the actions of people but that there is no single narrative that can be proved to be the correct one. This analogy from the study of history has relevance for social science in consumer behavior in that topics chosen for study differ in different time periods, while the same set of facts are not interpreted in the same way or always explained through the same conceptual lens of an established paradigm.

Narrative constructivism claims that anyone writing a narrative history (including those writing a historical review of a company's brands or a record of a shopping episode) should impose or impute a structure to what would otherwise be an amorphous collection of events. In other words, narratives are constructed, not discovered. But there are no amorphous collections of events in consumer actions. This is because the actions and social activities of consumers inevitably form narratives and the ongoing activities of rational people will always embody intelligible narratives. Actions in fact can only be understood if they are seen as intelligible so the problem is not one of imaginatively constructing a narrative but choosing the one that is most likely, given the evidence. This is not to suggest we have the ability to measure evidence on a ratio scale as happens in measuring a piece of string: weighing up the evidence involves judgment and is never an entirely objective process. If entirely objective, truth or falsity could be decided by the agreed facts, independently of anyone's feelings. If something is subjective this is not the case.

Consumer choices reflect, at least partially, the consumer's values (which on many occasions can be hedonistic) against which the consumer weighs up various considerations or types of evidence to affect a trade-off. This is also true of managerial judgments and court judgments (Cohen 1986). Not that the consumer's values completely determine his or her choices: values typically underdetermine (i.e. do not fully determine) choices. They are seldom so consciously articulated for this to be the case. Also, we cannot just claim self-interest is going to be the overriding value, as several rival values might collectively overturn self-interest. Nor can any researcher claim that tracking truth with integrity is the absolute, superordinate value since there is the desire to be proved right and to please bosses and other academics, and these conflicting goals can force trade-offs (e.g. between telling the truth and passing over an opportunity to shine) and bias the treatment of evidence. In any case, it should be said that researchers do not seek 'truth' per se but true explanations, since seeking the true facts is simply instrumental to achieving valid explanations of behavior.

If interpretation can be so decisive in sifting the evidence and reaching conclusions, the question arises as to whether we are seeking one true interpretation or believe this is no more attainable than finding the Holy

Grail. The debate between the *singularist* (who seeks the one 'true' interpretation) and the *multiplist* (who denies there is one true interpretation)
echoes the debate between narrative constructionism and narrative realism
since realism offers some support for singularism, whereas constructionism
is supportive of multiplism. The realist insists that doing research, along
the lines marketers do in getting out a historical review of a market, aims at
finding out what actually happened, and when, where, how and who was
involved. The constructionist, on the other hand, does not accept that history discovers any actuality but merely throws up an interpretation which,
given the evidence, is the one most compelling at the time: there is no past
except that which is constructed by those looking at the past.

The third position is that of *narrativism*. This falls between narrative
realism and narrative constructivism. The argument of those subscribing
to narrativism is that people like consumers live out intelligible lives and
we try to piece together a narrative that best captures what appears to be
going on, for example in a shopping episode. The structure or pattern we
impute to this follows the same structure as that embodied in the activities
of those whom we are currently studying, but there can still be no finality
of interpretation.

We are never certain that a particular interpretation of behavior or of
behavioral research findings is actually the truth as we do not have tucked
away somewhere the real truth against which to test the interpretation.
Research findings provide guidance on consumer behavior but, if implementation of the advice is to be a success, there is a need to judge applicability and the need to flesh out the advice in a creative way. It is like having
research findings about what seems to make for a successful science fiction
movie – more than such findings are needed for successful implementation.

In his book *What is History?*, Carr (1964) argued that there are basic
facts (the Second World War is a fact, or facts like sales over the years,
market share and so on) and there are historical facts. Basic facts are the
basis for constructing historical facts. Carr is thus a narrative realist when it
comes to basic facts but a narrative constructionist when it comes to historical facts. The constructionist rejects Carr's distinction on the grounds that
basic facts are interpreted facts since there are no 'unvarnished' (unconceptualized) facts about the world. This is so in the sense that facts are
concept-dependent, although there is likely to be more varnish on historical facts than basic facts. It was Nietzsche (1844–1900) who said that there
are no facts, only interpretations. A modern rendition of this is to say that
there are plenty of facts but to identify a fact necessitates an interpretation.
This does not mean that there is always a need to do so: many things are
recognized instantly without further ado and without invoking any process
that might be labeled interpretation.

BASIC STANCES IN THE SOCIAL SCIENCES

The big split in the social sciences is between those who search for causal
laws ('scientific' explanation) and those who claim such laws apply only

to involuntary movements like a blink – an involuntary, non-intentional action. This contrasts with voluntary behavior like the wink. In other words, the split is between those who impute some causal mechanism to be at work and those who do not. Somewhat reflecting this debate are the various basic, theoretical orientations of researchers in studying the consumer:

1. As simply responding to the push and pull of past impressed events and immediate stimuli. This covers:
   (a) Classical (Pavlovian) conditioning and operant conditioning
   (b) Sociological or anthropological studies that focus exclusively (most do not) on the search for external causes of behavior like culture, or environmental influences.
2. As rationally reflective. This covers:
   (a) Economics, which assumes that people act according to rational self-interest
   (b) Cognitive psychology, which focuses on how information is processed to arrive at intelligible answers.
3. As a social being guided by social norms. This is one viewpoint in social psychology and sociology.
4. As acting in response to unconscious desires and beliefs. This is the psychoanalytic approach.
5. As largely genetically determined, as in psychometrics and evolutionary psychology.
6. As acting as a free agent for reasons (wants and beliefs) that may go beyond mere self-interest. This is ethnopsychology or folk psychology, which is the psychology of the culture and not a psychology confined to a small class of experts (Bruner 1990). Although 'reasons' and 'motives' are sometimes used synonymously, motives refer to general dispositional tendencies (e.g. a dispositional tendency to avoid risk) activated by certain types of stimuli (e.g. investment opportunities), while reasons consist of beliefs and wants/desires.

CONCLUSION

In the Schumpeter section of *The Economist* (26 September 2009: 82), the author of the section argues that business schools need to change their tone more than their syllabuses; that, in particular, they should foster the twin virtues of skepticism and cynicism. Perspectivism cultivates these two virtues by rejecting the notion of universal laws in social science and rejecting certainty in social science findings. Instead of a claim to absolute truth, there is simply the acknowledgement of trying to track truth through a multiperspective approach that requires a tolerance for pluralism in methodology. There is a need here to distinguish between practical certainty and logical certainty. Natural scientists argue that there is practical certainty as to the truth of scientific laws. But if truth demands logical certainty then nothing is immune from doubt. It is the same with interpretation: there is no logical certainty but commonly there is practical certainty.

As the philosopher Von Wright (1971) sees it, the only thing that comes near a law-like statement explaining action is the economist's 'principle of rationality', asserting that people rationally choose the best means to maximize their goals. But this principle is a rule and not a law of nature in that, like all rules, it can be broken without anyone believing that it is thereby falsified. In any case rationality is a continuum ranging from perfect rationality to flawed rationality and on to irrationality. There are still those who espouse the notion that we should be seeking universal laws in all the social sciences. It is agreed that predicting individual behavior is beyond us but this should not apply to behavior in groups. But as McGuire (2000), the Yale social psychologist, says, those who seek universal laws find themselves confined to 'testing hypotheses' that are really truisms requiring no investigation to establish their truth, like saying no one likes to be humiliated or that, if I stare at the sky in the street, others will look up also. This is not to be dismissive of truisms since selecting the right truism is often the basis of wisdom as 'more people fail by ignoring the obvious than failing to penetrate the obscure'.

McGuire's alternative to the 'positivist view' – which asserts that all disciplines aspiring to be a science must adopt the natural sciences as their model and apply its methods – is 'perspectivism'. Perspectivism acknowledges that there are no laws of social behavior or of intentional action and no hypothesis is perfectly true (as we inevitably misrepresent reality to some extent) even if it is sometimes true enough. Context is, for example, always important as to how a stimulus might be interpreted. The same product may be sold in Neiman Marcus and in T.J. Maxx but perceptions will differ for the two different contexts. If we include the individual consumer's personality, knowledge and experience as part of the context then this, too, is a factor in how things are perceived. McGuire argues that context moderates against universals being able to explain the individual case but recommends exploring the pattern of contexts in which a hypothesis does or does not obtain and identifying the reasons why it does or does not. To fall back on demanding universals misses the nuances of a situation.

Flyvbjerg (2003), like McGuire, denies the possibility of laws in the social sciences on the grounds that findings are context-dependent. At the individual level people are not tokens of each other. We may be able to conceive of universal laws but conceivability does not imply possibility. Word meanings are tied to context, just as the word 'novel' can refer to a work of fiction or something original. Think of the two meanings of the words 'look down' in the sentence: 'A man should only look down on another man in order to pick him up.' The *indexicality* of a word or phrase is that part of its meaning that is tied to context. When meanings are ambiguous, it is often the context that is not clear to the reader or respondent.

In sum there are no universal laws in social science, which means research findings provide only *generalizations* that apply to a defined specified group in a specific context. Generalizations are selective inclusions and selective exclusions. But when applied in the appropriate context, they help in answering 'what if' questions. When we hypothesize what might have happened if this or that action had been taken, the answers amount to untestable counterfactual propositions, although social science findings may be more supportive of one answer than another. Similarly, when we ask 'what is likely to happen?' social science findings offer guidance but never certainty.

We can never be absolutely sure theories or models are true, however much they are corroborated. Even with experiments we cannot be certain that we can distinguish between cause and coexistence since it is a big assumption that the control and experimental groups are alike in all *relevant* respects. Similarly, there are always rival hypotheses that have not been eliminated. Nor can we be sure that a theory that has failed a test is necessarily untrue. We neither prove nor disprove any theory in any *absolute* sense. This claim about absolute proof and disproof underpins the doctrine of *fallibilism*, which asserts that there is no certainty: all knowledge is subject to modification and change. But as the British philosopher A.J. Ayer once said: 'It is in demanding impossible standards of perfection that the skeptic feels secure.' Factual knowledge at best can only be probable, in that we cannot prove the contrary to be absolutely impossible. There are always potential alternatives for any theory we regard as true. As Fay (1996) says, getting out theories or models in social science is analogous to map-making in that no mapmaker believes there is a unique pre-mapped world waiting to be discovered. This is a very fine analogy.

Statistical generalization, by definition, is unlikely to have direct applicability to the unique situation except in suggesting something to consider. Thus, even if we knew that 90 percent of new products fail, this particular statistical generalization tells us nothing about the likelihood of our individual product's success: the product may fail or it may not, but the fact that 90 percent of new products have failed in the past is irrelevant to whether an individual product will fail, particularly if the generalization is based on products outside the markets of interest. But it does give us pause to think. The significance of any finding does not depend on its contribution to a universal law but on whether it contributes to dealing with our concerns. This means that techniques like ethnogeny (see later) are useful for managers who are not concerned with developing universal laws.

Those about to study any of the behavioral sciences should respect but never worship at the feet of any proponent of a particular perspective or scientific paradigm. If the history of the behavioral sciences is anything to go by, social science paradigms come and go, leaving a legacy that offers insight but no certitude. Jerry Fodor (2011), essentially a philosopher but also one of the founding fathers of cognitive psychology, is particularly scathing of the current state of the psychological sciences – if somewhat overcritical:

> In philosophy, ever since Plato, the mainstream opinion has been that the mind is the organ of thought; thinking is what the mind is for, and we act as we do because we think what we do. But psychologists, for the last hundred years or so, have mostly viewed that sort of 'intellectualism' as an embarrassing remnant of the Enlightenment: behaviorists say that the question of what minds are for doesn't arise, since there aren't any. Freudians say that the myth that we think is a sort of cover story that the mind tells itself to avoid having to confess its libidinous urges. Associationists say we don't need a mind to think with ('we don't need an "executive" ' is how they put it) because *ideas think themselves* in virtue of the mechanical connections among them. And neuropsychologists say that since the mind is the brain we don't need the one because we have the other. That this bundle of muddle is recommended as the hard-headed, scientific way to do psychology is, I think, among the wonders of the age.
>
> (Fodor 2011)

This book is also critical of much that passes as valid reasoning in the social sciences. I think the criticism is defensible but this does not prove it to be altogether damning as undermining a claim may not necessarily destroy it at its foundations. I am also conscious of the fact that my own claims may have weaknesses and deficiencies of which I am not aware. Human beings are all error-prone and I ask the reader to remember this and not let my slips in logic go unnoticed but to have expectations that I will on occasion say some silly things. This is the way to sharpen our minds.

Chapter 2

Ethnopsychology (Folk Psychology)

THE NATURE AND ROLE OF FOLK PSYCHOLOGY

Folk psychology explains action in terms of reasons for action, imputing to human action the perspective of a free agent acting on the basis of wants and beliefs leading to intention and action.

Few would subscribe to the doctrine of 'solipsism', which asserts that the individual human mind has no grounds for believing in anything but itself – that we can only be aware of our own mental states and actions. We are in fact aware of possessing a *folk psychology* that allows us to interpret the actions of others and understand the reasons for those actions. It is folk psychology that tells us that consumers are likely to subscribe to the notion that every product has a 'fair' price, around which the consumer has expectations as to what he or she is likely to pay. Yet talk about folk psychology is likely to arouse scorn among psychologists on the grounds that it does not qualify as a science, as its claims have not emanated from any scientific investigation. This is true, although it is not clear whether, to date, the social sciences have told us *more* about the human condition than have novelists, historians and poets with their 'folk psychology' insights into human nature. Noam Chomsky, the Massachusetts Institute of Technology (MIT) linguist, once made a famous remark that when it comes to understanding how people think the science of psychology might never outperform what people learn from a good novel. But social science has systematized and validated a good deal of knowledge about human behavior and often presented us with deeper knowledge than that contained in folk psychology. Folk psychology cannot, however, be dismissed.

Most of what we say about human behavior is based on folk psychology, while perhaps most of what our politicians have to say about how people will react to a piece of legislation or about the dysfunctional behavioral consequences arising from some proposed legislation is seldom based on anything approaching evidence but is assumed true because 'we just know how people behave'. We find ourselves falling back on folk psychology to fill gaps in academic psychology, while social scientists often translate their research findings into folk psychology to 'sell' their claims to the general public. Translating findings into folk psychology is what often makes behavioral claims intelligible. But this is not a one-way street. Folk psychology borrows concepts from academic psychology (just think of all those terms from psychoanalytic psychology used in everyday conversation, such as ego, the Oedipus complex and the unconscious) when these are thought to have more explanatory force in the context.

Folk psychology reminds us of how much is believed to be common in human nature. One such commonality is the general belief that we live in a world of causes; that 'stuff' does not simply happen but has a causal ancestry. This recognition, if not inherent, arises from experience and is built into our expectations.

MEANING OF ACTION VERSUS CAUSES

Identifying and knowing the *meaning* of an action is what folk psychology is about. It is the meaning of an action in the sense of its purpose or significance that is sought. But not all social scientists find that knowing the significance of an action from the point of view of the agent (consumer) is sufficient for their purposes and want to know something about background causes. In this case, the cause(s) selected from some causal chain or background set of causes will depend on our concerns and what appears to be actionable for our purposes. We say 'cause(s)' rather than 'cause' since there is always the possibility of multiple causality or *equifinality*, which implies alternative causal paths leading to the same effect.

In thinking about causes, social scientists are sensitive to the distinction between correlation and causation in that two variables can be highly correlated (e.g. the number of storks born in Sweden and the birth rate have a perfect correlation) but have no causal connection. This is the straw-man used by many to dismiss high correlations, forgetting that causation brings about high correlation. On the other hand, laboratory-type experimentation is intended to distinguish spurious correlations from those that are causal. But experimentation does not *guarantee* that the relevant cause has been found, since experimentation cannot distinguish cause from what might be simply coexistence. Hard knowledge, as justified belief, is hard to establish.

In the social sciences we are more apt to talk about (a) contributory factors, (b) necessary factors and (c) sufficient factors in bringing about an effect and not the necessary and sufficient conditions we think of as defining cause. Mostly, research identifies contributory factors – that is, happenings that facilitate an occurrence – and commonsensical necessary factors since a necessary factor for success is, by definition, a sufficient reason for failure. To claim that a given event (e.g. buying) would not have happened if X (a want for the product) were not present is to say that the absence of a 'want' for the product is a sufficient reason for not buying it. To state a sufficient condition 'X' is to say: if 'X' then always 'Y'. Universal laws in the natural sciences aim to state sufficient conditions for the effect to occur: 'If metals are heated, they always expand.' There are no such universal laws in social science.

However, in folk psychology, the notion of human action being the cause of events is basic to allocating praise or blame and holding people accountable. Some illusion about what caused what is all-pervasive in social life. As Steven Pinker (2007), who was formerly at the MIT and is now at Harvard, says:

> The habit of hallucinating causal powers and forcing experience to fit them has shaped human cultures from time immemorial, producing our species' vast compendium of voodoo, astrology magic, prayer and idolatry, New Age nostrums, and other flimflam.
>
> (Pinker 2007: 217)

FOLK PSYCHOLOGY GUIDES DAY-TO-DAY INTERPRETATIONS OF BEHAVIOR

Folk psychology, not academic psychology, is what guides most interpretations of behavior. Whether it is generals, US presidents, CEOs or managers, it is folk psychology (refined as it is by experience) that is drawn upon in understanding the actions and behaviors of others and predicting the likely behavioral consequences of any decision. It is folk psychology that generally allows us to anticipate what others will do and to manipulate others into believing what we intend them to believe. It is folk psychology that leads us to see connections between a person's frustration and his anger or between sources of high credibility and their potential in persuading others.

Government policies typically rely on folk psychology and this can mislead. Thus the opening of pubs in England was extended on the reasonable assumption that being able to have a drink any time of the day would reduce binge drinking. This did not happen and seems to have made the problem worse. The financial crisis of 2008 arose from false assumptions about behavior in financial markets. The most flagrantly wrong assumption was in respect of house prices, not realizing that house prices would eventually far exceed what would be reasonable, while the indebtedness of the householders could not continue.

A great deal of our understanding of others comes from understanding relationships between expressed feelings and actions, like the relationship between expressed dislike and being non-supportive of those disliked. In fact we recognize, without any training in academic psychology, that a person's negative attitude to others colors his or her outlook towards them, leads to a bias in the selection of information about them and generally to viewing their actions through a distorted lens.

Ethnopsychology is the study of folk psychology in a systematic way. Consumers do grasp conceptual relationships like that between the absence of hope and corresponding despair and act on this basis, clutching at straws (paying for useless medicines or treatments for a terminal illness) to maintain hope and avoid despair. Ethnopsychology identifies and explicates such conceptual relationships, defines how words like 'want' and 'belief' are used and tries to systematize what we know about folk psychology.

If there are no universal laws in psychology this means that, before applying any findings from social science, there is a need to judge their applicability given the context. The applicability of the findings depends on the similarity of contexts; nonetheless, judging findings as applicable may simply be a matter of common sense which inevitably draws on folk psychology. In any case, context always needs to be considered. Even gestures and other forms of non-verbal behavior are not isolated signals as is often assumed but have to be interpreted within the context in which the behavior occurred.

Folk psychology is what the layperson employs to understand behavior; to judge, for example, whether the behavior in a movie is credible. Bogdan (2001) offers an evolutionary explanation of folk psychology, showing how the ability to interpret others would have evolved under communal, political, and epistemic pressures to help humans cope with social life. It is a survival tactic when life is social.

Those with Asperger's syndrome (synonymous with high-functioning autism) are deficient in social skills even though they may possess a high IQ. If we were to set out all that social science has taught us about how people act and react to others, the memorizing of this body of knowledge would not make up for a person's absence of folk psychology in respect to social skills. Memorization of appropriate responses in various situations would merely produce robot-like behavior. This is why all talk of building robots that will behave exactly like humans is a myth. Robots can surpass humans in many ways but will never have the social intelligence to behave like humans in novel situations. In particular, we are far from building robots that can bluff and deceive themselves and others. Whether in bargaining or in war, strategies depend somewhat on bluff and deception in a way that cannot be captured in the mathematics of game theory. However, subjecting everything to bargaining over time would undermine attempts at unity, just as increasing agreement over time tends to generate a conviction of rightness that rules out dissent.

Marketing needs to take account of folk psychology to understand the *perceptions* of the consumer. And it is consumer perceptions that are the reality of interest to those in marketing. These perceptions occur, however, within a perspective since a perspective is a sort of conceptual lens for viewing the aspects of reality that are of interest. But consumer perceptions frequently diverge from what the neutral observer would regard as the objective facts. If we put the Cadillac name and logo on the top models of Hyundai, it would change perceptions and be a great sales asset. Brand names change perceptions, sometimes even to the extent of the consumer seeing higher quality than exists, as is typically the case in buying clothing.

As we look at t-shirts, vests, socks and so on, they appear undifferentiated except for the brand name which allows a price premium. If even a placebo in a drug experiment is given a brand name, perceived effects of brand efficacy have been found to change. Logos make a brand more recognizable and can put a shine on the brand. Citigroup so prized its red umbrella logo that it claimed it was 'non-negotiable' in its split with Travelers Property Casualty Insurance in 2002, though it has now sold it back to them. The red umbrella is distinctive, sophisticated but, most importantly, signals its primary function. This does not mean all consumers want a logo on whatever they buy. A logo, however upmarket, will symbolize for some a non-exclusive rather than exclusive brand. Consumers are not tokens of each other in what they seek in a product-offering and this gives rise to the need to segment the market.

Company logos can be clever, with the cleverness going unnoticed. Thus the Amazon logo has a yellow swoosh that seems like a smile and links the 'a' to the 'z' to declare that the store has everything from 'a' to 'z'. 'Toblerone' is a chocolate bar made in Bern, Switzerland, with Bern called 'The City of Bears'. The Toblerone logo is seemingly a mountain, but embedded in the mountain is the silhouette of a bear. If you look carefully at the FedEx logo, there is an arrow between the last two letters, Ex. The Formula 1 logo is designed to convey the feeling of speed, which it does successfully, but if you look carefully between the F and the red stripes the white area represents a 1. We do not need to be told a logo can contribute to sales but this sort of cleverness may be too hidden to cause a buzz and act as a talking point.

Some researchers deny perception is a process; the consumer simply perceives something. If she sees her favorite packet of detergent on the shelf, she does not undertake any processing of the sensory input but just recognizes the packet. Perception can be viewed as simply being the conscious experience of what is perceived, though some psychologists might object that cognitive processes may still be at work behind the scenes. Logic can be used to *invent* a mental process, for example, that sensory input leads $\Rightarrow$ to conscious awareness of those inputs and this leads $\Rightarrow$ to interpretation of these inputs for sense-meaning. These stages sound logical but are they empirically true? Folk psychology is not one that focuses on inner goings-on in the mind so the folk psychology of students is often prepared to accept logical processes as descriptive of reality. But logic is purely a rational activity, while psychology is an empirical science. Yet in both folk psychology and scientific psychology there is a danger of conflating the two. Logic can invent processes that can happen but never or rarely do happen. Thus logic might suggest that before speaking I think about what to say and how I am going to say it. This could happen but rarely does. In general conversation, we just speak without mental reflection on what to say. It is the same with the claim that every stimulus of which we are conscious has to be interpreted. This is just not so. I see my car without any interpretation that it is my car, unless there is some ambiguity which may occur on occasion. Psychology is meant to be empirically grounded through systematic investigation, while folk psychology reflects the accumulated experience of those people with whom we interact.

ETHNOPSYCHOLOGY'S PERSPECTIVE AS SYSTEMATIZING FOLK PSYCHOLOGY

Ethnopsychology is the systematic study of folk psychology which, in turn, is the psychology people use in everyday dealings. Steve Jobs of Apple claimed his success was based on understanding technology *and popular culture*. He accepted the notion of 'latent wants' of which the consumer was not conscious until the product catering to the latent want was revealed. But if there is to be systematization of folk psychology, there is a need to provide conceptual clarity to basic folk psychology concepts like beliefs and wants/desires, intentions and actions. There are many philosophers intent on doing just that. Thus *beliefs* tell us how the world is and dispose us to accept statements that cohere with these beliefs. Beliefs can be distinguished from expressed opinions since many people express opinions (e.g. in interviews) that they do not believe but are socially appropriate replies or the views of a group to which they belong or aspire to belong. Many of our beliefs are not firmly grounded nor held with much conviction. Most beliefs are not in fact the result of heavy thinking, as most of our beliefs have little practical import and could be abandoned in an instant if we were pressed to do so. Beliefs that have been thought about may become internalized – that is, viewed as part of one's core being – but we suspect only relatively few of our beliefs have in fact been internalized. If this is so, many of our expressed beliefs may have little role to play in bringing about action as no feeling component will be present. We want the consumer to passionately believe something if it is to contribute to buying action.

Wants/desires, in contrast to beliefs, tell us how we would like the world to be: to want something is to have a disposition towards using, consuming or possessing that something. The central fact about such mental states as beliefs, wants and desires is what philosophers call their 'intentionality' – that is, they are *about* something. We have beliefs *about* what the world is like and we have wants *about* how we would like the world to be.

The difference between a 'want' and a 'desire' is that the word desire suggests a more intense want. Consistent with these definitions, Wollheim (1999) views beliefs as mapping the world to provide a picture of it, while wants and desires target things in the world at which to aim. Whenever the consumer speaks of something being good, it relates to desire in contrast to scientific language which typically relates to belief. That said, desires and beliefs form an interacting system in that strong beliefs influence desires, while strong desires influence beliefs. Thus if a consumer comes to believe strongly that a copper bracelet will reduce the pain of arthritis in her hand, she is likely to have the desire to buy one. On the other hand, if a consumer has a strong desire for a product to cure her terminal cancer, she is open to believing in any product that promises to do so. There are always certain situations where desire is such that we are likely to believe anything if it justifies satisfying our desires.

'Intentions' are our expectations as to actions to take. Intentions have been compared to going into gear, requiring the further step of having the 'will' to press the accelerator to follow through on intentions. Goals are the end states we seek by our actions. In rational decision-making, goals and values constitute criteria against which we evaluate alternative courses of action. But goals are chosen and pursued within a constraint, for example financial. A constraint is a rule that should not or cannot be violated but, unlike a goal, there is no point in overfulfilling it. Thus, a prospective buyer whose goal is buying a house will act within constraints centering on location, price, area, size, number of rooms and so on. Goals will direct which data are to be collected. This is because goals determine relevance. Values, though, are the highest level ends we seek and, as a consequence, implicitly act as part of the criteria we use in judging what decision or action to take.

Consumers, as purposive animals, are goal-seeking and seeking goals implies trying to coordinate wants and beliefs into a coherent system before taking action. But to make the connection between wants and beliefs (reasons) and corresponding action conceptually watertight demands more than this. In line with ethnopsychology, Collin (1985) points out, a person who wants goal (G) to be the case and who believes that performing the action (A) will bring about (G), will perform (A) providing:

(i)   He believes (G), the goal, will not come about without his action
(ii) He is able to do (A), the action, and knows this
(iii) The external conditions for doing (A), the action, are present
(iv) He knows of no better way of bringing about (G), the goal, than by doing (A), the action
(v)   He knows of no reason why he should not do (A), the action.

In ethnopsychology, human action is viewed as purposive, being directed by beliefs, wants/desires/values/goals which collectively constitute the reasons for action. Providing reasons for an action makes action meaningful. There is always dissatisfaction with explanations that fail to show how the actions of people are the actions of conscious human beings, reacting to an environment, trying to make sense of it and pursuing various goals in their actions with more or less success. But not all actions are purposive. We tap our fingers idly on the table, tap our foot to an imagined rhythm; these actions are in a sense sub-intentional, showing how the mind is bound up with the body and cannot be entirely divorced from it (O'Shaughnessy 1980).

'Reasoned action', preceded by deliberated decision-making, comes into its own when important choices have to be made and there is uncertainty over the costs and benefits of various options. But most actions are not based on any (highly conscious) deliberation to choose the best action-consequence sequence. As the philosopher Dretske (1988) says, much behavior is like shivering, perspiring, coughing, weeping, salivating, dreaming, choking, fumbling or emotional reactions like blushing or automatic reactions like withdrawing one's hand from a red-hot surface. Even behavior that is intentional may not be pre-planned. Thus 'impulse buying' does not evolve from any deliberation on action-consequence sequences but from a gut reaction for instant gratification. It is, in other words, unreflective, affect-driven (emotion-driven) action when faced with the desired object. Acting on impulse is, however, intentional in that consumers at the time of purchase had the intention of buying even if the intention was not preplanned and even if, after the purchase, there was regret.

Jerome Bruner's ethnopsychology

The psychologist Jerome Bruner (1990) makes the controversial claim that the boundaries that separate psychology, anthropology, sociology and philosophy are matters of administrative convenience and not intellectual substance. His own vision for psychology is that it joins forces with 'its sister interpretive disciplines in the humanities and the social sciences'. He seeks a cultural psychology that is organized around human 'meaning-making' and 'meaning-using' processes since these are what connect man to his culture. For Bruner it is culture and the quest for meaning (in the sense of the significance of things) within a cultural setting that are the proper 'causes' of human action. Culture, and the search for meaning, constitute the 'shaping hand' behind human action, with a person's biological make-up acting as a constraint. Steven Pinker might argue that biological make-up is a major constraint but acknowledge the more minor role of culture.

Bruner, one of the pioneers of cognitive psychology when at Harvard, claims the cognitive revolution in psychology started as an all-out effort to establish 'meaning' as the central concept of psychology but early on it became seduced by the metaphor of the mind as a computer. With the concept of 'mind' equated with a computer program, there was no place for any concept of mind involving intentional states like believing, desiring and seeking meaning. Even the concept of humans as 'agents' was attacked as if their behavior was completely determined by forces over which they had no control. Although cognitive psychologists accept the notion that behavior is goal-directed, the concept of 'agency' has been typically eschewed as implying that people act purely for reasons – that is, under the sway of intentional states. Although cognitive psychologists have no objection to speaking of humans acting 'as if' they are acting on the basis of intentional states, typically they reject the idea that this is a factual state of affairs.

The debate occurs also in philosophy. Folk psychology, unlike folk physics, has a good record in revealing how humans tick. What is called the *philosophy of action* starts with Aristotle's claim that we are free and responsible agents because we act for reasons. Traditionally, reasons for action are equated with wants and beliefs, with wants and beliefs employed to both explain motivation and justify action. David Velleman (2000) holds this traditional view, as perhaps do most philosophers. For him, if the consumer knows what he or she is doing, then he or she is acting freely. As always in philosophy there are dissenters, like Jonathan Dancy (2000), for whom the reasons for doing things are to be found in environmental factors ('states of affairs') and not just in the mind. This is a debate which is reflected in the different perspectives we find in the social sciences.

Bruner (1990), in support of ethnopsychology, argues that psychology must link up with culture because human actions are tied to culturally shared meanings and concepts: to shared 'modes of discourse' by which differences in meaning and interpretation are negotiated among people and because, most important of all, actions are tied to a culture's account of what makes human beings tick. The culture's account of what makes humans tick is what we have been calling 'folk psychology', though Bruner prefers the term *ethnopsychology* to remind us that he is talking about the discipline of folk psychology. Bruner argues that it is through folk psychology that people 'anticipate and judge one another, draw conclusions about the worthwhileness of their lives and so on'. Human beings react to one another in terms of their own psychology (folk psychology) rather than the psychologists' psychology, so we need to study this to give meaning to human experience.

Folk psychology, it is argued, must be the basis of any cultural psychology, together with its basic premise that people have beliefs and wants that activate behavior. A culturally oriented psychology would not dismiss what people have to say about their mental states, nor just accept such statements as predictive of behavior. What would be central to psychology would be the recognition that the relationship between expressed feelings like anger or mental states like attitudes and actions is, in the ordinary conduct of life, interpretable. For Bruner, cultural psychology that is tied to folk psychology should be the major thrust of psychology. It should be an interpretive psychology in much the same way that history, anthropology and linguistics are interpretive disciplines. Such a psychology, he argues, need not be unprincipled or without methods, even hard-nosed ones. What it would seek, however, are the *rules* that people bring to bear in creating meaning or understanding the significance of things in cultural contexts.

This focus by Bruner on 'meaning' as the key property of action is a focus shared by several 'schools' in social science. *Ethogeny*, for example, focuses on how action is made meaningful by those who carry out the action and those who observe the action being carried out. Observing the action carried out goes beyond just seeing the action carried out, since learning to observe involves learning to infer. Observation is concept-regulated in that we see what we have been taught to see by our vocabulary of concepts. The concepts enriching observation suggest consequences, just as the concept of shopping and observing an episode of 'shopping' allows us to infer likely consequences regarding the behavior of the shopper, even if the inference is never what the logician would describe as logically waterproof or valid. Inferences terminate in making assertions and lying behind these assertions are resulting beliefs. To criticize a concept such as, for example, the product life cycle, always involves consideration of the concept's inferential relationships: that is, what can be inferred about relationships with other concepts like the notion of an 'ideal type'. An ideal type is a socially constructed 'pure type' that highlights certain aspects of a social phenomenon that may not actually exist. Thus the product life cycle could be viewed as a an ideal type against which to compare real product life cycles to explain why the real life cycle did not follow the pattern of the ideal type. If the product life cycle concept is to have explanatory value, it would have to go beyond the metaphor of birth, growth, maturity and decline. In fact, many new products fail to have a life cycle as described because they die too soon after birth to have a life. In 2011, Microsoft withdrew its Kin mobile phones only 48 days after they went on sale. Hewlett-Packard similarly withdrew its touch-Pad tablet after 48 days. Goods and services are not biological organisms. We would need to know the external factors or processes acting as causal mechanisms in bringing about the sequence. To show sales varying with time is not enough, since time in itself is not a forcing variable. There is no reason why any shape of curve may not apply to a particular product, though there are reasons for thinking the textbook shape of the product life cycle makes most sense.

To apply one concept rather than another (the concept of 'want' rather than the concept of 'need') is to endorse as more applicable the consequences stemming from applying the concept selected (the concept of 'need' obliges us to endorse the notion of an absolute requirement). The logician talks of the 'truth conditions' lying behind a concept. These are the necessary and sufficient conditions for the application of the concept (Brandom 2009). Truth conditions are an ideal approach to concept analysis but seldom set out in practice.

There are social sciences that have links with folk psychology which are considered later in the text. *Ethnomethodology* studies the 'folk methods' used by people in everyday life to give meaning to the roles they and others play in life and to the nature of the institutions that surround them. *Symbolic interactionism*, while viewing interaction between people as symbolic exchanges (i.e. as exchanges that symbolize something) aims at discovering the ways by which such exchanges are rendered meaningful. In cultural anthropology, Geertz focuses on symbols and how they function to mediate meanings. Although all these approaches may differ somewhat in what they look for, they share a notion that the meaning of action involves understanding the point of the action: its significance and the wants and beliefs that guide and shape it. Understanding customers in this way is more important than just watching competition which is simply a source for imitation not in-house innovation.

Those promoting ethnopsychology who come from linguistic philosophy are likely to deny that academic psychology has anything to say, over and above the humanities, about our everyday understanding of others. The philosopher Ludwig Wittgenstein (1889–1951) argued that all significant thought was linguistic in character so that the improvement in thought implied the further ability and capacity to use language. There are, he argued, different 'language games' for different forms of life like mathematics, art, religion, physics, psychology and so on (including shopping), with different reasoning governing the different types of thought. The notion of people thinking and acting differently, when in the language game of acting as consumers as opposed to doing their daily job, has only been implicitly acknowledged though it provides a rationale for consumer behavior having its own specific domain.

Those studying consumer behavior deny that academic psychology has nothing distinctive to say over and above a systematic reformulation of folk psychology. In fact those developing ethnopsychology (i.e. those systematizing folk psychology) are happy to draw on concepts from social science if these better capture the reality behind and beyond folk psychology. The study of consumer behavior embraces many perspectives and methods with the implicit adoption of multiperspectivism and methodological pluralism.

If ethnopsychology is an interpretive discipline and hermeneutics the study of methods of interpretation, then ethnopsychology is a hermeneutic discipline in that it focuses on the interpretation of behavior in contrast to laboratory experimentation or quantitative methods.

As we have seen, Bruner (1990) regrets the move of cognitive psychology from the search for 'meaning' in the sense of personal significance and/or intentions lying behind action, to viewing the mind as a computer. In doing this, Bruner (1990) is implicitly rejecting the philosophy of *naturalism* with its central thesis that the search for causal explanation in the social sciences should always be the default position:

> To insist upon explanation in terms of 'causes' simply bars us from trying to understand how human beings interpret their worlds and how we interpret their acts of interpretation.
>
> (Bruner 1990: xiii)

We see the significance of things for us through our capacity for 'reflexive consciousness' – the consciousness of consciousness! It is this reflexive consciousness that helps us develop our understanding of others – an understanding we call folk psychology (Humphrey 1983). Even by the end of the second year of a child's existence, it seems a consciousness of consciousness has started to develop in the ability to infer the thoughts and feelings of others.

THE CONCEPT OF INTENTION

Interpretive methods in ethnopsychology commonly embrace not just identifying the relevant wants and beliefs or searching for meaning in the sense of the action's significance but also seeking to identify an agent's intentions. The search for intentions is not unproblematic. As Krausz (1993) reminds us, the original intentions of an author (or consumer) may be ambiguous and incongruous, while some texts may be collectively and not individually created. (In hermeneutics, everything put forward for analysis is a 'text' put forward for interpretation.) Intentions and knowledge of contextual factors do not necessarily reveal the wants and beliefs lying behind an action since the same intention can arise from very different wants and beliefs. Thus knowing that a consumer intends to buy a smartphone does not in itself reveal the relevant wants and beliefs.

Dennett's intentional stance

As already stated, although cognitive psychology accepts the notion of behavior being goal-directed, it generally eschews talk of agency where people are viewed as free agents being guided by intentional states arising from wants and beliefs – unless it describes a purely normative or stipulated scenario like Dennett's intentional stance.

Dennett (1989), a philosopher with a particular interest in consciousness and intentional behavior, describes his intentional stance as follows.

> Here is how it works: first you decide to treat the object whose behavior is to be predicted as a rational agent; then you figure out what beliefs that agent ought to have, given its place in the world and its purpose. Then you figure out what desires it ought to have, on the same considerations, and finally you predict that this rational agent will act to further its goals in the light of its beliefs. A little practical reasoning from the chosen set of beliefs and desires will in most instances yield a decision about what the agent ought to do; that is what you predict the agent will do.
>
> (Dennett 1989: 17)

Dennett (1996) also talks of humans having 'Popperian' minds (after Sir Karl Popper, the philosopher of science) in that we spend much of our time generating and testing ideas and learning by experimenting with inner representations. This seems an echo of George Kelly's (1963) 'constructive alternativism', put forward in his *A Theory of Personality*, part of which is captured in the following quotation.

> Might not the individual man, each in his own personal way, assume more of the stature of a scientist, ever seeking to predict and control the course of events, with which he is involved? Would he not have his theories, test his hypotheses, and weigh his experimental evidence? And, if so, might not the difference between the personal viewpoints of

different men correspond to the differences between theoretical points of view of different scientists?

(Kelly 1963: 5)

This perspective – man as the scientist – has not, as far as I know, been applied to consumer behavior but it has potential for explaining some types of behavior.

ETHNOPSYCHOLOGY'S FOCUS ON THE SEARCH FOR MEANING

As we have seen, for Bruner the quest for meaning or personal significance is what lies behind action. If the mind is equated with a computer program (as in cognitive psychology), there is no need for 'mind' in the sense of intentional states such as believing, wanting, intending or grasping meaning. Bruner claims ethnopsychology must be the basis for a 'cultural' psychology, a basic premise of which is that people act intentionally in accordance with their beliefs and wants to give meaning to their actions. This is also the view endorsed in philosophy's *theory of action*.

In claiming psychology should be a cultural psychology, Bruner in the process contrasts the perspective of people as 'atomic' individuals (a position taken in individual psychology) with the concept of *agency* or *agents* who are socially and culturally involved in making their own decisions and taking their own actions. When we ask in ethnopsychology what something means to the consumer, we are generally referring to the significance of that something for the consumer. To say that something has high meaning for the consumer implies that she *believes* it has high *significance* for her *wants* (goals or values). The notion of 'high meaning' in this context relates high meaning to a person's reasons, defined as embracing wants and beliefs. For the philosopher Charles Taylor (1983), the crucial difference between men and machines is not consciousness, but this significance factor:

> We also enjoy consciousness, because we are capable of focusing on the significance things have for us...Once you do see the importance of the significance feature, it is evident that computing machines can at best go some of the way to explaining human computation, let alone intelligent, adaptive performance generally.
>
> (Taylor 1983: 157–160)

Philosophy's theory of action also equates the meaning of an action with the reasons for carrying out the action. Actions are explained by the reasons for the action (the reason-giving explanation), showing the action to be purposeful and intelligible given the circumstances and the agent's wants, beliefs and intentions. As we have said above, reasons for action relate to the meaning of the action because taking an action is like saying we believe the action is meaningful or significant for our wants/goals/purposes. Interpreting the meaning of action in terms of significance and intentions, while explicating the reasons (wants, beliefs and intentions) for the action, may be all that is required to explain buying in the way most useful to marketing management. In other words, seeking a causal explanation may go beyond the needs of management, even though it is desirable for the social scientist. This is because the type and depth of explanation we seek depends on our purposes. If we can gauge the relevant wants and beliefs in the context, we have a general format for making actions intelligible.

No action in itself points unambiguously to the wants (motives), beliefs and intentions that lie behind it. This is why the concept of 'revealed preference' so prized by economists is of little value to the marketing manager who wants to know the reasons for preference. Given the three elements of wants, beliefs and action, we generally need two of the three to determine the reasons behind the action. Pollsters in elections are apt to forget this and believe they can gauge motives (wants) and beliefs from knowing which way people voted. Those social scientists that similarly focus on attitude measures, based on beliefs alone, are making the same mistake unless on occasion the purchase is purely belief-driven rather than also affect-driven. There are also those 'consumer watchers' who hang around supermarkets observing consumer behavior in order to spot trends and identify motives, but again focusing purely on what actions are taken has not led to much success in prediction.

We would expect ethnopsychology to be endorsed by academics in marketing where talk about wants and beliefs is pervasive. But the urge to join the ranks of 'scientific' psychology has led to the most abstract, idiosyncratic models of the consumer's information processing system or a focus on beliefs alone since attitude measures are most commonly based on summaries of belief statements. Beliefs alone are not likely to be predictive unless wants cohere. Thus the non-religious accuse religious believers of not acting in line with their beliefs. But unless motives and wants/desires are in line with the action that the beliefs endorse, action is inhibited. Similarly, wants alone do not direct action since there is a need to take account of beliefs. To repeat: of the three elements – beliefs, wants and action – we need at least two of them for prediction to be warranted. A set of religious beliefs about moral behavior simply constitutes a *normative* model of behavior, not a *descriptive* model. Sometimes, of course, beliefs can be so emotionally compelling that wants are brought into line with them and buying is *belief-driven*, or wants can be so emotionally demanding that supportive beliefs (rationalizations) emerge and buying is *affect-driven* ('affect' in psychology being equated with 'feeling' or 'emotion'). But these extremes, while important to recognize, are not typical.

The philosopher Jerry Fodor (1981), like Bruner, never abandons the need for psychology to explain human action (voluntary behavior) in terms of wants and beliefs as is done in 'folk' psychology. It is the type of explanation managers understand. But if this system of explanation were adopted by marketing academics for some purposes, there would be a need to refine folk psychology concepts like 'wants' and 'beliefs'. This is happening through the efforts of philosophers and those seeking to build the discipline of ethnopsychology. Conceptual analysis of folk psychology concepts yields insights that make us sensitive to the nice distinctions in the language. But there is a need to sharpen concepts in marketing generally. The level of discourse in the marketing literature is not that much more precise than would be expected in day-to-day conversation.

ETHNOPSYCHOLOGY AS A CULTURAL PSYCHOLOGY

Each person's folk psychology is more in tune with his own culture than alien cultures. Although we speculate about the motives and beliefs of other people to understand their actions, more commonly we assume people in other cultures act in ways that mirror our own social conventions. This explains why we can be lost in predicting the behavior of those in alien cultures (Millikan 2004). There is evidence that countries that trust each other tend to trade more with each other and the same is true of cross-border investment: culturally based trust can shape trade and investment patterns (Guiso et al. 2005). Understanding and speaking the other's language contributes to creating that trust.

ETHNOPSYCHOLOGY AND SOCIAL SCIENCE

Auyang (2000) takes to task critics of ethnopsychology who criticize it in the name of science when what they themselves are promoting is not science, like physics, but the dogma of *scientism* that fallaciously and wantonly extrapolates claims about the scope of science and its methods that actually undermine the scientific spirit. This is a harsh verdict, prompted by pretentious claims in many social science texts about social science being able to explain, predict and control behavior. This is to confuse a *normative* goal with what is feasible. In any case, this is not to suggest that approaching the consumer from the perspective of ethnopsychology means we ignore concepts developed elsewhere by social scientists. We can listen to the consumer before (anticipatory), during (contemporaneous) and after buying (retrospective) and get a deeper understanding through the directions given to us by these concepts which essentially sensitize us to things to look for (see O'Shaughnessy 1986).

What social science offers are sensitizing concepts, not universal laws of human action. These sensitizing concepts help guide fruitful observation since we see what we are taught to see through concepts. Furthermore, the range of studies conducted in consumer behavior makes us sensitive to aspects of consumer behavior requiring explanation that were not obvious before we became acquainted with these studies.

Heider (1958) argues, again like Bruner, that humans act and react to each other in terms of their own psychology rather than the psychologist's psychology and this must be taken into account in any methodology that is meant to lead to a human psychology. The methodology adopted by any discipline should be tied to the type of understanding sought, which means the type of questions the discipline seeks to answer. Ethnopsychology is applicable to many questions asked by marketing managers and this attests to its relevance.

Differences in subject matter and questions asked may demand differences in methodology. This means there is a need to justify why, for example, mathematical physics should be adopted as the model for psychology. It is just not true that causal-type explanations are needed for every purpose or to answer all the questions raised in marketing. Nor is the *rational choice model* of the economist necessarily enlightening when interest lies in behavior that is primarily self-expressive (an end in itself as with many sporting activities), or behavior tied to social norms, roles played or moral rules. Social norms and habits are not considered relevant in economics, where the only things assumed to impinge on the consumer are technology and prices whereas in practice human attachments often take precedence over self-interest.

HOW DOES ETHNOPSYCHOLOGY INTERPRET AND HELP IN PREDICTING THE ACTIONS OF OTHERS?

Goldman (1995), a philosopher of action theory, offers three methods by which people interpret the actions of others.

First, there is interpretation based on the assumption that people conform to an ideal or normative model of inference and choice. Dennett (1986) gets near to this notion of rationality in his concept of an *intentional stance* in interpreting behavior based on postulates of ideal rationality. This ideal rationality presupposes norms based on formal logic, or in quantitative modeling the calculus of probability or Bayesian decision theory. Goldman undermines this ideal rationality as a basis for ethnopsychology by pointing to work that undercuts the thesis, such as the work of Tversky and Kahneman (1983). They show that people typically violate the probability calculus, while experimental findings suggest that people think in ways that contravene accepted norms of rationality. On the other hand, the argument that the norms of ideal rationality just need to be watered down, as proposed by Cherniak's concept of minimal rationality (1986), is flawed since Goldman claims Cherniak's notion of minimal rationality is much too vague. The adherence to social norms is a voluntary act. Being constrained by social norms occurs only if we acknowledge such norms as binding, whereas to be compelled by causal factors, such as lack of resources or ability, is to be constrained by the facts.

Second, there is interpretation of behavior against an assumed set of lawlike generalizations that relate stimulus inputs to mental states or mental states to other mental states and mental states to action. Goldman points out that there is no universal set of 'laws' shared by people in general, though people may *act* as if valid generalizations about human behavior exist. People use folk psychology generalizations (e.g. people are likely to scratch my back if I scratch theirs) to interpret behavior and there may be more agreement within a culture on such interpretations than is generally assumed. But most of the generalizations people make are not explicit but implied or suggested, which makes it difficult to spot inconsistencies. A person may condemn the manufacture of fur coats but not leather coats. Is he or she being inconsistent or is it suggested that fur coats lead to animals being slaughtered while this is not so with leather? We never do know the whole set of implications of our beliefs and are generally not smart enough to recognize all the inconsistencies among our beliefs. It may also be that the evidence against a belief is strong but not for some people as the relevant evidence may not be easy to discern or to judge.

Everyone has some ability to predict behavior and emotional responses, given the situation. This is illustrated by an experiment carried out by Kahneman and Tversky (1982). The subjects in the experiment were given a scenario involving a Mr Crane and Mr Tees. These two gentlemen were scheduled to leave the airport at the same time but on different flights. They travelled to the airport in the same limousine, were caught in the same traffic jam and arrived at the airport 30 minutes late for their flights. Mr Crane was told his flight had left on time but Mr Tees was told that his had been delayed and had just left. The subjects in the experiment were asked: 'Who was more upset, Mr Crane or Mr Tees?' Not surprisingly, 96 percent believed Mr Tees would be more upset. We know that people are not tokens of each other but this does not rule out their many similarities in interpreting human behavior.

Third, there is interpretation based on *simulation* whereby people understand others by mentally simulating (imitating or reproducing) the situation of others and interpreting accordingly. Simulation is much more effective if analysts know something about the personality or characteristics of those being studied and are steeped in knowledge of the context. Otherwise, the simulation approach has to assume that others are like us in the relevant aspects. Folk psychology embraces roughly the second and this third method for interpreting the behavior of others.

Motivation, as in mainstream psychology, is a topic in ethnopsychology. Strictly speaking, motivation is a process, namely the process of providing others with a motive(s) for doing something. However, motivation is also used as a pretentious synonym for motive or motives. This practice of equating 'motivation' and 'motive' is now so well established that this book has just accepted this common usage.

A motive in folk psychology often has overtones of something hidden and impure, not just some internal state that activates behavior. Thus a consumer may attribute an underhand motive to a seller, believing that any discount offered is a cover for something underhand. In politics, being suspicious of motives is all-pervasive, and consequently rejects that which may be beneficial regardless of the motives of the politician. Because we cannot deduce motives from action alone, every single action of a rival politician is made to appear deviously motivated – and is believed by the party faithful.

The layperson is apt to refer to reasons for action in terms of the goals/wants and beliefs of the individual. In contrast, the psychological study of motivation presupposes that there are general things that can be said about the motives of people, for example that people are generally disposed to seek a common set of goals or at the very least to avoid punishment and seek reward. In other words, motives, in psychology, refer to general dispositional tendencies, activated by certain types of stimuli to achieve certain general goals, like self-preservation, satisfying hunger or thirst, or to achieve power or the admiration of others.

FOLK PSYCHOLOGY SEEKS TO MAKE ACTION INTELLIGIBLE

No marketing manager could or does rely on social science findings for all the answers he seeks and it is the insights from folk psychology that are often decisive. Folk psychology interprets action in terms of reasons for the action. It does this without subscribing to the assumption that reasons must necessarily be rational. It is only necessary that they be *intelligible* to make sense of them. Folk psychology does not answer all the questions that might be raised about behavior and has nothing much to say about abnormal behavior or mental illness, while we may need to ask about the causes of action, going beyond the want/belief /intention format.

The various actions people take like shopping are actions to be understood in terms of wants, beliefs (particularly about consequences), decisions and intentions. This is true even if we view shopping as including activities like browsing, just looking, seeking bargains or special deals. But the criteria for applying action concepts involve more than looking at physical movement. A wink (a voluntary action) is not the same as a blink (an involuntary movement) even if they cannot be distinguished physically. To say someone is shopping goes beyond physical movements. What counts as shopping depends on the socially constructed, shared rules of society as to what falls under the concept of shopping.

In any case, not all action is conscious action. Many things are done non-consciously: a matter of habit, indoctrination, conditioning, or simply a reaction to non-consciously absorbed cues when we are in effect on automatic pilot. While the overall action of going to play a particular tune on the piano by a pianist may be a deliberate act, the sequence of actual notes played happens automatically without conscious control or attention. The notion of two complementary processes occurring within the same episode – one lacking conscious control and the other where conscious control initiates and guides action – is a claim made by Norman and Shallice (1986). This is something not sufficiently recognized in the consumer buying literature.

Not all actions are intentional even though they are not involuntary movements either. Thus I non-intentionally read print material on a billboard or on the television screen though this does not qualify as involuntary activity (La Berge 1975).

Ethnopsychology explains intentional action by showing the action to be part of a purposeful narrative which is intelligible and meaningful in the circumstances. A common interpretive approach is premised on actions being *rule-regulated*, with people nonetheless having reasons for their actions. People have been viewed as chess players writ large (Peters 1960). Like chess players writ large, there are overall rules involved in shopping but, like individual chess moves, individual shopping moves cannot be predicted in advance. But the overall rules of chess have been deliberately created, are universal and define what we mean by chess, so the analogy with shopping is far from perfect.

As already claimed, between stimuli and response action, no conscious reflection need intervene at all. Consumers are on occasions more reactive than proactive, simply reacting to the meaning (significance for them) of the situation facing them. As people do not in general have a preference for hard thinking, following social norms or advice is very tempting.

THE REASON-GIVING EXPLANATION

The best argument for taking action is that it is the right thing to do in the circumstances so it is not surprising that we view others as likely to take action in line with what they think is right in the circumstances. In daily life we thus seek reasons for people's actions. The reason-giving explanation is the natural starting point for explaining human action, not only in courts of law but also in social science and history. Having reasons to act leads to intentions or a commitment to action. Those supportive of this paradigm of ethnopsychology argue that, if we are to capture the salient features of mental life, those studying human action must frame their explanations in terms of reasons using the concepts of beliefs and wants (or cognates of these terms). Experienced marketing managers can be very skilled in answering questions about buyer behavior in their markets because they have sensitivity to likely reasons for action and come to recognize certain patterns of behavior as related to future actions.

As we have said, psychologists eschew the reason-giving type of explanation on the grounds that:

(a) It does not lend itself to theory development as per the natural sciences. Psychologists argue that such teleological explanations (those based on the goals/wants sought) were abandoned with Isaac Newton when the focus shifted to causal explanation. Radical behaviorism (see later) in particular eschews teleological explanations, explaining behavior purely in terms of past reinforcements. The continued selection of effective actions in behaviorism is viewed as resulting from automatic reinforcements. When the same actions are constantly repeated, they become habitual when faced with the same set of circumstances. But the question arises whether behaviorism or the natural sciences is the most suitable model for understanding human action as opposed to mere physical movement. Researchers who confine their methods to those of the natural sciences limit the questions that can be asked and the behavior that can be explained for the purpose at hand.

(b) The reason-giving explanation is not one that is falsifiable and susceptibility to falsification is the mark of scientific explanation. This criticism is questionable since reason-giving explanations can be tested against different types of evidence.

(c) Reason-giving explanations inhibit the search for causal laws or the factors causing the action (e.g. poverty causes crime) expressed as functional relationships. In reply, it is claimed that external causes do enter into reason-giving explanations, but to restrict explanations to just push-forces or forcing variables like poverty will always result in the explanation being inadequate unless the findings can be related to wants and beliefs. Thus we can still ask 'why' poverty causes crime to try and identify the motives and beliefs at work.

(d) Reasons do not capture the unconscious influences or all the other influences at work. This is so. Unconscious influences can be important, and we are not aware of all the influences affecting us. Thus it seems people clean up more thoroughly if there is a whiff of cleaning fluid in the air or behave more competitively if there is a briefcase in sight (Carey 2007).

In spite of these limitations, it is still true that, for buyer action to be intelligible, explanations must directly or indirectly be tied to wants and beliefs as knowledge of the wants and beliefs lying behind action is needed to give meaning to the action. Reasons give meaning to action because wants and beliefs are tied to the rationality principle, namely: 'If any person wants to achieve goal "A" and believes that action "B" is a way to achieve goal "A" in the circumstances, then that person will be predisposed to take action "B", other things remaining equal.' Both wants and beliefs are involved. This is important to say when many approaches assume, as we have seen, one or the other is all that is needed for explanation. Attitude measures built up from beliefs are unlikely to be predictive without knowing wants. Motivation concepts like 'achievement need' are unlikely to be predictive in themselves without knowledge of beliefs and so on.

INTER-SUBJECTIVE UNDERSTANDING

If consumers were completely illogical, with no reasons for their actions, marketers would have no idea where to start in order to discover what is wanted or why it is wanted. The prediction of buying action rests on taking it for granted that buyers will tend to buy the offering that comes closest to what they believe they want, other things remaining equal. The use of the word 'offering' rather than product is to remind us that consumers buy not just a product per se but the total offering made up of product, price, distribution and promotional image, any of which can constitute the major competitive advantage, while the right mix of all these might be needed to meet customer expectations. We might remind ourselves that distribution outlets, too, has their own demands. Many a clothing company distributing to retail outlets have 'gone to the wall' through a failure to meet the desire of retailers to have exclusive lines within a certain catchment area. A policy of selling to any outlet that is simply creditworthy will not do. To avoid price wars with neighboring stores over the same brands, stores want to cut exclusive deals with designers or manufacturers. A set of brands exclusive to the store can be its critical advantage, providing excitement at the point of sale.

Predicting buying action presupposes some inter-subjective understanding. But it is easier to predict what the consumer does not want than what he or she does want. We usually have no problem predicting what consumers will not want: that they will not want to eat mud pies, would not want to return to sundials for telling the time but would like to have self-cleaning spectacles, cheaper air fares, cheaper gasoline prices and cars that can slide sideways from awkward parking slots.

MOTIVES AND SELF-INTEREST

Unlike economics, ethnopsychology does not assume that the reasons for choosing action 'A' rather than 'B' will always be self-interested, since reasons can be tied more to social appropriateness and personal integrity than to what is most efficient for achieving narrow (material) self-interest. Conscious reflection allows consumers to put desires at a distance to evaluate them, while intentional actions or choices made are not just a dependent variable to be predicted from knowledge of the relative strength of wants. Consumers do not always act on the strongest desires but may exercise self-control to 'savor' the long-term payoff. In the process of wanting-to-want something above instant gratification, the 'higher' want may be adopted.

The strongest motive is that which is stronger than any other single motive, but it need not be stronger than any two or more motives in alliance. The relative strength of all the reasons (wants/desires and beliefs) to do X rather than Y depends on what other desires people have and on beliefs about how satisfactions will be changed by choosing to satisfy X rather than Y. This is important to recognize since searching simply for the most dominant motive may be insufficient. If the consumer deliberates at all, she commonly contrasts what she wants most to do with what she believes she should do, whether for reasons of duty or practical necessity.

If we have a motive (or desire) to do X (buy brand X)
And
We have the ability (mental, physical and financial)
And
The opportunity (e.g. brand availability) to do X
And

The belief that doing X makes most sense in the circumstances, then we come to have an expectation of doing X which in turn:

Leads to
An intention to do X that, other things remaining equal
Leads to
The 'will' to do X and the actual doing of X.
Motive + ability + opportunity + beliefs about means, lie behind a *deliberated* purchase.

Although, as shorthand, we speak of a motive for doing something, in practice there are likely to be several motives at work. Thus a mother may take her children to church, not only to affirm a belief in God and to acknowledge a faith, but also as an attempt to bring up her children as good citizens and to show unity with others in the community. Similarly, people can take the same action for very different reasons, just as consumers can buy an identical make of car for different reasons.

The relative importance of 'motive' versus 'belief' can vary widely, though without a motive (desire/want) there is no voluntary action. Although a reason for action involves both belief and want (or desire if the want is intense), either belief or desire may occasionally be more determining of what is bought. In fact the phrase 'impulse buy' suggests that affect-driven choice (desire) in this instance is dominant. The extent of affect-driven choices is probably understated, as consumers like to rationalize their reasons for buying rather than admit to affect-driven buying. Emphasizing that our buying had utilitarian purposes in mind, rather than purely expressive, typically projects more of an image of being rational.

Traditionally there is controversy among philosophers over whether wants or beliefs are generally more dominant, with Kant (1724–1804) arguing that people can act against their present desires and Hume (1711–76) arguing that all actions occur at one time, instead of another, because a particular desire has the most force at the time. But the more defensible answer is that, in general, both are needed.

If desire, as an intense want, consists of the anticipation of *sensory pleasure*, desire is not, as is sometimes claimed, the only or dominant motive at work. Kagan (1999), a Harvard psychologist, rejects the very notion of human action being mostly motivated by a (narrow hedonistic) desire for sensory pleasure and argues that one universal motive is a wish to regard 'self' as possessing good qualities. Advertising occasionally assumes this. As we shall see later, one finding in social science is that human beings act to avoid experiencing *regret* after buying. Fear of regret may overcome the rush to seek instant gratification. Fear of regret and fear of being ripped off are both fears of losses. People are inhibited from actions likely to bring about guilt, embarrassment or shame, contributing to what Kagan calls a motive for virtue. Adherence to moral norms is tied to feelings of self-respect, while the violation of these norms gives rise to the emotion of guilt.

Consumers may take account of factors such as preservation of the environment and choose manufacturers who exhibit social responsibility such as those who do not exploit child labor, pollute the environment and so on. This is forgotten by writers like Henderson (2001) who claims the 'fad' for corporate social responsibility is doing actual harm, in that it poisons opinion against market capitalism, raises costs and prices and distracts from the goal of profit maximization.

It may violate a person's sense of integrity to accept an unfair transaction with consumers asking what something is worth in an objective sense rather than just what it is worth to them. A consumer may forgo buying, not because the utility of the product to her is less than the price to be paid, but because the price is considered a 'rip-off' (Frank 1988).

Consumers are emotional beings and emotions are not just turned on or off by narrow hedonistic desires for possessions but are influenced by anything that concerns them which, because of our common humanity, may be the plight of others. Folk psychology recognizes that the display of emotion indicates concern. Hence when President Obama did not initially show emotion in respect to the BP oil spill, it was assumed by many he was not concerned. Hence the emotion later, shown in 'jumping on' BP and referring to it as British Petroleum (a name that had been dropped in 1996) to suggest its foreign origins even though a large share of the company was owned by American investors. Folk psychology recognizes that associations are powerful in mobilizing attitudes, so that unkind letters on Obama in my local newspaper talk of President Barak *Hussein* Obama to suggest his connection to Islam.

Emotions inform our thinking, while energizing and intensifying motivation. As the expression goes, emotion puts fire in the belly and provides the energy to battle on and to reverse wavering loyalty. Yet there is no definition of emotion in folk psychology or mainstream psychology that unambiguously differentiates emotion; there is no definite set of features common to all the emotions. The terms often used for emotions are more in the nature of linguistic constructs rather than designated objective properties. Emotions simply have a family resemblance in that any two emotions have certain attributes in common while other pairs of emotions share other attributes. This is not surprising since most behavioral concepts do not have definitions that provide all the necessary and sufficient conditions for something to fall under the concept.

MEANING AS DIRECTING ACTION

'Action concepts' are 'doings' like buying, not 'happenings' like a fall from a horse (Fay 1999). Action concepts express behavior that is done for a purpose and that purpose is tied to the meaning of the action. Those who focus on the meaning of action talk of meaning directing action. 'Meaning' is more than a motive as it involves a set of beliefs about the significance of things. It is not something distinct from wants and beliefs but a convenient way of capturing in one construct the idea of wants, beliefs and the intentions directing action.

Operative reasons and auxiliary reasons, conclusive and absolute reasons

There are operative reasons and auxiliary reasons in buying. *Operative* reasons for buying cover functions sought, while *auxiliary* reasons comprise the various ways for fulfilling the functions sought. Different markets compete whenever they tempt buyers to change their operative reasons (e.g. to buy a new golf cart instead of taking a holiday cruise) but brands compete by focusing on auxiliary reasons (e.g. by showing the firm's brand best matches these auxiliary reasons).

There are conclusive and absolute reasons for buying. A *conclusive* reason for buying is a sufficient reason for choosing one product or brand rather than another, given the circumstances. An *absolute* reason is a sufficient reason for choosing one product or brand rather than another, *regardless of circumstances*. A conclusive reason does not override all other possible reasons but an absolute reason does. A conclusive reason for choosing brand XYZ may be its price but, given a change in circumstances (such as an increase in income), price may no longer be a conclusive reason to buy. Reasons for buying may be conclusive but rarely if ever absolute. Invariably some change in the conditions of purchase will lead a buyer to change her mind as to which product or brand to buy. We assume 'loyal' buyers have absolute reasons for staying with a brand when in fact they only have conclusive reasons. In fact, in most cases, it is better to think of firms *renting allegiance* of their customers as a reminder that, typically, if a critical advantage no longer holds, neither will loyalty. There is always a danger among marketing managers of the 'self-aggrandizement effect'. When things are going well and spirits are high there can be the illusion of control or the belief that management has control over all marketing variables when in fact marketers can only influence product, price, promotion and distribution.

CATEGORIES OF REASONS

Darwall (1983), a philosopher of action, distinguishes three sets of reasons, any of which might be quoted as lying behind action:

- The *real* reasons why someone acted as they did.
- The individual's *expressed* reasons for acting as they did.
- *Justificatory* reasons for the individual to so act, that is, the normative reasons that might justify action.

Darwall's argument focuses on justificatory reasons. He claims there is an intimate relationship between something being a justificatory reason and its capacity to motivate even if only under ideal conditions. In fact, a salesperson setting out justificatory reasons why someone should buy a product can often be the trigger to buying. He argues that there are inter-subjective values like justice, respect for privacy, seeing meaning to life and so on that are basic to the idea of community. Such values translate into a set of shared, objective, justificatory reasons for action. They emotionally motivate in that there is a connection between upholding societal values and having a sense of self-worth and self-respect, while actively promoting such values expresses our identification with others and they with us. As Darwall says, if we were always to act on the strongest desire, then the very notion of settling trade-offs by reasoning about the matter would probably make little sense: the strongest desire, however, may not be the desire to which we give greatest priority. The strongest desire in life is survival but at the battlefront this may not be given the highest priority. Similarly, the consumer may give as her strongest desire the need to shine socially among her peer group but in practice gives greatest priority to looking after her children.

Darwall's fundamental point is that *practical* reasons are at base *impartial* rather than entirely self-centered. This is because thinking about justificatory reasons can lead to new desires. For example, I may have no active desire to support 'animal rights', yet seeing a film on cruelty to animals might activate a desire to do something about it. People (including people as consumers) can be moved by new considerations without there being any active antecedent want. As the Harvard philosopher Quine (1987) points out, self-interest, however enlightened, affords no general rational basis for altruism. Yet there is altruism, stemming, partly at least, from the relationship between acting morally and maintaining self-respect: the capacity to care is tied to our emotional nature.

In interpreting action, ethnopsychology points to reasons, but what sort of reasons? Answers to the question: 'Why did she buy that particular brand of detergent?' involve several types of reason. Thus a researcher might locate the reason in the external world by saying that it was prompted by the discounted brand of detergent being the last one on the shelf. A second reason might concern the consumer's internal goals, namely that she bought it to fulfill her goal of doing all the laundry the next day. A third reason might invoke a moral principle in saying it was wrong to leave dirty clothes hanging around. All these reasons can enter into a reason-giving explanation, as there can be several reasons (motives) involved. It is wrong to assume only a single motive will be at work.

The reason-giving explanation is composed of wants and beliefs: the consumer wanted the detergent to do her laundry the next day as she hated to leave dirty clothes hanging around and believed that the particular brand of detergent was the best for her purposes and also believed the price at which it was being offered was a bargain too good to miss. In framing a reason-giving explanation we start with knowledge of a set of choices under consideration as these provide the set of contrasts and visual cues for understanding the action chosen. But if the reason-giving explanation is to capture real reasons (and not just any reasons) there is a need to record the mental dynamics of deliberation by listening as the consumer talks 'off the top of her head' as she goes about buying. If we want to know what is on the consumer's mind, just listen. When a topic is constantly mentioned, then that topic is one of concern for that person. We will argue later in the text that matters of concern are emotionally impregnated and tied to values.

Ideally in ethnopsychology, explanation takes the form of a narrative, interpreting the cognitive and affective components that led to the intention to buy: before buying, during buying and after buying. In this way the logic of the explanation is revealed (Lewis 1973). Interpretation is aided by mentally simulating what has occurred to ensure the sequence in the narrative captures the temporal and actual detail of the decision. K. A. Ericsson and the Nobel Laureate Herbert A. Simon (1980) claim that people who are asked to think their thoughts aloud are likely to supply reliable data, given no intent to deceive. However, there is more likelihood of bias if people are asked to recall from long-term memory – hence the need to record at the time of buying.

Another way of categorizing reasons is on the basis of the choice criteria employed in the buying decision. Unless we are picking a brand at random, we all have reasons for choosing one brand rather than another which implies criteria against which to compare options. Choice criteria can be complex or be a single criterion such as which brand has most immediate appeal. It can apply just to the product itself or to all elements of the offering: product, price, promotion and distribution. Emotion influences the weighting of choice criteria, which points to the need to give emotional significance to the choice criteria that support the firm's competitive position. As we listen to the consumer before, during and after buying, we can gauge the beliefs and the choice criteria she employs in choosing what she wants. There are six categories of decision criteria.

- *Technical* criteria: These criteria embrace the physical attributes and performance characteristics that are sought by the consumer.
- *Legalistic* criteria: These are imposed by or emanate from outside agencies (e.g. government insistence on wearing a seatbelt while driving or regulations on smoking in public places or what food a restaurant can provide).
- *Integrative* criteria: These criteria reflect the consumer's concern with being better integrated with self or with community.
- *Adaptive* criteria: These criteria refer to the adaptations that occur in coming to terms with risk, decision uncertainty and information overload.
- *Economic* criteria: These criteria are used to rank alternatives on the basis of the relative economic sacrifice being demanded.
- *Intrinsic likeability/pleasure* criteria: These criteria refer to likeability stemming from aesthetics, for example.

These criteria, whether technical, economic, legalistic, integrative, adaptive or likeability, may singly or in combination be reflected in the indicators or proxies that are used to judge the magnitude of their presence (O'Shaughnessy 1986). Consumers regard certain indicators as *prognomic*, that is, as justifying the expectation that they will reflect the true position. In certain cases, a consumer might simply use the brand name as prognomic.

These choice criteria are universal in all decision-making but need to be interpreted for different applications, in that the interpretation of the criteria for industrial buying will differ from consumer buying. They can in fact be applied to all decisions made by the consumer. This includes choice of store:

- Technical, for example quality of goods stocked, assortment and ease of movement within the store
- Economic, for example general level of prices and proximity of store
- Legalistic, for example outlet not banned to consumer as certain outlets are to troops in foreign countries
- Integrative, for example store offers a comfort zone and opportunity for socialization
- Adaptive, for example accepts all returns with receipt
- Intrinsic liking, for example atmospherics, personalized service.

The choice criteria can be applied as a checklist in all decisions. This is useful since all too often there is a lack of recognition that all the criteria might apply and missing one out might result in a suboptimum decision.

STATUS OF FOLK PSYCHOLOGY

There is a major debate over the status of folk psychology that reflects the debate over positivist and perspectivism approaches to social science. The positivist (or in philosophy the logical empiricist – the successor to the logical positivist of the 1930s) favors the establishment of knowledge through the methods used in the natural sciences and, like naturalism (already mentioned), seeks a causal explanation though social science is apt to avoid the term 'cause' for something less demanding like 'contributory factor' or 'forcing variable'. On the other hand, perspectivism claims there are many legitimate ways of viewing a topic and many methods of inquiry that can be equally defensible given our purposes.

Before we embark on any empirical study there is a need for pre-experimental thinking about hypotheses. Folk psychology at present provides many of these. It is not clear where hypotheses about buying action would arise when hypotheses are couched in terms of neuroscience. Auyang (2001) believes that to take away our common sense psychological concepts would eliminate our understanding of mind and that any scientific study of mind should focus on sharpening the meanings of the mental concepts of folk psychology, such as believing and desiring, instead of seeking to eliminate such terms. This is the general position in ethnopsychology. Fodor (1987) goes so far as to argue that to give up our common sense folk psychology that employs the belief-desire format would be an intellectual catastrophe. For Fodor (1981) the core of mental life is 'propositional attitudes', so-called because they express a proposition in the form of she believes *that*, she hopes *that*, he decided *that*, he desires *that* and so on. In philosophy, all psychological states are propositional attitudes because they are assertions *about* something, just as beliefs are statements about how we think the world is and wants are about how we would like the world to be. Thus to restate Fodor, the consumer has beliefs about, has hopes about, makes decisions about and has desires about.

Fodor claims, however, that brains, like computers, are symbol crunchers and the interplay of the propositional attitudes of beliefs, wants, hopes and any other terms in folk psychology make up the language of the brain and are reflected at the level of brain functioning. While agreeing with Fodor about the importance of folk psychology, many philosophers dislike this computer metaphor. Block (1980), for example, claims that viewing the mind as no more than a way of processing information is just dotty. The British linguistic philosopher John Searle (1981) argues that describing mental life in terms of symbol manipulation completely omits understanding: the mind viewed as computer software is a mind without understanding and a mind without understanding is no mind at all. The symbols in processing must have meaning (significance) for the person whose mind it is. In other words, for Searle, there must be *semantic* manipulation for understanding and not just syntactic manipulation. This criticism is fundamental since semantic manipulation means the employment of concepts. Minds are more than computer programs that run on biological hardware (Shapiro 2004). Nonetheless, the mind categorized as a computational system is a defensible perspective in psychology. IBM's Watson supercomputer has shown a remarkable capacity to understand complexities and even ambiguities of meaning. But for all the power of the metaphor of the mind being as software to the brain, computers are at their best when the context is precise and unambiguous. What distinguishes computers is their vast memory storage and they will inevitably displace many workers in law offices, hospitals and so on whose job it is to search for answers to memory-questions. On the other hand, people can make subtle connections and interpretations and deal with rich, vague and ambiguous contexts.

Beliefs, as already defined, tell us how the world is and wants tell us how we would like the world to be. Beliefs, even though sometimes overridden by the emotions, generally track truth as a matter of survival. While it is wants that motivate, beliefs do the steering. But controversies remain. Bittner (2003) would have us locate reasons for action entirely outside the mind on the grounds that reason-giving explanations in terms of wants and beliefs are too vague and obscure. He claims it is difficult to make sense of the motivating-steering distinction since, if a desire moves us to act, it moves us to act in a certain way. This is erroneous thinking in that a desire/want is simply a dispositional/tendency state that has to be supplemented by beliefs about options. The error lies in assuming that a want on its own is more than a disposition to seek a broad goal. If I am hungry I desire something to satisfy my hunger and am predisposed to seek that something. However, beliefs about my tastes and what is available within my price bracket are needed to actually make a specific choice.

CONCLUSION

Ethnopsychology is the systematization of folk psychology or the psychology people use in everyday dealings. Marketing needs to take account of folk psychology to understand the consumer's psychology. Humans act and react to each other in terms of their own psychology rather than the psychologists' psychology and their buying decisions are inevitably influenced by the perspectives generated by folk psychology. To be intelligible, buying action must directly or indirectly be tied to wants and beliefs since knowledge of the wants and beliefs lying behind any action is needed to give meaning to the action. Consumer wants and beliefs are tied to the meaning (significance) of things for them and buying choices reflect this. But if a reason-giving explanation is to capture real reasons (and not just any reasons) there is a need to record the mental dynamics of deliberation by listening as the consumer talks 'off the top of her head' as she goes about buying. The explanation takes the form of a narrative, interpreting the cognitive and affective components that led to the intention to buy: before buying, during buying and after buying. In this way the logic of the explanation is revealed. Interpretation is aided by mentally simulating what has occurred in the narrative to ensure that the sequence in the narrative captures the temporal and actual details of the decision.

DISCUSSION QUESTIONS ON CHAPTER 2 (ETHNOPSYCHOLOGY)

1. 'There is no escaping folk psychology for the marketing manager as the social sciences have a long way to go before they can answer all the questions that need answering in consumer behavior.' Discuss.
2. If ethnopsychology explains consumer actions in terms of wants, beliefs and intentions/actions, show why 'attitude measures' based purely on belief statements are likely to be inadequate for prediction.
3. Are the choice criteria discussed in the text also choice criteria that can be used in all decision-making as a checklist?
4. 'If a consumer acts for a reason, this makes the action intelligible. It does not make the action a rational one.' Discuss.
5. How do you think hermeneutics might help in interpreting a text/protocol detailing a consumer's thoughts before buying, during buying and after buying?

Chapter 3

Ethnopsychology Continued: Application

CHARTING THE BUYING PROCESS (SEE FIGURE 3.1)

If the question 'Why do people buy?' seems somewhat rhetorical, it is only because we seldom look beyond accepting buying as just part of living or a matter of necessity. But to claim we buy as a matter of necessity does scant justice to the variety of consumer goals, wants and beliefs at work. Ethnopsychology has done much to clean up the concepts in everyday use, particularly by analytic philosophers in that branch of philosophy known as *conceptual analysis*. Conceptual analysis points to many statements that are true or false simply as a result of the meaning of the concepts in the statement, for example a consistent service is a reliable service. That said, we would agree with Quine (1951) who shows that new facts might make us change our mind as to what statements are simply conceptual truths.

Figure 3.1 is a model that emerged from asking students in marketing over many years to record a buying episode, asking a consumer to talk spontaneously about the product: (i) before buying (the anticipatory account); (ii) during buying (the contemporaneous account); (iii) after buying (the retrospective account). Each record of an episode of buying was described as a consumer protocol statement.

CONSUMER GOALS/WANTS (SEE FIGURE 3.1)

Goals. Buying is a purposive activity, motivated and directed by the belief that the consequences of buying make life that much better. If asked about life goals, respondents tend to say that the ultimate goal of life is happiness, since happiness is regarded as the final end goal. This is not surprising. In the US, since the American Revolution, happiness is supposed to be within the reach of everyone. And everyone wants it, though without knowing how it is to be achieved or even recognized unless it is merely the subjective feeling that things are going well. It seems a person can have everything he or she could want and yet not be happy – or is it simply that there is something missing but we do not know what it is? Happiness is the total good, an end in itself, so it makes no sense to ask why we seek it.

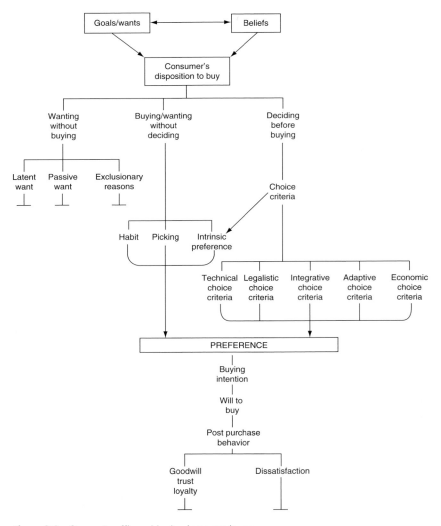

Figure 3.1 Concepts affirmed by buying experience

But this ultimate goal offers no guidance as to how it might be achieved and certainly no guidance to consumers on what they should buy to help achieve it. The evidence suggests individual happiness is fairly stable over time in that each person appears to have an innate set position to which they snap back after every bad or good experience (McMahon 2005). Consumers do, however, have implicit life goals that reflect a vision of the good life and buying action tracks this vision. This vision arises because people are sensitive to contrasts in the human condition, preferring to be:

- Healthy, not ill
- Respected, not despised
- Full of life, excited, not miserable and sluggish
- Fulfilled, not craving fulfillment
- Physically secure, not physically threatened
- Loved and admired, not hated and shunned
- Achieving, not sliding backwards
- Being in control of life, not at the mercy of others
- An insider, not an outsider looking in
- Confident, not insecure
- Serene/relaxed, not tense and anxious
- Beautiful, not ugly
- Rich, not poor
- Clean, not dirty
- Knowledgeable, not ignorant
- Entertained, enjoying life, not bored.

The agreeable polar extremes represent the *preferred life vision*. This list is likely to contain most of the higher level goals expressed by consumers but it is not likely to be exhaustive. Consumers are not tokens of each other and some consumers may subscribe to a list of purely materialistic goals aiming for a completely hedonistic lifestyle. But it is a more inclusive list than that usually put forward in the consumer behavior literature (see Kahle et al. 1986).

Leymore (1975) argues that consumer advertising should strongly link its appeals to such goals on the grounds that effective advertising must always offer (however obliquely) the possibility of enhancing the target audience's chances of achieving life goals. This is recognized in advertising whenever advertising shows how the 'good life' is enhanced by the use of the product. It justifies advertising focusing on consumer experiences and satisfactions with the product, rather than on the product itself. Consumer sensory experience of a product can be highly memorable and be a leading factor in buying the product again. Many companies today offer a more inclusive pleasure-package by offering 'experiences', for example Tiger Beer offers faithful customers access to concerts. Experiences can embrace learning skills, such as at Sheraton's Nha Trang hotel in Vietnam which offers a fully equipped cooking school for guests. Of particular interest is the growth of brand-sponsored online customer groups to foster bonding to the brand.

The degree of satisfaction provided by an offering does not distinguish between the satisfaction emanating from tangible features of the offering, whether in respect to product, price, promotion, or distribution, and the satisfaction generated by the *symbolic* aspects of the offering. Hence attaching to a product an aura of status, beauty, friendliness, excitement or other pleasant associations adds to its desirability. Upmarket possessions generally, illustrated by designer labels, can signal to others substance and status and induce corresponding reactions. But is Leymore right in focusing exclusively on goals or values at the highest level? It could be argued that the goals to which advertising should most directly appeal are the more specific goals of the target audience, which may constitute a specific subculture.

In marketing we want every customer, after buying, using or consuming our offering to have no reservations whatever about the product. In fact, one normative goal of all marketing managers is to reach the stage where all customers buy and consume their product *without reservations* about having bought the best product for the purposes they have in mind.

With multiple life goals constituting the preferred life vision, the consumer cannot seek all of them with equal vigor. The consumer, as a matter of necessity, has to order them, subordinating one to the other, so that at any one time, the consumer has preferences for one life goal over another (e.g. beauty over additional knowledge). This ordering of goals reflects the consumer's *value system*, which is another way of saying consumers have a basic structure of higher level preferences against which they determine goal priorities.

When the value systems of consumers differ, this typically results in different lifestyles. 'Typically' because it is possible for the same lifestyle to be sought by people with different value systems. This is not to suggest consumers are conscious of their value systems. They may not be. We infer value systems from the trade-offs made in choosing this product rather than that, not generally from directly questioning respondents about their values, which is not something they may have thought about.

The adoption of any one lifestyle imposes a loss to the consumer that the rejected way of life might have provided. When people cannot make up their minds about trade-offs it is because they are still deciding priorities or they cannot visualize the consequences of buying one product rather than another. Sometimes one goal may be manifestly subordinate to another as when the goal of being healthy is given priority over more social involvement. But not always; a sufficient number of lower level goals may collectively receive priority just as long-term health may be sacrificed to achieve the numerous instant gratifications with which it conflicts.

Value systems are largely culturally determined because living in society suggests what problems are key and what conduct generates social approval. The desire for social approval and the ability of social groups to bestow such approval is present in all societies. If advertising is offering a solution to meeting the consumer's goals, it will receive attention from consumers if the advertised solution can be shown to:

(a) Be realizable (not utopian)
(b) Have recognizable progress towards goals
(c) Have a socially approved solution.

For instance, if consumers have come to believe that good health or fitness is realizable and to some extent within their control (through diet and exercise), progress is recognizable (e.g. reduction of weight and cholesterol level) and society reinforces the pursuit of such goals, renewed attention will be given to personal fitness. Consumers do on occasion implicitly question what we would call their values, in some cases with a soul-searching that can lead to a reformulation of what they want out of life. It is because people feel they lack sources of advice on how to live life at its best that advertising has been able to fill the void by 'showing' how others get more out of life.

Having goals implies a disposition to seek the state of affairs described by the goals. But the state of affairs described by goals typically underdetermines (i.e. does not completely determine) what activities are undertaken, including what products are sought. Goals simply give the direction, not the 'how', of what to buy. There is rarely a one-to-one correspondence between goals and specific wants; goals are much too general for this purpose. Thus the goal of good health is identified with being free from bodily ailments and feeling fit but there are innumerable activities and products that relate to this purpose. The individual purchase is seldom an isolated event but part of an overall lifestyle. This is why those studying consumer behavior do not confine themselves just to the act of choosing, buying and consuming the product, but also consider the lifestyle of the target audience.

Consumer wants. Consumer wants are shaped by what the consumer believes to be both a desirable and feasible way of life that tracks the preferred life vision. However, if consumers only have a general sense of their goals and possess a flexible value system (which is usually the case) they are open to persuasion as to what products to buy. In fact, the consumer, within constraints, is generally open to persuasion right to the point of sale.

Shopping is a learning experience and consumers can continue to learn right to the point of sale. Consumers are rarely experts but simply collect enough product/brand information to state a preference. This does not mean that they would not like to be experts but sacrifices are involved in that becoming an expert requires time and effort or it may be beyond them. However, not being experts, consumers have less confidence in their judgments. In fact, where buying involves deliberation, consumers are uneasy about trade-offs as there is no objective way of doing the weighting of considerations against values. Even when satisfied with past choices, consumers recognize that things could have changed. New facts, new appeals that bring the consumer's attention to the potential of the product may swing the sale right up to the point of buying. There are many contextual or situational factors within a store such as the store ambience or atmospherics and special promotions that can give rise to an unplanned purchase. Until people have tried all brands, they cannot be absolutely convinced about their preferences but this need not worry them.

To want a particular product is to have a disposition towards using, consuming, or possessing that product. Wants are a disposition to possess the object of the want. Thus, to know someone wants a car is to know he or she is a 'suspect' for buying a car since having the want means the person is disposed towards possessing the car and this in turn suggests the possibility of future buying. Wants express goals since goals subsume wants. If consumers are free to choose, they will choose only that which is wanted (or likely to be wanted), which leads to the marketing truism that wanting something is a necessary condition for being predisposed to buy something and not wanting something is a sufficient condition for not buying it.

Customer orientation is the perspective advocated in marketing which views marketing's job as providing its target group of customers with what they say they want. But it is customer orientation within constraints, since, for example, if asked, customers would not want to pay anything and would prefer the product to be free. Also, professionals like doctors, professors and so on have a responsibility to provide what is needed rather than just responding to expressed wants. Students as consumers evokes the image of students seeking deals and being concerned with the goal of earning power and not with learning or being partners in an environment of learning. In addition to this, a more complete perspective recognizes that consumers are not necessarily conscious of their wants but that wants on occasion need to be activated. No one was demanding zippers, televisions, iPods and automobiles before they were invented and offered to the public. Consumers are not all-knowing about what they want or the products they actually buy. In fact, they may know little about competing brands and possess not perfect but flawed rationality. Even when supplied with exactly what they want, consumers often find, during usage, it is not exactly what they should have sought.

Once we accept that a preferred life vision or lifestyle finds expression in many equally acceptable ways, it follows that many wants are substitutable without any sense of corresponding loss. Persuasion can in such cases lead to the substitution of one want for another want. Even where a want has crystallized into wanting a particular product class, the want can still remain vague on specifics until the time for purchase when consumers look around at what is available. Consumers more often know what they do not want but otherwise, within constraints, generally remain open to persuasion.

Both desires and needs are special types of want. A 'desire' is an intense want which the consumer is acutely aware of not having realized. We usually think of desire as tied to the seeking of pleasure. But 'desire' cannot be equated with mere pleasure-seeking since most things in life that we desire are not sought for pleasure though, like our desire for peace in the world, the achievement might be pleasurable. A 'need' is a want that is a basic requirement for living. Most wants are neither felt as strongly as desires nor felt as needs but are just plain wants: most wants are neither longings for the gratification of desire nor pangs of hunger compelling satisfaction but simply enter as input into some choice process. What is distinctive about pure pleasure-seeking is that it is an end in itself and not instrumental for achieving other goals.

In mathematics, a continuum is a continuous variable with the same underlying metric. 'Satisfaction' is often taken as a continuum ranging from dissatisfaction to mere satisfaction, contentment, enthusiasm and on to delight. This raises the question as to what is the underlying metric. It is assumed to be feelings, but are feelings just feelings? Not so. Feeling 'delight' is an emotion, being 'content' is an overall feeling, while feeling 'dissatisfied' is a feeling that is more an 'inclination' to act. When a common inclination among the target audience is dissatisfaction combined with a desire to complain, complaints should all be taken seriously as they are an important source of information and an opportunity to exercise justice if the complaint is justified.

If a want tells us how we would like the world to be then the 'want' has content in the sense of a visualization of the benefits anticipated if it is met. This concept of a want thus carries with it a number of implications:

- The consumer is not always conscious of his or her wants until a stimulus like advertising facilitates recall or activates the want.
- The consumer may buy a product in anticipation of wanting it so reminding the consumer to plan to buy for the future can help generate sales.
- Consumers may want something they do not need (e.g. cigarettes) but they can also need something they do not want (unpleasant medicines) since a need that is not being met (e.g. need for exercise) may not always manifest itself in a want to remedy the deficiency.
- Active wants take account of feasibility so that expressed wants may not be active and so not necessarily the last word. A consumer may rule out wants for products that are beyond his or her budget or wants for products that are not available. But wants that are currently non-realizable may remain active and prompt action to remedy the situation (e.g. saving for a down payment on a house). In any case, it is important to facilitate the attainment of wants, for example (say) through the provision of credit.
- A want can be described as a 'cluster concept'; that is, a want can be thought of as a cluster of attributes not all of which must be possessed by any offering for the consumer to feel the want is being met.
- Consumers may have a dormant want for what at the conscious level they do not believe they want, and may think they want what in fact they do not want. Wanting something is neither a necessary nor sufficient condition for the object possessing actual worth for the consumer. What consumers might want with perfect understanding of their goals (and needs) may differ widely from what is currently wanted.
- Product wants change as the lifestyles of consumers change. Some wants disappear, just as the change in lifestyle from formal to informal attire radically reduced the demand for men's and women's hats and gloves. Informality is tied to the desire for convenience since informality in dress and at dinner takes less effort.

- Old wants are replaced by new wants when new products come along that perform functions better. Think of today's products that were unknown until around the middle of the last century, such as television, penicillin, ballpoint pens, the pill, credit cards, panty hose (tights), dishwashers, clothes dryers and air conditioners. Entirely new wants also arise. An increase in income, for example, makes realizable what may previously have been considered a pipe dream (such as possession of an automobile), while additionally leading to a demand for a better match between what is wanted and what is offered. This, in turn, leads to increasing segmentation of markets.

CONSUMER BELIEFS

If a consumer wants a specific product, it implies a belief that the product can provide some, or most or all, of the benefits anticipated. A belief tells us how we think the world is and is a disposition to accept that certain statements (e.g. about a product) are more likely to be true than false (or vice versa) or that certain things (e.g. buying) should be done (or not done). Beliefs are the principal guides to what actions should be taken to satisfy wants. Hence advertising tries to link its appeals to generally held beliefs or beliefs that can be changed. Thus, many advertisements for deodorants and so on exploit the commonly held belief that others are likely to reject us on the most trivial of grounds, so that 'image management' rather than real worth is what counts. Image management is not confined to what one *says* but to everything one *does* down to the clothes one wears.

The term perception is often used as a synonym for belief in folk psychology – and in marketing – when we wish to avoid the suggestion that beliefs are necessarily conscious beliefs. Thus to say the consumer perceives no difference between two rival brands carries less of a suggestion of conscious prior awareness than to say the consumer believes there is no difference between the two brands.

The standard view of perception is that it is a process of becoming aware of something and then interpreting what it is. But Bennett, a neuroscientist, and Hacker (2003), a philosopher, will have none of this. While perceiving can be used to refer to the act of perceiving or the internal mental state that results, Bennett and Hacker deny that the neural processes underlying perception constitute any *process* of perception, as perception occurs instantaneously: as soon as one sees something, one has seen that something. Most of us in the social sciences who have been brought up on the notion of perception as a process find ourselves slipping back to this way of thinking even if we have been put right by Bennett and Hacker. Perception on their view is more a *recognitional capacity* rather than an interpretive process.

Beliefs can control and inform action all the way from shaping wants into specific product preferences to guiding post-purchase actions like returning the product as unsatisfactory. A consumer may believe he or she has a particular want. But even if that want amounts to a strong desire for something, it does not follow that the consumer will rush out and act on the want. Beliefs as to the consequences of acting on the want typically come to mind – a belief about the consequences of buying and about the consequences of buying in relation to the satisfaction or frustration of other wants. A mark of rational decision-making is taking account of likely consequences.

Beliefs about products possess content in terms of which product attributes (e.g. furniture covers made of plastic) produce what effects (e.g. looking cheap). It is beliefs about the effect of a product having or not having a certain feature (e.g. a diesel engine) at a certain level (e.g. size of engine) that influences the consumer's choice criteria.

Initially, when a purchase is first contemplated, the beliefs that guide and constrain the consumer may be relatively few. Information search by the consumer is one way of acquiring additional beliefs to narrow the search for what is wanted. But information search requires effort so consumers not uncommonly remain ignorant of what they should know for rational decision-making. Also, unpalatable information may be avoided ('just cannot bear to read it') if it is likely to cause discomfort (e.g. getting on the scales each morning). Information search, too, can be hobbled by stress that occurs when the decision-maker believes it is not possible to avoid extremely negative outcomes (Janis and Mann 1977). It is also true that a person's perspective influences the sources chosen as reliable. Stalin was told on several occasions, mainly by the British, the exact date for the German invasion but he interpreted the sheer quantity of such reports as proof that it was a misinformation campaign by the British. It is often claimed that national intelligence services have an institutional bias towards information obtained through spies, collaborators, phone taps and other forms of secret information as opposed to believing what may be more common knowledge. They may often be right, but the evidence suggests they can also be very wrong. Much the same ignoring of intelligence occurs under various US administrations. Paul Pillar (2011), who served twenty-eight years at the Central Intelligence Agency (CIA) and the National Intelligence Council, shows how little impact intelligence analysis has, given that both presidents and their advisers distort and misuse the intelligence function. Before 9/11, the CIA constantly and loudly provided clear, strong, evidentially-based warnings about Al-Qaeda's intent to cause mass casualties through attacks on the US mainland. Little notice was taken of such warnings.

One limit on acting rationally is the absence of valid information. Mark Twain once wrote something to the effect that the trouble with the world is not that people know too little, but they know so many things that just aren't so. But initial beliefs can determine a purchase if the want for the product category is there. A purchase may, for example, be prompted by an advertisement if the advertised product (such as a dress) is believed to be the best one to buy. Initial beliefs may also direct shopping strategy. As one respondent worded it: 'Everyone thinks I am lucky to have a whole apartment to furnish from scratch but it is, in fact, a rather anxious time with no room for mistakes and no chance of extravagances so I will need to shop around to make sure I will have no regrets.'

Initial beliefs can range from general ideas about what is wanted to highly specific beliefs about a product class ('I wanted a wool carpet as past experience had shown me that wool is the only material that wears really well') to specific beliefs about brands ('Sony is a good name'). This is so because consumers start the buying process with different levels of experience.

We have spoken of beliefs 'coming to mind' as if only conscious beliefs influence behavior. This is not so. Implicit in every act of buying are beliefs we take for granted. Some may never have been thought about even though if examined they would be readily endorsed. For example, consumers in the US make the assumption that stores will not be out of stock the next time they visit and act accordingly. Where experience shows such assumptions to be untrue, buying patterns change radically. Implicit assumptions that would be endorsed if raised are *latent beliefs*. But there are other beliefs that might not be openly endorsed if exposed. Such beliefs may reflect on the consumer's self-image or they may be socially imprudent. Thus even at the trivial level, few consumers come right out and say they bought something because they believe it signals to the world their good taste and affluence. But such beliefs can often be read between the lines when people talk about their purchase.

Beliefs are held with different degrees of certainty and seldom held with complete certitude. Probably most beliefs are adopted without serious consideration and so are easily changed. As a consequence, beliefs about products and brands are seldom incorrigible and immutable but are open to correction and change through learning. In fact, as Mortimer Adler (1985), a popular writer on philosophy, points out, when truths are necessary truths (e.g. parallel lines never meet) we do not preface such truths by saying we believe them to be true. Beliefs are often qualified by saying I believe this is *probably* so. We use the term 'probable' in general conversation simply to qualify the force of an assertion and not to make any prediction. If I speak of something being highly probable, it not only suggests what is likely to happen but gives a suggestion of firm backing. The mathematical treatment of 'probability' is a natural extension of the term's use in daily life. If a consumer knows about the high probability of a drug harming him but consumes it nonetheless, he is *reckless*. If he pays no regard to the harmful effects he is regarded as *negligent*.

If beliefs are, for all practical purposes, neither incorrigible nor immutable and beliefs enter into buying, then new information via (say) advertising always holds out the possibility of changing behavior. This is a statement of the obvious yet it seems to run into conflict with the finding that an advertisement need not necessarily be believed to be effective. This is puzzling until it is appreciated that the opposite of belief is not disbelief (which is a form of belief itself) but *doubt*. Consumers who buy a product on the basis of advertising they completely disbelieve are likely to be very few indeed. When their numbers appear to be high it is likely that they doubt the claims made rather than completely disbelieving them. I may doubt the claims made in an advertisement but still buy as I may be anxious or even desperate for a solution to my problem.

While doubt is the opposite of belief, the opposite of doubt is *credulity*. While having doubt is rational when the evidence is thin or ambiguous, the credulous consumer is one who is easily taken in through being too trusting and not weighing up the evidence. It often happens that statements made by politicians to the converted are taken to be obvious truths rather than requiring empirical or theoretical support (e.g. 'The more the government tries to create jobs, the fewer the jobs that get created'). If people are wedded to a certain perspective, they are apt to assimilate just about anything as true if it coheres with that perspective.

The *coherence theory of truth* is a theory of warranted assertibility and is all-pervasive in that coherence with an existing viewpoint is typically the criterion for accepting something as true or rejecting it as false. Coherence in the coherence theory of truth is more demanding than mere consistency, involving as it does relationships that are explanatory and inferential. A current ad (2011) for the Subaru car offers to give $250 to the buyer's favorite charity on buying the car. This may suggest something ethically positive about the car manufacturer but it would cohere with my perspective to suggest the buyer would prefer a $250 cash payment to do with what he wants. Politicians seldom ask 'Is it true?' but ask themselves 'Will it persuade?' It is more likely to persuade if it coheres with the perspective or set of beliefs of the target audience. It is difficult to be on the side of truth when it can damage self-interest. But assertions need to be challenged by asking: What follows if such assertions are true? What evidence would be relevant to such a claim? Or are the assertions just definitionally or conceptually true – that is, just truisms?

Thagard's (2000) notion of coherence is a situation where the various elements fit together by being connected in some way, while at the same time avoiding inconsistencies and incompatibilities. Seeking coherence in everyday life, Thagard argues, means fitting something puzzling into a coherent pattern of mental representation made up of concepts, beliefs, goals/wants and actions. In other words, it means fitting something into a perspective already adopted. Thagard would argue that coherence is a necessary condition for something to have meaning for the individual.

In philosophy, the coherence theory of truth goes with 'idealism', where the reality of interest is the reality of the mental since there is nothing outside the mind for coherence to correspond to. In contrast, the *correspondence theory of truth* accords with 'empiricism' in arguing that a claim is true only if it corresponds to facts in the world; that is, something is true only if the world is as the claim says it is. Thagard finds the distinction between the coherence and correspondence theories not quite as rigid or strong as it appears since he argues that we have no means other than coherence to infer whether something does in fact correspond to the world. On the other hand, Thagard acknowledges that coherence-based reasoning is pervasive in human thinking and there is an echo here of those who stress the role of pattern-recognition in making things meaningful. Thagard would claim that buyers find satisfaction when an offering has the coherence that is sought. When there is coherence about a purchase, buyers feel a general sense of well-being whereas a lack of coherence with other beliefs and purchases contributes to anxiety and unpleasant surprise. The elements of any offering (product, price, promotion and distribution) should cohere both among themselves and the functions for which they are being bought. If Thagard is right, coherence is something that is sought in buying and key to making things meaningful. Thagard spends his major efforts trying to explicate the various kinds of coherence since it is not always obvious what type of coherence is being sought.

'Rooms to Go' sell package sets for rooms, from sofas to lamps. In accepting such 'all-in-one' sets, consumers are in effect delegating the job of selecting a coherent set of furniture to the seller. Not every consumer has what it takes to make what are essentially aesthetic and not just utilitarian decisions. We know, too, that juries make sense of a mass of evidence by pulling it together into a coherent narrative. They then use that narrative to evaluate the stories told by prosecutor and the defense. According to Pennington and Hastie (1993), it is on the basis of this evaluation that jurors accept or reject what they were told.

Needless to say there are other theories, such as the *pragmatic theory* of truth which says we believe something is true if it works or has practical results such as having predictive value, making us satisfied and so on, while the *performance theory* of truth claims that calling something true is merely a 'speech act' – simply an agreement with what has been stated (a position adopted by some postmodernists).

There are additional reasons why the claims of an advertisement may be doubted but the consumer still buys:

- The consumer may have doubts about the promise proclaimed by an ad but still goes ahead and buys because, if the promise holds, it means a lot to the consumer.
- The disputed claims may be irrelevant to the consumer's want; it is the other attributes of the product that elicit purchase.
- A less exaggerated form of the claim is believed which is enough to stimulate purchase.
- The purchase involves little risk or potential regret and the consumer believes he or she should give the product a try.
- The claims have high meaning or significance for the consumer so buying offers hope.

This leads to a consideration of the evidential support that consumers are likely to have for their beliefs. It would be expected that consumer certitude in respect to their beliefs would be directly related to the evidence in support of them. The relationship, however, is far from perfect. Consumers harbor and cherish many beliefs about products and brands for which they could produce little or no evidence. When acquiring information is costly in time and effort, buying decisions may be based on impression. One purpose of advertising is to reduce the cost and effort of acquiring information, though the information provided by advertising is unlikely to be objectively balanced. In any case, consumer beliefs, within limits, can be formed, changed or reinforced by persuasion. On some occasions, accepting the best information on, for example, our medical condition could lead us to abandon hope. Since the abandonment of hope results in a state of *despair*, we are all too willing to cling to hope by grasping at straws or perhaps indulging in fantasies about miracle cures. In any case, there are many sellers out there willing to exploit this fact by promising cures that are simply worthless.

Wants and beliefs form an *interacting system*, since wanting something to be true can influence whether a person holds certain beliefs. Similarly, passionately believing something to be true goes a long way towards adopting wants that are supportive of that belief. Thus if the consumer believes passionately that orange juice can ward off many diseases, she is likely to want to buy orange juice.

THE INTERACTING NATURE OF GOALS, WANTS AND BELIEFS (FIGURE 3.1)

Buying actions are meant to cohere and harmonize with the goals, wants and beliefs of the consumer. Buying actions are undertaken only as long as the consumer believes they are in line with wants/goals. The consumer has a plurality of wants/goals and the means at his disposal, like money, can act as a constraint which implies choices have to be made. Consumer goals and wants are also circumscribed by beliefs in that beliefs about what is and what is not feasible can affect the choice of goals and wants. On the other hand, goals and wants activate beliefs since the beliefs reflected in the consumer's value system determine trade-offs in setting goal priorities. Buying actions in fact depend on and influence beliefs, since buying is justified by antecedent beliefs which in turn may be modified as a result of the buying actions taken.

Consumer reasons for contemplating buying can always be expressed in terms of the wants and beliefs: consumer purchases are always perceived to be articulations of wants and applications of beliefs. Reasons that favor buying lead to an intention to buy. The mental process leading from wants and beliefs to intention to buy is a form of practical reasoning along the lines first suggested by Aristotle and developed more recently by philosophers Anscombe (1972) and Von Wright (1983). With regard to Anscombe, it was her book on *intention* that resulted in the topic (discussed earlier) called 'action theory'.

At the very simplest level, the following is illustrative of practical action:

Goals:	to be knowledgeable, not ignorant, and to make sense of the world around.
First premise:	I want to keep abreast of the news.
Second premise:	Unless I buy and read a newspaper I will not be able to keep abreast of the news.
Conclusion:	Therefore, I must buy and read a newspaper.

The goal expresses a vision of being knowledgeable rather than ignorant. The first premise expresses a 'want'. The second premise expresses a 'belief' about the (causal) relationship between keeping abreast of the news and the buying of a newspaper. The conclusion prescribes the action to be taken. The 'want' provides the motive while 'beliefs' steer the buying action taken. This is a simplistic view, however, of most buying decision processes in that it ignores many complexities, whereas few of us overtly undertake such a mental process.

While folk psychology provides a conceptual lens for imputing an interpretation in terms of wants and beliefs to human behavior, we use the term 'impute' more fittingly when we interpret behavior through a social science paradigm that offers more direction and focus than does folk psychology.

The focus resulting in Figure 3.1 was on reasons and the reason-giving explanation. In the process there emerged a contribution to ethnopsychology and an application of hermeneutics in the recording of consumers as they went about buying. One of the findings was the six criteria (already discussed) used in buying: a set of categories that are exhaustive and mutually exclusive when used in evaluating a decision.

Verbal protocols are most useful for generating reasons for buying and for discovering the inferences most likely to be made. As already stated, Ericsson and Simon (1980) claim verbal reports are most fruitful if buyers are simply asked to report their thoughts as they happen rather than be asked later to remember what they thought. A great variety of ways have been invented for analyzing 'thinking aloud' protocols and their strengths and limitations are well known. Thus verbal protocols offer limited guidance when the interest lies (as in cognitive psychology) in the mental process itself. As Baron (1988) says, asking a respondent what comes to mind when given the word 'table', the word 'chair' might come to mind but not any description of the mental process that occurs in a task like this. Thinking processes are very tied to the nature of the task at hand rather than to the nature of the mind. Needless to say, it is also true that not all information that might be relevant is necessarily available to conscious memory.

CONSUMER'S DISPOSITION TO BUY (FIGURE 3.1)

Goals/wants and beliefs are jointly involved in generating a disposition to buy. We use the word 'disposition' because wants and beliefs in themselves are not sufficient to activate buying. Thus my goal/want is to possess a sports car and I believe that the BMW sports car is ideal and I also believe I can afford the car. However, I may still not buy it since there can be wanting without buying.

WANTING WITHOUT BUYING (FIGURE 3.1)

The premise behind Figure 3.1 is that people have a vision of the good life that manifests itself in a set of goals/wants and beliefs. The consumer's bundle of wants is not a random collection but a coordinated system that represents a specification of the good life for them. At the top of Figure 3.1 are the goals/wants that dispose consumers to buy (as discussed earlier). However, consumers can be disposed towards buying a product without actually doing so. In Figure 3.1, this is labeled 'Wanting without buying'. Consumers want many products without any intention of buying because:

- The 'want' for the product may be *latent* or dormant because consumers are not aware of what a certain product can do to enrich their lives.
- The 'want' for the product may be *passive* until the consumer is made more aware of the potential benefits of a product.
- Consumers may be held back from buying by *exclusionary* reasons that take them, temporarily or permanently, out of the market through, for example, shortage of money, promises to parents or significant others and so on.

In calculating market potential, there is this need to take account of the extent to which marketing can activate latent and passive wants to increase market penetration and the extent to which market penetration is potentially dampened by exclusionary reasons.

BUYING WITHOUT DECIDING (FIGURE 3.1)

The next category is 'Buying without deciding'. Here the consumer proceeds to buying without undertaking any deliberation of the pros and cons of buying. If we define decision-making as involving deliberation of the pros and cons, making a decision is something distinct from mere choosing.

In buying from *habit*, consumers simply buy on the basis of past choices and do not undertake the deliberation of the pros and cons of alternatives that signifies decision-making. Many grocery products are chosen on the basis of what has been bought before. But many other products are often bought on habit as well. Thus when a consumer is replacing an old product, she might buy the same brand (e.g. of car), seeing no need to look elsewhere. Practically every decision we make, whether about what products to buy or what time to rise in the morning, sets a precedent for making the same decision in similar circumstances. But the habitual buying of the same brand should not be confused with loyalty to the brand. Some of us have bought Microsoft operating systems over many years but only because we are not aware of adequate substitutes. In fact, if we consider Microsoft has a monopoly, the use of the term 'loyalty' has no meaning in this context. Sometimes we continue buying the same brand because of the information fatigue involved in considering rival brands; falling back on the familiar is rather reassuring. Yet habitually buying the same brand does suggest sufficient satisfaction to continue purchasing the product. A seller in fact seeking to *convert* such consumers may have problems getting their attention and demonstrating that what they have to offer justifies the costs of change. Also firms seek to cement habitual buying through 'loyalty cards' that reward each purchase. Interestingly for many firms, 'loyalty cards' are not issued to ensure patronage but to obtain information on the customer and her purchases when she swipes the card at checkouts. This facilitates more focused marketing and segmentation.

Consumers may avoid decision-deliberation by just *picking* a brand as one picks a cigarette out of a packet: an instant choice bereft of reflection. The *Yellow Pages*, which simply lists suppliers, assumes that many buyers merely pick rather than inquire further.

Finally, many purchases are made purely on the basis of *intrinsic liking*, where the consumer follows the rule: I like it, therefore I choose it. The problem for the producer lies in identifying what will catch the fancy of the target set of consumers since tastes can vary widely. Clothes are obviously one category of purchase that is apt to be bought on this basis but so also are cars when there is an assumption that all the makes are of equal reliability. There is commonly an emotional urge, when we see something we particularly like, to want it immediately. The desire for this *instant gratification* is particularly highlighted in behaviorism (Chapter 4) but also in behavioral economics (Chapter 10).

DECIDING BEFORE BUYING (FIGURE 3.1)

The final category, 'Deciding before buying', describes those who deliberate the pros and cons before buying and hence can justifiably be regarded as undertaking decision-making. We assume too readily that the rational buyer in a problematic buying situation will do an information search and use such information to judge what or whether to buy. But in so many buying situations there is no perceived uncertainty, while the costs in time and resources weigh against undertaking an information search and time-consuming decision-making. There is also the question as to whether further study will result in understanding. Hence it is wrong to claim that consumers generally decide before choosing.

Those who undertake decision-making implicitly or explicitly use one or more of the six choice criteria discussed earlier. Although we typically think of beautiful things moving us emotionally, every one of the criteria is capable of arousing us emotionally because it is our concerns that lie behind emotional arousal and any of these six criteria may on occasion be of great concern.

Providing we recognize that there will be some reinterpretation of the criteria for applications to areas of life beyond buying, the criteria have general applicability to all decision-making. Thus take the subject of capital punishment, which arouses so much emotion. Often it is evaluated purely in terms of *technical* criteria: does it work, in the sense of does it deter? But the other five criteria are relevant. There are *legalistic* criteria in that capital punishment for many people violates human rights or at least violates guidelines issued by international bodies like the United Nations. There are *integrative* criteria in that capital punishment is divisive, with some claiming it falls disproportionately on minority groups or, in contrast, that without capital punishment, people would feel like taking the law into their own hands in the interests of 'justice'. There are *adaptive* criteria in that there is always some uncertainty that an innocent person may be executed. There are also *economic* criteria in judging relative costs in relation to benefits. Capital punishment should save money ('If you can't save souls, save money') but in practice the cost of constant appeals over decades can be more expensive than the cost of incarceration over a lifetime. There is finally the criterion of *intrinsic liking* in that the very idea of taking the life of another is repugnant or at least distasteful to many people.

In using protocol statements recording 'off-the-top-of-the-head' thoughts of the consumer before buying, during buying and after buying, there is recognition of the value of *listening* to members of the target market. If we wish to know what consumers want, believe and think, there is no adequate substitute for listening to the consumer's own testimony, not channeled by a set of predetermined questions and answers.

PREFERENCE (FIGURE 3.1)

Whether it is a case of buying without deciding or deciding before buying, the output is a preference (comparative desire) where consumers state their choice. We expect preferences to be transitive; that is, if I prefer A to B and B to C, I would prefer A to C. But an intransitive preference (preferring C to A) is irrational only if it can be shown that A is better in all respects and at all times and on all occasions. Intransitive preferences involve inconsistency only when it can be shown that the judgments cannot be simultaneously maintained without contradiction. But preferences are not absolute but vary over time and occasion for buying.

BUYING INTENTION (FIGURE 3.1)

Consumers can have a brand preference without any intention to buy since intention is a commitment to action. Buying intentions can lead to other intentions just as my intention to buy a computer may lead to my intention to buy a printer or to intentions about where to shop and how to pay. All voluntary buying is accompanied by an intention to buy, though not necessarily with a *planned intention* to buy. The consumer may buy on impulse. An 'impulse' is a strong notional want that finds expression in a response to some stimuli without the consumer being acutely conscious of exactly what is being sought. With impulse, intention is not part of any plan. The intention is *in the action*, just as there is intention in the action of putting my foot on the brake in an emergency to prevent an accident.

WILL TO BUY (FIGURE 3.1)

An intention to buy is not a promise to buy. It is not equivalent to saying 'I will' or 'I promise to buy brand *B* tomorrow'. However, an expressed intention to buy *B* does contain a resolve to buy *B* since buying intentions and actual purchase are linked much more closely than wants and buys. Nonetheless, expressed intentions are contingent, like saying: 'If the buying situation envisaged is the same next week, I will buy brand *B*.' Forming an intention is like going into gear in driving a car but the *will* (endeavoring) is needed to take the final step of pressing the accelerator. Yet intentions typically possess inertia; that is, they have a certain stability that inhibits reconsideration.

Intentions are not blind compulsory forces but usually emanate from reasons. The more powerful the reasons, the more likely is the fulfilling of the intention, unless it is frustrated by situational factors like non-availability or nuances of context, such as the rudeness of a salesperson.

POST-PURCHASE BEHAVIOR (FIGURE 3.1)

Post-purchase behavior may reflect satisfaction leading to trust and goodwill or to dissatisfaction leading to complaints and perhaps bad-mouthing the product. When a purchase is a new buy, there will be immediate post-purchase feelings and feelings that come after using the product. Immediately after buying there can be the search for reassurance about having bought wisely. There can also be dissatisfaction because of last-minute happenings, such as buying a new car and finding no gasoline in the tank. But in speaking of post-purchase behavior, the focus is on long-term satisfaction with the product as a basis for generating goodwill, trust and ultimately loyalty.

It is a truism to say that consumers come to know better what they want after buying, possessing, using and consuming the product. Experience with a product throws up knowledge about additional benefits and deficiencies that were not anticipated (Gardial et al. 1994). A product can be found to have worthwhile features not sought at the time of purchase but sought thereafter (e.g. wash-and-wear trousers) or a product can live up to expectations in terms of technical performance but still prove to have major flaws (e.g. a luxury soap that does not dry one's skin – the reason for purchasing – but lasts only two weeks). A purchase can perform outstandingly on all the criteria that entered into the decision to buy it but may still be regretted. The consumer may have judged wisely but used an erroneous framework, for example, about his or her future life. This is not uncommon in buying a house, where its location and size seem no longer to fit the new job and lifestyle. Alternatively, the consumer may have erred by drawing on too narrow a range of experience. Thus the consumer may have bought a Toshiba computer on the strength of being highly satisfied with a Toshiba television (or vice versa) but the result may be disappointment. It may even be that certain things were wrongly taken for granted; for example, the dissatisfied European customer of satellite television who assumed that he would be able to see all European television channels, that reception would always be excellent and that foreign programming was going to be superior to that in his own country! Post-purchase evaluation can still be ambiguous and this is common with many over-the-counter drugs. By and large, though, consumers seek confirmation that their choice was superior to the alternatives to avoid the discomfort of not having chosen wisely. Because habitual buying is so common, many, if not most, purchases do not give rise to feelings of doubt. If the purchase decision was important, difficult and irrevocable (e.g. buying a house) there are likely to be post-purchase attempts to justify the wisdom of the purchase. Even when consumers are unable to buy the best, they may rationalize that they would have bought what they did regardless of wealth. But with increases in wealth such rationalizations disappear as consumers are less prepared to make do with second best. In any case, the consumer has to interpret experience with a product and experience is not unambiguous so that interpretations can be influenced by marketing communications (Hoch and Deighton 1989).

Unexpected positive benefits are evaluated more positively than expected benefits, while unexpected negative experiences with a product are evaluated more negatively than expected negative experience. Post-purchase satisfaction is influenced by the effort (physical, mental and emotional) that went into obtaining the product in that disappointment is greater when one fails after trying hard. Also, when you have had to buy something (e.g. because others insisted), there is less pleasure in the purchase and a strong tendency to look for defects, so more dissatisfaction can be expected.

IDENTIFYING CHOICE CRITERIA

The choice criteria used by consumers can be discovered through the use of protocols. In the protocol, a sample of consumers is asked to give a continuous verbal report: that is, to think aloud:

- before buying (the anticipatory account)
- during buying (the contemporaneous account)
- after buying (the retrospective account).

All thoughts that occur to them are recorded. The record of this verbal report is called a *protocol*. Such protocols are sometimes used to study mental processes but here we are just concerned with using them to identify wants, beliefs and choice criteria and anything about the decision-making process that can be captured. Sometimes the buying decision takes place over a long period of time and it may not be possible to conveniently record the whole buying episode but resort may have to be made to recording different consumers at the different stages of before, during and after.

At the time of taking the protocol, any situational factors that might have unconsciously influenced the consumer should be recorded. Similarly, it is useful to note the consumer's actions since sometimes thought manifests itself in what consumers do and not just in what they say.

The meaning of the situation for the individual emerges in the form of the reasons given to justify decisions or actions taken. But when consumers are simply asked about their reasons, not all the answers reflect the real reasons since some will be rationalizations or socially appropriate, prudent replies. If we want to capture as many of the real reasons as possible, it is more likely to happen if we record at the time what people have to say ('off the top of their heads') before buying, during buying and after buying. It is better to just let consumers talk rather than question them or ask them to recall later what went through their minds. Verbal reports are less useful when subjects are asked to remember what they thought, rather than report their thoughts as they happen.

The whole process of protocol recording and analysis should be based on rules that guide objectivity; rules such as: (a) meticulous observation and recording of what is said without any leading questions being put to the respondent; (b) even-handed review of the social science literature for concepts and findings that would seem to be relevant to the analysis; (c) scrupulous attention to the evidence contained in the protocol and the observations made at the time, regardless of whether these support the analyst's evolving interpretation; (d) choosing among rival interpretations on the basis of the best information and evidence available; (e) a resolution not to go beyond the evidence in suggesting marketing implications.

It is sometimes suggested that the consumers' own account of their reasons for buying should be taken as decisive. This is the doctrine of 'privileged access' but it should not be taken to be universal. An observer or protocol interpreter may have insight that the respondent lacks. If humans are rational animals, they are often also rationalizing animals, protecting their egos.

Within any particular segment, a fairly small sample will quickly yield the choice criteria being used. However, if interest lies in discovering how the various choice criteria are weighted, then a proper sampling procedure should be instituted.

Interpretation of action: meaning and explanation

With regard to the interpretation of protocol statements, Hollis (1996), a philosopher, regards the question of how actions are to be interpreted as ambiguous. This is true, though all questions are ambiguous until you know what the questioner is getting at. This is apt to be forgotten by those preparing questionnaires or those at interviews who find it clever to ask the interviewee, 'Tell me, what makes Mr Doe, Mr Doe?' as happens in one current advertisement.

For Hollis, the interpretation of action must capture both meaning and explanation.

> With respect to *meaning*, interpretation covers:
>
> *Overt meaning*, for example: 'What did he succeed in saying?'
> This is the *action's meaning*.
> *Covert meaning*, for example: 'What did he intend to say and intend in saying it?'
> This is the *actor's meaning*.
> With respect to *explanation*, interpretation involves:
> *Overt explanation*, for example: 'Why was the utterance apt?'
> This is the legitimating reason(s).
> *Covert explanation*, for example: 'What was his motive in uttering the text?'
> This is the *actor's real reason*(s)

(Hollis 1996: 251)

Table 3.1 is a summary. Hollis argues that a complete interpretation of action involves answering all four parts and not just the first three, which cover significance and intentions: motive must be considered for an interpretation to be complete. In answering the four parts of the question, the interpreter needs to take account of context. Thus in answering the first part ('What did he succeed in saying?'), Hollis argues that the interpreter ideally cites both the social norms in respect to what a person must, can or may do in the context and any expressive elements that take account of the context. The question arises as to whether a complete interpretation of an action is needed given our purposes.

Group decision-making

Hollis acknowledges that things are less simple in group decision-making because it is the participants who decide the rules of their relationship rather than being guided by societal norms. Debate about what any decision-making unit (DMU) will do is complicated not only by the uncertainty inherent in all decision-making but because of the politics involved

Table 3.1 Summary of Hollis

	Overt	Covert
What?	Action's meaning	Actor's intention
Why?	Legitimating reasons	Actor's real reasons (motive)

(After Hollis 1996).

in trying to achieve alliances among participants with varying motives or interests. In organizational buying, participants are likely to be constrained by rules (such as zero tolerance of gifts from suppliers) and are formally accountable for their decisions. Showing the collective rationality of a group decision, argues Hollis, is to show its rationality, namely by demonstrating why it was rational for the participants to have pooled their different interests and reached the decision they did, taking into account the complexity of the buy, its centrality to the user and the perceived risk involved.

In many spheres of life, there is a danger of groupthink where the group makes wrong or faulty decisions because group pressures lead to the ignoring of alternatives or even to irrational actions that can dehumanize other groups. This can happen in a group concerned with buying. Janis (1982), who invented the term 'groupthink', listed eight symptoms of groupthink in a group that is trying to make a decision. These are the illusion of invulnerability; collective rationalization; belief in inherent morality; stereotyped views of out-groups; direct pressure on dissenters; self-censorship; the illusion of unanimity; and self-appointed 'mind guards'. Groupthink is most likely in highly cohesive groups under pressure to make a unanimous decision. But the more tightly integrated a group is and the more the support of each for the other, the greater is the resistance of the whole group to change.

In marketing, the concept of the DMU is mainly considered in industrial marketing and often treated as if all organizational decision-making has close commonality in all buying decisions. Yet there is light industry, taking small manufactured articles and assembling them into other products; there is heavy industry involving the use of large machines to make objects such as locomotives; there is the chemical industry manufacturing drugs, paints, explosives, pesticides, fertilizers, plastics and so on, with some production processes being more like large-scale versions of laboratory processes. And what about agriculture, fishing and services generally? In one of the earliest contingency approaches to organization, Joan Woodward (1965) sought to show the relationships between organization structure and type of industry, which she divided into: (a) unit and small batch production; (b) large batch and mass production; and (c) process production, as in the chemical industry. If decisions on organization structure differ with the type of industry, it is reasonable to assume there are likely to be differences in buying decision processes.

Appendix 3A

Student Project: Obtaining a Script or Protocol of a Buying Episode

1. Approach a member of the target customer group who is about to make a purchase and ask if she or he would mind talking about the purchase and the talk being recorded:

   - Before they buy (the anticipatory account)
   - During buying (the contemporaneous account)
   - After buying (the retrospective account)
   - Some purchases are made over a period of time. Where this occurs, there is often a need to record different respondents at different stages in buying.

2. Record at each stage whatever the consumer has to say. Just let the consumer talk 'off the top of her head'; that is, just ask him or her to voice what comes to mind. Do not ask questions or in some other way prompt them to say something they might not have thought about, since this might bias their actions or what they have to say. On the other hand, note at the time anything about the context that might have influenced the respondent of which he or she might not have been aware.

3. The record you make constitutes a script or 'protocol' of the buying episode. Analyze this protocol in terms of the model (Figure 3.1). This analysis will cover: (a) your inferences and interpretations from the data as to what preferred vision and system of values are operative; (b) the wants and beliefs that entered into the decision process; and (c) the decision process itself. In carrying out this analysis, read through the whole protocol so as to see the parts in relation to the whole in an iterative process (see section below on hermeneutics). When the buying episode is a learning experience for the consumer, there might be discrepancies between wants, beliefs and choice criteria stated in the anticipatory account and those exhibited during and after the purchase. Draw attention to this when later showing the analysis to the respondent for comment.

4. Write up the implications of your analysis for developing a marketing strategy on the assumption that the findings would be valid for all those consumers within the market segment. Quite a small sample of respondents is likely to be all that would be needed to provide information on choice criteria. However (not being requested here), the usual sampling is needed to discover: (a) the distribution of choice criteria weightings; and (b) the variety of surrogate or prognomic indicators used to gauge the presence of the attributes of interest.
5. Check the seller's current strategy to see what advice might be offered.

HERMENEUTICS

Hermeneutics has a role to play in the analysis of protocol statements. In fact we would expect ethnopsychology to draw extensively on hermeneutics, which is concerned with the nature of interpretation, initially to do with the interpretation of the scriptures and the interpretation of various philosophical traditions. In claiming all human activities, actions and institutions can be viewed as a *text* to be interpreted, it is surprising that there is no specific hermeneutics school among consumer behavior researchers. But this does not mean hermeneutics is ignored; rather that it finds expression in certain traditions in sociology and anthropology.

The name Hermes, as the messenger of the Greek gods, is the source of the word hermeneutics. Derived from the Greek hermeneia meaning 'interpretation', it has become an umbrella term for all interpretive approaches to social science. In medieval times, hermeneutics ascribed to the Bible four levels of meaning: literal meaning; allegorical meaning; tropological (moral) meaning and anagogical (eschatological). But one of the demands of the Reformation was for literal meaning, rejecting the exclusivity of using 'tradition' for the interpretation of the scriptures. The problem with any demand for a literal meaning is that, in the case of the Bible, it first has to be interpreted before moving on to a translation, and interpretation is influenced by the translator's perspective. There is no such thing as just one defensible interpretation.

While called the 'art of interpretation' by Schleiermacher (1768–1834), and the 'art or technique of understanding and interpretation' by Gadamer (1900–2002), the term has been expanded beyond studies of rhetoric and scripture to treating everything as a text for hermeneutic study, so even science can be viewed as studying the text of nature.

It was once thought that hermeneutics could, like the natural sciences, be an objective search for truth, but no longer. What distinguishes interpretation from deductive inference is that interpretation always involves some conjecture. While some interpretations are better than others in the sense that they make most sense and account for more of the relevant 'facts' with the minimum of conjecture, there can be no one, final, true interpretation.

As to hermeneutic methods, it was Schleiermacher (1768–1834), the Plato scholar and Protestant theologian, who developed the concept of the hermeneutic circle in which the parts of the text are interpreted in reference to the whole and the whole understood by reference to the parts. On the question of where to start in the circle, Schleiermacher argued that the problem should be resolved intuitively, leaping into the circle, moving from the parts to the whole and the whole to the parts. Schleiermacher saw a text as being interpreted from two points of view: from the point of view of the language in which it is written and the psychological point of view which relates to the author.

Schleiermacher promoted the view that understanding in the human realm was concerned with the field of meaning and this should be distinguished from science, which is concerned with explaining nature. He argued that the interpretation of human action is not something to be investigated by the methods of science. Human actions, he argued, are motivated by reason and are to be understood through dialogue. We might add that systematic interpretation of a text's concepts or categories requires both identifying *sense-meaning* and trying to gauge *referential-meaning*; that is, the aspect of reality to which it refers. Schleiermacher expanded hermeneutics by adding a psychological dimension to hermeneutic interpretation. This was the psychological claim that understanding a written text requires *empathy* or putting oneself in the mind of the author, justified on the grounds that there is 'a little of everyone in all of us'.

But it was Dilthey (1833–1911), the biographer of Schleiermacher, who argued that the hermeneutic methods could be applied to the whole human world: to understand a human being means identifying the reasons for his or her actions and conceptualizing the world as he or she does (Palmer 1969). This 'conceptualizing the world as he or she does' is equivalent to understanding the perspectives of others – if we really want to understand them. The concepts we use in conversing with others – like the words table, chair, bacon, eggs – are not the categories used by the natural sciences, as they are not intent on explaining the world but simply concerned with giving it meaning (significance).

Dilthey viewed history as a text to be deciphered and used hermeneutics for his own study of history, claiming that the social sciences cannot use the same methods as the natural sciences but need to employ empathy (*verstehen*). Dilthey views *verstehen* or empathy as the essence of interpretation and grounds the human sciences in interpretation. Still later, the German sociologist Max Weber (1864–1920) was to introduce the social sciences to hermeneutics, also stressing *verstehen* (empathy in the sense of 'putting oneself in another's shoes') as the approach to the social sciences.

For Heidegger (1889–1976), hermeneutics had a more profound meaning. Heidegger moved away from any concern with psychology to grounding every text in the question of the meaning of 'being in the world' whose very strangeness cries out for interpretation. Heidegger argued that the hermeneutic circle was not something solved by any intuitive leap into the circle but as interplay between the traditions reflected in the text and the interpreter. Heidegger's reformulation of the hermeneutic circle led

Hans-Georg Gadamer (1900–2002), his former student, to argue that everyone enters the hermeneutic process with prejudices. As Gadamer says, the mind is not a tabula rasa – a clean slate that records all experiences without distortion. He rejects the claim that prejudices are necessarily negative. The belief that this is so has prevented us from seeing that understanding always involves pre-judgment or 'prejudice'. There are in fact legitimate 'prejudices' based on the recognition of authority, a form of which is tradition. The notion of bringing to bear an existing point of view on any inquiry, or in interpreting findings, echoes 'perspectivism' which argues that every study is carried out through the conceptual lens provided by some perspective.

Gadamer is the major figure in twentieth-century hermeneutics, a position established by his book *Truth and Method* (1960). Gadamer claims the interpreter's own slant on a tradition (perspective) is part of the interpreter's 'horizon' that is set against the different 'horizon' of the text. What is needed is a *fusion of horizons*. In other words, there is a need to fuse the two different perspectives, leading to a more open perspective. This process of fusing perspectives or horizons is never final even if there is sufficient closure to proceed. However, the notion of 'fusing horizons' is confusing if it suggests the two horizons should become a single unity, as this is not what Gadamer had in mind. He realizes tension will remain when the horizons (perspectives) are very different. For Gadamer, it is not sufficient to master meanings-in-use in respect to the concepts of an alien culture. The real need is for enlightenment and insight into the culture by fusing its concepts with one's own way of thinking. The resulting interplay of the interpreter's own perspective and the other's perspective is what gives depth of understanding. Cultural concepts (including one's own culture) form a network for making inferences and familiarity with making inferences within the network of concepts makes for depth of understanding. Yet confidence in roaming round the network of cultural concepts does not entail having mastery of it. Thinking in depth with marketing concepts does not come from simply learning the concepts but from constant use of the concepts in one's work and conversation.

The notion that a legitimate 'prejudice' could be based on tradition (a position held in religion by the Catholic Church) is disputed by Jürgen Habermas (1981) and supporters of so-called 'critical theory'. Habermas agrees about the usefulness of Gadamer's hermeneutics for the humanities but argues that suggesting legitimacy can equate with tradition downplays the way tradition can be a source of power that distorts processes of communication. Drawing on the perspective of psychoanalysis, Habermas created a sketch of what he called a 'depth-hermeneutical' discipline where the focus returned to the text, without talk of belonging to a tradition.

Paul Ricoeur (1981), a postmodernist, takes a different view of the function of hermeneutics, arguing that it should be concerned with uncovering what is *not* said rather than being focused on the recovery of meanings. This is what Ricoeur calls the 'hermeneutics of suspicion', which has roots in

Nietzsche, Marx and Freud, where the goal is to 'liberate' by unmasking the hidden meanings that social and legal practices mask. The hermeneutics of suspicion can be viewed as an attack on the belief in objective truth, since claims to objective truth can be fronts for vested interests.

Hermeneutics has had an impact on the social sciences, and for the anthropologist Clifford Geertz (1987) (see Chapter 13) it is central to ethnographic interpretation and to understanding the modes of thought of people in another culture. He talks about doing *ethnography* as analogous to reading a faded manuscript in a foreign language: full of ambiguities and vagueness that leads to complications. The term ethnography (sometimes just called 'fieldwork') was first used by social anthropologists to cover a method of describing cultural groups resulting from extended observation. Case studies are commonly used in gathering information by direct observation or personal (participant) observation over an extended period of time. *Participant* observation is just that: no acting as a 'fly on the wall' but as a member of the group immersed in its activities. Some researchers draw on structural-functionalism (see Chapter 12) as a guiding perspective but many do not. Unstructured interviews are common, as are other qualitative techniques. Because different investigators can come up with different interpretations, there is the constant problem of demonstrating the reliability and validity of any ethnographic study. Reliability refers to the dependability of the method to produce consistent results, while validity refers to whether the data are a true reflection of the population being studied.

Appendix 3B

An Illustrative Analysis of Protocols in Respect to Obtaining a Homeowner's Mortgage

(Note: In analyzing a protocol, students should be encouraged to apply any sensitizing concepts learnt in subsequent chapters.)

GOALS

Preferred life vision: to have the physical security and experience of owning a chosen home rather than be dependent on the whim of landlords.

Social goals: to signal to others achievement, upward mobility, the desire to put down roots, be part of a community and to be accepted as a 'somebody'.

WANT(S)

Borrowers want a loan for the purchase of a home at minimum sacrifice to themselves in terms of:

- The time required to obtain the loan
- The mental and corporeal effort needed to understand the various options available, their implications and the procedures involved
- The emotional stress accompanying the uncertainties attendant on seeking a mortgage from 'strangers' (usually) within the time constraints
- Present and future cash outlays.

COMMONLY HELD BELIEFS

About commercial banks and costs/interest rates:

- Banks are premium price lenders.
- Banks are not competitive on the rates they charge.

- It costs more to borrow from a bank.
- Banks are bureaucratic organizations that have fixed policies and so are not flexible.
- Banks are out to get the maximum profit.

About commercial banks and service:

- Commercial banks are tied to big business and have little interest in making loans to individual homebuyers.
- A large commercial bank, however, will be dependable, efficient and trustworthy, though if its staff is from New York City, it is likely to be impersonal with little in common with the average borrower.
- The local branch of a large New York City commercial bank is likely to be a more attractive lender, though perhaps not as accommodating as the local Savings and Loan Bank.

About mortgage firms and brokers (views here are more mixed):

- Mortgage firms are lenders of last resort.
- Mortgage firms are not a safe alternative to banks.
- Mortgage firms work with several banks and are not just tied to one. As a consequence they are able to carry a lower rate and work quicker.
- As a whole, mortgage firms are neither credible nor attractive to deal with.
- Brokers are needed only when there is difficulty in getting a loan.

About realtors (estate agents) and loans:

- No settled or firm views about realtors by respondents.

CHOICE CRITERIA APPLIED
Technical criteria

- The core-use function: to provide funds to meet purchase costs within time and cost constraints. Loan costs are always considered key. The time factor is crucial since the property might be sold to some other buyer if there is delay.
- Ancillary use-functions: provision of funds for purposes ancillary to the purchase of the property, such as mortgage insurance.
- Convenience-in-use functions: the lender can reduce the mental and physical effort and emotional stress associated with obtaining a mortgage: reducing/simplifying the paperwork involved; reducing the uncertainty about the costs involved, the pros and cons of the options available and the likelihood of getting a loan; making available a personal banker to whom all queries can be addressed and whose job it is to keep the prospective borrower informed.
- Professional efficiency and competence are important given the nature of the purchase.

Economic criteria

- The most important item of information sought by the borrower is the amount to be repaid each month for different time loans. Because this is not a one-off cost but a continuing contractual payment, it is the most important feature of any loan as far as the borrower is concerned. This does not mean that the borrower will select the lender who can quote the lowest figures. Within limits, many borrowers will trade-off reduced costs for other assurances and services associated with loans. What trade-offs will be made cannot be determined by asking respondents about the relative importance of interest rates versus speed in handling the application and so on. This is not really a meaningful question when divorced from the specific quantities involved.
- One-off costs are important since homebuyers seeking mortgages are usually working on a limited budget. However, much of the anxiety associated with such costs results from their being perceived as hidden costs that could be beyond what was expected and allowed for in the budget.
- The other sacrifices involved in obtaining a loan – the time, the effort and the general hassle – assume an importance that is disproportionate to the hours taken up by the activity. This is because all delays in obtaining a loan postpone the gratification of owning the new home and symbolize the possibility of rejection and missing out to another buyer who can come up with the money sooner. While in a sober moment the borrower will claim that only the bottom line monthly payments count, a firm that promises and is perceived as more likely to reduce the time, effort and hassle of obtaining a loan will create for itself a market segment where pricing, within strict limits, is not the absolute criterion.

Adaptive criteria

Borrowers are concerned with reducing uncertainty, fear of regret, information overload and avoiding the emotional discomfort associated with making a mistake and a decision they might regret. Adaptive criteria loom large in choosing a lender – more than would be anticipated from asking people before they enter into the process of obtaining a loan.

Adaptive criteria emerge through:

Uncertainty over lack of information:

- Different interest rates among lenders from different loan terms
- The relationship between interest rates and points and between discount points and points for originating the loan
- Fixed versus variable rates
- Closing costs
- Insurance costs and the distinction between mortgage insurance and hazard insurance
- What loan the borrower is qualified to obtain
- The trustworthiness/meaning of advertised rates.

Uncertainty over procedures:

- Length of the process
- How to keep abreast of progress on the loan
- Lender obligations in respect of charges
- Whether it is worth shopping around.

Uncertainty over performance to be expected:

- The borrower's own performance over payments to be met and over closing costs
- The lender's performance over size of loan, meeting time constraints, ethical matters like the lender keeping promises and not trying to rip the borrower off.

Uncertainty as to future preferences:

- Whether wise to tie oneself to such payments given the uncertainty about future conditions
- Whether lender is sufficiently established to remain in business for period of loan, to remove uncertainty of payment terms changing
- Whether interest rates in the future will be above/below current rates.

Integrative criteria

- Borrowers, like consumers generally, are concerned with how the choice of supplier/offering integrates them better into the community and with self
- Protecting self-esteem by avoiding risk of a rejection and backing off from any proceedings that cast doubt on the borrower's standing
- Developing supportive interpersonal relations by choosing a friendly bank or a bank where someone is known and liked and by dealing with a local bank rather than a big city bank
- Avoiding institutions viewed as bureaucratic, those using a hard sell or full of faceless bureaucrats
- Preferring to deal with one 'understanding' person rather than a group of anonymous bureaucrats; seeking institutions that have an image of caring
- Promoting what seems fair: everything upfront; rejecting institutions that indulge in sharp practices such as demanding fees, not previously mentioned and not going ahead with firms whose ads are misleading.

POWER BALANCE IN BORROWER DECISION-MAKING

The borrower has high involvement with this product because of the risks involved. Interest rates will be of first concern but the mortgage decision is also an emotionally charged, ego-involving activity and choosing a lender will not just be based on the objective facts but also on felt expectations as to how the borrowing process and subsequent dealings with the lender will be personally experienced.

What distinguishes mortgage buying from most buying is the imbalance of power between buyer (borrower) and seller (lender) as perceived by the borrower. The borrower perceives the lender as having the most power when it comes to negotiation. This is because:

- Lenders are fairly certain about the overall behavior of borrowers but borrowers will be uncertain about the likely demands of lenders. When the other party is fairly certain about your behavior but you are uncertain about theirs, this pushes the balance of power in their favor.
- Borrowers are all too conscious of their ignorance when it comes to mortgage options and mortgage procedures and are very conscious of the fact that only the lender can deal with what are critical uncertainties for them. This knowledge imbalance enhances the borrower's perceptions of being the less powerful partner in the relationship.
- It is the lender who controls the resources (money) urgently needed by the borrower within some time constraint. In return the borrower simply promises to pay back the money and pledges his future home as security. At the negotiation stage both the promise and the pledge seem less substantial, which again enhances perceptions of lender power.
- The borrower is dependent on the lender not just for a loan but for the satisfaction of being accepted as worthy of a loan. A loan rejection symbolizes a negative judgment as to the applicant's prospects of repaying the loan, which is a blow to self-esteem. The borrower's sense of this outcome being possible again enhances the perceived power of the lender.

BORROWER BEHAVIOR

First-time borrowers are likely to feel obliged to explore alternative sources of funds in spite of the costs involved such as time, money, emotional upset and information overload. But first-time buyers who have already established a friendly relationship with a credible lender will wish to go with that lender and avoid the hassle of shopping around.

Second-time borrowers will have a disposition to 'repeat-buy' from the initial lenders if the relationship has gone smoothly

Borrowers in an unbalanced power relationship will in general seek to 'lean over backwards' to be on the good side of the lender but this is not a satisfying posture. As a consequence, the borrower can be expected on occasion to 'let off steam' in an emotional outburst or escape altogether by turning to some other lender.

Some borrowers will reduce the risk of rejection by not even trying to obtain a loan from any institution perceived to be highly selective and elitist.

LENDER BEHAVIOR

The behavior of the borrower is likely to convey to the lender the borrower's perception of the lender's higher relative power. This may unintentionally lead the lender to dominate the relationship with less regard for the need to cultivate a warm and caring image. Some salespeople may enjoy being perceived as more powerful and increase that power by creating additional uncertainties, for example 'Yours is a special case' or 'There'll be a problem getting this through' – or simply by using lots of technical jargon. Everything should be done to reduce this perception of a power imbalance if the process of obtaining a loan is to run smoothly.

SOME MARKETING IMPLICATIONS

Every borrower wants to borrow the amount needed in the minimum time with the minimum cost to himself or herself in terms of both money and costs incurred by way of mental and physical effort and emotional strain. Different borrowers will attach different values to the various features of what they seek and so seek different configurations of benefits. Bank X should design its offerings for those segments of the market composed of prospective borrowers whose buying criteria correspond most closely to Bank X's key thrust (its distinctive know-how) and core competences (its actual capabilities), so as to be in the best position to service these segments. Bank X has the know-how and capabilities to cater in service to each of the four choice criteria at work:

- Technical criteria: The service of speeding up the process of obtaining a loan
- Economic criteria: The service of reducing the time, effort and hassle required to obtain a loan
- Adaptive criteria: The service of reducing the confusion and uncertainty over procedure and performances expected of others
- Integrative criteria: The service of acting with fairness and being supportive by providing a personalized system or caring organization.

SUGGESTIONS FOR MARKETING STRATEGY

Competitive strategy: The competitive strategy should be one of market share advancement through catering more closely to the 'service' segment of the mortgage market. Service is Bank X's critical advantage in the sense that service is of central importance to a large segment of borrowers and is scarce among lenders (judging from remarks of potential borrowers). Furthermore, service can be a sustainable advantage for Bank X in that it will continue to be sought and the bank that first goes all out on service can stay ahead both in reputation for service and in service techniques.

Core segmentation strategy: Bank X should position itself in the service segment, with the buying inducement being the additional service offered by Bank X. What is desirable by way of service is suggested by our discussion of the borrower's choice criteria but what is practically feasible and commercially viable is to be decided by Bank X itself. Service to borrowers should span:

- Pre-sales service, including the pre-qualifying proposal, property loans and so on. There is a need for a more comprehensive 'reach out' program. The process itself needs to ensure a smooth coordinated efficient yet caring process that meets time schedules with minimum demands being made of the prospective borrower.
- Post-sales service to provide reassurance and encourage word-of-mouth recommendation. Whenever adaptive criteria enter into decision-making, buyers are apt to seek advice or just copy those with the relevant experience who are considered 'in the know'. The aim should be to try and ensure that borrowers who take out a loan have no reservations about having to deal with Bank X. If prospects do not follow the advice of others in choosing Bank X, they will surely follow the advice to avoid Bank X if the experience of others is bad. While a good reputation invites interest, a bad reputation destroys interest.

In the process of obtaining a loan, both lender and borrowers have expectations of each other based on: what is considered 'reasonable'; what has been promised; and what is believed to be the norm established by competition. The expectations of borrower and lender must complement each other if frustration or withdrawal from the process is not to occur. Prospective borrowers expect searching personal questions. Although such questions need to be asked in a respectful way (since they draw attention to the power imbalance), they are unlikely to be resented. What will be resented is a lack of professionalism (efficiency) and a lack of courtesy. It is the lender who creates expectations (e.g. about time to complete) and if promises are not kept frustration results. Even when nothing concrete is said, expectations are still created. Thus it is common practice to call on prospects in their own home to help them fill in the initial application form. This in itself raises high expectations about subsequent service. Emotional reactions are intensified when early stages of the process are highly rewarding and later stages present delays and other problems. One other reason why unfulfilled expectations are so emotionally charged is that the prospect is usually both a man and his wife and both feel an obligation to protect the other from a sense of powerlessness in negotiation. Which partner is dominant (if any) is usually apparent from who talks and initiates action and who looks at the other most, but in any case, it is an error for any loan officer to ignore either partner. The ideal loan process should be as much a move towards the borrower perceiving more of a power equalization as the process should be an act of affiliation. To ensure service standards are met, there will be a need to monitor the service to see if it comes up to standard. Without such a system there can be no real guidance.

Customer targets: All prospective borrowers who value the service dimension of the offering are 'suspects' for Bank X's offering, but primary 'prospects' are:

- Young professional couples buying a home for the first time
- Those repeating the process, particularly current customers.

Secondary prospects are non-professional couples disposed towards valuing service and current customers of Bank X.

Pricing: Of major concern to the borrower is the amount of monthly repayment. And things of major concern are emotionally charged. Not surprisingly, borrowers are first attracted to those who offer the lowest interest rate since interest rates are the only indicator initially available to operate as a guide. Even if the prospect is suspicious of advertised interest rates, they are still likely to investigate. But an advertised low rate signals that the lender is interested in prospective borrowers who are price-sensitive. The lender is in effect saying: 'If you are trying to get the cheapest loan you can, we are the people to consult.' This is effective as few can resist a likely bargain. Price is something the borrower can immediately understand while, in contrast, comparisons on service are difficult to make. This means Bank X is at a disadvantage in the propaganda war, particularly as Bank X is perceived as a premium price lender. This high price image is one of the two major impediments in pursuing market penetration. The other impediment is its image of being an elitist, inflexible, somewhat bureaucratic lender unlikely to show much interest or concern for the small mortgage borrower. It is interesting that bureaucracy should be so disliked, not because it acts irrationally but because it acts with mechanical rationality.

Positioning: Bank X should position itself as the service bank with the best overall deal. No one at Bank X should be encouraged to enter into a discussion about interest rates and so on until the prospect's problem is understood and the loan officer has had the opportunity to discuss Bank X's offering as a whole. A typical answer to the price query is: 'There are many lenders out there who will quote you a low rate without knowing your circumstances and without telling you about their hidden costs and the demands they'll make on you. Bank X does not behave that way.'

What Bank X has above all else is credibility. They are perceived as likely to be highly efficient (if somewhat impersonal) and trustworthy. This is the most important asset of all since it means their claims and promises are likely to be taken seriously.

What Bank X must prepare is answers to the price objection – as a guide:

- Describe the overall service provided and the guarantees given.
- Warn of risks associated with low price operators.
- Get prospects to take small steps towards Bank X. One of the most effective steps is to ask them to talk to a recent client like themselves. Such 'reference selling' can be a key tactic in swinging a sale.

Distribution: The current system of having a selective distribution system composed mainly of realtors who are members of Bank X is the right way to go. But more needs to be done:

- Encourage realtors to 'sell' Bank X to prospective borrowers. Break down the attributes of the Bank X offering to show features additional to those offered by the competition – features unique to Bank X yet of central importance to anyone seeking a loan. Socially validating the choice by showing that people like them have taken out loans at the bank.
- Use the realtor outlet to educate the borrower on what Bank X has to offer. Every one of Bank X's realtors should be able to tell borrowers not only (as now) the amount for which they qualify but also pre-qualify them for a loan with Bank X while they are looking for a home. Additionally, borrowers can be shown a video that describes the whole process to be gone through in obtaining a loan with a description of the possible ways of short-circuiting the procedures in certain circumstances. Prospects can be assured that no one gets turned down who meets the requirements as listed. The basic idea is to pre-equip prospects with the knowledge that will allow them to act in a confident manner with Bank X, so once again reducing the perceived power gap in the relationship.
- Bank X to have a pull strategy to get their clients to use their realtors. The more Bank X helps its realtors the more it helps itself. The more realtors are induced to 'invest' in Bank X, the more they will sell its services. What should be considered is not just cooperative advertising but some tangible incentive for prospective borrowers to call on realtor members to discuss home buying. Bank X might organize seminars for prospects in which Bank X's services are discussed. This is one way of dispelling the 'impersonal' image. Also, those made familiar with and unafraid of the supplier of a service will tend to stick with it.

Advertising: The major goal of any advertising campaign should be to attract new borrowers by dramatizing the importance and uniqueness of Bank X's services while dispelling the image of Bank X as being expensive and impersonal. The overall format of such advertising should link the message to the preferred life vision of experiencing home ownership and the independence and community identification that goes with it. The subsidiary goal in an appropriate promotion is to retain customer loyalty by (for example) periodically reminding existing customers of their good standing and the availability of future funding.

Chapter 4

Behaviorism

CONDITIONING

Behaviorism is the perspective that all animal (including human) behavior is the result of past and present conditioning; a perspective that eschews quoting mental happenings as causal factors. Every perspective, paradigm or model is a way of seeing, and a way of not-seeing in that it can block out alternative viewpoints. It reminds us of those drawings in Gestalt psychology. From one viewpoint we see a very old lady, but from another view we see a young girl. We are unable to see both at the same time. There is always a danger of distorting whatever has to be explained (the *explicandum*) to fit one's perspective or scientific paradigm. This was certainly true of behaviorism, which dominated psychology until the 1950/60s. All human and animal behavior was made to fit the mechanism of *operant conditioning*. But this does not mean that behaviorism is an obsolete paradigm (as is often suggested) but simply that it does not explain all that needs to be explained given our different purposes.

CLASSICAL CONDITIONING VERSUS OPERANT CONDITIONING

Classical conditioning: There are two forms of conditioning. The earliest was Pavlovian or classical conditioning. In Pavlov's well-known experiment, when the sound of a bell was paired with food, the food reliably produced salivation in the dogs based on a *reflex* response. After some trials, the bell itself (without any sight of food) was sufficient to produce salivation. Pavlovian conditioning is an S>R (stimulus>response) psychology. Pavlov spoke of the unconditional stimulus (the food) and the conditional stimulus (the bell). The transformation of these two terms into 'unconditioned' and 'conditioned' does not sufficiently capture the original meaning but they have become so established that we are now stuck with them.

Pavlov's contribution to conditioning was not confined, as is popularly supposed, to demonstrating a conditioned stimulus and response. He developed and demonstrated the concepts of extinction, higher order conditioning, generalization and discrimination learning.

Extinction occurs if the bell continues to be presented but without any subsequent presentation of food. There is, in other words, a diminution or extinction of the salivary response to presenting just the bell itself. *Higher-order* or *second-order* conditioning occurs when the initial conditioned stimulus, the bell (or whatever) that elicits the response of salivation, is later paired with a new stimulus (e.g. a light). If the light by itself later elicits salivation, then this is called *higher-order conditioning*. This demonstrates that, in bringing about a Pavlovian conditioned response, it is not necessary to use an unconditioned stimulus.

Generalization or *stimulus generalization* occurs when we (e.g. consumers) generalize from highly positive or negative experiences. To use a well-quoted example, we will generalize to avoid touching all hot coals as a result of once being burnt by touching hot coals. In this way we are saved from the effort of learning anew when we are faced with the same stimulus. Similarly, the consumer learns to generalize from shopping experiences and from using the product. Sellers try to exploit consumer generalization by giving, say, a brand extension a similar appearance or providing it with the dominant characteristic of the successful original product so that favorable attitudes are carried over to the brand extension.

The consumer falls back on generalizations from experience to determine responses next time around without undertaking any additional learning. Generalizations can extend to other products under the same brand name or produced by the same company. This is one of the advantages of extending the brand name or company name to a whole range of products: the association rubs off. But conversely, it means that a bad experience can be similarly generalized to condemn the whole range of products under that brand name. There is also the very real problem of brand extension diluting the brand: what can be said about the brand overall is diluted when covering only what is common to both brand and its extensions. Tylenol, as a brand name, is diluted by a broadened product line, having at the same time separate identities for each separate product falling under the brand name. If Mercedes had reserved the name for its top-of-the-range cars with their elegant designs the name would be still more prestigious than it is today.

While a company will try to create a distinctive brand, it is the consumer who finally decides. This is made clear when we look at the film industry. Not all studios can be regarded as distinctive brands: although some, like Metro Goldwyn Mayer, were once prominent brands, only a few like Disney have remained on top. A distinctive brand is distinguished by its independent power to draw custom, as when a film fan would once say: 'It will be a good film as it is a Metro Goldwyn Mayer film.' Films can be brands, such as *Harry Potter* and the *James Bond* movies, as can the actors and directors; but not all actors and directors qualify. A seller might speak of 'my brands', but if they are not treated as such by the consumer they are often regarded as merely another commodity product.

Discrimination learning or *stimulus discrimination* occurs when we learn, for example, from experience to discriminate between hot and merely warm coals or between qualities of leather or good and bad medical treatment. This ability to discriminate means the consumer is able to mould responses that take note of the differences. But as Pavlov discovered, asking his subjects to make discriminations that were mentally taxing led to frustration, with the likelihood of generating aggressive behavior. Discriminations involved in understanding product instructions can at times be similarly taxing, leading to frustrations. Vagueness and ambiguity abound in instructions as every instruction covers, by definition, all instructions not specifically excluded. Many of us can remember our particular frustrations in the 1970s with Japanese technical manuals that were obviously written by non-native speakers of English. This undoubtedly cost the Japanese a lot of business.

In classical conditioning the move towards a conditioned response is *interpreted* as an unconscious process. It is doubtful if many today accept the view that *all* conditioning occurs without conscious awareness. Thus Pavlov's dogs did not attempt to eat the bell when there was no food but simply salivated – an appropriate response to the expectation of food. Classical conditioning in marketing is manifested in ads whose main appeal is via *association*: the ad is associated with something that resonates with the target audience, such as nostalgic symbols or beautiful women.

Operant conditioning: The second form of conditioning is operant conditioning. In the 1890s E. L Thorndike invented the puzzle box for the study of animal learning. When in the box, the animal could see food but was unable to obtain it until it pushed a lever. This led Thorndike to a theory of conditioning that did not rely on any reflex. The stimulus and response were associated purely through the consequences of the animal's response – in this case the pleasure arising from escaping from the box and eating the food. This was an application of Thorndike's Law of Effect, which states that acts followed by good (satisfying) consequences will be repeated, while those followed by negative (discomforting) consequences will not be repeated – a common sense assertion that folk psychology would endorse.

Both the Pavlov and the Thorndike procedures came to be called the stimulus > response approach or the S-R paradigm in psychology. Yet the two are different and come from different intellectual traditions. Pavlov built on the concepts and methods of *reflexology* to understand how humans and other animals respond to a novel stimulus. In the Law of Effect, Thorndike was stating how an animal's responses in a novel situation were predicted by the *consequences* of its behavior. Pavlov sought a physical model of the mind, with the *reflex* being the basic unit of analysis. Thorndike simply sought to portray a *functional* explanation of the mind; that is, to show the contribution of the mind to behavior. This notion of the mind being a factor in generating behavior was anathema to many because the inner workings of the mind were not open to inspection.

The emergence of what we now call *behaviorism* arose with the work of John Broadus Watson (1878–1958), who sought to expunge all introspection and mentalist concepts from scientific psychology. Behaviorism rejects explanations of behavior that draw on inner workings of the mind and seeks to explain behavior purely in terms of the organism's conditioning via experience. This was in line with the 'logical positivism' of the 1930s, which eschewed all talk in science of things that were unobservable such as mental happenings, since true science was to be constructed from observable data. Watson rejected Thorndike's Law of Effect on the ground that it introduced subjective concepts like 'satisfaction' and 'discomfort'. On the other hand, conditioning for him was the key to behavior. Watson argued that behind all behavior lay causal stimuli, and accepted that causal-type explanations are incompatible with teleological explanations (explanations in terms of functions served, purposes and goals). The notion that for every physical event there is a *physical* cause is still generally endorsed by behaviorism. Teleological explanations, in contrast, assume that certain phenomena like human actions are best explained in terms of functions performed or in terms of purposes or reasons rather than in quoting any physical factors as the cause of behavior.

Watson would have rejected the reason-giving explanation that assumes human action to be purposive behavior and explains behavior this way. It would be rejected on the grounds of being a non-scientific explanation. Finding out about people's goals or purposes was not, for Watson, the method of science. As Watson eschewed the notion of purpose, the consequence was that the dependent variable in all his studies was *physical movement*, not actions. 'I raise my arm' is a purposeful action which contrasts with saying 'my arm rose' which is simply a physical movement. This means, in the case of Watson's behaviorism, that the predicted behavior (the dependent variable) is not intentional action but physical movement.

It was under Watson that the name behaviorism came into being. But with its focus on physical movements, it was called 'molecular' behaviorism. This contrasts with *molar* behaviorism, which claims certain types of physical movements can be judged to be acts. It was molar behaviorism that finally won out with its focus on acts, and not just movement.

Behaviorism, as advanced by Burrhus Frederic Skinner (1904–90), dominated psychology after the Second World War. Skinner's particular form of behaviorism is referred to as *radical behaviorism* since, unlike Watson, Skinner viewed private (covert) events like thinking and feeling as mental events and, as such, part of behavior, to be explained by environmental factors.

Skinner explained learning as arising from reinforcements. All animals spontaneously produce novel behaviors and those behaviors that are *positively* reinforced are likely to recur in the future in similar circumstances or contexts. Although Skinner's subjects were primarily rats and pigeons, Skinner claimed and sought to extend his findings to people. The focus was on *operant conditioning*. Operant conditioning asserts that we emit behavior all the time and emitted behaviors that are reinforced recur, while those that are not reinforced die away. According to operant conditioning, all behavior is contingent on (dependent upon) being reinforced. Reinforcement is anything in the environment that increases the probability of a response and a reinforcer is anything that increases the probability of the occurrence of a given class of responses. The term 'reinforcer' is distinguished from 'reward' because what might be considered a reward by an observer might not work to strengthen the emitted behavior. If a pigeon pecks a key and receives food and the key-pecking always increases, food is the reinforcer. If pecking does not increase then food (normally viewed as a reward) is not a reinforcer in this instance. Behaviorism focuses on reinforcement and eschews punishment. What is called *negative reinforcement* is not punishment but simply the *withdrawal* of a punisher and is therefore a reinforcement of behavior. The withdrawal of a penalty for spending over one's credit limit is a negative reinforcer that could result in more being purchased on credit.

If we accept the assumption of consumers as free agents it is all too easy to dismiss environmental reinforcing influences. In fact we often talk about people changing their behavior as if the 'change' were the result of mental adjustments, when it may be circumstances that have changed which in turn lead to the change in people's behavior. Consider the effect of 9/11 and the financial meltdown on consumer behavior – even in respect of home improvements, there was a move away from major, expensive projects to minor projects like painting walls and other essential maintenance. But it was not just a matter of scaling down; new interests developed, as illustrated at the time by the immense interest in The Museum of American Finance's program entitled 'tracking the credit crisis'.

Skinner, like Watson, rejected Thorndike's mental concepts of 'satisfaction' and 'discomfort' but not the Law of Effect, simply substituting 'positive' and 'negative reinforcement' for satisfying and discomforting happenings. Positive and negative reinforcements are things that were observable. In contrast, we cannot observe satisfying and discomforting happenings in the mind. In Skinner's revised version of the Law of Effect, a response followed by a positive reinforcer is strengthened in that it is more likely to reoccur in the future. Thus in the air miles program, credit card use is followed by the reinforcer of air miles. Skinner regarded his version of the Law of Effect as the central law of learning. Behavior conditioned through the Law of Effect, or Skinner's version of it, first waits for the behavior to be *emitted* before there can be reinforcement. With Pavlov, there was the need for a stimulus like food together with a reflex response.

Skinner showed the dysfunctional consequences of *delayed* reinforcement in that reinforcement can come too late to be effective in conditioning behavior. Hence the rule: when the desired behavior is emitted, employ immediate reinforcement. He demonstrated how a little ingenuity can be used to ensure immediate feedback. And this is important, as feedback or knowledge-of-results can be a powerful reinforcer (going on the scales each morning to help control weight) so immediate feedback on performance is to be encouraged. (The old adage 'practice makes perfect' should be modified to 'practice makes perfect providing we give knowledge of results'.) Industrial engineering consultants, after putting in a financial incentive scheme, try feedback each hour of the day, namely data on the extra pay earned (the reinforcer).

But how are we to define and recognize a reinforcer? Skinner's definition of reinforcement makes operant conditioning unfalsifiable. This is because, if we argue that the characteristic of a reinforcer is its power to strengthen the behavior emitted, this would *not* define a reinforcer independently of its effect on behavior. If the alleged reinforcer does not work, by definition it is not a reinforcer so it is impossible to specify in advance what will be a reinforcer. A Skinnerian believes he gets round this problem by appealing to the *trans-situational characteristics* of a reinforcer in that many reinforcers strengthen behavior in a wide variety of species and situations. But while no one doubts that all organisms are sensitive to the consequences of what they do, we are as yet unable to specify the mechanisms that lie behind this sensitivity.

Skinner's operant conditioning is not a S(stimulus)>R(response) model, since in operant conditioning behavior is viewed as being acquired, shaped and maintained by stimuli following responses, not by stimuli preceding responses. More precisely, we speak of *discriminative stimuli* to refer only to stimuli in the presence of which responses are reinforced. Responses are strengthened whenever they are followed by positive reinforcement and weakened when they are not followed by reinforcement. Skinner viewed operant conditioning as subsuming classical conditioning and an advance on classical conditioning because it came to grips with the two fundamental problems:

- To account for human creativity (novelty in behavior); and
- To account for the fact that people are motivated by future goals.

Skinner felt operant conditioning solved both these problems.

It was perhaps Skinner's explanation of *superstitious* behavior (e.g. wearing a particular piece of clothing for bombing missions or in competitive games) in terms of operant conditioning that gave him visibility with the general public. Superstition is pervasive among groups such as actors and soldiers engaged in battle where outcomes are highly uncertain and so 'luck' is perceived as playing a huge part in success. A fighter pilot who wears a medallion and comes home safely may see his wearing the medallion not as superstition but as a bringer of luck. Skinner's explanatory perspective sees the behavior of all living things as a consequence of environmental influences.

The behaviorist completely rejected the nineteenth-century *introspectionist* perspective (a perspective dependent on introspection to understand human behavior) in order to produce an objective explanation of behavior that rejected subjective (phenomenal) states of mind in explaining behavior. Mental states reflected in mental constructs like 'attitude' and 'motive' were too subjective for use in a science purporting to be objective. Yet people differ from pigeons (Skinner's usual subjects) as people are language-users with a language that employs mental concepts. It is not clear that people, as language users, behave like pigeons when it comes to reinforcements.

Learning: Behaviorism is regarded as a psychology of *learning*, claiming that we learn what we are reinforced to learn. Learning will occur most quickly when the reinforcement is immediate and continued. An obvious example is the way attaining good grades encourages further learning to maintain the reinforcement. However, there is quick cessation of the behavior when reinforcement stops.

However, there are forms of learning that operant conditioning fails to explain. Thus we now know that chimpanzees, when carried around by someone who hides food in a number of places, will later go directly to each of these locations to retrieve the food (Balda and Kamil 1992). This is the sort of learning in animals which conditioning has difficulty explaining. Also it is often pointed out that when people win on the lottery or the races, instead of reinforcing the behavior, they may cease gambling altogether. The fear of making a loss is greater than the anticipation of making a gain.

Learning via conditioning (whether classical or operant (instrumental) conditioning) is not the only way of learning. In fact, many psychologists regard it as the most trivial type of learning. There is, for example, *incidental* learning or learning that occurs without reward, effort or purpose which can happen through, say, watching television. There is learning from observing others leading to *imitation* or *modeling* the behavior of others, as when consumers copy a celebrity in buying the same brand of perfume. There is also *cognitive* learning when the consumer learns from consumer reports, teachers and books, while there is the related learning through the *solving* of *problems*. This latter relates to trial and error learning. Trial and error learning is sometimes contrasted with the notion of 'hill climbing learning' where, unlike with trial and error learning, there is a way of estimating whether we are closer to our goal or not – we can tell if we are getting closer to the top of the hill. It is also contrasted with the 'means–end' approach where we focus on what means are needed to achieve goals, considering the 'performance gap' between present state and goal state. The trial and error approach necessitates only recognition of the goal, the 'hill climbing' approach necessitates knowing also about closeness to the goal, while the 'ends–means' approach additionally necessitates having information about the type of difference that exists between present state and goal state as well. We have no studies indicating the incidence of these three methods of problem solving. (Note: The notion of trial and error ignores any distinction between an error and a mistake. But it might on occasion be useful to distinguish between making an 'error' and making a 'mistake'. Making an error suggests violating a relevant rule, while making a mistake simply suggests taking an action with a regrettable outcome.)

Extinction is the process of eliminating the occurrence of a conditioned response, typically by withholding the reinforcer (such as a discounted price) that was involved in its acquisition.

ESCHEWING HAPPENINGS IN THE MIND

Skinner's behaviorism eschews explanations of behavior through happenings in the mind such as beliefs, attitudes, motives and so on. A 'motive' to Skinner is some property of the stimulus by which it gains control over the behavior. While initially denying the very existence of subjective entities, Skinner later spoke of behavior being both overt (public) and covert (private) with all thoughts being regarded as covert (private) events. Skinner spurns looking at mental events as a stage along a causal chain of S > O > R (stimulus → organism (mental event) → response) on the grounds that, if the mental event ('mental way-station') itself fails to divert attention from the first stage (the stimulus), it would surely divert attention from the last stage (the response).

The explanatory basis for behaviorism is, as already stated, the Law of Effect which claims we repeat acts that are followed by positive consequences and avoid acts that are followed by negative consequences. What makes behaviorism meaningful to marketers is that common sense (folk psychology) endorses the Law of Effect and many behaviorist propositions such as:

- The greater the number of rival brands, the less dependent is the consumer on any one brand. This is why new entrants into a market are not usually welcomed by current suppliers. (This is true as a general rule but when a radical innovation is introduced into the market, the innovator may welcome another entrant since this can give credibility/legitimacy to what the product has to offer.)
- The more the brand 'XYZ' provides additional sources of reinforcement for consumer 'A', the more dependent is consumer 'A' on brand 'XYZ'. Thus a brand that appeals to all the senses can offer more reinforcement than a brand that appeals to just, for example, sight.
- The less satisfied consumer 'A' is with brand 'XYZ', the less the likelihood of 'A' continuing to buy brand 'XYZ' if other brands are available. This makes it important to know how relatively satisfied current customers are with their choices vis-à-vis rival brands.
- The greater the superiority of brand 'XYZ' in terms of offering reinforcement over its rivals, the more consumers will choose it.
- Consumers, other things remaining equal, buy the brands that yield most for the least cost.
- Consumers repeat buy whatever has proved the best reinforcer, other things remaining equal.
- Present stimuli (e.g. shopping at a particular store) associated with past reinforcement will evoke similar buying to that in the past.
- Repeat buying occurs only as long as the practice continues to be reinforced.
- Consumers display 'emotional' behavior when their actions (e.g. looking for a favorite brand), previously rewarded in a similar situation, suddenly go unrewarded (e.g. a store is out of stock).

It will be noted that some of the above could be regarded as simply conceptual truths.

Operant conditioning can also be used to offer advice to management in supervising the sales force with such propositions as the following:

- Avoid giving the same reward to all but instead ensure that rewards are tied to each person's performance.
- Ensure everyone is aware of what is expected of them. Without such standards, there can be neither guidance nor meaningful feedback.
- Respond to differences in performances, otherwise there is no reinforcement for high performance.
- Explain to subordinates what they are doing wrong; criticize what is wrong, not the person. Otherwise correct behavior is not being encouraged and good behavior is in danger of being extinguished.
- Never reprimand while others are present since this is a double punishment.
- Always avoid humiliating a subordinate since humiliation is punishment without encouraging better performance.
- Reinforcement by way of praise should not be overdone, otherwise it appears the person doing the praising has 'no measure of the man' so the praise becomes worthless and not reinforcing.

PARTIAL REINFORCEMENT

One important behaviorist concept is *partial reinforcement* and its effect on extinguishing a response. If behavior is reinforced every time it is emitted, the behavior is likely to cease quickly after the reinforcement is withdrawn. But if reinforcement is partial, only occurring sometimes when the behavior is emitted (e.g. periodically finding a bargain in a certain store), the behavior persists longer (e.g. we still visit the shop in hope of a bargain). Thus with the 'intermittent schedule' of reinforcement, learning takes longer but lasts longer. (However, when it comes to people as opposed to pigeons, the typical subjects used by Skinner, much depends on the information already possessed (beliefs) in that I may know there are going to be no more bargains.)

CRITICISMS OF BEHAVIORISM

Today non-behaviorists try to link the environment (the external stimulus) to behavior (response) through mental (hypothetical) constructs such as attitude, beliefs, emotion and motives. But Skinner challenges us with the problem of how mental states like motive and attitude *cause* physical movement. In philosophy this is the 'mind–body problem'. However, in taking a perspective that ignores cognitive processes altogether, behaviorism ignores many basic questions about human behavior. Yet behaviorism, particularly under the name of 'behavior modification', plays an important role in changing behaviors like compulsive-obsessive behavior. It is still the only approach shown to be helpful with autism, which involves language diffi-culties, social skills deficits and an obsession with order (Schreibman 2006).

Skinner's behaviorism points to the limits of self-knowledge. For Skin-ner, the limits have to do with language in that a necessary condition for knowledge of one's thinking (private events) is to have competence in a language of private events. This seems reasonable but is a matter of con-troversy, with some psychologists arguing that people are born knowing a pre-verbal language, with thought couched in this pre-verbal language before being clothed in words, whether English, Chinese or Apache (Pinker 1994). But the notion of a pre-verbal language would be a language that was pre-concept-use. This will not do, as humans think with concepts since a culture's concepts are what break up the world into categories.

As the philosopher Sidney Morgenbesser (a friend known for his wit) once said, after listening to Skinner in a talk given at Columbia: 'Let me see if I understand your thesis, you think we shouldn't anthropomorphize people?' (Ryerson 2004). This reminds us that human behavior and animal behavior differs as the following well-known rhetorical question suggests: if both your spouse and your dog are put into the trunk (boot) of the car for an hour, which would still be really happy to see you?

Behaviorism offers, as we have seen, important insights for marketing. Some academics have made serious attempts to expand behaviorism by eschewing its dogmatic rejection of all reference to mental happenings like 'intention' (Foxall 1990). But for many marketers, operant conditioning has the defect of assuming consumers do not adopt new and appropri-ate behaviors in new situations. More critically, it seems crass to believe that new behavior in new environments does not occur unless the present behavior is linked to it by a continuous chain of reinforcement. 'Extinc-tion' may in fact not be a cessation of learning as suggested but an instance of new learning. Some critics, while agreeing that behaviorism, based on the concept of reinforcement, may not be falsifiable, argue that predictions from behaviorism can still be tested and these have been found wanting. Behaviorism in ignoring the role of mental states inevitably fails to recog-nize that the specific characteristics of any mental state arise from a whole background of beliefs, emotions, desires and other mental states and not just from a reinforcement history.

Animals are the typical subjects in conditioning experiments but even animals are something more than 'hard-wired' organisms, simply respond-ing to reinforcements. Rumbaugh and Washburn (2003) use the example of Lana, a chimpanzee, being potty-trained using a reward for urinat-ing into a pan. Behaviorism suggests that Lana's urination response in the potty would become stronger with reinforcement but her urination response in the potty got smaller each time she used it: Lana had learnt that she got more total reward for the much smaller urinations than she would otherwise. But for behaviorists, it is not clear that this is not a case of reinforcement since any reinforcement for urinating in the pan would encourage her also to go to the potty more often!

Nicholas Humphrey (1983), a behavioral psychologist at Cambridge, sums up the limitations of behaviorism:

> Indeed I venture to suggest that if a rat's knowledge of the behaviour of other rats were limited to everything which behaviourists have discovered about rats to date, the rat would show so little understanding of its fellows that it would bungle disastrously every social interaction it engaged in; the prospects for a man similarly constrained would be still more dismal.
>
> (Humphrey 1983: 31)

Purposeful behavior is not the same as purposive behavior. We speak of animals such as young gulls aiming to obtain food by pecking at their mothers' beaks; of robins attacking other birds in order to drive away competitors; and ants cleaning their nests by removing the remains of dead ants. These are purposeful behaviors but not purposive as they are programed responses. Young gulls peck at any long dotted object even if it does not yield food; robins attack just any red lump; while ants are reacting to a chemical as they drag away anything smelling of oleic acid (Radner 1996). What distinguishes purposive behavior in humans is that it can ignore all features of the stimuli that are irrelevant to goal achievement and be able to visualize different ways of achieving goals while considering consequences. Thus, while a large win on the lottery would seemingly reinforce further engaging in the behavior, an individual may desist and just be happy with the one win.

Kagan (2006), a Harvard psychologist, in commenting on his initial commitment to behaviorism regards it now as 'bizarre' that he and other behaviorists actually believed that all behavior could be explained as an acquired association between an event and a reaction. Since it was assumed there was a biological continuity across animal species, the claim was extended to both humans and animals. The notion of universal law-like explanations of behavior was accepted as it was assumed there was a deterministic relation between a conditioned stimulus and conditioned response. There was this firm belief (or more correctly 'faith') that he and other behaviorists could achieve just about any behavioral change through the power of conditioning.

Kagan points out that hard evidence does not shift beliefs when the beliefs are basic to the accepted orthodoxy. It is somewhat similar with animals. Experiments show that rats do not learn an association between light and a subsequent feeling of illness but easily learn an association between a distinct taste and the subsequent, unpleasant sensations. There is a failure of many behaviorists to face up to the implications of such studies – that each animal has biological preferences that cannot always be ignored. As Kagan says, we may condition sexual arousal to the perfume worn by a romantic partner but not to the color of the pillow on which the lovers rest. If this is true it suggests the conditioned stimulus needs to be perceptually tied to the unconditioned stimulus. Color, like much else, does not project the same meaning regardless of context. Thus red on a woman's lips can be inviting and attractive but red in a wound not so welcome. It is interesting that the two most popular colors for cars in the US are white (the number one choice) and black (the number two choice).

Kagan credits behaviorists with three non-trivial advances:

(a) The discovery of principles of conditioning going beyond Pavlov's findings
(b) The significance of the conditioning stimulus, particularly its unexpectedness
(c) The special biological properties of each species.

Around 1964, the limited explanatory scope of behaviorism led to diminishing interest in it. But behaviorism is by no means extinct. Under the title of *behavior analysis* there are those who still claim, in line with logical positivism, that it is the only true science of behavior, denying it is a discipline within psychology. For these adherents of the true faith, it is not psychology but an alternative to psychology, since psychology focuses on mental goings-on (Baum 2007). Baum denies vigorously that behavior cannot be adequately explained without resorting to intentional terms as alleged by Foxall (2007). But this raises the question as to what constitutes an adequate explanation: adequate for what purpose(s) and in what situations? No paradigm that views the mind as *epiphenomena* can possibly come to grips with all the questions that might be asked about human behavior. Epiphenomenalism claims that mental phenomena are caused by physical forces in the brain but do not in themselves have any effects. Happenings in the brain are like shadows, caused by physical phenomena but having no effects themselves. What depth and breadth of explanation can be given by a focus purely on 'reinforcement and consequences'? Baum's behaviorism, as a discipline, is in danger of becoming sterile in the sense of not having the seeds within it for further development. The advent of cognitive behaviorism from around 1975 has been one attempt to put new life into a comatose paradigm. Foxall realizes behaviorism needs to be re-conceptualized and is trying to save behaviorism from its own dogmatic follies.

HULL'S DRIVE-REDUCTION THEORY

Some who called themselves behaviorists sought explanatory mechanisms to account for conditioning. Under such explanatory mechanisms come *drive-reduction theories*, where being motivated equates with a drive to change a state of physiological 'disequilibrium' to behavior that restores equilibrium. Equilibrium implies stability or some degree of overall integration within the self, viewed as being achieved when opposing forces within the individual balance themselves out.

Hull's (1943) drive-reduction theory is the most well known of attempts to account for conditioning. Hull's drive-reduction theory assumes an organism is in a state of homeostasis or equilibrium until some internal metabolic deficiency or chemical imbalance becomes a (causal) 'drive', driving the organism into a state of tension and trial-and-error learning until equilibrium is restored. On this basis, a drive is something we feel that incites behavior. Hull thus sought to give a physiological foundation to behaviorism. Only a few biological 'drives' (like hunger, thirst and sex) were thought necessary to account for all behavior on the grounds that other 'motives' were derivative and acquired through these basic drives. The 'drive state' at any one time depends on the extent to which the organism is deprived. Hull's drive-reduction theory does not use terms like 'wants', though on this theory a person would only want something to the extent that it had led in the past to drive-reduction.

It was once popular in basic marketing texts to talk of restoring equilibrium through satisfying wants and so forth but it is less so today. It may make some sense when applied to the biological needs of hunger and thirst, but no other wants can be traced to physiological disequilibrium. In any case, if a 'need' is a necessary human requirement like safety, it is wrong to suggest that all needs are accompanied by some sense of disequilibrium or discomfort. It is wrong to talk of all motivation as a 'drive' towards behavior restoring equilibrium since the consumer can act to buy a chocolate bar without any sense of being driven. The notion of being driven has a deterministic ring about it (if drive 'A' then always behavior 'B' as a consequent) that is inconsistent with much of what we know about consumers choosing and deciding. Satiety is usually equated with equilibrium but some of our most important motives, such as wanting respect, power and in particular status, seem insatiable while other motives seem connected more with dispassionate deliberation and choice than any physiological disequilibrium. As Robinson (1985) says, if we take satiety as the equivalence of physiological equilibrium, many of life's goals (e.g. friendship, power) are not things with which we become satiated, unlike the biological examples Hull considers. According to Robinson, drive-reduction theories do not say where in the system and in what manner equilibrium states reveal themselves. Any stimulation results in disequilibrium from a resting state so that a resting state is not any more normal than a state of arousal.

In most of our day-to-day buying, we have no sense of being 'driven' or feel any suppressed tension, nor do we normally feel a sense of being in an equilibrium state after buying. Although, as already stated, it is not uncommon in texts on consumer behavior to talk about 'drives' as Hull did, it is gravely wrong.

Harlow (1953) showed that, for monkeys at least, problem solving could be self-rewarding, so monkeys continue on such tasks even without reinforcement. This curiosity motive is difficult to reconcile with the homeostatic (equilibrium) assumption lying behind drive theory. Hebb (1955) has also challenged the homeostatic assumption. In studies on sensory deprivation, it was shown that a certain level of arousal is necessary for the optimal functioning of the central nervous system. If deprived of such arousal, the organism seeks stimulation.

Dretske (1988) makes the point that, while a drive can be the cause of movement, unlike a desire, it is not *for* anything. This means we cannot explain behavior by an appeal to drives in the same way that we can explain actions by an appeal to wants and beliefs. The concept of drives lacks the intentional properties of reasons for action.

SOCIAL CONDITIONING AND PERSUASION (?)

The rest of this chapter is devoted to the notion of 'social conditioning' as espoused by Robert Cialdini (1984), a psychologist whose books on influence and persuasion are probably the most popular in the field. Discussing Cialdini's principles of social conditioning allows us to detail much that is of interest to marketers, though it is doubtful whether Skinner would regard Cialdini's exposition as a manifestation of operant conditioning in its purest form. Consumers on occasion have to be persuaders and are always being subject to persuasive appeals. In any case, if we are to understand the consumer there is a need to understand how he or she responds to various persuasive messages. Some of the principles discussed below may require little in the way of practice to apply them, whereas others (particularly the material on persuasion later in this book) involve skills that are acquired through practice.

This section also uses Cialdini's exposition as an opportunity to set forth alternative explanations of his claims that, while supportive of Cialdini, draw on explanations from other social science paradigms. This is to demonstrate that drawing on other paradigms can be corroborating and need not compete in offering conflicting explanations.

Persuasion in the classical literature is associated with the Sophists, who were more interested in persuasion than in the search for truth. From this has come the word 'sophistry', meaning the art of getting compliance through misleading arguments. In interpreting persuasive processes in selling and elsewhere, behaviorists perceive conditioning to be at work. Cialdini, though not a card-carrying behaviorist, is one psychologist who talks about the 'principles' of persuasion which he identifies with tactics for inducing *automatic compliance* in face-to-face dealings. For him, some of the best tactics of persuasion are those that induce, through *social conditioning*, an automatic 'gut' reaction to comply. Cialdini uses the metaphor of 'mechanisms' in arguing that compliance follows as a sort of knee-jerk reaction. Cialdini does not, though, adhere entirely to behaviorist principles in that, on occasion, he expands on a behaviorist explanation by employing mental constructs that would be anathema to Skinner.

Principles of compliance: Cialdini's 'principles' of compliance cover: commitment/consistency; reciprocation; social proof; authority liking; and scarcity.

The commitment/consistency principle: there are two forms of *inconsistency* in logic: a contrary statement and a contradictory statement. In the *contrary* case, a person makes two statements, at least one of which must be false. Thus Joan bought her watch ABC in Macy's versus Joan bought her watch ABC in Target are contrary statements. Alternatively, a person can make two statements in which one statement contradicts the other. Thus Joan bought a watch versus Joan did not buy a watch are contradictory statements. We all, at some time or another, make inconsistent statements because we do not see the implications of all our beliefs. Thus the American electorate is highly supportive of Medicare, a government health care program for those over sixty-five years, but claims to abhor any notion of creating a so-called 'socialist medical' system. American values often conflict with a government foreign policy that supports tyrannical dictatorships. Anyhow, drawing out the logical implications of *all* our beliefs is just not feasible. If it were easy to do so, we would all be good mathematicians since most mathematical truths can be deduced from a few axioms, like the Peano axioms for arithmetic for example, where every number has an immediate successor.

Cialdini is supportive of *consistency theory* which argues that everyone aspires to be, and wants to appear to be, consistent as this is seen as reflecting integrity and personal and intellectual strength. Pointing out a person's inconsistencies can lead that person to make changes in his beliefs. However, Cialdini accepts that rigid consistency can also be a defense against having to think. But is there *always* automatic compliance to avoid inconsistency? Many believe they should not smoke and find it inconsistent with their beliefs to continue smoking, but they continue to smoke. People emphatically endorse the principle that the end does not justify the means but many are quite happy about using torture if it helps obtain information from the enemy. While agreeing that everyone is innocent until proven guilty, many have been happy to exclude those in Guantanamo Bay.

Nonetheless, it is true that commitment to a position is likely to induce behavior consistent with that commitment, particularly if that commitment has been made publicly. Salespeople try to get commitment early on: 'If I can get you that price will you then buy?' This is a common tactic for car salespeople, followed by trying to get the prospect's signed statement to that effect. If the prospect makes the commitment, the pressure is on to abide by that commitment so as to be consistent. The tactic is also employed on salespeople by managers: salespeople are induced to make a commitment in writing to achieve sales goals in order to make them more motivated to achieve them. As commitments change, self-image may change in unison. For example, building up a commitment to support solar heating can lead to a self-image of being a person who supports the conservation movement. Commitment can be further encouraged here by complimenting a person for being public-spirited. Some views of self may be easily abandoned but others, like being a good citizen, housewife or parent, may be central to one's feelings of identity and so important to self-motivation.

Cialdini argues that the commitments that are most effective in changing self-image and future behavior are:

- Those that are made in public
- Have not been easy to make
- Are actively advocated.

The more trouble something is to obtain, the more the commitment to its value. Jobs that have difficult hurdles to jump or schools that have demanding entry qualifications are more valued as a consequence. Similarly, doctors and service providers who have waiting lists give off an aura of being special. Religious groups recognize the importance of getting commitment for true conversions, as does Weight Watchers. People want to be consistent after making a commitment since such consistency helps them uphold a favorable self-image. Being inconsistent makes us appear less attractive, consistency being a mark of commitment.

In marketing, a contribution to generating commitment is to ask people to write down what they particularly like about the product or what they approve of in personal service or what pleased them about what happened. Material incentives offered for expressing a commitment are not as effective as commitment achieved through self-persuasion, which results in the commitment being internalized. Self-persuasion can come about through *talking* oneself into it, as this is a process of self-persuasion.

That people like to be consistent is used to explain why seeking a little favor (e.g. asking a retailer to put up a poster) facilitates asking for a big favor later on (e.g. placing an order). Because being consistent helps people maintain a positive view of themselves, once people show some commitment by acceding to a small request, they are more apt to go along with larger requests. Asking for small favors as a basis for inducing a big favor is known as the 'foot-in-the-door technique'. But is it not quite a stretch to speak of 'commitment' if one accedes to a small request as the motive may be nothing more than getting rid of a persistent request? Cialdini would argue that the acceding acts like a commitment.

The reciprocity principle: there is a social obligation to repay favors in kind. As Cialdini says, the principle of reciprocity explains why 'free' inspections, or giving small gifts, tend to facilitate a sale. It is seldom that we receive a request from a charity for a donation without some small gift, typically address labels. People subscribe to benevolent appeals for the police, not generally from some belief in the cause but in the hope that the car sticker they receive from donating will get them off with a caution instead of a ticket in the event of a speeding offense. The principle may even explain why, when a brand has earned the customer's trust, customers reciprocate with loyalty. (Though not necessarily, as there can be trust without loyalty in that I may trust my financial advisor but feel no loyalty, while

I may both trust and be loyal to my doctor.) It explains the 'door-in-the-face' technique whereby a salesperson first asks a very big favor which is refused. The salesperson then asks a much smaller favor which is accepted. This happens because the very act of making it a small favor is a sort of concession that brings into play the norm of reciprocity. But also at work is the contrast effect between the large original request and the minor one. Trusting a product contrasts with suspicion of a product; many a purchase is inhibited by the consumer's suspicion that all is not what is claimed. A major problem in promoting 'a bargain' lies in removing suspicion as to whether it is in fact a genuine bargain. There is a general suspicion of the products offered by financial institutions.

Small courtesies invite reciprocal acts even if the small courtesy is simply a greeting or the provision of free coffee and doughnuts. All salespeople and service staff need to be taught this. Just going out of one's way to be polite and helpful induces a desire to respond in kind, perhaps by buying. We are reminded of lobbyists who contribute money to election campaigns. They expect support for their proposals or less opposition in return. Such lobbying is defended on the grounds of 'free speech'. There are no objections here providing there is no passing of money or the use of other material incentives. This makes it bribery. For presidential or congressional candidates to claim they are willing to accept money from lobbyists, but at the same time claim it will in no way influence them, is either dishonest or naïve. If there were no temptation or opportunity to bribe or indulge in unethical behavior, there would be merit in being virtuous but the temptation can be huge. Thus as an example, one British Member of Parliament received just ten thousand pounds in return for putting forward an amendment to a piece of legislation that would have saved Mobil Oil millions in taxes. And think of all the money made by the false labeling of food products!

Many seem to believe that the principle of reciprocity also works with God – if they undertake enough prayer or make sacrifices, God will reciprocate. If God does not reciprocate, some get angry as if they have some entitlement. Certainly all known prehistoric civilizations offered sacrifices to the gods in the hope of some sort of return. The principle of reciprocity is considered by some social scientists to be the very basis of all social cooperation: that cooperation emanates not from disguised self-interest but from the universal presence of 'strong reciprocators' in every social group (Gintis et al. 2005). This position can be defended. We could look at unrequited love as a case of non-reciprocity leading to a sense of emotional loss.

Although the principle of reciprocity is not generally associated with people who try to get even for some injury or insult, the very words 'get even' suggest a desire to reciprocate in kind for a wrong done by another. As President Kennedy was reputed to have said: 'Don't get mad, get even.'

The social proof or social validation principle: people typically look to others to see what is socially correct. What others believe and do can become the standards to follow. We follow the crowd in applauding the players after a show and do similarly in all aspects of social life. This is particularly true if the group is our social milieu. Sharing of values and beliefs with those in our social milieu makes for solidarity and mutual attractiveness. It has been facilitated by the Internet with the advent of emails, public blog sites, chat rooms, Facebook, Twitter and so on. The Internet, it is argued, has been as instrumental to the circulation of information as electricity to the transmission of energy. Computers have largely replaced people as the informational memory of the organization: 'computers transform the professional knowledge of each person into assets of the company' (Cohen 2003).

Cialdini argues that social proof is most powerful for those who feel unfamiliar or unsure in a social situation. This is because such people feel a need to look beyond themselves for evidence of what to believe and how to behave. We are less certain about what is socially appropriate than whether something is a dog or a cat. There are more problems with *social-reality-testing* than with *physical-reality-testing* since consumers trust their senses more than they trust their knowledge of socially acceptable behavior. In any case, the persuader is much more effective if the message being communicated is said to be socially validated.

The authority principle: as Cialdini says, we are socially indoctrinated to respect authority and, other things remaining equal, to obey that authority. In life generally, to question the expert authority appears unreasonable. To violate legitimate authority results in feelings of guilt. People are still on the whole conditioned to obey authority figures like teachers and bosses and this is why advertisers seek the support of relevant authority figures. There are occasions where we bow to authority figures either because they are legitimate authorities like the police or because of their accepted expertise, for example a doctor in medicine. Unfortunately, we are also apt to go along with people who have the wrong sort of expertise for the problem at hand simply because they are well known. There are implicit or explicit rules in every society as to what constitutes a legitimate authority and so commands respect.

Celebrities can often be aspirational figures. Thus presidential candidates seek the endorsement of film stars, knowing that the endorsement can count. But that endorsement can count, not because voters really believe the film star has expertise in national policies but simply because the appeal associates them with a celebrity figure with whom they identify. But the endorsement of a product by some celebrity might work because the target audience does believe the user-endorser has experience with the product. It is also common in advertising to claim that the bulk of consumers endorse this brand or that. This can be effective since consumers seek a socially endorsed product. Thus orders for the B&P Company's skincare products multiplied many times after the actress Rene Russo praised the product in a magazine article in 2000.

The scarcity principle: economics has always stressed the relation between the scarcity of a product and the price that can be demanded. As Cialdini says, opportunities to buy always appear more valuable when the opportunity is fleeting. Madoff, who pulled off the biggest Ponzi scam in history, made getting into the scheme hard, as if he were offering a favor. Companies can do the same. Hublot, a watchmaker, 'rationed' the watch to jewelers, delivering just ten watches when fifteen had been ordered on the grounds that buyers want exclusivity since desire blossoms when people cannot get what they want. Whenever we have to make considerable effort or sacrifice to obtain some scarce good, the motivation to obtain that good is strengthened as otherwise the sunk costs of the sacrifice would appear to be in vain. On the other hand, when some 'good' is not just scarce but out of reach for the consumer, we can have the *sour grapes effect*, where we claim not to want it – not uncommon in love relationships. As Elster (1999) says, 'as in the story of the fox and the sour grapes, people adjust by changing their desires rather than their beliefs'.

Cialdini explains the efficacy of the scarcity principle on the grounds that, as an opportunity becomes less available, our freedom to choose is reduced and we all hate to lose the freedoms we have come to expect. Thus it is more persuasive to tell homeowners what they could lose financially from having inadequate insulation than to tell homeowners how much they could save with such insulation. This is tied to the general finding that we are more concerned about losses than corresponding gains. This makes it easier for legislators to retain their seats – and for manufacturers to find it easier to retain customers than to convert from rivals. It is one reason why those with more to lose from a particular piece of legislation are more emotionally aroused by its suggested passage than those who will materially gain by it.

Consumers may use the scarcity of an item to judge its worth. This applies even to information itself in that information obtained that is not generally available is considered more valuable. The banning of a book or the banning of the love choice of one's children can intensify the desire. We value things more that have just become scarce than when scarcity is a constant factor. This explains the frequent use of such appeals as 'last few'; 'last chance to buy'; 'only one per customer'; 'limited edition'. Those selling houses talk about its being a window of opportunity in that present interest rates are low but forecasted to go up, which means missing out. Manufacturers proclaim an inability to meet consumer demand as a way of increasing the demand still further. It is common to create an atmosphere of competition for the item to make people keener, as occurs (before the glut of houses) in inviting prospective buyers to an open house and to have someone show a keen interest in purchasing it to arouse buying interest on the part of the others. Consumers may desire something simply because they cannot have it. Brehm (1966), in an experiment, eliminated certain options from being chosen and found they were then valued more highly.

The liking principle: this is the sixth and last principle mentioned by Cialdini. We grow to like (non-threatening) things that become familiar to us and people become familiar and liked through *supportive interaction* through time. As we say, people can grow on you. The interaction needs to be supportive, as occurs in cooperative endeavors, since contact alone will not help if it is disagreeable. Perhaps liking, as the result of supportive inter-action, reflects the power of association in that someone associated with pleasant happenings will also share the pleasantness. But there is another factor at work in that we all tend to modify our beliefs to come closer to the assumed perspective of our audience, which can lead to much more open-mindedness. People who mix with people of different views and converse with them find any original extremism diminishes.

As people desire to be associated with powerful figures, the powerful find it easier, other things remaining equal, to get people to like them, while the views of the powerful are likely to get more attention. Cialdini points out that many sales training programs urge trainees to 'mirror and match' the customer's body posture, mood, and verbal style as these lead to positive results. Mutual liking encourages the doing of mutual favors and biasing decisions in favor of those we like.

In describing the six methods of persuasion above, comment has been added by the author that might not be endorsed by behaviorism. In making these comments, there is an acceptance that social conditioning might not be the sole or even the major mechanism at work and other approaches might be equally as explanatory. This leads us to consider alternative explanatory paradigms.

ALTERNATIVE EXPLANATORY INTERPRETATIONS

Is the Cialdini explanation in terms of social conditioning the most use-ful? There are other psychological perspectives, paradigms or theories that explain the same phenomena as Cialdini's so-called social condition-ing. Cialdini regards his six mechanisms as ways of inducing *automatic* compliance in face-to-face dealings. He assumes the mechanisms oper-ate through social conditioning to evoke automatic compliance. If these mechanisms do induce automatic compliance, they would be *causally deter-ministic* and very powerful indeed. But the 'compliance' can be explained on other grounds. These other grounds draw on paradigms discussed in later chapters, except for ethnopsychology, and so would naturally fall into other chapters of this book. But there are two reasons for discussing these in this chapter:

- To show different approaches can corroborate Cialdini's claims
- How looking at some phenomena from multiple perspectives and arriv-ing at the same conclusion adds greatly to our confidence in the conclusions. Different perspectives have different attractions but may also have different limitations.

EXPLAINING THROUGH THE REASON-GIVING EXPLANATION

The reason-giving explanation comes under ethnopsychology. While it is not difficult to visualize social conditioning as entering into the six mechanisms, it is also easy to view the six mechanisms as simply providing reasons for just wanting to comply since we may simply have *reasons* for:

- Reciprocating favors
- Wanting to be consistent and adhering to commitments
- Seeking a bargain
- Endorsing what is socially validated
- Going along with people we like
- Wanting to believe and obey authority figures.

The reason-giving explanation is very different from claiming the presence of conditioning mechanisms powerful enough to induce automatic compliance, bypassing conscious reflection. The six mechanisms, if viewed as reasons, are never absolute or even sufficient to guarantee compliance but are conditional on context or circumstances. Only radical behaviorism views conditioning as entirely unconscious resulting in automatic response, otherwise these 'mechanisms' can be interpreted as 'good' reasons for compliance. The six mechanisms, as reasons, can persuade but do not compel compliance.

EXPLAINING THROUGH EMOTIONAL MECHANISMS

Emotion could provide the motivation behind compliance. Most studies of emotion in psychology have been carried out by social psychologists and this is where (in Chapter 11) there is the fullest discussion of emotion. It could be argued that the 'power' of Cialdini's mechanisms to 'entrap' consumers into compliance arises not from any rigid, ingrained social conditioning but from their deeper ties to the emotions. In just assuming conditioning, not enough attention is paid to arousing the customer's emotions through exploiting her concerns.

Emotions are aroused when the consumer's concerns are involved in that events threaten these concerns or present an opportunity to promote them. It is emotion that energizes the motivation to comply if the emotion is acutely felt. Emotion motivates the process of motivation. Listening or seeing what people get emotional about is a guide to their concerns, while knowing people's major concerns is a guide to what they are likely to get emotional about. Resisting the six mechanisms entails emotional costs. Emotions are aroused if the things being said or done are of sufficient concern to the consumer as to give rise to highly negative or positive evaluations. Even then the evaluation may not result in compliance since attempted manipulation using the six mechanisms above can backfire, leading to anger and indignation rather than compliance. Emotions nonetheless can help explain the six mechanisms:

- Adhering to the principle of reciprocity avoids the potential for *embarrassment* since adhering to what is socially appropriate avoids the embarrassment of violating social norms

- Adhering to the principle of being consistent and abiding by commitments avoids the potential for *embarrassment* and *shame*
- Adhering to the principle of scarcity reduces the *fear* of losing out
- Adhering to the principle of social proof (social validation) reduces the sense of taking a *risk* and increases the feeling of *social solidarity*
- Adhering to the principle of liking enhances emotional *bonding* and the resulting sense of *affiliation* with those with whom we identify
- Adhering to what authority or expert figures assert reduces the *fear* of going against the judgments of those in power or of greater status and/or knowledge.

Thinking itself can arouse the emotions as when we look back on an embarrassing experience or just think about jumping off a cliff or out of an airplane. The fact that images of past events or imagined events can affect behavior is another illustration of the *semantic autonomy* of words or the causal powers of thought alone. This is why ads may ask the target audience to simply imagine what it would be like (what it would REALLY be like) to drive the car shown along the highway in the way shown. Pictures may not only be worth a thousand words but can emotionally move the target audience much more than words.

FIVE SOURCES OF INFLUENCE AND POWER AS EXPLANATIONS

The study of influence and power is more common in sociology than elsewhere. We can view Cialdini's six mechanisms in terms of five sources of influence and power. Power is closely tied to coercion, while the other sources reflect influence. These five sources are generic categories, embracing Cialdini's mechanisms as subsets.

Coercion: While coercion is not part of salesmanship, coercion is a mechanism for achieving compliance. But coercion achieves, within the limits of what is practically or legally feasible, only minimal compliance – enough to ward off punishment. The appeal is to *fear* based on intimidation, with security being the incentive for compliance. Applying coercion is different from applying legal sanctions in that sanctions are accepted as legitimate, while coercion is not.

Patronage: Patronage obtains agreement through appeals to *self-interest* based on expectations of material gain. Patronage in the sense of offering material rewards is probably the most common way of achieving compliance. But allegiance is rented with the likelihood of loyalty being small. But there can be loyalty to a product based on identifications, which can be broken. Thus the loyalty of beer drinkers in St. Louis to its home-brewed beer, Anheuser-Busch, was unquestioned until the firm was taken over by Belgium's InBev. The new home beer is becoming Schlafly Beer, a local start-up whose sales have jumped 30 percent since the takeover.

Legitimacy: Legitimacy brings about compliance by its foundation in social norms, enforced by social pressure, with the incentive to comply tied with the desire for *social acceptance*.

Attractiveness: Attractiveness can bring about compliance: (a) physical attractiveness is the popular exemplar of someone perceived as attractive. Physical attractiveness facilitates compliance, as the physically attractive are apt to impress people as being more intelligent, socially skilled and adjusted, as well as possessing other socially desirable characteristics. But physical attractiveness is not the only basis for finding someone attractive to deal with. Attractiveness can arise also from (b) similarity of background; (c) establishing common ground such as having the same hobbies or anything else that indicates having things in common; or (d) liking arising from supportive interaction through time with the customer and salesperson showing that liking. Being supportive of a buyer's self-image/self-esteem produces the likelihood of identifying with the seller to the extent of wanting to go along with his or her requests and opinions. Another way of appearing attractive to the other party is to imperfectly and slowly copy the movements of the other person. Subtle mimicry brings about a bonding with the other party, cementing an interaction through common ground. But mimicry must be subtle (following the other person slowly and after a time interval) or it degenerates into mockery. The incentive to comply follows from liking the other party through similarity or behavior that suggests friendliness and equality, together with a manner that comes across 'as if revealing all'. Similarity is important whether because people seem more disposed to buy from people like themselves or hire people like themselves. Of course, there are many ways people can be similar but a convergence of values seems to be important.

All that said, it is often difficult to predict whether an ad or a person will be found attractive by the majority of the target audience. Will the audience like it or not? This is a question that worries everyone, not only in the advertising business but in the entertainment and selling business.

Credibility: Credibility is reflected in the source's perceived *trustworthiness*/reliability and technical expertise. The consumer views a source as trustworthy if it is felt it can be depended on in terms of its communications. Perceptions of trustworthiness make it easier to trust that someone. The sources of communication are likely to be viewed as trustworthy if they cohere with the values and experience of the target audience or past communications have proved to be reliable. Credible appeals resonate with the target audience so the message is internalized. The incentive to go along with such messages is the desire for true beliefs since true beliefs can be vital to success or even survival. But the consumer, like people generally, cannot just decide to believe because they want to do so. We cannot just decide black is white or vice versa or that we like something when we don't.

Yet throughout the ages people have been tortured because their torturers seem to think beliefs are freely chosen. On the other hand, many of the consumer's beliefs are not well anchored in commitment so are much easier to engage. Beliefs about social norms are more easily changed than beliefs that cohere with physical reality.

Source credibility can be diminished or undermined. In politics, negative advertising is one (often effective) way. This is essentially character assassination or *ad hominem* nastiness where the person is attacked, rather than the person's argument or policies. Some political commentators make a good living from doing nothing but this. Attaching a label to someone saying he or she is a socialist or a fascist or a racist or an anti-semite is a basic of political advertising. It does not matter much what the label is, providing it has very negative connotations for the target audience. There are always similarities between any two people so finding that someone has something in common with Hitler or Stalin is easy and easily exploited. In line with the adage 'no smoke without fire', people believe there must be something to it. It explains why negative advertising can be effective. You attribute hated qualities to your opponent, generating an appeal to solidarity against the person possessing such negative attributes. It seems we are far more aware of the things we hate rather than the things we love. Negative advertising chooses an emotionally arousing symbol or image which is then attached to one's rival. It is taken for granted that most of the target audience will never move beyond the emotion aroused by the image and not ask questions about whether it is true; the emotion distracts from doing this. Shared enemies or opponents in ideology can be a good basis for bonding, as can a shared emotional experience, just as soldiers bond in face-to-face fighting with the enemy. Political discussions among supporters of one party are not concerned with voicing evidentially supported claims but with bonding, increasing solidarity through sentiments that all the group share. People, as the anthropologist Mary Douglas (1996) says, are more conscious of their hatreds than their loves and more bonded by what they hate than what they love. If negative advertising remains unchallenged, there is a danger of the audience accepting it as true. But there are also dangers for the sponsors in that they lose something if they get associated too closely with just making attacks.

Perceived credibility need not be based on evidence. It is because consumers generally have neither the time nor often the ability to check things that they tend to follow the coherence theory of truth; truth being what coheres with what is already believed. Much that consumers accept by way of advice adheres to a coherence theory of truth: it makes sense to them and to those giving the advice. In political marketing this means that anything is likely to be believed if it coheres with one's political ideology or prejudices. This is not to suggest that a coherence theory of truth cannot be valid. Many scientific findings are accepted chiefly on the ground that they cohere with what is already known or cohere with expectations but coherence here is well grounded.

LINKING MOTIVES TO PERSUASIVE APPEALS

There is still another psychological perspective to explain why Cialdini's six mechanisms work, without resorting to the notion of conditioning. This third way is to interpret motives at work and link these motives to corresponding persuasive appeals. The personal and professional goals/motives of consumers can be committed to memory by remembering five Is:

Image projected: Buyers are more persuaded if seller communications are supportive of the image they wish to project. If a potential customer presents herself as an experienced buyer concerned about others showing respect, then sales appeals should address this 'need'.

Interpersonal relationships: All those concerned with buying want to bolster interpersonal relations. Salespeople contribute to persuading the customer by telling the potential customer when other people in the customer's reference group are enthusiastic about the product. This reminds us of the importance of face-to-face selling when we are being told personal calls are being replaced by cheaper telephone calls. The conventional wisdom is that the difference in performance between the lowest sales performance and the best varies by a factor of three.

Integrity sought: Buyers want to act in a way that is supportive of personal integrity. A consumer may be attracted to solar heating but the added argument about solar heating being a highly responsible thing to do may be the final trigger that is needed.

Innovation risk avoidance: There is risk attached to anything bought for the first time. Buyers seek to avoid unnecessary risk and anticipated feelings of regret. It is more persuasive to diminish a sense of possible loss than to enhance a corresponding gain. Thus an investment advisor is better (if possible) stressing preservation of the amount invested before talking about potential gains.

Investment payoff: Buyers seek a payoff from buying whether in psychological or material terms. If buying can be shown to put the customer in a good light or contribute to advancing the interests of themselves or significant others, this helps the sale. Thus telling buyers that his boss or others felt he made a good buying decision provides reassurance and a basis for further sales.

Table 4.1 shows how these five Is relate to Cialdini's mechanisms and the sources of influence.

CONCLUSION

There are no non-trivial, universal laws when it comes to human behavior because behavior is affected by various contextual/situational factors (including individual personalities). There is the oft-repeated study of Princeton seminary students who, after listening and discussing the story of the Good Samaritan, were six times less likely to go to the aid of someone in distress, slumped in a doorway, if they were told they were going to

Table 4.1 Compliance mechanisms, Motivational appeal, Influence sources

Compliance mechanisms	Motivational appeal	Influence sources
(Cialdini's six mechanisms)	(The five Is)	(Sources)
Consistency/commitment	Image projected	Credibility
Reciprocity	Integrity sought	Legitimacy
Social validation	Interpersonal relations	Legitimacy
Authority/expertise	Innovation risk avoidance	Credibility
Scarcity	Investment payoff	Patronage
Liking	Image projected	Attractiveness

be late for an appointment. The notion that social scientists have proven something beyond doubt is nonsense. He or she may be convinced but 'being convinced' is a psychological notion, while proof lies in the objective realm of logic and evidence. But social scientists yearn for universals and those who claim to have discovered universals generate most interest. After all, there is considerable difference in interest between saying some dreams are manifestations of secret fears or wishes and saying *all* dreams are secret fears or wishes. Only the universal creates real excitement. But if we had to give one general lesson (not a law) that we learn from behaviorism, it is the desire for instant gratification. Anything about a seller's offering that necessitates postponement of that gratification is a disincentive. The consumer only needs a trivial reason to do what she feels like doing anyway to achieve instant gratification.

Behaviorism is far from being dead or obsolete. What a study of behaviorism does is draw attention to the influence of external environmental factors in providing positive and negative reinforcements that condition a good deal of behavior. Behaviorism has developed many methodologies for molding behavior. Some of these have been discussed in this chapter. In respect to consumer behavior, marketeers need to look at all elements of their marketing strategy to ensure they provide power enhancement for the brand or positive reinforcements for:

- Attracting new customers
- Converting from rivals
- Increasing the level of individual business, or simply
- Maintaining existing customers.

CASE: PEPSICO

During 2011, PepsiCo increased revenue by around 9 percent, helped by a boom in emerging markets. But this statistic can be misleading in that the market share for its drinks business, embracing for instance Pepsi and the sports drink Gatorade, has been declining. This decline has affected the value of its snack business Frito-Lay, which includes Walkers, Doritos and Tostitos.

Four years ago, the CEO, Indra Nooyi, with a background in strategic planning, set about producing more healthy drinks so that the company's fizzy drinks were less sugary and its snacks less salty (by 25 percent) and less fatty (by 15 percent). This was part of an overall strategy to move the company into marketing healthier, more nutritious foods, which in turn led to the takeover of Quaker Oats and Tropicana. The mission was to increase the revenue from such products from around $10 billion to $30 billion. But since taking over the business in 2006, things have not gone well for Ms Nooyi. While the shares of Coca-Cola, its nearest rival, have increased by 50 percent, Pepsi's shares have declined by 7 percent. It has been suggested that splitting PepsiCo into two companies, one focusing on drinks and the other on snacks, is one way to go. This would facilitate better coordination within each division as well as highlighting the winners and losers to investors. But other outside commentators point to the change in emphasis from tasty to health-centered products as being the source of the decline. The aim should be to give the target audience what it wants rather than what is better for it health-wise.

Case questions

- How might behaviorism explain the change to healthier products being largely responsible for the decline in market share?
- What might behaviorism suggest as a better way of achieving the CEO's move to healthier products?

Fill out the following elements of corporate strategy and identify what behaviorism might claim to be a likely problem. (A strategy is defined as a broad conception of how resources are to be deployed to overcome resistance to the achievement of objectives. While objectives focus on future states, strategies focus on the paths by which to get there.)

Corporate strategy involves:

1. Defining the business of the firm. The definition of the firm's business that has come to be adopted is the product/market scope definition, which defines the firm's business in terms of: (a) customer targets; (b) functions served or benefits offered; (c) technology employed.
2. Investment objectives. Investment objectives can be in terms of: (a) growth; (b) hold/defend; (c) turnabout/turnaround; (d) harvest (wind down); (e) divest; (f) liquidate.
3. Horizontal strategy. An organization's horizontal strategy occurs in a multi-business company when it seeks to coordinate the goals and strategies of the related businesses and exploit any synergies among them. The interrelationships with the potential for synergy can be: (a) tangible, in that there is a sharing of activities to reap economies of scale resulting from similar technologies and so on; (b) intangible, when there is a transference of skills and know-how from one business to another; (c) competitor, when multipoint competition occurs

as happens when attacking one competitor in one class of business has implications for the firm's other businesses since the competitor may respond by attacking the firm's other businesses instead of the one doing the attacking.

DISCUSSION QUESTIONS ON CHAPTER 4 (BEHAVIORISM)

1. Why do behaviorists (adhering to operant conditioning) see advertising as concerned with retaining customers and downplay advertising's role in attracting new customers and converting from rivals?
2. How might operant conditioning and the formation of habits be related?
3. How does operant conditioning explain the incentive nature of getting air miles from using your credit card?
4. At one time it was common for retailers to have a couple of periods a year in which they had sales. Now we find some department stores will have some different items on sale every week. Explain this in terms of operant conditioning.
5. 'Cialdini's social conditioning was social but would not satisfy the criteria for conditioning.' Discuss.

Chapter 5

Psychoanalytic Psychology

BASIC CLAIMS

Sigmund Freud (1856–1939) is the father of psychoanalytic psychology as well as psychoanalysis. Psychoanalysis is tied to psychoanalytic psychology: witness how the *Journal of Psychoanalytic Psychology* describes itself as 'the intersection of psychoanalysis and psychology'. *Psychoanalytic* psychology denies that mental life is dominated by the conscious mind; Freud questioned the degree to which we know the motives lying behind our actions while arguing that people's real motives and intentions remain hidden. *Psychoanalysis*, in turn, consists of both a set of techniques for discovering and exploring the underlying motives lying behind human behavior and as treatment for various mental disorders like neurosis.

The paradigm of psychoanalytic psychology (Freudian psychology) imputes to behavior a perspective that makes claims for the role of the *unconscious* lying behind human behavior, an unconscious defined as consisting of happenings in the mind, of which the subject is entirely unaware. But there is an inherent vagueness in the way the concept of 'unconsciousness' is used in psychology generally. Searle (1992), a well-known analytic philosopher, argues that all talk in psychology about unconscious mental states and processes is simply talk about *dispositional* states; that is, we are disposed to believe this or want that, while talk about unconscious mental states that are, even in principle, inaccessible can be shown to be incoherent. The term 'unconscious' in psychology, at a minimum, means 'outside of awareness', as perhaps are dispositional states, so Searle's view is defensible. However, the definition of being 'outside awareness' is deficient since not all things outside awareness are unconscious happenings; some automatic behavior, like some hand movements in talking, takes place without conscious awareness.

In Freudian psychology, the unconscious is home to unconscious pressing motives (desires) and unconscious beliefs that play a *causal* role in bringing about behavior. For Freud, neither beliefs nor desires need be conscious beliefs or conscious desires in order to play a causal role in activating behavior. Freudian psychology undermines the view of humans as conscious rational beings who can examine their beliefs and wants, assess their meaning and consider the pros and cons in weighing the evidence. We all accept that there are causes of behavior of which we are unaware and this is where psychoanalytic psychology finds its opportunity: to unmask the 'real motives' behind behavior. The psychoanalytic approach in marketing is associated with the notion of *unconscious meanings* being attached to products so that advertisers can design appeals that tap these meanings to appeal to basic motivations.

Psychoanalytic psychology seeks the unconscious causes, reasons and meanings that motivate behavior. The notion of the unconscious, as mental processes that operate below the threshold of consciousness, came to maturation with Freud but it had a long ancestry, with philosophers such as Plato, Leibniz and Schopenhauer, and Romanticism in the eighteenth and nineteenth centuries, all having an interest in it. Freudian concepts, such as rationalization, denial, childhood emotional experiences manifesting themselves in adult behavior and sexuality as a major motive, are today taken for granted as part of folk psychology.

A *rationalization* is an *ex post facto* justification for some action, while the true motives remain concealed. There can be many social reasons for not revealing our true motives since not all motives are socially acceptable. When the magazine *Playboy* was launched, it allowed its male readers to rationalize buying it for the sophistication of the articles it contained rather than for the sexuality of the nude women within. The Freudian notion of *denial* has been frequently quoted to explain why warnings (like those of Raghuram G. Rajan of the University of Chicago Booth School of Business) about the likelihood of a financial meltdown in 2008 were dismissed, since such warnings were too frightening to contemplate. Interestingly, Plato (429–347 BC), long before Freud, regarded sexual desire as the lead player in our appetites as did his fellow Greeks. If some of Freud's ideas now sound commonplace, his views at the time (like Darwin's) were a blow to self-esteem, particularly Freudian notions like the power of the unconscious, infant sexuality, the death drive and the masochistic pleasure in humiliation and pain (Cohen 2005). It was only later in his work that he put emphasis on aggressive 'drives'. From Freud's perspective, unconscious motivated dispositions are the basic motivators and Freud denied they could be manipulated by rewards and punishments (so much for behaviorism!)

The goal of psychoanalysis is to empower the individual to gain control over the unconscious self by bringing into consciousness his or her repressed desires and fears. This contrasts with paradigms where intentional action is considered conscious, purposive action on the grounds that having an intention implies having a goal in mind, while to act on an intention means believing that such action will lead to achieving the goal. In mainstream psychology and neuroscience, however, there is also no support for the view of consumers being always consciously aware as they go about their business. Kagan (1989), a Harvard psychologist, casts doubt on the pervasiveness of the degree of consciousness that the concept of 'conscious action' implies – whether it always implies reflection/deliberation before acting. For Kagan, consciousness is analogous to fire station personnel who only spring into action to fight fires when the alarm goes off. This is now a common view among many psychologists. Similarly, he argues that some problem of concern has to arise before we spring into conscious deliberation. Since emotion is aroused when happenings greatly concern us, it could be argued that emotion is involved in all conscious action. Mostly we, even as consumers, are on 'automatic pilot' until aroused. It is thus a mistake to view the consumer as being involved in constant decision-making or consciously aware of what is going on. How much thinking is involved in habitual buying, which describes for many consumers most of their purchases?

PSYCHOANALYSIS TODAY

Psychoanalysis seems to have been superseded in psychiatry by pharmacology, with psychiatrists referring to themselves as *psychopharmacologists*, starting with the development of Thorazine in the 1950s and later with the advent of Prozac at the end of the 1980s. The move from talk-therapy to prescription drugs followed naturally from the perspective of psychiatry today that chemical imbalances were the cause of mental illness, though in truth there is no consensus on whether imbalances are causes of mental illness or simply symptoms. With a focus on the elimination of symptoms, there has been diminishing interest in analyzing the life histories of patients, substituting for analysis an approach that focuses on symptoms and drugs that are claimed to be effective in relieving such symptoms. Consumers turn to medicine for cures for mental illness as they do not feel qualified to do other than accept expert advice.

If prescription drugs are effective in restoring mental health, what role is there for psychoanalysis? And does the success of drugs not suggest that mental illness is at base a physical illness? The answers to these questions for many psychiatrists have led Freudian approaches to almost disappear in psychiatry. In fact there are psychiatrists today who know less about Freud and his theories than mainstream psychologists. Yet most categories of mental illness in the *Diagnostic and Statistical Manual of Mental Disorders (DSM)* are not grounded in medical science but the opinion of psychiatrists called upon to subscribe to the book (Angell 2011). This, together with the dominance of pharmaceutical companies in determining what is prescribed, suggests that psychiatry itself is not in a healthy state.

But not everyone in the field of mental health subscribes to the theory that mental health is caused by chemical imbalances. Daniel Carlat (2011) is one psychiatrist who denies this claim. Carlat regards the chemical imbalance theory as a convenient myth to destigmatize mental illness. While traditionally a drug was developed to treat an illness, it is claimed an illness is now *postulated* to fit a drug. Kirsch (2011), a British psychologist, reported that his research in respect to antidepressants led him to conclude that the relatively *small difference* in effectiveness between drugs and placebos in clinical trials might not be a real drug effect at all since we might have been simply comparing 'regular' placebo with 'extra-strength' placebo. But other researchers reviewing his work claim his calculations underestimate the mean drug-placebo effect (2.68, not 1.8). Still, a constant criticism of drug treatments for mental illness is that it is not clear that medication is a great success as drugs do not work for many patients, with a consequent high dropout and relapse rate. Drugs often have unpleasant side-effects with doctors then having to prescribe more drugs to ease or combat the side-effects. Mental illness is diagnosed on *subjective* manifestations not, as in medicine generally, by objective manifestations of disease like abnormal laboratory tests. In contrast, others argue that, although pharmopsychiatry may be primitive when it comes to the causal mechanisms of mental illness, on the whole the drugs do work – antipsychotics for schizophrenia, benzo-diaz for anxiety disorders and stimulants for attention deficit hyperactivity disorder (ADHD) – over and above results obtained with placebos.

Psychoanalytic procedures have not been discarded in psychotherapy (Engel 2008) or in marketing. There are some psychotherapists and some marketing academics whose basic orientation is Freudian. The Freudian paradigm views the unconscious as a storehouse of motivation; a moti-vation that enters into dreams, fantasies, slips-of-the-tongue and neurotic symptoms. Dreams are a form of consciousness when consciousness is viewed as a continuum ranging from being fully aware and goal-oriented, to being hardly awake, to merely dreaming.

Freud's *methods* concentrated on dreams (initially) and the unstructured, free-association interview; the Freudian *focus* was on the unconscious and the 'irrational' elements in behavior while the Freudian *legacy* is the large body of literature stemming from his work and the impact he has had on mainstream psychology and educated people everywhere.

Freud claimed we can access the unconscious via hypnosis, slips of the tongue, depth interviewing and, most important of all, the analysis of dreams. Freud was later in life to discard hypnosis and dreams (once regarded as the royal road to tapping the unconscious) for accessing the unconscious in favor of the method of free association interviews where patients were asked to say whatever comes into their heads. This is still the basic tool of psychoanalysis.

Many ideas associated with Freud are found in earlier writers. Montaigne (1533–1592), whose writings were familiar to Freud, believed dreams revealed the dreamer's inner wishes and, like Freud, believed in the crucial importance of our earliest years when habits are being formed. As for the 'unconscious', this was part of the Romantic movement in psychology and philosophy in the late eighteenth and early nineteenth centuries, while the notion of hidden motives links to Nietzsche (1844–1900).

Biopsychiatrists are apt to treat Freud as unworthy of more than a passing reference to illustrate past error in the field. Crews (1998) (not a psychiatrist but an early devotee of Freud who only later became a severe critic) is vehemently critical of Freud. He claims Freud invented the data on which his major theories were based and that he lied about the outcome of treatments based on these theories – that he was merely a master of image-management. In a more recent book *Follies of the Wise* (2006), Crews claims Freud just made it up as he went along and there is no historical evidence that Freud cured any of his patients. Freud, to Crews, is just a fraud, with his writings full of untestable theories, conceptual confusion and the ignoring of counterexamples that amounts to chronic untruthfulness – all simply aimed at parting credulous patients from their money. Wilcocks (2001), another Freud critic, accuses Freud of near-criminal incompetence and dishonesty and claims his writings are those of a confused cocaine-intoxicated man. But for others Freud is an interpreter of behavior of the highest order (Elliott 1998). Bass (2001), a sympathetic writer, argues that Freud, in his later work, was rethinking the basic mechanism of psychic defense as disavowal rather than repression that promised to be much more fruitful. Many marketing academics endorse the more favorable assessments of Freud and reject the notion of being just a charlatan. In the history of psychology, Freud holds a notable place because he introduced a perspective that integrated a number of otherwise miscellaneous topics into a coherent whole, like personality development and structure, the unconscious, dream interpretation and infantile sexuality. His model of mind (see below) in terms of ego, superego and id has yet to be superseded.

Psychoanalytic psychology is no longer regarded as a general psychology but a psychology dealing with questions on unconscious inner conflicts as people strive towards achieving goals – inner conflicts that can give rise to mental illness. Of course, inner conflicts are seldom serious. Thus all buying gives rise to conflict as it is an approach-avoidance situation – the conflict, for example, between wanting the product (the approach) and paying for it (the avoidance). Such conflicts temporarily frustrate but are hardly likely to cause much mental anguish. Consumers also face an approach-approach situation where both alternatives are equally attractive but this, too, is simply likely to give rise to temporary indecision. The avoidance-avoidance situation arises when both alternatives are unattractive. This 'devil and the deep blue sea' situation suggests a need to escape, but most dilemmas like this are usually false in that there are additional options.

Freud's theory of personality is a model of the mind, structured by three elements: the *id* (the seat of unconscious passions, the primitive urges of the flesh), the *superego* (society's social constraints or a person's conscience) and the *ego* (the public and consciously known self, represented by reason). The id, the ego and the superego determine human behavior through their conflicting interactions. Freud took for granted that the ego and superego remain largely unconscious, with the id being incessant in its demands and with reason never able to achieve a position of dominance.

Kagan (2006) claims Freud had three original ideas:

- That early family experiences which frustrated biological impulses for pleasure give rise to unconscious states that could affect later development of personality and encourage neurotic symptoms. Freud viewed the human personality as developing during childhood in five stages: (a) *oral* stage at age one to two years when pleasure is associated with nursing and nurturing things into the body via the mouth; (b) *anal* stage around the second to third year is associated with toilet training and self-control, with excessive punishment for accidents or, alternatively, overindulgence leading to problems later in life; (c) *phallic* (or Oedipal stage) from age three to six associated with pleasurable feelings in the genitals and an Oedipus complex; (d) *latency* stage at around age six associated with early sexual feelings and socialization; (e) *genital* stage in adolescence associated with maturing sexually, moving away from self-centeredness towards social integration. Social integration implies the individual fits into relevant social groups so that mutual support, obligations and expectations are met.

- Too much or too little sexual pleasure is harmful.
- Revealing upsetting beliefs or wishes in the unconscious, through the therapist's free-association sessions, releases the energy used to suppress the upsetting wishes and beliefs. Anxiety is reduced by removing from the unconscious the repressed wishes. For Freud, people have a fixed amount of energy which he labeled the 'libido' and this supply could be depleted through the repression of sexual impulses.

Freudian psychology can be interpreted as dealing with the effects of repressed desires and neurotic beliefs; the id being equated with suppressed but pressing desires; the superego with beliefs about social appropriateness and what constitutes moral behavior and the ego with checking and screening desires to ensure they cohere with an acceptable self-image. The ego's job is to reconcile the competing demands of the id and the superego. Viewed this way, Freud's conceptualization of the mind is intelligible, while no recent model of the mind has entirely displaced the Freudian perspective on how the mind is structured.

It was mainly Freud's theory of dreams that gave him visibility and attracted criticism, essentially because of Freud's emphasis on sexual symbolism. Though Freud employed the term 'sexual' for any bodily pleasure, symbolism in dreams he saw as confined to the genital organs, sexual processes and intercourse. For Freud, the relationship between the manifest content and the latent content of dreams was primarily symbolic and this made it possible to interpret a dream without questioning the dreamer. In any case, he argued that unacceptable beliefs and desires can be discovered, confronted and exposed through rational argument, with the result that they lose their power over the individual. Rational thinking on an issue need not follow the stereotype of being divorced from emotion in that emotions can be an important type of evidence. Thus the consumer, in choosing an item of clothing, may find herself thrilled with a particular dress and this emotion is highly relevant to her decision on whether to buy.

Dreams were considered the most important because they are places where socially unacceptable thoughts are most likely to occur, often in coded form. Freudian therapy (contrary to critics) does assume self-knowledge is possible since knowing about one's inner desires and feelings is a way to cure neurosis. Freud, however, undermines trust in self-knowledge since what we think to be our real motives may not be the real ones at work. This is so because the conscious mind does not have access to the unconscious, or the irrational part of self.

Defense mechanisms are unconscious strategies of self-deception, the purpose of which for Freud was to protect the ego. For example, *rationalizations* protect the ego against harsher aspects of reality. Rationalizations occur in buying and can be a problem when asking buyers about their reasons. Reasons for buying, given *ex post facto* by respondents, commonly seem like rationalizations to justify choices rather than explain them. Buyers may work back to think of justifying reasons for buying when in fact they simply acted on impulse. Consumers may not be able to justify to themselves the buying of some product but think of a reason which allows them to go ahead. Rationalization is not the only defense mechanism. According to the psychoanalytic perspective, there is *projection* which ascribes to others one's own deficient characteristics to protect oneself from anxiety. There can also be the defense mechanisms of *repression* where the unpleasant is pushed into the unconscious. Finally there are the defense mechanisms of *aggression*, and *regression* in going back to childish behaviors or modes of functioning.

An unconscious motive in Freud is one forbidden by the superego and not acknowledged by the conscious self. Freud's concept of the unconscious is unlike the concept of a *subconscious* or what Freud called the 'preconscious' level, which is the level of mental life assumed to exist immediately below the threshold of consciousness.

On the general topic of *self-deception*, it is not an aberration but something we all do on occasion even if it simply involves setting one's watch five minutes fast to deceive ourselves about the time. The benefits of self-deception may sometimes outweigh the cost as, say, in the case of the wives of miners lost in a mine disaster who deceive themselves about the chances of their husbands being saved. Such deception allows hope, which avoids the opposite of hope which is despair, giving time for these wives to slowly adjust to the truth.

Subliminal perception is associated with the subconscious and refers to the effects of stimuli that are too short to be perceived. However, the perceptual threshold differs from one person to another, as this ability forms a normal distribution for the population at large. But subliminal perception involves a contradiction as people are unable to see optical displays that generate no visual experience. On the other hand, optical displays do activate neural processes that could potentially affect behavior but may not be sufficient for commercial exploitation (Greenwald et al. 1996). Subliminal advertising aims to affect a person's behavior by a below-threshold level (of seeing) stimulus. There is no evidence it is more effective than when the stimulus is consciously apprehended.

There have been many deviations from Freud by his followers. Adler and Jung, together with Wilhelm Stekel and Wilhelm Reich, were all cast out from Freud's circle for doctrinal deviations; that is, perspectives that deviated from Freud's. Alfred Adler (1870–1937) was convinced that the 'will to power' was as important as the sex drive in human motivation and believed that the frustration of the 'will to power' gives rise to feelings of inadequacy and neurotic behavior. Whatever the de jure power an individual possesses the de facto power is always much less since every powerful individual is constrained by obligations to others and accountability to some wider set of stake-owners. Believing that the sex drive in human motivation is in general dominant does not rule out the possibility that the will to power can on occasion be the dominant motive. But Freud obviously thought that to accept the will to power as an equally dominant motivator would undermine the neat coherence of his overall theory.

Freud was the mentor of Carl Jung (1875–1861) but Jung later became Freud's rival. Jung was unable to accept Freud's perspective on the unconscious. He believed that Freud's conception of the unconscious as a place of repressed urges and denied emotions was incomplete and too focused on neurosis. He viewed the unconscious as a repository of *archetypes* pervading all human experience. Jung's characterization of an archetype was not simply the original model formed (as in popular usage) but as the set of unconscious, inherited images and ideas that are the constituents of the collective unconscious. His notion of archetypes appearing in myths led him to the view that the creation of symbols was a major characteristic of humans. As the 'union of rational and irrational truth', the production of symbols was the most important function of the unconscious. For Jung, dreams offered a symbolic narrative emanating from the depths of the psyche or true being. Yet, unlike Freud, he viewed dreams as 'inferior expressions of unconscious content' as opposed to using an active imagination in developing 'waking dreams' through introspection (Jung 2009).

Jung's central themes were that humans shared a pool of wisdom that he called the *collective unconscious* together with the concept of an archetype or inborn images held in common by all people, like the Hero, the Evil One and the Wise Old Man. Advertising sometimes seeks to link brands to archetypes, so the notion is by no means dead.

PSYCHOANALYTICALLY INFORMED RESEARCH IN MARKETING

Psychoanalytically informed research into consumer behavior is advocated by Holbrook (1988) (among others) to 'move beyond the relatively surface level of meaning accessible to the ethnographer to explore the psychoanalytic interpretation of consumption'. None of us would deny the need to move beyond the 'relatively surface level of meaning' and Holbrook is right in arguing that we should not abandon psychoanalytic approaches if they offer an additional insight or a defensible perspective.

Although marketing uses techniques with links to Freud, the impact of Freudian ideas on marketing (except for the exploitation of sex) has not been extensive – though not for want of trying. Advertisers find psychoanalytic 'theory' insufficiently operational, though this can be debated (see the case study at the end of this chapter). In any case, a purely psychoanalytic interpretation of buying behavior would be a very partial reading even though a Freudian perspective is still of interest for stimulating ideas – if not an authoritative source of valid theory.

In applying psychoanalytic psychology to marketing, the focus has been on identifying the unconscious meaning or significance of a product or brand so that the seller can develop advertising and sales appeals that tap into the buyer's deepest motivations. Freudian psychology holds that things like goods and services can symbolize ('stand for') other things and, as a consequence, attract to themselves the emotions attached to what they symbolize. This is a very defensible position and most in advertising would acknowledge this.

Leo Bogart (2003) points out that, while the sociologist Paul Lazarsfeld stressed quantitative methods, he was steeped in the psychoanalytic interpretation of human motivation and behavior (his mother Sophie was in fact a psychoanalyst). Most people in marketing at Columbia Business School at that time knew Lazarsfeld through John Howard and, listening to Lazarsfeld, were in no doubts about the Freudian influence. His technique of *reason analysis* (see Lazarsfeld 1970; Stephen Cole, 1972) was one of the inputs that influenced my *Why People Buy* (O'Shaughnessy 1987), illustrated in Chapter 3.

MOTIVATION RESEARCH

Freud in marketing is associated with motivation research, popularized, if not entirely pioneered, by Ernest Dichter in the 1950s and 1960s. But, while never claiming to be a full-blooded Freudian, Dichter in motivation research did seek to exploit the techniques and insights of psychoanalysis. Dichter was trained as a psychoanalyst so it was not surprising that he stressed emotion and unconscious motivation, viewing the consumer as acting on impulses and fears. He promoted focus groups and depth interviewing and qualitative research generally (Samuel 2011). It was Paul Lazarsfeld who first helped Dichter find a job at a marketing research firm in Manhattan. He had been Dichter's statistics teacher, though Dichter came to regard Lazarsfeld's work as naïve empiricism. An exemplar of Dichter's motivation research is his claim that, in baking a cake or loaf, using mixes that simply necessitate the adding of water is threatening to the housewife on the grounds that her role is marginalized. The recommendation was for the cook to add eggs, regarded as a symbol of fertility. An example of his reframing was for the advertiser to promote self-indulgent products as 'rewards' well-deserved to assuage any feelings of guilt. It was the rise of quantitative techniques, aided by the computer, such as the use of the Markov chain and linear programming in advertising, that made Dichter's approach seem unscientific, though these two particular techniques did not live up to expectations. But the notion of behavior being influenced by emotion and the unconscious has survived even in cognitive neuroscience.

Levy (1999) claims the origin of the term 'motivation research' arose during a conversation with the research director of the *Chicago Tribune*, at the same time pointing out that motivation research is now applied to the 'commercial application of qualitative research' (p.103). This is true. When we speak of motivation research in marketing today, we are more likely to refer to all forms or ways of seeking motives or reasons for buying. This is in line with Tadajewski (2006), who traces the historical path that links together traditional motivation research, interpretive consumer research and consumer culture theory concerned with sociological processes and structures.

The techniques extensively employed in motivation research are 'depth' interviewing, projective techniques and focus groups, augmented by the employment of concepts like the ego and the unconscious. Contrary to popular opinion, Dichter distanced himself from a focus on purely sexual motivations. He presented himself, not as someone exclusively Freudian, but as someone eclectic in the theories and tools he used. He put emphasis on the actual observation of behavior, employing the camera where possible. Anyone who has the opportunity to examine a Dichter market research study is likely to be more impressed with the motivational insights than with the Freudian imputations. (The author employed Dichter's company services when a market research manager.) For Dichter, motivation research was not built chiefly on imputing Freudian concepts to consumer behavior. For some marketers, motivation research was (and is) less an imputation of Freud to consumer behavior than the use of abduction, defined as moving back from the problematic facts to infer the best explanation of those facts (Lipton 1991), like Sherlock Holmes. But this can be misleading unless we recognize that the facts will be selected and interpreted in accordance with the paradigm adopted and the Freudian paradigm is the major perspective.

Projective *techniques*, like the well-known Rorschach (ink spot) test, assume that the more ambiguous the stimulus, the greater the scope offered for respondents to project onto their answers their real motivations and beliefs – what is dominant in their inner thoughts reflecting their deepest motives or chief concerns. These techniques are used to uncover the unconscious meanings of, for example, brands or products. There is an analogy with dreams in that, in a dream, we seem to provide a narrative for some sequence of images and that narrative may reflect unconscious motives as claimed by Freud. Projective techniques are a standard tool, common in all types of consumer research.

Focus groups are most commonly used to generate motivation research-type data, usually employing projective techniques like the Thematic

Apperception Test (TAT), where those in the focus group are asked for their views on, say, what the people in a drawing might be talking about in discussing the product of interest. Thus one focus group used to supplement protocol statements (see Chapter 3), with which the author was involved, concerned choosing a home mortgage. We gave each participant a pictorial drawing of a man and a woman, with the participants being told that the man and the woman were talking about home mortgages and asked them to say what was likely being discussed. Focus groups were used by Waste Management Company to elicit views on garbage haulers and found many negative associations, such as being tied to the Mafia. The company set out to change this perspective to that of an environmental services company.

There are several types of projective techniques, all based on the assumption that the vaguer the stimulus the greater the scope for the respondents to project their basic motivations on to their answers, on the grounds that what concerns people is most likely to be retrieved. This notion that what concerns us is easily retrieved or ever-present in the mind manifests itself when listening to people whose conversation keeps coming back to what is occupying them. If something consistently occupies our thoughts it is because it is of concern and something that is of concern has emotional roots.

PROJECTIVE TECHNIQUES

Projective techniques cover a number of procedures but all assume that a vagueness of stimuli is most likely to arouse thoughts that are uppermost in our minds and so concern us.

- *Association techniques*, such as word association tests, where the subject is presented with a word and asked to say immediately what comes to mind
- *Construction techniques*, such as TAT, which focus on picture interpretations where the respondent is asked to construct a story about a picture
- *Completion techniques*, such as sentence completion, where the subject is asked to complete a sentence at high speed
- *Expressive techniques*, such as play therapy, where the emphasis is on the way subjects express their emotions as they play.

Construction techniques such as TAT and completion techniques are those most commonly employed in marketing research.

Kagan (2006) makes an uncommon criticism of TAT, the projective technique (widely used in marketing) where respondents are asked to tell stories on the basis of pictorial material shown to them. As with all projective techniques, it is assumed a vague stimulus will prompt replies that reveal salient preoccupations, including motives. Kagan argues that psychologists using TAT refuse to acknowledge the problems that arise from the enormous variation in the verbal fluency of respondents, resulting often in a failure to find words to communicate the respondent's notions, for example, of love, ambition and failure. This applies to many market research studies. Familiarity with relevant concepts and verbal fluency are the skills needed to express what concerns respondents. There is also the problem of whether a respondent's narrative does in fact reflect purely preoccupations or, alternatively, a cognitive bias that leads the respondent to analyze and focus simply on an ambiguous or novel feature which then motivates the respondent's story. Whatever the limitations of focus groups, they can yield impressive insights even if by no means drawn from a representative sample. Those who have children who are siblings closely related in age might use the TAT test to reveal motivations – the result is apt to confirm what experience of your children has taught you!

MODERN RESURRECTIONS OF FREUDIAN INFLUENCE

In this postmodern climate, it is not surprising to see a resurrection of Freudian influence. Ideas seldom die but instead hibernate for a more favorable climate. One prominent example is Clotaire Rapaille, a psychiatrist who employs the psychoanalytic methods of Freud and Jung to reveal unconscious desires that are alleged to transcend time and fashion (Gross 2004). He draws on the notion of 'archetype', formulated by Jung who defined an archetype as an innate image held in common by all people. In claiming certain archetypes were common to all people, Jung took an archetype as residing in the collective unconscious in contrast to the personal unconscious mind. The archetype concept is an echo of the doctrine of innate ideas promoted by Plato or, more recently, the notion of animal instincts. But more important was the claim by Jung that archetypes are expressions of universal psychological needs.

Rapaille, whose Florida company is called Archetype Discoveries Worldwide, claims the consumer has deeply held preferences that reflect archetypes. Preferences are discovered through a variation of Freud's dream analysis. But Rapaille does not fall back on Jung's list of archetypes in guiding the discovery of universal preferences but on universal unconscious desires which, in his approach, could include a house, a car and even a jacket. His focus is on discovering core preferences in a product that do not change: he is not in the business of spotting trends. Consumers, for him, make their decisions from the 'gut', not the brain. Thus consumers want to live in a house that is an archetype, own a car that is an archetype, wear a jacket that is an archetype and so on. All these claims are difficult to establish empirically. Rapaille persuaded Procter & Gamble that Americans care more about the aroma of coffee than the taste, and want their cheese refrigerated rather than runny. He persuaded Chrysler that consumers prefer automobiles that resemble armored tanks on the outside and a cozy living room on the inside. (The result is the *original* version of the Chrysler 300.) These may seem reasonable observations of some subset of consumers, but are certainly not true of all car buyers, which is the assumption being made.

Rapaille says he is not in the business of spotting trends. Yet trend spotting can be decisive; for example Mott's, known for their juices and apple sauce, have maintained their success by spotting trends. Thus in the 1960s they spotted the trend of women being concerned with their figures so produced low-calorie juices and adult foods. Today Mott's is capitalizing on a trend of mothers looking for quick healthy snacks for their children.

How does one test Rapaille's system? First we test by observation. We find lots of consumers who do not think aroma is everything in coffee (I don't) or want their cars to resemble armored tanks (I hate the design of the *original* version of the Chrysler 300). Do all buyers of the Hummer seek a sense of dominance? Would this be the only or the most dominant choice criterion? Contrary to Rapaille, choices are not all affect-driven but can be belief-driven or affect- and belief-driven, concerned with technical factors (use-functions and convenience-in-use functions), economic factors, factors suggesting better self-integration and social integration, legalistic factors (rules imposed from outside) and adaptive factors concerned with adapting to information overload and risk. This may be denied, by falling back on the untestable claim that people do not *really* know what determines their buying. Does this mean always? Sometimes? Often? The claim itself is in need of unpacking. It seems to be a case of believing that there is a universal explanation of buying decisions corresponding to the notion of there being universal laws in consumer behavior, beyond the trivial. There are not.

If every consumer in buying is seeking to satisfy the same innate, primeval instinct, it would imply that this instinct is present in everyone and arises without learning. This has not been demonstrated. What is surprising is that the management of firms, who seek evidence to justify all production decisions, seem willing to accept an advertising rationale or buyer behavior model that has no evidential support, beyond the assurance of the consultant 'that he knows from his wide experience that it works'. There is a common myth about a 'hot button' that needs to be identified and pressed for buying action to be assured, with this button to be discovered, hidden in the psyche, awaiting Freudian interpretation. A firm may possess a sufficient advantage, at a particular time, to win in a particular competitive environment but there is no such thing as a winning advantage that is universal and timeless.

We speak of something being necessary for success (e.g. resources of various sorts) because the absence of a necessary condition for success is a sufficient reason for failure. Thus, since oxygen is a necessary condition for human life, its absence would be a sufficient condition for life to cease. But in marketing we identify more correctly factors that make a contribution (albeit an important contribution) to success. In any case, stating a necessary condition for success does not in itself indicate the magnitude of its contribution to the outcome. This is why not all necessary conditions for success are equivalent to *critical success factors*. Thus possessing a field sales force may be a necessary condition for success but does not constitute a

critical success factor since recruiting a sales force may not present a problem. On the other hand, critical success factors in service industries can be
recruitment and training. Although the service industries are characterizing
society today, it should be asked: how much of what they do still connects
directly or indirectly to serving production?

The Zaltman Metaphor Elicitation Technique (ZMET) is another example of a revival of Freud, though Zaltman, at the Harvard Business School,
does not quote Freud as an influence (Zaltman 2003). Zaltman claims, as
do some psychologists, such as Wilson (2002), that only about 5 percent of
our thinking occurs in the conscious mind. This is not based on hard evidence and it is difficult to see how it might be established. There is also the
vagueness in the claim. Would we say, for example, that when we are on
'automatic pilot', which we often are, thinking is going on in the unconscious? In fact the whole notion of unconscious thinking is dubious since
thinking involves thinking with concepts which implies some degree of
consciousness. It is meaningless to talk about unconscious thinking as if the
unconscious possessed a corresponding language of its own. Nevertheless,
this claim about only 5 percent of our thinking occurring in the conscious
mind is basic to Zaltman's position.

Zaltman's (2002) ZMET has received much publicity (Eakin 2002). Like
Freudians, Zaltman claims people's deepest thoughts are non-conscious and
it is these thoughts that account for their behavior in the marketplace.
For him, at least 95 percent of the thinking that 'drives' behavior occurs
unconsciously and much of what we think of as conscious is really an after-
the-fact construction (rationalization) (Useem 2003). Not only is it not clear
how Zaltman gets the figure of 95 percent, it is not even clear what he
regards as a decision. In any case, he claims consumers commonly act for
reasons of which they are not conscious. This is so. Consumers often act
for reasons of which they are not conscious and this has to be kept in mind
by those who try to fit all human decision-making into some variation of
the economist's 'rational choice model' (see later Chapter 9).

Consumer decision-making is not monolithic. In fact consumers make
choices without going through any of the stages or rule-following procedures we imagine to be needed to make a meaningful decision. If consumers
were known to follow specific rules, it would be possible to draw up
rules that are likely to be far more reliable since random biases would
be eliminated. For example, in studying the selection process for salespeople, we might try to identify the rules being used by interviewers to
achieve a more reliable selection process. The approach is called 'bootstrap-
ping' (analogous to pulling oneself up by one's bootstraps) and is one of
the approaches employed by specialists in *artificial intelligence*. Although
artificial intelligence is concerned largely with the goal of establishing
human-like thinking in computers, progress so far has been limited.

Basic to ZMET is the claim that unconscious thoughts are primarily
visual. But to quote Bennett, a neuroscientist, and Hacker, an analytic
philosopher (2003) (see Chapter 8), to recall an image of brand XYZ is

not to start thinking in images since images are not an expression of one's thought but an aid to thought – simply an accompaniment (Bennett and Hacker 2003). We do not *think* just using images. It is concepts (since these reflect the categories into which we break up the world) that are basic to all thinking. In conscious abstract thought we think linguistically and there is no evidence to demonstrate that visuals must be implanted in sentences for understanding.

The very essence of language-using human beings is thinking with concepts. If we lack the relevant concepts, we lack the corresponding thinking. Thinking is not restricted to images (Kosslyn 1980). This does not mean that before children learn a language they do not recognize (and think about?) differences in objects, while adults do employ quasi-pictorial representations but use such representations in cognitive processing (thinking with language). When consumers recall (whether aided or unaided) a particular brand, what they recall are beliefs, claims (assertions) *and* images of the brand and it is these which are used in cognitive processing. Both imagery representations and propositional representations (involving concepts) are typically recalled. It seems that the relative speed with which the two types of information (images and propositions) are processed determines which type of information dominates consumer thinking about (brand) image. The image the consumer recalls may be vivid but it cannot be analyzed to reveal what the consumer does not already know. I may have a vivid image of the car I have just test-driven but if I have forgotten the particular make I cannot just read it off from that vivid image.

How visuals in the unconscious make up for a lack of conceptual language is difficult to see since not all concepts can be represented in visuals. The answer perhaps for Zaltman is that the unconscious is a hidden store of visual metaphors that influence behavior. But do not metaphors involve concepts? It is true that Freud interpreted dreams as metaphoric and, as Prinz (2002) says, there may be good theoretical reasons for postulating representations that exist outside consciousness. But even if we were to accept that thought-equivalents may be represented in some way in the unconscious, it is by no means obvious that the process involves visual imagery.

As a matter of definition, we have no conscious access to the unconscious so claims about unconscious thought are purely speculative. Even as we talk, it is a mystery to all of us how, in speaking, things just come out in a meaningful flow. General Motors utilizes metaphor in its *Value-Cues Research*. In one of General Motors' studies, consumers were asked to view photographs of 'friendly' watches to help identify dominant design features. Apparently, these are a large face that is easy to read and robust to abuse, and one that appears to be 'fun', as judged by color, shape and designs that make you smile, look comfortable and so on. It is not quite clear how these features might be weighted or whether they would be surprising to a manufacturer of watches.

In probing the unconscious mind, Zaltman conducts in-depth, one-to-one interviews to obtain the consumer's perspective on how he or she experiences the problem addressed by a new offering. Additionally, he uses *metaphor-elicitation techniques* that draw out subconscious thoughts by, say, asking the respondent to bring in photographs that depict their thoughts and feelings about the product. No one denies the role of metaphor in conscious thinking or speaking. Gibbs (1994), a cognitive psychologist, claims that much of our language is metaphorically structured, as is much of our cognition. Gibbs's work promotes the important role of the metaphor in conscious thinking. But this does not imply a universal inner language of thought. As Jonathan Cohen (1987) says in respect of cognitive psychology and its metaphor of the mind being a computer: 'the computational hypothesis gives no support to the doctrine of a tacit, universal language of thought' (p. 230). It would indeed be difficult to demonstrate the unconscious existence of 'sentence-tokens' in 'mentalize'. Much of our conceptualization of experience is metaphorical and a great deal of thinking is metaphorical mappings from dissimilar sources. However, it does not follow from this that our unconscious thoughts are visual. It is not even clear what evidence might be quoted to establish the validity of Zaltman's claim. Yet ZMET, as a technique, relies on this claim about visual images.

Metaphors can act as models for imputing a structure to data and are common in trying to come to grips with something new. But Zaltman goes well beyond this. Participants in ZMET studies collect pictures from magazines, catalogues or anywhere else that might capture their feelings about the product or brand and later create a 'digital collage' with these images and record a short text about its meaning. The digital collage of images becomes a metaphor for the feelings and meanings evoked. In one study on Coca-Cola, Zaltman's team arrived at the conclusion that Coca-Cola evokes not just feelings of invigoration and sociability, as has been traditionally claimed, but 'feelings of calm, solicitude and relaxation as well'. He believes this finding distinguishes his method. If he is suggesting no other method would capture such a finding he is wrong. Those same feelings were found in a study based on just listening to subjects (schoolchildren) 'talk off the top of their heads' before buying, during buying and after buying Coca-Cola. The study used the label 'hedonic tone' or achieving inner harmony (a move away from tension), as reflected in such statements as: 'After drinking I felt calm and relaxed' (O'Shaughnessy and Holbrook 1988).

Zaltman does not overtly draw on Freud but cites a debt to neuroscientists as well as semiotics as sources of his method. Cognitive neuroscience does claim that much takes place at the non-conscious level, together with the notion that things are initiated in the brain before happening in consciousness. This latter claim is examined in Chapter 9 where the meaning of such neurological findings is discussed. In any case, it does not license the claim that thought is visual while semiotics, defined as the study of all signs and the meanings they convey, is neutral on the matter. Zaltman, like Rapaille, claims to be influenced by Jung, who did a good deal of work on word association, dream symbolism and religion, but Jung also saw the unconscious as a source of spiritual insight. Jung in fact developed a number of concepts, not just the concept of the archetypes: concepts like the collective unconscious, anima, and stressed the two dimensions of personality (extroverted, introverted), as well as classifying mental functions into thinking, feeling, sensation and intuition. On the other hand, Jung is also known for his support of phrenology, astrology and alchemy!

Zaltman believes, like Rapaille, that the vast majority of consumers buy for the same 'reason'. If by 'reason' it is meant that consumers seek the same thing, this may be true at the abstract level but it is not helpful since it would not be predictive of brands bought: beliefs will differ as to the weighting of attributes and judgment on the extent to which a brand has the attributes being sought. In any case, consumers do not always buy the same product for even the same technical function, for example the consumer can buy Kleenex tissues for very different purposes. Zaltman talks about the four core metaphors that are nearly universal and involved in the purchase and consumption of many products. This, too, finds an echo in Jung's archetypes.

Whatever ZMET turns out to be, its antecedents are tied to Freud and not neuroscience, though the latter has more sales appeal. ZMET cannot be regarded as a receiving-set tuned into the unconscious, capable of catching, through its methods, relevant wavelengths emanating from consumer feelings. More fundamentally, we cannot infer from the consumer's actions alone the conscious or unconscious feelings, wants and beliefs that enter into buying decisions.

A good deal of human action is, as the philosopher Wittgenstein argued, unreflective in the sense that it is not consciously directed but an immediate response to the situation, so we may go along with gut liking, acting on the basis of the likeability heuristic and so on. Buying action may occur in the absence of any conscious deliberation about what we are doing. Being consciously aware of something suggests being reflective on that something and being reflective does not occupy most of our time. Although consumers often act on gut feelings, just following the likeability heuristic (choosing on the basis of liking), or may even pick a brand at random, they do, more typically, think about what they want, while the means they choose to satisfy that want depend on beliefs, even if those beliefs are not formally articulated.

The ZMET consumer groups who did the collecting discussed the 'images' during a two-hour private interview with a ZMET 'specialist' before going on to create 'a digital collage with their images and recorded a short text about its meaning'. What sort of successes would certify someone as a specialist or what sort of training would make someone a specialist? It is not clear how anyone could be an expert in interpreting the data selected by the volunteer groups or how generalizing from such a non-random sample of data could be defended as a valid method of generalizing. Theoretically, interpretations of the images would be legion unless there is theoretical guidance available, going well beyond simplistic, dogmatic assertions about our deepest thoughts being unconscious and that these thoughts are primarily visual. The 'experts' impute an interpretation based on whatever ZMET suggests by way of theory. But whatever the interpretation of the studies, inferences made (as with motivation research) depend crucially on the skills of the interpreter as is true of motivation research. One is reminded of a comment made by Leo Bogart (2003) on Dichter, the father of motivation research:

> Dichter ran his business from a castle on the Hudson in upper Westchester County. His former employees generally conceded that the 'depth interviews' they collected served more to illustrate observations and insights that the master had spun a priori than as evidence from which to pursue a subsequent analysis.
>
> (Bogart 2003: 163–4)

Could not the same thing be said about Zaltman and Rapaille? Bogart uses the term 'a priori' in this quote. The term 'a priori' contrasts with 'a posteriori' to refer to conclusions that do not arise from any empirical source but are true as a matter of definition while, in contrast, a posteriori conclusions are built up from empirical data. A priori knowledge consists of facts that could not be otherwise while a posteriori knowledge is dependent on events in the world.

Hacking (1995), a philosopher of science, also makes a comment that is highly relevant:

> To say that remembering is often of scenes, views, and feelings is not to imply that we remember in images or reproduce, internally, an image of a scene or an afterimage or interpretation of a feeling. We may do so, but we need not. Empirical psychology teaches that people are very different in the extent to which they (say they) visualize or form images.
>
> (Hacking, 1995: 252)

But what if Zaltman is ahead of the game – what are the implications? If Zaltman is right about the visual images in unconscious thought influencing behavior, it would suggest that advertising which draws on metaphor, particularly pictorial metaphor, will have less difficulty in getting the attention and interest of the target audience. One pictorial metaphor, attacking the alleged high prices of a competitor, showed pigs eating the money being paid out. Whatever the fact of the matter, ZMET highlights the importance of visual metaphors in persuasion and few would quarrel with that. A current ad for 'Post-it Super Sticky Notes', for example, shows a Post-it on the wall with a drawing of a bone on it and a little Jack Russell dog with its teeth sunk into the note but suspended there on the wall, the note holding the dog up. But, as language users, humans think with concepts and it is difficult to even know what it means to say that at the unconscious level humans think in images.

It is interesting to note two contrasting reviews of Zaltman's book. Morris Holbrook, a friend and my former colleague, says the difference between prior efforts and Zaltman's consolidation is that, unlike many previous explorations, *How Customers Think* insistently addresses the concerns of marketing practitioners (Holbrook 2003). This is true, but it does not make ZMET valid. In contrast, Winston Fletcher (2003), chairman of the Royal Institution (UK), starts his review by saying that if he were an academic in a management faculty, he would be sorely tempted to buy every copy of *How Customers Think* and dump the lot in the Atlantic. He views the book as simply an exercise in repackaging and contrasts the book unfavorably with Vance Packard's *The Hidden Persuaders*, written nearly fifty years ago. Packard's book is indeed still well worth reading even if he overrated the efficacy of motivation research.

Once we acknowledge that we are not aware of our deepest motivations (as we do not have access to the non-conscious processes that underlie many of our decisions), it follows that there will always be attempts to delve into the 'unconscious' mind. Lear (1988) offers a sympathetic account of Freud. He argues that the real attack on Freud is on the idea that humans have unconscious motivation; that there is 'method in our madness' even when our actions appear weird and bizarre. To a sympathetic audience most things sound reasonable.

FANTASIES, FEELINGS AND FUN

Holbrook (2008), and in earlier work with co-authors, developed an approach tied to the psychoanalytic paradigm. Hirschman and Holbrook (1982) introduced the concept of *hedonic consumption*, a situation where consumers decide on an offering because they are seeking a multi-sensory experience and emotional involvement in product usage. As Montaigne (1533–1592) once said: 'In every pleasure known to man the very pursuit of it is pleasurable.' Humans are not just thinking (sapient) beings but are also beings that feel (sentient beings). In a sapient state, people are rational but in a sentient state there is the joy of sensuous pleasure. For sentient human beings, what is good is what is pleasurable. And sensuous pleasure may on occasion be all that is sought, though we should not confuse all pleasure with sensuous pleasure. The brain entertains all sorts of pleasures, down to just walking in the countryside, anticipating/contemplating a good meal as well as the intellectual pleasures arising from seeking understanding. There are thus pleasures when in a sapient state so that seeking pleasure does not necessitate ignoring sapience in favor of sentience.

The approach explores the various aspects of consumption experience under what Holbrook calls the three Fs, specifically: Fantasies, Feelings and Fun (FFF). *Fantasies* he defines as 'all those conscious and unconscious aspects of thought that reflect how we subjectively experience the world of consumption'. 'Fantasies' are 'make-beliefs' and 'wishes' are assumed to be 'non-realizable wants'. 'I believe that Crest toothpaste will fight cavities; but in my dreams, I imagine that it will make me a handsome stud with gleaming white teeth that will appeal to beautiful women everywhere.' Perhaps President Nixon was appealing to fantasies when he said other politicians promise you the moon, I'm the first one able to deliver it. For Holbrook, feelings encompass the full spectrum of emotional responses that arise in a consumption experience. But while all emotions give rise to feelings, can we say that all feelings are emotional? Are all feelings of pain emotional? Emotion, as a term in general usage, does not embrace the concept of pain per se, though pain can give rise to emotions like anger and resentment.

Holbrook defines *fun* as those aspects of playful leisure activities that are pursued for their own sake as ends in themselves. In other words, having fun is *expressive behavior*. Expressive behavior is an end in itself so that I might behave like the mountaineer who, when asked why he tries to climb Everest, replied 'because it is there'. A fine exemplar of expressive behavior is reaffirming one's marriage vows since it is purely symbolic. Expressive behavior expresses our personality, hopes and dreams, which may be far removed from the desire for hedonistic pleasure. In 1900, Ernest Shackleton, the Antarctic explorer, placed the following ad in London newspapers and received lots of volunteers:

> Men wanted for hazardous journey. Small wages, bitter cold, long months of complete darkness, safe return doubtful. Honour and recognition in case of success.

Some may have volunteered in the hope of achieving recognition and honor but certainly not for pleasure.

Holbrook quotes Disney, Starbucks and Benihana of Tokyo among others as focusing on the experience of using their products. Howard Shultz who created Starbucks went all out to make the Starbucks coffee house feel like a continental coffee house and make the total experience of drinking coffee at Starbucks a completely different feel so consumers would not use prices at Dunkin' Donuts as their anchor prices. What consumers want are products, communications and marketing campaigns that dazzle the senses, touch their hearts and stimulate their minds, where quality can be taken for granted. But not all self-expressive behavior is necessarily positive or benign in that an obsessive focus on pleasure-seeking can be expressive of a hedonistic lifestyle.

Holbrook contrasts the FFF approach with the decision-oriented view:

- Decision-oriented view: tangible offer, cost measured purely in money terms, informational advertising, the buying proposition proposing reasons for buying, while the retailer is just viewed as a purchase 'facilitator.'
- Experiential (FFF) view: intangible offerings with subjective meanings like television programs; cost measure in time. Transformational advertising with the retailer viewed as a source of shopping experience.

In the 2010 advertising for Subaru (as reported in *Bloomberg Businessweek*, May 24 – May 30, p. 18) the Holbrook perspective finds expression with the marketing director saying: 'Subaruers are customers who are not buying things, but experiences' and a research commentator saying that Subaru advertising 'plays up fun, the adventure you can have with a Subaru'. Experiences enjoyed in using the media would in particular be expected to affect choice of media, and according to one study this is so (Peck 2010). It is the positive, meaningful experiences that are apt to motivate readers and users of the media to patronize it, experiences like: 'I feel less stress after reading it', 'I lose myself in the pleasure of reading this magazine'. Viewer experience lies behind audience affiliation to various media. Similarly, associating some medium with negative experiences puts people off using it.

Holbrook more than anyone has been concerned with aesthetics and likings. The look of a product can be the deciding factor in any purchase. Kleenex has recently paid particular attention to aesthetics: in 2005 it introduced an oval-shaped package and later embossed wallpaper patterns and so on. Kleenex rightly regards the packaging as part of the product being promoted. Kia Motors hopes this can be true for cars since its new Optima has been designed to sell with visual appeal being its critical advantage. Consumers commonly use no more than likeability ('the likeability heuristic') to determine their choice. Enjoyment from the pleasurable, the aesthetic and the fun of sports can be an end in itself and there is seldom any point in inquiring further since to ask why something is enjoyable simply leads to synonyms for enjoyment, for example saying it is exciting or fascinating. To say that we cannot understand why people take drugs like marijuana and cocaine is to ignore pleasure and just focus on the dangers inherent in doing so. If consumers are asked to provide reasons for their liking, these reasons would simply describe the type of enjoyment anticipated: the answer would not tell the questioner why the consumer likes what she likes. Because 'liking' something is so pervasive throughout all buying and is so subjective, it is an important factor in making prediction of sales difficult. Film producers do not deliberately make films that are unsuccessful but simply find it difficult to say what will appeal on a wide scale. It is the same with many other products and advertisements. I find many ads very unappealing, such as the commercial for Pringles with the actors shown stuffing their mouths with crisps in a way that repels, though no doubt the ad gets attention! And getting attention has been a crucial goal in commercials to reduce skipping of commercials from pre-recorded programs or changing to another program when they appear. Not surprisingly, the 'art' of getting attention has improved over the years but an ad may get initial attention without the brand name or the message even registering.

The doctrine of the three Fs is tied to the claim for the importance of *novelty* in our lives, but is it true that the three Fs are relevant for every situation, such as dealing with bank withdrawals or deposits? We might argue, in line with Holbrook, that it is not only wants/desires and beliefs that are tied to motivation but also fantasies and wishes. Here Velleman (2000) substitutes 'fantasies' for the role of 'belief' and 'wishes' for the role of 'desires' in action. Wishes, unlike wants, are unrestricted as to feasibility – we can just go ahead and wish for anything we like, regardless of whether it is obtainable or whether it even exists. Consumers recognize that meeting their actual 'wishes' is seldom feasible so what consumers say they want takes some account of feasibility.

Satisfying 'wants' is far less demanding than trying to satisfy 'wishes'. What consumers might 'wish for' is not part of their expectations. Nonetheless, surveys might ask consumers about their wishes since the wishes of yesterday might be the 'wants' that can be met today.

As we reflect on words in the mind, they can have *semantic* autonomy as if having a life of their own, conjuring up images that can be emotionally impelling. Emotional images that have semantic autonomy distract us from deliberating their validity. This leads to consumers (and voters) acting not through reflection but in reaction to the emotional images. We can live the life created by the images since these images have attractive sense-meanings even if they have no counterpart in the life we live; we are just carried along by a dream that has the desired reality. In marketing we speak of fantasy consumption when consumers vicariously live the life they desire through books, television, films or whatever. We might also argue that subscribers to Facebook can indulge in the fantasy of being a celebrity. But fantasy consumption does not capture the role of 'wishes' in firming up the fantasies. One of the most popular painters 'for the masses' is Thomas Kinkade, whose paintings project magical scenes of cottages, rivers and fields clothed in twilight that stimulate the wish to be part of that scene, to live in the fantasy world 'out there somewhere'. But all this talk of images influencing the consumer is different from the claim that consumers think with images rather than concepts.

As Velleman says, fantasies and wishes are able to motivate behavior expressive of emotion. Also, when consumers fantasize about being other people, it is not a case of saying 'I will behave as if I am that celebrity' but rather 'I am that celebrity' and accordingly adopting the behavior of the celebrity, for example buying brands associated with the celebrity. Fantasizing about having supernatural abilities (some psychiatrists have suggested) is a way of surviving a crushing sense of powerlessness. While fantasizing about being someone else is a way of imagining, Velleman argues that talking to ourselves is not imagining conversing with someone else but wishing that we were conversing with that someone else. In fantasizing, people can reify an idea in that we act as though it were real when it is just metaphorical or hypothetical, just as the term 'death panels' in criticizing the proposed health bill became real to many people.

CONCLUSION

A view initiated by the philosopher Wittgenstein is that psychoanalysis is an interpretive system, unlike the natural sciences that seek law-like generalizations. This is a useful way to approach psychoanalytic psychology (Rycroft 1995) even if it is not what Freud wanted. If we accept Kuhn's

(1973) claim that an existing paradigm will continue to be used until a better paradigm comes along to replace it, then Freud's system of the mind is not likely to be relegated to history any time soon. As Horgan's (1999) *The Undiscovered Mind* demonstrates, we are a very long way from having a 'unified theory' of the mind. As for Freud in psychiatry (as opposed to psychotherapy), Paul McHugh (2007), a distinguished psychiatrist at Johns Hopkins University, claims Freud is 'deader than Elvis' and that no psychiatrist today investigating psychiatric disorders is dancing to Freud's tunes. This is a harsh verdict that ignores the usefulness of Freudian concepts in explaining behavior.

The term 'unified theory' is commonly encountered today. It is a term going back to Einstein, who sought in his later years a unified theory encompassing all of nature's laws in science. He failed and was sidelined by mainstream physicists whose focus was on particle physics, not on (for them) some heroic but pointless pursuit. But, as we said earlier, ideas do not die but hibernate for a more favorable climate and today we have a revival of interest by physicists studying string theory in the notion of a unified theory of science so as to come to grips with the questions of the origins of the universe. On this basis, if ideas simply hibernate for more favorable times, we would predict a resurrection of Freudianism as well as Marxism with more attractive labeling and packaging. Such overarching theories are too attractive to a segment of political consumers to fall by the wayside. Marxism claims to explain how the whole world works and, as a secular religion, prescribes how the world should work. As logical positivism in the 1930s allowed us to save our mental energies by dispensing with metaphysics, religion and anything that was not empirically verifiable or conceptually true, Marxism promises us a mastery of history and economics without studying either. In the past it proved to be snake oil for the masses, but it will be claimed its failure arose from being adopted by ill-educated peasants who just failed to understand its subtleties!

CASE: COKE EXPERIENCE

The following quotes are from children, no older than fifteen years of age, on the Coke-buying experience. They have been extracted from:

- Unstructured free association interviews with the children
- Asking them to write about buying a Coke
- In-depth interviews with individual children
- Asking several focus groups of six children to each say what comes to mind when viewing a vague sketch of someone of their own age choosing a bottle of Coke.

'I am now going to flick on the TV, open the blinds and make sure the mood is right. I'll put my Max Headroom sunglasses on and think to myself: catch the wave, Coke.'

'I take my favorite glass and some ice and make it nice and cold.'

'I am going to drink now in the privacy of my room, sit on the bed, leaning against the wall.'

'How I enjoy putting it in a glass of ice and hear a cracking sound and smelling the aroma of the contents.'

'I don't guzzle but drink it slowly to admire the flavor.'

'What a treat my taste buds are having – and thanking me with every sip.'

'As I sip there is a tingly feeling all over my body.'

'The feeling as it slithers down my throat.'

'How I love swishing it around the can and letting it fizz again.'

'I chew on the ice and hear a cracking sound as I taste the Coke in the ice.'

'After I finish I start feeling energetic.'

'After drinking I feel calm and relaxed.'

'I felt so revived, I could tackle the whole world with full energy.'

'I buy a Coke not just to relieve my thirst but to give me a lift when I'm tired and need to be refreshed.'

'The caffeine in the sugar in the Coke sets me jumping so whenever I play a sport it helps me play better.'

'Classic Coke has the original formula which is best as other cokes contain preservatives. Classic Coke is not watery and has no unpleasant after taste.'

'Coke rids me of all that tension.'

'Choosing a Coke is difficult as I have to decide against other cokes that I might enjoy better.'

'The design and color of the bottle itself is important. I would never buy a plain and tacky bottle of soda.'

'I like a colorful can.'

'Cherry really gives it life and restfulness and a delicious cherry flavor that Coke and Pepsi do not have.'

'Friends must approve. I could never buy a soda that wasn't popular with them.'

'I look at the price and see if it is really worth the money.'

Case questions

1. Identify the elements of fantasy, feelings and fun that are suggested in these quotes.
2. Categorize various motives for buying Coke in this sample of schoolchildren.
3. What unconscious meanings do you think Coke can have for these children?
4. What can Coke symbolize to some of these children and what emotions are evoked?
5. What elements of their behavior might be regarded by the economist as 'irrational'?

6. What persuasive advertising appeals and methods of execution would you suggest for this target audience using the categories shown below?

Persuasive appeals

1. Emotional appeals: whenever some stimulus exemplifies something of concern in the preferred life vision, or is opposed to it, an emotional response is likely. Emotional advertising seeks to induce a highly positive or negative evaluation. Fantasies generated by advertising have the capacity to stimulate the emotions as they can be known to be false but felt to be true.
2. Dogmatic appeals. The dogmatic assertion ('No one beats our prices') can be very persuasive when put across by a confident speaker in a self-assured way. The aim is to convey conviction and lend credibility to the message.
3. Rational, reason-giving appeals. If the emotional appeal focuses on 'feel' and the dogmatic assertion on 'do', the rational, reason-giving appeal focuses on 'learn/think'. Rational, reason-giving appeals say why the message is right, correct or true. They need not ignore the emotional. However, the logic may not meet all the requirements of the logician as the argument will accept the existing prejudices of the audience while the move from such premises to conclusion is of an acceptable kind, not a rigorous deductive logic.

Methods of Execution

1. Entertainment and humor
   Those watching television are generally interested in being entertained, not in doing heavy thinking. Entertaining advertisements can distract the viewer from counter-arguments; when liked, they can pass on some of that liking to the product. Humor is attention-getting but tricky to orchestrate and does not seem to travel well.
2. Evidential and factual
   Evidential and factual advertising is common in industrial and service marketing. Long messages can be persuasive here in suggesting something substantive is on offer.
3. Use of celebrities
   A high percentage of ads on television in the US use celebrities. This can seemingly demonstrate the brand as socially appropriate and a good quality product, while the buyer can have a sense of sharing something with their favorite star. Celebrities can thus help to sell a product if the target audience identifies with them.
4. Slice of life advertising
   A play is a slice of life and a slice of life advertisement is a miniature play involving some incident that demonstrates the use of the product. However, members of the target audience must be able to self-categorize

with those in the advertisement: we can fit the label but reject the stereotype. Slice of life advertising can induce self-persuasion through the mechanism of self-imagining.

5. Comparative advertising

   Comparative advertising is a common tactic for new entrants to the market or to regain market share with an improved product. It can be very effective though disliked by advertising agencies. But knocking the competitor is not free of risk, even of law suits. Also, what is being pushed is not always what consumers are seeking so they may not be influenced by the differences stressed.

6. Symbolism

   Much image advertising relies on emotional symbolism. This is because image advertising is not concerned with leading the target audience to some conclusion through an inference process but to conjuring up a certain perspective so as to get the audience to reinterpret something about the brand. Emotional symbolism tied to values is very common and can be effective – witness the Marlboro ad. Slogans are also commonly used here as they can resonate emotionally with the target audience via a link to their system of values.

DISCUSSION QUESTIONS CHAPTER 5 (PSYCHOANALYTIC PSYCHOLOGY)

1. 'The psychoanalytic approach cannot be ignored as it is the only approach that seeks motives of which the consumer is unaware and it is not in dispute that there are causes of behavior that lie in the unconscious.' Discuss
2. If the Freudian system is associated with the notion of unconscious meanings being attached to products, what exactly does this mean?
3. 'The techniques extensively employed in motivation research are depth interviewing, projective techniques and the use of focus groups. Such methods can be very fallible when it comes to unearthing hidden meanings and motives. This highlights the importance of interpretation and the insight of the analyst.' Discuss
4. Critique the notion, associated with Clotaire Rapaille, of unconscious desires that transcend time and fashion.
5. The book is very critical of Zaltman's ZMET. Can you think of a defense?

Chapter 6

Cognitive Psychology: The Basic Perspective

INTRODUCTION: HISTORICAL ANTECEDENTS

What makes a psychology cognitive is a focus on 'cognition': the faculty of knowing and perceiving. Cognition, as a faculty, contrasts with conation (the exercise of the will to action) and affective experiences (feelings/emotions). Cognitive psychology's domain embraces perceiving and knowing and the related processes of remembering, paying attention, language use, problem solving and manipulating things around us with, for example, our hands.

In Howard Gardner's seminal history of cognitive psychology, *The Mind's New Science: A History of the Cognitive Revolution* (1985), it is claimed that it was the computer metaphor started the cognitive revolution. This is denied by Jerome Bruner, who was one of the pioneers of the revolution at Harvard. Gardner studied under Bruner at Harvard and it was Jerome Bruner, together with George Miller, who established the Center for Cognitive Studies there.

Bruner (1990) claims that the cognitive revolution intended the notion of 'meaning' to be the central concept of psychology, the aim being to nudge psychology to join forces with the interpretive disciplines in the humanities and social sciences; such disciplines as ethnomethodology, ethnography, symbolic interactionism, action research, discourse analysis and cultural anthropology. But there was a change of direction from this original conception – a move from the search for 'meaning' (significance and/or intentions) to viewing the mind as software programs for the brain's hard drive. In John Horgan's *The Undiscovered Mind*, an interview with Gardner was surprisingly critical of cognitive science, which Gardner had done so much to popularize (Horgan 1999). Gardner argues that strictly scientific approaches to the mind have not advanced our understanding of psychology's core topics: consciousness, the self, free will and personality. He contended that psychologists may advance by following a more 'literary' style in both investigation and discourse. He is quoted as saying:

> By the way, 95 percent – you can quote me on this – 95 percent of psychologists are not deeply intuitive about others... They come

to psychology out of chemistry because they weren't good enough in chemistry.

(Horgan 1999: 73)

This last comment seems a little spiteful, particularly as in his (2004) book on persuasion there is no strong sense that Gardner is other than a card-carrying cognitive psychologist.

Behaviorism asserts that it is impossible to know what goes on in the mind as opposed to:

• Knowing what information is fed to the mind; and
• Observing behavior before and after some event.

However, cognitive psychology claims that this should not rule attempts to model the inner workings of the mind, since the physical world is always represented in consciousness by mental representations. Much depends, of course, on what is meant by 'mental representation'; after all, representation can simply be expressed in mathematical form. Much of economics today is expressed this way; while in physics, quantum mechanics has resisted all attempts at representation via *visualization* relying purely on the language of mathematics. Even if it means sacrificing the advantage of physical visualization, the symbolic perspective in cognitive psychology would also like to employ mathematical models to represent the symbol manipulation in mental processes. There is always a danger of such mathematical models being created that fail to spell out the referential-meanings of the variables. Thus to state 'let X equal the sum of all human knowledge' may sound meaningful but has in fact no referential-meaning.

COGNITIVE MODELING

Mainstream cognitive psychology imputes a model to behavior derived from the analogy of the computer; viewing the brain as hardware with the mind as software. There are two basic approaches to modeling representations based on whether brains are regarded as merely computers or, alternatively, as connectionist 'neural nets' (Gardenfors 2000). The computer model approach is the *information processing approach* which exploits the computer metaphor, picturing cognition as computation comprised of symbol manipulation. The consumer in decision-making becomes an information processor, in the same way that the computer is an information processor. The second approach is *connectionism*, which models *associations* using artificial neuron networks and views the mind as a constellation of sensory impressions. This chapter will mainly focus on the information processing approach which has been the chief interest in marketing.

William Lyons (2001), in his *Matters of the Mind*, explains why psychologists are anxious to view the mind as an information processor. Such a model allows clear autonomy of psychology from physiology and neuroscience (so there would be no question of putting the psychologist out of a job!), with the psychologist needing only to take account of input information (sensory impressions), internal processing of information (thinking) and output of information (verbalization of thought).

At the time of its emergence, the information processing view had the backing of philosophers of the caliber of Hilary Putnam (1973) at Harvard and Jerry Fodor (1981) as it seemed to solve the mind–body problem by viewing the human mind as a set of software programs realized by the brain's neural hardware. (The mind–body problem is concerned with the relationship between mind and body. The dualist view of mind asserts that mind and body are distinct things but this view is overthrown if mind is demonstrated to be simply software for the brain's hardware.)

Interestingly, Lyons believes, like most philosophers with an interest in the field, that the most useful explanation of human action will always be because of 'What I believed and wanted'. But cognitive psychologists are likely to eschew such *teleological* explanations couched in terms of reasons, rejecting any talk of people as *agents* guided in their actions by intentions or intentional states. This is in line with *logical empiricism* (today's successor to the logical positivism before the Second World War) that the methodology of the natural sciences is the way to go for the social sciences. To be called a science, there is a need to adopt the methods of the natural sciences. *Empiricism* should form the philosophical underpinnings as opposed to *rationalism* (where reason is given the primary role in thinking and developing explanations) or indeed *pragmatism* (just concerned with practical consequences: whether it works or not). But others argue that cognitive psychology, as practiced, falls short of logical empiricism's ideals in that mapping processes in the mind inevitably falls short of empirical verification of relevant occurrences in the mind, with the danger of conflating logic with psychology.

ARTIFICIAL INTELLIGENCE

We will not deal with the subject of 'artificial intelligence' (AI) as this approach deviates from the other cognitive approaches by focusing on the relationship between behavioral 'outputs' in relation to 'inputs' with no discussion of what happens in between. For some critics this simply amounts to reintroducing behaviorism in another form (Johnson and Erneling 1997). Alan Turing, a British mathematician, is generally regarded as pioneering artificial intelligence (AI) and the one who devised a test to establish whether a computer can be regarded as something that can 'think' (Christian 2011). He put forward the view that, if a computer is able to deceive people into thinking they are communicating with another person, then it would be impossible to tell whether or not the computer was 'thinking'. No computer has yet been developed that can deceive all those appointed as judges in the competition for the Loebner prize into believing a computer is human. Computers lend themselves to work that can be automated. A computer does not have motives and has no reasons for doing what it does but, on the other hand, it can persist without ever getting bored.

INFORMATION PROCESSING APPROACH

Cognitive psychologists who view the mind as an information processor see the psychologist's job as being, not to program the mind, but to work backwards from behavior to identify the likely 'programs' lying behind that behavior (Bruner 1990). Cognitive psychology proceeds by reconstruction (technically, *abduction*, moving back from effects to explanation). The aim is to show how various mental operations, lying behind behavior, are represented and carried out. In viewing people as information processing machines, cognitive psychology takes into account the input of information via sensory impressions: the internal processing of the information via thinking and the output of information via the verbalization of that thinking (Putnam 1975). Just as Hobbes (1588–1679) portrayed humans in terms of the technology of his day, namely self-maintaining mechanisms like the watch, cognitive psychologists espouse today's technology, namely the computer, as the metaphor of the mind.

In cognitive psychology, thinking is the focus, not action, as the computer metaphor better fits the notion of people as information processors than people taking action. The cognitive psychology paradigm sees human beings as constructing mental models (or representations) of, say, a bargaining situation, and mentally manipulating these models to find solutions to problems. The focus is entirely on understanding the mind's programs (software) and not on the 'hardware' of the brain itself. Cognitive psychology is primarily concerned with decision-processes, influenced only by instrumental thinking; that is, thinking with a purpose in mind (Baron 1988).

In the information processing approach, the approach to modeling decision-making follows a set sequence. *First* a *normative* decision model is devised that assumes the individual has the capacity to make optimum choices in line with the model. *Next*, it is shown that such a model is not something human beings are completely capable of following. For example, beliefs (cognitions) are viewed as organized in the mind into 'files' but these files of beliefs cannot always be related or matched by the decision-maker so, in the absence of this matching, inconsistencies can be found among the beliefs in different files.

In practice it is accepted that consumers, as do all people, use *heuristics* (rules of thumb) in decision-making rather than undertake complex deductive or computational processes, so one aim is to identify such heuristics. Heuristics are not regarded as non-rational but rather as a rational way of avoiding complete paralysis of action. The term 'heuristic' was coined by the Hungarian mathematician George Polya (1957) while at Stanford University, and originally meant 'serving to discover'. Heuristic reasoning aims to discover some tentative solution to a problem, a solution not regarded as likely to be the last word. The *final* step in mapping decision-making is to devise a *prescriptive model* (as opposed to the initial 'normative model') that people are more capable of following. A prescriptive model guides us on what to do or how to think about some issue, in contrast to a normative model that defines what is considered the optimal way of going about decision-making.

One normative model in cognitive psychology is the *expectancy-value theory* of motivation, which shares the major features of the subjective expected utility model in economics (see Chapter 9). Viewed as a model of motivation, it makes the assumption that people take account of probabilities as they go about decision-making. This is not always true in real life. If entrepreneurs, would-be professional athletes and climbers of Everest always took account of probabilities of success, the motivation to proceed would not be forthcoming. But such a normative model is a start in moving on to something more realistic with the adoption of a prescriptive model.

CRITICISM OF THE INFORMATION PROCESSING APPROACH

A typical criticism of the information processing approach is that consciousness is not captured by the computer metaphor; our intentions are something more than neural states, while people's emotional natures undermine the notion of the mind as just a calculating machine. A psychology confined to the computer metaphor cannot deal with subjective conscious experience, the emotions, self-consciousness or any feelings towards things that concern us. Thinking, in practice, cannot be confined to *syntactic* (the way words are arranged) manipulation of inputs, with *semantic* (meaning) processing entirely ignored.

Many agree with Searle (1994), another analytic philosopher, that a mind that is merely computer software is not a mind at all in any meaningful sense. As Searle and Freeman (1998) point out, some cognitive scientists, to help simplify things, have moved on to defining consciousness as no more than a qualitative feel. This, they argue, reflects a view of man as an unconscious zombie that behaves as if consciousness is an epiphenomenon, being caused but not, in turn, causing anything itself. If mind is an epiphenomenon, it is a sterile concept, with mind having no causal relevance to action so there is no point in studying it. But this accusation is denied by cognitive psychologists. It is apparent that the mind in consciousness is not simply an epiphenomenon, since burning my hand or having a headache, for example, can explain many subsequent actions. In fact, conscious experiences of all sorts can trigger action. Cognitive psychologists thus do not regard the mind as an epiphenomenon but as something causal of behavior. But cognitive psychologists are still in the dark about why cognitive functioning of the mind brings with it conscious experience – in spite of the many claims to have solved the problem. It may arise purely from the functional organization of the mind. We do not in fact know.

Jerome Bruner's (1990) assessment of the information processing approach in cognitive psychology is:

> But information processing cannot deal with anything beyond well-defined and arbitrary entries that can enter into specific relationships that are strictly governed by a program of elementary operations. Such a system cannot cope with vagueness, with polysemy, with metaphoric or connotative connections... It precludes such ill-formed questions as 'How is the world organized in the mind of a Muslim fundamentalist?' or 'How does the concept of Self differ in Homeric Greece and in the postindustrial world.
>
> (Bruner 1990: 5)

All this has not stopped cognitive psychologists. Just because cognitive psychology has a limited perspective (just like the other psychologies!) does not mean the perspective is of no practical significance.

Cognitive psychologists reject dualism (that mind and body are distinct entities), as social scientists do, and opt for the notion of the mind as software to the brain in action, accepting that most mental activity occurs at the unconscious level and metaphors play an important role in thinking. But dualism is not completely dead. Chalmers (1996) makes the best case to date for some modified form of mind–body dualism while also providing a penetrating review of the literature and controversies on the subject of consciousness. As Chalmers defines it, being conscious implies a mental state that has the qualitative feel of experiencing something: consciousness is equated with the subjective quality of experience, whether visual, auditory, tactile, taste, pain, bodily sensation, mental imagery, sense of self, emotions or conscious thought. This view of consciousness is controversial but often quoted in the absence of anything more profound.

The cognitive sciences have had much to say about cognition in general but little to say about consciousness. In psychology, consciousness is commonly viewed in terms of psychological properties of mind such as the ability to report on external events or access information from short-term and long-term memory but none of this *explains* consciousness. At present, we are at a loss as to how physical processes give rise to conscious experience. The *phenomenal* (subjective) perspective views mind as a consciously experienced mental state, while cognitive psychology views mental states as the cause of behavior whether those mental states are conscious or not. Thus we have those who view the conscious mind as distinguished by the way it feels, while others view the conscious mind as distinguished by what it does.

Social scientists whose interest lies in conscious experience will focus on the phenomenal (subjective) attributes of mind but if the interest lies in the causal role of the mind in bringing about action, interest will lie in psychological concepts like motivation. That said, many mental concepts have a foot in both camps, such as 'pain' which has both a conscious experience component and a psychological component, as when we discuss its causes and consequences.

Cognitive studies in marketing are seldom concerned with the issues raised above but just proceed without much debate or reminding the reader of what is being assumed.

THE ROLE OF HYPOTHETICAL CONSTRUCTS

Cognitive psychology studies mental happenings that can never be directly observed. Studying mental processes is not like studying observable processes, while there can be many rival mental processes to account for any set of experimental findings. *Constructs* as concepts developed to facilitate communication within a discipline, like 'cognition', are not at the same level of reality as words like 'trees' and 'house'. They are *hypothetical constructs*; that is, they are invented, hypothetical, man-made concepts to account for what is believed to be so. It is 'as if' people have attitudes, motives, desires, personalities and so on. In other words, people's behavior suggests something analogous to their having these things. If I say to my doctor that my symptoms are 'as if' someone were scratching my feet, I do not think that this is literally so but it is analogous to this being the case. It is the same with *hypothetical constructs* (those concepts constructed within the discipline) like 'attitude'. If I say my dog acts 'as if' it is a human being, there must be a common understanding of how a human being acts in such circumstances. To say consumers *generally* act 'as if' following the economist's rational choice model is in fact not true but what is true is that consumers are capable of acting in this way on occasion. All too often we confuse what is logically feasible or imagined to be feasible with what actually occurs – that is, we again confuse logic with empirical psychology.

MacCorquodale and Meehl (1948) distinguished the hypothetical construct from what they describe as an *intervening variable*. Hypothetical constructs are the abstractions representing the sense-meanings of terms, while the intervening variables provide the referent (referential-meaning), which is the operational definition or measure of the construct. Although the authors promoted the need for the intervening variable, they acknowledge that the hypothetical construct alone may have to assume the burden of explaining findings. This is frequently the case in cognitive psychology where it is not always possible to obtain operational measures for the various hypothetical constructs. There is a danger of models being created from constructs defined purely in terms of sense-meanings without having been given referential-meanings/operational meanings.

Hypothetical constructs like 'attitude' are an essential part of social science but, contrary to popular opinion, hypothetical constructs also find their way into the natural sciences. Thus scientists speak of particles that have never been observed, as in the case of the 'Higgs boson' particle after the physicist Peter Higgs who first proposed its existence. If indeed it does exist, it would represent a 'field' that exists everywhere, filling space and touching everything. None of the hypothetical constructs in social science are quite as expansive as this!

ATTITUDE AND OTHER MENTAL CONSTRUCTS

Social constructs (those concepts developed to describe and explain in social life) are dominant in social science as opposed to the natural sciences where concepts tend to be grounded in the natural world of substances. It could be argued that many social scientists have focused purely on the operational measures of concepts in order to make clear their referential-meaning, as opposed to first thinking deeply about the sense-meaning of a concept (i.e. thinking about its *construct validity*), to determine what can be inferred from it, what it develops from, what it is consistent with and incompatible with, as well as what we are being committed to by applying the concept. We should applaud those psychologists who investigate 'concept formation' which takes account of little else but how the concept is distinguished and developed. Clarity in sense-meaning should come before considering its operational definition (referential-meaning).

The concept (construct) of attitude has come to play a major role in marketing. An attitude is a predisposition to respond in a consistently favorable or unfavorable way to some person, item or thing. Katz (1960) argued that attitudes have four functions:

1. Utilitarian, in that a person may benefit from adopting a certain attitude;
2. Value-expressive, in that the attitude may project a person's core superordinate values;
3. Ego-defensive, in that the adoption of a certain attitude may be a tactic to protect one's ego;
4. Knowledge, in that adopting a certain attitude may reduce uncertainty.

It is not quite clear whether these functions cover all functions that involve other people, such as the adoption of an attitude to show support for group solidarity.

It is generally assumed that attitudes are learnt, though some evolutionary psychologists claim that hostility to those outside the 'tribe' is inherent as strangers, universally throughout cultures, appear threatening. Attitudes are also assumed to be targeted towards a specific object, though there is no reason why that object is not life itself, since there is no contradiction in current usage in saying of someone that he or she has a negative attitude to life. It is assumed that attitude responses are consistent in that if I have a negative attitude towards air travel today, it will be the same tomorrow and the day after. This again may be generally true, but not all attitudes are well grounded and some change easily. Attitudes also may *not* have cross-situational stability in the sense that my attitude towards alcohol is favorable when expressed at a party and unfavorable when expressed in front of my children.

It is common in the consumer behavior literature to talk of attitudes 'causing' actions. But a favorable or negative attitude towards some action like air travel is neither necessary nor sufficient to initiate action, or inhibit it in respect of air travel. Typically, attitude measures rest on tapping into a person's *beliefs* but it takes beliefs and *supportive* motives/wants to bring about action, unless the action is completely belief-driven such as for a suicide bomber. Highly negative or positive attitudes are simply a contributory factor, not a forcing variable. Thus I may have a highly negative attitude towards air travel but still travel by air as the alternatives displaced are poor substitutes in terms of time. In fact I can have highly positive attitudes towards all sorts of products but buy none of them as they do not fall into my list of wants.

We might note the use of the word 'predisposition' as the category to which the concept of 'attitude' belongs. An attitude is a predisposition to evaluate an event, person or thing in a certain way, which indicates that attitudes are triggered or aroused by some happening. It has to be triggered or aroused by some event to evoke a response but, as far as action is concerned, that trigger provides a motive.

Many models of buyer behavior are loaded with hypothetical constructs that have sense-meaning but no operational meaning or measure, which is another way of saying they have no referential-meaning in terms of observables. On the other hand, as argued earlier, the focus on obtaining operational definitions that capture referential-meanings is deficient if it occurs without first paying attention to core sense-meanings. Even when an attempt is made to obtain operational measures of the constructs to establish referential-meanings, the measures may capture a different concept than that originally proposed. We should all be on the lookout for this displacement. On the other hand, focusing purely on sense-meanings can result in models consisting of lots of little boxes linked with other boxes which claim to be mental processes but simply link a set of sense-meanings. The result is misleading boxology – misleading in the sense that it suggests substance where none may exist. Whenever concepts in social science are difficult to measure, such as beauty, taste, motive and so on, particular attention has to be paid to how the concept is indeed measured since such measures may not be useful for the purposes (if any) for which they are employed.

There are at present too many measures of 'attitude' reflecting different theoretical positions. It might be better to return to the basic concept of attitude as a 'predisposition to react to some person or thing' and measure it by using measures of 'gut' reaction in terms of like or dislike. This would cohere with Damasio's claim (see Chapter 8) about our reactions being first 'gut' reactions of like or dislike. However, the broader tripartite model of attitude as being composed of affect, cognition and conation has an academic usefulness that has tended to beat off criticism.

THE FALLACY OF WANT CREATION

A persistent question of a cognitive nature is whether advertising creates wants. There is an implicit image here of the consumer being motivationally empty until advertising comes along and induces a want. Certainly, consumers do buy products they were not actively seeking before being made aware of them. Some of these new products may simply be better solutions to old problems, in which case no new want is created. However, some new products perform a function not previously regarded as a problem until the new product solved it. Thus we have the recent spate of 'skin repair' products claiming to help speed the natural repair of damaged skin cells. While most consumers may not have been aware of the possibility of damaged skin cells, it cannot be denied that such products are purporting to meet the universal goals of health and beauty. In other words, the want for the product was latent or dormant until activated by the consumer being made aware of the product's function. It is like someone saying we look cold and our response being: 'Now that you mention it I am.' People are not always conscious of what they might want. The product function for which there is a latent want may not be the original designer-use function but some other function, just as Kleenex tissue is now more in demand for wiping noses than for cleaning car windows. Companies commonly find that consumers are using their products for some other purpose than was originally intended; it pays to check and see.

So-called created wants are not created out of nothing but reflect some non-conscious want. One recent innovation alerts the customer's smartphone whenever a purchase is made with their credit card. Given how many of us have had our card number stolen and used, this is something that is likely to be a latent want. Consumers will not in general knowingly go against their own perceived self-interest even though they are not necessarily able to spell out precisely what that self-interest is. 'In general' because it is not clear that a consumer might not interpret self-interest as instant gratification (e.g. using drugs) which may not serve long-term interests. Philosophers occasionally talk of our 'wanting-to-want', in the sense that I may 'want-to-want' to eat less and diet. We may look at such cases as reinforcing 'the will to do good'. Public service advertising may have the goal of helping this process: to get the target audience to 'want-to-want' to give up cigarettes as the first step in bringing about change.

There is also the possibility of consumers believing something to be true that is false and against their own self-interest to believe it. This is the concept of 'false consciousness' which Marxists (not Marx himself) introduced into social science. It sought to explain why the move towards Marxism was not occurring, with electorates moving back and forth from right to left and vice versa. It is true that people do vote for political programs that make false claims and which, though believed, are not in their interests to believe. The explanation on some occasions may lie in those promoting the program being a 'reference group' to which those believers aspire to belong or whose values they share. It was not uncommon between the First and Second World Wars for some members of the upper classes in the UK to actively support communist political programs, which made no sense except on the grounds of a sharing of values. Self-interest is not, for many, the superordinate value or goal in life.

What seems to be meant, however, by 'creating wants' is *not* that firms are capable of creating a demand for products that serve no purpose but that many wants of the consumer are 'artificial'. This is an old debate. In the first century AD, Seneca attributed the evils of civilization to the stimulation of artificial wants. This charge was resurrected in the nineteenth century by socialists claiming that all the evils of society were due to the inculcation of artificial needs. But is not any distinction between artificial and natural wants purely arbitrary, simply reflecting differences in values? Taking the argument to extremes, only the bare necessities of life can be defended as non-artificial, while everything else, including the whole of culture with a capital C, could be regarded as artificial.

PERCEPTIONS AND BRAND MEANING

Perceptions are what count in marketing and perceptions are a topic for cognitive psychology. Perceptions of brand image, price and brand availability – all relative to competition – influence consumers. In marketing, the aim is to build a brand image that resonates with the target customer group, with price and distribution matching the desired image. But cognitive psychology has not entirely accepted the claim that perceptions are completely determined by how we view reality; that beliefs permeate perception. In other words, cognitive psychology does not necessarily endorse that perspective determines perceptions. A major counterexample is the Müller–Lyer illusion in Figure 6.1.

Line Y looks longer than Line X, although they are the same. The question arises that, if beliefs or perspective infuse perception should not knowing about the Müller–Lyer illusion make the illusion go away? While our perspective does affect how we view reality so that, for example, we commonly see what we believe we should see, it is not the whole story,

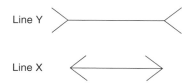

Figure 6.1   The Müller-Lyer illusion

as Figure 6.1 indicates. There are many such examples where, for example, the shape of a glass deceives us as to quantity held or the shape of plates deceive as to quantity of food the plate can hold and so on.

The cognitive psychologist is likely to subscribe to the *modularity theory*, according to which most cognitive processes are carried out by special-purpose computational modules, with the mind viewed as a bundle of domain-specific 'software' constituting the totality of an individual's available heuristics. It is these specialized modules, not minds or selves per se, that house beliefs. It is claimed that it is the left hemisphere of the brain that uses what information it has to deliver a coherent narrative to conscious awareness. (Is there not a faint echo here of the notion of a coherence theory of truth?)

A brand image is the collective interpretation of the associations, feelings and expectations conjured up by the brand. Thus the brand image of Brooks Brothers is an elite one whereby it manages to sell to actors like George Clooney and President Barack Obama, providing assurance to top executives as to the wisdom of their choice. Advertising has an important role in bringing about a favorable image. A favorable brand image symbolizes something positive for those in the relevant market segment and evokes a comfortable feeling of familiarity with pleasant emotional overtones.

The concept of the product class is a concept *type*, and any brand in the product class is a concept *token*. Most consumers form images of both the concept type and the concept token, though this does not mean we have mental images for all concepts. For example, how could one have a mental image of truth? We cannot. As already stated, the mind evokes both images and propositions or beliefs that can be true or false (Kosslyn 1980). Propositions and images are drawn upon in interpreting what the brand means to us, but in asking about brand image consumers are apt to focus on the propositions (beliefs about the brand) that are evoked by the brand, rather than describing some picture or image in the mind.

Concrete descriptors are interpreted faster than words that are abstract. The reason for this might be that concrete words are processed using a dual system through: (a) networks of associated words; (b) sensory images that are more easily evoked than abstractions. But an alternative explanation is that abstract words need more contextual information in order to retrieve the relevant information crucial to interpretation. The evidence for this is that, when abstract words appear in a meaningful context, they are readily comprehended (Schwanenflugel 1991).

Perceptions of a brand are tied somewhat to the meaning (significance) of a brand name which consists of:

- What the brand denotes (referential-meaning), in the sense of what it refers to. Thus the brand name Lexus refers to a car; something real and tangible. But the name itself may have no counterpart in the *real* physical world beyond its being the name of a brand. Thus I may call my brand of cereal the Unicorn brand, with a logo showing the mythical animal resembling a horse with a single horn projecting from its forehead. There may be no such animal in the real world but this does not mean the name 'Unicorn' has no referential-meaning in that it denotes something in mythology and associates the brand with that mythology. Companies strive for customer recognition of their logos, with their logos hopefully being all that is needed for company recognition.

- I may give a brand a proper name, like the Rolls-Royce car, which not only references the car firm itself but carries with it the sense-meaning aura of that proper name, as happens all the time with luxury items such as Cartier, Bulgari, Ralph Lauren and so on.
- Whatever sense-meanings or connotations are conjured up by the brand name in the minds of consumers, the referential-meaning may remain constant, while the connotation (sense-meaning) can change. This is because brand connotations often change without changing the referential-meaning. Therefore a series of happenings that impinge negatively on the reputational capital of a brand, as happened with Toyota and Goldman Sachs, can leave the referential-meaning unchanged but the sense-meaning diminished. Sometimes the referential-meaning remains constant and the brand name resists any new sense-meanings being attached to it. Thus a brand name with a lifeless image may resist attempts to raise that image by associating it with something exciting. While the referential-meaning of a brand can be universally agreed upon by all members of the target audience, this is not true of sense-meanings in that the sense-meaning conjured up in the mind by a brand can occasionally be idiosyncratic. It can also be tied to context (class of store, different times and different consumer moods). But an overall brand image is a reality and marketers are wise to take it into account and measure brand image for its target group in the context of interest.
- The brand name per se influences the connotations conjured up by the name. Typically, these connotations are:

  Functional: the various functions suggested by the name.

  Semantic: whatever words and their associations are conjured up by the name itself.

  Thematic: the feel and texture of the name.

As we have said, brand image, used without qualification, refers to the target audience's collective brand image. Since every consumer will have his or her own personal image of the brand, the collective brand image will only consist of the commonalities. This means the collective brand image is less rich in detail than it is at the individual level. In fact the collective brand image may amount to little more than an overall positive or negative appraisal with ideas for enhancing that image suggested by looking at the brand image at the individual level to seek suggestions that connect to many in the target group of consumers.

The collective brand image arises from cumulative interpretations of past promotions of the brand, word-of-mouth communications and actual experience with the brand. This explains why there is a need to spell out the desired brand image and the sort of promotion and experiences that will help ensure a favorable interpretation. A consistent brand image, symbolizing what the brand stands for, is crucial. The same is true in politics; a party or a politician must come across as standing for something that is worthy of our commitment. In any case, a brand image improves or erodes over time. The more memorable the initial image, the less is the erosion of that image.

All marketers seek to make their brand a *significant symbol* by checking whether its image resonates with the target audience by evoking pleasant feelings. But, as cognitive psychologists tell us, evoking a brand image is not equivalent to retrieving a picture from a mental file, since images are constructed during recall rather than retrieved from some mental filing system. A memorable image is a coherent one, accompanied by a consistent and novel message about the brand. The seller needs to ensure the image is memorable in this sense. The more the consumer's conscious awareness of the brand through exposure, whether through advertising or usage, the more easily are brands recalled and the more the imagery evolves into propositions or belief statements about the brand.

BRAND AWARENESS, BRAND FAMILIARITY AND THE REPEATED EXPOSURE EFFECT

While the term 'awareness' is sloppily used as a synonym for 'consciousness', we can in fact be aware of many things in the environment without being conscious of anything. Neuroscientists typically claim that much of what happens in the brain occurs without conscious awareness; that most choices are made subconsciously with gradations of awareness. This is the notion of people being on automatic pilot, guided by an unconscious system 90 percent of the time. We have used the term 'choices' instead of 'decisions'. This is because the term 'decision' suggests deliberation and so is more correctly reserved for occasions where there is deliberation (and hence consciousness).

With repeated exposure to the brand there comes increased *familiarity* and, other things remaining equal, the greater the familiarity, the more the liking. This is because the familiar constitutes an informational anchor in making life intelligible. This is the *repeated exposure effect*, leading to liking that helps mass advertising sell a brand through repeat ads even if the ads in themselves possess little persuasive content. It assumes, of course, that the consumer's impression of the brand is not just negative in the first place. We are all familiar with the expressions: 'He just grows on you' or 'He's not bad once you get to know him.' This is analogous to the repeated exposure effect.

The repeated exposure effect is what can make 'product positioning' in a movie effective. And product positioning or product placement in films has now become a fact of life. Product placement and branded entertainment generally have increased as marketers seek alternatives to the 30 second television commercial, which is all too easily avoided with zipping, muting and zapping. But the 30 second spot is in fact changing as attention-getting becomes more sophisticated and technology develops to make ads truly customized, not just by neighborhood or household but even, it is hoped, by viewing habits. Ads can now appear in strange places. We read about General Mills paying teachers $250 a month to have their cars become rolling ads for a breakfast cereal, Reese's Puffs.

Just as when we see something happening we believe it, when we are told something, it most likely goes directly into belief (Gilbert 1993). If we think about it, life would be impossibly complicated if we didn't accept much of what we are told without asking for supportive evidence. Claims, however, may be rejected instantly if they conflict with existing beliefs. But most assertions have no reason to be doubted. We accept what is said then evaluate it (if we do at all) to see if we should reject it. And under cognitive stress, we may not evaluate it at all. One aim of promotion is to ensure that the target audience's beliefs about the brand and imagery associated with the brand are positive so interpretations of persuasive communications are positive. Pleasant images associated with the brand induce affect (emotion)-driven choices, while positive beliefs help generate belief-driven choices. We would like to induce choices that are both affect-driven and belief-driven.

PRIMACY AND RECENCY EFFECTS

In speaking of persuasive communications, the question arises as to whether initial impressions (*primacy effect*) are more persuasive than last impressions (*recency effects*). The answer is that it depends on circumstances though both can be important. Thus, the first impressions and last impressions of service in a hotel can determine one's attitude towards the hotel. Whenever the first piece of evidence is given undue weight, it is known as the primacy effect. This bias can arise from its being the evidence first encountered, which can generate an implicit commitment if persuasive. The opposite bias is the recency effect where more weight is given to the last piece of evidence presented. This again can arise from being given more attention. Both biases can be related to the *availability heuristic* in that what comes to mind first is given undue weight.

BRAND PERSONA AND PERSONALITY

The *persona* is the public face an individual presents to the outside world. The public façade projected by the brand is the brand's persona; a consistent persona suggests the company's commitment to whatever the image suggests by way of benefits. That persona is sharpened by a reinforcing logo, brand name, appropriate packaging and characters (if not used as the logo) that the consumer can identify with. We can think of characters like the Jolly Green Giant, Speedy-Alka-Seltzer, Mr Clean, Mr Peanut with his top hat and cane and so on. Consumers feel particularly comfortable with a brand persona similar to the persona they themselves try to project. If a consumer likes to project an image of being solid and reliable, a product that projects a similar image will attract. Consumers generally feel comfortable with a persona that has an attractive image or fits the image they have of themselves (Birdwell 1968). Think of how the talking 'gecko' with the cockney accent and smartness gives an attractive image to Geico in selling car insurance. We might add that packaging can influence perceptions of a brand. Unfortunately too much packaging today is designed to just protect and in the process causes a great deal of difficulty in unwrapping. Many people have bought some alternative simply because opening the packaging was easier.

On the question of *personality*, developing an attractive brand personality can generate the feeling of the brand being a friend. We are told in psychology not to attribute to non-humans what may be specific human traits as this commits the *anthropomorphic* fallacy. But we do this all the time in marketing, particularly in developing a brand personality, as we want to humanize the brand. Brand personality is based on viewing the brand as a person or living thing. Consumers might be asked: if the brand were a living animal, what animal does it bring to mind? Or, if the brand were a human being, what characteristics would you attach to it? And so on. Or it is possible just to show some personality and say he or she epitomizes the brand. Jameson, the Irish whiskey, promotes the brand's personality as 'a serious whiskey that also knows how to have fun' in a television narrative that stresses the brand's authenticity and a heritage going back to the 1780s. Believing something is the real thing, not a replica but *authentic*, evokes very different imaginings and a very different view of what something is worth.

The development of an attractive brand personality can generate fantasies (fanciful beliefs) about what the brand can do for the consumer, as well as the feeling of the brand being a friend. Thus the Mercedes car may generate fantasies about increased status and comfort (more so if Mercedes had kept the brand limited to their pricier, more attractive models). On this basis, clubs can be formed for owners of a make of car, like the Mazda Miata (or any other product) which has clubs throughout the US.

The consumer may *know* certain claims to be false but *feel* they are true, particularly for brands that possess a nostalgic resonance. Brands have been created, like the PT Cruiser, simply to cater to such nostalgia. Lévi-Strauss has a certain aura based on being the first producer of jeans. Similarly, Coca-Cola has always stressed its history of being first, retaining the same logo from the very beginning in the 1870s. If brand 'persona' and brand 'personality' are regarded as favorable and memorable, these constitute an emotional anchor for enlisting support. A recent nostalgic tactic is for advertisers to resurrect past characters, personalities, jingles and so on that evoke nostalgic memories for times past. Given the inherent danger of such revivals being viewed as reviving brands too dated for today's tastes, the tactic has been supplemented by an updating of the logos, songs and actions susceptible to such judgments.

A brand name will always conjure up a certain set of beliefs about brand characteristics and what the brand symbolizes. There is no such thing as a name having no connotations or sense-meanings attached to it. To say that conjuring a name 'out of the blue' avoids any unpleasant connotations is not true. Computer-generated names do not escape having connotations. Perhaps more importantly, the connotations of a brand can resonate emotionally because of brand name associations, as do brands that have nostalgic appeal. Different brand connotations will be evoked for different people but there are likely to be certain core characteristics of the brand that members of the target audience are apt to share, such as the brand being upmarket, having high reliability, having a top reputation.

Connotations or sense-meanings of the brand name are also influenced by the sound of the name as well as by the product that bears the name. *Phonaesthetics* is the study of the inherent beauty (euphony) or unpleasantness (cacophony) of the sound of a name or other linguistic utterance. Phonaesthetics is often put forward to explain why some but not all celebrity names catch on. Certainly, euphony should be a consideration in choosing a brand name. Lamolay sounds better than Tarytak for a toilet paper even though it has the same number of letters.

Steven Pinker (2007) speaks of 'sound symbolism' where 'the pronunciation of a word reminds people of an aspect of the referent. Long words may be used for things that are big or coarse, staccato words for things that are sharp or quick, words pronounced deep in the mouth or throat for things that took place long ago or far way' (p. 300). Pinker points out how brands at one time were named after their founders, like Ford, or had a name that conveyed their immensity, like General Motors, or a name that identified the new technology like Microsoft, or a name connoting the quality they wished to project, like Impala, but today manufacturers often use neologisms vaguely suggesting qualities: names like Acura, Viagra and so on. This may be simply an attempt to adopt a unique name since the uniqueness of the name suggests the uniqueness of the brand. It may also be true that consumers regard the brand name as suggesting the brand's essence, which is another reason for asserting that a brand name may have no referential-meaning but will still have sense-meaning. Perhaps the technical names given to prescription drugs are meant mainly for the doctor or the notion that a too-simple name suggests a too-simple product. It might be added that marketing should also try to influence the names of departments within a company. If this had happened perhaps firms would have avoided speaking of the 'human resources department' which, though more descriptive of function than the former term 'personnel department', suggests employees are just another resource like production materials.

It is not always in line with a nation's cultural norms to try and impose the same brand name as that used in the home nation. Thus in China the brand name for Colgate toothpaste is replaced by a name that literally declares 'gets rid of dirt', while the substitute name for the detergent 'Tide' literally says 'revealing superior cleanliness' (Wines 2011).

BRAND EXTENSIONS DILUTE BRAND IMAGE

Companies want to exploit a brand name by putting the name on other products they produce. It is usually argued that any extension of the brand name to other products should be regarded as 'natural' by the consumer so acceptance follows. But the question arises as to what is considered 'natural'. After all, the Ralph Lauren brand name is not only put on clothing but other household products like furniture. We need to think about the sense-meaning of the brand name and its symbolism. With the name Ralph Lauren there is the sense-meaning of quality and the symbolism of status and being upmarket. In any case, as a matter of logic, brand extensions dilute the brand image, that is, using the brand name on other products produced by the firm weakens the image. This is because, as the brand name is extended to cover more products, less can be said about the brand as a whole. Thus I can say much more about an individual product like the Mazda Miata than I can say about the Mazda brand in general.

Diluting the authenticity of the brand can also arise from merchandising where the brand name is put on all sorts of accessories from perfume to toys, to watches, to sunglasses. Less can be said about the brand overall than about the individual brands, since the family brand name applied to all brands in the family is restricted to the commonalities of the whole family of brands. But this may not mean that the family brand name is tarnished. There are occasions when one of the brands produces a *halo effect* in that its prominence casts a halo over the other family members so they share in the glory. Of course this can work both ways, in that if one of the family brands has a poor reputation then this can affect perceptions of the other family members.

Auyang (2001) points out that the information content of a concept is a function of its power to discriminate. This is because concepts are mechanisms for dividing the world into categories. Thus the information content of the concept of 'convertible' is higher than the concept of a 'car' since the convertible discriminates more than does the word 'car'. This is so because the meaning of a concept depends on the range of entities to which it applies: the smaller the range, the less equivocal the meaning (both referential and sense-meaning). Auyang further points out that extending the range of entities to which a concept applies *devalues* the concept, as commonly happens with concepts in marketing and social science. Thus the term 'innovation' becomes devalued when defined to embrace every type of change or the most minor improvement in the product line (or even in the company). On these grounds, we devalue a brand name the more there are brand extensions, though this does not mean brand extensions are to be avoided.

Brand extensions are different from 'product enlargements' where the firm's product is augmented by new features. Sometimes *product enlargements* can be necessary for survival. Thus one chain of pubs in the UK, run by JD Wetherspoon, started to open its pubs early in the morning to serve breakfast in order to meet competition from firms like McDonalds. It is currently selling about 400,000 breakfasts a day, second only to McDonalds, and 600,000 cups of coffee, second only to Starbucks and Costa Coffee.

UNIVERSAL BRAND PERSONALITY DESCRIPTORS (?)

If a brand personality presents itself as a human personality, it might be expected that brands could be rated along personality traits or personality types developed for the assessment of people. Unfortunately, this would cover too broad a spectrum. As a consequence, specific shortlists have been devised, for example one that uses such dimensions as sincere, exciting, competent, rugged and sophisticated. In thinking about a brand's personality the first step should always be to state the objective in promoting the brand as a personality since the personality chosen must cohere with the rest of the marketing promotions. We may want to change the current perceptions of consumers or reinforce those perceptions. This may lead us to think more about appropriate characteristics than accept that existing lists have necessarily captured the personality characteristics we want the brand to convey. It may be much better to try and see if the firm's target group of customers share a common set of positive personality descriptors for the firm's brand. In any case, advertising, personal experience and social interactions do much to shape personality perceptions. Just as consumers, when asked about a brand's characteristics, often feed back what they have heard in ads, the same goes for a brand's personality descriptors.

In advertising we find ads that flatter their assumed target audience, as National, the car rental firm, tries to do in talking about their customers being 'business pros' and proceeding to flatter them for their prowess. But the voiceover in this case just sounds patronizing. It is easier in personal life to get one's way with flattery than it is in an ad. Appeals to vanity are, however, quite common. Every US president seemingly has to appeal to the country by talking about American 'exceptionalism', though there are millions of similarities and differences between the US and other Western democracies so the claim remains sufficiently vague to read any positive thoughts about the US into it.

PERCEPTUAL MAPS

Perceptual maps, employed in 'market structure analysis', are another cognitive technique. They show the position of the various brands in a market relative to the attribute dimensions that interest the consumer. The maps are used to identify competitors and rivals but also to make changes to the

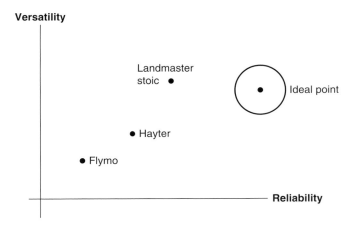

Figure 6.2   Market structure analysis (lawnmower market)

product, if necessary, and to discover any misperceptions that might be corrected. A perceptual map allows us to plot the preference or *ideal point* for a significant group of consumers (see Figure 6.2).

The relative position of the brands on the map is based on consumer interpretations of the degree of similarity and dissimilarity. While all brands on the map may be regarded as competitors, a firm's rivals are those on the perceptual map closest to the firm's own brand. In showing how the brands are related in the consumer's mind, there is generally a reliance on how consumers compare the similarity of different brands on each of their attributes. Similarity is something relative; it is not an attribute of a product, and what we take to be similar attributes may only haphazardly correspond to what is taken to be similar by other people. Everything depends on a person's frame of reference. Analysts identify the dimensions of most interest to the consumer by asking consumers about how they evaluate brands and, via the statistical technique of factor analysis, reduce the dimensions to just two factors. In Figure 6.2 the two dimensions are versatility and reliability for the lawnmower market. The consumer then plots the rival brands on the two dimensions on the map. Consumers can be asked their 'ideal point' for versatility and reliability so the manufacturer can use such information for future planning.

Alternatively, consumers may simply move the brands about on a map until they are satisfied that the *relative* position of the brands represents the respondent's perceptions of relative similarity. Just a map is given, without the axis being given names, with respondents simply asked to position the brands on the map according to perceptions of similarity. Later an attempt is made to identify the axis (attribute) dimensions, since these are needed to give real substance to the map. There is an assumption that the closer the positioning of two brands on the map, the more intense is the competition between them because closeness is directly tied to perceived similarity and familiarity to the likelihood of substitution. While competitors are defined as competing in the same market, rivals are those who compete in the same segment. Not surprisingly, it is argued that the closer the rivals are on the perceptual map the more likely the threat of substitution. But closeness does not *necessarily* imply likelihood of substitution, as sometimes the consumer prefers to forgo buying the product altogether. Thus one woman in talking during shopping refused a substitute yogurt for her favorite Danone yogurt even though it was perceived by her to be closest in taste.

We can use perceptual maps to plot consumer preferences. For example, in Figure 6.3 consumers of chocolate register their ideal balance of 'milkiness' and 'sweetness'. Consumers can put their ideal on the perceptual map. If we accept the procedure as a valid one, it offers help in the area of product improvement or new introductions.

The philosopher Nelson Goodman, in an article entitled 'The Seven Strictures on Similarity' (1969), was an early pioneer in discussing the problems involved in gauging similarity. In seeking to identify the dimensions of interest, the tendency is to list the shared attributes of the rival brands that might enter into evaluation. This seems reasonable and in line with Medin (1989), who argues that judgments of similarity between items increase as a function of the number of attributes they share and decrease

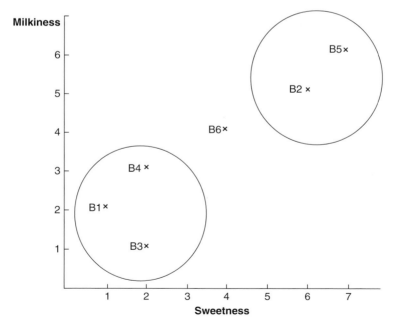

Figure 6.3 Preferences or ideal points of six consumers on the dimensions of milkiness and sweetness of chocolate bars

as a function of mismatching or distinctive attributes. But this proves to be too simplistic. As Aronson et al. (1994) say, interpretation of similarity for practical purposes (e.g. marketing) cannot be determined purely in terms of the number of matches of attributes among, for example, rival brands. This is true even if similarity is viewed as a function of attributes held in common, weighted for salience or importance, which is the definition favored by Tversky (1977). Tversky seems to assume that the question of selecting similar features is unproblematic. It is not. Any two brands have an infinite number of features in common that could be used in evaluation – if we think imaginatively enough. As Aronson et al. show, the key lies in determining what attributes are relevant for the purpose at hand. Simply using shared similarity as the sole criterion for grouping can lead to groupings where members of the group may not have any relevant attributes at all in common for the purpose at hand. This is made clear by Murphy and Medin (1985) who point out that even plums and lawnmowers have an infinite number of features in common.

Empirical facts need to be collected to establish how brands *actually* interrelate in the market. Such facts are needed to identify which attributes are to be counted as relevant for judgments of similarity when similarity is tied to purpose. In marketing, the purpose is that of gauging relative competitive postures. In doing this, it is common to assume we can short-circuit facts about the market. Theodore Levitt (1960) is a case in point when, in a classic article, he advocated defining a business in terms of the generic need for which the firm catered as the way to define the firm's competition. The trouble is that products can appear to serve the same generic need or overall function without being in competition. Thus sundials and watches serve the same generic need to measure time but they are not in the same market. The reply, that the primary function of a sundial is ornamental and not to measure time, implicitly concedes the need to fall back on collected facts about the market. The competitive arena is not identified by armchair reflection on the generic need served by the product but on empirical data collected on the market. Similarly, competitive brand clusters cannot be satisfactorily defined by any listing by consumers of attributes reflecting similarity. Nor does the solution lie in merely letting consumers position brands on the map (though this is helpful) on the assumption that this is how they actually perceive things. We need to know about actual choice behavior in the market.

We think of consumers as classifying new products on the basis of their defining features or characteristics, as we would still classify the Hummer as a car even if it appeared somewhat strange. But there is evidence from cognitive psychology that people commonly categorize on the basis of prototype or exemplars without resort to the individual comparison of attributes (Gibbs 1994). Thus if asked to classify birds, people think first of a prototype bird (such as a blackbird) and on this basis are unlikely to classify a kiwi as a bird as it has no wings. A layperson's classifications are not relevant to zoologists with their reliance on cladistic clustering algorithms that draw on evolutionary history. The layman does not possess the scientific concept of a bird for organizing into interwoven patterns of similarity and dissimilarity. They have a *prototype* in mind and judge similarity using this as a base. Or they may think in terms of *exemplars*. Exemplars, as opposed to prototypes, are actual illustrative examples, not composites like prototypes that take account of context. Recognizing this can alter classification. However, there can be problems in that it is by no means certain that the location of brands on a map in relation to some consumer prototype or exemplar will be the same as groupings that mirror perceived *competitive* sets by the consumer.

We need to research facts about the actual competitive sets in the market as perceived by consumers. Knowing these competitive sets, we can move back to attributes not vice versa in moving from attributes to competitive sets. We would quickly realize that competitive sets are not fixed but vary with context. Two brands may be close competitors on one use-occasion but not on another use-occasion. As Tversky (1977) points out, similarity cannot be assumed to be symmetrical in that the statement 'X is like Y' does not entail our claiming Y is like X. This means that the consumer may see Pepsi Lite as similar to Diet Coca-Cola but not see Diet Coca-Cola as similar to Pepsi Lite. In such a case, the consumer may not buy Pepsi Lite when Coca-Cola is unavailable (preferring not to buy at all) but buy Coca-Cola when Pepsi Lite is unavailable. The mind may interpret or infer what types of sets are likely but only research will give us the actual relevant sets.

Are we then saying that there can be no cognitive recognition of similarity by the marketer without investigation of market facts? Not quite perhaps since, according to the Gestalt principle of similarity, visual items that are like each other in respect to form, size, color or direction are perceived as forming a whole based on similarity among the parts. This would certainly seem to give substance to consumer groupings. However, such gestalt perceptions of similarity may or may not serve any particular purpose for marketing as they are not tied to buying goals. It is only by looking at the way competitive activity is organized and takes place in the market that we are properly able to identify relevant similarities. As Griffiths (1997) says, there is no such thing as overall similarity, only similarity in relation to a particular set of attributes, so the selection of relevant attributes is all important and this requires empirical investigation in the market itself.

REPOSITIONING IN THE MARKET

A brand might be repositioned in the market. Sometimes this is done by modifying the product to appeal to a broader target audience or (more in line with the notion of repositioning) sometimes to an entirely different audience, as happened when Tina Brown took over *Vanity Fair* magazine. This worked but repositioning failed in the case of *Harper's Bazaar* under Katherine Betts, who was forced to resign. In any case, repositioning may involve changing the perceived benefits of the product, whether these benefits are functional or symbolic, or promoting the brand for some use-occasion like a wine for formal dinners, or changing symbolic attributes like image, personality or persona. In repositioning, the aim is to change consumer perceptions of the brand to fit the new target group but changing perceptions of a brand is not necessarily repositioning in that I might simply be trying to get perceptions of the brand more in line with what suits the present segment, as occurs when a car manufacturer tries to change perceptions of the quality of his make of car.

If a company aims to expand market share by trying to attract new users to its established product line, clarity suggests that this should be distinguished from repositioning which involves altering the product somewhat to appeal to a new target group of customers. Thus Jell-O is currently aiming to sell its product as a treat for adults and not just as a children's snack. This is market expansion into new segments as additional to the segments now addressed.

If repositioning involves promoting new functions for the product, there is the problem of *functional fixedness* which Duncker (1945) defines as being inhibited from seeing new functions for a product when the current function for the product is well established. The problem lies in convincing consumers that the product is suited for the new function, given the fixedness of the old function, and is not inferior in performing the function to rival products but has something distinctive to offer. Unless consumers are actually seeking a product combining many functions, they can be suspicious of a product that may be seen as 'a jack of all trades and master of none'.

Somewhat related to functional fixedness is the concept of *retroactive interference* which occurs when any new learning interferes with the memory of what has been already learnt. Thus if the retrieval cue for a product is its original function, when that function is superseded by a different function, there can be retroactive interference. The case of Kentucky Fried Chicken illustrates the difficulties of trying to reposition a product. Given the desire to capture the market for a more healthy, lower calorie offering, the firm introduced its grilled chicken and sandwiches campaign with the slogan 'Unthink KFC' in May 2009. It was seen by many franchisees as an attempt to distance itself from its fried chicken business that had created its success. The campaign was dropped with the franchisees threatening to put out their own ads focusing on fried chicken using life-sized stand-ups of Colonel Sanders.

MISLEADING HIERARCHY OF EFFECTS MODELS

As we have said, cognitive psychology focuses on internal, mental processing with the consumer being viewed as an information processor. In explaining how advertising works, the aim is to identify the mediating mental processes between exposure to the advertisement and buying. One such explanation is the *hierarchy of effects* model which claims to depict the mental stages through which the buyer can be guided in creating a favorable attitude towards the product.

Hierarchy of effects models view advertising as having its impact on sales through consumer attitudes, establishing attitudes where none existed or reinforcing attitudes or pushing them in a direction in which they are already moving. Attitude is conceptualized as having three components:

- A cognitive (knowledge) component
- An affective (feeling, liking/disliking) component
- A conative (behavior) component.

There is nothing in these three components that captures the notion of 'wanting'. The word 'affect' will not do since it lacks any notion of the future state sought. Without incorporating 'want/desire', it is not clear how feelings and beliefs lead to action>intent. If an attitude is a predisposition to react in a positive or negative way to some object, person or thing, how do we establish that these three components are at work? We cannot look into the mind but assume on logical grounds that these three components must be at work. But psychological processes cannot be equated with what is logical. We must not conflate the logical with the psychological. This tripartite division in fact has no standing empirically but is just assumed because the process of going from the cognitive to the affective to the conative seems logical. Of course, we can frame a questionnaire where respondents tick answers suggesting such a hierarchy but this is simply a method artifact.

The aim in using the concept of attitude in marketing is to:

- Form attitudes where none before existed or
- Reinforce existing attitudes or
- Accelerate the movement of attitudes in the direction favored by the advertiser.

In advertising, the first hierarchy of effects model was Colley's (see Figure 6.4), which views the target audience as being moved along the following sequence of stages (Colley 1961):

- Awareness: developing consumer awareness of the brand
- Comprehension: consumer understanding of a product's benefits and so on
- Conviction: getting the target audience to take some form of buying action
- Action: getting members of the target audience convinced enough to want to buy the product.

The hierarchy of effects through which the consumer is said to pass is related to the components of attitude since each stage falls into one of the three components. This is shown in Figure 6.4 where Colley's model

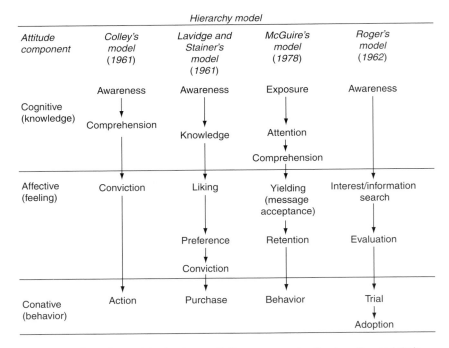

Hierarchy model

Attitude component	Colley's model (1961)	Lavidge and Stainer's model (1961)	McGuire's model (1978)	Roger's model (1962)
Cognitive (knowledge)	Awareness ↓ Comprehension	Awareness ↓ Knowledge	Exposure ↓ Attention ↓ Comprehension	Awareness
Affective (feeling)	Conviction	Liking ↓ Preference ↓ Conviction	Yielding (message acceptance) ↓ Retention	Interest/information search ↓ Evaluation
Conative (behavior)	Action	Purchase	Behavior	Trial ↓ Adoption

Figure 6.4 Hierarchy models showing mediating processes leading to action and their link with the alleged components of attitude

and the other advertising hierarchy models are shown in relation to the components of attitude when conceived in this tripartite way. In general, hierarchy models assume that the consumer first learns something about the product, then develops feelings towards it and then behaves consistently in the light of such knowledge and feelings. The formation of attitudes is thus considered key to understanding the persuasive process, with the various hierarchy of effects models being views about the mental processing steps that comprise attitude development: the mental processing steps comprising the cognitive and affective dimensions of attitude with the conative being identified with some behavioral outcome. Probably McGuire's information processing model is the one most grounded in cognitive psychology. Thus, unlike the others, he includes a *retention* stage, which is important since advertising is more directed at future action than action at the time of seeing the advertisement.

Even if all the various hierarchy models could be reconciled and shown to be descriptively correct, they would simply show the hurdles to be overcome by advertising but not *how* to overcome the hurdles. Even if advertisers believe that creating awareness and comprehension is technically solvable, they would still be faced with the problem of how to get conviction and action. Hierarchy models do not tell them this, beyond recognizing the need for some rewarding mechanism to be at work at each stage. But advertisers need to know about such mechanisms or the appropriate appeals that move the consumer from one stage to the next. Hierarchy models tell us where we are and where we have to go but not how to get there.

Further criticism of hierarchy models stems from an implicit recognition of the arbitrariness of the various stages described and the assumed uniformity of the choice process. On the surface, Colley's mental sequence of:

$$\text{Awareness} \Rightarrow \text{Comprehension} \Rightarrow \text{Conviction} \Rightarrow \text{Action}$$

would appear appropriate for activating a latent want. But creating awareness means nothing unless the product is shown to be relevant to meeting the consumer's goals. If the want is passive, awareness and comprehension have already occurred and the need is to change that part of the offering that is holding back buying or depreciating the factors inhibiting purchase.

Hierarchy models seem to have little relevance to maintaining buying habits or altering a picking situation so that the firm's brand is picked more frequently or bought exclusively. Similarly, if intrinsic liking alone determines choice, the model misrepresents the choice process. There is no meaningful evaluation here or deep deliberation (as implied by terms like 'comprehension') since intrinsic choice may consist simply of:

$$\text{I see} \Rightarrow \text{I like} \Rightarrow \text{I buy}$$

A communication (e.g. from one's physician) *can* be persuasive even if arguments are not learned, remembered and fully understood: impression and faith (unshakable belief) often substitute. For extrinsic preference, the model also shows weaknesses. Comprehension is interpreted to mean absorbing facts about the product or brand. But if integrative criteria (e.g. the desire for group acceptance) dominate choice, is 'getting comprehension' a meaningful description of the job to be done? If adaptive criteria (e.g. worry over making a mistake) dominate, is 'getting conviction' particularly relevant? The term 'conviction' suggests being rationally convinced. If so, this ignores the fact that many products are bought on the basis of advice or the brand's reputation/image, or through following the lead of others in the hope (but without conviction) that we have chosen wisely.

Each of the hierarchy models presupposes that consumers first learn something about a product or brand before liking or disliking it. This ignores the work of Damasio, the neuroscientist, who shows that perceiving anything involves an immediate 'gut feel' of like or dislike without any evaluation, which may come later. Just because we can separate the cognitive and the affective at the conceptual level does not mean that they reflect separate mental steps. The various hierarchies simply represent different logical refinements of the process or different interpretations of processing stages using the computer as an analogy.

The hierarchy of effects models mislead if treated as universally valid. If a particular stage is not a necessary step for the target audience to go through, resources could be wasted in focusing on it. For example, an advertising campaign launched to generate comprehension errs if buying action can be prompted by some personality recommending the product. Also, an emphasis on creating awareness and comprehension can misdirect if it tempts advertisers into always putting across more and more product information. Buyers are not just persuaded by technical and economic facts and neither are such facts always primary for the buyer.

An answer to some of this criticism is to accept that the standard learning hierarchies illustrated in Figure 6.4, taking the form of learn⇒feel⇒do, are more applicable to situations where the buyer has high involvement with the purchase and consequent involvement with the advertisement for the product. But this still assumes these are separate mental stages when they need not be.

Herbert Krugman (1965) argued that, in respect to television advertising, there was learning without involvement. As a consequence of what amounts to simple incidental learning, defenses were down when receiving the message. Although Krugman's article was not a piece of research but more an observation or hypothesis, it had such intuitive appeal (coinciding as it did with the idea of the viewer being just a 'couch potato') that many marketers have come to accept the idea of the passive viewer. But more recently, research has supported the idea of an active rather than passive viewer. But how can something like this be demonstrated either way? Psychological theory is neutral and statistical generalizations are not likely to cover a random, unbiased sample. All we can say is that some viewers may be passive and some may be active.

The term 'involvement', as defined by Krugman, is essentially the same as the term 'symbolic meaning' used in some branches of sociology. When such sociologists say that 'meaning' directs behavior, they are saying in effect that it is beliefs about what something signifies for a person's wants that determine his or her actions. If buyers are highly involved with an advertisement for a product, it is the same as saying they believe the advertisement has significance for their wants. The concept of meaning in the sense described has the advantage of combining both wants and beliefs, that is, reasons for action or non-action, in the one word.

The acceptance of Krugman's concept of involvement, when linked to the recognition that consumers do not all follow the same sequence of stages in attitude formation, has led to the development of additional hierarchies to replace the single process view. Thus Ray (1982) posits three distinct hierarchies. These are shown in Figure 6.5:

(i) The standard learning hierarchy of learn⇒feel⇒do.
(ii) The dissonance-attribution hierarchy of do⇒feel⇒learn, where the action comes first followed by the affective (evaluative) and then by the cognitive.

(iii) The low-involvement hierarchy of learn⇒do⇒feel where some learning occurs first then the conative and then the affective. This model reflects Krugman's view and has received some support in the literature but also some skepticism. This is not surprising since it is difficult to visualize learning enough about a product to actually buy it without having feelings towards it.

The conditions listed by Ray under which each of the processes is said to arise are also given in Figure 6.5. Ray does not claim that these conditions are either necessary or sufficient for each stage in the process to be carried along. Figure 6.5 simply shows the *logical* link between situations and processes though it is the *empirical* link that needs to be firmly established. As with the standard hierarchy, it is not clear how the target audience moves from one stage to the next. There is the assumption that marketers know the full potential of each of their promotional tools and so can devise appropriate strategies for moving the target audience through any hierarchy adopted.

Many of the same criticisms made of the standard learning hierarchy also apply to all hierarchies made of constructs similar to those of awareness, comprehension and conviction. We must ask whether these constructs are sufficiently operational and comprehensive enough for

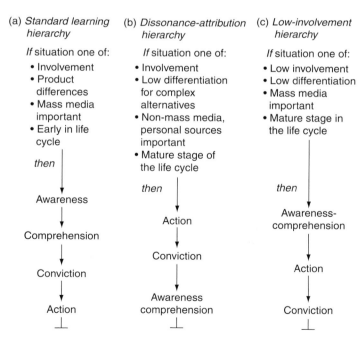

Figure 6.5   Decision-process hierarchies
Source: after Ray (1982).

depicting the relevant process of attitude formation and coming to buying action. Even if we accept that awareness/comprehension ('learning'), conviction ('feel') and action ('do') are distinct mental processes, there are additional possible hierarchies:

Ray's hierarchies	Additional hierarchies
(i) Learn⇒feel⇒do	(iv) Feel⇒learn⇒do
(ii) Do⇒feel⇒learn	(v) Feel⇒do⇒learn
(iii) Learn⇒do⇒feel	(vi) Do⇒learn⇒feel

Ray would probably argue that his three hierarchies have some theoretical backing but since the other possible hierarchies are easy to visualize as occurring in our mental processing, they should not be ignored as too remote to consider.

There is this assumed uniformity of the choice process. The standard learn⇒feel⇒do sequence assumes a very rational approach and high involvement with the purchase. High or deep involvement with a purchase implies concern with the purchase in that the product is of central importance to the consumer and risk is attached to buying. High or deep involvement endures only so long as the product remains of central importance and there is risk attached to buying. High involvement motivates by tapping the emotions, thus focusing attention on obtaining the product and making the product easier to 'sell'. Are all the stages necessary and is the standard sequence invariable? The answer to both questions is 'no', hence the creation of additional hierarchies to replace the single process view. The logical possibilities are the following hierarchies:

- Learn (about product)⇒feel⇒do(act)
- Feel⇒learn⇒do
- Do (act)⇒feel⇒learn
- Learn⇒do⇒feel
- Feel⇒do⇒learn
- Do⇒learn⇒feel

It is simplistic to assert that the persuader need only consider the hierarchies to decide whether to use the cognitive route to attitude change, or the affective route or the conative route, since persuasion is a mixture of rational reason-giving, emotional fellowship and trials. The concept of involvement is not some dichotomy into high/low but a continuum so that boundary areas are somewhat arbitrary. Whether these mental steps actually occur, as opposed to being logical stages that can manifest themselves (when respondents are encouraged to do so), is a matter of dispute. But are we not confusing a logical process with some actual mental process? Do we really learn without first instantly forming an affective response? Or can we not just go from feel to do? Not all advertising would be interested in moving along some hierarchy, for interest might simply focus on retaining current customers.

For Ray, the hierarchies are very much tied to promotional strategies and budgeting in that each hierarchy stage is tied to some component or components of the communications mix. Ray argues for what he calls a 'balanced, multi-communications-tool approach', choosing whatever tool will do the job most effectively, within some budget constraint, while at the same time recognizing a *compensation principle* to be at work in that setting extreme targets (e.g. stressing *zero* cigarette tar as the advertising theme) tends to have corresponding mental reactions (e.g. less credibility about the cigarette's taste). Of course, not all advertising is concerned with moving along some hierarchy, for the focus might be simply on retaining current customers. Also, there is the problem that arises when different members of the target segment are at different stages of the same hierarchy or at different stages of different hierarchies which may necessitate different campaigns.

One prominent advertising agency that has promoted the notion of hierarchy endorses the view that the learn⇒feel⇒do and the feel⇒learn⇒do operate in conditions of high involvement, with the first sequence being attributed to the consumer as 'thinker' and the second to the consumer as 'feeler'. The 'thinker' sequence suggests providing information that allows for a rational decision-making process. The feeler sequence suggests emotional appeals as being more effective. The do⇒learn⇒feel and the do⇒feel⇒learn are seen as operating in conditions of low involvement, with the first sequence being attributed to the consumer as 'doer' and the second to the consumer as 'reactor'. Given the low involvement, brand familiarity might be all that is needed. Accordingly, the claim is made that the advertising message should vary with each category as the receptiveness to different appeals will necessarily differ. It seems a logical approach that offers a solution to an important problem. But logical sequences do not necessarily mirror the empirical facts. Again are, for example, learn, feel and do, distinct mental activities? Is marketing right to assume they are the normative mental processes?

The logical attraction of distinct processes does not mean that these occur as distinct mental processes. Might they not occur simultaneously so that catering to distinct stages is misleading? It would be equally easy to talk of 'speaking' as consisting of the logical sequence: Reflect⇒Choose Words⇒Speak, except we are all too aware of how talking occurs without any notion of a mental process, though on occasion we might follow such a sequence in planning a talk. Can we not just make up lots of logical mental sequences? Thus the following has a logic that seems plausible: Awareness⇒Conscious awareness⇒Interest⇒Attention (sustained interest)⇒Intention⇒Buying action. It is doubtful that these are mentally distinct stages as opposed to being words in the language that relate conceptually. There is this implicit assumption that our concepts and conceptual relationships have a counterpart in mental events. This is to confuse logic with psychology, which is a common fallacy in the consumer behavior literature that has a cognitive orientation.

Logic, unlike psychology, is not an empirical discipline though interestingly some adherents of the 'philosophy of mind' have aspirations to work with the psychological disciplines in developing the joint discipline of cognitive science. This runs contrary to the 'linguistic turn' in analytic philosophy because cognitive science seeks to explain mental structures independent of linguistic expression. Analytic philosophy started with Gottlob Frege's new logic in the nineteenth century. Its emphasis was on advancing knowledge through the deeper understanding of concepts.

Many consumer decisions are probably simply: I like, therefore, I'll buy. Expressed liking may be the main coordinating principle that runs through many otherwise diverse purchases. But even supposing these conceptual chains do represent mental stages, what are the mechanisms that propel movement from one stage to the next? A logical order based on conceptual understanding does not imply any compelling evolutionary order. What appears to be a logical order to the language user does not necessarily have any counterpart in mental stages.

INTERPRETATION OF ADS: TRANSPARENT VERSUS LEGIBLE ADS

While ads do not need to be transparently clear, they need do to be legible if the target audience is to persevere in probing for the right 'decoding'. Cognitive psychology suggests that advertisers overestimate the copywriter's ability to provide ads able to promote a dominant or preferred interpretation and underestimate the extent to which the target audience makes sense of ads in ways that relate directly to their concerns.

Sometimes the need to get attention conflicts with achieving clarity of message. One ad for the 2011 Grand Cherokee shows the front part of the Jeep with the caption: 'Plastic Cannot Be Forged'. The association of the word 'forged' in memory is the association with 'counterfeiting', not with 'beating into shape' which was the intended meaning. Presumably the ad is saying the Jeep is not plastic but metal and suggesting its rivals are plastic (more vulnerable in an accident). But it needs to be said more head-on as few would take the trouble to get the full message – unless the ambiguity is deliberate to stimulate attention through curiosity. This suggests the need to pre-test ads for interpretations that are likely to evoke concerns of the target audience. This is particularly so for ads tapping the emotions. Since the subject matter of most commercial ads does not link with our deep concerns, there is a need to associate the ad with the concerns of the target audience. When poorly done the ad just comes across as 'corny' and even embarrassing. Putting across an emotional message is particularly difficult for commercial products or commercial advertising generally. Usually this is done through association, as the Subaru car in current advertising is associated with compelling events and emotional situations that pull at the heart strings.

Aberrant decoding, which occurs when a different code is applied in decoding from that used in encoding, is common in interpreting advertising and in interpreting aesthetic artifacts. But ensuring interpretation is in line with sender intentions is not confined to just choosing the right signs but also to taking account of context. This means taking into account preceding messages, environmental factors and mental states such as mood. This is illustrated by the President Richard Nixon White House tapes; without background context, the broken sentences would be difficult to understand.

Strongly shared codes may lead, on occasion, to interpretations that are erroneously made to fit the code as in Jerzy Koskinski's *Being There*, where even the most idiotic remarks were taken as wisdom. The apparent sharing of a common code may give rise to anthropomorphism or the predilection to attribute human characteristics to lower organisms or inanimate objects. Anthropomorphism extends to inanimate products, particularly to active machines like computers. Interaction with the computers (the Joseph Weizenbaum's computer program is an example) can lead a few people to fantasize that they are interacting with real people. Perhaps most of all we attribute human characteristics to animals and act accordingly. We find it irresistible to claim a dog is depressed or anxious, happy or sad because interpretation of the dog's behavior is based on assuming dog and man share the same code of non-verbal behavior.

ATTITUDE MEASURES AND PREDICTION

The most common way of measuring attitudes is through the use of questionnaires inquiring about beliefs on the grounds that attitudes arise from beliefs. In fact, it is commonly taken for granted that underlying attitudes are the beliefs we have about the object of the attitude. This points to the limitation of attitude measures for predicting behavior since beliefs alone will be a poor predictor unless we can take for granted what the consumer wants or the action is purely belief-driven. Thus I may have a very favorable attitude to eating broccoli for health reasons but do not follow up on my beliefs because of its taste. Of wants, beliefs and action, we need two out of the three in order to have reasonable success in prediction. Not surprisingly, attitudes have not been a success in prediction without using measures of attitude that take corresponding wants for granted, such as the context implying what the want will be.

In everyday life we tend to gauge attitudes from behavior but this can be misleading. Thus we might interpret behavior as indicating affection when people are just pretending to love someone when they actually hate them. To *pretend* involves the intention to pretend in that if the intention is absent we are simply left with imagining and not pretending. The trouble with most questionnaires is that, when they are not designed as open questionnaires, they are designed to elicit answers that can be easily coded for statistical analysis. In this way, a good deal of the richness of potential answers is lost. Also, the immediate, spontaneous answers generated may not be the opinions arising after time for reflection. Questionnaires can be designed to arouse the emotions with *leading* questions like: 'Do you feel the government should stop wasting your money on social programs?' Political fundraising letters often arrive in the guise of a survey. The questions are loaded to arouse emotion enough to persuade the respondent to send a donation. It is a way of getting at the voter without head-on propaganda but more subtly arouses basic dispositions into action against the alleged sins of the political party in office. The worst of political propaganda was described by Aldous Huxley as making 'one set of people forget that certain other sets of people are human'. What is also often forgotten is that questions are neither true nor false but ambiguous unless you know what the questioner is getting at.

Here are some of the 'theory'-based methods used to gauge attitudes:

TORA: This is Fishbein's (1983) 'theory of reasoned action' (the so-called TORA model). Fishbein's theory of reasoned action is an extension of the multiattribute model to relate attitudes to intentions. This is an attempt to explain buying behavior as arising from: (i) attitude towards the brand, made up of beliefs about the brand and the evaluations of these beliefs; (ii) added to the beliefs about the expectations of others; (iii) motivation to comply, leading to intention and action.

More specifically, this model claims that intention to take an action is $f(A + P + M)$ where:

A = The individual's attitude towards taking that particular action. This is measured in a multiattribute way that takes account of beliefs about the consequences of taking the action and an evaluation of these consequences.

P = The individual's perceptions of the social and group norms relevant to the behavior, given the situation.

M = The individual's motivation to comply with these group norms.

When divorced from its algebraic formulation, this 'theory' is somewhat pedestrian and can be criticized for assuming that brand attitudes (A) are independent and not influenced by perceptions of social and group norms (P) and independent of the motivation to comply (M) with these norms. But can the perceptions of relevant social and group norms be independent of attitude and motivation, needing to be measured separately and so duplicating measures? Is not the motivation to comply influenced by the expectations of others? Is not motivation to comply inevitably part of any attitude measure that seeks to capture the intensity of attitude? Do not perceived opportunity to buy and the ability to buy in terms of resources affect intention to buy? Reminding ourselves that action emanates not just from beliefs but also from motives/wants, does motivation to comply embrace wanting what the action seeks to achieve? It is doubtful whether the Fishbein formulation takes sufficient account of a person's sense of integrity and perceptions of risk attached to the action, both of which can influence behavior. But one value in models such as TORA (and most mathematical models) is that they make clear what is being assumed and/or ignored. This helps knowledge progress.

TOVA: Another model is the theory of value assessment, which claims that an individual's attitude towards a product is based on the extent to which it promotes the values in which we believe, weighted by the relative importance of these values. Attitude is thus the degree to which the product furthers values, times the relative importance of each value to the consumer. This is done for each value at a time, summing up across all relevant values.

This incorporation of values is of interest, not only as a basis for predicting behavior at the macro level but as a basis for advertising appeals. All brand images and other symbolization are grounded in values. There are values that are universal in emotional appeal, like motherhood, but there are also the values of the target group to which appeals are made. It is these that are of most importance but the problem lies in establishing: (a) that the target group does indeed have distinct values; and (b) how to discover the most salient values distinguishing the group. It may be that such values are best discovered by being a participant observer within the group; listening and observing rather than going out with some questionnaire. But a central question still remains. While values might constitute some superordinate goal that gives some direction, can values direct specific choices? It is doubtful except under certain controlled experimental conditions.

Sum of sub-attitudes: Some measures of attitude are calculated by summing up the sub-attitudes of which the overall attitude is assumed to be composed, for example attitudes towards success, towards failure and towards the process itself. The assumption is that each sub-attitude is independent of the others, which is an empirical question to be answered by investigation.

Fishbein and Ajzen (1975) claim 'I intend to A' implies 'I believe I *will* do A'. But to use the verb 'will' instead of 'shall' implies determination on the part of the speaker – such commitment does not necessarily go along with intention. Juarrero agrees with Mele (1992) in inserting 'other things remaining equal' as a qualification. McGinn (1982), a psychologist and philosopher, with his focus on volition as the trigger to action, goes further in arguing that intention is like going into gear, but the will to act is like pressing the accelerator. Emmet (1985) claims 'setting oneself' to do something is a better candidate than act of will. But this seems a mere redescription of what is meant by an 'act of will'.

Any attitude measure will reflect whatever theoretical construct of attitude is adopted. It follows that, if different researchers hold different conceptualizations of attitude, their measures will reflect this. But it is not always true that different operational measures necessarily imply different concepts. When scientists use different tests for detecting, say, the presence of electrons, this does not imply they have different concepts of the electron. Everyone accepts, for example, that the electron is an elementary particle in that it cannot be broken down into smaller particles.

The problem is more acute if a social science construct is vague and so not easy to identify. For example, this is the case with 'emotional intelligence' (EI), which refers to the ability to identify, express, understand and assimilate our own emotions and the emotions of others into our thinking. But as Mathews et al. (2002) point out, the scientific evidence for a clearly identified construct of EI is sparse, though this has not prevented the most extravagant claims being made for it. We find this all the time in social science, extrapolating extravagant claims from some supposed implications of some hypothetical construct which has sense-meaning but with the referential-meaning depending on individual interpretations.

ELABORATION LIKELIHOOD MODEL AND CHANGING THE DIRECTION OF ATTITUDES

The *elaboration likelihood* (*cognitive*) *model* is another cognitive model. It is associated with psychologists Petty and Cacioppo (1979). It is concerned not with the development of attitudes where none exist but with changing the direction of attitudes. This is why it excited academics in marketing. The authors posit two routes to attitude change:

- Peripheral route, where persuasion is a form of short-term acceptance based on affective cues or what is socially acceptable, more attractive or superficially appealing. Not surprisingly, it becomes logical to argue that the peripheral route is more likely to occur when there is low involvement with the products.
- Central route, where persuasion is long lasting as there is true rational attitude change that comes from thoughtful reflection on the information received. Information is defined as communication or data that strengthens or changes beliefs. (This semantic notion of information contrasts with the syntactic notion of information used in computer science.) The central route presupposes the motivation to generate attention to the information because of its personal relevance. High involvement with the purchase is taken for granted. Also assumed is the ability to process the information and its believability. Reflection on the product may involve our imagining using the product and what it might do to enrich our lives. Again, it is logical to argue that the central route is more likely to be followed in the case of high involvement with a product.

What particular route is adopted depends on the receiver's *motivation and ability* to elaborate cognitively the information presented. What determines motivation to think about the informational content is the personal relevance of the issue.

In the Elaboration Likelihood Model, it is implicitly assumed that 'central route persuasion' arises as an *objective* property of the arguments used, just a matter of processing 'good' information, since Petty and Cacioppo argue that only the cognitive processing of strong arguments persuades in a fundamental way. The model suggests that social comparison with reference group norms does not influence the perceived validity of the messages being processed via the central route; that is, peripheral factors do not affect the perceived validity of the information being processed. However, the authors acknowledge that they do not know what makes an argument persuasive but define an argument as strong simply on the basis of its subjective effects, namely its rated persuasiveness together with its capacity to stimulate favorable thought in the recipient of the message. Thus persuasion is identified with information processing: information processing of 'good', 'valid' and 'sound' information with this good, valid and sound information being defined as that which persuades.

In denying that what is considered good, valid and sound is in any way tied to social norms and conventions, the authors are regarding validity as an inherent, *objective property* of the information processed. But is validity a property of the information given or is it a function of the *perceptions* of the recipient doing the information processing? If it is just a function of the perceptions of the recipient, such perceptions will not be independent of social norms and conventions. There is also the question of whether the majority of consumers have the motivation and ability to process information via the central route. One piece of research relevant to these questions resulted in the following findings (Deanna Kuhn 1991):

- The subjects in the study (a wide cross-section of people in the US) commonly viewed pseudo-evidence (just the plausibility of the argument) to be as powerful in persuading them as genuine evidence when it came to establishing the correctness of ideas or hypotheses.
- Subjects commonly were unable to envision alternatives or counter arguments to their own 'theory', just continuing to stick to positions they thought others would endorse.
- Even when subjects did entertain alternative explanations, they sought more to rebut them than to seriously consider them as rival explanations. Predisposition to certain beliefs made it difficult to entertain other explanations.
- Subjects whose disposition was to see positions as either right or wrong or to see all alternative explanations as equally defensible, saw little value in even engaging in argument.

The study found that only 9 to 20 percent of subjects had the necessary understanding needed to generate and evaluate alternatives to reach a reasoned judgment, with the author of the study arguing that without such understanding 'people have little incentive or disposition to develop argumentative skills'.

Psychologists interested in reasoning skills claim that people do not normally use logic to solve problems (Watson and Johnson-Laird 1972).

Of course, we must use some logic to cope with life but we seem to use it sparingly.

It is difficult to believe that there are no communications that are deeply persuasive based on the peripheral route. Thus in accepting the Elaboration Likelihood Model, we are, for example, either assuming that religious conversions are just short-term conversions or that long-term religious conversions, based on strong convictions, cannot arise from or be primarily influenced by: (a) the attractiveness of the communication source; (b) what is socially endorsed; (c) the pain/pleasure attached to agreeing with the position advocated.

One reason for the support of the Elaboration Likelihood Model is its seeming backing for the distinction between *normative conformity*, where conformity comes about through wanting to adhere to social norms, and *informational conformity*, where conformity arises from reflecting on the evidence. But adhering to what is socially appropriate or socially dictated does not necessarily mean adopting some peripheral route to persuasion but can arise from a good deal of hard thinking as to what would be the prudent thing to do. On the other hand, informational conformity may simply mean following the actions of those considered to have the best information (e.g. as occurs in buying shares) without doing any deep reflection on relevant information which may be beyond the lay person's comprehension. Also, in the message-dense advertising environment, who has the time to think deeply about some issue? There is time-pressure, information-overload, and general lack of expertise in assessing the validity of information which leads to the use of heuristics (rules of thumb) in decision-making.

Most academics would *like* to think there is such a thing as an Olympian evaluation of information leading to real persuasion (rationally convincing) when consumers are highly involved with the issue. But perhaps philosophers Cohen and Nagel (1934) were right when they said in their classic 1934 textbook on logic and scientific method something to the effect that the factual persuasiveness of arguments is more often brought about by properly chosen words, which through association have powerful emotional influences, than through logically unassailable arguments.

Physical reality testing may be demanding for the non-expert in considering the validity of information but consumers feel a particular need to do *social reality testing* to gauge a product's social acceptability. It is doubtful that messages that go against the social norms of a group will be acceptable. Some psychologists believe that all arguments, if they are to be effective, should be pro-normative.

Chapter 7

Cognitive Psychology Continued: Cognitive Psychology in Marketing

MEANS–END DECISION-MAKING

It is commonly assumed that the consumer knows what she wants and we accordingly interpret her decisions as a means–end process. Hare (1979), an Oxford philosopher, denies this is typical and points to the pitfalls in the means–end approach ('choose means adapted to goals') where it is assumed the consumer's goals are clear-cut and the means selected are those that best meet the goals. As Hare says, there is real difficulty in saying *how much* of the end in question is *required*. The consumer may have a good idea of what capacity of refrigerator she wants but not the size of car engine. There is also difficulty in gauging how much of the end in question is being *provided*. The consumer can easily see she is getting a bottle of dishwashing liquid but not how much cleaning power she is getting. Finally, there is the difficulty of undertaking trade-offs when goals (ends) conflict. Thus manufacturers need to know how much convenience, space and so on the consumer is prepared to sacrifice for a lower price. *Conjoint analysis* is the statistical technique meant to solve this problem but it assumes the whole is a sum of the parts and fails to come to grips with non-measurable goals like beauty. Looking at parts in isolation without a visualization of the whole misses the notion of the system to which the purchase belongs. Given that any system is a set of interdependent parts which together form a unitary whole for achieving ends, the consumer needs to assess the contribution of the part to the whole.

Hare claims that these difficulties are inherent when we insist on a prior statement of *precise* ends. He argues against attempting any precise statement of exactly what is wanted in favor of finding out what is available and then evaluating these options. Asking the consumer to evaluate rival brands has the advantage of not tying up in advance exactly what is being sought and avoids the problem of trying to put a price on, say, comfort in order to make trade-offs using the common metric of money. As an alternative to conjoint analysis (which makes many dubious assumptions about the independence of factors), we might just provide ten packages/configurations to choose from. This is commonly what consumers do when they visit a store to see what is available. Wiggins (1978), however, defends the need for the consumer to set goals. He says:

> It is the search for the best specification of what would honor or answer to the relevant concerns. Till the specification is available there is no room for the questions of means. When this specification is reached means–end deliberation can start.
>
> (Wiggins 1978: 145)

Wiggins is consistent with those (like the author) who in writing on management argue that, if management set the wrong objectives, they solve the wrong problem, and this can be far more wasteful of resources than solving the right problem in an inefficient way. This advice has links to what the statistician John Tukey (who coined the word 'bit' for binary digit and the word 'software' for computer programs) used to say: it is better to have an approximate answer to the right question than an exact answer to the wrong one. But in respect of actual consumer behavior, it is normative advice as it ignores how often consumers can specify only vaguely what their relevant concerns are, with specific goals only becoming clearer as they look around at what is available. Wiggins goes on to say that, even if we seek precise specification, we find ourselves modifying our aspirations by what is available, as difficulties which turn up in the means–end deliberation may send us back a finite number of times to the problem of a better or more practical specification.

Which advice is best depends on context, though Wiggins's advice is more in the nature of normative advice to the consumer than what actually occurs. Hare's advice is more practical. With new purchases, consumers often do need to shop around to see what is available, rent (if possible) rather than immediately buy, or buy in small trial sizes and indulge in other tactics that gain experience without undertaking any major commitment. In interpreting buyer responses, we cannot just assume that consumers know exactly what they want even if they talk as though they do.

We know a good deal about *shopping* behavior from *behavioral tracking* which includes: (i) the use of cameras that follow the customer from the time she enters the store, recording all activities right to checkout; (ii) Web coupons that are embedded in the bar codes notifying the retailer of the search used in finding the product. These Web coupons can contain a good deal of information about the customer which is passed over to the retailer when the coupon is used. RevTrax is one firm that tracks Web-based coupons for retailers. The coupons the consumer gets over the Web may contain specific information about the keywords the customer used to retrieve the coupons, and other data; (iii) mobile market researchers who send messages to cell phones when the shopper is, for example, examining an item of clothing. But the mere observation of what actions are taken has strict limits in that the meaning of the action has to be interpreted in the absence of knowing also about wants and beliefs.

THE PERSUASIVE COMMUNICATION APPROACH

This is another cognitive approach to persuasion that sees persuasion as involving the:

a. Individual receiver of the communication
b. Communication/information source
c. Content/presentation of the message.

The persuasive communication approach can be viewed as focusing on the 'acceptance' stage in the hierarchy of effects model, though without any commitment to underwriting such a model.

Individual receiver

There are a number of background factors about the nature of the consumer that have to be taken into account in planning any promotional campaign such as advertising.

Attention is selective so there is a problem of first getting attention for any form of promotion. There has been an increasing focus on attention-getting in commercials to discourage the consumer from zipping, zapping and muting advertisements, but there is still the need for the persuasive element.

Attention is basic in that it is the process that opens the consumer to information. Attention is selective, not just because our interests dictate this but also because we see what we have been taught to see. The more the conceptual deprivation, the less we see as we do not have the vocabulary for naming the things before us, no more than we see that much less than a car mechanic as we look at a car engine. Consumers with a broad education find things around them much more meaningful as more things can be given a name and understood.

Repetition of a message (if initially liked) leads to ⇒familiarity⇒consistency of image⇒acceptance as true. This sequence suggests that repetition of some assertion comes to be believed and accepted though we suspect that variety in an ad is needed to prevent wear-out and retain interest.

Distraction (e.g. music in the background) interferes with the development of counter-arguments as the consumer watches and listens. Not infrequently, though, background 'music' can drown out the message. Humor in an advertisement can be a distraction (useful if the seller has a need to distract the prospect from unfavorable aspects of the offering). It has already been claimed that words can have a semantic autonomy so that when emotional messages enter the mind, emotion can distract from any evaluation of the reality so the consumer acts in accordance with the message.

Existing beliefs, self-esteem, age and mood are all relevant to the acceptance of the message. Messages that conflict with strongly held beliefs or which undermine self-esteem, or that seem more appropriate to another age group, or are communicated when the audience is in a bad mood, are unlikely to be accepted.

Good arguments are only good from a certain point of view. People must be on the right *wavelength* to accept the message. If we have the same perspective as that of our audience then 'rational' arguments can be the way to go in the sense that, if we agree premises, logic has a strong role to play. But if we have to change the way people look at an issue, to induce the right perspective in the first place, then indirect means of persuasion are needed since a more direct approach will be resisted. The indirect approach involves vivid imagery, metaphor and so on that stick in the mind to challenge the existing perspective. Not surprisingly, conceptual changes accompany a change in perspective as concepts mediate between the mind and the world: they are tied to the world by representing it and are linked to the mind by being constituents of it.

Metaphor (e.g. the mind is a computer) defamiliarizes that which is familiar, encouraging a new perspective. The metaphor need not be verbal. In advertising, some of the best metaphors are visual metaphors. And for this reason visual metaphors are becoming more common in advertising.

Reframing or redefining the situation. Shifts can occur in perspectives via reframing the issue, for example reframing the issue of banning smoking as an attack on individual freedom; or redefining the situation, for example an investment as opposed to being a payment. Simply asking questions can be a way of reframing or redefining by redirecting thoughts, for example: 'Do you want more government interference?' Even the choice of words can conjure up fresh perspectives: warm person versus just a person.

Manipulation of expectations via comparisons, for example showing the very expensive option first so that the other options seem a good buy. This relates to the concept of *anchor points* in that the expensive item becomes the anchor that influences subsequent perceptions of price. In labor negotiation, both parties set anchors far away from what they expect to achieve in the hope that this influences the other party to come up with some offer that is a better deal than would be the case without the high initial anchor points. Expectations can be the anchor points.

Court a viewpoint (perspective) and a standard of truth by which the advertisement's own message follows in a manner acceptable to the target audience. This means the advertiser must know the target audience as all the advertiser's efforts are directed at this audience. It does not matter whether other audiences, like academics, voice criticism of the ad or argue that it is meaningless to them or that it is not attention-grabbing if the target audience is drawn to the ad and is influenced by it.

THE COMMUNICATION SOURCE

The credibility and attractiveness of the communication source is vital for successful communications. A *credible* source is perceived as trustworthy and as possessing technical expertise. The appeal is to *values* so the message becomes *internalized*. An *attractive* source relates to liking, not just through physical presence but commonality of values and background, perhaps occurring as a result of supportive interaction through time. Perceptions of attractiveness, within broad limits, vary. This complicates the evaluation of ads since not all members of the target audience will have the same perspective on attractiveness. The appeal is to self-image/self-esteem so that the acceptance of the message is tied to the receiver's identification with the communication source: as the source changes his or her mind, so does the receiver change her mind in concert. This can be a problem for a company.

Credibility and attractiveness are fleshed out to explain even success in organizations (Pffefer 2010). There is a need first to 'manage upwards', which requires playing the role of supplicant to the bosses as one subtly flatters them in looking for help. Attractiveness in particular is the asset here with the promise of being a supportive follower. The next strategy is to network so you are the 'node' at the center. In establishing oneself as the link to various parts of the company, supportive interaction moves in the direction of increased liking which, when combined with expertise, enhances one's relative stature. Finally, there is the matter of loyalty to the company boss which makes you a particularly attractive candidate for promotion as witness to the fact that four out of five CEO appointments go to insiders.

Celebrities and other spokespersons in advertising should have credibility and attractiveness as well as adding something of their persona to the brand so that people fantasize that using the product equates with some of the persona rubbing off on them. Spokespersons can add to their credibility by disproving expectations, such as by not trying to sell too hard. All aspects of an ad (unless fear appeals which ignores attractiveness) should meet the criteria of having credibility and attractiveness.

Content/presentation of the message

There is *latitude of acceptance* for any message. Outside that latitude, consumers will reject the message. In other words, not every message is accepted, however attractive and credible the source.

A *one-sided presentation* appeals to the already-converted but a *two-sided appeal* (but leaning towards the advertiser's position) is better, unless speaking to the already converted whose views are simply being reinforced. This is the problem for a lot of political heavyweights. In being so one-sided they are loved by their core adherents but manage to convert few people from the other side which may be essential to winning an election. News programs that are heavily slanted to some ideological position nonetheless seek to give the appearance of adopting a two-sided presentation as this gives the impression of being balanced. Some advice:

- In a *message-dense environment*, it is better to make one's conclusions clear if misunderstanding is to be avoided.
- *Printed* messages tend to be looked at more and better understood.
- A *liked* message is more persuasive in an audio or visual medium than the written medium.
- *Long* messages suggest substantive content and can be persuasive due simply to this fact.
- Getting the target audience to *imagine* using, possessing or consuming the product can lead to more direct self-persuasion.

We now turn to a number of theories and models about the consumer's mental processing, covering consistency theory, attribution theory and self-perception theory.

CONSISTENCY THEORY

Consumers value the experience as well as the appearance of being consistent. This is not to suggest people are always consistent. They are not. But they are not always conscious of being inconsistent; people harbor many contradictory beliefs until the conflict is brought to their attention.

There are several models explaining this striving for consistency:

1. *Balance model.* Feelings are not always consistent with beliefs and people seek a balance between their feelings (affects) and their beliefs (cognitions). They want their beliefs and feelings brought into line so conflict is avoided. In changing one we can affect the other. Balance 'theory' claims that a state of imbalance between feelings and cognitions (beliefs) initiates attempts to remove the imbalance by changing feelings (emotions/affects) to come into line with beliefs (cognitions) or, alternatively, bring beliefs in line with feelings. These ways of achieving a balance between feelings and beliefs can be undertaken by advertising. Consumers commonly *feel* something to be true but believe this is just not so. This commonly occurs in respect to religion: our emotions and commitments encourage us to feel certain religious claims must be true yet we do not believe these claims are rationally defensible. Consumers do not like conflict between their beliefs and feelings ('I feel this pill must be doing me good, but I don't believe it is') and will try to resolve the conflict. This, of course, assumes the conflict is apparent when we often avoid facing up to such conflicts by not entertaining both the conflicting beliefs and feelings at the same time.
2. *Congruity model.* People want their attitude towards the source of a communication and their attitude towards things linked to the source to be

congruent. We typically feel uncomfortable when our friends say something with which we violently disagree and we try to seek agreement. Perhaps this is why we agree with the notion of avoiding religion and politics at social occasions. In any case, in wanting our beliefs about a product to be congruent with the views of positive reference groups or some celebrity we admire, we find ourselves moving towards their position. We might remind ourselves that identifying a positive reference group is not always obvious in that youth are often a positive reference group in fashion for some older people. This is one reason for using admired groups or celebrities to promote our brand. But sometimes testimonials from actual customers are judged to have more credibility. Thus Nutrisystem and some other companies that have traditionally used celebrities to promote weight control foods now use mostly real customers to 'inspire others', in part because celebrities can be a risky proposition with their lives and appearance constantly being dissected by the news media.

3. *Cognitive dissonance/attribution model.* Cognitive dissonance is a concept that belongs more to social psychology but can be discussed here. It refers to the feelings of discomfort arising from having inconsistent cognitions (beliefs) or discomfort arising from conflict between our beliefs and our actions. After purchasing an expensive product, we often find ourselves going out of our way to look at the alternatives displaced to ensure we have bought the best. The seller can reduce such discomfort by:

- Depreciating the loss or enhancing the gain;
- Reassuring consumers on the wisdom of their choice after purchase.

Cognitive dissonance has great intuitive appeal, so much so that it has entered into the layperson's vocabulary. Yet it has proved difficult to test in that any results can be used in support and *attribution theory* sometimes substitutes as an alternative explanation.

ATTRIBUTION THEORY

Attribution theory reminds us how we attribute causes to explain a person's behavior. Thus we say someone is in a bad mood to explain his irascible behavior or claim an elderly person is senile to explain what is causing problems in understanding. Whereas the layperson looks for reasons (wants and beliefs) to explain 'normal' behavior, he or she seeks causes of abnormal behavior. The *attribution error* lies in understating or underestimating the influence of external factors on the actions of others, while the *self-serving error* lies in attributing one's personal success to oneself and one's failure to external factors, which can lead to denying any individual responsibility for what occurs. Thus the ad that attributes failure in love to the absence of a good aftershave is exploiting this tendency to commit the self-serving error. It is argued that we are by nature 'hard wired' to seek causes.

We certainly do look for causes and in religious societies God often fulfils that role, so that one well-known televangelist attributed the 9/11 terrorist attack to God's disapproval of America's evil ways! But for something to be so inherent as to be hardwired, it must be present in everyone and shown to arise without learning. This is difficult to demonstrate. However, people do, as a common observation, look for causes of their behavior and do attribute success to personal factors and failure to external causes. But not always. Some people are all too willing to see failure as being caused by their own deficiencies.

SELF-PERCEPTION THEORY

Self-perception is our perception of our own state of mind and behavior. Self-perceptions influence behavior. If we have a perception of ourselves as being inherently incompetent in mathematics, this is likely to impede our overcoming the deficiency. While attribution theory argues that people observe others and make inferences about other people's underlying motivations, consistent with the observed behavior, *self-perception* theories go beyond attribution theory in arguing that people analyze their own behavior, much like an outside observer, and as a result of these observations make judgments about their own motivations and infer their own attitudes from their behavior. If I drink Folgers's coffee every morning, I infer I have a favorable attitude towards Folgers's coffee. This has an important implication if valid, as it suggests that attitudes do not come first to cause behavior but arise from observation of our behavioral reaction to some stimulus. Although we often do infer beliefs from our actions, we can also infer our feelings. As an example, we have all had the experience of being surprised at our emotional reaction to some event, even though we were not previously aware that the event was of great concern to us. We infer from this emotional reaction that we are concerned and have congruent feelings to match.

The potential importance of self-perception theory lies in changing attitudes, since if our attitudes are determined by our behavior, then induced behavior modification will bring about changes in attitude. Thus when the law bans racist behavior, attitudes tend to change in line with the law. As we accept the law our behavior changes and so do our attitudes. To those who say that the law can do nothing to change attitudes, self-perception theory (and the history of civil rights) tells us otherwise. Nonetheless, while a change in behavior can result in the creation of an attitude, it is also true that attitudes can influence behavior, for example when my negative attitudes towards environmental polluters induce me to withhold my patronage of such firms. Attitudes and behavior form an interacting system in that attitudes influence behavior but behavior influences attitudes, just as mental illness can cause physical illness and physical illness can cause mental illness. In speaking of the etiology of mental problems ('etiology' is medical science's word for cause or the origins of diseases), Hacking (1995) reminds us how often causes are just assumed to be known, though, for example, the belief that early abuse is the cause of adult dysfunction is far closer to being an act of faith than an item of knowledge. Thus Hacking quotes one study in New Zealand that found that the psychiatric problems in adult women correlated less well with early abuse than with straightforward poverty.

Bennett and Hacker (2003) deny that people develop beliefs on the basis of observing their own behavior since people 'introspect' how things are and need not wait to hear what their behavior has to say in order to find out what they think. We go along with Bennett and Hacker in arguing that it would indeed be odd if our beliefs about our motivations and attitudes had to be always inferred from observing our own behavior, since we think of ourselves as knowing these things and strive for consistency between motivations, beliefs and behavior. That said, this is not always so. Thus we may not be clear on occasions which of two brands we prefer if both have seemingly equal pluses and minuses. We might observe that we gravitate more to one brand rather than another and infer this to be the implicit favorite. In such a situation, self-perception theory would seem to play an explanatory role. Sometimes we do indeed infer our beliefs from our actions, but it is far truer that consumers infer beliefs from their own reflections, social interactions and experiences which may take no account of their behavior.

Self-perception theory has been used to explain the effectiveness of the so-called 'foot-in-the-door' technique used in selling, whereby getting acceptance of a small request facilitates getting acceptance of a big request. It is argued that the person responding to the request infers that his or her acceptance of the small request implies he or she has a favorable attitude towards such requests. Is this always the explanation? I might agree to the big request because I would not wish to destroy the goodwill I had created by agreeing to the small request. Similarly, self-perception theory is used to explain the effectiveness of the 'door-in-the-face' technique whereby a large request is rejected but later a small request is accepted on the grounds that the person does not like to feel he or she is being miserly. Again, there are other explanations. For example, the principle of reciprocity might suggest to those accepting the small request that the seller has made a concession that requires some form of reciprocation.

DECISION PROCESSES

As might be expected given the importance of the consumer's decision-making, there are many theories and models of: (a) decision processes; (b) decision-making strategies. This section considers decision processes.

Decision-making, as a social science area of study, is generally regarded as falling within the field of cognitive psychology, which undertakes a sort of 'reverse-engineering' in working back from what we do to how we do it. As well as the study of actual decision-making there is 'decision theory', which seeks both to describe and explain decision-making: studying such things as problem solving, choice behavior, utility theory, game theory and so on. Not surprisingly, marketing academics who are drawn to cognitive psychology are also interested in decision theory.

A lot of buying does not necessitate much in the way of decision-making or deliberation, or even acute awareness of what is happening, until something happens to jolt the buyer into more conscious thinking. A decision is not just simply a choice but a *deliberated* choice that involves the weighing up of alternatives: the pros and cons. Where there is deliberation on which brand to buy (or any other aspect of buying and consuming), there is a weighing up of these pros and cons. Such deliberation typically occurs in buying when there are risks or uncertainties attached to buying and the importance of the purchase justifies the effort involved. But inherent buying risks and uncertainties may or may not arouse anxiety or any other emotion. A consumer may spend a good deal of time deciding on which television to buy without any accompanying anxiety about making a serious error.

The consumer behavior literature has focused on decision *processes* and decision *strategies*, not on actual decision content. The decision *process* leading up to buying is generally viewed as a logical process. Thus a typical suggested sequence is the following:

Buying problem → want-recognition → search-for-alternatives → information-on-alternatives → evoked set of options → subset of options → the evaluation of the subset of options → decision/selection → post-purchase behavior.

It is not uncommon to claim that the consumer, before any search of alternatives, first feels a sense of deprivation and this constitutes a 'problem' for the consumer. But what the consumer thinks or feels may or may not amount to any felt sense of deprivation. In any case, a sense of deprivation or perception of some difficulty is *not* the identification of a problem since the problem needs first to be diagnosed and to diagnose a problem is to classify how it might be solved. This depends on what the consumer believes counts as a solution to the sensed difficulty, he or she has encountered. We cannot identify a problem without first understanding what would count as a solution: the consumer cannot understand what her problem is without understanding what would count as solving it. If my computer breaks down, this constitutes a difficulty, but to diagnose the problem is to suggest where the solution might lie; that is, unless we pass the difficulty over to some expert to define what the problem is. This is not to suggest there is always a problem diagnosis since a consumer may simply fall back on experience to recognize and choose what he or she wants without feeling any need to diagnose the problem. Thus if the consumer finds that she has run out of milk (the difficulty), there is generally no diagnosis but simply a recognition of the need to visit the store for a carton of milk.

If the consumer senses a difficulty and does not know what sort of problem it is (common when we go and see a medical doctor), he or she first needs someone more knowledgeable to diagnose the problem. In considering alternatives, the options may constitute an *awareness set* (all the relevant brands of which the consumer is potentially aware) or *evoked set* of brands that just spring to mind or a *consideration set* from which the consumer just chooses. All this sounds like a logical progression but how empirically based is it? A logical process is not necessarily something that is factually so. The incidence of such sequences of events is not known, nor can it be inferred from laboratory tests which might suggest such a sequence. Would it be so odd or non-rational to go straight to a consideration set? Not all buying is the buying of new products that might entail thought and inquiry. For many products that are new to us (particularly in respect of services) we might simply ask 'advice' and then follow it. There are many sources of information, from the news media to the Internet, but personal sources are probably most common when hiring a service provider. One problem with the Internet as a source of information can be bias. If Google has enough information about your search habits, its software directs you to information that fits your perspective, so if it appears you deny global warming, you will be fed information that reinforces that view. Google, the largest advertising platform in the world, can be viewed not so much as pushing products towards consumers as pulling consumers towards specific brands or products. It is estimated there are around 500 companies that have the ability to track every move a consumer makes on the Internet to mine the information collected. Your click on the 'like' button for a product on Facebook may in fact lead to the ad appearing on the Facebook pages of your friends.

The non-necessity of much deliberation or information search is acknowledged in the literature, with a sharp distinction being made between high involvement with a product versus low involvement, with high involvement assumed to justify a fairly rational process of deliberation and information search. This justification seems reasonable until we are faced with the fact that a consumer may have high involvement with a purchase, such as buying a house or a new car, and yet in no way follow a thorough decision process because of information overload, time pressure and the sense of non-understanding anyway. We commonly avoid rational procedures through using heuristics (rules of thumb), such as relying on a builder's reputation or assuming that all top makes of new car are reliable and therefore just looking at a few of the top brands and buying the car that most appeals aesthetically. We are reminded here that around 25 percent of adults in Western societies are functionally illiterate and unable to undertake much by way of investigation. I suspect this explains quite a bit of habitual buying, in that keeping abreast of product innovations may be seen as requiring functional literacy. This may also explain the finding that those who already have expertise with a product are likely to seek more information than newcomers about a proposed purchase. However, findings like this have to be treated with caution, since they do not necessarily carry over to all products or have stability through time. We cannot always assume that research findings have external validity beyond the experimental group to other populations of interest or that the incidence of taking certain buying action after some influencing intervention will continue in other populations.

The concept of *involvement* is commonly quoted in explaining aspects of consumer behavior. Although marketing texts may talk of high (and low or in between) involvement *products*, involvement is not a function of the type of product bought but a function of the consumer, in that what purchases a particular buyer regards as high involvement depends on the consumer not the product per se. When we speak of a purchase having high involvement for a consumer, this is the same as saying the consumer believes the purchase has high meaning or significance in terms of his or her wants. But this begs the question as to when a purchase symbolizes high involvement for the consumer. It is not just a matter of the purchase being important in the life of the consumer: centrality is necessary but not sufficient. There must also be a risk (for example, because of the product's high price) attached to the purchase. High centrality and perceived high risk attached to the purchase make the product highly meaningful for the buyer and imply high involvement by the consumer in the purchase. Risks cover financial risks, performance risk failures, social appropriateness and the risk that an upgrade may come along making the present product out of date. In fact, trying to make the older product obsolete in terms of style or function is a common strategy by for example car manufacturers and firms like Microsoft.

When products are made to appear out of date despite being perfectly good functionally, the term *psychological obsolescence* is used. We just grow tired of them or feel they have become rather dated. But, of course, many products such as slide rules, typewriters and fountain pens are displaced by products that perform better functionally. Innovation is typically the source of a product's decline. The growth of the Internet has brought with it the decline of dealers of all sorts, such as retailers selling electronic equipment, travel agencies, auction houses (the eBay effect), even realtors. The introduction of the smartphone seriously affected the sales of point-and-shoot cameras, GPS systems, and will even perhaps affect the sales of wristwatches and alarm clocks. What is interesting is that multifunction devices like the smartphone are often treated as less effective at the level of the individual function ('jack of all trades, master of none') but not so this time. The smartphone is so convenient that it has become more desirable than a single-function device, as in the case of the Flip video camera that it is gradually displacing.

Consumer behavior is intelligible (or we could not even begin to understand it) but cannot necessarily be decomposed into a set of highly rational processes without sacrificing reality for intellectual rigor. There is a surfeit of information sources that might be consulted or that might influence passively but for the marketer the problem lies in reaching the target consumer with information that has credibility (particularly trustworthiness) and attractiveness. The consumer does use criteria in evaluating alternatives though it may amount to no more than an application of the likeability heuristic (rule of thumb): 'I like, therefore, I buy.' Likeability may be all that is needed in buying from a salesperson though this has much more to do with how the salesperson makes people feel than how she might look. Likeable people seem to have openness 'as if revealing all' and a willingness to connect in friendship. But likeability may not just reflect personal attractiveness since I may like a politician's values and ideas but looks may be secondary.

Post-purchase behavior depends on post-purchase experience so that if post-purchase experience exceeds expectations the consumer is happy to repeat the purchase if the 'need' arises. But sometimes post-purchase experience must extend to the time of repeat purchase. Thus a consumer may be very satisfied with a new electric toothbrush until the battery fails before even replacing the brush for a second time. No repeat purchase is considered. This is why, in forecasting the long-term sales of a product, it is important to establish the likelihood of repeat sales. *Expectations* can be viewed as the standard against which evaluation takes place, since without standards there can be no guidance. In rational buying we are meant to consider all the major consequences arising from buying. In fact, thinking about consequences is viewed as the hallmark of rational decision-making but consumers often lack the experience and knowledge to allow them to do this effectively.

Velleman's model of the decision process

Not surprisingly, there are many rival logical processes to that given above since there are no universal sequences for every type of decision, no more than there are universal laws in social science. David Velleman (1989), for example, suggests the following decision process:

- Ruling out of options disliked
- Reflection on the descriptive image evoked of each alternative considered, and its fit to the descriptive image of the consumer and the context or situation in which he or she will be using the product
- Rationalization to justify an emerging *implicit favorite*
- Formation of intention to buy the emerging favorite.

Whether a consumer does or does not have an implicit favorite before buying, she is likely to think up additional reasons to reinforce and justify her final favorite.

The Montgomery model

All decisions are made within a social milieu and this is recognized in Montgomery's (1984) model which claims that the desire to justify to others and to self-justify a decision can result in a process of cognitively restructuring information in making the decision so that the alternative chosen is presented as dominating its rivals. He argues that people try to avoid calculating trade-offs by thinking of reasons why one or more dimensions can be completely ignored, so that if there is a conflict between price and quality the consumer might claim quality is the same whatever the brand and so choose on price. This can arise because there is a particular problem in gauging quality when the consumer relies purely on visual inspection. It could prevent the consumer from buying if it were not for warranties, guarantees, acceptance of returns or faith in certain brand names. Sometimes it is the seller who worries about quality, as occurs in health insurance when the insurance company does not know the true health state of an applicant for insurance. Any serious lack of information on the part of either buyer or seller undermines the standard models in economics.

Montgomery's description of the decision process echoes Velleman's. He argues that information search prior to the decision passes through four stages:

- Screening where the (conjunctive) rule operates to eliminate options not having certain attributes, such as being able to justify the option to one's social milieu
- Choice of a promising alternative defined as that which most commands attention
- Dominance building, in which the promising alternative becomes the dominant alternative (what is known elsewhere as the 'implicit favorite model') through confirmation bias when assessing the evidence
- Restructuring the problem to choose a new promising alternative if the dominance structuring that has already occurred fails for some reason.

Confirmation bias is common in assessing evidence; if the information we have coheres with what we want to do, we discontinue our search, whereas if it goes against what we want, we continue searching. In life generally, we are apt to close out information that might be emotionally upsetting unless such information is a necessity for what we want to do. At the trivial level, how many people refuse to go on the scales each morning because they fear what their weight might be, though without such feedback weight goals are meaningless?

Klein's recognition-primed decision model

A contrasting model that has empirical support is concerned with the situation where decisions have to be made quickly under pressure and where there is no time for any dispassionate evaluation of options. Klein's (1993) *recognition-primed decision model* accepts that experts, like firefighters, make decisions on the basis of instant recognition of the problem and which problems go with which solutions. In other words, the occurrence or set of events is immediately categorized as such and such a problem requiring such and such a solution. Whenever we encounter a perceived difficulty, we diagnose the difficulty which means classifying the perceived difficulty according to the type of solution required. Experts have learnt to classify difficulties or diagnose the difficulty according to the type of solution required. Thus they work back from perceived difficulty to problem diagnosis, which involves saying where the solution may lie. This model has applications in consumer behavior as well.

A consumer's perspective or a scientist's paradigm or a predisposition towards a certain outcome can give rise to *confirmation* bias, whereby relevant facts are ignored or redescribed and reinterpreted in a distorted way. This is true not just for consumers but also for academics who can cling to a particular perspective regardless of the evidence. They do the same thing when undertaking statistical analysis, employing technique after technique until results are statistically significant. Garcia and Koelling (1966) undermined behaviorist learning theory but the findings were dismissed by one prominent learning theorist as 'no more likely than birdshit in a cuckoo clock' (quoted by Frank, 1988: 149). There are still groups that deny the germ theory of disease (check this on the Internet) and there are even flat earth adherents finding alternative hypotheses for facts that suggest that this is nonsense.

DECISION-MAKING STRATEGIES

There are not just theories or models of consumer decision processes but also of decision-making strategies. It is these that have been of more interest to marketers.

The strategies approach is based on the assumption that consumers follow a number of decision-making strategies in buying. These strategies by and large have not emerged from extensive empirical research but are strategies that seem logical. But the strategies consumers actually employ cannot be equated with what is the most logical strategy or what emerges in a laboratory. This is because the laboratory situation can unconsciously ensure that 'logical' strategies are chosen, as Harré and Secord (1973) show. Respondents recognize the logical thing to do and tend to underwrite it. Both professors and students understand logical strategies so they are easily endorsed as valid descriptions of consumer behavior.

One such strategy is expressed in the multiattribute model or compensatory model. It is compensatory because it assumes a brand's weakness on one attribute can be compensated for by strength on another. The consumer is viewed as acting 'as if' he or she weights each attribute, such as durability, economy, taste or whatever, and rates each brand on the basis of how much it has of the attribute. The overall relative scores resulting from the sum of the weights multiplied by the ratings give the relative evaluation of each brand.

The model is illustrated in Table 7.1, which shows the choice criteria in column 1, the choice criteria weights in column 2 out of a total of 10, ratings of the two brands in column 3 on a 5-point scale, while column 4 shows column 2 × column 3 (weights times ratings) with the sum of the

Table 7.1 Multiattribute model applied to brands of lawnmower

Choice Criteria	Criteria Weights	Brand Ratings		Col.(2) × Col.(3)	
		Hayter	Stoic	Hayter	Stoic
(1)	(2)	(3)		(4)	
Technical					
Powerful	2	1	3	2	6
Rotary	2	3	3	6	6
Starting convenience	1	3	3	3	3
Economic					
Price around $1,000	1	1	1	1	1
Maintenance	1	3	3	3	3
Trade-in price	1	3	3	3	3
Adaptive					
Reputation of brand	1	3	2	3	2
Bought by experts	1	1	3	1	3
Totals				22	27

scores shown at the bottom. The sums 22 and 27 can be interpreted as the relative attitude scores of the two brands. There is no doubt that consumers, when in a situation that induces a highly rational approach (e.g. in experiments with MBA students), are able to act as if following such a model. In fact any choice may be interpreted as following this model. For example, suppose the buyer in Table 7.1 simply chose the lawnmower on the basis of brand name alone. It could still be interpreted as following the compensatory model; just giving the whole weight to the brand name.

The multiattribute model was first used in social science as a way of describing attitudinal structure. As already stated, it is known as a *compensatory* model because several attributes are involved, with a brand's weakness on one attribute being compensated for by strength on another attribute. The list of attributes should be those reflecting bases for variations in choice and should preferably be obtained from consumers themselves. The attributes need to be independent (to prevent double counting) and free of vagueness and ambiguity. This may not be difficult to do when the attributes are physically based but can be more problematic when the attributes are abstract, such as brand image and the status potential of each brand of, for example, car. In any case, the consumer calculates the overall relative scores for various alternatives.

Can it really be argued that consumers behave 'as if' following the multiattribute model? There is confusion here between what consumers would find it logically possible to do and what they actually do. It is easy to design experiments that guide answers into something approaching employing such a model, but this establishes nothing beyond stating a possibility, not a probability.

It is interesting to speculate where consumers would not follow the multiattribute model even if the model were valid. Those buying on habit, or just liking or picking are not engaged in much deliberation and can be said to choose rather than decide. To what extent buying in these cases can be said to be mindless or the consumer viewed as on automatic pilot is debatable. Routine, habitual buying might be without thought, but with intrinsic liking it depends on whether such likings can be said to be instantaneous, occurring without reflection. Picking involves some deliberation in initially choosing brands from which to pick and/or making sure differences among brands do not justify deliberation.

Deliberation in buying consists of canvassing reasons and assessing them to reach a decision. In the process, reasons that were initially given little consideration may come to be weighted heavily, so that views about product attributes and combinations of attributes can change. This is not only because deliberation involves some rational calculation, but also because it puts us in touch with our gut feelings (emotions) about the salience of various product attributes.

Rational deliberation, contrary to the stereotype, is not necessarily cold since it is rational to take account of emotions (such as anticipated future regret if a mistake is made), while an emotional attachment to a product can be sensibly quoted to justify a purchase (e.g. of a sports car). But emotions can distort deliberation by affecting confidence. Thus, when we are in a state of excitement (e.g. in seeing the house of our dreams) there is a heightened sense of confidence in decision-making with little sense of the risk until the excitement wears off.

We commonly assume that consumer decision-making, as practical reasoning, is means–end reasoning. We have already discussed the limitations of this approach. It is an oversimplification as it suggests that wants (ends) are already in place and fixed, and that exactly what is sought is known and observable. In fact, rationality involves reflecting on the wants themselves and modifying them if there are good reasons to do so. Thus, as I think about future wants, I may change my mind about a second car being an SUV. Reason *proscribes* rather than *prescribes*, pointing, for example, to inconsistencies between immediate desires and long-term goals and distinguishing real differences from distinctions without a difference. The actual trade-offs themselves are difficult to measure as well as being value-laden. If the consumer's values form a coherent set for the purpose of buying, the weighing of options and trade-offs is made easier. When value systems are vague and the outcomes sought are vague, decision criteria are correspondingly vague and, unless such vagueness is recognized and corrected, deliberation will inevitably be perfunctory and open to manipulation by persuasive communications. The process of deliberation is a learning process that moves from some initial (antecedent) set of wants and beliefs to a new or modified set. Thus beliefs about what is practically feasible can affect wants (the 'sour grapes' phenomenon) in that consumers may end up desiring only what they know is possible for them.

In experiments on decision-making strategies where we have several hypotheses, statistical analysis such as significance testing is generally undertaken to decide between rival hypotheses. But these statistical techniques are commonly also used to make statements about the objective strength of evidence even though they are not designed for this purpose. Bayesian analysis would seem more appropriate, though the incorporation of subjective beliefs into such an analysis has proved unacceptable to many scientists. In statistical inference we ask: (a) what do the data lead me to believe? (b) what action should I take given the data? (c) how should I interpret the data as evidence for favoring one hypothesis over another? It is this latter question that gives the most problems (Taper and Lele 2004).

Although we all endorse the logic that standards of evidence should be raised when the consequences of being wrong are great, as can happen in buying, this often does not happen. People instead go on gathering evidence when the results are not to their liking and cut short the search when the evidence corroborates what they already think or want to believe. Statistical techniques operate, by convention, to bring closure in research when there appears no end to the disputes over the degree of support for some hypotheses but this may be done at the expense of not trying to eliminate major rival explanations of the data.

RATIONALITY IN CONSUMER DECISION-MAKING

Marketing commonly accepts the convenient assumption of high rationality on the part of the consumer. But even if consumers, on average, were capable of being highly rational, the costs in terms of time spent in thinking and information collection would be a limitation. Consumers have 'bounded rationality' with limitations of memory, information access and intelligence. This is not to suggest that everything depends on what is in consciousness. A major claim of cognitive psychologists is that much of our total behavior is governed by *implicit* knowledge rather than conscious knowledge. This is in line with Sir Francis Galton, the anthropologist, in the nineteenth century who claimed that we would be at the level of idiots if our brain work had to depend on what was completely in consciousness. Thus consumers may not be aware of how packaging or brand image influences their choices. This means that the reasons people give for their actions, even when reasons are real (and not just rationalizations), can be incomplete.

There is short-term memory (STM) or working memory which, as the name suggests, is limited in capacity and also in duration. It contrasts with long-term memory (LTM) which has neither of these limitations. Any information coming in from the outside goes through short-term memory and into long-term memory, while information in long-term memory has to be retrieved by short-term memory if it is to be used. Retrieval is helped through repetition of the information, associating lists of facts with some code words or through what psychologists call 'elaboration' whereby the information is related to other things in memory. In general, the more information in the consumer's memory and the more it is based on learning with understanding (as opposed to learning by rote), the better will be the deliberations carried out by the consumer.

Deliberation characterizes a real decision. This means we cannot predict our own decisions or they would cease to be decisions. But perhaps an outsider on occasions can predict if they sense a disposition to choose some implicit favorite. It is believed that thinking in decision-making is largely determined by the contents of primary or working memory, but this can be misleading unless it is realized that much in working memory is at the time recalled from long-term memory. If the content of working memory is in consciousness, it implies that decisions are impacted only by what we are conscious of at the time we make the decision. This in itself does seem to limit the consumer's ability to reach an optimum decision.

Consumers, as pointed out, when in a situation that induces a rational approach (such as in experiments with students) can act as if following a model along the lines of the multiattribute model. But we could also work back to an infinite set of mental process models from which the decision could have arisen; the multiattribute is selected because it seems to be rational. In fact, it is not even clear whether consumers, as a rule, undertake comparative evaluations of brands on the basis of their attributes (Foxall 1990). The multiattribute model is a theory of *best* action, not a theory of *rational* action since there is no rational consideration of beliefs and goals; both are taken for granted.

While acknowledging the model is not exactly true to life, it is argued that it is 'as if' consumers behave in this way just as attitudes are 'as if' dispositions to react. But in the case of attitudes, there is a basis for believing we have attitudes. We have criteria for claiming we all have attitudes towards things but, unless we can demonstrate that consumers follow the multiattribute model in the real world, outside an experiment that directs them to act that way, what purpose does it serve? The answer is that such normative models allow a contrast to be made with real world decision-making. But to claim that it is 'as if' this is what happens is to claim it is in some way analogous to what happens but this cannot just be asserted; there must be behavioral evidence in support. This is true even when the list of attributes is reduced to those reflecting a basis for variations in choice and where the attributes are independent (to prevent double counting) and free of vagueness and ambiguity.

It is all too common in experiments to assume the concepts employed are unproblematic, neither vague nor ambiguous. In fact, of course, one way to get support for a proposition is through vagueness and ambiguity, as when the politician says he or she is in favor of justice and prosperity for all. Who isn't, until spelt out? If a politician makes a statement with which every person agrees, it is surely because of its vagueness or ambiguity. A word is vague when it does not have clear boundaries, while a word is ambiguous if it can be confused, in the context, with a different concept. Manufacturers may find obscurity favors them. Thus one recommendation of the US government was to 'eat less meat' as a dietary recommendation in the fight against heart disease. Lobbying efforts had this changed to 'choose meats that will reduce your saturated fat intake', knowing consumers are quite clear about what red meat is but are generally in the dark about saturated fat.

Apart from the high rationality and the time involved in the multiattribute strategy, an expressive object like a work of art functions as a whole and we cannot break it down into parts and demonstrate that the whole is simply the function of the parts. Parts only have significance as part of the whole and the meaning of each part can only be given significance when visualized as part of a whole. Attributes can emerge that do not emerge when attributes are simply considered in isolation. In any case, the overall value to the consumer equals not only the values of the various attributes combined but additionally the value of their *being combined* in that particular way, as with a painting.

The multiattribute model has aptly been called a 'kitchen scales model', a metaphor used by Dancy (2005) to describe any additive approach to overall value. Our awareness of the product as an overall system can dissolve if we are simply asked to attend to individual elements. Listing the elements of the whole offering does not capture the whole system. In any case, there is the problem of which attributes are considered since even the simplest product can consist of too large a number of attributes to be evaluated. Thus one shirt manufacturer tells us that all of the following are important: made of a two-fold poplin, quality material such as sea island cotton; two-piece collar for better fit and longer wear; soft collar for comfort; single needle seaming for extra strength; four-hole button and buttons cross-stitched; spacing of upper buttons on shirt and so on. Would asking consumers to consider these and weight them for relative importance be predictive of anything at all? How many men buying a shirt look other than at the manufacturer's name, collar size, color and style and general appearance?

The multiattribute model is sometimes put forward as showing how, not really how well, people make decisions. It is meant to be descriptive of the process of decision-making where trade-offs have to be made. Assuming this is so, the claim is then made that we are able to change or at least modify the attitudes of the consumer by: (a) influencing the list of attributes considered by the consumer; (b) influencing the weights given to the various attributes by, say, changing beliefs about consequences. This model, like many models of decision-making, reflects our desire to mold behavior into something highly rational (and therefore easily teachable), when in fact behavior may be intelligible without approximating the norms of rationality. Consumers are unlikely, if ever, to think of a potential purchase as a sum of attributes but of something that is either expressive and/or serves some function.

The philosopher Toulmin (1964) suggests the study of jurisprudence or the study of the procedures by which claims-at-law are put forward, disputed and determined and the concepts that are involved, is of more practical use than believing our understanding of decision-making is more likely to arise through logic. Toulmin is conscious of our confusing logical models with psychological reality.

Consumers often do not think of a particular product at all until they see something that activates their desire for it. A common assumption is that marketing is concerned with catering to the articulated needs and the wants/desires of consumers. As an unqualified assertion this evokes the image of the consumer as a bundle of needs and wants that act as a filter for determining what they will buy. But, as has been said already, the motivational capacities of consumers are not made up of a fixed set of needs and wants; consumers have latent or dormant wants that are activated on being shown what something can do to enrich their lives. If sellers could create wants without there being an underlying appetite for the product, we could just sell consumers anything at all. We would certainly not have a problem in getting children to eat healthy foods. Consumers have the capacity to imagine what it would be like to possess/use/consume a product, never used or thought about before. And they use this imagination in checking whether something new is likely to enrich their lives. Entrepreneurship is tied to catering to latent wants that are discovered outside the articulated wants of the consumer. Just as the picture in photography is latent until the developer is put on, a want can be latent until developed by the marketer. Steve Jobs of Apple had a gift of inventing the most easy-to-use, convenient-in-use products that consumers didn't even know they wanted or needed. Digital music players, iPhone, iPod, iPad, Smartphones, Facebook and so on were not being demanded before they were invented but this did not mean there was not a latent want for such products.

Products are sold under description and that description can be decisive in whether something is perceived as desirable and appropriate for the buying situation. This is not to suggest that the consumer only has an understanding of a product through its description, just that the consumer understands products through invoking descriptions that fit the product. This is not something recognized in economics. How something is described influences perceptions and beliefs about the desirability of the product. How often have we been deceived by the description of an item on a restaurant menu that excites our taste buds but may not be what we expected in reality? We believe or want something under description and this description can blind us to other descriptions of the same thing. Consultants, whether industrial or medical, often pride themselves on presenting the options to the customer, together with their pros and cons, as if this were proof of trustworthiness. This is just not so since everything depends on how the options are described. A medical consultant, for example, usually has no difficulty in steering the patient into choosing the preferred alternative.

While we can deceive someone into buying something, this is different from saying that sellers create wants as opposed to activating a latent want. We see things from a perspective and, when we believe something or want something, it is from the perspective of a desirable description. The idea that people know exactly what they want, even in advance of experience, without even knowing how things will be presented or described, lies behind representing buying deliberations as following models such as the multiattribute model.

As Scriven (1992), another philosopher, points out, the weightings of attributes cannot be given the significance intended because relative importance is controlled by the number of criteria involved. This is an important point though apt to be ignored in the literature. For example, assume the weights given to the criteria for each product attribute ranged from 1 to 5, while the ratings given to the alternatives for the amount possessed of an attribute ranged from 1 to10. The most important criterion can only contribute a maximum of 50 points to any one of the products being evaluated. This maximum of '50' can be completely swamped by the accumulation of only five minor criteria, each weighted only 1 but each rated a '10' for the alternative being evaluated. There is also the question of interaction effects given that the whole is something more than the sum of the parts.

It is difficult to believe the claim that consumers build up to what they want from a list of individual attributes. To list all the attributes of a car would quickly be overwhelming. An offering is a system, that is, a set of interdependent parts that together form a unitary whole for meeting some want or function(s). This means that any attribute only has meaning in terms of the visualized whole. A buyer cannot just think about the size of the car engine he wants unless he already has in mind a vision of the whole car of which the engine will be a part. Also, buying something new is a learning experience which means the attributes consumers initially claim to be seeking may be considerably modified or abandoned as they learn more about what they really want. Buying, as opposed to filling in questionnaires about buying, can be an emotional experience (even just looking at the packaging) that colors outlooks and prejudices decisions.

Few of those buying an infrequently bought product or buying for the first time know exactly what they want and they do not have fully ordered preferences. An expressed pre-purchase preference may be no more than a *ceteris paribus*, saying buying will proceed, all else being equal. Buying is a learning experience and initial preferences can be outweighed or overridden as learning takes place. As Underhill (1999) says, more and more purchasing decisions are being made in the store itself, with shoppers being susceptible to impressions and information acquired while in the store, rather than being dependent on advertising. This is certainly true of the supermarket. Although Underhill talks of doing anthropology, there is nothing in his methodology that would not come under industrial engineering (or work study in the UK) but what he has to say is sensible and backed by empirical facts.

In questionnaires about their future buying, consumers are often asked about preferences for experiences they have not tried, in conditions outside the emotional context of buying. Consumers are not given courses on determining how to decide so their approaches are far from optimal. Luce et al. (2001) claim that 'importance' is not the only dimension along which people respond to product attributes and that *emotionality* is a separable dimension influencing the responses to product attributes. They are right: emotion cannot be captured in any cost/benefit function. They remind us of other studies showing that anticipated post-decisional regret influences the outcomes of any decision and that concerns about justifying one's decision to others are major reasons why trade-offs between attributes can be such a problem for decision-makers.

Conjoint analysis, ninety-five already mentioned, is used for measuring the relative importance of various attributes in undertaking trade-offs. This again makes the assumption that consumers know what attributes they will want and what they want is some sum of tangible attributes (Green 1990). Before me is a home buyers' checklist. Under the headings of location; development and community; nearby facilities and services; home construction; and home amenities, there are over ninety-five factors to consider. Some trade-offs! As Luce et al. say, the output of a conjoint analysis is a utility estimate assigned to each level of each tested attribute with the utility scales in common units across attributes, allowing for relative attribute importance judgments. Velleman (2000) makes the point that, even if we could establish the equivalence of value between a helping of financial benefit and a helping of physical well-being, these measures of financial benefit and physical benefit would not reflect potential interactions between the values of the underlying commodities. Even when consumers know what combinations they want, their preferences are rarely absolute but conditional. The relative utilities of different attributes are seldom likely to be stable and constant, but vary with context and even, on occasion, mood. Thus the 9/11 attacks had a depressing effect on the public mood in the US.

In any case, as already said, an expressive artifact like a work of art acts as a whole and cannot be taken apart to demonstrate that the whole is simply the sum of the parts; the meaning of each part can only be given significance when visualized as part of a whole. That said, there are seldom research findings that are context- or *field-invariant*, they are instead dependent on context, which means a judgment has to be made as to the generality of the findings. One aim of research is to find out what is field-invariant and what features are context-dependent. The explanation is among several rivals and the evidence does not unequivocally tell us which to accept though, in the light of our data, there are those more deserving of consideration than others.

Rex Brown (2006), a philosopher, agrees on the need to take account of the context in which decisions are made; a context that includes the knowledge a person brings to the decision. In the social sciences, any depth of explanation or understanding of a situation is tied to context. This context-dependency undercuts efforts to find laws that can take account of the richness of contexts.

At the individual level, prediction has to contend with the fact that we are not tokens of each other, not even in terms of our reaction to medical treatments. But prediction in buying and in social life generally is helped, as MacIntyre (1981) says, by:

- Statistical regularities that are unlikely to change, for example more people catch colds in winter; past weather patterns and so on
- Stable 'causal'-type associations like the level of education and the type of magazine read
- Social conventions, for example the persistence of social conventions like weddings and wearing ties at work
- Much buying is tied to habit.

THE IMPLICIT FAVORITE MODEL AND SATISFICING BEHAVIOR

Two alternatives to the multiattribute model are commonly quoted in the literature: the 'satisficing model' and the 'implicit favorite model', though neither of these is incompatible with the multiattribute model. With the *implicit favorite model*, which has echoes of both Montgomery and Valleman, consumers do not enter into the difficult task of seriously evaluating alternatives until the 'best' can be identified, but have an 'implicit favorite' which is the tentative preferred alternative. The rest of the decision process becomes essentially a confirmation process with the decision-maker simply selecting or weighing evidence to support the implicit favorite or thinking up additional reasons to reinforce the implicit choice. The implicit favorite model operates also in 'legal realism', where it is claimed that judges first make an 'all things considered' judgment about who ought to win, then rationalize the choice in some legal rule. To the legal realist, legal rules serve not for pre-decision guidance but for *ex post facto* legitimization of decisions reached.

The *satisficing model* was first proposed by Herbert Simon in opposition to the economist's notion of our maximizing utility and assumes people have 'bounded' or limited rationality and so settle for the first solution to their problem that is good enough. Perhaps most purchases are not of sufficient importance to justify more time and effort.

NON-COMPENSATORY STRATEGIES

- There are non-compensatory strategies which, unlike the multiattribute (compensatory) model, do not assume that a brand's weakness on one attribute can be compensated for by strength on another. Under the *conjunctive* rule the consumer insists on minimum acceptable levels for each attribute of interest. Thus we would insist on a dress or shirt or pair of shoes of the right size and this automatically rules out other sizes. The rule establishes a cut-off value for the most important attribute and allows all competing products that meet the cut-off value to go on to the next attribute, to meet, in turn, its cut-off point and so on. For example, in buying a computer the conjunctive rule could be: 'must have an Intel processor as standard; speed at least XY MHz; at least Z megabytes of internal memory; not less than TK megabytes of hard disk memory; fax capabilities. But are rules like this unconditional? The buyer is likely to insist on a high performance level only when prepared to pay a corresponding price. Like most rules, there is usually an implicit 'other things remaining equal'.

- The conjunctive rule is reflected in the 'elimination-by-aspects heuristic' attributable to Tversky (1972). Tversky argues that, in making complex decisions, we look for favorable attributes (aspects), rate one at a time, across all the choice alternatives, while defining the minimum values of the attributes required. We eliminate all options in the choice or evoked set that lack the most important single attribute and carry on doing this with the next most important attribute and so on. Tversky claims this approach is encouraged by advertisers who in their promotions try to persuade consumers to focus on specific aspects of the brand they are promoting. We can imagine a serious consumer doing this in, say, buying a house but is this process as rational as it seems? In making a decision on the basis of one or more outstanding attributes, the consumer may be ignoring a whole host of smaller attribute differences which collectively might favor some entirely different option.

- An offering is acceptable under the disjunctive rule if it exceeds the minimum level on at least one criterion or attribute of interest, for example 'exceeds Z megabytes of internal memory'. Both the conjunctive and disjunctive rules are attempts to reduce the total set of options to consider. Where the purchase is important, too many options create information overload as the wide range of choices is intimidating. The phrase 'information overload' originated in 1970 with Alvin Tofler, an American writer on the digital revolution, but perhaps a better phrase than information *overload* is information *fatigue*, defined in terms of the mental exhaustion arising from the exposure to too much information that can result in indifference or apathy. Information fatigue complicates deliberations in decision-making, making it more burdensome and resulting in the search for easy answers.

- With the *lexicographic* rule the consumer ranks attributes in terms of relative importance. If a product is clearly superior on the most important attribute, that product is selected or, if no product (or brand) dominates, the procedure is repeated until a product is superior. The lexicographic rule does have the advantage of leading to a unique choice. It assumes that alternatives are first compared on the most important attribute or dimension. Any product or brand that is 'in a class of its own' on the most important dimension is selected. If several brands are equally good on the particular dimension, the next most important dimension or attribute is considered and so on.

- There are also partially compensatory strategies in that strategies are evaluated against each other: two competing products may be evaluated across all attributes and the product that has the higher values across all attributes is chosen or, alternatively, another competing product is added and evaluated to arrive at the best, or all products are compared to cut-off values for each relevant attribute, with the product chosen being the one that has the most 'good' features that exceed cut-off values. Of course, after using conjunctive and disjunctive rules, consumers could use both compensatory and/or lexicographic rules.

- Even where rationality comes into its own in proscribing options, deficiencies in decision-making can arise in receiving information through functional illiteracy, expectations, wishful thinking or time pressure. Deficiencies can also arise in processing information through lack of competence, faulty reasoning habits, wishful thinking, erroneous beliefs, emotions, the overweighting of more recent events and just plain fatigue. Choices are not necessarily in line with the relative strength of wants. Typically, wants are not so much compelling forces as key information that is taken into account. However, the strongest desires start with an advantage as their pursuit seems to promise instant gratification.

- The decision strategies discussed above are easy to teach and make sense in their logic. But logic is not psychology. Anyone teaching them as representing how consumers actually behave in the supermarket should reflect on his or her own behavior as a check as he or she goes about buying. It is not difficult to think of additional strategies that are plausible and logical but the real question is the extent to which such strategies are in fact used. Unless such strategies are those that nature dictates (like nature determines our basic needs), we cannot just assume they actually reflect what occurs. To assume that this is so is to assume people are tokens of each other instead of distinct individuals with their own idiosyncrasies. It is not difficult to think of logical strategies, and that because they are logical they are rational and because they are rational they must be the reality! This is fallacious thinking.

Does a very wide choice overwhelm?

One area of study raises the problem of choosing or deciding when confronted with a wide range of choices. Some researchers have concluded that an overload of options can lead to decision paralysis or poor choices (Tugend 2010). This seems reasonable as we have already argued that there is the possibility of information overload or fatigue. The same article quotes one well-known experiment demonstrating this. This was a field experiment in a gourmet market with the researchers selling samples of Wilkin & Sons jams and switching from a selection of twenty-four jams to a group of six jams every few hours. On average each customer tasted two jams regardless of the size of the assortment and each was given a coupon for $1 off one Wilkin & Sons jam. Sixty percent of customers were attracted to the large assortment and only 40 percent stopped by when the assortment was small. However, 30 percent who sampled from the small assortment decided to buy jam, while only 3 percent of those faced with two dozen jams purchased a jar. The conclusion was that, while a wide choice was preferred in theory, beyond a certain point a wide choice might be 'debilitating'. But is this explanation better than rival hypotheses that could be put forward? After all, it does not explain why more customers were attracted to the larger assortment and this is important. If a man is choosing a tie, he wants to choose from a very wide selection and is unlikely to buy at all if the selection is narrow. From the action taken, motives cannot just be taken for granted. I would suggest a larger number were attracted because they were curious at the novelty of such a large selection of jams. Many visitors go to a motor show because they are curious to see all the new cars. But fewer visitors buy proportionately at motor shows than visitors to car dealerships with a more limited display. The large selection of twenty-four jams aroused curiosity through its novelty but most visitors had no disposition to buy as did those visitors to the display of six jams. In other words their non-buying had nothing to do with decision paralysis or being 'debilitated'. The vast majority of consumers when overwhelmed with a wide choice:

(a) Seek advice
(b) Simply pick at random
(c) Follow the conjunctive or disjunctive rule in reducing the alternatives to a manageable number.

As Damasio shows (see Chapter 8), decision paralysis can occur when the emotional part of the brain has been damaged but otherwise emotion operates to bring about closure on options chosen. In other words, when faced with a vast array of options, the emotions quickly act as if following the conjunctive rule. It might also be pointed out that a wide choice may be a necessary condition for buying. This is particularly so in retailing where the retail buyer wants to feel he can offer a wide choice. I never feel any decision paralysis when faced with over a hundred different makes and styles of shirts as is common in department stores.

Yet there is a problem when a manufacturer brings out numerous versions of a brand based on minor differences in features (Austen 2011). This is the case with Research in Motion's (RIM) BlackBerry line where the line has been extended by varying the features on different BlackBerrys. There are BlackBerrys with touch screens and without touch screens, some that flip, some with full keyboards, all at varying prices. In just four years, RIM has introduced thirty-seven models. If this does not inhibit consumer buying, the product four-digit model numbers will. We might compare RIM's fertility with the much bigger Apple which has only introduced four iPhones since 2008. Even experts cannot keep abreast of RIM's pro-lific model range with all the minor differences. Yet the extensive product line has not stemmed RIM's continuing loss of market share. Does this case not support the claim that many options can overwhelm the consumer? It does, but this can be attributed to the fact that no consumer wants to have to master a whole catalogue of complex products with just minor differences before deciding which to buy. Offering a wide product line may not be overwhelming when the consumer is quickly able to master the differences and reach a few from which to choose. This is the case with choosing from a wide selection of shirts or other apparel.

In the same review by Tugend, one researcher argues it can be just as wrong to assume too many choices are bad as to assume more choices are always better, though decision-makers are more likely to delay a purchase when there is much more choice. He points to the information provided to the customer, the consumer's individual expertise and the relative importance of the choice to the consumer as factors affecting his or her behavior when faced with a very wide assortment. He stresses the importance of separating choice overload from information overload as we need to answer how we are affected by the number of choices and how much from the lack of information or prior understanding of the options. This distinction is in itself not without vagueness since the number of choices on offer is in fact information that cannot be entirely separated from information on the choices themselves. What is perhaps less controversial is that too many choices can lead to post-purchase cognitive dissonance.

PROGNOMIC INDICATORS

Why should buyers believe that the products they are about to buy have the benefits they seek in the quantity they want? More often than not they have bought the brand or make before and regard the next purchase as identical. But there are problems with new or infrequent buys when inspection is not all-revealing. The buyer may be obliged to use surrogate indicators or proxies of the attributes sought (O'Shaughnessy 1986). Consumers, as stated earlier in the book, regard certain indicators as *prognomic*, that is, as justifying the expectation that they will reflect the true position. Thus I may judge the quality of a carpet by its feel; the material of which it is made; its thickness; the closeness of the pile as well as the name of the manufacturer and the retail store stocking it. But one woman in a protocol simply based her choice on what the retailer used as floor carpet on the grounds that the retailer would have chosen wisely. With sunglasses, I may judge their optical properties by trying them on to see if I have comfortable vision without frowning or a narrowing of the eyes as I look towards the sun, as well as looking at the brand name and price. But this may not indicate value for money, since brand name and presentation still count. Thus in one evaluation of *functional* performance in the UK, Yellow Glasses at $15 were rated 10/10, while Chanel, rated 9/10, were priced at over $300, though it was difficult to see any superiority in even the appearance of the two products. If a company promotes the brand's low price, it needs to be a low cost producer. But more importantly, promoting 'price' as the competitive advantage induces the consumer to think of price as the major feature and this undermines brand image. That said, if a company is interested in profit, its brand must be perceived as standing for something that has real significance for the consumer. And this could be price as in the case of the retailer T.J. Maxx.

In many product categories brand name can be the key prognomic indicator that benefits as promised will be realized. In choosing a service, the perceived knowledge, attractiveness and competence of the service provider may be prognomic of satisfaction with the service. In any case, the use of surrogate indicators can give rise to the *halo effect*, or the tendency to allow one outstanding feature (and this could be the brand name) to influence the evaluation of the other features (top brand name, therefore all else must be top class). The halo effect is one of the factors that may lie behind the effectiveness of advertising based on association of the brand with compelling images.

Even when consumers apply the same choice criteria and weightings, the process may not lead to the same preference or choice since applying the criteria is a *skill* and not a straightforward process of measurement. We may accurately gauge the sacrifice but estimating potential benefits is something else. Consumers who seek prestige from a car purchase will differ somewhat in deciding which of the makes is most likely to provide this. The consumer has to estimate such benefits from seeing the product, the promotional material, and from tapping information sources.

The prognomic indicators consumers use to make inferences need to be identified by the marketer. Thus consumers may associate plastic parts with cheapness and have all sorts of indicators to suggest low quality in foods. In one focus group, transparency and homogeneity in honey suggested artificiality of manufacture, which inhibited purchasing the brand. This suggests that a firm's indicators should be in line with the *symbolization* consumers use to indicate what they seek. A firm may even be providing the highest quality but the consumers' prognomic indicators fail to capture this.

The output of a buying decision is a *preference*, which is a comparative desire. As stated earlier, we expect preferences to be transitive; that is, if I prefer A to B and B to C, I would prefer A to C. But an intransitive preference (preferring C to A) is irrational only if it can be shown that A is better in all respects and at all times and on all occasions. Intransitive preferences involve inconsistency only when it can be shown that the judgments cannot be simultaneously maintained without contradiction. But preferences are not absolute but vary over time and occasion.

INTENTION TO BUY

This section repeats to some extent what has already been said about the notion of intention. Consumers can have a brand preference without any intention to buy since intention is a tentative commitment to action. Initial buying intentions can lead to other intentions, just as my intention to buy a computer may lead to my intention to buy a printer or to intentions about where to shop and how to pay. All voluntary buying is accompanied by an intention to buy, though not necessarily with a *planned* intention to buy. The consumer may buy on impulse. An 'impulse' is a strong notional want that finds expression in a response to some stimuli without the consumer being acutely conscious of exactly what is being sought. With impulse, while intention is not part of any plan, intention is in the action itself, just as there is intention in the action of putting my foot on the brake in an emergency to prevent an accident. Philosophers also talk of *sub-intentional* action as when we fidget, drum fingers idly on the table or even when we unconsciously move our arms and hands about when talking. They are sub-intentional because they are done without direction or purpose.

An intention to buy is not a promise to buy. It is not equivalent to saying 'I will' or 'I promise to buy brand B tomorrow'. However, an expressed intention to buy B does contain a resolve to buy B since buying intentions and actual purchase are linked much more closely than wants and buys. Nonetheless, expressed intentions are contingent, like saying: 'If the buying situation envisaged is the same next week, I will buy brand B.' We agree with the claim that forming an intention is like going into gear in driving a car but the *will* (endeavoring) is needed to take the final step of pressing the accelerator. Intentions typically possess inertia, that is, have a certain stability that inhibits reconsideration.

Intentions are not blind compulsory forces but emanate from reasons and, the more powerful the reasons, the more likely is the fulfilling of the intention, unless frustrated by situational factors like non-availability or the nuances of context, like the rudeness of a salesperson.

Cognitive psychology makes no distinction between 'motivated' and 'willed' behavior. The term 'will' is typically eschewed because of its association with 'volition' used in the sense of something in the mind putting muscles into action. But the concept of the 'will' as a self-promise ('I will') to indicate firmness of resolve seems a useful concept for marketing as an improvement on using only 'buying intention' in forecasting future sales.

POST-PURCHASE BEHAVIOR

When a purchase is a new buy, there will be post-purchase feelings and also the feeling that comes after using the product. Immediately after buying there can be cognitive dissonance, with the search for reassurance about having bought wisely. But in speaking of post-purchase behavior the focus is on long-term satisfaction with the product as a basis for generating goodwill, trust and repeat buying. The seller is not generally just interested in a one-off sale but in securing a customer: not the same thing. Market success in itself does not imply customer satisfaction. We are reminded that one survey found that Facebook ranked second from the bottom in customer satisfaction, while another survey found that only 30 percent of BlackBerry users (41 percent of the smartphone market) at the time were satisfied with the product. But satisfaction is relative to expectations. This is often forgotten in listing the relative satisfaction with different makes of, say, cars. It is common to point out that a low-priced car was rated higher in satisfaction than a high-priced car. But would the buyer of the high-priced car not have higher relative expectations than the buyer of the low-priced car?

Much depends on consumer expectations, with expectations being influenced by how much was promised by the seller. The extent to which the consumer is disappointed depends on the extent to which expectations are not realized. Sellers who teach their potential customers to expect a lot but give much less are likely to fail in getting repeat business. The aim of any business should be to get their customers to buy and rebuy, without reservations, which means meeting or exceeding customer expectations.

It is a truism to say that consumers come to know better what they want after buying, possessing, using and consuming the product. Experience with a product throws up knowledge about additional benefits and deficiencies not anticipated (Gardial et al. 1994). A purchase can perform outstandingly on all the criteria that entered into the decision to buy it but may still be regretted. The consumer may have judged wisely but used an erroneous framework, for example about his or her future lifestyle. We assume that post-purchase evaluation is likely to be more thorough for customers with high involvement with the purchase than in the case of low involvement. In any case, evaluation can still be ambiguous and this is common with many over-the-counter drugs. By and large, consumers are apt to seek confirmation that their choice was superior to the alternatives displaced in order to avoid the discomfort of not having chosen wisely. This *confirmation bias* helps the manufacturer. Because habitual buying is so common, many, if not most, purchases do not give rise to feelings of doubt or dissonance. If the purchase decision was important, difficult and perceived as irrevocable (e.g. buying a house) there are likely to be post-purchase attempts, through selective perception and interpretation, to justify the wisdom of the purchase. Even when consumers are unable to buy the best, they may rationalize that they would have bought what they did regardless of wealth. But with increases in wealth such rationalizations disappear as consumers are less prepared to make do with second best. In any case, the consumer has to interpret experience with a product, and experience is not unambiguous so that interpretations can be influenced by marketing communications (Hoch 1989).

Unexpected positive benefits are evaluated more positively than expected benefits, while unexpected negative experiences with a product are evaluated most negatively of all. Post-purchase satisfaction is influenced by the effort (physical, mental and emotional) that went into obtaining the product in that disappointment is greater when one fails after trying hard. This is something to be remembered by sellers who, in exploiting the principle of scarcity, make obtaining the product a major hurdle. Also, when you have had to buy something at the insistence of others, there is less pleasure in the purchase and a strong tendency to look for defects, therefore more dissatisfaction can be expected.

THE CONNECTIONIST PARADIGM

A few words on the so-called connectionist paradigm. The more recent connectionist paradigm in cognitive psychology takes meanings of things in consciousness and seeks to integrate them into structures. In connectionist models there is no one place labeled 'long-term memory' or domain-specific long-term memory stores. There are no stores stocked with memory at all. It has been found that people generally have a poor memory of the exact basis on which their knowledge is based and are only likely to retain the substance of what is said or read. It is their *meanings (significances)* that are stored and integrated into related structures. If this claim is valid, it has important implications for advertising.

In computer science, the connectionist approach dominates in *parallel distributed processing*, so it is not surprising that it is being used in cognitive psychology. It is something different. Cognitive psychology is not generally involved with physiology and the physical and chemical properties of the nervous system. This may change as the new 'connectionist' models in computer science question the sharp distinction between software and hardware. Connectionist models are designed so they learn to perform.

The information processing approach is weak at modeling concept learning (basic for understanding key cognitive phenomena). The connectionist approaches also have the same problem and, also like the information processing approach, have difficulty handling emotion and motivation, though these are basic to explaining intentional action. Fodor (2004) is dismissive of both approaches. He rejects the notion that brains are either like computers or like connectionist neural nets. While he upholds the idea of the mind being a representational system on the grounds that mental activity (thinking) necessarily involves mental representation, he conceives representational systems as similar to a language with a syntactic and semantic structure. We return to the question of mental representation when we consider the criticisms put forward by a neuroscientist (Bennett) and a philosopher (Hacker) (Chapter 8).

PROBLEMS IN ADOPTING COGNITIVE MODELS

There is a need (as stated earlier) in adopting any cognitive model to check models that bring together decision variables into an overall information processing system, with each variable in a box linked to other boxes, when the linkages suggest causal linkages but are typically purely conceptual (hypothetical constructs), with the variables linked merely through sense-meanings, with no concrete references (no referential-meanings). In other words, the link is conceptual and not causal. Just because a mental process appears rational does not mean the process describes mental reality. This is again to conflate psychology with logic. There is no way to test such models because the constructs, while having sense-meaning, typically have no concrete physical reference. In other words, the meanings of the constructs or concepts are not represented by observational measures which allow testing.

Even when such constructs are given an operational definition and measure, the measure may not capture the full meaning and implications of the construct. Operational measures provide referential-meaning, while definition of the hypothetical construct itself embraces sense-meaning. In contrasting the sense-meaning of a construct with an operational measure that does not fully capture it, we speak of the sense-meaning having 'surplus value' over the measure. Turning a weakness into an opportunity, it is argued that this 'surplus value' allows the researcher to generate additional hypotheses than would otherwise be the case.

Sometimes cognitive models link together variables that come from different theoretical paradigms. This linking together may (misleadingly) give the impression that the various constructs drawn from various theories are pieces in a jigsaw puzzle which, when put together, constitute a complete explanation of, say, the buying decision. In fact the concepts may overlap or be at different levels of abstraction so that there is no jigsaw but what amounts to different perspectives of the same terrain from different angles. This criticism is not meant to condemn the linking of behavioral concepts as this inevitably occurs in showing relationships. But thoughtless linking together of concepts/constructs developed in social science can be very misleading.

OTHER NOTIONS IN COGNITIVE PSYCHOLOGY

Starting with Chomsky (1968) and the notion of an inherited module for mastering a language syntax, many cognitive psychologists hold that the human mind is modular, with modules for reasoning, modules for perceiving and modules for seemingly every mental ability including, for a very few, an innate God-module, located in the frontal lobe of the brain. (The term 'module' was first put forward by Fodor for a relatively circumscribed faculty.) For example, psychologist and anthropologist Scott Altran (2004), while dismissive of any God-module, subscribes to the basic notion of modularity.

Cognitive scientists sometimes use the metaphor of cognitive 'architecture' or cognitive 'landscape'. Such descriptions of cognitive architecture or landscape are fairly speculative, far removed from constituting a category of scientific explanatory theory. Except perhaps for language, the existence of modules as mental structures, situated in different parts of the brain, is mainly guesswork. What is less speculative is that different parts of the brain have different functions: the front part enabling us to think;

the middle part enables us to move, speak and feel, while the back part enables us to understand what we see. Brain injuries have taught us many such things.

In the early days of computers, the terms used to describe the workings of the brain, like 'memory', were used to describe the computer. Now computer terminology is used in talk about the brain, with the use of terms like inputs, accessing and retrieval systems. But at some point the metaphor breaks down in imputing the computer model to brain functioning. Brains do not have the same flexibility as computers so that 'circuits' that deal with vision cannot just be switched over to deal with hearing. With humans (unlike computers) there is *declarative* learning which is the explicit learning to remember objects and events and *procedural* learning which is the learning that unconsciously occurs in learning how to perform a skill.

LIMITATIONS OF COGNITIVE PSYCHOLOGY

Cognitive psychology as a perspective or scientific paradigm has made a contribution to the study of consumer behavior. But the information processing approach is under attack, as many question the extent to which everyone perceives, thinks and reasons in the same way in any given situation. The approach cannot cope with a brain obliged to come to grips (as it does) with vague information, not formally organized but disordered. Additionally, the information processing approach fails to consider the role of symbols, emotion and motivation in energizing action. The cognitive psychology paradigm is far removed from viewing human beings as influenced by the significance or *meaning* of the situation for them even if the approach was initially sensitive to the concept of meaning.

INDIFFERENCE AND INCOMMENSURABILITY IN CHOOSING

Consumer choice may be stymied in cognitive processing through 'incommensurability' or 'indifference'. Elster (1999) distinguishes 'indifference' from 'incommensurability'. If the consumer is indifferent as to whether to buy A or B, a one dollar discount on A would lead her to buy A. 'Indifference' is an important concept for marketers since it explains why the simple addition of a feature (such as packaging nuts in 100-calorie bags) can lead to a highly profitable increase in sales. Indifference typically gives rise to 'picking behavior' where choice is random, analogous to picking a cigarette out of a packet of cigarettes. Markets are full of consumers who are indifferent to the various brands on offer, particularly when they look vaguely alike with similar names, so that a feature-advantage or a unique claim on the packaging may be all that is needed to swing the sale, or some change in another aspect of the offering such as distribution. Similarly, a consumer who would otherwise be indifferent as to which brand to buy, buys the brand whose name she recognizes: the name makes a difference. The individuals who win the gold medals at the Olympics only need to be just ahead of rivals to win. It is often the same in business; the winner need not be that far ahead but the question becomes one of sustaining the advantage.

If the buyer remains indecisive in spite of the discount, the two brands are incommensurate. Incommensurability implies the absence of a common metric for deciding which is best. Incommensurability does not imply products, models or theories are not comparable but that it is impossible to weight the attributes of the alternatives on a common scale, like the money scale, to obtain a conclusive answer. Options can be *compared*. It is always possible to make comparisons even though the comparison may not be sufficient to decide conclusively. Different cultures may on some level be incommensurable but this does not rule out critical comparisons of cultures as no culture is entirely unintelligible. With regard to comparing cultures, any significant comparison will inevitably be against a background of one's own culture providing the standard (criteria). Incommensurability just makes the grounds for preference inconclusive. It does not mean that the grounds for preference must lead to indecisiveness; being '*inconclusive*' is a logical notion, but being '*indecisive*' is a psychological notion. In interviews, consumers will willingly admit that the evidence for preferring brand A to brand B is inconclusive but still do not admit to being indecisive about their final choice. Comparisons imply the presence of criteria as a basis for making the comparison. Marketing promotions aim to implant criteria that favor their own brand.

Berry and Mirabito (2006) distinguish between 'customer-need-centered' and 'customer-desire-centered' marketing. Need-centered marketing aims at helping customers improve their lives over the long term, in contrast to desire-centered marketing which is concerned with satisfying customers' immediate wants in the sense that customers dictate and marketers oblige. They assert that desire-centered marketing can never be as effective as satisfying customers' needs! This is an empirical proposition that cannot just be asserted as true. As there are no accepted lists of universal needs, beyond talking of absolute requirements, the authors talk of 'need' as that which enhances quality of life, as measured by the percentage of time a person spends in a state of well-being. This does not get us very far in thinking about what products to produce except to avoid products that cater to instant gratification. But who would want to avoid buying real bargains that intrinsically provide instant gratification – as does buying ice cream? The view of human needs in this argument bears little resemblance to how the term 'needs' is used in our various 'language games'.

CONSUMER WELL-BEING

More importantly, whatever we know about well-being and contentment is not directly tied to possessions but to ensuring we are fully *absorbed* in whatever we do. This is the lesson we draw from the work of Csikszentmihalyi (1990) and other psychologists who study this field. Academics in marketing tend to talk of marketing satisfying needs when they mean 'needs and wants' – perhaps because it sounds more respectable.

Csikszentmihalyi (1990) provides a more intellectually defensible view. He talks about what he calls 'flow', defined as a state of contentment or happiness. He views enjoyment as optimal experience but distinguishes enjoyment from mere pleasure, which he sees as resulting from a reflex response built into the genes for the preservation of the species. Just as the pleasure obtained from eating when hungry ensures the body will get the nourishment it needs, the pleasure that arises from meeting social expectations is related to the continuance of the 'tribe' for collective security. (It should be noted that desire-centered marketing would embrace both of these 'pleasures'.) Though pleasurable experiences can on occasion be optimal experiences (enjoyment), pleasure is generally evanescent. Only if the pleasurable experience involves intensity of attention, sense of achievement and psychological growth does pleasure become enjoyment.

Csikszentmihalyi (2000) argues that humans have a need to keep consciousness in an ordered state and this experiential need to keep consciousness tuned is what influences a good deal of consumer behavior. Sometimes it does not matter what we are shopping for, 'as consuming is a way to respond to the void in consciousness when there is nothing else to do'. This insightful analysis is backed by empirical data, in contrast to the speculative claims of Berry and Mirabito.

There has been increasing interest in the notion of happiness. Derek Bok (2010), the former president of Harvard, and his wife Sissela Bok (2010) have both written books on the subject. An important distinction is that between subjective happiness as revealed by surveys and objective (correlated) measures such as standard of living. Derek Bok points out that reported (subjective) happiness has not increased over the last fifty years in spite of a real increase in per capita income. One explanation is that people judge their happiness relative to others. This means that acquiring more possessions has more to do with our competitive natures than with increasing happiness. People in the top income quartile throughout the world are, however, on average, significantly more satisfied with their lives than the bottom quartile. However, greater economic equality in a country is not correlated with higher average happiness. Yet Bok believes in pushing for equality of opportunity even if lack of such opportunity does not make for unhappiness. He believes we should attack 'happiness destroyers' like inadequate medical services, unemployment, chronic pain and the decline of the two-parent families. He argues that happiness, which is tied heavily to family life and personal relationships, is a more significant national goal for society than increasing GDP. We should, he says, resist the temptation of claiming (untruly) that government never achieves anything positive since the general belief that the government cannot achieve anything of significance is a source of unhappiness in society. Sissela Bok debates the question of whether happiness is purely a matter of subjective pleasure and so experiential, or whether it refers to what is happening to us and what we are doing. In any case, she argues that the pursuit of happiness is sub-ordinated to morality, agreeing with Aristotle that morality of character is necessary for someone to be called happy.

NON-CONSCIOUS KNOWLEDGE AND BEHAVIOR

Cognitive psychologists point out that much behavior is governed by implicit, non-conscious knowledge rather than conscious knowledge. Think, for example, of all the body movements that occur at the non-conscious level such as hand gestures and head movements but also actions that are non-consciously performed, such as tying one's bow tie. In fact, deliberately trying to *consciously* perform some of these actions, like tying one's bow tie, often results in failure. Consumers are seldom aware of how packaging or brand image influences their choice of brand, even though brand image can be a critical advantage in getting the consumer to feel the brand is 'in a class of its own'. Kleenex in 2010 bolstered sales of its facial tissue with packages looking like wedges of fruit more suited to a picnic table than the bedroom. Surprisingly, the innovation did not canni-balize on sales of the established Kleenex boxes. The increasing sales came from existing customers and attracting new customers. The fear of can-nibalization is ever present when bringing out a cheaper version of the parent brand. In 2003, Northwest Airlines rejected a proposal to bring out a discount carrier because it feared cannibalizing existing business.

People do not necessarily know what causes their behavior or their men-tal states, while conscious knowledge alone does not initiate all mental activity. We 'know more than we can tell'. Accurate self-knowledge is not guaranteed by introspection on happenings in the mind since these can be misinterpreted.

Episodic knowledge is knowledge of events and this comes to mind more easily than the language meaning or semantic knowledge of objects and their properties. But there is always the caveat 'other things remain equal', since an object or its properties with emotional significance will be recalled more easily than some event of no emotional significance. In any case, the ease with which episodes are recalled has led to many 'slice of life' ads with episodic narratives embedded with semantic material.

FLAWED RATIONALITY

Definitions of rationality in decision-making vary. The definition in eco-nomics defines rationality as that decision which maximizes utility or self-interest. The *efficient* achievement of a single goal is equated with tech-nical rationality, while the maximum achievement of a plurality of goals is economic rationality. This tells us next to nothing about how to under-take rational decision-making, which needs to take account of ends and not just means. Some judge rationality of actions as simply those actions that are consistent with objectives. Others focus on the method of arriving at a decision, with validity depending on the method's objectivity and being shown to be helpful in achieving ends. In marketing, many equate rationality with some procedure like that of the multiattribute model. Others insist on the beliefs entering into the decision being sound and in line with long-term interests and would reject rationality being demonstrated by just having an ordered set of preferences, or action just being goal-directed.

Rationality in decision-making in marketing suggests establishing goals; identifying the most appropriate alternative courses of action to achieve those goals; collecting and assessing the evidential support for these courses of action and choosing that course of action that promises to maximize goal achievement. These are hard demands for the consumer as many buying decisions are just made on the basis of social appropriateness or the result of unexamined advice, or even on the basis of the feelings aroused by imagining buying, possessing and consuming the product.

Rationality in decision-making is far from perfect and one of the main contributions of cognitive psychology to marketing has been the highlighting of *flawed rationality*. If perfect rationality in buying is buying only what serves long-term best interests, buying does not reflect perfect rationality. In fact, buyers are not always aware of what their long-term interests are. They do not have complete information about options and their consequences for future satisfaction but have to cope with data that are incomplete, ambiguous and inconsistent, or based on second-hand opinions that can lead to suboptimum purchases. But to define *irrationality* as anything less than perfect rationality is bizarre. A better definition is that which views irrationality as deliberately harming one's well-being without a compensating reason (like cutting off one's leg without a medical reason). On this definition, buyers are not irrational but have flawed rationality. *Flawed rationality* is not an occasional aberration but something characteristic of human beings. Cognitive rationality does not ensure we can avoid 'crooked thinking'.

Gilovich (1991) argues that our judgments become distorted through cognitive processes that normally help us accurately perceive and understand the world. Here are some of his examples translated into marketing:

- Consumers expect every brand in a product category to have the attributes commonly associated with that category so that we expect, say, every germ-killing mouthwash to taste unpleasant. It can be difficult to position a brand by declaring a particular attribute (e.g. low calorie chocolate) to be its competitive advantage when that attribute is not considered an element of that category of product.
- Buyers tend to overextend a belief about how an attribute should manifest itself and expect, say, a product that is claimed to be durable to look robust so that a light vacuum cleaner may be rejected because it is not perceived as durable enough. This is what actually did happen in

the introductory launch of one vacuum cleaner, which was sold on its lightness.

- Buyers pay most attention to confirmatory evidence of what they want to believe. This may arise from wishful thinking or because confirmatory evidence is cognitively simpler to deal with. Related to this confirmatory bias is *defensive avoidance* where people avoid thinking out the consequences of unwelcome information, for example about the true interest charges on credit cards.
- Buyers tend to manipulate ambiguous evidence to fit expectations, for example the expectation that all Japanese cars are reliable. Consumers search for certainty and closure so that manipulating the facts to meet expectations is one way to meet this goal.
- Buyers tend to estimate risk, not by its objective likelihood, but by the availability heuristic, which is tied to how dramatic the event was when first encountered. Thus the risk of airplane crashes seems much higher after news about a crash. It appears consumers will pay more for air-travel insurance against death through 'terrorist acts' than they will pay for insurance against death from all possible causes! Does this sound rational? Some events are more available in the mind because the event is: (a) recent or ongoing; (b) emotional or (c) just inherently easier to think about. The availability heuristic is associated with Tversky and Kahneman (1973), who demonstrated that what comes to the mind most easily tends to be given undue weight, just as publicity given to a series of muggings in the street leads people to overestimate the likelihood of being mugged in the street. The availability heuristic might be involved in shaping national mood in that a series of negative events can create a depressed mood.

Other generalizations that we look for in imputing cognitive psychology models to behavior are:

- When a post-purchase experience, bad or good, stands out, it is a two-sided event in that in both cases a poor experience and a good experience are likely to be well remembered.
- When brands are similar on some dominant attribute (such as the tube in which the toothpaste is packaged), it is the similarities among the brands that are noticed. This bias can make brands appear undifferentiated. It is important for the seller to highlight and emphasize the differences in offerings. Thus one brand of printer places great emphasis on the sameness of its printer to rival printers but then points out that running costs are much less.
- When consumers have a prior preference for a brand, it influences not only the kind of information collected but also the amount of information collected. If the early information supports the prior preference, the information search ceases, while, if it does not, the search is likely to continue to seek confirmatory evidence, including approaching 'advisors'

most likely to give it. We see this happening in governments intent on finding justification for what they intend to do anyway. Consumers seek, at best, only enough information to be confident in making a choice and not to become experts.

- Consumers tend to be overconfident in buying if their confidence is high and under-confident if their confidence is low. Overconfidence leads to less scrutiny of buying options, while under-confidence leads to indecision. Salespeople are aware of these phenomena and make a real effort at trying to put people into a confident mood. It might be added that, if we are making some overall judgment about a product or a person, the tendency is to be overconfident.
- Strong desires lead to self-deception or possibly wishful thinking, both being the distortion of beliefs arising through strong desires. Self-deceivers hold beliefs in conflict with the evidence in their possession. Self-deception is commonly employed to evade threats to self-esteem but is also employed when consumers are overwhelmed by the attractive features of a product and buy it without taking account of functional suitability.
- People conserve 'cognitive energy' by using rules of thumb or mental shortcuts to save time and effort. Subsequently, they rationalize about their behavior to make it appear more rational than it was. A good deal of deceptive advertising exploits such tendencies. But sometimes when the choice that was made was affect-driven (emotion-driven), the consumer feels the need to justify the implicit favorite on more substantive grounds and moves to reasons more easily defended. If a choice is affect-driven then emotion takes over, while a belief-driven decision is tied to beliefs that can be dispassionately assessed.
- Buyers dislike losses more than they like equivalent gains so that it is more painful to discover one has paid an excess of $10 than it is pleasurable to be given an unexpected rebate of $10. This dispositional tendency contributes to the persistence of habits and 'loyalty' to political parties since it seems preferable to go with 'the devil we know than the devil we don't know'.
- How a problem is formulated or an issue is framed influences choices, so that a 3 percent surcharge on the use of a credit card generates a different (less favorable) response than offering 3 percent off for paying cash. Because consumers prefer information that is positive rather than stressing the negative, they favor the ad that says 90 percent fat free rather than one saying 10 percent fat. Similarly, to say something is an investment rather than a cost shifts perspectives towards buying since an investment is something positive. The reframing of an issue is a major device in persuasion and critical in political propaganda.
- Consumers make insufficient adjustment up or down from an initial starting point in determining what is an equitable price. The original starting price becomes an 'anchor' against which further prices are compared. Thus when students reject the claim that the average price of

textbooks is $100 or reject the claim that the average price is around $10, the average price they estimate as more realistic will be relatively high or low depending on the original price given them. This has implications for pricing and is taken into account in wage and price negotiations. The extravagant demands in compensation for small injuries can be explained this way in that it is hoped the initial demand gives the 'jury' a fix for setting a more reasonable figure. High anchor prices are common in guiding insecure consumers to choose a middle-priced brand that is more than they would otherwise pay. Even a realtor is apt to show prospects the highest-priced houses first to give them a 'fix' as to prices.

There is difficulty in incorporating flawed rationality into predictive models of behavior because we do not know the specific conditions that activate these dispositional tendencies. What we might do is conduct research in the domain of interest (e.g. the market of interest) to discover which flaws in rationality arise sufficiently to demand marketing's attention.

THE COGNITIVE VERSUS THE PSYCHOANALYTIC PARADIGM IN THERAPY

Therapy can be regarded as a product bought by the consumer. With regard to therapy, the paradigm of cognitive psychology conflicts with the psychoanalytic paradigm. In reviewing this conflict we get an even more subtle sense of the limitations of cognitive psychology as a field of firm knowledge. The Freudian methodology of going back to early life experiences is challenged by 'cognitive behavior therapy' (CBT), which denies any need to return to the early origins or sources of an individual's problems. CBT centers on getting patients to accept a certain story or narrative of their life that is positive, by focusing on positive thinking to ward off fearful and negative thoughts. The CBT approach aims at correcting 'cognitive distortions', such as irrational perspectives that have led the patient to reach beliefs that are dysfunctional to living a normal life. CBT claims there is no convincing evidence that understanding the origins of a patient's problems is necessary. Agreements between therapist and patient about what caused the patient's problems can be effective simply by showing cause and effect sequences that make sense to the patient. They need not be valid cause and effect relationships. This is contested by traditional psychotherapists and has given rise to an approach known as cognitive analytic therapy (CAT), which spends the first four sessions on identifying childhood 'causal' factors.

A more recent development of cognitive therapy is the more specific cognitive-bias modification (CBM) where the aim is to identify and remove the bias that distorts behavior. The assumption is that many mental problems arise from automatic, unconscious biases in thinking. No therapist here since the patient simply sits in front of a computer screen performing a program that in a subtle way changes harmful biases. Thus a patient with an anxiety neurosis has an attitudinal bias towards perceived threats and in therapy is confronted on the computer screen with pictures and words, some neutral, some threatening. The patient will focus on the threatening signals but the program obliges him to complete tasks that necessitate working constantly with the neutral words and pictures to change the inclination to focus on what is threatening. Apparently the patient is helped considerably after just a relatively few fifteen-minute sessions.

Although CBT often claims a high success rate, James (2009) quotes evidence to suggest that the long-term success rate is low at best as patients relapse into depression or anxiety. Initially patients acknowledge less intense symptoms but, months later, there is a return to the original symptoms. There is a need for more evidence using control and experimental groups. Thus psychiatrists many years ago used to claim they cured two out of every three patients they treated. But by using a control group made up of similarly ill people who never went to a psychiatrist, two out of every three were cured anyway.

THE MYTH OF THE CALCULATING MACHINE MODEL OF THE CONSUMER

The calculating machine model of the decision-maker is a myth. The myth of pure rationality arose from the Enlightenment in eighteenth-century Europe. This is the period that Kant (1724–1804) called the 'Dare to know' period, which was shaped by optimism about the possibilities of reason in controlling human life. The Enlightenment writers deeply distrusted emotion, which was associated with the backward, the primitive and the superstitious. The Enlightenment's advocacy of the sovereignty of reason holds sway when it is assumed emotion has no role to play. But there is no such thing as major decision-making without an emotional component: without the emotion there would be decision-paralysis. Textbook exercises, where we choose, via money metric, the alternative that yields maximum profit, are deceptive in that the superordinate value of profit maximization is laid down, and trade-offs can be converted into a common money scale. In practice, goals and values are multiple and competing, and trade-offs are not measurable on a common scale. However, where value priorities are uncertain (and they can be), indecision is the rule since, when values are unclear, trade-offs can be less confidently made.

CASE: KNO

Osman Rashid is a co-founder and CEO of Kno, whose aim is to bring the e-book revolution to college textbooks. Before co-founding Kno, he had co-founded Chegg which was set up to rent paperback textbooks to students. Rashid left Chegg to co-found Kno because he believed the move to digital books to be inevitable. After abandoning plans to develop its own 'tablet', Kno chose the iPad, but Apple's terms (30 percent of revenues generated) led Kno to switch in 2011 to selling its catalogue through Facebook. Users can download a textbook on a tablet or PC and, through Facebook, readers can connect to each other. There are already rival companies like Inkling that have made agreements with several publishers to develop interactive digital textbooks, while some publishers have decided to develop interactive versions of their most popular texts.

Case questions

1. Rashid sees an inevitable move by textbook consumers to digital books. Test this assertion in terms of the decision-process models in the text, such as Velleman's and Montgomery's. If these models have some validity, what obstacles will need to be overcome if digital texts are to replace buying textbooks or renting?
2. Apply the multiattribute model as a decision strategy. Are there any benefits in doing this? What heuristics of flawed rationality might Rashid have to take into account?

DISCUSSION QUESTIONS ON CHAPTER 6 (COGNITIVE PSYCHOLOGY)

1. Contrast the view of consumer decision-making in the multiattribute model with the idea that buyers simply have felt expectations as to how buying brand X rather than brand Y will be personally experienced.
2. What sort of evidence would you accept for claiming consumers have: (i) a self-concept; (ii) self-esteem; (iii) an ideal self-image?
3. In the text it is argued that saying a product has high meaning for the consumer is equivalent to saying that the consumer is highly involved with the product. As involvement is related in the text to centrality and risk, how can these two elements of involvement be related to meaning?
4. You have probably noticed that sellers of prestige brands that are bought to signal status never claim their customers buy for such unsavory reasons but rather for the quality of what they have to offer. The same goes for those selling services. Thus, headmasters and presidents of prestigious schools and universities always claim those 'buying' are influenced by tangible quality factors and not by the hope of benefiting from the status that rubs off from attending and the entry into some 'old boy network'. If this is genuinely self-deception, what are the dangers from the point of view of marketing?
5. Think about how you selected your university. Was it nearer the 'implicit favorite model', the multiattribute model, one of the non-compensatory models or near to none of these?

Chapter 8

Cognitive Neuroscience (and a Comment on Evolutionary Psychology or Sociobiology)

THE SOMATIC MARKER VIEW OF RATIONALITY

Cognitive neuroscientists impute significance to neurological phenomena for explaining human behavior. Cognitive neuroscience endorses the claim made in earlier chapters that unconscious states influence behavior and decisions can be rationalizations for conclusions already determined at the unconscious level. But cognitive neuroscience has neither ignored nor neglected emotion and deficiencies in rationality.

One basic research area in neuroscience has been to identify the various functions of the brain and their locations in the brain, helped by technologies like magnetic resonance imaging (MRI) machines. A major approach has been to study patients with brain damage since, if damage to one part of the brain affects functioning elsewhere, it suggests a causal connection. What has become apparent is the high amount of specialization in the brain; the brain being a constellation of specialized modules, each carrying out a special skill. All this is important for the surgeon undertaking brain surgery but, from a psychological point of view, there is a neglect of research identifying the mechanisms lying behind the functions performed by the brain. Yet how things work is more important for psychology than knowing where functions are located in the brain. Capturing an image of the brain is just a snapshot of the brain and tells us little about how the brain functions.

Cognitive neuroscience is full of technical jargon. This can mislead the reader into thinking something profound and novel is being said. Thus Churchland (1995) proposes to explain mental abilities by 'multidimensional vector space' which Fodor (1998) depicts as 'techno-hype' that simply expresses in connectionist jargon ordinary psychological concepts. As Aristotle pointed out, it is absurd to explain the obvious in terms of the obscure since explanations should aim to take the obscure and make it evident.

Antonio Damasio (1989), a cognitive neuroscientist, states there are 'pre-organized' mechanisms in the brain that are involved in instantly classifying happenings as 'good' or 'bad'. With increasing experience, the repertoire of things categorized as 'good' or 'bad' grows exponentially. If a given entity is classified as 'good' or 'bad' there is a tendency to classify any *contiguous* entity as also 'good' or 'bad'. This offers support for the power of association – in, for example, employing attractive associations/images in advertising to boost brand image. The rule for any ad is to avoid associations that could be viewed negatively by the target audience, unless the ad is using a fear appeal. Persuasive associations can arise from *associating* a brand with social norms, values, valued images, status and prestige, and appeals to solidarity with others. An evaluation of all such persuasive tactics in advertising has been written elsewhere (O'Shaughnessy and O'Shaughnessy 2004).

Employing the association of a brand or product with positive, valued images tends to go with the soft sell approach, as the aim is to deftly fuse the associations with the brand even if the associations just evoke a fantasy of sharing. However, it would be wrong to assume that effective advertising can amount to nothing more than selecting the right things with which to associate a brand. We commonly find in advertising that the associations selected could have been equally chosen for a rival brand without a mention of a competitive advantage that might distinguish the brand. The hope is that, if the advertiser has got in first with the association, the association has already become attached. While pleasing associations can be crucial and decisive where brands are otherwise undifferentiated, elsewhere substance can be decisive. The philosopher Heidegger (1962), in his *Being and Time*, would agree that how things function and how we can figure out how to use things are the major concerns as we go about living, not the perceptual properties of things!

For Damasio, the purpose of all reasoning is *deciding* but this depends on how we define 'deciding': doing deductive logic is reasoning but not deciding in any meaningful sense. Choosing without deliberation of the pros and cons is not 'deciding'. In any case, Damasio posits two views on deciding. The first is the 'high reason' view, associated with classical economics, where people examine all alternatives and their consequences to arrive at a preference that maximizes *subjective expected utility* (SEU). Damasio ridicules this 'high reason' view assumed in economics, equating it with the way patients with prefrontal damage go about deciding, than with how normal people decide. This criticism is in line, among others, with Herbert Simon's 'bounded rationality' (Simon 1957). Models of rational decision-making in economics and elsewhere seem to assume agents with perfect knowledge and unlimited time. Herbert Simon's notion of bounded rationality disputed this view. Bounded rationality stresses the limitations of the human mind and, as such, cannot be equated with simply optimizing under constraints or recognition of fallacies in reasoning.

The second view Damasio calls the *somatic-marker* view of rationality. According to Damasio, when options come to mind and bad outcomes (negative consequences) are connected to an option, this instantly generates an unpleasant gut feeling. If good outcomes are connected to a particular option, this generates a pleasant gut reaction. The feeling is 'somatic' because it relates to the body and is a 'marker' because it 'marks' an image, however fleetingly. An unpleasant 'gut feeling' in turn brings about an immediate 'gut' rejection of the option, whereas if it were a pleasant gut feeling, it would bring about an immediate gut acceptance. In the rejection case, marketers would claim that the consumer is acting in line with the conjunctive rule to eliminate alternatives that lack the necessary feature(s) for acceptance. But the Damasio position is scientifically based. Somatic markers act as sentinels, producing speedy responses ahead of any reasoned response. Such a speedy response can be illustrated by the reaction to an oncoming car, where stopping to deliberate could be fatal.

When a negative somatic marker is juxtaposed to a likely future outcome the juxtaposition acts as an alarm bell. When a positive somatic marker is juxtaposed instead, it becomes a beacon of incentive. Somatic markers connect classes of stimuli with specific somatic states. This somatic marker view applies to Damasio's broadly based view of decision-making, not necessarily covering only situations where the deliberation of alternatives occurs.

When the immediate 'gut feeling' propels a positive response, *likeability* comes into play with the consumer predisposed to choose on the basis of liking. Choosing on the basis of liking alone is an *affect-driven choice*, where consumers are said to follow the likeability heuristic in making their choice. On the other hand, when the immediate gut feeling propels a negative response, there is no further consideration of the merits of the option at that time. Anything – item, event or person – can be rejected out of hand through a gut reaction of dislike. This mirrors the notion of a negative attitude leading to rejection and this is why the concept of positive and negative somatic markers is very useful for those in marketing since it gives physiological support to the concept of attitude as a predisposition to react positively or negatively to some item, event or thing. It might be argued, as in this book, that this is how attitude should be conceptualized and measured.

*f*MRI AND PET SCAN STUDIES

Damasio started an interest in the potential of brain scans in psychology, using magnetic-resonance imaging (MRI) and positron emission tomography (PET scans). MRI predates *f*MRI (functional magnetic-resonance imaging). *f*MRI is an advance in being able to record activity and not just the anatomy of the brain. These various instruments show what parts of the brain are active or responding to a particular stimulus when we are engaged in thinking.

It is no longer rare to take brain scans of a sample of consumers and correlate their brain activity with the viewing of various ads or brands. In a review article, Thompson quotes Montague, a neuroscientist at Baylor College of Medicine, as saying: 'My God, if you combine making the can red with making it less sweet, you can measure this in a scanner and see the result. If I were Pepsi, I'd go in there and I'd start scanning people' (Thompson, 2003). But the problem lies not in recording brain activity corresponding to some stimuli but in gauging what it all *means* since the meaning of brain scans is unclear and interpretations vary widely. As there is no way an examination of a person's neural processes by means of PET scans and so on enables us to investigate someone's reasoning or what they are thinking, interpretation becomes decisive.

One study using MRI brain scans distinguished songs that became 'hits' by showing that these 'sparked' greater activity in teenagers' brains than did flops (Saadi 2011). Can we interpret this as saying that such greater activity in the brain will always distinguish future hits from flops? More importantly, are such brain scans more predictive of success than asking the teenagers to rate the songs on a scale of 0 to 5 according to how much the song excited them? After all, if we say MRI scans are better predictors, we must state what they are better than by showing the scans to be better than the alternative methods displaced. In the same mini-article, a spokesperson for NeuroFocus, which specializes in neuromarketing, is quoted as saying: 'We're not omnipotent but we can shine light in the darkest parts of a consumer's mind, and that's worth something.' MRI brain scans that are simply recording brain activity are in this way equated with penetrating the deepest recesses of the *mind* and knowing what goes on there!

Any ad or piece of rhetoric can be viewed as a text, with the term *exegesis* employed to mean the critical interpreting of a text. It is argued that words in a text have *semantic autonomy* in the sense that words, sentences and paragraphs or speech carry meanings that are independent of the creator of, say, an ad. Put another way, as words enter the mind they seemingly can have a life of their own and a corresponding reality removed from factual reality. The ad or rhetoric has the potential to shape reality in thought. It is this semantic autonomy of language that can divorce language from its source and evoke ambiguities and create new meanings. If this is endorsed by postmodernists, it should not as a consequence prompt dismissal. Ads do have semantic autonomy and consumers interpret them, drawing not just on the literal meaning of words used, but on their own experience, wishes and contextual understandings that have nuances unique to the individual interpreter. Words that have a semantic autonomy can prompt thoughts that arouse action divorced from deliberation on evidential support. Important meanings can be implicit in the text outside the author's intentions.

To return to the article by Thompson, subjects were asked to rate a series of products on the basis of liking. The brains of the subjects were later scanned in an MRI machine, with Clint Kilts, the investigator, showing them pictures of the same products again. Whenever a subject saw the product he had previously identified as one he 'truly loved', his brain showed increased activity in the medial prefrontal cortex, which is associated with the emotions. The investigator concluded that, when this part of the brain 'fired' on seeing the product, it was likely to be because the product 'clicks' *with self-image*. This interpretation is postulating a causal relationship between the social construct of 'self-image' and a specific happening in the brain. This is a far more ambitious claim than it appears. Establishing such a relationship is the dream of all those who advocate *reductionism*, reducing psychology to neuroscience, while at the same time establishing the *construct validity* of social creations like self-image through establishing corresponding brain indicators. In practice we are very far from defining social constructs like self-image, free will and so on in terms of biological processes. This has, however, not stopped one chemical company from claiming in its ads that 'love' is simply a chemical reaction! Construct validity, which is concerned with the soundness of a social science concept, is a key question that is not always easy to establish. It would indeed be a remarkable breakthrough to demonstrate that the constructs created by social scientists such as attitude and self-image are something more than 'as if' existing but do have identifiable counterparts in nature, namely in the brain.

The author of the review article maintains *f*MRI scanning is seen as offering the promise of concrete fact – an unbiased glimpse at the consumer's mind in action. But the only thing that could possibly be labeled a 'fact' is 'a something' on the MRI scan. All the rest is speculation. The magic button in all this is identified as the medial prefrontal cortex: 'if that area is firing, a consumer isn't deliberating, he's itching to buy. At that point, it's intuitive. You say: "I'm going to do it" ' (p. 57). This claim raises very questionable assumptions. No one to date even claims each and every emotion can be shown to have a distinctive brain pattern. In fact, a specific brain pattern may indicate many types of emotion. As the author says at the end of the article many scientists are skeptical of 'neuromarketing'; just because we get neurons firing does not mean that we know what the mind is doing. The fundamental question is: what does this firing mean? Answering this question is basic to any interpretation of the phenomena. In any case, brain scans, as one leading neuroscientist says, can tell us little about our personhood.

In another study, researchers monitored brain scans in sixty-seven consumers after they were given a blind taste test of Coca-Cola and Pepsi (Blakeslee 2004a). We are told that each soft drink lit up the brain's 'reward system' (we apparently now know for sure that some part of the brain is its reward system!) and the participants were equally split as to which drink they preferred. However, on being informed which brand they were drinking, activity in a different set of brain locations 'linked to brand loyalty' (note how the consumers' usual preferences were equated here with the more demanding concept of brand loyalty) overrode their original preferences. This is greeted with surprise; that consumers did not choose on the basis of taste alone but more on the basis of brand. Those in marketing would not be surprised.

The only thing surprising is that there was surprise, as this is a finding well known for at least sixty years of blind taste tests. It is interesting how researchers fail to reach out to other disciplines for relevant findings. Reactions to 'neuromarketing' are similar to the reactions to subliminal perception studies in the 1950s: an exaggerated fear of being manipulated. In fact, the whole area at present is so full of speculative interpretations that not much reliance can be placed on any claims made beyond the firings in the brain.

In still another study, reported by Blakeslee (2004b), women participants ticked off their answers to a structured questionnaire whose answers reflected the respondent's trust in a retail outlet ('XYZ always treats me fairly'; 'XYZ is a name I can always trust') and the respondent's loyalty to the store ('XYZ is the perfect store for me': 'I can't imagine a world without XYZ'). From these answers, those with seemingly a strong emotional attachment to the store were found to be those whose areas of the brain associated with memory and emotion (the orbitofrontal cortex, the temporal pole and the amygdala) lit up. Women who were not strongly attached to the store showed little or no activation. The author asserts that, using such brain-imaging technology, marketers hope to glean what buyers really want instead of what they might say in a focus group. They hope to create loyal customers by 'hooking up to their amygdala'. The researchers quote Daniel Kahneman, whose work (with the late Amos Tversky) won him the 2002 Nobel Prize, who said that the emotions are important determinants of economic behavior, more so than rationality.

One article by a medical doctor argues that inside the human brain is the reward circuit. When someone anticipates a reward, this reward center lights up 'like a Christmas tree', so if we want to see how a new product is perceived we can place a prospect in an MRI scanner and study the activity in their brain's reward center (Friedman 2006). (Note how the concept of perception is reduced to this activity in the brain.) In a study of DaimlerChrysler cars, the hypothesis put forward was that because sports cars are such social status symbols, they would be perceived as the most rewarding and so produce the greatest activation in the reward circuit. This hypothesis was corroborated. The author goes on to claim that the proposition 'a sports car is sexy' has literally been encoded in the average male brain! Surprisingly, this is viewed as a legitimate inference from the activation observed. The author believes that, if things like mpg, safety features and so on do not excite a man's reward circuit, the new car will 'remain an engineer's dream'. Thus activating the reward center becomes a *necessary* condition for success, that is, a sufficient reason for failure! This is just plain silly, contradicting common sense as well as all sorts of research into car preferences and car buying decisions.

There are many odd claims made from brain scans. Sam Harris (2011) points out that neuroimaging studies show that the same regions of the brain are active both when people judge the truth or falsity of a statement ('Prince William married Kate Middleton') and when making ethical statements ('The killing of civilians in wartime is never justified'). The conclusion drawn from this is that the distinction between fact and values is illusory. But this would also imply that, if the same region of the brain is active when angry and when joyous then the distinction between the two is illusory. It is as if the whole neurological and psychological story is captured by activity within a certain location in the brain.

There are few, if any, people in consumer marketing who would quarrel with stressing the importance of emotion but the uses of brain-imaging technologies are being grossly oversold. Many years ago, much the same claims were made for lie detector tests (commonly used not just by the police but by advertising agencies to judge reactions to ads) on the grounds that they could detect the emotional reactions of consumers. The problem will always be to interpret the meaning (significance) of the brain 'lighting up'. It may at best indicate brand recognition and/or brand resonance. Going beyond this is pure speculation. Areas of the brain lighting up do not prove that the subject trusts the brand or has loyalty to the brand in the sense of 'sticking to it through thick and thin'. It is, of course, true that when we are emotionally aroused there are happenings in the brain. The pleasurable experience of beautiful music, good food or sex seems to trigger the same chemical reaction in the brain, as well as physical effects like changes in heart rate and temperature, while regions of the brain linked to pleasure release dopamine. But a specific one-to-one correspondence between external stimuli and these happenings is something else.

A letter from Dr Emilio Bizzi of the McGovern Institute For Brain Research concludes that the consensus view at a symposium on the use of fMRI was that 'one should be careful not to invest too much faith in the capacity of brain imaging to reveal individuals' true motives and motivations – the technology is not ready for use, despite optimism about its commercial potential' (Bizzi 2007: 10).

The fMRI work is allied to the search for locations in the brain that are causal sources of behavior: a project that has links to the discredited phrenology in the nineteenth century which aimed to locate mental and personality faculties through examining bumps in the skull. This is not to suggest that there are no distinct mental faculties. We know that one sort of brain injury damages one faculty, like memory, while another sort of brain injury affects the sense of smell and so on. But this sort of *subtractive* approach to investigating brain functioning is unlikely to tell the whole story. In any case to what extent is there a distinct relationship between a specific physiological state and a specific emotional mental state, except in the most general terms? What we can say is that an emotional state acts as a motivational state in initiating action, though the motivational state has to be sufficiently intense to overcome any counterbalancing thoughts suggesting forbearance. Forbearance is helped by thinking about implications for the future and 'savoring' that future.

Sinha et al. (1992) found systematic differences in physiology between several negative emotions like anger and fear; basic physiological emotions that are also present in animals. There are other studies along the same lines (e.g. Levenson et al. 1990). In particular, Goleman (1995) argues that the emotions prepare the body for different kinds of response and certain discrete emotions have distinct physiological aspects. Thus, in anger, the blood flows to the hands; in fear, the blood goes to the large skeletal muscles; in happiness there is an increased level of activity in the brain center that inhibits negative feelings; in sadness, there is a drop in energy level. Anger and fear are basic emotions that we share with all animals and there is a corresponding physiological aspect. On the other hand, there is no evidence that the more important self-assessment emotions of guilt, shame, pride and the emotions to which they are linked, such as humiliation, have a distinct counterpart in the neurological system. These emotions are of social/cultural origin and are more important to marketers. However, the absence of evidence that identifies such emotions by using physiological measures is just that: no evidence.

More recently, efforts have been made to chart the brain's main connections in order to establish the parts of the brain that work together in networks and measure the variability from one person to the next rather than simply employing scanners to discover which areas of the brain light up on undertaking different tasks (Anderson 2011). It is too early to know what the future holds for this approach.

DOES THE FUTURE LIE WITH COGNITIVE NEUROSCIENCE?

Churchland, a philosopher who focuses on neuroscience, believes the future lies with neuroscience, which he claims will supersede psychology (including folk psychology) (Churchland 1989). Since psychological mental states can be viewed in terms of playing a causal role (for example, negative attitudes leading to rejection) we would like to quote specific neurophysiological states as responsible for the psychological state. In this way we *reductively* explain the psychological state. Churchland is a reductionist. A reductionist aims to reduce one science to a more fundamental one by showing that the key concepts of the one can be expressed in the language of the other. The aim is thus to reduce biology to cellular phenomena and then to biochemical phenomena and so on to physical phenomena. Churchland thus would seek to reduce psychology to neuroscience. He is an advocate of 'eliminative reduction', replacing psychological explanations of human behavior with neuroscientific theory. In his view, folk psychology and also all empirical psychology consist simply of vacuous concepts. In contrast, Fodor (1975), the philosopher and a specialist in the area of cognitive science, believes folk psychology in its essentials will be validated by any future 'scientific' psychology as folk psychology reflects the mind's characteristics.

It may be that explanations of action in terms of wants and beliefs or conditioning could in principle be explained in neurological terms, but this reductive explanation would neither be as enlightening nor as useful as, say, the reason-giving explanation. At present we have no clear notion of how electrical charges in the nerve cells of the brain are linked to beliefs, wants and feelings or to the constructs of academic psychology. We might set out some cognitive model showing how, possibly, certain mental states cause certain types of behavior, but without the neurological understanding there will always be an explanatory gap in any behavior explanation. But whether this is important or not depends on what would constitute a satisfactory explanation for our purposes. For scientists seeking to remove all mysteries about the mind, Churchland's normative ideal has appeal even though, if universal discoveries are to be found, it assumes people are to some extent tokens of each other at the neurological level. At present, it is not even clear how subjective states like pain and pleasure, the smell of a rose, the sight of beauty can be reduced to molecules and neurons.

We are a long way from explaining consciousness or conscious experience in terms of physical happenings. Consciousness may have a physical basis without consciousness being necessarily determined by that physical basis (Chalmers 1996). Writers on consciousness tell us a good deal about the correlates of consciousness, but the real phenomenon to be explained is how lots of firing neurons in some kind of network manage to produce consciousness. This remains a mystery.

THE BENNETT AND HACKER CRITIQUE OF COGNITIVE NEUROSCIENCE

Cognitive neuroscience is sharply criticized in *Philosophical Foundations of Neuroscience* by Bennett and Hacker (2003). This critiques the conceptual foundations of cognitive neuroscience. Anyone reading the book learns much about cognitive neuroscience – and about conceptual analysis. The book reviews cognitive neuroscience and its current limitations. Marketing needs conceptual analysis as it is stymied (as is much of social science) by conceptual confusion. As Bennett and Hacker (2003) say:

> Conceptual questions antecede matters of truth and falsehood. They are questions concerning our forms of representation, not questions concerning the truth or falsehood of empirical statements.
>
> (Bennett and Hacker 2003: 2)

Hacker, an Oxford philosopher, is a well-known scholar on Wittgenstein, while Bennett is a professor of neuroscience. It is a book that bucks current trends (it attacks the most received of wisdom) with erudition (the book is profoundly erudite). If readers believe that many aspects of marketing suffer from conceptual confusion, hidden by a dash of technological sophistication, they are in good company, as this is the charge made in this book against cognitive neuroscience – with the difference that the technological achievements of non-cognitive neuroscience are admitted to be substantial. Critics will rightly claim that the book has a behaviorist bias but it is still a book to be reckoned with by those in the field.

Conceptual confusion differs from errors of fact. Factual errors imply false beliefs whereas conceptual confusion gives rise to *incoherence* arising from things not being logically connected. Bennett and Hacker's accusations are pertinent also to cognitive psychology, since cognitive psychology draws many of its concepts from the same pool of concepts as cognitive neuroscience. In fact the authors define cognitive neuroscience as operating across the boundary of the two fields of neurophysiology and psychology.

Disagreement among psychologists often arises from the same concept being used to describe very different types of phenomena. The word 'aggressive', for example, is used to cover many types of behavior. This leads Kagan (2006), after a lifetime as a Harvard psychologist, to suggest that social scientists should generally reject context-free concepts, to speak in full sentences to embrace the context of the concept. There is no longer a single word to represent a concept like 'attitude', but, instead, a full statement of concept/context – for example, 'the white middle class mother's attitude to cloth diapers in the Spring of 2006 in the town of Dallas'. As Kagan says, the belief that contextually unspecified concepts would be theoretically useful has not fared well. This verdict would be endorsed by many in the field of consumer behavior but following the advice of Kagan will not be easy.

Concepts in social science are not like trees, part of nature, but man-made (social) constructs that may or may not fit nature. As Kagan says, 'rejection' is a symbolic invention of the mind and not a *property* of social experience. Alternatively, if the word is a concept in daily use there is the danger of its referent being too broad for scientific purposes. Kagan recommends inventing new words that have unequivocal meaning-in-use rather than falling back on laypersons' language. He notes how physicists invented the new words 'boson' and 'gluon' to describe atomic events to avoid inappropriate connotations. While it is true these terms have no *referential* meaning, it is surely true they retain sense-meaning in that words always come with connotations attached – for example boson, unlike gluon, suggests something to do with boats, while gluon, unlike boson, conjures up images of sticky things.

Kagan implicitly takes to task those researchers who start with a lot of abstract concepts semantically linked together through sense-meanings, and, if they seem valid, construct a coherent semantic argument in support without giving referential-meaning to the concepts via operational (empirically derived) measures. This failure has been common in consumer research, stretching back to what is now regarded as a seminal work in the field, namely Howard and Sheth's (1968) *The Theory of Buyer Behavior*. It is usually claimed that Farley and Ring (1970) tested the model, providing operational measures of the concepts with results consistent with the relationships shown in the Howard-Sheth model. This is misleading since their operational measures were too remote from the sense-meanings described in the Howard-Sheth model; the consistency that was found was simply the result of the operational measures themselves being conceptually related in line with the findings. It is not enough for the variables in a model to cohere among themselves; the model must be checked against the real world. Kagan's approach is different and far more defensible. He recommends proceeding from observational data to appropriate concepts:

> I was critical of concepts that bubbled up from intuition rather than plucked from the red-hot kiln of direct observation...I cannot think of one theoretically important psychological concept originating in intuition, without the support of reliable observations, that survived more than twenty-five years'...Psychologists like abstract words – 'emotion,' 'memory' and 'learning' – that bury the natural phenomena under a blanket of semantic networks. Too many investigators begin their research with concepts like 'intelligence' or 'reactivity' and look for evidence to prove their existence.
>
> (Kagan 2006: 179)

Constructs inferred from direct observations, he argues, are the ones that have proved most fruitful. This would, on the surface, seem good advice but direct observation might cover too narrow a domain, while constructs arising from reflection are unlikely to be entirely remote from reality as Kagan seems to imply. A model arising from systematic self-reflection will have some contact with reality, while something purely descriptive will still be a selection from an interpreted reality. The gulf between model and reality in any particular case may not be as wide as most of us think. A more relevant criticism is that direct observation is not free of potential bias. Observation is concept-loaded in the sense that the concepts we possess guide our observations. We are apt to see what we have been trained to look for. This is what we mean by the 'trained mind'. The hope is that we have the right training to observe and in observing arrive at meaningful concepts. As we all know from watching detective films, the layperson does not see what is identified by the forensic scientist.

To return to Bennett and Hacker, it seems like every major figure in cognitive science comes in for criticism. But unlike David Hackett Fischer's *Historians' Fallacies*, which accuses the most famous of historians of fallacious reasoning (Fischer 1970), or Harrè and Secord's *The Explanation of Social Behavior* which describes cognitive psychology as analogous to alchemy (Harrè and Secord 1973), this book is concerned with the concepts of cognitive neuroscience, arguing that cognitive neuroscience frequently and systematically confuses conceptual and empirical questions.

The philosophical methodology employed in the book is *analytic philosophy*, an umbrella term that covers a variety of philosophical techniques. In particular, it embraces *conceptual analysis* which focuses on the meaning-in-use of various concepts within some particular 'language game' or way of life. Conceptual analysis is a key part of the linguistic turn started by Wittgenstein, who invented the phrase 'language game' to draw attention to the fact that language use cannot be detached from the activities of which it is part. The linguistic turn in social science claims there can be no apprehending of 'reality' except through the intervention of language because all perceptions, concepts and claims to truth are constructed in language. Language is the medium through which we describe and study reality. In conceptual analysis, concept elucidation is achieved by focusing on the rule-governed use of words, in contrast to linguistic analysis which focuses on the analysis of sentences.

The crucial argument of the two authors is that cognitive neuroscientists and cognitive psychologists take words like sensation, perception, image, belief, consciousness, mind, memory, imagination and emotion in the way they are used by the layperson without analyzing how these words are used in various situations or even trying to capture other than the layman's meaning. It might be added that neuroscience nonetheless has its share of jargon. But as the authors say, conceptual analysis cannot be ignored since conceptual questions come before matters of truth or falsity. The empirical science of cognitive neuroscience seeks to explain the *neural* conditions that make perceptual, cognitive, cogitative, affective and volitional functions possible and the neural processes that occur when such capacities are exercised. When these empirical issues are addressed without ensuring conceptual clarity, misconceived questions and misdirected research arise.

THE MEREOLOGICAL FALLACY

Michael Gazzaniga (2005), together with linguist George A. Miller, pioneered cognitive neuroscience. The story goes that he coined the term 'neuroscience' with George Miller in the 1970s in the back of a New York taxi. Bennett and Hacker, in discussing Gazzaniga's book *The Ethical Brain*, report him as saying that cognitive neuroscience is 'even shedding light on how moral beliefs take shape in our brain'(Zimmer 2005). Gazzaniga talks of the brain's interpreter producing rational explanations of otherwise inexplicable feelings. In Gazzaniga's (2008) most recent book *Human*, he argues that the distinguishing characteristic of human beings is the ability to inhibit automatic responses (desire for instant gratification) in favor of responses arising from reasoned deliberation.

Gazzaniga's claims are an anathema to Bennett and Hacker who label such statements as subscribing to the 'mereological fallacy': a fallacy going back to Descartes. It was Descartes (1596–1650) who ascribed psychological attributes to the mind as if the mind were a distinct entity: an entity that thinks, perceives and believes on its own. But the mind is not any kind of thing and certainly not software in the brain as cognitive psychologists assume: to have a mind, they argue, is simply to have the *capacities* of intellect, particularly the conceptual capacities of a language-user which makes self-awareness and self-reflection possible.

Self-reflection is important since whatever might be promoted by the unconscious automatic brain, can be subject to self-reflection and, as a consequence, rejected or accepted (Damasio 2010). Fixed abilities are capacities that can be contrasted with dispositions, which relate more to cognitive style and which are not fixed but generally learnt. Thus attitudes are generally learnt. Capacities, as Bennett and Hacker say, are not space-occupying entities, any more than the 'horsepower' of a car is something physical. Human beings, not brains, have minds. Thus they deny that minds are simply the software of the brain as claimed by cognitive psychologists. It is simplistic to view the mind as machine-like and machines as mind-like. If computers seem to act like free human agents, it is simply because this was the intention of a human designer.

Bennett and Hacker argue that, while cognitive neuroscientists reject Cartesian dualism (an immaterial mind that is separate from a material body), at the same time they ascribe psychological attributes to the brain. Bennett and Hacker claim that cognitive neuroscience is overtly anti-Cartesian but essentially Cartesian in retaining the same form of Cartesian explanation, allocating to the brain the same psychological functions that dualism allocated to the mind. This is the *mereological fallacy* (ascribing to the mind properties that can only be ascribed intelligibly to the person as a whole) since human beings, not their brains, can intelligibly be said to see, hear, smell and taste things, perceive and make decisions. Rockwell (2005) would agree, arguing that mental phenomena arise not merely from brain activity but from an interacting nexus of body, brain and the environment. Similarly, Pfeifer and Bongard (2005) show that thought is not independent of body but is both constrained and enabled by it while even the thoughts we have are founded in our embodiment. It is human beings who think, reason and decide, not their brains: a brain is simply a necessary condition for us to perceive, think and feel.

There is a growing field called *embodied cognition* which accepts the role of the whole body in cognition. A question that immediately arises is whether this view is adopting a too holistic view of the functioning of the human organism. Some scientists do in fact claim that every single organ or cell in the body is involved in storing our memories, activating our emotions and helping to create our personality; that our memories and attributes are embedded, not just in our brain but throughout our whole body so that consciousness, say, emerges using every living cell in the body acting in unison (Penman 2008). Similarly, one Dutch scientist, Nils B. Jostmann, is quoted as saying: 'How we process information is related not just to our brains but to our entire body. We use every system available to us to come to a conclusion that makes sense of what's going on' (Angier 2010). By way of evidence, there are more than seventy documented cases where transplant patients are reputed to have taken on some of the personality traits of the organ donor.

Bennett and Hacker deny there are symbols in the brain that, by their array or arrangement, express a proposition or sentence. What goes on in the brain are simply neural processes which need to occur in order for the person to be undertaking the relevant mental processes. To say the brain perceives, feels, thinks, desires, or that 'unconscious' mental acts of the brain cause bodily movements that constitute voluntary action, makes no sense. Brains are not autonomous living creatures that act in ways that logically warrant the ascription of psychological properties. We do not even know what sort of evidence would show the brain as possessing such properties/attributes and by just assuming it does, cognitive neuroscientists are asking the wrong questions and misdirecting research.

Is contemporary cognitive neuroscience as conceptually deficient as Bennett and Hacker suggest? Are not cognitive neuroscientists simply employing figurative uses of speech; namely, employing the trope of synecdoche (the substitution of a part for the whole – for example, sail for ship)? This will not do, as the authors show; cognitive scientists carry on as if the brain does all these things. If Gilbert Ryle (1949) dismissed Cartesian dualism – the mind as separate from the body – as 'the ghost in the machine', Bennett and Hacker would claim cognitive neuroscientists are substituting 'the little man in the machine' for the 'ghost in the machine': the dualism of mind and body being replaced by brain and body. Psychological predicates apply to the whole living being, not to its parts.

But perhaps cognitive neuroscientists are using terms like 'belief' and 'perception' in a technical neuroscience sense? The authors will have none of this either, pointing out that the words used by cognitive neuroscientists are used with the same meaning as non-neuroscientists: they are not homonyms (using the same word but with a different meaning), otherwise cognitive neuroscientists would not go on to draw the type of inferences from them that they do.

THE INTERNAL REPRESENTATION MYTH

Cognitive scientists speak of 'internal representations' and 'mental maps' on the grounds that there must be a symbolic representation of the outside world embedded in the brain. While Bennett and Hacker acknowledge that it is harmless in some cases to talk of mapping features of the perceptual field on to topographically related groups of cells, it is invalid to talk of such maps playing a crucial role in representing the world by the brain, as playing the same role as an atlas. We may correlate a person's expressed thoughts with corresponding specific brain activity detected by PET or *f*MRI scans but this in no way shows the brain is thinking – it simply shows, no more, no less, that a certain part of the person's cortex is active when the person is thinking. The neural events in the brain may correlate with seeing, thinking or whatever a person says he is doing, but the brain is not an organ of perception and it is conceptually confusing to talk of the brain as 'seeing things': it does not. It is the person who does the seeing.

A widespread notion in the behavioral literature is that when we look at an object outside ourselves, we form a mirror image in the brain. This notion is almost taken as gospel in consumer behavior. Mental images or representations are viewed as private inner pictures, as copies of antecedent impressions which can be scanned and examined with their features being discerned or overlooked as with a physical picture. Bennett and Hacker regard it as a serious error to suppose that to perceive something is to have an image in the mind of whatever is perceived: we only perceive an image or representation if we are perceiving paintings or photographs of objects. To recall an image of brand XYZ is not to start thinking in images since images are not an expression of one's thought but an aid to thought, simply an accompaniment. We do not think in images; this is not to suggest that when something is consciously experienced it has no cognitive counterpart, but this is something different from *thinking* in images. This undermines the claims made by Zaltman (see earlier in Chapter 5).

Thus we might have:

- Immediate perception: it is a car
- Reflection on that perception: I have a positive sensation on seeing that it is a friend's car
- Inference from that perception: my friend must be nearby.

To see a Coca-Cola bottle is not to *see* an image of a bottle in the mind, and to hear an ad on television for Coca-Cola is not to *see* an image or representation of what is said or sung. If I am asked how I know it is a Coca-Cola bottle, I simply reply that I can just see it is. Of course the consumer, like everyone else, conjures up images and sometimes images just come to mind regardless, as when the image of a certain make of car comes to mind, providing a positive (I like) or negative (I dislike) brand image. This is not the same as *seeing* an image of the car in my mind when it is before me or *thinking* in images.

If perceiving a product requires an internal picture, image or representation, it would have to be *constructed* and the puzzle is, as the authors say, how the brain could produce such coherent images, correctly associating the shape, motion, depth and color of the perceived object and not jumbling them up. While it is true that, to see anything at all, separate groups of neurons must be simultaneously active, this gives no license to claim that when we perceive things in the environment the mind perceives an internal picture or representation of the world. Representational theories conceptualize the mind as *looking in* on mental representations but, as Bennett and Hacker say, there can be no such thing as the brain *representing* information; it is simply not intelligible to assume there can be symbolic descriptions of, say, a visual scene in the brain. There is no such thing as a description or internal representation in the brain.

A pattern of neural firing that is a causal response to a stimulus in the visual field is not a description of the stimulus or anything else. For patterns of neural firings are no more symbols than are rings in the trunk of an oak tree, or molecules in a material subjected to carbon dating... A symbol is used only if the user means something by it – but brains cannot mean anything.

(Bennett and Hacker 2003: 145–6)

The authors say the term 'representation' is a weed in the neuroscientific garden, not a tool – and 'the sooner it is uprooted the better' (2006: 143) Cognitive neuroscientists should stop referring to correlates of features in the visual scene as either 'representations' or 'symbols' and not base their explanations of perceptual processes by espousing the mereological fallacy.

SEMANTIC VERSUS PERCEPTUAL REPRESENTATIONS

Of relevance here is Kagan's point that the promotion of theory, ignoring the facts on the ground, is flawed. One cannot create realistic models in an observational vacuum. Kagan contrasts 'semantic' versus 'perceptual' representations; important for those in marketing. He quotes, as an example, the word 'heavy' in discussing semantic representation. 'Heavy', as a *semantic representation*, has branches stemming from nodes for boulders, arcane arguments, serious plays and so on. Heavy has an opposite ('light') and is part of a hierarchy of concepts ('magnitude' being higher in the hierarchy). It is the actual context that determines which route we go. On the other hand, there is no *perceptual representation* of the word 'heavy', no opposite, and it is not part of any hierarchy. There are only representations of objects with this property. Infants below eight months have only perceptual knowledge but no semantic concepts, so such a child staring at the divide between sky and sea has a perceptual representation without any semantic component. This distinction is important as many consumers have only a perceptual representation of some feature of a product. Without the semantic representation they not only have less understanding of that feature but are less likely to even notice it. There can be too much attention to the perceptual at the expense of the semantic when it comes to advertising. Kagan points out that it is the right hemisphere of the brain that plays the more significant role in perceptual matters and the left a larger role in semantic matters.

PSYCHOLOGICAL ATTRIBUTES

Bennett and Hacker remind us that psychological mental attributes like attitude are not the names of inner entities and their objective meaning is only grasped by their conceptual connection with behavioral criteria and not their link to 'inner' experiences. The individual herself knows she has a pain, but I infer she has a pain from her behavior (including her saying so) or indirectly assume it from having noticed she is taking analgesics. It is pointless to regard beliefs or attitudes as *real mental entities* and speculate about their non-conceptual (that is, their empirical) connections with other mental entities (as commonly occurs in the consumer behavior literature) as there are no such mental entities. We infer a person's beliefs, wants and attitudes from behavior (including what a person says). We should not treat beliefs, wants, attitudes, self-image, motives and so on as real physical, material entities located somewhere in the brain as some advocates of cognitive neuroscience seem to suggest.

All this is different from recognizing *conceptual* connections (as opposed to physical connections) between various psychological concepts. Making conceptual connections can result in many conceptual truths, for example saying the greater the source credibility, the greater its influence. Similarly we can say a lack of credibility implies a lack of trust and so more risk. It is not uncommon in the behavioral literature to treat a conceptual truth as if it were an empirical hypothesis put forward for testing. Conceptual truths are true by the relationship between words (e.g. the opposite of belief is not disbelief, which is a form of belief itself, but doubt), while hypotheses require empirical support. Conceptual truths can give rise to truisms, while selection of the right truism is often equated with wisdom.

FEELINGS

Bennett and Hacker take Damasio to task for talking as if feelings were private mental experiences that the individual can observe (Damasio 1994). They argue that to feel guilt, shame and so on is not to observe anything at all but simply to have the feelings. We may apply psychological attributes or properties to ourselves without evidential grounds (for example, we feel ill or depressed) but need to apply them to others on the basis of behavioral criteria (such as expressed inability to feel pleasure, changes in appetite, sleep patterns, low energy levels).

The authors claim the notion of feelings needs to be unpacked into:

- Sensations, for example feeling a pain
- Emotions, for example feeling angry
- Inclinations to act, for example in feeling like going out to dine
- Perceptions, for example feeling the leather chair in the dark
- Overall physical or psychological conditions, for example feeling contented.

To anyone studying consumer behavior these distinctions are not merely academic hair-splitting but can be crucial. It is an example of conceptual confusion to treat all feelings as being of the same nature.

Bennett and Hacker maintain that people do not express beliefs about their feelings on the basis of observing their own behavior as they can 'introspect' how things are and need not wait to hear what they have to say in order to find out what they think. This claim would seem to run counter to *self-perception theory* in psychology. It was argued earlier that on occasion we do infer our beliefs and our feelings from observing our reactions to certain events, just as one respondent said he discovered his patriotism only when the country's soldiers went to fight a war he personally had deplored. An emotional reaction tells us what concerns us and what concerns us might come as a surprise. How often have we all found ourselves moved by some event which tells us something about what we believe? Similarly the consumer may find her positive emotional response to seeing herself in a dress leads her to believe that this is perfect for her. But such cases may be infrequent exceptions to Bennett and Hacker's claim. On the whole, observing our own behavior is not the main source of our beliefs.

FALSE NOTIONS OF INTROSPECTION

Bennett and Hacker dismiss the notion of introspection being a sort of 'inner eye' into mental goings on, asserting that introspection is a form of reflexive thought, a way to self-knowledge, particularly about one's moods, feelings and emotions and in no way a form of perception. People cannot be said to have access to anything inner at all: we may say a person has pains but not that he has access to his pains. But whatever the nature of introspection, it is important in understanding others. Nicholas Humphrey (1983), an experimental psychologist at Cambridge, sees it as the foundation of folk psychology and thinking up hypotheses about human behavior:

> Without introspection to guide me, the task of deciphering the behavior of my fellow men would be quite beyond my powers.
>
> (Humphrey 1983: 33)

SENSATIONS AND PERCEPTIONS

Bennett and Hacker's discussion of sensation and perception is a demonstration of the usefulness of conceptual analysis. It is common to claim that perceiving entails having sensations; that sensation is an essential input to perception. In fact, the view of perception as a process (which Bennett and Hacker deny) claims the process consists of three steps: sensation ⇒selection⇒sense-making (interpretation)⇒perception. A view going back to the seventeenth century is that perception is the cause of all ideas and impressions. But we are not in fact conscious of any such mental processes but just assume they occur. It is true that this so-called process of perception is a logical one but this does not mean it represents distinct mental stages. It is once again a confusion of logic with psychology. Bennett and Hacker deny perception is a process, arguing that sensation is distinct from perception, while sense-making (interpretation) occurs only if the immediate perception raises doubts or questions about what is being sensed.

Of course, there are perceptual biases in that consumers are selective in what they see, hear, touch, feel and smell, while perceptions are very concept-dependent. In Gestalt psychology, the focus is mainly on perception and the rules by which forms or shapes are perceived as unitary wholes.

It was founded in Germany early in the nineteenth century (*Gestalt* is German for 'form' or 'shape'), with the claim that psychological phenomena are always viewed as organized wholes. Thus, according to the principle of closure, a figure will be seen as a square even if all four lines are not completed. We know we respond well to grouping so we like things that are similarly colored to go together. In systems theory we talk about *redundancy* which reflects this principle of closure: Gd Sv Th Q is immediately read as God Save the Queen. We are all familiar with the drawing of a woman who can be seen as either young or old but not both at the same time. Gestalt psychologists do not regard learning as primarily the result of association between stimuli and responses, as claimed by behaviorists, but as a result of insightfully reorganizing some whole. It is a psychology that views problem solving as a kind of perceptual process with the problem solver finally seeing the relationships between means and ends. If, in line with Bennett and Hacker, there is no process of perception but instant apprehension, it might be better to substitute 'insightful reflection' for perceptual processes. In other words we should distinguish 'insightful reflection' from perception since there is no perceptual process. Gestalt psychology recognizes the notion of changing perspectives and implicitly supports the notion that perspective affects perception. It is not unusual to come across the claim that Gestalt psychology has outlived its usefulness but it still has a role to play in the field of consumer behavior.

If a 'sensation' covers *things* like tickles, pains and twinges, and perception is of *qualities* such as colors, sounds, smells, tastes and entities we can touch, perceptual qualities cannot be sensations. Just to see an object per se is not to have any sort of sensation; seeing, for example, the red coloring of a Coca Cola bottle is not something that happens in the brain but in the supermarket or wherever. This is not to suggest that seeing something cannot arouse a sensation like a pain but that seeing is not intertwined with sensation. To have a sensation is not to perceive: perception is not involved in having a sensation. Objects perceived exist whether perceived or not, while a sensation occurs only when felt and, unlike a perception, it is as it is felt to be. There can be sensation in a perceptual organ as when our eyes are irritated but this has nothing to do with the exercise of a perceptual faculty.

This view of sensation as something distinct from the senses like seeing and hearing contrasts with one view expressed by Steven Pinker (2007) in claiming that language is 'notoriously poor, for instance, at conveying the subtlety and richness of sensations like smells and sounds' (p. 276). It is certainly true that language seems very inadequate for describing smells and sounds but this is not helped by regarding them as sensations. The appeal to the senses can change mood or emotions, just as the bagpipes can rally the troops in battle, the sense of smell can arouse memories, the sense of touch employed in touching clothing can be pleasing, while the consumer's sight is a major source of pleasure when looking at products and the environs. Marketers do appreciate this, but many of us believe that the exploitation of the senses in marketing still does not go far enough.

Sensations, whether internally or externally induced, typically give rise to behavior, just as an itch stimulates scratching. Sensations are hedonic in being either pleasant or unpleasant. On the other hand, perception bestows pleasure or displeasure. It is because perception produces pleasure or displeasure that there is a bias in perception towards that which gives pleasure and against that which gives displeasure. Skill in perception can be improved but it makes no sense to talk about acquiring skill in feeling sensations or even to talk about such feelings being incorrect: sensations are just as they are felt to be. Contrary to what is assumed, sensations do not involve any interpretive or inference process; neither are they the conclusions of unconscious inferences.

Perception is a primary source of knowledge and the senses involved in perception are cognitive faculties, crucial to knowledge acquisition. Given that the objects of perception are out there in the environment and not in our heads, it makes no sense to say that perceiving takes place in the brain. Of the five senses involved in the acquisition of knowledge, namely sight (recognition), hearing (distinguishing), taste (distinguishing), smell (detecting) and feel (discerning), only feel (tactile perception) is not confined to one organ. While we have eyes for sight, ears for hearing, palate for taste and nose for smell, perceiving something through feel can come from any part of the body. The product that appeals to all the senses has a better chance of creating the most pleasurable impact and being more desirable.

COGNITIVE POWERS

Bennett and Hacker reject any claim that knowledge is a 'mental' state; being in a state of anxiety can be interrupted but we cannot interrupt someone in 'knowing'. Yet in the consumer behavior literature, knowing is often spoken of as a mental state. 'Knowledge' instead is a kind of ability, making it possible to act on information. Abilities can be innate like the ability to breathe or acquired like the ability to read. 'Knowing how' to do something implies knowing the way to do something which means being able to distinguish between doing it correctly and incorrectly. The authors criticize philosopher Gilbert Ryle (who first talked about the difference between 'knowing that' and 'knowing how') for saying 'knowing how' is essentially different from 'knowing that' on the grounds that these are not so much different forms of knowledge as different forms which knowledge may take: to know how to do something is to know the way to do it and to know the way to do it is to 'know that' and so be able to say that it is done this way or that. This argument rests on the authors' claim that knowledge is a kind of ability and 'knowing that' and 'knowing how' are simply different forms of ability. This is a defensible claim but, even if accepted, the Ryle distinction is still very important. Ryle would not accept that 'knowing how' implies being able to say what is correct and incorrect. He might argue that a salesperson may be a superb salesperson but be unable to articulate, except at the broadest level, correct and incorrect selling tactics since in selling, as is common elsewhere, there are many different ways of 'knowing how', each equally as effective. On the other hand, we could know a good deal about the interpersonal influence process (knowing that) but not know how to put it into effect in selling (knowing how), since selling skills need to be *practiced*. Equally we may know 'how' without 'knowing that', just as we may 'know how' to ride a bicycle without being able to write down instructions that would allow a non-cyclist to read them and then be able to ride a bicycle.

One of the problems with courses on organizational behavior in business schools is that the focus is on 'knowing that' without practice in 'knowing how'. Cognitive psychologists do make a distinction between learning facts and the learning of a skill. As we learn a skill we become faster at it and also more precise while requiring less effort. On the other hand, we cannot practice rote-learning and expect to improve our minds by doing so in the way we improve the body through exercise.

Bennett and Hacker contend that it is false to maintain that, in remembering some fact (like a brand name), we are aware or conscious of remembering anything. In contrast, LeDoux in *The Emotional Brain* (1998) argues that to remember is to be conscious of some past experience. But, as the authors say, remembering need not be of anything past; what one remembers need not be an experience at all, while to remember feeling unwell last week is not to be conscious of feeling ill last week but to merely *know* that I was unwell then. Memory is *knowledge retained*, not knowledge stored in the brain (a notion going back to Plato) and it is confusing to claim that declarative memories (knowing that) and non-declarative memories (knowing how to do things) are stored in different brain areas, though it is correct to say that the capacity to remember various kinds of things is causally dependent on different areas of the brain and on the synaptic adjustments in these areas. Also, though memory consists of ability it is not ability for reproducing copies of antecedent images, impressions or ideas.

It is natural to suppose that, as we acquire knowledge, it is stored in the brain in the form of a representational image or at least an encoded description. But the metaphor of 'storage' must not be taken literally since it is an error to suppose that in order to remember we must have stored the facts in the brain since the neural storage of semantic images or representations makes no sense. How could a person look into his own brain and read some 'neuralize'? A neural causal correlate may occur but this is not a form of storing information nor does it need to involve any encoding. One only stores information if one writes it down but we cannot, except in the metaphorical sense, store information in the brain.

To remember a brand name is to be able to recognize that name and this implies *recognition ability*. Marketers need to do all they can to help their target audience to recognize the brand name. It is the neural prerequisites of this that requires research by cognitive scientists but talk of storing does not help. Memory is not a representation of what is remembered and neither is a belief a representation of what is believed. What would count as a neural representation of the remembered facts about a product? Remembering need in no way entail 'exciting' a brain trace to re-create a 'reproductive mnemonic experience' and there is no sense to the notion of our encoding or representing factual information in the neurons and synapses of the brain. The fact that neuroscientists have found that damage to the hippocampus deprives that individual of the ability to recollect for longer than thirty seconds anything that is later learned or experienced, simply suggests that the retention of certain synaptic connections and the creation of certain recurrent firing patterns are a necessary condition for a person to recall something. However, these synaptic connections and firing patterns cannot be claimed to represent memory or what is remembered. In any case, the notion of 'recall' is not unproblematic, in that people trying to recall may forget, fantasize and distort. This is true whether the recall is unaided or, as is often the case in market research, aided in the sense that some guidance is offered.

COGITATIVE POWERS

Cogitative powers of meditation or reflection cover belief, thought and imagination. Bennett and Hacker argue that *believing* applies to a person, not her brain and, while believing can be fervent and rigid, it cannot be right or wrong as beliefs themselves can be. Thinking does not always involve believing: we can engage in thinking but not believing and can be interrupted in thinking but not in believing.

The authors explicate different kinds of thinking: thinking as attending to the task at hand; thinking as intelligently engaging in an activity, adjusting to circumstances; thinking as intelligent speech; thinking as recollecting; thinking as a way of viewing an issue; thinking as reasoned problem solving; thinking as idle rumination and imagining. This wide variety of thinking is, they claim, ignored by neuroscientists, who concentrate on just one or perhaps two of these. Experimenters who use PET and fMRI technology try to identify the locus of thought in the brain, asking the subject to think of something, and then generalizing from the study to all thinking, while they seem oblivious to the different kinds of thinking. If findings from different studies do not cohere, it may simply be that different types of thinking are involved.

There is a connection between the *imagination* and the power to summon up visual or auditory images and it is appealing to think such images are the same as physical images, only mental. But, the authors argue, mental images are not necessary for imagining since we can just imagine descriptions of what it would be like, say, to go on a holiday to Rome. A powerful *imagination* is not the ability to conjure up striking images but an ability to think of unusual, unthought-of possibilities. The imagination is not a cognitive faculty concerned with truth or falsity but a cogitative faculty concerned with meditation or reflecting. The imagination is one attribute that distinguishes humans from other animals. But does a definition of imagination that embraces 'unthought-of possibilities' coincide with popular usage which would seem to accept imagination as able to 'conjure up striking images', as when we refer to the imagination of a child? Does not 'unthought-of possibilities' refer in fact to *creativity* or at least to a creative imagination?

The capacity to visualize or conjure up visual images is of considerable interest to neuroscientists as it seems to involve the excitation of the same neural system as would a visual experience. But seeing an object is not to form an image of it but simply to see it: what is perceived is not an image unless we are imagining the object. To talk of seeing something in the mind's eye is not to see at all but simply to visualize: imagining or recollecting it. It is true that one may recollect how many windows are in one's house by visualizing the house and each of its rooms and counting them but mental images are distinct from perceptions of the same thing as they do not occupy the same logical space. Cognitive scientists are wrong to characterize mental images as 'internal representations'; mental images are direct 'messages' without a medium. Mental images are not representations: to make a representation of how one visualizes something is to describe it as one imagines it. It is certainly not to conjure up any image.

BENNETT AND HACKER ON EMOTIONS

Emotions arise from the appraisal of people, events and attributes in terms of a person's concerns. As Bennett and Hacker say, such concerns may go beyond personal welfare. Typifying emotions are love, hope, fear, anger, indignation, resentment, envy, jealousy as well as the self-assessment emotions of pride, shame, humiliation, regret, remorse and guilt. The emotions link to beliefs, desires, aversions, volition, motivation, to the imagination and our fantasies. There is no single emotion that serves as a conceptual prototype for emotions in general.

The authors distinguish the *cause* of emotion from the *object* of the emotion. What a person is frightened *by* (such as a loud noise at night) is the cause of her fear but what one is frightened *of* (someone breaking into the house) is its object. Neuroscience does not distinguish the causes of emotion from the object of the emotion; though the cause of my anger is some insult, the object of my anger is some person. Emotions have specific objects (anger is directed at someone or something) and emotions are typically motives for action. In saying emotions specify motives, we are saying they indicate concerns and the type of beliefs at work.

Bennett and Hacker claim emotions like humility, respect, admiration, contempt and gratitude are not associated with emotional upsets. But is this really true? Would we classify these as emotions unless they were intense enough to prompt action? It is certainly true that we can be subject to each of these states, without any manifestation of emotion but it is also true that, if felt deeply, they have an emotional aspect.

Bennett and Hacker point to serious limitations in trying to understand human emotions by experimenting on (non-language using) animals (as in LeDoux's work). They deny emotions equate with either brain states or somatic reactions, even though both views are current. While brain states may be essential for feeling an emotion and somatic responses may characterize an emotion perturbation, they are not emotions per se. Wrongly, many neuroscientists like Damasio subscribe to the discredited James-Lange theory of emotions (summed up in the saying: 'We do not weep because we are sad but rather we are sad because we weep' – the application of the word emotion follows the physical event instead of the emotion resulting in the physical). As a consequence, neuroscientists neglect or ignore *emotional attitudes* (for example, *continuing* to feel proud of something) as well as the motivation and cogitative aspects of emotions. This concept of 'emotional attitudes' is new to the literature on emotion but it echoes the distinction between 'standing wants' and 'occurrent wants' (Goldman 1970). Standing wants, like emotional attitudes, reflect permanent or semi-permanent dispositions, while occurrent wants, like emotions that are not emotional attitudes, are those that reflect existing circumstances such as a want for a taxi to get to the airport. Sellers should seek to establish among the target audience an emotional attitude towards their brand and to have a standing want for it.

Damasio and LeDoux, in line with the James-Lange theory, distinguish emotion from feeling an emotion, claiming an emotion is a *bodily response* to a mental image and the feeling of emotion is a *cognitive* response to that bodily condition. For Damasio, an emotion is a collection of changes in body states, linked to particular mental images that have activated part of the brain system. This distinction between 'having and feeling' an emotion is denied by Bennett and Hacker and the reasoning that lies behind it: feeling an emotion, they claim, is not a cognitive response to a bodily condition as feelings of emotion are not about the body but about the *object* of the emotion. This seems the more defensible position.

Damasio's somatic marker thesis refers to the emotional gut reaction that arises from highly positive or negative appraisals: 'somatic' because it relates to bodily feelings and a 'marker' because it marks the receipt of an image. This is misconceived according to the authors in that it suggests emotions are somatic images that tell us what is good and bad. But bodily reactions are not ersatz guides to what to do and do not inform us about good and evil. This distorts what Damasio is saying. Damasio does not use 'good' and 'bad' in the ethical sense of good and evil, but in respect to consequences that can be good or bad in terms of what concerns us; ethical issues being just one of our concerns. Terms like 'good' and 'bad' have an evaluative meaning and a descriptive meaning and the descriptive meaning varies with subject, just as a good wine is different from talking about a good book. What constitutes a good car is not the same as what constitutes a good haircut or a good computer, so the criteria of 'good' will differ from product to product and even, within limits, among buyers themselves. Even within a market segment consumers will vary in what they want and sellers exploit this when positioning their own brand within the segment and (hopefully) in the mind of the consumer.

Continuing to stress the distinction between the cause and the object of emotion, Bennett and Hacker argue that Damasio's view is flawed on the grounds that emotion cannot be individuated by somatic changes caused by the thought about an object since there is a need to take account of the appropriate objects of the relevant emotions, just as something dangerous and threatening is the object of the emotion of fear. This is so; emotions cannot be distinguished and labeled on the basis of somatic markers. But Damasio does not claim that somatic markers distinguish (individuate) all the various emotions but that somatic markers separate incoming images into liked or disliked as a basis for decision: negative somatic markers set off alarm bells, while positive somatic markers encourage action in line with the positive (unconscious) appraisal.

In further attacking the Damasio position, Bennett and Hacker claim that somatic changes do not always follow negative/positive appraisals in that, for example, thinking the rate of inflation is likely to rise may involve no somatic changes in spite of the fear that inflation will occur. This is hardly convincing. Damasio is talking about the recognition/response phenomena that bypasses consciousness, not what occurs after reflection. Indeed there can be just recognition and purchase response as occurs in what we call impulse buying. In any case, whether a person experiences the emotion of fear depends on:

- The perceived severity and nearness of the threat
- The perceived probability that the threat will occur
- The perceived ability of coping behavior to remove the threat
- The perceived ability to carry out the coping behavior.

As a result we can be *fearful* of inflation but not experience the emotion of *fear*.

CATEGORIES OF ACTION

For Bennett and Hacker, volitional categories of action (i.e. those that are 'willed') can be voluntary, involuntary and non-voluntary; intentional and unintentional, deliberate or impulsive; attentive and careless. A fully voluntary action is an action a person controls from its inception to its continuation and termination. Actions such as the expressive gestures made with the hands as one talks are voluntary without being intentional, while actions can be voluntary which throw up consequences that were not intended. These distinctions can be important. Non-voluntary is distinguished from involuntary behavior like the automatic reflex because non-voluntary action can be the result of external pressures, like adhering reluctantly to the office dress code. Involuntary action can occur such as turning away when we watch ads on television that are just annoying and irrelevant to what we see ourselves as buying.

DOES ACTION BEGIN BEFORE CONSCIOUSNESS OF IT?

A recent claim is that all voluntary action begins in the brain independently of any relevant conscious acts of volition. Libet's (1993) work is the main reference. He conceives voluntary action (erroneously according to Bennett and Hacker) as bodily movement caused by an act of volition and concludes that such antecedent volition is started by the brain ahead of any conscious awareness of a desire to move. Libet thus views voluntary control as restricted to inhibiting or permitting movement that is already ongoing. The authors say this assertion is confused since it is not necessary for an act to be voluntary for it to be preceded by a feeling of desiring, wanting or intending or by any urge to do it. It is also not necessary for a person to think of himself as having moved involuntarily just because he moves without feeling an urge to move or feeling a desire to move. As a person begins to type he or she feels no urges, desires or intentions. While I can say whether my movements are voluntary or involuntary, the grounds would not relate to my feeling some urge, desire and intention before making a move.

If the consumer acts to buy a certain product, because she feels an urge to do so, this 'because' is not causal. Libet, it is argued, misconceives the nature of voluntary action:

> The fact that the neurons in the supplementary motor cortex fire 350 ms before the feeling is allegedly apprehended does not show that the brain 'unconsciously decided' to move before the agent did. It merely shows that the neuronal processes that activate the muscles began before the time at which the agent reported a 'feeling of desire' or 'feeling an urge to move' to have occurred. But, to repeat, a voluntary movement is not a movement caused by a felt urge, any more than to refrain voluntarily from moving is to feel an urge not to move which prevents one from moving.
>
> (Bennett and Hacker 2003: 230)

This quote is also a blow to those in consumer behavior who still persist in talking about wants arising from equilibrium imbalance or a feeling of discomfort.

When the consumer shops, there is no requirement that 'she *feel* an intention' (there is no such thing) nor does she necessarily need to 'feel a desire' but simply to act in accordance with her overall shopping plan with the ongoing movements she makes being accordingly voluntary and intentional. There is a faint echo here of the consumer switched to automatic pilot.

CONSCIOUSNESS

Bennett and Hacker remind us that saying the brain is conscious only makes sense in a synecdochical (synecdoche = part used to represent the whole) use of words as consciousness is not something that can be ascribed to the brain but applies only to the individual: one sees with one's eyes but one is not conscious with one's brain. We judge a person conscious, not by looking at or into his brain but by his responses to his environment. While the brain itself is necessary to consciousness as oxygen is to fire, the brain neither perceives nor fails to perceive things in the environment. Being conscious of something amounts to becoming conscious of that something and being conscious of that something can be equated with getting knowledge.

Consciousness can be transitive or intransitive. *Intransitive* consciousness has no object at all but simply implies being awake as opposed to being unconscious or asleep. Intransitive consciousness receives much attention in discussions on consciousness. In contrast, *transitive* consciousness is neglected. Transitive consciousness is conscious that something is this or that, so we can speak of perceptual, somatic and affective consciousness.

- *Perceptual* consciousness, as occurs in being conscious of the sound of music. Only those things we perceive and realize we perceive are objects of which we are conscious. We are not conscious of many things we see. Much of what we see we hardly notice, never mind paying attention to it. This is true of most of the ads we see. Getting attention recognizes the need not just for awareness but *conscious* awareness of the ad. Where there is consciousness there will be awareness of some sort but not necessarily awareness of what we want the consumer to be aware of. Awareness is a state whereby some mental content is available for verbal report but the advertiser wants that mental content to relate to his ad.
- *Somatic* consciousness refers to being conscious of sensations like pain, not objects perceived. On the other hand, there is no difference between feeling a sensation like pain and being conscious of a pain: feeling implies consciousness. This means an ad aimed at arousing the emotions generates feeling and feeling requires consciousness.
- *Affective* consciousness covers emotion and mood where emotion may erupt with only conscious recognition of it at the time. This means we may not be aware that an ad, a product or a person has aroused us emotionally so just asking someone about whether something has been emotionally arousing could be misleading. If this is so, it is important since a good deal of research on emotion assumes subjects do know of an emotion erupting.

As with other mental states, we can speak of transitive consciousness being dispositional or occurrent. Occurrent transitive consciousness implies being *currently* conscious of the object (e.g. a high price) as opposed to a dispositional transitive consciousness which implies being predisposed to being continually conscious of the object (of high prices). To say Richard is angry is to describe a temporary (occurrent) state, as opposed to saying Richard is an introvert which is a dispositional state.

In consumer behavior we would like to identify *dispositional transitive consciousness*, whether about prices or anything else, since the presence of a dispositional transitive consciousness makes it easier to get attention. The consumer is primed to pay attention. Because we cannot be conscious of many things simultaneously, nor remain conscious of things which no longer concern us, there is always a problem of getting attention to what we say, do or advertise. In looking back at old commercials and print ads, there is no doubt that tactics for getting attention have become much more effective. Sometimes we talk mistakenly of factors that shape the process of perception, like stimulus characteristics, when what we are really talking about are things that get the consumer's attention. There is no process of perception.

Marketers err when they talk of 'arousing awareness' and would be better off speaking (as other disciplines do) of *raising consciousness* since people may be aware of many things around them but not conscious of any of them: being 'conscious of' includes both 'awareness' and 'reflecting on'. The viewer is aware of the many ads that appear on television but not conscious of many of them. This is particularly so, given the advent of multitasking where the viewer can be watching television while at the same time reading a newspaper or magazine, talking on the phone or even surfing the net. We cannot give equal attention to all, so the problem is, as the media world says, how to get the viewer 'engaged', which captures the notion of getting the viewer's attention. To be perceptually conscious of some product, the product must catch and hold our attention. Even if the ad engages our attention, it is common for it to be remembered but not the brand being advertised. This is encouraged by creating ads that could just as easily be an ad for a rival's brand. Over-concern with tactics to attract attention can get the tactic remembered but not the brand and what it can do to enrich our lives.

CONSCIOUSNESS, CONSCIOUS EXPERIENCE AND MENTAL STATES

Extending the concept of consciousness to all perception, as many cognitive scientists do, with all uses of the term 'perceiving' characterized as 'experience', the question becomes: how can happenings in a material world create something as distinct from matter as experience? This question has led to a focus in neuroscience on conscious experience or the mental state of a person while conscious. Yet, as Bennett and Hacker say, many psychological attributes cannot be categorized as forms of conscious experience: attributes like thinking, knowing and believing. In any case, a 'conscious experience' is not an experience with the property of being conscious; it is the person who has the experience who is conscious and conscious of the experience, with that experience embracing not just what is perceived but sensations and emotions as well. Bennett and Hacker reject the notion that all cases of perceiving something are necessarily cases of being conscious of that something (i.e. being aware and reflecting on that something), while that of which we become conscious is an object, not in fact a subject of consciousness.

The authors distinguish 'beliefs' from 'what is believed' in that I can *passionately* believe that H.P. printers are the best on the market but I cannot say that what I believe is passionate. The concept of an unconscious belief, as commonly described, is misconceived in that a so-called unconscious belief is simply something I believe but am unwilling to acknowledge to myself or to others. It is wrong thus to view beliefs not currently present in the mind as 'unconscious' beliefs. Another misuse of 'unconscious' occurs in talking of the activities of the brain as being 'unconscious'. The work of the brain is not done consciously, nor can it be said that the work of the brain is done unconsciously, for the brain is not a conscious creature with the capacity to be conscious. It is the individual who can be said to do things consciously or unconsciously. Many things we do (as shoppers) can be carried out without thought. However, this does not imply that the conscious thinking that would be needed for a novice is the same thinking that also goes on 'unconsciously' for the non-novice; it need not go on at all since the relevant skill has been acquired – just as an adult who has the established synaptic connections in the brain in place can take in a sentence at a time without talk of things happening unconsciously.

QUALIA OR THE PHENOMENAL ASPECTS OF EXPERIENCE

Qualia is a term used to cover *qualitative* conscious states. The experiential qualitative properties of sensations, feelings, perceptions, thoughts and desires are referred to in the literature as *qualia*. Qualia are the phenomenal or subjective aspects of experiences though we have no distinct language for describing qualia or these phenomenal qualities. We are all familiar with the convoluted language used to describe the qualities of wine. Although, say, sweetness is a distinct sort of sensation there is very little to say about it except to compare it with the sweetness of some other product. We might say something has the smell of roses or ammonia, being unable to describe any intrinsic properties. Because enjoyment is an experience that is an end in itself, we can do no more than state the type of enjoyment it was, such as saying it was exciting or thrilling. This has been a limitation for determining what the consumer seeks in terms of enjoyment or pleasure.

As we have seen, consciousness is usually conceived in terms of having qualia, though for Bennett and Hacker this is in error. In fact it is the psychological (as opposed to the phenomenal) aspects of mind that have been of most interest, topics such as awareness, attention and self-consciousness, not what has been called the *phenomenal consciousness* that covers subjective experience or qualia. We often ask others how some experience felt on the assumption that every experience has a distinct qualitative (phenomenal) quality. This is not always so. How does it feel to believe in Pythagoras's theorem? There are instances where there is this qualitative feel to experience, as when a born-blind person can suddenly see, or the experience is novel, or experiences are contrasting, or we are experiencing the sensation of pain, but it would be odd to ask a person how it feels to see a mundane article like a kitchen table.

It is not true that every experience has a different qualitative feel to it and it is also not true that the difference between products can always be stated in terms of 'feel'. The difference between products is seldom that product A feels different from product B: does the house insurance policy feel different to the title deeds to the house? For the vast range of things that come under the rubric of experience, there isn't any 'way it feels' to have them. Rival products in the same segment may have differences but this does not necessarily mean different qualitative feelings. A person may see a number of products without any of them evoking any feeling at all. While every experience has the potential to evoke a negative or positive attitudinal response, it is false to claim that this is true of all experiences. Experiences are distinguished by what they are experiences *of*, not by reference to how they feel. Consumers differ among themselves too much to distinguish products by the feel of the reaction (if there is any at all). The qualitative character of my experience on seeing the same new make of car may be different from that of my friend in that I find the car exciting and my friend finds it pedestrian, but it can also happen that both of us like the car equally. If, however, I have had no experience with a particular car, the experiences of my friend with that make of car are highly likely to have an effect on how I myself will experience the car. Just to know that one's friend has enjoyed a film is an important factor in how you will enjoy the film.

All this is another reason why word-of-mouth can be so important. And companies know it. Procter & Gamble's Vocalpoint program employs 600,000 mothers across the US, within the age group twenty-eight to forty-five, to spread the word about new products to others. These are not a random group of women but women selected because they belong to a social network, talking to twenty-five to thirty other women a day in contrast to the average mother who talks to only about five. The mothers are recruited through banner ads on Internet sites such as iVillage and referrals, and are paid by way of samples. It seems to be effective in that sales of Dawn in test markets using Vocalpoint were double when compared with markets not using Vocalpoint (Berner 2006).

The character of an experience is often said to be indescribable. As Bennett and Hacker say, this requires being unpacked if we are to investigate the consumer's experience since we need to:

- Distinguish between the object of the experience (such as the new car) and the properties of the object of the experience (qualities of the car)
- Describe those properties (qualities or attributes) of the experience (on seeing the new car)
- Distinguish a description of the experience from describing the qualities of the experience.

If there is a hedonic tone to the experience we can describe that tone, for example saying things about the new car that gave pleasure or enjoyment. But as the authors point out, this is not what people usually mean when they say an experience is indescribable. What is meant is the difficulty of describing the attributes (properties, qualities) of the objects of experience. We can talk about enjoying a film in terms of its being exciting but not about the nature of the excitement, no more than we can describe the different aromas of coffee. This is because the form of description being demanded is inapplicable to the characterization of qualities of things such as their smell or taste.

Describing a material object is to describe its properties (qualities, attributes) but this is not open to us when describing the properties themselves. We can describe a coffee as dense and rich but we cannot go further to describe the qualities of these properties. Or we say the coffee has a delightful smell but cannot describe the smell itself, except by comparison with something else. Hence the description of anything is never a perfect substitute for the experience itself. This is important for marketing since it points to the limitations of description. The finest description of driving that new car will never substitute for the actual experience of driving the car itself (and car manufacturers know this). We try to project what the properties of a product have to offer by providing consumers with a sample (for example, of the food product), by showing the reactions of consumers on consuming or using the product. If we do not recognize all of this, we find ourselves struggling to describe the qualities of a property, which is a non-starter.

Perceptual qualities such as sound, smell and taste are defined and understood by reference to *public* samples and these samples become the standard for the correct use of a word expressing a perceptual quality. The public samples are needed in promoting perceptual qualities. In contrast, *sensation concepts* such as pain cannot be defined by reference to public samples but are learned and understood as extensions of natural behavior in response to pain, tickles and itches. Illustrations of the appropriate behavior are needed, for example in promoting a product that relieves such sensations. This is often forgotten. These sensation concepts are what the authors called Janus-faced in that you can know personally when you are in pain but can only know that others are in pain by assessing their public behavior.

What all this means is that if we are to establish meaningful correlations between a person's perceptual experiences and neural events, there is a presupposition that we have established:

- Exactly what people perceive
- Whether different people perceive the same thing in the same way.

Even then, the differences that show up in *neural* events will demonstrate simply that there is diversity in the neural events in different people, corresponding to their exposure to what might be the same stimulus: it will not demonstrate that these different people see things differently.

As was said earlier, to see a Coca-Cola bottle on the store shelf is not to see an image of the bottle in the mind as there is no image of the bottle appearing in the brain or anywhere else: one only sees an image if one is looking at an image of the bottle in an ad or when one vividly imagines the bottle. The discoveries in visual theory explain the neural processes that are required for an individual to see, not for the brain to see – and these explanations do not bridge any gap between brain processes and consciousness for there is no such gap to bridge. The neural factors and processes that form the causal background for perception are not perceptible to us. The neural processes that underlie perception do not constitute any process of perception: as soon as one has seen, one has seen.

It is often said that much of what the brain does is hidden from consciousness when (neurological experiments being an exception) all that our brains do is hidden from consciousness. There is no such thing as being conscious of one's consciousness but merely our being conscious of something specific.

SELF-CONSCIOUSNESS AND TALK ABOUT SELF AND EGO

The concept of 'self-consciousness', Bennett and Hacker argue, can be used in several senses:

- Being embarrassed about the attention of others
- Being deliberative
- Being introspective as to one's attitudes, motives or reactions to some event.

There is a need to state which of these we are talking about. Self-consciousness does not refer to consciousness of self but either to the introspective person or to a person's ability to reflect and take into account his thinking and facts about himself.

The authors criticize the way the term 'an ego' is used in psychology. *Ego* is one of the most widely used terms in social science as we talk about ego-centric, egoist, egocentrism, ego-boosters, ego-defensive motives, ego-ideal, alter-ego, ego-likeness and even the ego-depletion theory of self-control. Ego itself is used in several senses:

- The central core of a person's being, around which all psychic activities revolve
- The 'self' with which an individual is most concerned and which constitutes the self-interested part of one's personality
- The psychoanalytic theory sense in that Freud talked of the ego as the realistic part of the mind, having to deal with demands of the pleasure-seeking 'id' and the puritanical 'superego'.

Bennett and Hacker attack talk of 'an ego' or 'a self' on the grounds that the subject of experience is not some entity dominated by the 'I' or 'self' but the living human being. They agree, however, that much talk about self is fairly innocuous as in 'my former self' or my 'sense of self' but they object to the concept of 'a self', conceived as an inner subject and owner of experience. This all relates back to their accusation of the mereological fallacy. The self is identical with me and not some entity which I am alleged to have: to speak of myself is not to refer to some self whom I have but simply to speak of the human being I am.

Bennett and Hacker would reject the concept of 'a self' as a fruitful hypothetical construct on the grounds that it misdirects inquiries. Asking about a person's 'true self' or the inner search for self, presupposes we have a conception of what would count as having found that self. We don't. This is valid criticism. However, within the 'language games' in which the term ego or self is used, it is simply drawing attention to that self-interested, status-conscious, emotionally vulnerable side of our nature. This practice is legitimate.

Philosophers do debate whether there is such a thing as 'self', though Descartes believed it was the one thing of which we could be certain. Some argue, as do Bennett and Hacker, that the notion of 'a self' is an illusion since it simply refers to the publicly observable human being and nothing more. As for the 'self' or 'ego' being the core of one's being, this would suggest belief in the persistence of the same self over time when in fact our subjective experience does not suggest it need exist beyond the immediate present (Strawson 2009). For Strawson, there is really no point in inventing the hypothetical construct of 'a self' since it is in no way distinct from 'human being': only human beings persist in time and are subject to a constantly changing sequence of experiences. But social scientists have found it useful to distinguish between the sense of 'I' that refers to the inner subject and the 'I' that refers to the observable person. Strawson we suspect leans towards a positivist view that would reject all hypothetical constructs that cannot be defined in observational language.

In answer to those cognitive neuroscientists and some philosophers who claim that all mental states, events and processes can be reduced to neural states, events and processes, Bennett and Hacker maintain that minds are not made of anything since all talk of mind is a way of talking about the specific *human capacities* of thought, memory and will and the exercise of these capacities: we are no more a collection of cells than a painting is a collection of brush strokes and no amount of neural knowledge will be sufficient to discriminate between copying one's name, forging a name, signing a check and so forth. There are no correspondence rules for identifying what someone believes with some corresponding set of specific neural conditions – or that people believing the same thing cannot have different neural structures.

Consistent with this position, the authors reject the reductionist position that there will be an *eliminative reduction* of psychological explanations of human behavior by reducing such explanations to neuroscientific theory. And they firmly reject the claim that psychological concepts are vacuous, fictitious entities, to be relegated to the dustbin of history along with concepts like phlogiston. If this were in fact true the subject matter of psychology would not exist, no more than there could be a *scientific* study of witchcraft when there are no witches or, alternatively, of ghosts when there are no ghosts.

As Bennett and Hacker say, nothing in the real world answers to the concept of phlogiston but it is just not true that nothing answers to our ordinary psychological concepts as there are criteria for the use of psychological constructs, as there are even for folk psychology concepts, and these criteria are met daily in our lives. Nonetheless, psychological hypothetical constructs are not concepts of imperceptible real entities, like genes or viruses. They are in fact not concepts of entities or kinds of things at all since beliefs, thoughts, hopes, fears, expectations and so on are abstractions from believings, thinkings, hopings, fearings and expectings – and often these things are observable, as when we hear a person's beliefs as he expresses them. We need no theory, folk theories or psychological theories to hear or read the expressed thoughts of others.

Bennett and Hacker criticize those who claim ethnopsychology (folk psychology) is trying or claiming to state laws. To say 'people who suffer a sharp pain wince' is not to state any causal law but is simply a logical criterion for being in pain (it is a type of pain behavior). Even saying injury causes pain or being denied food for any length of time results in hunger are dubious candidates for being laws since injury is simply a circumstance in which pain-behavior is a criterion of pain, while the deprivation of food is a situation in which the desire for food is a sign of hunger. Furthermore, to say 'angry people tend to get impatient' is merely a characterization of one form that anger can take: anger is not the cause of impatience but is something that manifests itself in impatience. If we accept this clarification as valid, it avoids some of the debates in the buyer behavior literature. Readers will recognize that there is an echo here of the earlier discussion on conceptual truths.

REASONS VERSUS CAUSES

Bennett and Hacker hold the position that the relation between reasons and action is conceptual and not causal. This is an important debate in the philosophy of science since accepting that reasons are causes is a triumph for the philosophy of *naturalism* which regards the natural world as the whole of reality for scientific purposes and limits knowledge to natural events and causal relationships. It is argued that everything can be explained in physical terms. In opposition, some philosophers have argued that there can be no explanation in purely physical terms for the emergence of conscious experience or that phenomenal feel.

Neuroscientists, the authors argue, are in error in supposing human action is caused by volitions, intentions or decisions. Wanting, intending and deciding are not causes of action or bodily movements. This is not to suggest that we do not take action because we want to and believe it is right. The important point is that this 'because' is not causal. If it were, action would occur without doing anything else but reaching a decision based on wants and beliefs. Specifying the relevant wants and beliefs gives reasons for acting and is not the cause of anything done voluntarily. Beliefs inform our expectations as to what the world is like, while wants tell us about how we would like the world to be. Reason-giving explanations work by explaining human action, by quoting the wants and beliefs and the reasoning people go through. Rational explanations view behavior as goal-directed. Such goal-ascription explanations are teleological in that they specify the action's purpose to account for it. Voluntary actions like buying are goal-directed in that such actions create conditions for bringing about the buyer's goal or removing the conditions that are impeding the realization of the goal. In contrast, neuroscience explanations are likely to quote the neural conditions for behavior. But neuroscience, it is argued, explains incapacitation, not normal behavior.

Bennett and Hacker claim the connection between reasons and action is conceptual (not causal) since to grasp the connection is not to understand any law-like generalization but simply to grasp the concepts of belief, want, intention and action. The reason-giving explanation applies to practical reasoning whereby people typically do what they have good reasons for doing. Even empirical psychology, though it undeniably throws light on various elements of human behavior, supplements but does not displace ordinary explanations of human behavior and the same applies to neuroscience. We only have to listen to the defense and prosecution in a court of law or the ordinary conversation of social scientists to see how behavior is normally explained.

When a consumer justifies her purchase in saying she desired to perform function X (cleaning clothes) and believed brand Y (Tide) was best for performing that function and hence she bought it, this may on occasion be an *ex post facto* reconstruction to justify to others the buying of Y (Tide). What may have actually happened is that she just liked Y (Tide) best so practical reasoning was simply embarked upon to justify what she intended to do anyway. This can indeed happen on occasion though the actual incidence is unknown. As Ruth Millikan (2004) states:

> Just as in mathematical reasoning you are likely to start with something you would like to prove, in practical reasoning you begin with something you would like to do or to have done and then attempt to construct something like a proof, a path from premises you have to a conclusion you would like to reach. And you do this largely by controlled trial and error. You start with what you would like to prove and work backward, trying to find plausible steps that might lead to that conclusion, and you start also with things you already know to be true and work forward to see where these things might lead.
>
> (Millikan 2004: 205)

Sehon (2005) agrees that reason-giving explanations are not causal but teleological (purposive), simply giving the purpose or goal of the behavior without reference to any causal antecedents. As a consequence, they are answering a different question from one focusing on causes of behavior. This brings us back to the claim that different paradigms and methodologies are associated with answering different questions. But the position espoused by Bennett and Hacker, Sehon and many others is controversial in philosophy. In fact Brown (2001), a philosopher of science, argues that philosophers generally hold that 'reasons are causes' and reason explanations are 'causal explanations' of action (p. 152). Fay's view on reasons as causes is more nuanced than Brown's (Fay 1996). He argues, in line with Bennett and Hacker, that reasons in themselves cannot possibly be the cause of anything as the content of thought is neither a state, nor an event, nor a process. Those who argue like this usually go on to claim reasons are simply *justifications* for action. But Fay does not go down this route, arguing that the real (causal) reasons for action must be understood to mean the *practical reasoning process* that prompted (caused) the person to act. He agrees that the reasoning process that causes the person to act may not always be conscious or amenable to recall or even capable of verbalization. This is an original approach that needs thinking about. Not being 'amenable to recall' is recognized in marketing and acknowledged when we say respondents may rationalize when the real reasons are lost in time.

In accepting that there is no 'unvarnished' view of the world, we have slipped, according to Bennett and Hacker, into accepting that all observation is theory-laden. As the authors say, this is false since to observe, say, that there is a car in the road is not theory-laden. Most of our observations are of this nature. They are not theory-laden but it could be claimed that they are concept-dependent. The concepts we possess limit somewhat what we perceive.

A relevant notion here is that of consumer optimism as measured by The Conference Board's consumer confidence index in the US. This has proved to be a useful index for forecasting the level of consumer spending. There is a relationship between consumer optimism and consumer spending, suggesting consumer optimism might act as a causal contributory factor. But for full understanding we would need to go further to reveal the practical reasoning processes of the optimistic versus the pessimistic consumer. We seldom do spell out the practical reasoning or the causal chain even when much depends on it. For example, a current position in politics is that a reduction in the deficit by Congress or Parliament will so stimulate business and consumer optimism that spending will increase and the unemployment problem disappear. This claim has become a mantra based more on faith than on evidence. It was John Maynard Keynes who once said that those who tell us that the path of escape is to be found in strict economy ... are the voices of fools and madmen. But Keynes is an example of how ideas (in his *The General Theory of Employment, Interest and Money*) can follow a life cycle in once being popular and later suffering a steep decline and, something we forget about products, then being resurrected at another time. Governments gave up on the Keynesian notion that it was possible to secure both growth and full employment by keeping purchasing power in circulation. Friedrich Hayek with his free market ideas displaced Keynes though the recent financial meltdown has led to a revival of Keynes (Wapshott 2011).

COMMENT ON THE BENNETT AND HACKER CONTRIBUTION

Bennett and Hacker offer a different perspective on many issues in neuroscience and in the process review some key claims in cognitive neuroscience. Their conclusions arise from an application of conceptual analysis. But on the basis of conceptual analysis alone, it is difficult to see how these criticisms could be made so assertively: it is not always easy to distinguish the purely logical from what might demand empirical support. The answer lies in the substantial knowledge of the current state of cognitive neuroscience displayed in their book. Not surprising since Bennett is a neuroscientist.

Traditionally, conceptual analysis has been viewed as analogous to geometry in that it exercises reason alone. But Quine (1953), the Harvard philosopher, attacks the sharp distinction made between truths of fact justified by observation and conceptual truths justified by logic alone. There is no incontestable distinction between analytic (linguistic/conceptual/definitional) truth and truth about matters of fact (synthetic/contingent truth). To Quine there are no analytic statements (definitional or conceptual truths) that in principle could *never* be rejected in the light of future knowledge. This is logically so, but what might be logically true may be too rare to matter. Many philosophers deny the universality of the Quine claim, while Kripke has put forward the notion of 'necessity' to vindicate conceptual analysis (Hughes 2004). In line with Kripke, we no longer equate necessary propositions with purely conceptual (linguistic) propositions but substitute a more metaphysical account of necessity so we identify *necessarily true statements* with those that would be true in every possible world and necessarily false propositions with those that would be false in every possible world. This approach would give us a non-conceptual notion of necessity. To many this whole debate seems to be academic hair-splitting in that most concepts are not in any immediate danger of being superseded and certainly not during the stage of conceptual analysis.

ANOTHER VIEW OF NEUROSCIENCE

It is interesting to see how Kagan (2006), after his retirement from Harvard, views neuroscience in his survey of academic psychology over the last fifty years. Kagan does not equate mind with brain and argues that a complete understanding of the brain is not synonymous with a full understanding of mind. Reminding us that when he started his career, behaviorism and

Freudianism were in the ascendancy, he points out that, while behavior-ism vastly underestimated the limits biology places on our being able to engineer desired behaviors and could not explain human language skills, Freudian analysis tends to be too speculative and vague. Both survived because, he claims, they fitted the perspective or preconceptions researchers had of what a scientific account of mind should look like. But it is Kagan's views on neuroscience that are of interest.

Kagan's review of cognitive neuroscience is highly pertinent. As he says, traditional psychological puzzles in neuroscience are being reduced to asking: 'What is happening in the brain when language, memory and decisions are ongoing processes?' He is highly critical of the many claims made. Kagan mentions an article in the official journal of the Royal Society in the UK which offered the prediction that one day scientists will be able to identify the particular brain state that precedes each freely willed decision or action. Kagan dismisses this claim, arguing there cannot be a unique brain state across all individuals that precedes 'the selection of a salad over a soup'. Just because every decision arises from brain activity, it does not necessarily follow that a specific psychological state correlates with a distinct brain activity. The evidence does not support the notion that particular mental states are tied to fixed places in the brain, though some scientists persist in research that presupposes otherwise. Although seeing a human face almost invariably activates a cortical site in the posterior part of the brain, namely the fusiform gyrus, a picture of a spider will also activate this site if the person is afraid of spiders, while even photographs of cars will activate the site for those who love cars. Any set of brain characteristics permits more than just one inference as to psychological state. Pictures of angry faces, unexpected but desirable events, as well as an attractive nude, all produce similar patterns of activation in the amygdala and other parts of the brain. This should be borne in mind when we read claims that suggest that a certain activation of one location in the brain is tied to just one interpretation of the stimulus.

Thus Kagan states:

> Reflection on all the evidence reveals that the primary cause of amygdala activation is an unexpected event whether snake or a friend not seen for years.

> (Kagan 2006: 92)

If a brain site does not give rise to increased activity in reacting to some stimulus, this does not prove that it did not enter into the person's reaction since inhibition of the site may be part of the reaction. Kagan is insistent that a more accurate understanding of the relationship between brain and mind will depend on the acceptance that such relationships are always dependent on the context in which the individual is acting. But if the notion of *context* includes not just situation but consumer attributes and the nature of the stimulus, this makes following Kagan's advice a very tall order. In any case, the varying contextual factors are what make the very possibility of discovering universal laws, as in physics, a mirage for social science.

REDUCTIONISM (AGAIN)

Reducing psychological states to neurological brain states falls under 'reductionism'. As stated earlier, Bennett and Hacker are critical of both the desirability and feasibility of reductionism. Interestingly, so is Gazzaniga, that pioneer of neuroscience, who argues that, while the brain enables the mind, mental activity is not reducible to neural events. Similarly, Kagan points out that the dream (fantasy?) of reducing psychological states and behavior to the activity of 'tiny' neurons emerged a century ago. But if there is reductionism in the natural sciences, why can we not reduce psychology to neuroscience? That this may be feasible is what motivates those seeking to attribute psychological states to profiles of brain activity, implying that the brain state is a proxy for the psychological state. Kagan argues that distinct terminology for mind and brain states will always be necessary because everything has both a referential-meaning and a sense-meaning. Referential-meaning is the thing to which the item (brand) refers, while the sense-meaning is all the thoughts that are evoked by the name. These thoughts will consist of the patterns of associations that define the product and distinguish the brand. Not surprisingly, sense-meanings differ widely among individuals (think of the many sense-meanings of the word Conservative or Liberal) and for the same individual depending on context.

It is in fact not possible to use measures of brain activity as a proxy for, say, states of fear or anxiety since there are multiple forms of these emotional states. This does not mean Kagan dismisses biological material in order to keep psychology from vanishing into neuroscience. He agrees that adding biological information on brain activity can add to a more profound understanding of behavior in that brain measures may one day provide some notion of the meaningfulness of different brain patterns. But how to translate a biological measure into a meaningful psychological one is a major hurdle. And he insists that people do have freedom to decide and that their decision is not knowable from measurements of their brains.

Kagan is acutely conscious of how the prevailing *zeitgeist* determines whether ideas are accepted. Thus he argues that behaviorism took hold because politically liberal Americans were disposed to believe that *experience* was the sculptor of development. Similarly, the Freudian perspective was welcome because, with the availability of contraceptives, people felt freer about their sexuality. In describing the discomfort of guilt or shame as simply arising from a conflict between the id and superego that could be erased by psychoanalysis, people had a sense of liberation. Kagan even attributes a prize he won in psychology to a popular desire to believe his thesis about the preservation of personality traits from childhood to adulthood. Also, the same zeitgeist may be the source and support of our current dominant paradigms because they fit the historical moment.

NEUROSCIENCE AND DECISION-MAKING

Jonah Lehrer (2009) makes many insightful comments on neuroscience and decision-making in marketing. He introduces the concepts of 'negativity bias' and 'loss aversion'. *Negativity bias* covers the propensity of the human brain to register negative information more strongly than positive information. This reinforces the finding that negative information about a brand takes a long time to overcome so a company should avoid tarnishing its reputation. Consumers, like everyone else, are also *loss averse*. Different parts of the brain are activated if a potential *loss* is in the mid-term or long-term future, rather than here and now. Very distant potential losses tempt the consumer to spend today and neglect thinking about the future. Paying by credit card makes a transaction abstract and in the process alters 'the calculus of our financial decision' since paying with cash seems more of a loss with your 'wallet literally lighter'.

A NOTE ON EVOLUTIONARY PSYCHOLOGY (SOCIOBIOLOGY)

If cognitive neuroscience (and cognitive psychology) claims the mind is the brain in action, it implies that one way to understand ourselves is to observe the brain in action by employing the latest brain scanning technology. Evolutionary psychology, on the other hand, draws on Darwinism to tell us not only how the human race came into being but also what molds human behavior. Both approaches, however, share a biological basis so that the two together are grouped under the label 'biologism'. After all, if the brain is something that has evolved from natural selection as the mechanism of evolution, and the mind is simply the brain in action, then the mind and all those things humans choose to do can be explained by evolution. This is the perspective of evolutionary psychology.

Evolutionary psychology (EP) or, as it was originally called, *sociobiology* is the one subdivision of the social sciences that has not been covered in this text with a separate chapter. It has been popularized by academics like E.O. Wilson and Steven Pinker. It does not justify a separate chapter because it has had little impact in research on consumer behavior, though many of the quoted views of Steven Pinker in this book would fall into the category of evolutionary psychology. Pinker argues that all our mental faculties arise from natural selection and we ignore our evolved brains at our peril as the evolved brain acts as a constraint on what can be achieved by those who believe all behavior can be molded by environmental interventions. In his most recent book he argues that evolutionary psychology provides the best explanation of why things throughout the ages have got better, showing that the historical trends in violence throughout the world have been downwards (Pinker 2011). He points out that, while humans have an inclination towards violence, they also have an inclination to empathy, to cooperation and self-control.

Like rational choice theory (RCT) in economics, EP does not take into account any phenomena beyond the desires of the single individual. The notion of the consumer as an agent with a free will is not considered under the deterministic perspective of evolutionary psychology (EP). It has been placed at the end of this chapter because it assumes that most neuro-cognitive mechanisms, lying behind mental states, are the result of *evolutionary adaptations* to ancestral environments. Looking back through evolution for likely causes of behavior would seemingly require the employment of *abduction*, which is described as inference to the best explanation of the facts presented to us, or more commonly as the method of Sherlock Holmes. But trying to construct evolutionary history to explain some phenomena makes solving a Sherlock Holmes murder seem simple.

Since it is claimed that for 90 percent of the time the human animal has been on this earth it has been in hunter-gatherer societies (there are still hunter-gatherer societies in different parts of the world), this type of society is regarded as the starting point for the evolution of humans because so much is traced back to the influencing conditions of that time. Much speculation is inevitable here.

EP claims to be able to explain the 'universals' in cultural living such as female sexual coyness and male promiscuity. It is argued that we have propensities for certain wants and these are evolutionary adaptations. It accepts the evolutionary basis of innate behavior and tries to theorize as to how it might have arisen. Only by assuming that the psychology of humans is rooted in evolution does a problematic situation arise. The metaphor of the 'selfish gene' is used though this has created the misleading impression of genes with motivations and intentions (substituting the man-in-the-gene for Ryle's dismissal of dualism as the man-in-the-machine). But to speak of the 'selfish gene' is not to claim that genes have motivations, but to suggest that natural selection is a process of evolutionary change rooted in competition among genes.

Robert Wright (2009) combines evolutionary theory with game theory to explain religious developments. He claims evolution resulted in people recognizing mutually advantageous exchanges or, in the language of game theory, non-zero-sum interactions. Religious doctrines became more tolerant of other faiths wherever tolerance helped smooth the way for mutually beneficial economic and political exchanges that were seemingly a win for both sides (the win–win situation). But toleration of religious differences can be a denial of the importance to us of those differences. While toleration is an incomplete form of unification, it does mean covering up differences and stressing what is held in common. Moore (1994), a historian, argues differently in his book *Selling God*. For him, it was competition among religions that pushed religions into being viewed by 'buyers' as simply rival products and this made for inter-religious tolerance, – thus not arising, as Wright claims, from the role of non-zero-sum dynamics. Wright even sees our ability to put ourselves in another's shoes, which facilitates non-zero-sum dynamics, as an aspect of our 'moral imagination' which has an evolutionary basis. But stripped of its jargon, Wright's thesis is little more than that people will act in their own interests, while many believe that evolutionary psychology and game theory are elastic enough for all of us to interpret them in any way we think fit.

EP has yet to have an impact in the social sciences, perhaps because the strong claims made by its advocates seem implausible and the hard evidence missing. In one of the latest books, Gad Saad (2011) argues that most of the things we do as consumers are related to sex. With men looking for attractive, fertile females and women looking for the socially powerful, it is not surprising if women focus on their looks and men on advancing their status. Saad, like other evolutionary psychologists, sees the roots of human behavior in biology and natural selection but sees these forces as serving functions. Thus, long hair in women serves the function of signaling health and youth, with the employment of cosmetics to mimic the signs of sexual arousal, while high heels serve the function of making the woman's gait more attractive and feminine. Perfectly symmetrical faces point to good genes, while a deep male voice is linked to reproductive fitness. A waist to hip ratio of 0:7 (the hourglass figure) for women is tied to fertility. Gift-giving strengthens bonds between people though usually between people who can reciprocate. The major criticism here is in claiming that the evolutionary causal origins of human behavior give rise to purposeful manifest behavior. This gives too much of a deterministic stance to behavior without our really having the methodological tools to provide strong evidence in support.

Sometimes the explanations appear bizarre. Nicholas Wade (2006) explains dialects as having evolved to distinguish friend from foe! There are simpler, less far-fetched explanations. Even the notion of our psychological make-up coming about thousands of years ago, to meet the demands on our hunter-gatherer ancestors, is itself somewhat speculative. Buller (2004), a philosopher specializing in the area, claims in fact that our minds are *not* adapted to the so-called Pleistocene age but are continually adapting, over both evolutionary time and individual lifetimes. He examines the most highly publicized 'discoveries' and concludes that none are actually supported by the evidence. If we look at many of the claims, they are simply the *logical* implications that arise from the assumption that evolutionary theory is true without providing corroborating evidence. Such explanations are 'just so stories'; *post hoc* speculations, accepting all behavior as arising from natural selection to serve some function.

In one book of essays written by biologists, sociologists, anthropologists and psychologists, evolutionary psychology is criticized as a flagrant abuse of Darwinism with the aim of promoting a conservative, political viewpoint and to suggest biology as reigning supreme among the social sciences (Rose and Rose 2000). It is no coincidence that the resurrection of Darwinism has coincided with the revival of free-market economics and the two views are related in the public imagination. But the criticism in the book's essays is a little overblown, which indicates the controversial nature of evolutionary psychology. We know so little about the conditions of human evolution that claims made by evolutionary psychologists about universal human traits have to be justified on other grounds. As already pointed out, claims are often straightforward deductions from the acceptance of evolutionary theory as valid, like the claim that women are naturally less promiscuous than men. This is a direct deduction from the fact that promiscuity for women confers no evolutionary advantage whereas it does for a man. But can this today be said to be a universal trait in that since the 1960s women have indeed become more sexually assertive?

CASE: REALEYES

The marketing manager of a firm marketing jewelry is interested in using the services of Realeyes, a London company which specializes in eye-spying webcams combined with emotion identification. As consumers browse a website, their eye movements can be followed. Image-processing software combined with the tiny cameras in computers allow a record to be made of the consumer browsing an ad and the facial expressions that tie to the eye movements. Realeyes claims to be able to gauge the browser's emotional state by plotting the position of facial features like mouth, eyebrows and so on. Noting the position of facial features combined with eye movement tracking and employing quantitative techniques in analysis is claimed to produce measures of interest in the ad and the emotional states aroused by it.

Case questions

1. Would it be useful to the manager to first evaluate this system by examining the basics that need to be in place for the outputs to have the significance claimed? Although you agree that a pragmatic evaluation that demonstrates the applicability and success of the research method may be needed, you argue that basic assumptions should first be examined to see if it is worth going forward.
2. 'Although the techniques used by Realeyes produce data, the question is, what is the meaning of the data if they are to become information.' Discuss.

DISCUSSION QUESTIONS ON CHAPTER 8 (COGNITIVE NEUROSCIENCE)

1. If Damasio is right and we instantly perceive any happenings as 'good' or 'bad', does this perception not satisfy the definition of an attitude as 'a predisposition to respond in a consistently favorable or unfavorable

way to some person, item or thing'? If so, why do we have so many different conceptualizations of 'attitude'?

2. Take some of the mental processes discussed and identify any that are more accurately described as logical rather than mental processes.

3. If we knew that certain mental processes did occur in deciding which product to buy, explain the utility of knowing this.

4. Defend the proposition that conceptual clarity comes before quantification or mathematical modeling.

5. The notion of perception is a process that involves having a corresponding image in the mind of what is being perceived. Why can this be misleading in conducting thinking about how consumers choose?

6. What critiques of Bennett and Hacker strike you as significant for understanding the consumer and which do you feel have been more like academic hair-splitting? Or are all the points they make of potential significance?

Chapter 9

Microeconomics (Rational Choice Theory)

RATIONALITY IN ECONOMICS

The discipline of economics assumes people are highly rational in choosing means to satisfy self-interests. This is the perspective that *rational choice theory* (RCT) imputes to behavior, with consumers assumed to possess perfect information about alternatives and their consequences. The consumer arrives at his or her optimum choice via the *rationality principle*, interpreted as the maximization of utility or subjective value. RCT assumes that action is explained in terms of consumers seeking to get what they want in the most rational way.

Consumers undertake *practical thinking* when wants and beliefs serve as reasons for an intention to buy: I want to get rid of this headache; I believe that aspirin will cure my headache; my intention is to buy aspirin and swallow two tablets. The contents of my want(s), beliefs and intentions cohere rationally. This is an *instrumental* view of rationality in that it focuses on rational means to achieve what one wants to achieve. Being rational in RCT is also instrumental rationality in being exclusively focused with choosing the best means for ends already in being.

Standard economic theory views people as 'utility' maximizers who are rational to the extent that they select the most efficient means of achieving the goal of maximizing utility for them (Hollis 1996). The concept of utility equates with the notion of subjective value or subjective desirability. Utility does not equate with 'satisfaction', which is more of a feeling that comes from progressing towards meeting one's goals. The most common explication of RCT is the notion of RCT explaining rational behavior in terms of *maximizing expected utility*. Expected utility applies to choices with probabilistic (uncertain) consequences. It is the average utility expected if we repeatedly made the same choice with probabilities remaining the same.

Although maximizing utility can be defined as maximizing whatever we want to maximize, such a definition would make the term 'utility' operationally vacuous. As a consequence, rational choice theory confines utility to what self-interest determines. This means that rational choice theory (RCT) can be interpreted as concerned with maximizing self-interest. Self-interest is a key motivator in that trying to get someone to understand something or do something is a major hurdle when self-interest dictates the adoption of a contrary viewpoint or some other action. Consumers weigh the costs and benefits of various actions and choose those that maximize the net benefits for them.

Whatever we might say about other motives that might prevail, maximizing self-interest or expected utility is perhaps the most defensible of the single-motive assumptions. Much more questionable are the assumptions that:

(a) There are no other major motives at work
(b) Consumers possess perfect information about alternatives
(c) Each person's 'wants' can be ranked according to their contribution to utility as subjectively assessed.

These assumptions can be very remote from reality. How many consumers, for example, waste money by choosing brand names over private labels or generics because they lack information that would tell them there was no significant difference? How many credit card holders do not know the 'usury' charges for late payments? How many consumers pay for credit card theft insurance, not realizing the most they are liable for is $50? How many consumers realize the foolishness of taking out extended warranty contracts with their outrageous profit margins? How many consumers cannot resist a sale and buy far more than they will ever need or use? How many consumers who swear by copper bracelets or magnets know that they are useless for curing arthritis? As Grayling (2003) points out, 50 million Americans claim to be allergic to something or other and spend $10 billion annually on remedies in the belief that the environment is a hostile, toxic place, with pathogens, pollutants, parasites, processed food and chemical additives steadily eroding the health and well-being of the nation. This is odd given that we live in an era which has never been healthier – and safer, despite terrorism. Grayling says this testifies to a human need to be afraid of something. Even if this is not quite the position, it does seem humans are innately vigilant to potential threats even if these threats have an exceedingly low probability of actually happening.

But not all buying is dominated by brand names that are heavily promoted. In respect to *private label*, which is the store's own label (sometimes called a 'generic'), private label packaged goods have been growing faster than branded products. In fact Wal-Mart's own Ol'Roy Dog Food, which is a dry dog food made specifically for Wal-Mart, is the top-selling dog food in the US. The explanation is a testament to the credibility of Wal-Mart's guaranteeing the product and its in-store promotion with a vast array of bright red Ol'Roy bags in every Wal-Mart store – and last but not least, dogs seem to like it!

PERVASIVENESS OF RCT IN SOCIAL SCIENCE

It is an indicator of how specialized consumer researchers have become that some talk as if rational choice theory (RCT) is just part of history, ignored today. (This would not be true of those who did their PhD in marketing at a major business school in the US where there is a strong emphasis on economics for the training it gives in mathematical model building.) That said, the ignoring of RCT is far from being true throughout academic marketing and is certainly not true of the quantitative model builders in marketing. As Ho et al. (2006) say:

> Marketing models are usually applications of standard economic theories, which rely on strong assumptions of rationality of consumers and firms.
>
> (Ho et al. 2006)

Ho et al. also point out that the new subject of behavioral economics (see Chapter 10), however, accepts that actions can be irrational and deals with the likely consequences of such actions while at the same time exploring other implications of this irrationality (p. 307).

RCT describes economic man as profit maximizing, efficient and rational in going about his business. But people often do not act rationally in promoting their best interests and do not behave in line with the 'laws' of classical economics. One problem lies in our being unable to obtain and process all the information relevant to a decision. Those who place great faith in the free market are assuming highly rational market participants possessing all relevant information, which is just not the case. The emerging discipline of behavioral economics (Chapter 10) recognizes that economic decisions do not emerge from deep rational analysis but are influenced by emotional attitudes such as *risk aversion*. Typically it appears that people reject a 50/50 probability of gaining/losing money if the amount to be gained is less than double the sum to be lost. In other words, one claim is that the potential payoff needs to be at least double the potential loss.

The RCT perspective enters into much of marketing. Even in saying that it is marketing's job to identify wants and cater to them, we are implicitly taking for granted the economist's paradigm that consumers know what they want, and can rank these wants, with advertising being concerned with simply establishing visibility, showing that the product matches the want in order to activate it. There is no sense here of activating latent wants, or the influence that descriptive words and images in an ad can have on choices.

Two recent attempts at paradigm change in marketing stress marketing's legacy from economics. Hill (2003) in promoting his 'sensory perspective' talks about how twentieth-century marketing was dominated by a rational, utilitarian orientation – reason-based, neoclassical economics being the underlying dogma. Vargo and Lusch (2004) in providing the evolutionary development of their service perspective, argue that the models on which much of economics and marketing are based were developed when the focus was on efficiencies, and quote marketing academics like Fred Webster (1992) with approval, who point out that the historical marketing management function was based on the microeconomic maximization paradigm.

Alan Ryan (2003), an Oxford philosopher and social scientist, in a review of Amartya Sen's (2003) *Rationality and Freedom*, maintains that, because of the prestige of economics, social sciences like sociology, law and political science have been applying the analytical methods of economics to their own disciplines, happily adopting the label 'rational choice theory'. Ryan claims RCT appeals to academics in the social sciences who yearn for the kind of consensus they see among economists about the standards for good professional work. He might also have included history and biology even while acknowledging that biology is not destiny. In the case of biology, Glimcher (2003) points out that biologists have returned to economics on the assumption that the decisions an animal makes, given the environment in which the animal evolved, may more nearly approximate optimal courses of action than do the decisions of humans operating in modern society. Economic models, he argues, have allowed us to predict and define the behavior of animals with tremendous precision. Ferling (2003), in history, argues that political behavior owes much to economic considerations and most people customarily embrace ideas that cohere with their personal interests, especially pecuniary considerations. Even in theology, rational choice theory is by no means ignored but shown to be predictive, as in Young's (1997) *Rational Choice Theory and Religion*.

Hollis (1996) provides us with a more extended definition and view of RCT in the following quotation:

> Austerely as consistency among preferences, together with correctness in the calculations which link preferences to actions...Preference itself is more like an avowal of a ranking than a desire for a feeling of satisfaction...preferences are simply imputed to an agent by reading them off behavior as revealed in the actual choices made. It is hard to see how action can be explained by just considering preferences [p. 3]....In any case, people do not always act rationally, using the test of what one would predict from the axioms of rational choice.
>
> (Hollis 1996: 3–5)

If we take the behavior of any group, whether consumers, politicians or laborers, it is not driven by just a single motive like self-interest. The same goes for individuals. Motives are multiple and conflicting. If we interpret all motives as self-serving (by simply interpreting all actions as such), then all the work on human motivation can be dismissed. On the other hand, as Ryan states, the assumption of some degree of rationality is a condition for being able to offer an explanation of human behavior and RCT is the best developed *overarching* theory that is currently on offer.

Perhaps, more specifically, we have to assume behavior to be intelligible to be understood.

THE NATURE AND LIMITATIONS OF RCT

Rational choice theory (RCT) is not a causal theory: it makes no claim about self-interest causing behavior. It is a combination of competence and performance theories. *Performance theory* in RCT is made up of theories about *instrumental* rationality which is concerned with drawing up rules for choosing the best means to achieve ends. Such instrumental rationality leads to a consideration of *competence theories* in that a person's competence is tied to mastery of the rules or norms of rationality that are applicable to the activity being undertaken.

Competence theory is concerned with developing *criteria* to judge the *mastery* of the rules. Thus 'decision theory' and 'game theory' seek rules for identifying utility-maximizing strategies by simulating the thought processes of perfectly rational agents seeking the best course of action. Although decision theory is typically defined to include game theory, decision theory is best reserved for decision-making in situations where decisions need to take account of the reliability of information, the probabilities of various outcomes and so on, confining game theory to laying out rational strategies, under conditions constrained by the agent's interdependency with other utility-maximizers.

The simplest case of decision-making is where there is certainty as to options (alternatives) and consequences. In such cases it is logically evident which action produces the greatest net utility, that is, the greatest realization of preferences. Decision-makers, under conditions of certainty, possess perfect information about options (alternatives) and their consequences, while preferences (desires/wants) can be ranked according to their contribution to utility. But the more realistic economic models take account of risk and uncertainty. With risk, the probabilities of various consequences can be calculated. However, if there is absolute *uncertainty*, prediction of consequences is ruled out. In practice, it is assumed there is no complete or absolute uncertainty, on the grounds that there is seldom complete ignorance because we always have subjective estimates or *subjective probabilities* about outcomes. In this way decision-making under uncertainty is incorporated into decision-making under risk.

When economists talk of expectations (expectancies) they refer to whatever they believe will happen based on (subjective) probability estimates. In *subjective probabilities* we assign a probability number to a belief. Subjective probability contrasts with probabilities based on the limit that observed (empirical) frequencies would approach (the *relative frequency view of probability*) in the very long run or those based on *logical* possibilities like saying logic would suggest that an unbiased penny will, if tossed, come out as 50 percent heads and 50 percent tails over long-run trials. Subjective probability estimates emanate from all the beliefs and knowledge of the person who is making the estimate and may or may not have an empirical base but just be guesstimates.

What is generally claimed (but not supported in the National Aeronautics and Space Administration (NASA) example below) is that subjective probabilities tend to overestimate the probability of events that are rare or infrequent. Also, in making probability estimates consumers are over-confident if confidence is high as judgments are more subject to bias – like relying on evidence that is supportive of their beliefs. This explains why salespeople are likely to be more successful with the over-confident. On the other hand, people are under-confident in making probability estimates when confidence is lacking. We may change a person's level of confidence by exploring with him or her the pros and cons (reasons) for their position.

Expectations enter into decision-making. Expectations become the *standard* against which to compare results. At the time of writing, the media report a study that purports to show women are more dissatisfied with their lives now than fifty or so years ago. Does this mean women's 'liberation' has failed as was suggested? Satisfaction/dissatisfaction cannot be measured in any absolute sense (i.e. on a ratio scale) but against some standard and that standard is expectations. People are only disappointed in the extent to which their expectations are not met. Women's expectations were perhaps raised to a level where disappointment was inevitable.

Subjective probabilities, as opposed to probabilities based on past data (the relative frequency view), are so common in marketing science decision-making and in life that we hardly question the method. The question is whether such probabilities are reliable or possess predictive validity. In fact, actual subjective probabilities vary with the method used to elicit them. Commenting on this, Elster (1989) points out that if we were truly measuring something in a person's mind, the result should not depend on the method of measurement. Since it does, the probability is an artifact of the procedure. Kahneman and Tversky (1972) maintain that people do not even have a consistent view of what different probabilities mean and actual subjective probabilities are no foundation for mathematical modeling meant to reflect the real world. Mathematical modelers prefer to ignore this claim which is so destructive of much of what they hold to be scientific.

Does the decision calculus embodying subjective probability 'work' in that predictions are correct? Subjective interpretations of probability vary from one individual to another. Thus one classic case is recorded by Richard Feynman, the Nobel Laureate in physics, when he served on the NASA Commission inquiring into the *Challenger* disaster in 1986. He asked both NASA engineers and managers to estimate the risk of disastrous failure in each space shuttle mission. The managers estimated it to be one disaster in 100,000 missions, while for the engineers it was one disaster in 100 missions – a factor of 1,000 between the two estimates (Dyson 2011). The engineers gave the better estimates, not the managers. It didn't even seem in this case that probabilities were overestimated as is generally claimed.

There is no way to resolve such differences except by changing to another type of probability (such as the relative frequency view of probability). Therefore it cannot be asserted that the technique is always reliable so its predictive validity is automatically suspect. What we know about subjective probabilities does not increase our confidence in their validity. Thus Tversky and Kahneman (1973) found that subjective probability estimates relate, for example, to the availability of items in memory with the result that people (say) overestimate sensational cases (e.g. of airplane crashes). This phenomenon is now known as the 'availability principle'. The availability principle explains why pricing an item, say, at $8.99 instead of $9 is effective in getting consumers to talk and think of the price as being around $8 since the '8' is what is immediately available in the mind. It is interesting to note how often what the boss brings up relates to what he or she has recently read. Senior citizens are acutely aware that they might get critically ill which makes them an easy target for critical illness insurance.

It could be argued that subjective probabilities reflect experience and knowledge. More specifically, it is claimed a subjective probability is likely to embody enough relevant experience and observations to make the decision. But how can these observations be verified unless set out? The point is that thinking about subjective probabilities should be a rational process whereby something is discovered as a result. There is a need to consider the evidence lying behind the subjective probability, if there is any.

Managers will always have reasons for supporting the probabilities they offer but such reasons may or may not be reasons that would be accepted as supporting evidence. Could it be that subjective probability estimates arise from thought experiments? Kuhn (1977) points out that, if thought experiments are to be successful, nothing about the imagined situation must be entirely unfamiliar or strange. If I were to plot the probabilities of getting various levels of sales from various levels of expenditure on advertising, would they have any predictive value – particularly when I have had no experience of such levels of advertising? Of course, if the results turn out to be only as meaningful as a set of random numbers of buses, it could always be claimed that the analyst just did not have the relevant experience! Thought experiments embody no new information about the world so the addition to knowledge is limited to deductions and corrections of conceptual errors. Subjective probabilities ought to reflect relevant experience in the same way (say) that I might judge the probable conduct of a friend of long standing.

We all have to deal with uncertainty as a fact of life but many philosophers are questioning whether probability theory will remain the dominant methodology by which to tackle uncertainty. Many of us suspect that much of this questioning arises from an inability to discover the scope of probability application since, for example, probability theory does not apply to propositions known to be partially true. But instead of asking what probability is, we might ask in what senses in everyday life we use the word probability. It was common at one time to ask, as Plato did, 'what is the state?', as if the word 'state' had some meaning divorced from its usage. We may not be able to define the 'true nature' of probability but we can establish its meaning-in-use.

Elster (1989) makes the point that we simply hate to admit uncertainty and indeterminacy in decision-making. Rather than accept the limits to reason, we prefer 'the rituals of reason' and, wanting to have reasons for what we do, we create reasons where none exist. Many of us would endorse this judgment.

But subjective probabilities may be a fact of life for the consumer as subjective probabilities manifest themselves in the form of consumer expectations. The consumer may believe that brand X has more appeal (i.e. promises higher utility) than brand Y but suspects there is a higher probability (hence higher expectations) of getting the benefits associated with brand Y and this is taken into account. She has knowledge, say, about brand Y because she habitually buys brand Y and knows it well, whereas brand X is new to her. Ideally she would compute the utility of each choice and implicitly multiply the utility of the outcomes (consequences) by their probability of happening. She then adds up the expected utilities for each of the different outcomes, repeating the procedure for each option so as to choose the alternative which yields the highest expected utility. If this is what she actually does(?), she is following the rule of RCT, namely maximizing expected utility.

The economist's 'rationality principle' assumes that people do take the action that best promotes their goals. This principle, embodied in *expected* utility theory, has been the major paradigm in decision-making under conditions of risk since the Second World War. When first developed by Von Neumann and Morgenstern (1947), *expected* utility theory was put forward as a *normative* theory of rationality though it is now considered *descriptive* as well. In support it could be claimed that all normative theories to an extent describe aspects of the real world. As Harman (1986), a Princeton philosopher, says, it is hard to come up with any normative model without considering how you think people might behave. Similarly, any actual description of decision-making involves a certain amount of idealization and such idealization is normative to some extent.

The RCT paradigm assumes that, in choosing from among alternatives, the focus is on differences in outcomes/consequences (the *cancellation principle*); that choices are transitive in that if I prefer A to B and B to C, I will prefer A to C (the *transitivity principle*) and the decision-maker is not affected by the way alternatives are presented (the *invariance principle*). All these principles have been challenged by economists themselves, showing they can be violated for good reasons. For example, Maurice Allais (1953) challenged the cancellation principle as did Daniel Ellsberg (1961). Similarly, there have been challenges to the transitivity principle, for example Arrow's (1951) theorem. Tversky (1969) showed how the transitivity rule (if I prefer A to B and B to C, I should prefer A to C) is violated through the overweighting and underweighting of utility. Preferences in fact are not stable but often in a state of flux and change over time so are likely to violate any assumption as to consistent preference ordering. We cannot imagine anyone in consumer marketing subscribing to the invariance principle since all marketers know that how things are 'packaged' or presented can be all-important.

Probabilities, based on relative frequencies, are not usually available to the decision-maker. In any case, as Nozick (1993) points out, there are problems with the relative frequency view of probability as there is always a problem of providing justification for using what occurs in a hypothetical infinite sequence of events to guide us in one particular finite case. Savage, a pioneer on the topic of subjective probabilities, would dismiss this worry in arguing that, instead of worrying over justifying why we should act on probabilities, we should instead define probabilities in terms of how we should act. This is done by employing *subjective expected utility* (SEU) developed by Savage (1954).

The concept of subjective probabilities is particularly controversial in the philosophy of mathematics but not in marketing, management science or economics (see Kyburg 1983 for his critique of the use of subjective probabilities). However, the question still remains: why is it rational to act in the individual case on what is most probable when this probability applies only to the *distribution* of cases? The answer is that it is assumed the individual case is not a one-off but one of a long series. This is often not so in marketing. There may be a probability of 80 percent that a newly launched product will die in infancy but that particular statistic has no effect on whether this newly launched product will be a failure or a success. The best that such statistics can do is act as a warning sign. For the statistician all knowledge that is obtained from observation is uncertain and can only be justifiably employed in decision-making if the degree of uncertainty is known. Statistical methodology can in fact be viewed as focusing on the quantification of uncertainty.

There have been other developments, making expected utility theory a family of theories, not just one unified theory. Luce (1959) developed stochastic (implying the presence of randomness) models of choice, treating preferences as though they have a random component, as one way of coping with the problem of why it is still rational to prefer fish today and salad tomorrow. Luce would treat fish and salad choices as probabilistic, rather than fixed choices that occur 100 percent of the time.

With regard to expectations, economists subscribing to *adaptive expectations* view the decision-maker as constantly *updating* expectations on the basis of experience while, alternatively, economists subscribing to *rational expectations* claim that decision-makers have expectations which they perceive as being borne out on average and so treat deviations from expectations as random events. Adaptive expectations lost a lot of its attraction when this perspective on investor behavior performed badly in predicting inflation in the early 1970s. Rational expectations, too, had its failures when, for example, it predicted wrongly that monetary policy did not affect employment.

Rational expectations combined with the *efficient market hypothesis* (EMH) paints a very different picture of the market from that of John Maynard Keynes, who saw the market as susceptible to waves of unreasoning consumer optimism and pessimism arising from uncertainty about what is happening in the market. The EMH as applied to financial markets claims that the prices prevailing at any one time in a market make it impossible to earn abnormal economic profits by trading in the market given any specified amount of information, since all such information will have been taken into account.

Economists focus on *revealed preference*, that is, preferences revealed by market choice. This frustrates any attempt to explain the motivation lying behind choices, beyond assuming it is to maximize expected utility. It appears to be a rejection of mental constructs. But not quite, since the economist still refers to mental constructs like subjective expectations, whether rational or adaptive.

'Deliberation' on alternatives leading to trade-offs among the options considered characterizes decision-making as traditionally conceived, but on this view decision-making is not as pervasive as commonly assumed. We can choose without deliberation in that choices can be based on habit or (random) picking or just intrinsic liking that involves no uncertainties, with no need for deliberation over trade-offs. The likeability heuristic (rule of thumb) in particular is prevalent whether in choosing what to eat, whom to employ, what to buy or how to vote. At its core is a positive or negative attitude; liking or not-liking some item, person or thing.

Some psychologists but not economists see people in general as on 'automatic pilot', being only motivated into deliberation when some difficulty signals a problem needing to be solved (Kagan, 1989). Otherwise, they let their minds wander, daydreaming, fantasizing but certainly not concentrating on the matter at hand. Mindfulness, in the sense of being consciously aware of happenings around us, is not some equilibrium state to which we always return after some slip of attention.

There is a general assumption in economics that there is little variation in ultimate values or end-wants among people, which allows economic theorists to model changes in behavior as arising purely from external factors such as varying circumstances, different incomes, and prices. It is this stress on external factors in determining behavior that links economics to behaviorism and some of the other social sciences.

FINANCIAL PRODUCTS AND MATHEMATICAL MODELS

For many economists, economic theory reduces to mathematical analysis. But mathematical economics has lost a good deal of credibility with the meltdown in the financial markets, given the belief of many economists that the problem of avoiding an economic depression had been solved. While past celebrated figures in economics like the British economists Keynes, Marshall and Hicks had mathematical backgrounds, there was not the same notion of mathematical model building which characterizes today's economists.

As in marketing science, the focus in today's economics has been on prediction and not on explanation. This is another way of saying that *instrumentalism* has been the guiding philosophy. John Dewey (1859–1952), the philosopher, developed a version of *pragmatism* called *instrumentalism*, which prizes prediction above all else: any scientific theory on this basis is simply an instrument for producing new predictions or techniques for controlling happenings. This gets round the problem of considering whether a theory is tracking truth by simply ignoring the need for any theory. We say *tracking truth* because science is essentially a continuing exploration of puzzles rather than settled answers. Beliefs reflect this tracking of truth though our feelings often suggest we have found it!

Instrumentalism is the approach advocated in economics by Milton Friedman. Causal explanations are eschewed. As far as there has been any interest in causal analysis, it has remained at the level of *concomitant variations*, an exemplar of which is regression and correlation analysis in statistics. The method of concomitant variation assesses the variation between factors that may be causally related. It suggests the possibility of causation, for example, by establishing a high correlation between the independent variable(s) (the 'cause') and the dependent variable(s) (the 'effect'). A high correlation may, of course, have little or no causal significance. On the other hand, causation may be the reason for the high correlation so the finding of a high correlation must be considered. More limiting is the assumption in mathematical economics that consumers in the market are governed by and influenced only by rational behavior and that free competition and full information are always present! In any case having 'full' information, contrary to much current wisdom, is not in itself sufficient for making an optimal decision. Information is like headlights to the night driver: it illuminates the road ahead but does not rule out the need for good judgment.

Even when there is an interest by economists in identifying 'causes', the conceptualization of 'cause' promoted by *scientific realism*, though the most fundamental concept of cause, is not the one captured by economists or by mathematical modelers in marketing. Those subscribing to scientific realism conceptualize 'causes' as mechanisms, structures or powers that cause the effects of interest. They seek something more than a view of cause as epitomized by the billiard ball analogy or a bee sting. The realist does not look for single causes linked to single effects but argues that any effect is more likely to result from complex interrelations among *background* causal mechanisms. For the realist, the causes of any effect are usually complex, *unobservable* structures and processes. The realist is not viewing cause as some immediate antecedent event but as something that, like lung cancer, can result from causal factors (such as smoking) that only slowly take their effect. These causal structures and processes can be out of phase with the events they cause, with the consequence that causal relationships are often hidden. This comes about because the world is composed of open systems, not closed ones; open to intervening and countervailing causes, resulting in instability in cause-and-effect relationships. The result is that prediction is always problematic as we can never be sure which set of generative mechanisms are at work. A further problem occurs when there are several variables causing the results of interest. In this case, how are we to assign the relative importance of each in determining the total variation when there are interaction effects? The statistician here falls back on multivariate statistics for at least some help.

Accepting that prediction is problematic (except in the 'closed system' of the laboratory), the realist does not consider prediction the acid test of theory but seeks explanations in terms of causal necessity. But professional expertise often dictates where to look for cause, in that people look for causes within their own area of expertise. The causes sought by the behavior researcher may have little significance for the marketing manager because he or she either does not see that cause as actionable (e.g. culture) or requires education as to why it is in fact significant.

Mathematical model building is often regarded as an application of *positivism* in marketing. But positivism (or today's update 'logical empiricism') champions empirical investigation and the methods of the natural sciences, while a large proportion of mathematical models are not built up from empirical inquiry, as demanded by positivism or logical empiricism, but fall under *rationalism* in that they are based on reason alone. Thus, from reason alone we can state that there are infinitely many prime numbers. Some knowledge, like mathematical knowledge, is only in fact discoverable through logical reasoning.

Handy and Harwood (1973), writing in support of the positivist tradition of the 1930s, argue that rationalism is the dominant orientation among formal mathematical model builders, giving rise to models like 'game theory' and 'utility theory' that confuse warranted assertions about the particular model with warranted assertions about some aspect of human behavior. They take such model builders to task for not investigating the presumed connections between the model and observed behavior with any degree of thoroughness: typically it is the internal aspects of the model that are examined rather than matching the model to actual behavior. Handy and Harwood assert that internal tests are seldom adequate since assumptions can often seem unchallengeable, reasoning absolutely sound and conclusions inescapable, when, in instance after instance, the assumptions are later shown to be unfounded, the facts proved wrong, and errors in reasoning detected. They take econometricians to task for often 'obtaining plausible numbers to provide ceremonial adequacy for a theory'. A little cleverness 'will get you almost any result you want' and that is why 'few econometricians have ever been forced by the facts to abandon any firmly held belief'.

These criticisms are valid and cannot just be dismissed. They are being endorsed more and more since the financial meltdown. As Paul Krugman (2009), who won the Nobel Memorial Prize in Economics in 2008, says about economics: 'As I see it, the economics profession went astray because economists, as a group, mistook beauty, clad in impressive-looking mathematics, for truth.' Krugman quotes the critic H.L. Mencken: 'There is always an easy solution to every human problem – neat, plausible and wrong.' This criticism made of mathematical model builders in economics is also made of mathematical model builders in marketing. That said, without being able to put numbers onto things, we enhance the risk of our pronouncements being vague and ambiguous. We need something more than just 'some' or 'many' by way of quantification if we are to gauge relative importance and relevance to the context.

In the same article, Krugman contrasts Milton Friedman's perspective of monetarism with the perspective of J.M. Keynes in macroeconomics. Monetarism claims that the only government intervention needed in financial markets to prevent a depression was instructing central banks to ensure the nation's money supply (defined as the sum of cash in circulation together with bank deposits) was growing on a steady path. The Keynesian view of financial markets as a 'casino' was replaced by the *efficient market hypothesis* (EMH), advanced by Eugene Fama of the University of Chicago, which implied that CEOs should focus on maximizing the share prices of the company. There is no place in this perspective for a fiscal stimulus as advocated by Keynes for a depression economy. For Krugman himself, Keynesian economics 'remains the best framework for making sense of recessions and depressions'. Yet Krugman acknowledges that the current New Keynesian models leave no room for a crisis like that happening at the time of writing (2009) because they, too, generally accept the efficient-market view of the financial section of the economy. But Keynes, we might recall, did in fact recommend building up government revenue reserves during good times in order to keep purchasing power in circulation during bad times.

The study of financial markets and the consumer in the role of investor emerged in the 1970s to be incorporated into economics under the rubric of financial economics. The dominating perspective in financial economics covering financial products has been the *rational expectations hypothesis* (REH) and the assumption of efficient markets. The prevailing view has been of perfectly rational consumers and perfectly efficient markets. The REH views the market economy as a mechanism governed, like any physical system, by universal economic laws. In the 2008 financial crisis these 'rational investors' assumed the probability of a fall in house prices to be virtually zero.

REH was meant to reflect rational behavior in a scientific way and caught on among economists because the premise of economic laws and identical expectations among consumers as investors lent itself to techniques of mathematical model building. The EMH, when applied to financial markets, assumes, as already stated, that prices prevailing in any market prevent abnormal profits being made by trading in that market because all have the same information, that is, stocks and other financial products were optimally priced. In other words, financial markets always result in correct prices and reflect fundamental asset values. This follows from the assumption of financial markets consisting of highly competitive and rational consumers who would determine prices that captured all relevant information in the most accessible way.

The notion of the stock market being efficient was supported by the *random walk* theory that viewed stock prices as following a random walk through stocks that could be captured in statistical analysis. The acceptance of this view led to the popularity with investors (consumers) of index funds or mutual stocks that incorporated large diversified baskets of stock. The notion of stock prices following a random walk was destructive of the notion of stock prices reflecting fundamental values to be revealed by 'fundamental analysis' which is still advocated by many investment houses. In practice, we cannot predict that markets will automatically self-correct, any more than we can depend on enlightened self-interest to propel national interests. There can be price movements (called 'fat tails') much wider than would be suggested by random walk theory, tied as it is to the Bell curve in statistics. There can be causes at work that can change the underlying reality, not captured by random walk theory. What is often ignored are government policies (e.g. on taxes) which can influence those in the market to act in ways contrary to those suggested by the EMH. One big development as a consequence in finance has been *risk management* whereby options like securities known as *derivatives* have been developed to help the investor manage risk.

The *Capital Asset Pricing Model* (CAPM), an elegant mathematical theory of stock prices, is based on the assumption that consumers as investors make optimal investment decisions given the information that is available. No need here for marketers to be talking about alternative pricing strategies. All relevant information 'out there' would already be manifest in the price. Certainly, no manufacturer could get away with pricing as occurs at present with mobile phones, where the price of the replacement battery can be (as I discovered) the same as the price of the whole phone (including battery). This allowed economists to claim that market prices are more or less correct. Deviations from these 'equilibrium' prices would not last long. If the price of a share fell too low or rose too high, investors would recognize this and their actions would return the price to the equilibrium level.

On the assumption of rational buyers and efficient markets, economists built mathematical models and computer simulations, inevitably with an anti-regulation bias. Computer simulations seem particularly apt since the analyst can bring out the implications of a model's assumptions without sanitizing the results. Though these models have not had predictive success, 'falsification' has not led to a complete loss of faith in such tools.

In fact, in spite of the financial meltdown influenced by reliance on such theories, until better models come along (from behavioral economics?) they are unlikely to be pushed onto the scrapheap of mistaken ideas. The claim that unregulated free markets are the best of all possible worlds and that there can be mathematical models, applying to human behavior, that are universal in nature, remains an article of faith. One influential mathematical model was that developed by David X. Li whose 'Gaussian copula function' seemingly allowed the most complex of risks to be accurately modeled, leading traders to market large quantities of new financial products. It might be added that all these mathematical models could be played about with to suggest that an increase in lending was safe. Unfortunately, financial markets did not behave in accordance with Li's model but contributed to bringing down the financial system and the collapse of financial economics. Li's model made no allowance for 'black swans', or exceptional events, while changing contexts render universal laws infeasible when it comes to human behavior. The financial 'meltdown' in 2008–9 put paid to all such claims.

There have been attempts at building new paradigms, such as the *adaptive market hypothesis*, which, while denying perfect rationality, does not assume buyers are completely irrational. Behavior can be intelligible without being perfectly rational or irrational. No mathematical model can do justice to the complexity and variation in human behavior but, on the other hand, they do help us think about what variables are likely to be at work and how they might interact. The growth of mortgage-backed securities, subprime loans and the vastly expanded credit market altered the landscape, making standard solutions inapplicable to the new context. Aiding this were new financial products like *derivatives* (already mentioned) which are securities whose market value is derived from the price of other financial products or *credit default swaps* which 'protected' investors against the possibility of some bond defaulting.

Anatole Kaletsky (2009), a biographer of Keynes, argues that three ideas transformed economics in the 1980s: the first idea was the rational expectations concept, the second idea was the assumption of efficient markets and the third idea was the need to transform economics into mathematics, expressing simple assumptions about human behavior in algebraic formulae, ignoring problems that could not be tackled mathematically. But the economists reversed the methods of the physical sciences which use their models to draw out conclusions that are tested against reality. In contrast, if reality disagrees with the economist's model, it is reality that economists seek to change. For Kaletsky, the economist's mathematical model is apt to take little or no account of reality.

EQUITY AND RATIONAL CHOICE THEORY

An important consideration in consumer behavior is the matter of *equity*. If we use rational choice theory (RCT) to interpret consumer behavior that is concerned with realizing equity in commercial transactions, RCT fails. For the economy as a whole there is the criterion of the Pareto-efficient state where it is impossible for anybody to be made better off without making someone else worse off. However, achieving such a state would not achieve equity either. Equity-seeking behavior is, in general, *expressive* behavior where the consumer is more concerned with symbolizing the pursuit of equity than calculating whether benefits will be greater than costs. We can have instrumental reasons for buying where we aim to choose the best means for achieving ends but we can also have expressive reasons where the action taken can be an end in itself. Children and, usually, adults at play provide an exemplar of expressive behavior.

Many consumers contribute to humanitarian causes which they know have no chance of success. People donate money and labor to causes they know are hopeless simply because they have a need to express support. *Expressive behavior* can be symbolic, showing our concern even if it has no material function. Thus the lone cyclist riding all over America in honor of those killed in 9/11 is not creating material benefit but taking action expressive of feelings. Language, when purely expressive, is used to express feelings.

THE CONCEPT OF EQUITY

While equity is used in a number of senses, all involve the notion of *fair* dealing. In recognizing the insufficiency of general rules to cover all individual cases, Aristotle fell back on the concept of equity as being concerned with what is 'just' – not legally just, but as a correction to legal justice. This concept of equity carries the notion of a fairness that goes beyond legal requirements. The perception of fairness is important to consumers. Thus there was outrage when the Bank of America tried to impose a $5 a month fee for debit card use. The anger was exacerbated because of the lack of trust in banks which have little reputational capital left after the financial meltdown. We speak of equity in advocating equal opportunity and affirmative action for women and disadvantaged minorities as well as in democracy where it is interpreted as the government showing equal concern for each and every citizen.

In health care, equity, as an ethical principle, has led to attempts at eradicating systematic disparities in access to medical treatment, not by appeal to 'natural justice', but by appeal to human rights as defined by the United Nations. For the consumer, equity is also concerned with fairness; fairness in commercial transactions. And the demand for fairness seems to be 'hardwired' and hence a universal desire. Experiments have shown that if we give a capuchin monkey a cucumber slice, she is prepared to trade a small pebble for it. But if a second monkey nearby receives an obviously more desirable grape for the same pebble, the first monkey will reject the cucumber and might even throw it out of the cage! Although speculating about the motives of monkeys may seem like a case of anthropomorphism, most would interpret the monkey's behavior as a case of suppressing the desire for food to declare a more important desire, namely the desire for fairness. What would undermine behaviorism, though, is the suggestion that the monkeys' behavior was conscious as behaviorism sees conditioning as acting unconsciously.

Ethical principles, though propagated as universal, are usually provided with exceptions. Thus the principle of freedom of speech, the first of the ten amendments to the US Constitution, is not an absolute right in that there are still libel laws, 'hate speech' and so on which are prohibited under the law. Yet, in general, the individual case is treated as a member of a class where the particularizing features of the case are ignored.

It is not hard, in the abstract, to get sellers or consumers to accept good ethical precepts but it is more difficult to get them to apply them. In philosophy, there is the claim that we are not able to draw moral (logically derived) conclusions from facts alone. It was David Hume (1711–76) in his *A Treatise of Human Nature* who first argued that we could never justify an inference that proceeds from an 'is' to an 'ought', that is, that proceeds from a description of 'what is' to a prescription of how things ought to be: statements about facts cannot justify claims about values. G.E. Moore (1873–1958) in his *Principia Ethica* (1903) elaborated in arguing that it was a mistake to define 'good' in a way that ties it to any natural property. Ethical concepts cannot be defined in terms of natural properties. To do so would commit the *naturalistic fallacy*. More recently, the *naturalistic fallacy* has evolved to mean drawing a conclusion about what we 'ought' to do from the 'facts' alone, giving rise to the slogan: 'ought' cannot be deduced from 'is'. But for those studying ethics, this slogan has provided little guidance as to what is the ethical thing to do. That said, the word 'ought' need not refer to any moral imperative as when we say the consumer 'ought' to check the product before buying. A more controversial claim is that 'ought' implies 'can' in that the word would appear empty otherwise. But there are situations where some purpose is served in saying 'ought', while at the same time denying 'can'.

For many philosophers, the world of facts described in science and the world of values described by ethics are forever distinct. Does this mean that if I know a product is unsafe, I cannot conclude I ought to tell the relevant authorities? It would be argued that 'unsafe' is a value judgment not some fact so the distinction between fact and value remains intact. It is not suggested that no action should be taken on the facts revealed but that what action we take cannot be logically deduced from the facts as there are many alternative courses of action. But there are also situations where the move from an 'is' to a specific 'ought' seems justified as when I accept the fact that I am in pain and feel it *ought* to be treated.

Equity, as a principle, falls under the concept of *objective-relativism* which claims that, while the right ethical decision is relative to the situation, the decision can still be objectively right or objectively wrong as in the case of contradictory proverbs. The contradiction is reconciled by recognizing that, while their appropriate application is relative to circumstances, the application is objective and not a subjective matter in that we have no problem in saying which proverb applies in what situation.

This is true of equity. It also has application to generalizations from social science findings. Just as proverbs can be contradictory (my favorite example: too many cooks spoil the broth versus many hands make light work) but we can still determine which proverb is apt given the context. Both principles of marketing and social science findings depend on context for their applicability. In other words, we should not simply dismiss some findings but see where they might be applicable. This is the pragmatic approach. The appropriateness of a principle is tied to the situation; that is, whether the principle is applicable or not depends on the context which suggests whether it can be validly applied. It even applies to the 'canons of construction' in law where for every canon one might seek to apply there is an equal and opposite canon (Llewellyn 1960).

In the 24 July 2006 edition of *Fortune*, the magazine headline was 'Sorry, Jack! Welch's Rules for Winning Don't Work Anymore (But We've Got 7 New Ones That Do)'. But there have never been universal rules of business strategy, any more than there are universal laws in social science, since, in both cases, context is decisive and contexts change. The *Harvard Business Review* exploits this fact in taking the existing wisdom and, with many examples from industry, suggesting it is no longer true. But we can always show exceptions to any universal panaceas for success, the new wisdom later becoming the new candidate for demolition. Although seldom acknowledged, there seems to be an implicit belief in the business world in the existence of a 'one best way', though given any objective there will be many means to achieve the same end.

Although there may be no uniformity of judgment as to what is 'fair' or 'unfair', this does not imply that decisions on equity in individual cases are arbitrary. One approach is to argue that ethical claims are concerned with human well-being and can be evaluated in terms of being reasonable or unreasonable by reference to social norms.

Every buyer is disposed to reject an offer that is perceived as violating the norms of what is considered fair or just, even if self-interest would dictate otherwise. On the other hand, a commitment by the seller to fairness is part of the seller's ethical responsibility which is to ensure company policies and actions do not threaten individual and public well-being – do not intentionally deceive – while compensating for injuries that occur in carrying on business. Seller violations of equity norms destroy trust in the seller, while undermining the seller's *reputational capital*. The slow response of Toyota to the problem of the accelerator pedal undermined Toyota's reputational capital in the area of quality which had been its critical advantage. Goldman Sachs is still trying to shake off its image as a nasty and rapacious predator whose chief goal is to single-mindedly enhance the wealth of its financiers (not investors) above all else. This image will affect the type of recruits it attracts. It is interesting to note that Goldman Sachs promotes itself in the following way: 'Our clients' interests always come first.' As one commentator says: 'in the light of the Penn Central scandal, this principle looked as if it had been mostly honoured in the breach' (Cohan 2011). In 2010, the Securities and Exchange Commission charged Goldman Sachs with selling securities that they knew would fail and then betting against them!.

The approach to equity in the marketing literature is one of trying to fit equity into the RCT framework of gains and losses. This will not do. It is an illicit graft in the sense that equity issues and calculations of tangible gains and losses do not gel.

JUSTICE AND EQUITY

How does the concept of justice fit the concept of equity? The doctrine of justice as advocated by Rawls (1971) is coterminous with fairness and can be seen as advancing a claim for the primacy of distributive justice in settling claims over what is just. On the other hand, the notions of fair trading, fair wages and fair treatment use the term 'fair' to denote justice in transactions rather than distribution. Although the term justice may be equated with equity, it is more properly a goal of political activity, most directly applied to setting up and evaluating legal systems.

Rawls (1971) in his *Theory of Justice* articulates the principles of justice (pp. 259–65) that might underlie a democratic state. In order to arrive at these, Rawls revives the notion of a social contract, while arguing that people would prefer to live in a society where there was equal liberty with a minimum of social and economic inequities. For Rawls, justice requires that society be governed by the principles that free rational individuals would endorse from a position of equality. His first principle of justice would guarantee basic liberties for all, while his second principle would afford everyone fair and equal opportunities to develop their own capacities and talents. His third and final principle would require economic inequalities be so arranged as to provide maximum benefits for society's least advantaged. He rejects *utilitarianism* on the grounds that it allows the welfare of some people to be pushed aside for the greater good of society. His 'just' social contract is one we would agree on, providing we did not know in advance what it would mean to us individually. This echoes Adam Smith's doctrine of the 'impartial spectator' whose assumed disinterested judgment we should use to distinguish right from wrong in any given situation or society (Raphael and Macfie 1984). The concept of the impartial spectator is useful for judging the relative merits in an equity dispute. However, to many this would seem more properly to be the domain of ethical theory. In practice, the most important ethical questions tend to be complicated, with consequences difficult to foresee and probabilities difficult to establish. This is why so many ethical issues are shelved and judgment suspended.

Needless to say, Rawls's theory of justice has given rise to alternative views. Harvard philosopher Robert Nozick's (1975) libertarian view, called 'entitlement theory', would guarantee absolute property rights and unregulated economic liberties within an ultra-minimal state; a state that would provide no public goods or services or even benefits for the incapacitated. Public goods have two distinguishing features: one person's use does not prevent the use by others (e.g. public parks) and, second, it is difficult to prevent people using public goods for nothing (Cassidy 2009). Nozick's philosophy carries great weight with some politicians in the US today, where his view on the role of government resonates.

The latest contribution is from Amartya Sen (2010), a Nobel Laureate in economics, specializing in welfare economics. Sen greatly expanded the scope of *social choice theory*, defined as the study of decisions by groups of people (including societies), which aims to develop a foundation for reaching a collective decision, given the differences in preferences and values among members of the group. Majority rule will not do. As the economist Kenneth Arrow shows, majority rule encounters problems of inconsistency in ordering different preferences. Social choice theory arrives at social choices or decisions by calculating the effects on people's well-being that arise from alternative social policies. Sen rejects the notion of measuring personal well-being by the satisfaction of desires or preferences since preferences often arise from mistaken beliefs or are adaptations to miserable or forced circumstances. Similarly, he rejects measuring well-being by income and wealth. Instead of measuring utility or one's resources, well-being should be evaluated according to 'capabilities for functioning' that allow people to exercise effective freedoms to choose to do what they value. Capabilities include having adequate nutrition; health and personal safety; freedom from fear; literacy; and being able to appear in public without shame. Sen's social justice would focus on providing adequate capabilities for functioning in a context of real opportunities. Sen, like Adam Smith and Rawls, pushes the notion of the 'impartial spectator' in assessing laws, policies and actions. But Sen considers Rawls's theory as an 'ideal' unable to cope with real-world issues addressing existing injustices. This seems too harsh a judgment for those of us who see a motivating vision in any 'ideal' theory.

ETHICAL THEORY AND EQUITY

Issues of equity theory shade into broader ethical issues, for example the ethics of human organs harvested from prisoners or bought from the impoverished elsewhere in the world, or the more mundane lack of ethics in pricing, information provision and product safety. More typical are deceptions in advertising. There are numerous examples. Nivea was ordered to withdraw its DNAge face cream for misleading claims, while in 2005 L'Oréal was accused of misleading claims about its anti-creasing cream being able to rapidly reduce wrinkles. Currently, there is the problem of functional foods where foods are claimed to have curative properties. This extension of foods into functions normally reserved for drugs has led the Food and Drug Administration (FDA) in the US to revise the rules for nutritional claims on food labels. For example, General Mills has been taken to task for claiming its popular breakfast cereal *Cheerios* has been 'clinically proven to lower cholesterol'. But often the deception is more subtle, as when the car dealer posts two prices: (i) the manufacturer's suggested retail price; and (ii) the dealer's invoice price. The buyer often focuses on the dealer's invoice price even though both prices are purely artificial, chosen by the car manufacturer and dealer to facilitate their negotiation with the prospect. As for financial services, Madoff, siphoning off billions in his Ponzi scheme, was merely the most egregious case. But deception on the part of politicians is considered so common that someone once defined a gaffe as a politician who tells the truth to the public.

Pharmaceutical companies and financial institutions are often accused of getting away with deception through consumers not being knowledgeable enough to make a sound judgment on their products. This is the problem. Far from being all-knowledgeable, the consumer has often to rely on companies telling the truth. When the consumer is not expert enough to judge, the temptation to deceive is hard to resist. The danger in all these claims to health benefits is that they might encourage consumers to believe there is no need to consult doctors. But, of course, consumers themselves can exhibit unethical behavior, a classical example being 'deshopping' where something is bought with the intention of using it once and then returning it for a refund.

With respect to deception, there has been a growth of lawsuits over ads whose assertions require proof or are just not true. Firms are filing lawsuits to force competitors to withdraw or amend some ads. Thus AT&T sued Verizon Wireless over an ad it used that falsely suggested AT&T had no cell phone coverage in certain areas on the map. This filing of a lawsuit is one way of announcing to the world the competitor's lack of honesty. Advertising is a promise and, like all promises, builds up expectations. When consumer expectations are not realized there is disappointment that can lead to a backlash against the product advertised. Hence overpromising has inherent dangers which advertising agencies may ignore at a cost.

Although we are not able to uphold ethical or moral standards by the methods of science, we are typically in a position to show the dysfunctional consequences of having no ethical or moral standards. The word 'ethics' is from the Greek *ethikos*, and 'moral' from the Latin *moralis*. In Anglo-American philosophy it was once common to make a sharp distinction between talking about morals and talking about ethics, with morals reserved for first-order questions about good and evil as well as relations between humans generally. Ethics was a second-order discipline concerned with analyzing ethical concepts and not with answering moral questions at all. But from the late 1950s, philosophers have increasingly used their philosophical expertise to comment on all manner of moral and ethical issues. Some ethical standards can be better defended than others in terms of (say) basic 'needs' for: (a) survival; (b) to belong; (c) order and (d) security. As Rapoport (1953) says, there is no point in trying to justify our pursuit of these four invariant needs.

While the philosophy of science is concerned with reasoning in scientific investigations, ethics is concerned with the *justification* of actions that may be harmful to innocent others. In ethics there are the 'minimalists' like Milton Friedman (1962) who claim business ethics should be minimal, while others appeal to higher standards of social responsibility. But James Kuhn (2008), Emeritus Professor of Ethics at Columbia, points out that, contrary to popular opinion, Friedman claims that an equitable society is a necessary condition for free markets and, since a necessary condition for success is a sufficient reason for failure, Friedman in effect places the highest value on achieving an equitable society. In support, James Kuhn says:

> Only if the moral foundations of a market are behaviorally present in and among participants, can a free, competitive-market exist and deliver its promised benefit [p. 6] ... a general trustworthiness among those interacting in markets may contribute more to ease commercial relationships – as well as economic efficiency – than does single-minded pursuit of self-interest.

(Kuhn 1995: 6–13)

This does not explain why deceiving the consumer is ethically wrong. And deception is prevalent. Weiss (2006) calls the investment practices of Wall Street a cesspool of unethical behavior – helped by the consumer signing papers he does not read, buying investment products he does not understand from brokers whose backgrounds are unknown. To answer this question – why deceiving the consumer is ethically wrong – we are tempted to look to ethical theory. An ethically good action, like a good product, meets some criteria of 'goodness' but the criteria in the two cases are not comparable.

Excluding Divine Law, there are four ethical theories: the *deontological* (Kantian) approach which focuses on the acts themselves, insisting they conform to some moral absolutist position ('Thou shalt not kill ... under any conditions'). The approach is both prescriptive and of universal scope though it is difficult to think of something that is always wrong in all circumstances. The next is the *consequentialist* tradition which focuses on consequences, as with *utilitarianism* which is a consequentialist theory. The right action here is that which generates the highest expected utility for all. A recent variation is Sam Harris's definition of the 'good' as promoting the well-being of conscious creatures (Harris 2011). The next is the *contractarian* view which is Rawls's position (see earlier) rooted in fundamental individual rights emanating from a hypothetical (as if) contract with society. Finally there is *communitarianism* where moral justification is rooted in community tradition – what the virtuous person would do in that tradition. This view is reflected in the demand that the US not violate its traditional values by allowing its security agencies to indulge in torture. The most commonly drawn upon ethical theories are deontological ways of thinking (Thomas Nagel 1979) and the utilitarian/consequentialist tradition (Singer 1979).

Many philosophers argue that it is difficult to defend any ethical approach that does not take account of consequences. In fact, what may seem to be a deontological position may have been adopted for good consequentialist reasons. Yet utilitarianism occasionally has problems in its conflict with individual rights, with John Rawls proposing the fundamental right to equal liberty from which all other defensible rights can be deduced. What is all too common is to define unethical behavior only on the basis of the harm done through our actions, ignoring completely the good we failed to achieve through inaction.

Flanagan (1996), a philosopher, claims none of these ethical theories offer answers or much guidance in any ethical controversy because the wisdom we seek in ethics is often geographically local and temporarily local (p. 123), and morality resists theoretical unification under either a set of special-purpose rules or a single general-purpose rule (p. 127). Toulmin (2001), another philosopher, has this advice to those teaching ethics:

> doctors, nurses and paramedics taking courses in applied ethics found the abstractions of philosophical analysis too general and theoretical to be useful teaching tools. When required to master the definitions of 'deontology' and 'consequentialism', apprentice nurses dropped out in droves. Real-life cases they understood and enjoyed, but theoretical modes of analysis were less than ideal ways to resolve the quandaries of practice at the bedsides of individual patients.
>
> (Toulmin 2001: 121)

What these philosophers are reacting against is the notion that there are rules that can be mechanically applied to solve ethical problems. There is a temptation to suggest rules because rules are always welcome as a substitute for hard thinking. But just following rules blindly can lead to putting in standard solutions when standard conditions don't exist.

Courses on ethics are a latecomer to business schools, emerging in the 1970s, with the focus on the ethical justification of business structures; the ethical responsibilities of management; fairness in the workplace and so on. Courses, largely through case studies, sensitize students to the ethical responsibilities of corporations to consumers, workers, shareholders and the general public and, most important of all, talk about how to implement and monitor ethical behavior within the company. In brief, courses sensitize future managers to interpreting what activity constitutes unethical behavior. If done well, it induces a sensitivity to ethical norms so that breaking such norms becomes shameful.

Some academics reject the whole notion of employing principles and instead talk about 'particularism' (Dancy 2005). To allow generality, ethical principles assume sameness across situations which can be denied. In contrast, *particularism* advocates, in each case, forming new judgments tied to context. But does not particularism draw implicitly on generalities? We talk about the 'nomothetic' sciences seeking general laws and contrast this with 'ideographic' disciplines like history that set out to understand the unique and non-recurrent. Particularism is ideographic and, it could be argued, ideographic studies are important for customization. Ideographic studies take account of context so ideographic studies are basic for studying particular situations. But in all ideographic studies there is inevitably a tacit acceptance of generalizations. All problems have unique features that need to be considered but it does not follow from this that treating certain problems as belonging to a certain general class of problems and thus amenable to a certain type of treatment is impossible. In fact it is essential and the only way to interpret what we mean by experience. But generalizing from any set of observations is not error-free in that there are many competing generalizations that can be made from the same set of observations.

EQUITY IN THE CONSUMER BEHAVIOR LITERATURE

In the consumer behavior literature, equity is generally treated as a contributor to customer satisfaction. This seems logical since equity does enter into customer satisfaction. But the literature incorporates equity into the economist's cost–benefit function, which is wrong. This notion of cost–benefit arises when we seek to reduce everything to a money base. In such a case, utility theory is converted into a cost–benefit analysis which avoids confusing the market value of something with its subjective value. The trouble with the notion of 'utility' generally is that it cannot be measured on a ratio scale (like measuring a piece of cloth) because no one has succeeded in providing an agreed natural zero point for utility, though attempts have been made to get round the problem with the concept of *indifference curves*.

The following equity studies in marketing discussed below are within the loss/gain format of rational choice theory (RCT). Bolton and Lemon's study (1999) on 'payment equity' is clearly defined in terms of cost–benefit analysis:

> Payment equity is the customer's changing evaluation of fairness of the level of economic benefits derived from usage in relation to economic costs.

(Bolton and Lemon 1999: 3)

Tax et al. (1998) talk of equity in considering complaint-handling situations but equity issues are addressed within the cost–benefit framework. The authors argue that equity is a part of what they describe as psychic costs and psychic benefits, but this does not get away from the cost–benefit framework since everything that costs something has a psychic impact. Similarly, everything that throws off benefits will evoke favorable feelings or psychic benefits.

Szymanski and Henard (2001) found equity to be the most important antecedent to customer satisfaction and dissatisfaction. Dissatisfaction is likely to be felt more intensely than satisfaction and hence have more effect on repeat purchase. But what they have to say about equity is rooted in the cost–benefit calculations to maximize benefit. Positive emotional benefits arise from experiencing fair treatment, while negative emotional costs arise from experiencing unfair treatment. The authors argue that customer satisfaction has focused predominantly on modeling the effects of expectations, disconfirmation of expectations, performance, affect and equity:

(a) Expectations: consumers are assumed to assimilate satisfaction levels to expectation levels to avoid any cognitive dissonance that would arise when expectations and satisfaction levels diverge.

(b) Disconfirmation of expectations: the consumer is assumed to use expectations as the standard against which performance outcomes are assessed. Consumers are said to be satisfied when actual outcomes exceed expectations (positive disconfirmation), dissatisfied when expectations exceed outcomes (negative disconfirmation) and just satisfied (zero disconfirmation).

(c) Performance: assumed to directly affect satisfaction, in the sense of customers being more likely to be satisfied with the offering if it provides what they want in relation to the costs incurred.

(d) Affect: in that satisfaction is influenced by the affective component of the offering.

(e) Equity: in the sense of fairness, rightness or 'deservingness' judgments that consumers make about what they receive in relation to some reference group.

Although expectation has its roots in Tolman's purposive behaviorism, it is a foundational concept of RCT, with economists, as we have seen, subscribing either to adaptive expectations or rational expectations. Without standards there can be no guidance for making any sort of judgment and expectations constitute a standard for the consumer. No consumer purchases anything unless he or she has some idea of what to expect ('buying a pig in a poke' may occur but it is never something expected). Whatever the performance of the product, it will have to be judged before and after purchase against some standard/expectation. The same goes for affect and equity. However, the separation of affect and equity in the article is incoherent since affect studies inevitably overlap with equity considerations.

The Szymanski and Henard article is coupled with the notion of expectations about costs (in terms of performance, affect and equity), set against expectations of benefits. This is the cost–benefit format. When we talk about expectations, or better still exceeding expectations, this sets a standard that puts us high on the satisfaction scale but in the process makes the concept of satisfaction somewhat redundant. Meeting or exceeding expectations is more meaningful and operational than talking about satisfaction since satisfaction is a matter of degree: a product that pleases wins over a product that merely satisfies.

All the above studies are right in giving prominence to ethical issues as influencing consumer behavior and post-purchase reservations. But all the studies can be faulted for forcing equity considerations into the cost–material benefits framework. Elster (1999) makes the criticism explicit. Equity issues are typically emotional and Elster rejects any model of rational decision-making that seeks to fit emotional issues into a cost–benefit function. As Elster says:

> I am not saying that shame is a 'cost' that can be added to other costs of action. Just as emotions can override interest, interest can override emotions but that is not to say that emotions are arguments in a cost-benefit function. For some purposes, shame may be usefully modeled as a cost, but only as a rough approximation and in an 'as if' sense. A person, who thought of shame as a cost, similar to a parking fine, would probably not feel any. Similarly ... a person who thought of guilt as a cost that could be eliminated by taking a guilt-erasing pill would probably not feel any.
>
> (Elster 1999: 155)

TRUST AND LOYALTY

Trust: Violations of ethical norms of equity undermine trust and loyalty, both being factors in influencing consumer behavior. Because trust is part of everyone's vocabulary, it is usually regarded as unproblematic but it needs to be unpacked which means distinguishing it from similar concepts. Seligman (1997) distinguishes trust from 'confidence', 'faith' and 'familiarity'. Seligman points out that trust is necessary for the workings of society, and trustworthiness is the warrant for promise-keeping and promise-keeping assumes bonds of trust. He separates 'trust in people' from trust in 'abstract systems', though it could be argued that trust in abstract systems like mathematical models can and often does stem from trust in those developing or promoting the system.

Seligman rightly states that it is often more appropriate to speak of *confidence* in institutions and abstract systems than to talk of trust. This is because confidence is less demanding of attachment than trust. We can be confident a company will do the right thing if it is in their self-interest or because of legal and social pressures, without giving them our trust.

Trust resolves doubts about the other party. Trust can induce people to dispense with sensible buying 'principles' like checking on the standing and credibility of the other person. Trust, as Seligman notes, comes into interpersonal relations: (a) with 'role negotiability' (the other party could act otherwise); (b) when role expectations cannot be relied on; and (c) against a background of indeterminacy and ambiguity. Trust is neither faith nor confidence in the product or person, while mistrust cannot be equated simply with lack of confidence. We talk inappropriately about having trust in the other party, institution, product or brand when we simply mean there is a basis for having positive expectations.

Most business relations are based on contractual obligations, giving rise to mutual confidence about role expectations. Role expectations rely on social norms, not the law, for example the principle of reciprocity whereby people feel an obligation to return a favor of any kind. *Supportive* interaction through time gives rise to liking and with liking comes a sense of solidarity and trust. Trust leads us to accept, on occasion, unequal exchanges because we believe things will even out over time. But this belief is not essential since signaling trust and having a trusting relationship can bring its own reward.

Loyalty: When there is sentiment, nostalgia or positive emotion linked to trust, it becomes the basis for loyalty. Many marketers regard buying the same brand a number of times as operationally defining loyalty. I and many others like me have, over the years, bought upgrades of Microsoft Word, but feel no loyalty to Microsoft and would drop them in an instant if a feasible alternative came along. Operational measures that are this remote from the sense-meaning of the basic concept of loyalty are common in the marketing literature which indicates indifference to conceptual clarity. The measure misses the emotional element while failing to distinguish between habit and loyalty and the presence of feasible alternatives which loyalty presupposes. Loyalty to a monopolist makes no sense as there are no rivals to patronize. Sentiment for some item, person or thing is linked to loyalty as it is to liking. One recent development in market research is *sentiment analysis* whereby attention is paid to the language used in, say, online media like Twitter to discern a change in sentiment as a gauge of likely changes in behavior. This comes back to the recognition that every communication carries not only a message but also a tone – and tone can be very indicative of attitude.

A recent suggestion from a *Harvard Business Review* article, discussed by *Business Week* (30 January 2006, pp. 94–5), for measuring loyalty is simply to ask: 'On a scale of zero to 10, how likely is it that you would recommend us to your friends or colleagues?' *Promoters* are those who give high responses and *detractors* are those who give low responses: net promoter scores measure the difference between the two sets of scores and these correlate closely with a company's growth revenue. But this is surely a way of measuring the proportion of loyalty *suspects* not loyal customers, since a consumer can highly recommend a product because they trust it rather than because they are loyal to it. Loyalty can withstand more assaults than trust alone since trust is more easily undermined by the evidence. An example of loyalty is the child's attachment to its security blanket which it clings on to in preference to any identical replacement. Brand loyalty in this sense is more likely to be given to those providing personal services like a doctor or hairdresser. A man may have used Gillette razor blades all his adult life but have no problem moving to a rival like the Schick Quattro razor (or Wilkinson in the UK) that offers something additional. It is much wiser for Gillette to think of itself as *renting allegiance* for only as long as it has a superior product, than it is for Gillette to talk of possessing customer loyalty. If we look at the share of shoppers who claim they are extremely or likely to stick with the one brand when choosing, pet food (50 percent) comes first, followed by soft drinks/juices (40 percent), condiments, baby food, pasta sauce and breakfast foods (*Business Week*, 25 November 2002, p. 10). These are typical habitual buys rather than products likely to incite an emotional attachment.

Amazon.com talks about increasing customer loyalty through Amazon Prime, which is their ordering system whereby for $79 per year customers get free shipping and their orders delivered in two days. This is an exemplar of renting customer allegiance in that customers are attracted by the 'free' fast service and will spend more than before to make sure they can justify the $79. Take away the perceived money saving and the additional 'loyalty' will I suspect disappear.

In any case, it is totally inadequate to operationally define 'loyalty' by repeatedly buying the product. This would make me a loyal customer of Microsoft and lots of other quasi-monopolies as well as failing to capture the sense-meaning of loyalty. There is recognition that repeatedly buying the same brand is more in tune with habitual buying than with brand loyalty. A slightly better approach is to measure *attitudinal brand loyalty* by asking members of the target segment to rate the brands on the basis of liking and preference. But still more is needed to capture the trust and sentiment elements of brand loyalty. Performance of a brand and the centrality of the brand to the consumer contribute to loyalty but, as with political parties, neither is necessary nor sufficient for loyalty.

Violations of equity undermine trust and can destroy loyalty. But even if organizations follow the norms of equity with customers, yet behave outrageously with other stakeholders, there can be a backlash from customers. Customers do not simply look to how they are treated personally but are influenced by the total picture. If loyalty does involve trust and emotional attachment, then loyalty is not pervasive in markets except for personal loyalties to those who perform services for us. The term 'loyalty' belongs to social relationships even if it is used outside of social relations. This does not mean consumers cannot be loyal to a company or a product but it is not what we can take for granted – though we might expect more loyalty where we get the customer to view the product as a person, as may occur with products that can be set in motion.

Sellers should not look merely at costs and benefits but also take account of consumer perceptions of what is fair, since violation of what is considered fair can lead to the rejection of what the firm has to offer. This is so apparent that it amounts to a truism. What is perhaps lacking is the recognition of how important it is and the failure of sellers to collect information on consumer equity perceptions. These perceptions may surprise marketers by the presence of so much latent anger. Equity issues tap deeply into the emotions and can be decisive in continuing patronage. Also, unless companies take account of perceptions of fairness, they find a diminution of reputational capital as trust in their organization erodes. Both loyalty and trust are 'earned the hard way' and not to be jeopardized by consumer perceptions of 'sharp practice'.

That action is sufficiently rational to be intelligible is a necessary assumption for interpreting action. But economics has a narrow view (self-interest only, no altruism) of rationality. It assumes a rationality that makes it difficult to take account of ethical principles that are not self-interested; of altruistic actions; of actions undertaken as part of a social role; actions taken because they appear dignified and socially appropriate; and actions that are expressive rather than instrumental (Kirsh 1983). Where communal relationships are well established, people commonly act for others without expecting a favor in return and some people act in an altruistic way through a belief that this is the right thing to do morally.

WEBSITE REDESIGN CASE

A consultant on website redesign wrote to the ethicist employed by the *New York Times* (24 November 2009) that he was told by one of his clients that any generic picture of an African-American customer could deter others from patronizing the client's business. The client claimed that none of his customers was in fact African-American. The consultant asked the ethicist if race could be a factor in choice.

The ethicist, in reply, argued that race could be a factor only if germane to the product or service on offer like hair-care products developed for African-American hair. For the ethicist, the client using race to define a generic customer is simply racist, while to decline to use a photo of an African-American because it might deter others from buying is to 'yield to racism'.

Case questions

1. Would the adherents of rational choice theory offer the same advice given the facts presented in the case?
2. How would those single-mindedly pursuing rational choice theory justify avoiding any use of a picture of a generic African-American in this particular case?
3. If one looks at ads in the 1960s and compares them to today's ads, a striking feature is the employment of black Americans in sponsoring or promoting a product or as an illustrative customer of the product. How might you explain this?

DISCUSSION QUESTIONS ON CHAPTER 9 (RATIONAL CHOICE THEORY)

1. 'Rational choice theory is a theory of best action, not a theory of rational action.' Discuss.

2. Even if the consumer was given perfect information about the relevant set of options and their consequences, it would not necessarily result in an optimal decision. Discuss.

3. If you accept the notion of Kahneman and Tversky that people are more concerned with losses than with corresponding gains, what might this tell you about investor behavior? Would this help explain the roller-coaster behavior of the stock market in 2011?

4. Show how treating the consumer fairly ties into enlightened self-interest. How is it then that many financial institutions are notorious for not treating the customer fairly? Is deception incompatible in the long term with a firm's reputational capital?

5. Explain why a consumer can have trust in a company but is not loyal to that company. Why might you be more inclined to speak of renting the allegiance of your customer than talking about their loyalty?

6. Value Clothes' competitive advantage is 'value-for-money' in that it sells clothing that is both competitively fashionable yet at prices below the competition. The debate is over whether to prominently display the firm's name and logo on the front of their sports shirts and so on, as do Ralph Lauren and other prestigious manufacturers. Jim Brown, an economist by training, is all in favor, arguing there is nothing to lose and it could attract attention. Tim Evans, who has spent his business career in marketing, argues against such a policy in spite of its prevalence. He argues that stressing the value-for-money claim is incompatible with putting the firm's name and logo on the front of its jerseys, as it signals to the public at large that the wearer is wearing a cheap shirt. Recognizing that this is so, the potential customer will hesitate to buy, so sales will be reduced rather than increased. What do you think?

Chapter 10

Behavioral Economics

ECONOMICS AND PSYCHOLOGY

In the nineteenth century, economics and psychology were grouped together (as was the case with philosophy and religion) and studied together but, later, economics sought to separate itself from psychology. Today's psychology quickly disabuses us of any notion that economic criteria are the only criteria employed in making a decision. *The Economist* magazine once said something to the effect that in the affairs of man, wounded pride and xenophobia often trump economic reason. Why else would Russia terrorize its gas customers? Or Britons demonize the European Union? In a rational world China would not stir up Japanophobia and rich Saudis would not help Islamic extremists abroad. To economists, emotions are unlikely to be viewed as an early information system but something they hope will just go away. But the neglect of emotion is not the only sin of omission by economists. Criticism by economists themselves points to the failure of economists to pay attention to empirical, behavioral research and instead base their theories of markets on idealized market theory.

Top leaders, whether in government or business, who exclusively apply economic and technical criteria in dealing with people are likely to alienate, being perceived as callous or indifferent to human concerns. Leaders are not just expected to act decisively in the interests of the nation or organization but are also expected to exercise compassion. That said, the separation of economics from psychology resulted from a desire for an autonomous science of economics that did not fall back on mental constructs, so the term 'preference', for example, as a mental construct, became 'revealed preference': something empirically verifiable. But the many attacks on rational choice theory (RCT), as well as the thrashing given to the concept of rational economic man by psychologists of the caliber of Tversky and Kahneman and Herbert Simon, resulted in a movement to bring psychology and economics together under the rubric of *behavioral economics*. A whole multitude of well-known economists and psychologists are quoted in developing behavioral economics, such as Adam Smith, Herbert Simon, Amos Tversky and Daniel Kahneman (prospect theory) and (often forgotten) Arthur Cecil Pigou, a contemporary of Keynes at Cambridge, who concerned himself with the way economic psychology, like undue optimism or undue pessimism, could influence business cycles (Pigou 1929). George Loewenstein of Carnegie Mellon and Richard Thaler of the University of Chicago are commonly regarded as pioneers in the field, now joined by economists like David Laibson of Harvard, Colin Camerer of Caltech and Esther Duflo and Dan Ariely (formerly of the Massachusetts Institute of Technology) at Duke.

Behavioral economics seeks to explain what appear to be 'irrational' decisions in the economic arena. Thus as Loewenstein and Ubel (2010) say:

> Behavioral economics helps explain why, for example, people undersave for retirement, why they eat too much and exercise too little and why they buy energy-inefficient light bulbs and appliances. And, by understanding the causes of these problems, behavioral economics has spawned a number of creative interventions to deal with them.
>
> (Loewenstein and Ubel 2010)

Behavioral economics has been influenced primarily by cognitive and social psychology. Given that this is so, it does not have a distinct perspective except for its focus on economic behavior. But there are also behavioral economists interested in *neuroeconomics* or behavioral genetics which aims at understanding not just the psychological forces at work, but the underlying neural machinery, using technology like the *f*MRI scanner. Neuroeconomics shifts away from traditional economics and psychology to draw on biological models to undertake studies like finding the underlying biology of altruism and trust, notions ruled out in RCT. Behavioral genetics or neuroeconomics views what happens in a culture or the environment as possible triggers for genes that require activation. It is generally assumed that genes account for a large proportion of the differences between individuals, hence the search for genes underlying various diseases though this research so far has not been fruitful. One problem lies in the fact that genes do not work independently but act in conjunction with the environment. One route by which genes affect behavior is through *neurotransmitters*, consisting of chemicals that transport messages among nerve cells. But hormones also play a role in affecting behavior, for example oxytocin is claimed to promote trust. But there is little so far in behavioral genetics that has much significance for marketing. In this chapter we confine our discussion to mainstream behavioral economics and ignore neuroeconomics, which is still in its infancy.

One field of behavioral economics has been behavioral finance to explain things like speculative bubbles and other events that undermine the efficient market hypothesis. But the two authors of the quotation above go on to claim that behavioral economics is being asked to solve problems it was not meant to address and argue that behavioral economics should complement, not substitute for, more substantive economic interventions.

With respect to the claim that behavioral economics deals with economic decisions that appear 'irrational', justification of the term 'irrational' occurs only against the norm of rational choice theory. The fact that these so-called irrational decisions are explainable suggests that the behavior is in fact intelligible. Thus 'irrational' corporate takeovers have been explained by 'hubris', the concept of 'disaster myopia' and 'ambiguity aversion'. But true irrationality involves deliberately harming one's own interests without compensating reason. This is not the case here.

Traditionally, as already stated, empirical studies in economics (as opposed to the purely rational mathematical models) follow what John Stuart Mill in the nineteenth century called 'the method of concomitant variations' which assesses the variation among factors that may or may not be causally related. It finds its contemporary expression in the techniques of multivariate analysis in statistics. But those economists in the field of behavioral economics have been adept at adopting *experimental* approaches, modeled after experimental psychology, as they seek explanations of 'irrational' behavior. This is its major departure from mainstream economics where talk of experimental design and experimental and control groups is foreign.

One of the more popular books on behavioral economics designed for public consumption is Dan Ariely's *Predictably Irrational* (2008), and one of the most prominent economists supportive of behavioral economics is Larry Summers, ex-President of Harvard University and ex-senior economic adviser in the Obama administration.

Behavioral economics seeks to explain errors in judgment and reasoning among all economic agents (including consumers) that result in making non-rational decisions. It originated as a hybrid of economics and social or cognitive psychology. Behavioral economics, like the behaviorists, is acutely sensitive to the desire for instant gratification and the conflict between this notion and the forbearance needed to reap greater rewards in the future. In fact Adam Smith himself, and later the Cambridge economist Arthur Pigou, stressed the consumer's preference for instant gratification rather than deferring satisfaction. There is an acceptance that most actions are driven by immediate desires and are not the result of well thought out deliberations. Thus it is hardly rational to get into heavy debt with credit cards when orthodox economics claims that rational long-term self-interest guides behavior. Contrary to orthodox economics, there is a strong tendency to put off any action that requires an immediate unpalatable cost such as exercising and dieting, even though these things have a long-term payoff.

Not surprisingly, many of the concepts and findings of behavioral economics are to be found already in psychology and the consumer behavior literature, without having had the visibility they have received in behavioral economics. Thus, as we have seen in Chapter 6, cognitive psychologists have drawn attention, as now have behavioral economists, to the employment of heuristics in the making of decisions, often eschewing rational analysis. Heuristics can be defined as cognitive rules of thumb or mental shortcuts which consumers and people generally use every day in routine decision-making. The use of heuristics is both essential and inevitable to cope with life's problems (Herbert 2010).

The importance of how an issue, problem or product is described or 'framed' is also well established in the psychological literature, though behavioral economics has made it a major topic of interest. The inefficiencies of the market have been of interest to marketing academics, though not to the extent manifested in behavioral economists. Again in behavioral economics, a good deal of emphasis is placed on making things convenient because lacking convenience is a cost. For instance, poor families are deterred from applying for financial aid for their children because the application forms are much too complicated. (We are reminded that around 25 percent of adults are functionally illiterate.) There is also the recognition of how people will 'cut off their nose to spite their face'; that consumers are, for example, prepared to suffer a financial loss in casino-type games to exact revenge on a player perceived as acting unfairly. Behavioral economists have rediscovered the importance of 'association' in persuasion so that just labeling estate tax as the 'death tax' can radically change perspectives. (Interestingly, estate taxes have always been called 'death duties' in the UK, emphasizing the 'duty', not the tax.) If orthodox economics sees success solely in terms of producing something functionally better than rivals, behavioral economics knows, as marketing has known from its infancy, that how something is *framed* makes a great deal of difference to marketing success.

Kahneman (2011) has brought much of his work with Tversky together with his more recent views. His example of framing is particularly dramatic. Apparently, test surgery patients were more likely to choose surgery if informed that the survival rate was 90 percent than told the mortality rate was 10 percent. He uses the finding that people seek to avoid feelings of regret to argue that this can commonly result in people investing time and money into failing projects in which investment has already been made (the fallacy of sunk costs). But what is distinctive in his latest book is his model of man as comprising of two systems: System 1 and System 2. System 2 is the thinking mind which deliberates slowly and is associated with our stereotypical view of rational man. In contrast, System 1 is in charge when the mind acts automatically and effortlessly. System 1 acts on what is in immediate memory as well as learned patterns of association such as money and power. System 1 is the system that forms snap judgments and reactions. System 1 acts on what information it has and, if that information is not there, still supplies an answer based on related but often irrelevant data. This model seems to reflect the view of man as commonly on automatic pilot. Kahneman argues that someone's ability to switch on to System 2 as the need arises is the sign of an active mind and a predictor of success. This claim seems a conceptual truth given the conceptualizations of System 1 and System 2.

HERBERT SIMON'S BOUNDED RATIONALITY AND SATISFICING BEHAVIOR

Behavioral economics can be found early on in Herbert Simon's concept of 'bounded rationality'. This is the notion that people may not possess the cognitive resources to make optimum decisions. Even though they may aim to be rational, they lack what it takes to be so. Thus rational choice theory alone would not explain decisions made. Given this concept of 'bounded rationality' Simon questions the notion of maximizing. Simon (1957) invented the term 'satisficing' to describe the more typical behavior of people searching until they find a workable (satisfactory) solution rather than an optimum one. There are difficulties in optimizing. There is the information difficulty associated with knowing all the relevant alternatives and their consequences; there is the problem of limited resources and time pressures; and finally, the problem of choosing and sustaining the 'right' balance among multiple and conflicting goals. These concepts of Simon, bounded rationality and satisficing, have until recently had little impact on economists. For instance, bounded rationality was regarded as simply 'maximizing within constraints', though bounded rationality takes no account of maximizing. Richard Thaler was another early pioneer in behavioral economics, ignored by mainstream economists, though well known among decision theorists in business schools (Thaler 1985).

PROSPECT THEORY

Economists tended to follow Von Neumann and Morgenstern in believing decision-makers could form probabilistic views of the world in making decisions. Tversky and Kahneman dismissed this claim, arguing that when people are faced with alternatives with uncertain outcomes, they simply employ heuristics or rules of thumb as mental shortcuts. There is thus the so-called *representativeness-heuristic* which notes people's tendency to generalize from a sample which is taken as representative without the evidence to back this up. You only have to listen to politicians to see this happening where anecdotes substitute for sampling and are quoted as proof (often saying the exception 'proves the rule', interpreting 'proves' to mean corroborates when the 'proves' in the phrase is meant to be a synonym for 'test'). Even research social scientists often rush to generalize from small samples, though these are more likely than large samples to produce extreme, non-representative outcomes. In financial markets, the representativeness-heuristic prompts investors to make predictions from short-term market trends and to downplay the likelihood of a reversal. There is also the *availability heuristic* whereby what comes immediately to mind is what affects a decision. A recent air crash makes us all too aware of this possibility and puts many people off flying for quite some time. When an offering on television gives the price as $19.93, the consumer thinks in terms of the price being below $20 as this is what comes to mind and this helps sell the product. It is the same with all other prices that are not rounded off.

In *prospect theory*, Tversky and Kahneman challenge the very notion that economic decisions are made rationally. Prospect theory seeks to describe and explain how people handle uncertain rewards and risks. Although it has proved easy to show the deficiencies of RCT, it has been less easy to put forward an alternative as opposed to suggesting patches. Kahneman and Tversky's (1979) prospect theory is meant to be an exception. While RCT, with its concept of utility maximization, views decision-making in absolute terms, prospect theory claims people make decisions *relative* to how they perceive their current and future state.

Prospect theory is positioned as an alternative to RCT on how choices are made under conditions of risk, but draws on aspects of utility theory and Herbert Simon's notion of 'satisficing'. Both information search and thinking have costs, while there are often time pressures as well as memory limitations. Consumers can be incompetent, inefficient, forgetful, silly and with flawed rationality. Consumers are not always even consistent but tolerate a good deal of inconsistency in what they say and do. Reasons for this, suggested by cognitive psychologists, are that different (inconsistent) beliefs or cognitions are organized in the mind in different 'files' so that inconsistencies may not be recognized unless exposed. Prospect theory accounts for its findings by replacing utilities and probabilities with 'value functions' and 'decision weights' which need not obey the usual probability calculus. These two components of value functions and decision weights are combined. Critically, prospect theory modifies subjective expected utility (SEU) theory to account for a series of experimental results that show that the unmodified SEU model does not describe real behavior. In replacing the concept of utility with the concept of value, prospect theory provides a *value reference point* for evaluating gains and losses. It argues that gains and losses are evaluated in terms of that value reference point and that there is greater subjective value for the *first* marginal gain from the reference point than for subsequent gains.

The *isolation effect* states that there can be inconsistent preferences for identical objective outcomes based on how the outcomes are described or framed. (No one in marketing would doubt this.) The authors underwrite what everyone in consumer marketing knows: that the way alternatives or options are framed or presented heavily impacts the decisions people make. Consumer advertising aims at inducing a perspective favorable to a sale through the way it frames the offering. In particular, the framing of alternatives can change people's preferences regarding risk.

Tversky and Kahneman set out the following example. We are asked to imagine that the US is getting ready for the outbreak of an unusual Asian disease that is anticipated to kill 600 people. Two options are put forward to deal with the disease. Adopting Program A is likely to save 200 people. With Program B, there is a one-third probability of saving 600 people with a two-thirds probability that no one will be saved. In the study, 72 percent of respondents chose Program A although the actual predicted outcomes of the two programs are identical. Most preferred the certainty of 200 lives saved, reflecting their risk aversion.

A restatement of the problem was then put forward. This time there is a Program C where 400 people will die, and a Program D, where there is a one-third probability that no one will die and a two-thirds probability that 600 people will die. On this occasion 78 percent of respondents chose Program D despite identical outcomes. But this time the respondents chose the risk-taking option! How do the authors explain this? What was different in the two cases was that in the first case the problem was framed in terms of lives 'saved' while, in the second case, as lives 'lost', suggesting people are more likely to take risks to prevent lives being lost than to save lives.

According to prospect theory, people's perspective on their current and future state gets them to think of outcomes as additions to or deletions from their current wealth and they are more repelled by the idea of losing some of their wealth than they are attracted by a corresponding gain. This is in line with a rule in investment services that the client's capital should be preserved above all else: people are more concerned with losses than corresponding gains. We give unlikely events more weight than they deserve and *arbitrarily* give some events more weight than they deserve – at least in judging lotteries.

Prospect theory takes issue with the basic concept of expected utility:

- Prospect theory, as already pointed out, replaces the notion of utility with 'value'. Value is defined in terms of gains and losses (deviations from a value reference point). While the value function for losses is convex and relatively steep, the value function for gains is concave and not quite so steep. One implication is that people make decisions based on whether they consider each option a gain or a loss: losses loom larger than gains, for example a loss of $400 is felt more than a gain of $400. Hence the way an option is described can be of the utmost importance because how an option is actually described is influential in interpreting whether it is likely to be a gain or a loss. *Loss aversion*, as predicted by prospect theory, implies, for example, that a discount for paying cash will appeal more to consumers than a surcharge for using a credit card. A further implication of loss aversion is the *endowment effect* in which the value of something increases when it becomes part of the person's endowment. For example, when students were asked to say whether they would prefer a coffee mug or a bar of chocolate, they expressed a preference for the chocolate bar, but when given the coffee mug they were very reluctant to trade the coffee mug for a bar of chocolate. When people are asked to name a selling price for something they own, they often require much more than they would now be willing to pay to own the very same item. (But could this not arise from adopting a negotiation stance?) In any case, offering products on a trial basis often increases the value of the product to the trial users and so makes it more difficult for them to return the product. We can all think of examples of this. On the other hand, we might recall that consumers often do have post-purchase dissatisfaction and return products all the time, so the endowment concept needs further explication to demarcate its boundaries. By definition, whenever I purchase something I value it more than the seller or the price paid but I may be quite willing to immediately give it up if I see something I like better for the same price. There is also the phenomenon of *psychological obsolescence* where we just get tired of the same old thing. Another allied claim is that when something is the consumer's own selection this adds something over and above the non-selected (identical) product. Is this not perhaps an exaggeration of prospect theory in that I may take a long time selecting a shirt but not think the shirt is different from the other shirts that are like it? There may also be the emergence of cognitive dissonance when thinking of the other shirts. Satisfaction is not simply the absence of dissatisfaction, since satisfaction is something positive and not just non-dissatisfaction.

- Unlike expected utility, prospect theory predicts that preferences will depend on how a problem is framed (described).
- Prospect theory differs from expected utility theory in the way it handles the probabilities attached to particular outcomes, in that prospect theory postulates that decision weights tend to overweight small probabilities and underweight moderate and high probabilities. This is something well recognized in the marketing of insurance policies.
- Prospect theory predicts a 'certainty effect' in which a 'reduction of the probability of an outcome by a constant factor has more impact if the outcome was initially viewed as certain than if it was viewed as merely probable'. This illustrates how the extent to which we are disappointed is the extent to which our expectations are not realized: we are only disappointed to the extent that our expectations are let down. It is the problem with over-promising: we may be building up expectations that cannot be met. It is a problem for all presidential candidates who inevitably build up expectations that cannot be fulfilled.
- The pseudo-certainty effect – we like certainty even if more apparent than real. Thus instead of advertising a 25 percent reduction, a dry cleaner may offer to clean one shirt free with each order of three. The idea is that a free service will be more appealing than a discounted service, even if the free service does not represent a greater overall price reduction.

Does prospect theory entail universal laws? No; for example I may regret losing $50 at the races but find winning $50 more gratifying than the loss because it seems to suggest a skill at choosing the right horse. There is thus always the problem of context. Today, in ads for new proprietary drugs, we hear of the most frightening possible side effects (possible losses) which should put anyone off taking drugs. The fact that they do not is because, in the business of drug-taking, there is this sense that the risk is negligible or the drug would not be on the market. It is also not always clear in a sale whether someone sees herself as making a gain or avoiding a loss. In any case, prospect theory does not really come to grips with a central weakness of RCT in its ignoring emotional commitments to principled action. Not surprising, prospect theory is a lively field of research (Novemsky and Kahneman, 2005a).

The basic core of prospect theory has not gone unchallenged in academia, sometimes in a very fundamental way. Isaac Levi (1985) offers a radically different interpretation of the experimental base for the claims. Levi (1985), a philosopher at Columbia specializing in decision theory, questions prospect theory at its roots, namely the interpretations of the experiments that supply the phenomena that prospect theory attempts to incorporate. He demonstrates that similar results could have been produced if subjects simply took a different but equally defensible interpretation of the instructions. Considerations of equity could come under the notion of people being more concerned with losses such as loss of face, self-esteem and so on than with corresponding gains. Prospect theory is in fact more suited to tangible losses and tangible gains, and requires some stretching to explain consumer behavior in equity situations.

REGRET THEORY

Regret theory could also be regarded as an early contribution to behavioral economics. Regret theory takes account of the emotion of *regret*: an emotion relevant to decision-making. Anticipatory reasoning forms the basis of the theory. It is an economic theory of choice, independently proposed by David Bell (1982, 1985). Regret theory rests on two assumptions:

(1) Many people experience the 'sensations' people call regret and rejoicing. (This would be regarded by Bennett and Hacker as an inappropriate use of the word 'sensation' since it is doubtful if feelings of regret are in the same category as the true sensations of pain, tickles and itches. If we change the term 'sensations' to 'feelings' nothing is lost.)

(2) In making decisions under uncertainty, we try to anticipate and take account of those sensations (feelings). Thus if faced with a choice between $1000 for sure but getting $2000 if the unbiased coin lands on Heads, we typically choose the sure bet to avoid any regret we would feel if the coin had landed on Tails. This is the same risk aversion predicted by prospect theory, but regret theory predicts this choice by adding a new variable, regret, to the normal utility function of the economist. With the addition of this variable, regret theory is able to account for many of the same paradoxes as prospect theory. But if regret is an emotion is it not an illicit graft to try and enter it into the normal utility function?

Anticipation of regret is just one of many possible emotions that could account for the direction of a decision. In fact, lying behind the values exhibited in all consumer trade-offs is some tie to past emotional episodes and it is the emotions that avert paralysis in decision-making (De Sousa 1990).

Regret theory can be regarded as another 'patch' on RCT that is not fundamental enough. In any case, the anticipation of regret may be unwarranted. Consumers may regret years later that they actually feared regret and wish they had just indulged.

FOLLOWING THE CROWD: THE MAJORITY EFFECT

The focus of behavioral economists such as Robert Shiller of Yale relates more to crowd psychology. This is not surprising when the focus is on financial markets and the mass of investors. While a *group* is a plurality of individuals bound together for some purpose or possessing some criteria of membership, a *crowd* is a large but temporary gathering of people who respond collectively. People finding themselves one of a crowd are apt to follow the crowd rather than acting as individuals. People follow what might be called the 'default option', which may be the course of action presented to them by the crowd, rather than seeking the optimal choice. The default option has wide appeal.

We might remind ourselves of that well-known experiment that appears in every organizational behavior textbook. This is the experiment conducted by the psychologist Asch (1952) where subjects were invited to match the length of a given line with one of three unequal lines. The task was easy and participants left to themselves found it so. However, when a subject found himself in the company of others who, like himself, had to voice their opinions aloud, but had been instructed to agree on a judgment that was clearly wrong, there was a strong tendency for the odd man out to fall in line with the majority opinion. This *majority effect* is even more marked in circumstances where the discrimination is difficult.

Investors can be influenced by the majority effect. Investors are far from being super-rational but subject to 'irrational exuberance' and unjustified panic in their actions. This has often been borne out in recent years. People worry more about losses than corresponding gains and reach firm conclusions without a firm empirical base. Not many consumer decisions in financial markets are based on solid evidence since gathering evidence is not costless. But this does not mean that decisions are not deliberated but that consumers may follow a 'coherence theory of truth' in believing what they are doing coheres with what they already know, often the result of just going along with the crowd. Even those consumers (investors) who seek to be highly rational may find themselves pushed into herd-like behavior by social pressure.

Besides the unbelievably large financial incentives, a factor in the recent collapse of the economy was the slavish copying of others by traders and investors; a practice that has come to be called *herding*. Thus the VAR (*value-at-risk*) models, employed to monitor risk and prevent financial disasters by calculating the amount of capital to set aside for insurance against losses (on assets deemed to be risky), are commonly followed slavishly by risk managers, so that when the model says 'sell', all financial managers act so. This leads to what seems to be panic selling. What is forgotten is that all forecasting is to a large extent a projection of ignorance.

Behavioral economics shows consumers, as investors, to be over-confident when extrapolating positive trends into the future. On the other hand, losses lead them to adopt a very risk-averse posture not justified by any rational assessment. There is also a rejection of the Milton Friedman notion that financial markets are stable. On the contrary, the evidence suggests they are highly unstable. But following the herd may not be irrational imitation but possess some justification in terms of beliefs. Investors, for example, may believe that others are better informed than they are. If this imitation of the actions of others is widespread, investors end up doing the same thing; a process in economics known as an *information cascade*.

Confirmation bias is the bias towards discounting information that contradicts one's thinking and sticking to assumptions, despite evidence to the contrary. Confirmation bias can make it difficult to persuade someone to change his or her mind. This tendency is reinforced when evidence can be interpreted to suit either position. Thus the recall of a certain make of car is interpreted by those supportive as a sign of quick action by a reputable company and by those who are not supportive as simply a sign of a low-quality car. Confirmation bias is all pervasive in politics where everything the other side does is interpreted as dysfunctional in some way. There is the *overconfidence bias* in which investors overestimate their ability to analyze and assess the significance of information. It has been suggested that the overconfidence of CEOs is the reason for many unhappy mergers and acquisitions in that the CEO *feels* he can reap big profits from his ideas on turning around the company acquired. Overconfidence can lead to *disaster myopia* where we cannot imagine things going badly wrong. Finally there is the *focusing illusion*, which happens when, in focusing on a single change in the situation, people go on to mistakenly predict dramatic consequences in the overall position. This can be related to the *availability* principle whereby we are unduly influenced by what comes most easily to mind, for example the last airline crash or car call-back for a faulty pedal. Consumers are far from being highly rational as depicted by economists, if for no other reason than that consumer decision-making suffers from biases and a lack of information.

LE BON ON CROWDS

The seminal work on crowd psychology is *The Crowd*, first published in English in 1896 and written by the French psychologist Gustave Le Bon (2002). It more fittingly belongs to the chapter on social psychology (Chapter 11) but is discussed here because the subject has been highlighted in behavioral economics. It has remained a classic because it was the book that Hitler admired and used in rabble-rousing. It is also a book whose claims today find expression in political campaigns and political marketing as each of us will be able to match Le Bon's assertions against politicians' strategies for winning votes.

Le Bon was wedded to methodological holism which claims that the social whole cannot be understood by analysis of the individuals of which it is composed. In contrast, methodological individualism claims that social phenomena are explainable in terms of facts about the individuals of which the whole is composed.

Le Bon's claims still resonate today as insightful about crowd behavior. Some of the claims made by Le Bon about crowds, defined broadly to include many types of groups, are:

- The greater part of our actions is the result of hidden motives which escape our observation.
- Under certain circumstances, a crowd presents new characteristics from the individuals composing it.
- Individuals forming part of any crowd can acquire a sense of invincible power which enables them to behave in ways they would never do outside of the crowd. The emotion of the crowd is contagious and the crowd remains highly suggestible.
- Characteristics of crowds. Most commonly crowds are characterized by impulsiveness, suggestibility and credulity. The starting point is an illusion produced by vague reminiscences, with contagion following as the result of the repeated affirmation of this initial illusion.
- A crowd is only impressed by excessive sentiments. An orator wishing to move a crowd must make an abusive use of violent affirmations (i.e. dogmatic assertions). To exaggerate, to affirm, to resort to repetitions while never attempting to prove anything by reasoning – these are the methods of argument well known to persuasive speakers at public meetings. There is an intolerance, dictatorialness and conservatism about crowds, while personal interest is rarely a powerful motive with crowds, as it is with individuals. A long time is needed to eradicate well-established beliefs of crowds even though these beliefs may have been discredited years ago by the scientific community.
- The imaginative imagery of crowds is very active and very powerful. The images evoked in the mind by speakers and events such as an accident can be almost lifelike. The sentiments suggested by the images can be so strong that they tend, like habitual suggestions, to transform themselves into collective action.
- The crowd demands a godlike leader before all else. We need to appreciate the religious form, which the convictions of crowds always assume in the long run. Intolerance and fanaticism are the accompaniments of religious sentiment.
- Civilization is impossible without tradition, but progress is impossible without the destruction of tradition. The power of words is bound up with the images they evoke and this power is independent of their real

significance. Those words whose sense-meaning is the most ill-defined, like the word socialism, are often those that possess the most influence.

- Reason and argument are incapable of combating the powerful imagery of words and slogans. Such words may evoke grandiose and vague images but this very vagueness wraps them in obscurity and gives them their mysterious power. After all, anything can be read into them.
- The absolute translation of a language, especially a dead language, is totally impossible. Words have first to be interpreted, which results in our reading into a word the sense-meanings that are part of modern life. The sense-meaning of words like 'royalty' change over time so a literal translation can be misleading.
- The masses have never thirsted after truth but turn aside from evidence that is not to their taste. Whoever can supply them with illusions is easily their master. Logic and reason have no appeal. Crowds look for the ready-made phrase that dispenses with the need for reason. Instead, the arousing of faith has always been the function of the greatest leaders of crowds. It is in the interests of leaders to indulge in the most improbable exaggerations if they are to be successful.
- At the end of a certain time period, we have forgotten who the author of the repeated assertion is, and we finish by believing it.
- Great power is given to ideas that are propagated by affirmation (dogmatic assertion) followed by constant repetition facilitated by contagion. The movement from dogmatic assertion to constant repetition is propelled along by the prestige of the source. The source of prestige is typically the prestige possessed by some dead or fictive figure. The proof that success is one of the principal stepping stones to prestige is that the disappearance of the one is almost always followed by the disappearance of the other. Prestige lost by want of success disappears in a brief space of time. (It could be argued similarly that success is essential for the charismatic personality to continue to influence.)

ANIMAL SPIRITS

In a recent book, Akerlof and Shiller (2009) resurrect John Maynard Keynes's notion of *animal spirits* which gives rise to an urge to action rather than inaction. They argue that there are five classes of animal spirits present in consumers as investors:

1. *Confidence.* This can push us beyond rational expectations in the pricing of securities or other financial instruments. Confidence, whether high or low, builds on itself in a way resembling Keynes's multiplier effect.
2. *Fairness* or *equity*. This concept has already been discussed even if neglected in traditional economics. It can and does play a role in investor decision-making, particularly among the general public. The investment market segments developed by firms offering investment advice are likely to include segments based on ethical criteria, for

example companies committed to avoiding firms that pollute the environment or exploit workers in third world countries.

3. *Corruption* or bad faith. Corruption is one of the major reasons why many countries never realize their potential. Many investors seek investments that will not be supportive of regimes that are tyrannical and corrupt. Unfortunately, when corruption is widespread within a society, it comes to be regarded as socially acceptable, if not ethically right.

4. The *money illusion*. Money, as something physical, can give the illusion of constant value, particularly when inflation is low. One British prime minister, Harold Wilson, an economist by training, after a serious decline in the British pound, sought to cash in on this illusion in talking about the pound in our pockets being still a pound. (The ruse did not work!) Few investors take account of inflation in congratulating themselves on the payoff in their investments. Investors are very concerned with not losing the actual amount they invested so, if that investment is not below what they put in, they can be satisfied, forgetting to take account of inflation.

5. *Stories* or *narratives*. People fall victim to plausible narratives such as that house prices can only go up, when such narratives defy rational expectations. Unless economists take account of such unfounded beliefs, models predicting behavior are bound to fail.

These five factors and others are being used to explain happenings that puzzle economists or, more realistically, that are not explained by economic theory. Thus, contrary to what might be expected from economic theory, there is a long-run trade-off between unemployment and inflation that can mainly be explained by the concepts of equity (fairness) and the money illusion. In explaining the 2008 credit crisis, resort is made to a collapse of confidence, sudden change from optimistic to pessimistic narratives and corruption (bad faith). In explaining the wide swings in shares and house prices, resort is made to a combination of confidence, corruption and plausible narratives. The *plausible narrative* explains the irrational belief investors had in the Madoff claim to be getting an unerringly high return for his investors every year.

Behavioral economics has been used to influence public policy in getting consumers to save and make better choices in their investment portfolios. It has been used to study 'inter-temporal choices' which show that consumers have only a very hazy view of how their decisions today will play out in the future. But behavioral economics does not dismiss the rational expectations hypothesis (REH), in its claim that breakdowns in capitalism arise from market imperfections which can be avoided by making markets more perfect. Hence behavioral economics has been promoted (re-framed?) by some economists as something complementary to the traditional orthodoxy rather than challenging it. But economic man is less likely to be considered highly rational if following enlightened self-interest instead of unconstrained greed. People have to 'learn' to be rational when buying and selling in order to overcome their irrational instincts. Behavioral economics endorses this in arguing that humans are more apt to make decisions on a whim and prefer to indulge in the immediate pleasure of consuming over saving for the future.

The more fundamental attacks on REH and EMH are by those who criticize the very notion of economic behavior being captured by a set of mathematical relationships. Economics sees itself as following physics (or, more truly, a 'physics that never was') in demanding that all economic insights be expressed in mathematical form. The danger is of methodology dictating what questions are addressed and acting like the little boy with a hammer who finds that everything needs hammering.

DAN ARIELY'S STUDIES AS ILLUSTRATIVE OF BEHAVIORAL ECONOMICS

In his book *Predictably Irrational*: *The Hidden Forces that Shape our Decisions*, Dan Ariely (2008) maintains that, in economics, the foundational concept is 'rationality,' as it is basic to all its theories, predictions and recommendations. He challenges the notion of rational economic man by indicating that people are not only irrational but predictably irrational in that this irrationality happens the same way, time and time again. (This can be misleading if we interpret this as saying that each and every individual acts irrationally all the time, as opposed to saying that, within any group of individuals, there are always a significant percentage who act contrary to the norms of rational choice theory.)

Ariely agrees that if the findings of experiments were valid only in respect to the exact context in which they took place, they would be of limited value. Instead he assumes that the experimental findings discussed in his book illustrate general principles; that the findings do not just apply to the specific context in which the experiment took place but can be extrapolated to many contexts of life. This faith may be justified but this does not absolve us from reflecting on the context in which we propose to apply the findings to see if there are obvious contextual factors that rule against their applicability. Just as we can usually see where a proverb is inapplicable, we can often recognize where certain experimental findings are inapplicable.

The following are the conclusions of Ariely arising from his work, usually involving experiments employing university students as subjects. One has to assume a high uniformity in human behavior to believe that findings can always be extrapolated from experiments on university students to the population at large.

There are always alternative explanations of any findings. In fact all evidence should be regarded as comparative: one discusses evidence not for or against a single, isolated hypothesis but against rival hypotheses. Unfortunately, this basic notion in the philosophy of science is typically ignored in research in the social sciences. Confirming that a result is statistically significant is just not good enough, since we are really concerned with saying whether the major alternative hypotheses have been displaced.

Comments here are restricted to assessing the applicability of Ariely's findings to situations we know about. Every reader of his book should consider his or her own experience in testing whether the findings have wide validity in terms of their own experience. After all, your experience as a consumer should not be dismissed as it also needs to be explained. If managers did reflect on their own experience in critically examining social science findings, perhaps fewer claims would be accepted as gospel.

Although Ariely's thirteen findings are given below, such summaries cannot substitute for reading his book:

1. Consumers and humans generally judge a product *relative* to other things. We compare products with other products: jobs with jobs, holidays with holidays and wines with wines. In making comparisons we focus on comparing things that are easily comparable and avoid comparisons that are not so easily made. Most consumers do not know what they want until they see it relative to other things within some context. Thus if the televisions on display are a 36-inch Panasonic for $690, a 42-inch Toshiba for $850 and a 50-inch Philips for $1,480, these are compared relative to each other. In making such comparisons, the middle option is most likely to be chosen. The claim is that consumers will be more inclined to buy the middle choice, not the cheapest or the most expensive. This claim by Ariely does not give much weight to the influence of the various brand names in that I might just think that a 50-inch television by Philips at $1,480 is a bargain compared with a 42-inch Toshiba at $850. Ariely acknowledges that the more expensive might on occasion be perceived as so much better and that the consumer might save to buy it but that this is the exception. Ariely's studies demonstrate a tendency to avoid the cheapest and the most expensive, with the highest and lowest prices providing relative *anchor* points for making a decision. Ariely shows how just putting in a third option that is merely a decoy, not a serious option, will alter final choices. Thus the seller can introduce, as a decoy, a very high-priced model, making the lower-priced models appear more of a bargain. Realtors do this all the time by first displaying the relatively high-priced model then the middle-range models and then the cheapest, generally betting that a house in the middle range will be chosen. Similarly, consumers tend to choose in between the highest-priced and the lowest-priced entrées on a restaurant menu. But how common is this? It is certainly not universal. At the steak restaurant to which my wife and I go with two friends, there is a 6-inch steak, a 9-inch steak and a 12-inch steak. None of us chooses the middle-priced 9-inch steak as three of us regard the 6-inch steak as being quite adequate, while the fourth member of the group always chooses the

12-inch to put half into a 'doggie bag' for eating the next day! Not all decisions emanate from just looking at the choices; some stem from the reasons for the choices.

2. Ariely introduces the notion of 'arbitrary coherence' in respect to pricing in arguing that, while the initial price of a product may be somewhat arbitrary, once these prices are established in the mind of the consumer, they shape not only what the consumer is willing to pay for a product but also what they are willing to pay in the future for that product and related products. It appears *first* decisions about product prices influence a future sequence of decisions. Once we consider buying a certain product at a specific price, that price becomes an *anchor* in terms of looking at rival products. Older consumers regard plasma televisions today as cheap but gasoline as expensive, since past experience informs them to this effect. This is not to suggest that consumers do not over time adjust to the new prices and establish new anchor prices but there is reluctance about doing this.

Ariely asserts that supply and demand are not, as assumed by economists, independent, since experiments show how the price consumers are willing to pay can, within limits, be easily manipulated. Consumers, it appears, do not have a good grasp of their own preferences and the prices they are willing to pay for different offerings. Consumer price anchors come from the seller's suggested retail prices and other data from the seller which are all supply-side variables. It is not the consumers' willingness to pay per se that influences prices, but market prices themselves that affect the consumers' willingness to pay. Hence Ariely speaks of the 'fallacy of supply and demand'. He speculates that price sensitivity might be largely a result of remembering the prices paid in the past, together with a desire for coherence with past decisions – and not a reflection of our true preferences. If it is the memory of past price anchors that affects behavior, it is not clear that the opportunity to trade would be key to maximizing utility. Why? Because for Ariely price anchors may not reflect the relative utility for the consumer who is doing the trading, since the consumer may mistakenly trade something that gives lots of pleasure but for which he has a low price anchor for something that gives less pleasure but has a high initial price anchor.

Can we always be so dismissive of economic theory? It seems defensible to argue that supply and demand form an *interacting system*, with the suppliers' list prices influencing the consumer's initial anchor price but with consumer reaction to that price influencing the supplier's prices through time. In any case, there are no 'laws' of supply and demand because the claims are not falsifiable since there can be just about any shape, in theory, to supply and demand curves. The notion of the consumer accepting the prices being offered seems to assume a passive consumer and to ignore market dynamics. Thus the attempt to charge high prices for televisions in China was met with such resistance that Sony and Panasonic were obliged to reduce prices by

33 percent to 50 percent. In any case, it is not always the anchor price that is important in sales. When Chanel No. 5 was made available in drugstores to increase distribution and sales, the sales actually plummeted and only returned to previous levels after the product once again was sold just in exclusive department stores.

3. Ariely highlights the powerful attraction of something that is promoted as being 'free'. Any purchase is an approach/avoidance situation in that attractions are set against costs, but when something is free there is no loss (or regret) to consider arising from a poor decision. Ariely argues that people are innately afraid of suffering a loss and the attraction of something being 'free' is tied to this fear. Something being free, he claims, results in its being perceived as immensely more valuable than it really is. But is this always so? The adage about 'not looking a gift horse in the mouth' suggests we often do look suspiciously at something that is offered free as there are often strings attached. But Ariely is simply reminding us how the attraction of something being 'free' distracts the consumer from looking more carefully at the offering. Thus a mortgage without closing costs has great appeal but we may be maneuvered into accepting interest rates and fees that are 'off the wall' to get that which is free (gifts at perfume counters). Consumers often buy what they do not really want because some element of the offering is free. Consumers can easily discount their time while they line up for a free sample or fill in a complicated form for some tiny rebate. Yet promoting something as 'free' is a powerful motivator – the cola drink advertised as being free of calories (zero calories) is likely to sell many more tins than a cola that says it has 'one calorie'. If you want to draw a crowd, says Ariely, then say something is FREE. If you want to sell more of your product then make part of the purchase FREE.

4. Ariely regards all of us as simultaneously being in two different worlds. In one world, 'social norms' dominate and, in the other world, 'market norms'. Social norms, as influencing behavior, are not something considered by the economist, though in a social world it is not enough to meet goals in an efficient way since the means for achieving those goals must be socially appropriate. Goats may be a cheap way of keeping down the grass on our lawn but using goats in a suburban environment would not be considered socially appropriate. Social rewards strongly motivate behavior. Soldiers fight as a unit and for that unit, not a nation or a flag. Pride in serving the norms of the profession generally motivates a medical doctor and not just pay. Ariely shows in one experiment how participants worked harder under non-monetary social norms than they did for money. While not prepared to be paid below the market rate, US doctors worked for nothing in Haiti. Indeed there are many cases where people work harder for a cause than for cash. In respect to gift-giving, this normally adheres to the norms of the social world. However, the mention of cost can shift the gift into the realm of market norms; introducing market norms in

this way into social exchanges violates social norms and perhaps the relationship.

Gifts have symbolic meaning and create goodwill. Ariely illustrates this by drawing on ads that try to secure loyalty by an appeal to solidarity in proclaiming customers are 'family' or like 'friends' ('Like a good neighbor, State Farm is there'). One current bank ad portrays the bank as standing by its customers through both good and bad times. But, as Ariely says, it is difficult to treat a customer as a friend one minute and the next time (when they are behind in mortgage payments) treat him or her under the rules of the market. Treating employees as just another resource and getting rid of them as the need arises, undermines the social contract and morale and the loyalty of employees to the company. Ariely claims money to be the most expensive way to motivate people, while appeal to social norms such as pride in the job can be the cheapest. This claim by Ariely was at its loudest in the organizational behavior literature in the 1960s when financial incentives were being deplored for their non-contribution to group bonding and morale. Yet at the same time it was common for industrial engineering consultants to be getting a 100–200 percent increase in output for a 33 percent increase in pay. It is going beyond the evidence to make unqualified claims about the efficacy of social motivators. As Victor Vroom (1964), a professor of organizational behavior, was to say at the time:

> If one assumes that money constitutes a goal and that behavior is goal directed, it follows that persons should perform more effectively in a work role if their wages are directly linked to their performance than if their wages are independent of their performance. The results of a number of different kinds of research investigations are in essential agreement with this proposition.
>
> (Vroom 1964: 75)

5. Ariely considers the influence of emotional arousal. He concludes that every one of us under-predicts the effect of passion on our behavior and how emotions can take over the control of behavior, negating our superego and 'throwing caution to the wind'. This can be true, but surely the problem lies in predicting the action arising from an emotion. Thus pride may rule out our trying something again or, on the contrary, it might induce us to do so. In respect to sexual education, he argues that teenagers should be taught to walk away from the 'fire of passion' while they are still able to do so. This is because it is easier for them to deal with temptation before it occurs than afterwards. Teaching teenagers to just say 'No' assumes passion can be turned on and off like a tap. Similarly, we need to teach people not to drive when in an emotional state. The general lesson is that all of us are apt to make the wrong decision when gripped by intense emotions. But the word 'intense' emotion is needed since emotion, as the work of Damasio

and others shows, is a necessary condition for seriously deliberating the pros and cons of a decision and moving on to action when serious decisions have to be made. Without our emotions we would suffer decision-paralysis.

6. 'Self-control' has been another area of study for Ariely. Here we have a situation where the students in the first group had some flexibility in respect to three deadlines for delivering their papers; the second group was given a single deadline but otherwise had complete flexibility; the third group had the three deadlines dictated to them and therefore had no flexibility at all. It turned out that the class with the firm deadlines received the best grades; the class with no deadlines had the worst grades, while the class that chose their own three deadlines (but with penalties for failing to meet them) finished in the middle, in terms of their grades. Ariely argues that without pre-commitments (in this case on deadlines), we procrastinate. Yet in spite of his findings, he advocates giving people the opportunity to pre-commit to deadlines or in some other way getting round the desire for instant gratification and procrastination by, say, agreeing to an employer's saving his or her pay through automatic deduction from the employee's wages. Recommendations in the organizational behavior literature emphasize setting personal goals (without goals there can be no self-guidance) and feedback or knowledge of results (the old adage 'practice makes perfect' should be modified to practice makes perfect providing we have knowledge of results). Ariely discusses the problem of excessive individual debt, suggesting the development of a smart card with a spending 'governor' that sets limits to spending. He presented the idea to bankers who seemed supportive of the innovation but never followed it through and this surprises him. This is not really unexpected since, though desirable for some credit users and even technically feasible, it is unlikely to be a commercial success. We see the need for such a card at the national level but, at the individual level, consumers want to feel in control of their lives and feel free to change their mind rather than being committed to abide by target credit goals, set outside the contextual conditions that might occur in the future. Since Ariely wrote this, MasterCard has announced that Citigroup bank will issue a MasterCard, called inControl, to protect customers not only from thieves but from themselves. A cardholder can simply inform his or her bank to ensure they never spend above a certain sum. Some Barclaycard holders in the UK are already being issued with a similar card, called the 'financial chastity belt' by cynics. It will be interesting to see how successful the self-imposed restrictions are, though it would seem ideal for parents who provide their children with credit cards.

7. One study deals with the 'endowment effect' already discussed, which claims that when we own something the tendency is to value it more than other people would. Ariely asks: Why does the seller of a house usually value that property more than the potential buyer? But setting

a price higher than what a buyer would pay does not demonstrate a psychological gulf between seller and potential buyers. The seller usually gets a price suggestion from the realtor (estate agent in the UK) and perhaps sets it a little higher, knowing that the prospective buyer expects some reduction. Ariely acknowledges that if the consumer always overvalued what they had, there would be no such thing as an Antiques Roadshow. I would add that there would also be no such thing as a garage sale. We tire of things and it is naive to claim that the value we put on some item we own is stable. However, he still believes the ownership of something increases its value in the owner's eyes; that we are instantly attached to what we have. This certainly is the case when we have an emotional attachment to some nostalgic possession or to some puppy we have just bought. It is also true in the sense that anything we have just bought is to us worth more than we paid for it or otherwise we would not have bought it. Ariely also argues that we can begin to feel ownership (virtual ownership) even before we actually own it. This is the hope of the car salesperson who lets us drive the car he is hoping to sell us. But can the pleasurable experience of driving the car or imagining driving the car be completely equated with feelings of virtual ownership, as alleged, rather than getting switched on to the notion of the car doing more to enrich our lives than the money-cost? Is it true that driving the car conjures up emotions of ownership, and is this the forcing variable at work?

We can, of course, all think of instances where the endowment effect applies and Ariely's studies suggest such instances. He rightly quotes the prevalence of 'trial' promotions to induce purchase but, for many of us, the endorsement of the endowment effect by so many social scientists has more to do with its being part of 'prospect theory' and the credibility of its authors. The argument goes that we price some possession, such as our car, higher than the buyers because we think what we will suffer is a loss which is not compensated for by the money gained. This can be so but, as I look at my possessions, few fall into this category. Perhaps Ariely is right that downsizing to a smaller home is experienced as a loss and is painful for many people but this is because there is as a matter of fact a loss of benefits. But many living in a retirement community look forward to downsizing because looking after the bigger home has become too much of a burden.

8. People generally favor the notion of keeping options open but Ariely shows there is a tendency to keep options open for too long, and having too many options can be dysfunctional. Too many options can occur from taking on too many obligations to the situation of buying products which have too many functions for our purposes. It is argued that a major reason for this is that closing options is viewed as a loss which is unpleasant to contemplate. The economist is viewed as investigating all options before making a decision whereas Ariely is saying we should resist this irrational compulsion to keep all doors open but

close doors so as to be able to deal with what is important. We try to do too many things and end up with less.

Ariely here and elsewhere speaks of people being 'hardwired' to do irrational things. This is a poor metaphor unless evidence can be offered showing such behavior is present in everyone and, most important of all, arises without learning. No such evidence can be offered. Although Ariely does show in his experiments how students hate to close options, many of us believe that just as often consumers do not look at enough options. He also claims that choosing between two equally attractive options (remember the ass that starved between two bales of hay) is one of the most difficult decisions we can make. This is the approach-approach dilemma in psychology where, contrary to Ariely, it is claimed people quickly do come to a decision; the donkey does not die but decides quickly. The more difficult decisions to make are in the approach-avoidance and the avoidance-avoidance situations.

9. The concept of expectations has a long history in psychology and sociology since our reactions are tied to our expectations. In economics, expectations play a significant role. One experiment by Ariely was to determine whether people's expectations influence their views of subsequent events, for example whether bar patrons' expectations for a certain kind of beer would shape their perceptions of taste. He found expectations did have this result and concluded that, if people are informed that something is distasteful, the chances are high that they end up agreeing with you; not because experience has taught them that but because of the induced expectations. It seems that if we anticipate beforehand that some experience will be good or bad, it is generally perceived as good or bad. (But not always, by any means, in that I often have very low expectations of enjoying a film but find I have enjoyed it.) Telling the experimental group before they drank the beer that it was laced with vinegar affected their evaluation of its taste, while telling the control group after they had drunk the beer that it was laced with vinegar actually resulted in their liking the beer as much as did another control group who were not aware of any vinegar in the beer. All this is not surprising since if we expect a certain state of affairs, we look for confirmatory evidence, whether good or bad. As the personal investment in an issue increases, the more rigid the expectations and interpretation of the 'facts'. The lesson here is to build up high expectations (if such expectations can be met) of the quality of the food (or whatever) by, say, depth of description, leading the consumer to expect great things. Even the wine glasses at the meal, if elegant, can build up expectations about the wine so that it actually tastes better. For Ariely, providing information for enhancing anticipated pleasure is what marketing promotions are about; the 'bright red can, swirling script, and the myriad messages that have come down to consumers over the years (such as "Things go better with . . .") are as

much responsible for our love of Coke as the brown bubbly stuff itself" (p. 168). This is certainly not the gospel of traditional economics but it is that of marketing, where the *symbolic* is recognized as being just as important in appreciating a product as anything else. Ariely concludes that we tend to be trapped within a perspective which sets up expectations that blind us in objectively searching for the truth. But expectations are not always met by the seller; sometimes there is a reality that cannot be ignored and disappointment results. This leads to the marketing claim that we are only disappointed to the extent that our expectations are let down.

10. Ariely argues that many things can be perceived as effective simply by 'believing' in them. This is probably the case with the skin-care industry, which would collapse if consumers ceased believing its bogus claims. In the case of placebos it is the power of suggestion. The placebo effect suggests it is possible to get some consumers of an ineffective product to vouch for its effectiveness and to sing its praises. Ariely sees two mechanisms lying behind the expectations that make placebos effective: (i) belief/confidence/faith in the drug; (ii) classical conditioning in that the body builds up expectancy after repeated experiences so the product, without the key ingredient, can be effective.

   Ariely shows how the price of a product affects our response to it. As we accept a discount price, we discount perceptions of quality. As we have said before, the seller who emphasizes price is training consumers to think mainly of price. He shows how the level of pricing can drive the efficacy of placebos, painkillers and energy drinks. In one experiment, at a price of $2.50 for each pill, almost all participants experienced pain relief, but at a price of 10 cents per pill, only 50 percent did. Price thus can change the experience. It also seems that those who paid the full list price reported significantly better medical results than those who bought at a discounted price. Similarly, in the case of an energy drink, promising 'superior functionality', the students who bought and drank the higher-priced product claimed they suffered less fatigue than those students who bought and drank the discounted beverage. The higher price primed the students to expect more. It is interesting to speculate whether this would be true of textbooks in that few students would equate low price with poverty of content since this often suggests mass sales. Ariely concludes that the message on the packaging and the price can be so significant in building up expectations that these can be more important than the beverage inside in creating consumer satisfaction. Ariely ends the section (chapter) of the book by asking: 'If people actually get more satisfaction out of a product that has been hyped, has the marketer done anything worse than sell the sizzle along with the steak?'

11. Ariely's conclusions from experiments on 'honesty' are that many otherwise honest people will cheat if given the opportunity. Businesses

act similarly so we get the credit card companies ripping off their customers with usury-level interest rates. If external controls to enforce honesty have limited effectiveness, what is the answer? Getting people to read and reflect on moral benchmarks of some sort seems to help. Thus it appears that signing an honor code, as a moral reminder to students, seemed to eliminate much cheating among the students – at least in Ariely's experiment. Reminding people about what is ethical/moral at the time of temptation or in conditions of temptation can affect behavior. We are reminded here of how a cardboard shape of a policeman at the end of a supermarket aisle, or just of someone smiling, can reduce the amount of stealing. Many companies set out lists of ethical principles but they just become part of the wallpaper unless someone is delegated to ensure compliance. It is useful to remind people to ask themselves when considering some dubious action whether, if this were publicly revealed, they would feel ashamed. If so, then they should reconsider.

12. One interesting finding is how people who have no hesitation in helping themselves to cans of coke from the company refrigerator or in pilfering stationery and so on seem to recoil from actually stealing money. It seems that 'once cash is a step away, we will cheat by a factor bigger than we could ever imagine'.

13. In the final chapter Ariely concludes from experiments that people will sometimes sacrifice the product that would give them most pleasure in order to project a certain image to others. Thus in his experiments it seemed that when people order food among a group of friends, the aim is not just to order what they would most enjoy but also to project a positive image of themselves to friends. This may occur but does it continue over time? I go out with twelve friends once a week and have no sense at all of being influenced by wanting to project a positive image to my friends – and I see no one noticing what others order. Ariely would argue that I have no sense of ordering-to-project-an-image because the influence is unconscious, but under this claim anything can be asserted.

CRITICISM OF BEHAVIORAL ECONOMICS

As with cognitive psychology, there have been criticisms of generalizing from experimental findings on the grounds that, in the context of real market forces, behavior does not follow that of students in laboratory experiments. This is always a criticism of all findings from experiments in social science but it is wrong to suppose such findings do not offer insight. In fact we can often imagine when the findings are most applicable and the modifications that need to be made for real-world application. Behavioral economists themselves have been critical of the use of survey evidence because of the various biases to which surveys are prone, particularly the fact that respondents have no incentive to carefully examine their beliefs. But today many of these inherent difficulties with surveys have been identified and precautions taken, though nothing can compensate for dishonest replies. In any case, such criticisms have been taken to heart, with the increasing use of field studies rather than laboratory experiments employing students.

Perhaps the criticism that carries most weight with traditional economists is that economists are interested in how groups respond, not in the individual – it does not matter how you and I behave but how the whole group behaves. This raises the debate between methodological individualism and methodological holism. *Methodological individualism* is the claim that social phenomena are wholly explainable in terms of facts about individuals. The logical positivists of the 1930s were methodological individualists in that they recognized only individual particulars, denying that general abstract concepts like 'society', 'market', 'beauty' or 'goodness' offer any additional insight into the world. In economics, general equilibrium theorists sought to build up a theory of how the whole economy works from the behavior of individual consumers and firms. But this goal has come up against the criticism that the whole cannot be developed from the parts.

In contrast, *methodological holism* focuses on social wholes. Neither methodological individualism nor methodological holism has won universal acceptance since much depends on the problems being addressed. Psychologists implicitly adopt methodological individualism, while methodological holism has attractions for those social scientists whose interest lies in the behavior of groups. Diffusion theory in marketing focuses on the individual but is quoted in support of the product life cycle (PLC), which is a holistic phenomenon assumed to arise from the individual actions of decision-makers. What is true is that what is rational for the individual consumer may not be rational for society. Thus the individual self-interested consumer may not save on energy to the detriment of society. Or the individual voter may ensure little is spent on social goods leading to what the economist Kenneth Galbraith described as a society of private affluence and public squalor. Rational self-interest in the market can build up to a socially inferior outcome: what Cassidy (2009) calls a condition of *rational irrationality*.

Surowiecki (2004), in a book entitled *The Wisdom of Crowds: Why the Many Are Smarter than the Few*, offers support of methodological holism. Surowiecki says that in a wide variety of circumstances, even the smartest individual can be outperformed by the impersonal group. The judgment of the group can be better than the judgment of any individual within the group, even though the judgment of the group is determined by its individual members. This goes against orthodoxy which claims that group decision-making may be better but never better than the smartest individual in the group. But Surowiecki demolishes this claim: our prejudice against group-think or collective mediocrity in favor of the individual genius seems to be unfounded. Surowiecki is not claiming that the judgment of the group will always be best: there is indeed a danger of group-think unless certain conditions are satisfied, namely:

- Members of the group are willing to think for themselves
- Members of the group are more or less independent of each other
- The group is fairly decentralized
- There is a defensible way of aggregating opinions into a collective judgment
- The judgment sought is confined to cognitive and not moral judgments.

What is relevant here is the concept of shared mental models. Orasanu and Salas (1993) found that effective teams seemed to develop a shared mental model of other participants' knowledge, skill, anticipated behavior and needs. It would seem that the overlap or sharing of perspectives facilitates team working, while, it goes without saying, structural secrecy inhibits such sharing.

Finally, Faruk Gul and Wolfgang Pesendorfer (2005), two Princeton economists, make the following comment on criticisms of traditional economics by behavioral economists:

> Economics and psychology address different questions, utilize different abstractions, and address different types of empirical evidence. Neuroscience evidence cannot refute economic models because the latter make no assumptions and draw no conclusions about the physiology of the brain. Conversely, brain science cannot revolutionize economics because it has no vehicle for addressing concerns of economics.
>
> (Gul and Pesendorfer 2005)

Gul and Pesendorfer are arguing that economics and cognitive science offer different perspectives on economic phenomena. This is true. But is it true that neuroscience evidence cannot refute an economic model as opposed to just supplementing it? Does drawing on different types of evidence rule out such refutation? Archeology has often led us to revise the historical record even though the historians' record had drawn no conclusions on the basis of archeology. The real issue is which approach is more credible in answering certain economic questions. The authors are saying not just that the two approaches are asking different questions so both can be right, but that one cannot displace the other because each uses different types of evidence. But this claim assumes that the evidential base each uses is incommensurate or equally defensible. Many would deny this on the grounds that behavioral economics seeks a firmer empirical base for economics and, on this basis, can refute some of the claims of mainstream economics even if, for its purposes, mainstream economics is justified in remaining content with its assertions.

CASE: NETFLIX

Netflix has been a fast growing company. Founded by Reed Hastings in 1997, it offered movie DVDs through the mail and later added online movies. Thus in 2011, the consumer could be getting DVDs directly from Netflix or stream movies on to her computer or (by employing a router and Roku player), streaming the movies on to her television. Netflix had arrangements with film companies whereby it could stream in film titles from, say, DreamWorks Animation. As streaming got better with increased bandwidths, quality was assured and customers flocked to use Netflix. The customer could at any time view a movie from those he or she had chosen on the computer or television or through checking the Netflix inventory to find a movie not previously chosen. In any case, if there was a problem in streaming because of Hollywood licensing restrictions, many Netflix customers could locate those missing movies in the far greater selection on DVD.

Within the company, there was a constant debate over the amount of company resources to devote to the DVD business as opposed to streaming movies to customers over the Internet. There was a general consensus that the DVD business was at the decline stage of the product life cycle, while the future lay with video streaming for movies on demand. On this basis, Hastings set about moving away from DVDs-by-mail to devote more time and resources to the online business. In April 2011, Hastings separated the DVD service and renamed it Qwikster. In July 2011, customers were told that there would be an equal charge for the DVDs-by-mail product and for the streaming of films. The charge was to be $7.99 for each. The present charge was $9.99 for both. Hastings believed the price increase was needed to generate revenue to license additional material. Suppliers of movies had become more demanding in terms of charging more for their product.

Many customers both received DVDs-by-mail and also streamed in movies to their television. To them this new pricing represented an increase of about 60 percent, while in any case they did not want to deal with two separate accounts. Those customers who only bought into the streaming service saved $2 per month. But there was a loud outcry from the customers who subscribed to both services. Netflix was estimated to have lost 600,000 of its 24.6 million customers in the US and the stock fell 25 percent in after-hours trading. Nor were the customers who simply subscribed to the streaming service entirely satisfied in spite of a price reduction. There were complaints that the films on offer were becoming more and more mainstream, with fewer foreign films and films by independents. It offers only three operas on film, for example.

While many commentators were critical of Netflix for acting as it did, others argued that Hastings made the right business decision, with the price of either service still being a bargain. Three weeks after the price increase, Hastings reversed the decision to split the company but held firm on the price increase. He attributed the hostility to the price change to the angry mood of the country as manifested in the Tea Party and the Occupy Wall

Street movement. But he admitted the price increase was too big to be passed along all at once.

Case questions

1. Although classical economics would predict a fall-off in demand for such a large percentage increase, what would it not explain?
2. Although Netflix has rivals like Apple, Amazon and Hulu, given the overall service the Netflix package is still considered a good buy. If so, do you believe most of the lost customers will return?
3. Any marketing strategy is a thin conceptual creation that is fleshed out in detail as the implementation of the strategy is planned. What was wrong in the implementation of Hastings's strategy? What might behavioral economics contribute to this discussion?

DISCUSSION QUESTIONS ON CHAPTER 10 (BEHAVIORAL ECONOMICS)

1. 'Behavioral economics uses the term "irrational" for any behavior that deviates from rationality as defined by rational choice theory. This can be an impediment to understanding consumer behavior.' Discuss.
2. If traditional economics does not conduct its investigations into economic phenomena through experiments, with the usual control and experimental groups, how does traditional economics track the truth?
3. What distinguishes rational decision-making in mainstream economics from the claim that consumers typically employ heuristics?
4. 'Prospect theory seeks to describe and explain how people (including consumers) handle uncertain rewards and risks.' Discuss.
5. What do you think of the Keynesian notion of 'animal spirits' in explaining the behavior of consumers as investors?

Chapter 11

Social Psychology: Social Groups, Social Reference Groups and the Nature and Role of Emotion in Influencing Behavior

SOCIAL PSYCHOLOGY'S FOCUS

Social psychology investigates how individuals are influenced by interactions with others and by the actual or imagined presence of others. Much about the consumer's life is social and social influences need to be considered for understanding buying behavior. When we think about things that concern us, other people usually form the background.

One of the earliest theories in social psychology to be imputed to buyer behavior was cognitive dissonance (already discussed), developed in the 1950s by Leon Festinger.

Festinger (1957) maintained that, when people are confident about their proposed action (such as buying), they believe the action to be:

- Desirable
- Rationally defensible
- Socially appropriate.

If an action is desirable, rationally defensible and socially appropriate, the proposed buying action possesses *subjective validity* for the buyer. The need for the action to be socially appropriate is something not considered in economics but is basic in social psychology. However, it is not always clear that these criteria are employed whenever the consumer is confident she has made the right decision. Nonetheless, sellers who demonstrate to the satisfaction of the buyer that the purchase is desirable, rationally defensible and socially appropriate are likely to be persuasive. Hence sellers should set out to meet these criteria. When sellers meet expectations without post-purchase reservations, this translates into a post-purchase evaluation of the purchase as being desirable, rationally defensible and socially appropriate. The problem remains of uncovering the bases for subjective validity since

326

we want to know what our target customers think is desirable, rationally defensible and socially appropriate – and what is not. Social appropriateness does not necessarily have a cultural fixedness but can change, particularly with clothing. Who would have thought years ago that it would be acceptable to wear deliberately torn jeans? At one time, not too long ago, this would have symbolized poverty, not an anti-establishment sentiment or a display of freedom to choose one's own lifestyle.

SOCIAL INTERACTION, SOCIAL VALIDATION, SOCIAL GROUPS AND SOCIAL REFERENCE GROUPS

People desire their judgments to be socially validated and this explains the selling effectiveness of telling the customer which positive reference groups have bought the product. Alternatively, there are simply ads saying things like 'what doctors use themselves'; 'one million people can't be wrong'; 'the secret product that keeps the stars looking young' and so on.

Social *validation* is sought because consumers do not behave as isolated individuals but look to those with whom they socialize for advice. Traditionally, in the organizational behavior literature, a 'group' is a set of two or more individuals who are in reciprocal communication or association with each other for some purpose. There are the primary groups like work groups, family groups and social groups who have direct contact with each other, but also the more remote, secondary groups such as trade unions whose members associate with each other to further their common interests. In marketing, the groups of interest are social groups and reference groups.

Social groups are social communication networks. The informal word-of-mouth communication that occurs within groups may on occasion be far more influential than mass advertising in determining which brand of product is bought, because such communication carries more social validation, credibility and perhaps more pressure to conform. The advertising industry has tried to exploit the power of 'buzz' and viral marketing with the aim of getting consumers to spread messages to each other. Sometimes it is forgotten that the message must be relevant to the target audience's interests and concerns or the message will be neither absorbed nor passed on. Thus Volvo in 2004 ran spoof ads in Europe that claimed that thirty-two people in Dalaro, a small town in Sweden, had bought Volvo S40 sedans on a single day. This exploited the likelihood of people being curious about such a happening even if the concern was lacking. The house party is another form of generating word of mouth. House Party is one company that organizes such events. It seems companies are willing to spend around $250,000 for 2,000 house parties because such parties can be organized to target particular demographics. House parties are organized to generate interest in the product but do not necessarily get people to talk about the product after leaving the party unless the product has been shown to have the potential to enrich their lives.

Consumer buying cannot all be based on objective testing or personal experience so *advice* is what is sought. A person who is constantly sought for advice, on the principle of reciprocity, builds up social debts. Marketers stress the importance of cultivating word-of-mouth communication about a product. The most discussed products are those of immediate interest and concern such as movies and television shows, followed by food and dining products. Word-of-mouth research suggests the most criticized products are financial services. Research confirms that ads generate consumer interest but conversations and advice from friends tend to be more credible (Story 2006). There is recognition of the distinction between what can be best confirmed by the senses and what needs to be endorsed by those in our social milieu and this is where word of mouth plays a major role.

There has been a fragmentation of the media, with consumers getting information from many sources. Marketers have responded by using a wide variety of media. Not surprisingly there has been an upsurge of public relations (PR) whose goal is to secure positive coverage in the media for anything it is promoting. Although traditionally PR is associated with 'brand communications' using the press conference, sending novel news to journalists, setting up interviews and so on, a good deal of PR is 'in-house' working for charities and other not-for-profit organizations. PR has found it easy to get its messages (usually unaltered) into the local press if they are of interest to consumers. If an organization has a novel and interesting message to put across, it might be advisable to use PR first before going on to advertising. Or to get the message across first if it is likely to be controversial, as outsourcing has become.

There is the question of decision-making within the *family* unit. The focus has been on who has the final decision; who has concurring authority; the influence of the family life cycle and so on. But cultures will vary widely on the issue of influence, and it would be foolish to believe in any generalities without investigating one's own market where we might find few set patterns. Typically, researchers talk about who has the most power to make the decision, though often we agree to go along with the person in the family to whom the decision *means more* as they feel most concern about it. While certain purchases are jointly decided or dominated by one or other family member, most commonly the wife in Western societies takes on the role of gatekeeper who can screen which household products or brands are bought. But this classification ignores how we respond positively to family members to whom the purchase is most significant (has most meaning). We are all sensitive to the emotion that can be involved in buying a product and a family member who seems to feel most concern with a purchase can have most influence. In line with this is the finding that 70 percent of shower gels for men are bought by women. Procter & Gamble, in marketing their Old Spice shower gel for men, had the problem of marketing to women yet luring men away from their soap when shower gels had the image of being unmanly to many of the men targeted. The competing brand Axe promoted it by suggesting it was irresistible to all those scantily clad ladies. An ad was created for Old Spice with the slogan: 'Smell Like A Man, Man' and using a 'beef-cake' actor showing his body, ending by saying that if your man 'stopped using ladies scented body wash and switched to Old Spice, he could smell like he's me'. The appeal to men was that the shower gel was not that scented-ladies-stuff but something manly, while the appeal to women was the fantasy of something of the actor rubbing off on to her man. The ad was a success in terms of the sales generated, which is particularly surprising since Old Spice aftershave has the image of what grandfather used and the young tend to be put off by such associations.

Immersion in a group – identifying strongly with some group's interests – is apt to reduce an individual's self-awareness so less attention is focused on an individual's own feelings, beliefs and wants. This reduces an individual's own deliberation and encourages action in accordance with group pressures. This group pressure is facilitated by members being anxious to please the group because pleasing the group is regarded as the path to full acceptance. But sometimes going along with the group emerges not from just a desire to conform socially but because of a belief that the group knows best so the aim is not 'social conformity' but 'information conformity'. The identification with groups and the sense that mass judgment can't be wrong is one explanation of the *herd* instinct that periodically disrupts the stock market.

A *reference group* consists of those whose standards, as perceived by the individual consumer, are the standards that the individual feels the need to consider to guide his or her own behavior. The consumer need not be a member of a group but aspires to join it. Reference groups serve a comparative and a normative function. A group is a 'normative reference group' if the individual consumer uses the group to establish behavioral standards, for example in dress. A group is a 'comparative reference group' if it is used by the consumer as a basis of comparison to evaluate personal qualities and buying actions. A church group may be a comparative reference group.

There are 'positive' and 'negative' reference groups for every consumer: positive reference groups are those with which the individual identifies, accepts and wants to join or maintain membership, while negative reference groups are those privately rejected and used to define what he or she does not want to be. When all established politicians are viewed by voters as a negative reference group, contrasting candidates will be chosen, not infrequently with no political experience and strange views. Professors often go to some lengths to avoid looking like a Wall Street broker, as these tend to be a negative reference group when it comes to dressing. When the term reference group is used without any qualification, however, it is interpreted to mean some positive reference group.

The more attractive the reference group, the greater the motivation to adhere to the group's *norms*. 'Group norms' are the accepted standard ways of thinking, feeling or behaving that are shared by members of the group. They result from social interaction: the behavior of people within the social group determines social norms and, for example, what is fashionable or popular with the group.

Norms are both *descriptive* of behavior (that is, reflect similarities in behavior among members of the group) and *prescriptive* of behavior (they reflect shared beliefs about what constitutes appropriate opinions and behavior). One way to change people is to show that what they believe or the way they act is not in line with the social norms of their positive reference groups. A person who arrives at some conclusion which no one else in their social milieu believes will have little confidence in the validity of that conclusion and anyone who acts in a socially inappropriate way invites social disapproval. It is difficult to change behavior if that change conflicts with reference group norms.

Reference group influence can be exerted both for the product class bought and for the brand. In particular, if the product or brand is publicly 'consumed' (e.g. wearing clothes) the influence is likely to be stronger. Reference groups can on occasion influence which product is bought but not the brand, while, on other occasions, they can influence the brand bought but not the decision to buy the particular product. In any individual case there are always countervailing influences such as the urge for autonomy and to be in control of one's own life. With regard to the latter, if a person is ill he or she wants not only to be free from pain but to regain a sense of being in control of his or her own body.

Conformity to group norms is motivated both by social conformity and informational conformity. *Social conformity* stems from a desire to go along with positive reference groups, and *informational conformity* is conformity arising from a belief that others are more knowledgeable or wise on the issue. Even medical practitioners adhere to informational conformity when adopting the claims of salespeople who are assumed to possess more knowledge about the benefits of their company's drugs. Social conformity arises from the desire for acceptance. People want to harmonize their relations with others and social conformity is the result. When beliefs are not built on tangible, physical reality but relate to social reality (such as status symbols) where things are ambiguous, social conformity offers a safe anchor. Social conformity is more common if the purchase is socially visible, such as a car, or the product is for a social occasion, such as wine, or the purchase has relevance for the buyer's social group, such as clothing. *Informational conformity*, on the other hand, stems from the desire to make sense of the world around. In other words, while social (normative) conformity to group norms emanates from the desire to be accepted, informational conformity is a way of seeking a more accurate view of reality. Much conformity involves both informational and normative influence. Group influence can be powerful in both informational and social conformity since the attachment to various groups is one aspect of a person's social identity. One interesting group phenomenon is the so-called 'polarization effect'.

The *polarization effect* in group decision-making occurs when all those within the decision-making unit (DMU) are a little inclined, before they meet, to favor supplier/offering X. In coming together to express views, they move in the direction of actually choosing X; going from what was formerly just an inclination to making a definite choice because others are supportive of the choice. Salespeople can do a good deal to influence that initial tendency by finding out who is going to be involved in the decision (through what sociologists call the *snowball technique* of asking one and then another who will be involved until no more names are mentioned) and approaching each in turn. This does not mean that members of the DMU, in agreeing on what to do, must also agree on the reasons for doing it. As with individual consumers, members of the DMU can arrive at the same choices by different paths. Certain voters can act like a decision-making group in being inclined to one candidate and later becoming committed to that candidate when some message resonates in suggesting many others are of like mind.

An even more interesting concept in group behavior is the granfalloon effect. Those who regularly buy a brand may be induced to feel that other buyers of the brand are potential friends. This is what Pratkanis and Aronson (1991) refer to as the granfalloon effect. It is based on Tajfel's observation that labeling a group of people as having something in common gets them to act as if they had much in common or are friends (Tajfel 1981). The exploitation of this phenomenon occurs in the various car clubs, with manufacturers hosting 'reunions' and so on. 'Brandfests' provide an ideal opportunity for the manufacturer. Apple computers tries to get its customers to regard themselves as 'revolutionary' (in being discerning and on the cutting edge of technology). We also get the granfalloon effect in politics. Brett (2003) shows how the Liberals in Australia formed a party out of the middle class, who previously had simply viewed themselves as individuals, by appealing to them as having higher moral principles than everyone else. (This is similar to the so-called Moral Majority promoted in the US.) This 'moral middle class' was something created by appeals to their moral sense, rather than to their self-interest.

EMOTION: A MAJOR TOPIC FOR SOCIAL PSYCHOLOGISTS

One major limitation of cognitive psychology for marketing purposes is its neglect of emotion, though things are changing (Ortony et al. 1988) and there is progress even to the extent of the establishment of a journal with the title *Cognition and Emotion*. Emotion is important for marketing as it informs decision-making by highlighting what is important. Emotion strengthens and reinforces the process of motivation by energizing it. As the expression goes, it puts fire in the belly. Emotions are aroused when some happening is evaluated as of high concern; as so highly desirable or undesirable in terms of our concerns that an autonomic, physiological reaction occurs. Emotions are tied to values, as threats to our values are what concern us. Threats to values, like the value we put on maintaining a certain way of life, can be emotionally arousing. This does not mean that emotions just bubble up when anything at all concerns us since emotional reactions may not necessarily be that strong.

Social psychologists have shown a special interest in emotion. Other psychologists and sociologists have also shown an interest (as other chapters testify) though not always in the same way or with the same focus.

As the layman uses the word, 'emotion' is an umbrella term for feeling states resulting from highly charged happenings of concern to the individual. In psychology there are different conceptualizations of emotion without any being dismissive of this view, though some limit the focus. One way of limiting the focus has been to ignore neurotic conditions. There is a reason for this since it is seldom possible to extrapolate from emotions as commonly experienced to abnormal neurotic conditions. As Sims (1995), a psychiatrist, words it, there is less likely to be a continuum from emotions as popularly conceived to neurotic conditions. For example, we all experience 'anxiety' but this is different from having an anxiety *trait* which is defined as meeting all the vicissitudes of life with a habitual high degree of anxiety, typically associated with a personality disorder. Similarly, many upsets in brain functioning contribute to depression or an obsessive-compulsive syndrome but these are outside the typical psychological study of emotion (Kotulak 1996). But to complicate this, some psychologists see neurotic behavior as 'reasonable' within the bounds of social norms, and advocate simply retaining the term 'psychosis' for disorders 'characterized by profound disturbances of thought and emotion' (Vyse 1997).

Claiming the emotions are of central importance in all human actions, whether in buying, working or playing football, Elster (1989), a social science scholar at Columbia, argues that the nature, causes and consequences of the emotions are among the least understood aspects of human behavior. There is truth in this. A good deal of confusion surrounds the study of emotion and it is not surprising that some of the most outstanding contributions to the study of emotion have been made by philosophers. In fact the early academic literature on emotion was written by philosophers, for example Aristotle's *Rhetoric*; Descartes' *The Passions of the Soul*; Hobbes's *Ethics*; Hume's *A Treatise on Human Nature* and Adam Smith's *Theory of Moral Sentiments*. As Elster maintains, scientific psychology has been more successful in the study of biological (basic) emotions such as anger and fear than cultural emotions such as guilt, shame, envy, embarrassment and jealousy.

Emotion as a concept: It is difficult to make the concept of emotion precise when psychologists themselves differ. As one dictionary of psychology says: 'no other term in psychology shares its combination of non-definability with its frequency of use' (Reber, Allen and Reber 2009). Yet one important distinction, as Goldie (2000) points out, is frequently ignored. This is the distinction between emotion and *episodes* of emotional experience. As Goldie says, an emotion such as love or jealousy can last for years, while the eruption of emotional episodes will be relatively short-lived. An employee can, over time, build an enduring anger against her boss or the company for the way she has been treated and the anger can then suddenly erupt as an emotional episode. This is an important distinction since marketing managers need to be aware that relationships with customers can be damaged without, in the short term, there being any emotional manifestation (episode).

When definitions of emotion are precise, they commonly turn out to be mini-theories on the nature of emotion, with the particular definition of emotion acting as a premise for the explication of some favored theory. In fact some psychologists and philosophers argue that the phenomena grouped under the name 'emotion' are too varied to come under just one label. The lack of agreement on categories of emotion within cultures and across cultures is an additional factor that makes the study of emotion frustrating. One commonly accepted distinction is between basic (physiologically based) emotions like fear, anger, disgust and the self-assessment emotions such as pride, envy, shame, guilt and humiliation which are directed towards self, one's status and the need to believe in one's own self-worth.

Early writers on emotion such as Descartes (1596–1650) sought to compile lists of basic emotions. While such distinctions between emotions can appear clear in their respective abstract definitions, these distinctions are often difficult to make in observational terms. There have been many different lists of emotions but no general agreement. One popular attempt that appears in the marketing literature is that made by Plutchik. Plutchik (1980) identifies eight primary (basic) emotions, with all other emotions being regarded as combinations of these eight. They are: fear, surprise, sadness, disgust, anger, anticipation, acceptance and joy. Plutchik claims these primary emotions can be expressed at different degrees of arousal as follows:

Table 11.1 Plutchik's Table of Emotions

Primary Emotion	At Low Intensity	At High Intensity
Acceptance	Tolerance	Adoration
Fear	Timidity	Terror
Surprise	Uncertainty	Amazement
Sadness	Pensiveness	Grief
Disgust	Boredom	Loathing
Anger	Annoyance	Rage
Anticipation	Mindfulness	Vigilance
Joy	Serenity	Ecstasy

If Plutchik is talking about how we apply emotional labels then it is not easy to make sense of the above, if we are to avoid doing violence to the

English language. Sadness at low intensity is said to be 'pensiveness' but 'pensiveness' need not involve any sadness but may even have a hedonic tone. Similarly, however minor (low intensity) the 'disgust', it need not involve 'boredom' since disgust is always active toward whatever is inspiring the disgust, while boredom is always a passive turning away. There are hardly any of the emotions said to reflect the primary emotions at a low or high level which could not be similarly contested. In fact it is not even clear that the so-called emotion of 'acceptance' is a recognizable emotion at all. Plutchik is saying there are just these eight basic physiological states or feeling states, with other states being combinations of these basic eight. In saying this, Plutchik is going beyond what current knowledge can deliver. The fact that his list is so often quoted is testimony to the dearth of substantive theory on emotion.

Plutchik's list of emotions has been used to rate the emotional content of an ad. The scale that emerged was developed by taking each emotion and splitting it into subcategories that are claimed to range from *mild* to *moderate* to *intense*. Thus the *mild* subcategory of fear is 'threatened', the *moderate* 'frightened' and the *intense* 'intimidated'. None of these labels are fleshed out in operational measures on the assumption that every speaker of the language will construe them in the same way. In other words, the sense-meaning is such that the referential-meaning is assumed to be neither vague nor ambiguous. But surely if one feels threatened, one will be frightened and also feel intimidated? Similarly, the emotion of 'anger' is split into mild/hostile, moderate/annoyed and intense/irritated but it seems legitimate to claim the reverse is equally defensible. Plutchik's list is neither exhaustive nor mutually exclusive which is logically demanded for any classification. But even if we accept the list for the purpose of rating ads, it would seem preferable simply to ask respondents to rate the intensity of fear, anger, disgust and so on, on a scale from 0 to 10 without any pretence of putting dubious emotional labels on subdivisions.

An alternative method of gauging the emotions generated by an ad and used by some ad agencies is to use 'faces' that reflect emotions in that emotions tend to be associated with certain stereotypical facial expressions (see earlier). The respondent is asked to tick the face most reflective of his or her feelings on seeing the ad. If the expressions were other than stereotypical and were the actual faces of emotion, we might simply have an observer note the expression on the face of the subject and dispense with the ticking of faces. This would make the process more objective. The fact is, respondents do not typically display such stereotypical emotions through facial expressions on seeing the ad. This means the advertiser needs to establish the reliability and validity of this way of gauging emotional reactions. Reliability relates to consistency, while validity is the more important concept of correctness. We can have reliability without validity but we cannot have validity without reliability. It may be that advertising agencies have done such tests. What is certainly true is that advertisers would like their ads to produce certain specific emotions and want to know that this has been achieved by the ad.

One theory-grounded classification of the emotions is that put forward by Gordon (1987). He classifies emotions into *factive* and *epistemic*. Factive emotions are those like joy which necessitate the subject believing as a fact that the emotion-arousing event or situation has happened. If a customer is upset at, annoyed with, ashamed of, embarrassed by, amused by, pleased with and so on, she must believe as a fact that the state, event or situation which triggered her emotional state did in fact occur or does in fact exist. In contrast, epistemic emotions stem from uncertainty because the relevant facts are not yet known to the subject. For example, a person 'hopeful' of winning the next state lottery is acting as if she believed she could be a winner: she does not as yet know whether she has won. Hope is an epistemic emotion. The American dream of rags to riches is sufficiently fulfilled to keep that hope alive.

Gordon claims that the distinction between factive and epistemic emotions is preferable to talk of 'forward'- and 'backward'-looking emotions. This is because it is possible to speak (say) of someone desperately hoping the train arrived safely – the facts about the train's arrival are already known but not yet to the subject. The key distinction is knowledge possessed. A consumer can only have fear about a product's safety when she does not know as a fact that the product is safe or unsafe. To be in a state of fear about some possibility, for example the safety of some product, it is not necessary to even think the possibility likely. On the contrary, it is possible to be in a state of fear when the possibility feared is believed by the subject to be very unlikely or considered by others to be a delusion, as happens in hypochondria. Epistemic emotions may be without evidential support. Yet when an emotion is epistemic, we act as if we believe that our fears or hopes could be true.

Definitions of emotion: Before expressing irritation with the failure to agree on a definition of emotion, we should recognize that precise definitions of everyday concepts are seldom without exception (Flanagan 1996). Everyday concepts like emotion seldom have a *conjunctive* definition, that is, one that consists of all the necessary and sufficient conditions for the use of the term. Ludwig Wittgenstein pointed out that terms in everyday use (such as the word 'game') resist being defined by any single set of necessary and sufficient conditions. Activities classified as games have little or nothing in common: they are a *polymorphous* set which is one that can be defined neither in terms of necessary nor in terms of sufficient conditions for all uses of the term 'game'.

The inability to agree on conjunctive definitions for terms in everyday usage is pervasive in public debates, for example on what constitutes deception in advertising. Most advertising, as advocacy, is biased in that it does not provide all the needed information for making a rational decision and the information it does provide is typically stacked against making a fully informed decision. But is this deception? Everyday concepts have vague boundaries, with some instances of the concept illustrating usage better than others in that they are recalled more easily and with less effort. Nonetheless, attempts at defining individual emotions in a conjunctive way have not been entirely abandoned.

Instead of seeking a conjunctive definition, we might set out a list of attributes, with individual emotions being viewed as different combinations of these attributes. If we did, the different emotions, being different combinations from the same total set of attributes, would possess a family resemblance (Wittgenstein 1953). The majority of emotions do have a 'family resemblance', even if no single definition of emotion is universally accepted as supplying the 'essence' of emotion.

DEFINING EMOTIONS IN TERMS OF FAMILY RESEMBLANCE

Psychologists view emotions as *syndromes*, which implies that emotions have many elements without any one being regarded as the 'essence' of emotion. But collectively these elements do form a 'family resemblance' in looking at emotions. Given that this is so, what set of features sustains the family resemblance? Providing we accept that each and every emotion does not necessarily possess the same set of features, we might agree on the family resemblance being tied to something like the following set of characteristics:

1. Intentionality
2. Appraisal tied to our concerns
3. Autonomic physiological activity, arousal and feelings
4. Action tendency
5. Physiological expression.

Each of these characteristics is discussed below.

INTENTIONALITY OF EMOTIONAL STATES

Emotions differ from *visceral* feelings such as pain by having an object. Visceral feelings can give rise to emotion but are not themselves emotions per se. *Intentionality* is what characterizes most emotions. What is meant by the intentionality of emotional states is that emotions have an *object*. Thus we are angry at something or someone; we take pride in something; we love someone; we hate someone; we are ashamed of something; embarrassed by something or guilty about something and so on. It is hard to imagine a state of pride, anger or love without the state being directed at something. This intentionality of emotion is termed the 'aboutness' of emotion: emotions are *about something*. If we are to fully understand some emotional episode we need to identify the *object* of the emotion in sufficient detail to apprehend why he or she feels such emotion about the object. Emotion tends to attach itself to a singular object, such as the infant's emotional attachment to a specific security blanket which leads to the infant's rejection of other blankets which are objectively the same. Emotions, like love, can be very specific in intentionality.

Depression, happiness and boredom are commonly quoted as exceptions since they conflict with the claim that emotions always 'imply a certain relationship between a person and some object, like a person (including the self) or event whether real, remembered, or imagined' (Parkinson 1994). One answer is that depression, happiness and boredom are *moods* distinguished from emotions proper by being more diffuse and persistent and so having no definite object. But another answer is that, unless they are a psychopathological condition, they do have an object, that is, they are *about* something. Thus we are depressed about something, happy about something, bored about something. A diffuse reference need not be the case as when someone says she is happy at being promoted, or bored with her job or depressed about some failure.

APPRAISAL OF THE OBJECT OF EMOTION TIED TO OUR CONCERNS

The second feature that characterizes exemplars of emotion is that emotion involves an appraisal of the object of the emotion whether this is a situation, person, happening (real or imagined) or some combination of situation and physiological state. Getting emotional is tied to a highly positive or negative appraisal, involving something that concerns us. Appraisal may, on occasion, be linked to an attribution, as when personal failure is attributed to the tricky actions of others and, as a consequence, produces anger. Emotional reactions are tied to what concerns us or, we should add, what concerns significant others or situations with which we identify. What concerns us, in turn, is tied to our values (praiseworthy or not) which in turn are shaped by past emotional episodes. Values, emotions and what concerns us are thus interrelated.

Lazarus (1991), one expert on emotion, is adamant in regarding a highly positive or highly negative appraisal as the cause of all emotion. For him appraisal always precedes emotion. But what about when we stumble in walking or going down steps? There is an immediate autonomic physiological reaction of panic or fear. Is this not an emotional reaction without conscious appraisal? This simply demonstrates perhaps that appraisal need not be conscious but can occur at the non-conscious level. The response comes first and the conscious appraisal of what occurred (if it comes at all) follows. Thus we might find ourselves being immediately envious on seeing that a rival has been promoted, without any intervening thought of what it means personally. This would be consistent with Damasio's somatic marker view discussed earlier (Chapter 8) and below in this chapter.

Lazarus (1994) distinguishes primary from secondary appraisal. Primary appraisal is the 'process of sensing the significance of what is happening for personal well-being'. This is another way of saying 'sensing it concerns us'. This notion of primary appraisal links back to Arnold (1960), whose seminal work on emotion defined appraisal as the process by which the personal relevance of the emotional event is apprehended. Secondary appraisal, according to Lazarus, is concerned with the evaluation of possible ways of coping with the situation, given the personal and environmental resources available. Thus the primary appraisal of a purchase may be that it is a poor buy, but the secondary appraisal may dampen the emotion if it involves the recognition that it is easy to return the product to the seller.

Appraisal versus evaluation: The terms 'appraisal' and 'evaluation' are used as synonyms by Lazarus but the two can be distinguished. Evaluation is concerned with *ranking* items against criteria whereas appraisal is an assessment of the significance or personal meaning of the object for the individual. In any case, the phrase 'possible ways of *coping*' associated with secondary appraisal seems inappropriate to positive emotions like, for example, pride.

Appraisal as a logical component of emotion: In contrast to Lazarus, Parkinson (1995) claims that a highly positive or negative appraisal links to emotion, not causally (i.e. appraisal does not cause emotion), but by *logical* necessity: saying someone is angry simply implies (not causes) that he or she is taking offense at something someone has done or failed to do. For Parkinson, the appraisal pattern defines the type of emotion aroused. Parkinson points out that there are no research findings demonstrating that appraisal causes emotion. But this simply reflects the difficulty of separating stages in a causal chain when effects are so instantaneous. No evidence for something simply means no evidence available and does not prove one way or another. Parkinson's position is that held by some philosophers who claim that the relationship between reasons and action is conceptual and not causal.

Parkinson argues that an emotional reaction can follow an in-depth evaluation since the result can be emotionally disturbing. Thus it may be that the consumer is not *immediately* emotionally affected by being told tuition has risen, until she reflects on the matter and comes to realize it means giving up school or cutting out all expenditures beyond basic necessities. This, though, simply shifts the relevant appraisal to the appraisal of the evaluative findings.

Conceptualization versus appraisal: Psychologists attempt to specify both the eliciting conditions (contributory factors or causes) for emotion and the variables that influence their intensity. Instead of talking about identical appraisals giving rise to identical emotions (a common enough claim), Ortony et al. (1988) claim that it is the same *conceptualization* of the situation that gives rise to the same emotion. These social psychologists characterize emotions as *valenced reactions* to events, agents or objects, with the emotion's character being determined by the way in which the eliciting situation is construed (conceptualized). A valenced reaction, as used here, is a reaction emanating from the perceived positive or negative desirability of the event's consequences, the action or the situation's characteristics. (Valence is a term introduced into social psychology by Kurt

Lewin (1890–1947) to mean the psychological value of an object.) Under this view, 'conceptualizing' is the key cognitive antecedent to emotion.

The authors go on to argue that this is consistent with writers of novels producing in readers an awareness of a character's affective (emotional) state simply by putting across a certain characterization of the situation, leading millions of readers to infer similar emotions from the described situation. While research on emotion generally focuses on appraisal and arousal, Ortony et al. point out that this research offers no satisfactory account of how appraisal and arousal interact to produce emotion. Their own approach focuses on showing how people's construal or conceptualization of a situation can cause them to experience emotions. Given Kurt Lewin's attraction to Gestalt psychology, it is not surprising that conceptualizing rather than appraising should have such appeal to his admirers.

Although conceptualizing a situation carries the notion of grasping the whole thing, while appraising a situation only focuses on the situation's significance for the appraiser, the difference between appraising a situation and conceptualizing it may be of little significance as far as the generation of emotion is concerned. Thus appraising a situation as life threatening or conceptualizing the situation as life threatening would in both cases lead to the emotion of fear. But perhaps it could be argued that the appraisal of life threatening would be separately inferred from conceptualizing the situation. However, the term 'appraisal' does seem to be preferable since conceptualizing suggests conscious cognitive processing when there can be simply a gut emotional appraisal that need not involve any conscious process. In any case, to argue that two people who conceptualize a situation in the same way will have the same emotion is not a testable proposition since any failure to do so could always be explained away by saying the two people did not conceptualize the situation in the same way. There is really no way of making the notion of 'conceptualizing in the same way' sufficiently operational for unambiguous testing.

AUTONOMIC PHYSIOLOGICAL ACTIVITY, AROUSAL AND FEELINGS

The third family resemblance commonly exhibited in emotions is the presence of autonomic (spontaneous/involuntary) *physiological* activity. Emotions are accompanied by physiological activity that is typically a form of arousal though there are other forms of arousal than autonomic arousal since arousal can relate to either physiological or psychological activation. Autonomic (involuntary) physiological arousal is sensed in the subjective feelings that are associated with an emotion such as a feeling of fear.

Ortony and Taylor (1990) argue that each emotion is defined by its affective valence since emotions are valenced reactions to events, agents or objects. As valence is used for the psychological desirability of an object, affective valence refers to the desirability of the appraised object in terms of the positive or negative feelings aroused. To Ortony and Taylor the experience of positive or negative feelings is the basic feature of emotion.

Emotional feelings can be pleasant or unpleasant and it is commonly assumed that highly pleasant or unpleasant feelings imply being highly aroused. This need not be the case since the unpleasant feeling of boredom may not be accompanied by high arousal. Yet it may be that, for an emotion to be motivating, there must be both high arousal and high feelings of pleasantness or unpleasantness (Elster 1999b).

Goldie (2000) points out that most accounts of emotional episodes would be completely consistent with not experiencing emotion at all. Why? Because these accounts miss out feelings, specifically *feelings towards*. We can only 'act out of emotion' when we have a certain feeling towards the object. Without having certain feelings towards the object of concern there can be no emotion. Thus we can only act out of anger if we have a certain feeling towards some person or other object of the emotion. As he says, 'feeling towards' is thinking with feeling. Whatever feeling we have towards the object this feeling may be immune to beliefs. Thus a consumer may believe that she was lucky to have got the plasma television at the price she did, yet her feeling towards the retailer may still be hostile because the retailer refused to give her a rebate for today's price that had been further discounted: there is a sense that things were not done fairly. The intentionality of emotion and the appraisal of the object of the emotion imply some resulting feeling towards the object. For Goldie, without our having certain 'feelings towards' the object, there can be no accompanying emotion. In other words, *feelings towards* is a *necessary* condition for emotion to be aroused, that is, a *sufficient* condition for emotion not to occur. This is a valid claim even if a person is not reflectively aware of his or her feelings towards the object of the emotion.

The question arises as to whether people can be in an emotional state without actually *feeling* an autonomic physiological activity. Lyons (1980) says this can be so, since an increase in pulse rate, adrenaline secretion or a rise in blood pressure might go unnoticed. On the other hand, he agrees with what has been said, that someone is in an emotional state if, and only if, an evaluation (read appraisal) of an event is accompanied by an 'abnormal' (read 'autonomic') physiological state. Neither the evaluation nor the autonomic bodily effects is sufficient: only jointly do they produce an emotional state. For Lyons, appraisal and autonomic arousal explain how emotions are produced. To Lyons, an emotional state presupposes a very positive or very negative antecedent appraisal of an object, person (including the self) or event (real, remembered or imagined), while autonomic physiological effects are a necessary condition for the emotional experience. He argues that this is demonstrated by findings which show that the loss of bodily sensation is accompanied by a loss of emotion. He maintains, however, that the autonomic bodily effects need not actually be felt (e.g. an increase in blood pressure). People are not always conscious of being in an emotional state. This is true; but the question arises as to whether people can *believe* they are in an emotional state without feeling any bodily effects. There is doubt here. In any case, is there not something missing in just focusing on appraisal and autonomic physiological effects? Must not appraisal also involve a feeling towards something that *concerns* us so we have an appraisal that is highly negative or positive leading to autonomic physiological effects?

Carroll (1990) agrees that to be in an emotional state a person must undergo some 'concomitant physical agitation', registered as a sensation, and also have evaluative beliefs (read: beliefs based on appraisals) of the object of the emotion. However, unlike Lyons, Carroll claims there are counterexamples such as neurasthenia (a nervous debility), which do not seem to have any object. Also, dancing can be emotional even though based purely on rhythm and physiology, without any evaluation. But does neurasthenia really fall into the family of emotions as generally under-stood? And does not the emotional uplift we get from dancing involve some self-evaluation or self-appraisal of our dancing? Emotion can arise from appraisals of objects of our imaginings and fantasies which may not mirror any objective fact in the world 'out there'. Nonetheless, all highly positive or negative appraisals (evaluations, conceptualizations, perceptions) give rise to some feelings towards the object of the appraisal.

ACTION TENDENCY OF EMOTION

The fourth feature in family resemblance of various emotions is action ten-dency. For intentional, goal-oriented, *deliberate* buying action to take place there must be:

- Motivation, which could be emotional
- Beliefs about the desirability, social appropriateness and rational defensi-bility of the recommended action
- Ability to take the action (feasibility)
- Opportunity to act.

But action arising from being in an *emotional state* may *not* arise from this set of factors, as this assumes action is always the result of deliberation. Emotional action may, on occasion, be simply impulsive behavior. But emotion does give rise to an action tendency. Exemplars of emotion com-monly do involve impulses to behave in line with the emotion regardless of beliefs, ability or opportunity. Thus in anger, people have an inclination to harm or be aggressive; in fear an inclination to flight or fight and so on, without weighing up the pros and cons. Action tendencies result from highly positive or negative appraisals of things that concern us and emo-tional reactions may simply be a conditioned response if such reactions in the past (for example, aggression) have been reinforced. In any case, what must be acknowledged is that emotion alone can trigger action just as excitement at the point of sale can trigger an impulse buy.

But emotional reactions depend somewhat on how the things are pre-sented. While the logician, lawyer or economist might argue whether policies on returns, A and B, are equivalent in meaning, they can arouse very different emotions in the consumer depending on how they are worded and presented. Similarly, different policies may have the same logical consequences yet emotional reactions might differ. Elster (1999) gives as an example how workers may feel shame if the state subsidizes their wages but not if the state offers the company the equivalent in cheap energy so it can pay the higher wages.

McGaugh (2003) shows how a strong emotional reaction helps ensure a negative experience is vividly fixed in memory and in the process changes sense-meanings, for example about brand image. What is remembered relates to what concerns us and major concerns always have an affective tone. As consumers recall an experience, they also recall the relevant affective tone, which validates the memory's authenticity, but in doing so attach certain emotional sense-meanings to what is recalled. Since the affective tone of the 'same' experience can differ among consumers, concepts associated with that experience can differ in sense-meaning to different people. Or, alternatively, different concepts are associated with that experience by different people. Thus two consumers may experience the same poor service but one may take the incident 'in their stride' while the other reacts angrily: the first consumer may use concepts such as 'sluggish' to describe the service while the second consumer may speak of the service merely as very 'cavalier'. A service that is provided by a firm with a non-established reputation suffers most from a lapse of service as there is no previous reputational capital to challenge that experience.

For Lazarus (1991), every emotion has a *core relational theme*. This core relational theme points to underlying motivational tendencies. For instance, the core relational theme associated with frustration is aggression or hitting out (Carver and Scheier 1990). This is interesting since 'frustration' is so tied to being dissatisfied with a purchase. When people are asked to report on emotional episodes, it is found that certain *patterns* of emotion and action tendencies go together (Frijda et al. 1989). Apart from this finding, there is little empirical evidence relating specific emotion and specific action. This is not surprising since emotions, like motives or desires generally, provide only a vague directional push; unlike the specific direction provided by beliefs. Although beliefs and emotions do affect each other, this is only within limits. There are limits on the extent to which emotions influence beliefs (e.g. that black is actually white) and beliefs influence emotions (when believing it is unwise to hit back at the boss yet being unable to restrain oneself). Beliefs calculate the feasibility of actions and this may lead to a modification of the intensity of the emotion. A further complication in predicting action lies in the fact that opposing emotions can be at work, for example the emotion of anger can be suppressed by the fear of getting the sack or the fear of regret can suppress a strong desire for indulging in instant gratification.

Elster (1999) rejects the idea of there being any universal laws when it comes to the emotions, either in terms of predicting precisely what conditions necessarily bring about a specific emotion or in predicting the precise action resulting from a particular emotional state. As already mentioned, David Hume (1711–76) saw every human action as emerging from some passion (emotion) and denies that reason by itself ever moves a person to action. For Hume, beliefs simply suggest means to achieve the *goals of passion*. It was this position that Kant (1724–1804) attacked as subversive of morality on the grounds that moral imperatives to duty are reasons for action that can be divorced from desires. We will return to this debate later.

Function of emotions: Emotions serve many useful functions. First, emotions help us *survive* by directing attention to what is important for survival such as threats to life and limb. Thus today we react emotionally to the perception of danger in our children taking up smoking. Second, emotions provide *information to others* (e.g. that we are in an angry state) to influence, for example, the sales clerk's behavior and to ourselves so we know our likes, dislikes, values and concerns. *Emotional* tears (some tears like those arising from peeling an onion are not generated by emotion), for example, tell others that we are particularly moved by some event. Third, emotions contribute to *social control* in that violation of religious or legal laws arouses feelings of guilt; being caught doing something not socially endorsed and not knowing what to do leads to embarrassment, while violations of strong cultural norms leads to shame and regret. Four, the display of emotion plays a role in *persuasion* (e.g. in negotiations) by indicating consistency and degree of commitment to a particular position. But it goes without saying that emotions on occasion have dysfunctional consequences as when they distort judgment and lead to ill-considered action. Fifth, and most important from the point of view of marketing, the function of emotion is to make up for the *insufficiency of reason*.

Reasoning can *proscribe* by logically pointing to inconsistencies, clarifying thoughts and making legitimate inferences. But reason alone does not determine trade-offs when trade-offs cannot be measured in terms of some common metric such as money. Making trade-offs involves values/goals since values point to the relative importance of the trade-offs. But behind values are not just biologically pressing demands such as the need for survival but past emotional episodes that shape whatever it is that concerns us. Some emotional episodes can be the inherited myths of history that are exploited in emotional advertising by associating brands with great historical figures or events. As de Sousa (1990) says:

> Emotions, by being tied to values, determine what is considered important; what options are considered; the patterns of salience among options; the relative importance of attributes while limiting the inferences actually drawn from a potential infinity of possible inferences.
>
> (De Sousa 1990)

Reasoning tells consumers a great deal about the features of a product but it is the link between reason and emotion that decides the actual trade-offs made. If reasoning proscribes by telling us what not to do, it is values that dictate trade-offs to prescribe action; lying behind values are emotional episodes steeped in our personal histories.

We might remind ourselves again of the work of neurologist Antonio Damasio (1994), which we dealt with in Chapter 8 on Cognitive Neuroscience. He shows that emotions are necessary for *serious* decision-making. Without emotions consumers, in making *deliberated* decisions, would be unable to assign values to different options or product attributes. This implies decision paralysis since consumers would be unable to make up their minds. As explained in Chapter 8, Damasio uses the expression *somatic markers* in connection with the emotional gut feeling that arises from a highly positive or negative appraisal. It is 'somatic' because it relates to bodily feeling and it is a 'marker' because it marks an image, however fleetingly. Somatic markers are like 'sentinels' who raise the alarm to help survival. Negative somatic markers set off alarm bells, while positive somatic markers encourage action in line with any positive (non-conscious) appraisal.

With the recognition that emotional reactions can arise without any conscious cognitive participation, there is the implication that we can form instant attitudes about anything that concerns us. This rules out the notion, commonly claimed in the consumer behavior literature, that attitudes must *always* start with a *conscious* cognitive appraisal. There may be a cognitive appraisal but it need not be conscious. In fact the very idea that the consumer's attitude towards a brand can be best viewed as a tripartite concept, consisting of a fixed temporal sequence of cognitive (awareness and comprehension of the product) > affective (feeling/assessment of the brand) > conative (action), has been undermined. This again is one of those logical sequences that are passed off as empirically verified psychology. There is too much interdependence between the cognitive and the affective for such a division to be considered realistic. It also rules out the notion of *target* audiences being either passive or active. If something is of major concern (high involvement is involved) to a target audience, that audience will be *attentive*. If it is of no concern, that audience may still not be passive since the ad can still *entertain* even if it has nothing of substance to say to the audience.

Emotional sentiment and brand loyalty: To have an *emotional sentiment* towards a brand is to have a strong positive feeling of liking for that brand. Strong brand loyalty involves emotional sentiment. Exercising a choice makes for the expression of loyalty as it provides an opportunity to be against alternatives disliked. There are satisfactions associated with loyalty in suggesting commitment to a set of beliefs. But brand loyalty, whether to a product or even a political party, *seems* to be less common than in earlier times. Perhaps this has to do with more vigorous competition, information availability and a fast-moving, mobile society used to making changes. In any case, it is not wise to assume a core of loyal customers since most offerings simply *rent allegiance*, only for as long as that offering has a quasi-monopoly of something desired – that is, a critical advantage. But not always, since the original product can still remain on top as its features or attributes become the accepted standard for its product class. In this way, 'better' products can come along without displacing the original product that has a 'lock' on the market. If this is so, the seller of the competitive brand must answer the question: better for what? And they must highlight the extra benefit it has to offer.

Consumers do nonetheless have loyalties and not just to individuals, but on occasion to brands that have served them long and well. However, loyalties in general tend to be fickle. For example, at the time of writing, political party loyalty in the US and the UK is at an all-time low because of the quality of candidates and their offerings. Providers of land phones have been shaken by how many of their customers have moved on to competitors for slightly lower prices. Nonetheless some voters and consumers do have intense attachments to brands, particularly those that encourage, as Starbucks tried to do, a sense of *belonging* to a community based on the consumption of that brand of product. Every company would like its customers to have a sense of bonding with other users of the brand since this is one way of keeping (retaining) a customer. Other ways are by appealing to customers as if they are a group with common interests, getting them to participate in joint projects and asking their advice as Snapple does in encouraging its drinkers to forward ideas for new drinks. A consumer can have a positive attitude towards the brand and consistently repurchase it without having an ounce of emotional attachment to the brand, though both these things (positive attitude and repurchase) are likely to correlate with perceptions of high brand performance.

In contrast to *moods*, emotional sentiments are not persistent conscious states but dormant until aroused by the object of the sentiment. Emotional sentiment ties into emotional memory in that those memories have sentimental content. Every firm catering to the consumer should seek to develop an emotional sentiment for the firm's brand by fixing the brand in the consumer's memory as part of a valued way of life. It is the vestiges of emotional sentiment which allow the successful resurrection of old brand names, such as the revival of the name Bugatti. It is ignorance of the emotional sentiment that can attach to venerable brand names that leads to many such brands being dismissed as worthless assets. The emotional sentiment still attached to the name Pan Am is not simply that arising from the Lockerbie air disaster of terrorist origin, but from the way the name acted as an informational anchor for a certain way of life.

Loyalty to a brand, as said earlier, is not just a matter of habitually buying the same brand since not all habitual buys are grounded in the components of loyalty, namely trust and sentiment. Nor is it buying habitually together with the feeling of a commitment to the brand, since commitment may arise from sentiments other than loyalty. It is not uncommon to use service providers such as medical consultants and lawyers because they are perceived as having great competence and credibility but at the same time are regarded as unattractive and disliked. Yet the combination of trust and sentiment (loyalty) is the best barrier to brand switching by customers while facilitating word-of-mouth recommendations or, in the case of industrial markets, referrals. There may, of course, be no loyalty to any particular brand when the various brands in the market are perceived as mere tokens of each other, with differences marginal and of no significance to the consumer. This is not to suggest that meaningful differences will always be confined to the product itself since things like brand image and distribution and other aspects of the offering can be crucial. In any case, being a loyal customer does not imply just buying the one brand. Brands in different segments of the market may be bought simultaneously by the buyer for different use-occasions or for different family members. Thus a woman might want a fresh light perfume during the day and a strong sophisticated scent for the evening and buy separate brands for each of these occasions, with loyalty to each brand.

PHYSIOLOGICAL EXPRESSION

Physiological expression is the fifth and final common feature in exemplars of emotion, though not all those who study emotion would necessarily select these five features. Emotions can be accompanied by certain characteristic expressions such as facial expression, the pupils of the eyes, gestures, voice, bodily posture, weeping, blushing, frowning and so on. Thus we have one reviewer commenting on Bing Crosby's voice as 'like the sonic balm that had held together some of the parts of a world. It had created an impression – an illusion, perhaps – of shared feeling, of realized good humor, of benevolence and tolerance that could almost be taken for granted' (O'Brien 2001).

Physiological displays or expressions are commonly viewed as basic channels through which emotional information is communicated. But each in isolation yields no certain meaning since none should be regarded as an isolated signal box. Only in the context of some situation do they collectively act as a semi-reliable system of communication. They reinforce each other, just as encouraging people to have more animation on their faces results in their voices becoming more animated. Emotions like fear and joy appear in facial expression even if we might question whether these manifest themselves in only one form of facial expression. Those who are blind find in the voice (given some context) many of the emotions that are found by the sighted in the face. The voice can indicate the intensity of emotion. For example, the level of anger is typically reflected in the voice rather than the face.

Jonathan Cole (1998) illustrates what happens when there is a 'disconnect' between that part of the brain concerned with emotion and the experience of emotion itself. This happens in cases of Mobius syndrome where there is no ability to make facial expressions because sufferers have no ability to move their faces. Sufferers not only have a problem in reading emotions and adjusting to another's emotional state (important in human interaction) but, in the absence of sensing feelings from the face, emotions are less clearly experienced. Similarly, those suffering from Asperger's syndrome (a form of high-functioning autism) do not know how to 'read' non-verbal behavior. They tend to evaluate in black or white terms so that if someone smiles they must be a friend, or if they scowl they must be an enemy, and so on. Children who are quick to recognize emotion in others have more peer group popularity, while being popular, in turn, helps fine tune their recognition of emotion in others (Manstead 1992). It is such examples of so-called 'emotional intelligence' that are also important in business, even if there is debate about the construct validity of the notion of 'emotional intelligence'.

Sometimes the term *emotional display* is used rather than 'emotional expression' to avoid the suggestion of such being completely involuntary behavior. Harre (1995) regards all displays of emotion as expressions of *judgmental* appraisals with the consequence that people should look behind emotional displays to discover the kind of judgment being expressed. Thus, if we see a customer, colleague, subordinate or superior in some emotional display, we need to ask what judgmental appraisal lies behind it if we are to do anything about the situation. We consider emotional expressions/displays through interpretations of emotion from such emotional displays/expressions, though these can seldom be precise as they depend on the interpreter's imagination, experience and acquaintance with the subject.

Exemplars of emotion will stress one or a combination of the five characteristics discussed above: intentionality, appraisal, autonomic physiological reaction, action tendency and physiological expression. Thus the emotion 'disgust' puts emphasis on appraisal; the emotion 'anger' focuses on the internal physiological happening; the emotion 'desire' focuses on action tendency; while the emotion 'embarrassment' focuses on outward signs.

WHAT IS IT ABOUT THE OBJECT OF THE EMOTION THAT GENERATES STRONG APPRAISAL?

If a highly positive or negative appraisal (conscious or non-conscious) is an antecedent of all emotion, what is it about the object of the emotion that generates strong appraisals or evaluations? As de Sousa (1990) says, the attributes or properties of objects which tie to emotions are *axiological*, that is, related to values. He speaks of emotions being a kind of *perception* rather than a kind of appraisal because perception embraces a sort of instant non-conscious appraisal, without our being committed to the cognitive demands that might be suggested by talk about appraisal per se. And perceptions alone can guide action, which is one reason why wise people can make foolish decisions.

While de Sousa agrees that we think of emotions as grounded in (evaluative) beliefs about the object of the emotion, he argues that it is better to regard emotions as resulting from evoking not just beliefs but a 'whole paradigm scenario at a metalevel'. (The word 'paradigm' is used here, as is common in philosophy, in the sense of being illustrative, though in social science it is used today to represent an overall perspective, scientific or otherwise – that is, the conceptual lens through which we view our subject area.) Beliefs per se touch only the cognitive and not the axiological level that embraces values grounded in our emotional history. The objects of emotion are tied to values (the axiological level) by resonating with the emotional memories or experiences that constitute the paradigm scenarios or the 'little dramas in which our natural capacities for emotional response were first enlisted'.

In other words, strong appraisals or evaluations of things that concern us arise through the object of the emotion resonating with values linked to past (emotional) happenings. It is emotional experiences that most determine our system of values. Our deepest concerns act as guides to our desires (wants), but concerns at the highest level are those that uphold values that tie to emotional experiences. Thus an obituary of one army general points out he was a survivor of the disastrous battle of Arnhem in the Second World War, an experience we are told which left him with a strong emotional prejudice against all staff planners. But emotions can arise from less serious incidents in that the object of emotion can simply be a football game, with winning or losing subject to strong appraisals tied to the values of loyalty and upholding self-esteem.

What concerns us reflects our values. This is why we can be concerned about others when values are involved. Martha Nussbaum (2001) claims that emotions like grief, love and compassion are the very cornerstone of the humane society and arise from our seeing our concerns reflected in others who become beneficiaries of our concern. On the morning after 9/11, a newscaster focused on a scene outside the American Embassy in London where attached to one of the bouquets on the pavement was a note that read: 'To our best friends the Yanks. If you need help, just call.' Who could not be moved by that sentiment of compassion?

Although we talk about ideologies of different political parties, the real dispute is over values. We have been made more aware of the importance of values by the media and social critics. Even Disney's brand of entertainment has given rise to criticism for the values it portrays with the claim that Disney portrays the world in a distorted and ultraconservative way and manipulates children by giving them a false sense of reality (Giroux 2000). Companies are constantly being criticized for the values that their policies suggest, like using child labor or shifting manufacture to any part of the globe that offers the cheapest labor.

What has made the consideration of values in society acute is the recognition that values relating to family ties and community are weakening to be replaced by strong individualistic values, not those like self-reliance and achievement but emotional gratification, getting in touch with feelings, hedonistic consumerism and so on. When firms merge or are acquired there is typically a clash of values. Thus the corporate values of those who ran Mobil led to the provision of health care coverage to the partners of gay employees but this was not the same at Exxon. At the time of the merger of the two into Exxon Mobil, this and other clashes of values were causing a problem as the newly formed company sought to revoke for new employees the Mobil policy that provided such health care coverage. Of course, values do change and are changed. When new values are acquired, past treatments may be reviewed in terms of newly acquired values or value priorities with a sense of outrage not present at the time the behavior was taking place. Thus we condemn companies for their past treatment of workers (well illustrated by a trade union recruiting program about failure to join: 'If you don't come in Sunday, don't come in Monday') when these actions were the community values weighted differently at that time. The values emphasized will vary depending on role and circumstances at the time. Thus when a party is in government, the values pushed when in opposition may be forgotten. Tony Blair, the ex-prime minister of the UK and leader of the Labour Party, when in opposition pushed for a Freedom of Information Act. When in office, in spite of the passing of the Freedom of Information Act in 2000, the public's right in this respect was considerably eroded. As Anthony Lewis (1999), columnist of the *New York Times*, says: 'No First Amendment rights here . . . or other civil liberties.'

The arousal of emotion occurs when some internal or external stimulus is immediately appraised in the light of our concerns, either highly positively or highly negatively, accompanied by some autonomic physiological effects. The closer in proximity, and more real the object of the emotion, the more intense the emotion is likely to be. A certain level of intensity is required before it is experienced as emotion. A person's system of values link back to emotional episodes in early life so that threats to values arouse negative emotions like fear, while the advancement of values we hold dear is accompanied by positive emotions like joy. It is interesting how words classified as taboo in early life can still cause an emotional jolt in a more tolerant society, as did the name FCUK used to name French Connection UK, a clothing company. The name certainly got attention by obliging us to consider the sense-meaning. Maybe its young target audience was attracted but many consumers were emotionally outraged and boycotted the brand.

MEASURING EMOTION AND USING EMOTIONAL APPEALS

The typical market survey with its structured questionnaire seems the wrong vehicle for eliciting emotional responses so there is resort to other techniques such as the *benefit probe*. We can ask respondents to think of two *functional* benefits for each product benefit and two emotional benefits for each functional benefit. In another approach, some marketers calculate the *emotional bonding* with brands by the use of an emotional counterpart to the multiattribute model. Emotional feelings are listed then weighted for the relative importance for the product class. Then brands are rated according to their perceived possession of each of the emotions, with a final score being calculated. Current brands can then be rated against some emotional ideal to discover any emotional gaps to be filled via advertising. There is an assumption that the sense-meaning and the referential-meaning of emotion terms used are unproblematic, which is just not the case. There is a need to make clear this meaning for each emotion term used. Perhaps Gabriele Taylor's approach points the way to establishing such clear meanings (1985).

Surveys using questionnaires have many inherent weaknesses since respondents have many reasons for not answering truthfully, such as protecting self-image. Also, divorced from actual buying, the tendency is to answer questions according to the way logic would dictate. Anyone who moves away from single-source data will often have a problem in reconciling results. This is apart from all the problems of getting a representative sample. The problem of getting a random sample (as a means to obtaining a representative sample) is becoming more complicated in telephone surveys, given that about a quarter of potential respondents now only have cell phones. Even if their cell phone number is obtainable, it appears they are less likely to answer their phone or willing to answer questions. 'Robopolling', with its use of automated recordings, is being made obsolete. It is difficult for pollsters to 'rinse' dirty data to correct flaws in such data collection; even more so when we remember that only about 15 percent of the adult population seem prepared to participate in phone surveys.

Emotional appeals are increasing since they can change interpretations, create a certain perception or conjure up a certain experience. But emotionally directed advertising needs to tie into values and to those culturally induced emotional experiences from which systems of values are generated. Emotional appeals in recent years have even been used to sell paint. Valspar research noted how seemingly all ads for paint followed the same formula, boasting about their range of colors with an ad showing a young couple painting a wall. In focus groups, however, consumers talked about how they feel on finishing a project: the sense of achievement, the pride and the joy and so on. It is these sentiments that Valspar sought to exploit in its successful advertising campaign. Pictures can be very effective in evoking emotions and this is why the old-fashioned catalog is by no means dead.

Liking the ad is a contributory factor in liking the brand but is neither necessary nor sufficient for purchase as is demonstrated by comparative ads which can be effective though disliked. A comparative ad portrays the competing rival as inferior to the product or brand being promoted. One bank in a current ad campaign suggests rival banks are short-changing their customers by subtly deceiving them as to what they will get, and the ad uses children to drive the point home. This has been an effective campaign but at the expense of reducing the credibility of all banks. This can be a problem with comparative ads; they can undermine the industry image. Sometimes the attribute on which the comparative ad claims superiority may not be that important to the target audience but the advertiser may have hoped that the *halo effect* occurs where the attribute on which the

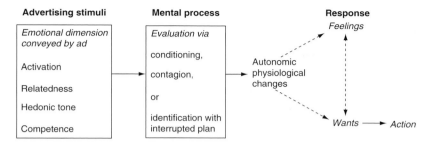

Figure 11.1   Emotion in advertisng

item is outstanding is generalized to other attributes so the target audience comes to assume the product is superior on other attributes.

One view of the relationship of advertising stimuli, mental process and response is that shown in Figure 11.1 (O'Shaughnessy 1995).

In Figure 11.1 it is argued that, typically, the *dimensions* associated with emotional stimuli are (Davitz 1969):

- *Activation*: associations of being alive and full of vitality as opposed to being bored and sluggish
- *Relatedness*: associations of warm, close, loving relationships with others as opposed to being lonely, isolated and an outsider
- *Hedonic tone*: association with achieving inner harmony and relaxation as opposed to being in a state of anxiety
- *Competence*: associations of being in control of life and having a sense of accomplishment as opposed to feeling unable to cope.

These dimensions are tied to values or the preferred life vision and when embodied in an advertisement can arouse emotion (however slight) through the mechanisms of conditioning, contagion or identification:

- Conditioning: conditioning can occur because events can have associations that stimulate a conditioned response (such as a loving mother).
- Contagion: behavior exhibited by others can be contagious. Thus everyone clapping or laughing serves to suggest some social consensus which becomes a cue for others to imitate: it is the thing to do to signify that one belongs. Anything that makes for similarity with the characters (like circumstances, age or background) increases emotional contagion. One advertisement that exploits contagion shows the product being demonstrated with the words 'I'm impressed' appearing on the screen.
- Identification: one form of identification in advertising is identification with someone's frustration arising from some *interrupted* plan. Thus in one advertisement we see the hostess's entertainment plans being interrupted by seeing that the wine glasses are 'spotty'. The audience identifies with the situation and the character's disappointment, and shares her glee when Cascade (a dishwasher detergent) remedies the situation. It is

not so much that we identify with the fictional characters in the television commercial than that we *assimilate* the situation, coming to see the situation both from the point of view of the characters in the situation and from the outside as well. We do not so much identify with the housewife in feeling her embarrassment but understand why she would be embarrassed because of our grasp of the situation. Without this capacity for understanding, no theatre would be possible.

Figure 11.1 illustrates the process. Not all of the physiological changes can be introspected as feelings, so a dotted line is shown going from the autonomic physiological changes to feelings. Similarly, autonomic physiological changes need not give rise to wants: not all emotions have an appetitive component. This latter point raises a related issue. Advertising may activate an emotion but the problem is to channel that emotion in the direction of buying the brand advertised. The target audience can be emotionally activated but not necessarily into buying the brand advertised. There is also the problem of ensuring advertising *connects to the experiences* that lie behind the values symbolized in the advertisement. Many marketers consider this the most difficult task of all in trying to generate emotion in advertising: the right emotional buttons are not always marked for pressing, though claims are made for focus groups and the use of psychographic data as useful for identifying emotions and values.

MOODS

Conditioning, contagion and identification suggest the mechanisms at work in producing a *national mood*. A mood, as an emotional state, differs from normal emotions in being diffused and attached to no specific object, being more a persistent feeling tied to personality or perceived quality of life rather than to any one event or situation. Moods can be the lingering effect of a series of events that are emotionally charged. There are times when sizable segments of the population can coalesce in a common mood. Thus national events such as the crime and unemployment figures and perceptions of the country's international stature (e.g. as judged in international sport competitions) can affect national mood. Knowledge of moods can be important since moods dispose us to make certain types of evaluation and to be even more selectively perceptive of the facts. Thus during a recession the mood is to evaluate certain types of expenditure as wasteful or as insensitive to the plight of others and to selectively pick product attributes that suggest good value for money. Shoppers in a good mood are more likely to buy and be satisfied with a store. When personal service staff uplift customer mood this can be a factor in disposing the customer to buy or repeat a buy.

There are certain anti-pleasure moods and suggested countermeasures (Gosling 1969):

Anti-pleasure mood	Advertisement countermeasures
Jangled nerves	Something soothing
Feel dull	Something exciting
Feel bored	Something amusing
Life unmanageable	Return to simpler life

The return to the simpler life gives rise to nostalgic feelings accompanied by a desire to relive earlier times. In times of rapid change, life can seem unmanageable, as the experiences and informational anchors that give people a sense of security and personal identity disappear. *Nostalgia* is one form of longing for something different from the present: longing for something lost like 'paradise' itself. Nostalgia is common during people's lives when careers have leveled off and values seem to be changing. However, what is nostalgic for one audience is not necessarily nostalgic for another, while the objects of nostalgia need not be just places but can be the celebrities who typified the past. This may account for the Ford Motor Company's use of the Beatles' song of 1965, *Help*, in its advertising and the return of old slogans like Timex's 'it takes a licking but it keeps on ticking' and the revival of certain brands and magazines. However, nostalgic advertising tends to give rise to an anti-nostalgic backlash in advertising appealing to the young, though if the young includes thirty-year-olds, the 1980s can be nostalgic for them.

The power of emotional bonding is best seen in the attachment to a brand that may be objectively undifferentiated from its rivals. This attachment is a feeling, typically built up from past pleasant associations with possessing, using or consuming the brand. Familiarity does not breed contempt of brands that have served the consumer well. On the contrary, it leads to increasing sentiment towards the brand. If, on some occasion, the brand is at a disadvantage (e.g. price remains higher than that of its rivals) and still the consumer sticks to it, this demonstrates the core concept of what we mean by loyalty. It is the loyalty of the child for its security blanket, refusing to accept a like substitute.

CHOICE CRITERIA AND EMOTION

One way of demonstrating the use of emotion in influencing the consumer is to take the six categories of choice criteria listed in Chapter 3, and show how emotion enters into each of the categories. Each category is capable of arousing the emotions providing it conjures up attributes of concern to the buyer. Below we sketch each category's emotion potential (O'Shaughnessy 1987).

1. *Technical criteria*: The core 'technical' function of a product is the primary purpose for which the product is designed. Thus the core function of a watch is to measure time. The very concept of a watch is defined by

its core function. We use words in advertising like 'state-of-the-art technology', 'smooth performance', 'fast results', 'dependable' and so on to excite interest and evoke positive emotional feelings towards the brand.

To call a watch 'good' is first and foremost to claim efficacy in its core function. But products have other technical functions besides the core function. There can be ancillary-use functions, and convenience-in-use functions. Ancillary-use functions are the permanent or optional technical features associated with the core function. An ancillary-use function of a detergent is to soften clothes, and that of a clock to speak the time. Advertisers use words like 'extra features' and 'enriched' to excite feelings of curiosity in ancillary use-functions. Convenience-in-use functions are the additions, modifications or packaging of a product that facilitate the performance of its core function such as the toothpaste tube-pump or power-steering on a car. Think of how often you find a toothbrush that has a handle too thick for the bathroom built-in holders, bread slices too wide for the standard toaster and cereal boxes that don't fit into kitchen cabinets and so on. Convenience-in-use also covers convenience in obtaining the product. This is still a problem when using the Internet or mobile phones. Many of the retailers' sites (particularly mobile sites) are much too complicated. Instead of having their technical staff show how 'easy' it is, sellers should always directly observe how a subset of customers goes about placing an order. Consumers seek a carefree, turnkey system where little or no learning is involved; anything less being potentially emotionally frustrating and off-putting. Advertisers promote such functions with emotionally charged words like 'fast'; 'easy access'; 'easily adjustable'; 'amazingly simple'; 'easy to follow; 'user-friendly' and 'light as a feather' to resonate with the emotions. Think of the extra cost per unit we seem prepared to pay for the convenience of having a small-sized container of the product when travelling.

Typically, competition in a mature market is no longer on the basis of core use-function since high performance in the core function is often taken for granted. Instead, competition is on other aspects of the offering, such as ancillary and convenience-in-use functions, price and distribution as well as brand image. Any technical function can arouse emotion because any technical function can be of high concern to the consumer. There is the excitement of anticipating high performance in a computer, the pleasure arising if performance turns out to be higher than expected . . . and disappointment if performance is below expectations. Often in talking about quality of a product the focus is purely on technical factors. Thus the criterion of quality in software tends to be functionality and convenience-in-use functions of efficiency, maintainability, portability and reliability.

2. *Economic/sacrifice criteria*: All buying is an approach/avoidance situation in that benefits are set against price paid and effort expended. Where we can have benefits for nothing because the product is free or benefits far outstrip costs, as with a bargain, the words 'free' or perceptions of

a bargain are emotionally gratifying. The buying effort expended is the effort involved in finding and choosing the product or in using the product. Marder (1997) distinguishes choice-effort from use-effort. Use-effort is reduced by convenience-in-use features and choice-effort by better distribution. If choice-effort is broadened to include taking the hassle out of buying, like the frustration that comes from waiting at the cash desk, there is considerable scope for choice-effort reduction. Underhill (1999) shows how stores can and should make shopping a more pleasurable experience. As Underhill says, no one knows how much a shopper will buy until the shopping experience is made as pleasurable as possible. We might add, no one knows what people might want until the most persuasive appeal has been made.

Price is always a concern. This is not surprising. As Brittan (1997) says: 'When you purchase any good, your enjoyment is reduced by the psychological cost of paying for it'. Consumers and marketers alike benefit if they explicitly seek pricing systems that let people enjoy things without having to think about paying for them which thereby dampens the enjoyment. And the possibility of enjoying things immediately is facilitated by installment buying like hire purchase. Hire purchase in fact could be said to have got the car industry into the mass market (Calder 1999). This should not blind us to the fact that there are always those who will pay a high price for the same functional performance if it signals, to all and sundry, wealth, status and good taste. There is also the matter of sacrifices to obtain that low price. There is one ad for British Airways appearing in an email that offers: 'Fly to London for less, stay in London for less than less . . . free hotel for two nights'. Unfortunately, there is a list of twenty-two terms and conditions – very off-putting and requiring far too much time to read and understand.

Emotionally *deal-sensitive* buyers switch among their favored set of brands depending on current prices in contrast to those who are *price-sensitive* in an absolute sense. Let us look at the factors that influence the maximum price that can be obtained by the seller:

- The centrality of the product for the function for which it is being bought
- The uniqueness of the product to the seller
- The social perceptions of the wisdom of paying the price being demanded
- The perceived fairness of the price
- The purchase location.

They are all factors that have emotional resonance. And contrary to the rules of rationality in economics, the framing of price is important, for example a 3 percent charge for using a credit card versus a 3 percent discount for cash. Being charged 3 percent for using a credit card is a much more emotional issue.

It seems that we find it less emotional to spend in a foreign currency as we are less conscious of the sacrifice. Club Med exploits this finding by having 'guests' buy beads to use rather than cash. At least one Florida developer attracts prospects by offering them hotel accommodation at an extremely low cost – and then even giving most of it back in 'village dollars' that are accepted in all the stores around the development. In this way, those accepting the offer spend time savoring the lifestyle without any sense of its costing them anything.

Consumers become emotional about 'hidden' charges (e.g. in hiring a car), with the 'all-inclusive' price having the additional advantage that it reduces the number of payment decisions which, in turn, reduces the emotional burden of payment. Prepaid cards such as domestic or mobile phone cards are ways of reducing the emotional burden (what Brittan calls the 'moral tax') of payment and the anxiety of uncertainty about the final bill. Emotive words in advertising covering economic criteria include 'fabulous bargain'; 'pays for itself'; 'no frills pricing'; and 'designer quality at affordable prices' and so on. Advertising anticipates emotional reaction to a premium price by stressing enhanced benefits such as 'you won't need to repair a quality garment', car or machine for years. This influences the inner dialogue consumers conduct when they want something emotionally but which reason refuses to authorize. Where the only interest lies in applying economic criteria and all trade-offs can be expressed in money terms, decision-making is reduced to calculation.

3. *Legalistic criteria*: Buyers are often guided by what authorities demand or want, that is, buyers take account of criteria decreed by others. Such buyers are said to take account of legalistic criteria. While some 'legalistic' criteria are imposed by legal regulations (seatbelts in cars, certain drugs by prescription only), there are also the requirements of others whose wishes the consumer feels obliged to consider. In supermarket shopping for groceries, the tastes of various family members might, for example, be considered. The paradigm case of legalistic criteria outside of the law is the husband shopping in the supermarket from a list written by his wife. On the list his wife has written: orange juice, lettuce, fish cakes and so on and the husband in his purchases is governed by that list. Children, too, have quite an influence. One study by J. Walter Thomson ad agency found that even children under twelve years of age played a decisive role in parental decisions, for example in 31 percent of all holiday destinations, 30 percent of all car models and 22 percent of all stereo brands (reported in 'Attention all Shoppers', *Time Magazine*, 2 August 1999, p. 36). While parents may be the ones who pay, children may be the key decision-makers.

Legalistic criteria can evoke emotion. Trying to buy something for someone else can be stressful (e.g. a wedding present) and any rules imposed from outside (even edicts on how much to spend) can give rise to frustration at not being completely in control. Being in control of one's life or events can be a key motivator. On the other hand, being successful at meeting the expectations of others like friends gives rise to a glow of accomplishment. All this is not to deny there can be a conflict of values in gift-giving between the desire to give what is desired and what would be more in tune with the giver's own values.

4. *Integrative criteria*: Integrative functions refer to the desire for social integration and also integration with self. Integrative criteria involve:

Social acceptance: How consumers think others might view them as a result of their possessions influences what is bought. Buying what is not socially endorsed by one's social milieu implies non-conformity and any kind of non-conformity is associated with potential embarrassment that can undermine confidence. Of course, there are consumers who reject conformity or just 'couldn't care a damn' what others think! This is their way of signaling individuality. Today's individualism is described as keeping *away* from the Joneses rather than keeping *up* with the Joneses though this usually means rejecting the larger culture for some subculture. Consumers may no longer be conforming to societal norms but their behavior is still *conformative* to their subculture. Elites, and not just out-groups, are involved in non-conformity as the elite may want to signal hostility to the majority just as much as punks and other out-groups (Hodge and Kress 1988). Those adopting deviant fashions, or challenging the prevalent ethic, follow the principle that influence can come about either from sticking rigidly to the rules or by the creation of new rules. Body tattoos for many people are an expression of deviant behavior but a badge of acceptance to others.

Self-identity and possessions: We might remind ourselves how gifts have a role to play in social acceptance and social integration. Gift-giving can enhance or highlight both a person's status and their social identity if the gift is large enough. The consumer's self-identity is assumed to be a primary motivation in that how people view themselves influences their choices. A female consumer who views herself as a liberated woman is less likely to be dissuaded by what has been typical socially appropriate behavior for women. But how people appear to classify us will inevitably be a part of how we view ourselves. Another view of self-identity is that people take their self-identity from their possessions (see, for example, Dittmar 1992). Dittmar views possessions as *material* symbols of identity; as *expressive* symbols of identity and as *reflections* of identity in terms of gender and social-material status. But it is a parochial view to equate self-identity with mere possessions as it is to equate self-identity with what we eat.

John Locke (1632–1704) introduced the word 'consciousness' to help in understanding personal identity. He argued that a person is identical with anything he is conscious of, which includes anything he can remember. This view seems consistent with the Roman poet Ovid who said: 'it is the mind that makes the man' – that minds define our personalities and abilities. Self-identity comes with a life history (Schiffer 1998). Many factors enter into self-identity, such as personal history, socio-economic status, religion and ethnicity, roles in life, occupation and so on. In fact Flanagan (1996) argues that the whole narrative of our lives and what concerns us enters into self-identity. Self-identity is something more than the sum of our appetites. As Erving Goffman (1971) says, no one's self-identity is limited to a singular 'core image', since people have many different sides to their personalities, revealed on different occasions. This is not to deny that consumers use goods as a way to express aspects of their *social* identity and to distinguish themselves from others 'in a world in which traditional social bonds and class boundaries are weakening' (Gronow 1997).

Another half-truth is that self-identity is more a matter of individual choice than social ascription. But self-identity is not developed in a vacuum: it is very much influenced by the way others view us in social interaction. There is a limit to the extent that consumers can express a completely distinct self-identity. In fact, is self-identity constant and stable given that we so often fantasize in assuming other identities such as in what we wear? There is the matter of time and financial resources while, as said earlier, someone who seemingly is non-conforming to societal norms may be conforming to the norms of his or her sub-cultural group. Sub-cultural social pressures are likely to produce a strong family resemblance in possessions among the members of the deviant subgroup. Products bought as symbolic possessions link to the emotions. Flanagan (1996) suggests such products are:

- Those such as photographs which symbolize the historical continuity of self, family and so on
- Those which express artistic or intellectual interests such as a book collection
- Those that signify wealth and symbolize status such as a sailing boat.

And, we might add,

- Products that express a preferred social persona such as being youthful, bohemian, establishment or whatever.

Self-*identity* is commonly interpreted as how we define ourselves, while self-*image* is what a person assumes himself to be. If there is a difference between the two, it is mainly one of emphasis, with self-identity focusing on attributes that distinguish us from others, while self-image is the overall view a person holds of himself. Sometimes the term 'self-identification' is used but this does not relate to self-identity but to the actual process by which a person comes to have admiration for another who possesses attributes that mirror one's own. We often identify with the organization, the football team or whatever, whereby the success or failure of the organization or football team merges with one's own personal success or failure.

Status, visibility, fashion or standing within one's social milieu: Although people crave social acceptance, they also aim for status in the group's 'pecking order', together with respect and social recognition. It was Simmel who first stressed the opposition between the individual and the wider social group (Wolf 1950). Humans need other people for emotional, intellectual and material sustenance but, at the same time, do not want to submerge their individuality and independence (Unger 1984). There is a constant tension provoked in trying to get the balance right that occurs throughout life. Consumers, in buying products, seek respect, status and visibility to rise above the crowd. Consumers do not want to be tokens of each other in their clothing or whatever. Status, social visibility and sex appeal are sources of power, a feeling of being in control of the world around. Status symbols enhance self-esteem and anything that adds to self-esteem is emotionally satisfying. Any formal association with a celebrity or an institution of status is a source of satisfaction and highly valued – as university fund-raisers know. Emotive words here are 'upscale'; 'caters to the discriminating few'; 'you'll join the ranks of'; 'exclusive' and so on. A novelty that becomes widespread ceases to be a novelty with the result that those seeking visibility and status supplant the old novelty by a 'genuine' new one. Attention is sustained by novelty and novelty also has the potential to entertain.

Fashion: Fashion occurs when, at a moment in time, consumers insist on the same thing, only to drop it shortly afterwards. Fashion satisfies the desire for status and novelty even if it only does so by recycling old (forgotten?) styles. Simmel points out that fashion enters into all aspects of our lives from clothes, to cars, to investing, to science and the selection of first names. Simmel views fashion as combining the novelty of esthetic charm and the play form of socializing. Consumers adopt fashions to fulfill attempts at image-management; to signal social aspirations and identifications. Fashion in clothing helps camouflage deficiencies and savor the emotional fantasy of being like some famous person or part of some lifestyle. Fashion is fed by the insatiable demand for novelty in stylistic innovations. Campbell (1987) argues that fashion functions as a substitute for taste in that fashion fulfills a social role originally played by standards of good taste and can be as socially binding as past standards of taste.

Fashion has expanded in scope more than ever with the demand for 'difference' in social identity. As Gronow (1997) says, one characteristic of modern consumer society is that the extension and social influence of fashion has greatly increased. He acknowledges that consumer demands are no longer determined by an 'economy of needs' but by an 'economy of desire and dreams' or the yearning for something new and unexperienced. Among the affluent of the world who have everything they need or want in terms of clothing, housing and other durables, wants move to the desire for new and rare experiences so that a Christmas present becomes the experience of, for example, driving a tank (as has happened in the UK and also the US). Gronow reminds us that all conscious experiences reach beyond themselves, with each thought reminding us of other thoughts. This 'overflow 'of thought leads to fantasies about the pleasures of buying, particularly buying things for personal adornment – and, he might have added, the pleasures of anticipating some experience.

Personal integrity: Kagan (1999) rejects the notion of human action being mostly motivated by a desire for sensory pleasure but claims there is a universal motive to regard the self as possessing good qualities. People are inhibited from actions which are likely to bring about guilt, embarrassment or shame, contributing to what Kagan calls a motive for virtue. People have a sense of being moral agents. Adherence to ethics or moral norms is tied to self-respect, while the violation of social norms gives rise to the emotion of shame. Whenever some decision-maker is concerned over the ethics of some proposed course of action, he or she should ask themselves if what is proposed were to be publicly revealed, would they feel ashamed? If the answer is 'yes', they have an ethical issue. In their buying, a growing number of consumers take account of the environment and choose manufacturers who exhibit social responsibility such as those who are not exploiting child labor, polluting the environment and so on. It also violates integrity to accept an unfair transaction so consumers may ask what something is worth in some objective sense rather than just what it is worth to them. A consumer may forgo buying, not because the utility of the product to her is less than the price to be paid, but because the price is considered a 'rip-off'. People will not willingly be cheated or be seen as being willing to be so. This seems to be part of our evolutionary inheritance (Wright 1994).

5. *Adaptive criteria*: Adaptive criteria reflect the desire to minimize risk, reduce the anxiety of uncertainty or fear of regret (Bell 1982, 1985). Risks can be:

(a) Financial
(b) Physical, since products can be harmful or dangerous
(c) Social, in that significant others may not approve
(d) Performance, which may be deficient
(e) Hassle involved in, say, returning the product.

Many products cannot be completely evaluated prior to purchase. Inspection of the product may give some certainties (that the product has particular features) and may provide some idea about quality but there are often uncertainties about effectiveness (such as when buying financial products). A significant purchase with a high risk attached to it (what marketers call a 'high involvement purchase') arouses anxiety, fear of making a mistake or coming to regret the decision. We might add that uncertainty about positive events can evoke curiosity as well as hope. It is uncertainty about negative events that is likely to lead to anxiety and fear.

Consumers adopt several heuristics or rules of thumb for dealing with uncertainty. The easiest is simply to sidestep responsibility by trusting the advice of others. Consumers often pay dearly for some expert to make the decision for them. This commonly happens with financial services and in matters of taste. Older adults are more limited in their information processing capacity (they easily become mentally overloaded) and are likely to collect and evaluate less information and so be more inclined to rely on 'expert' advice (Park and Gutchess 1999). Consumers, like people in general, are conditioned to some extent into accepting the advice of people in authority, whether they are teachers, doctors, policemen or those regarded as authorities on matters of taste or a line of products. In fact the advice may come from someone who simply projects a relevant authority figure, such as when the actor Robert Young on television was recommending Sanka, a caffeine-free coffee, while wearing the white coat of a doctor he played in a television series (*Marcus Welby MD*).

Making the habitual buy or letting others decide releases time to come to grips with other problems and relieves the burden of decision. Other heuristics are to imitate those assumed to be 'in the know'; seeking guarantees; buying on reputation or buying on brand image; sampling; diversifying to spread risks; or buying on the basis of just liking. Most of these heuristics or rules of thumb are perceived as indicators of the attributes sought, just as a buyer might view a high price as an indicator of quality, with quality defined as embracing all attributes of a product which relate to satisfying a given set of requirements. (Note this definition of quality would include the symbolic features of a product.) Emotive ad words here are: 'you can't lose'; 'we stand behind our claims'; 'genuine'; 'authentic'; 'proven'; 'pure'; 'nothing artificial'; 'we provide training and support services in' and so on. Where consumers are in a state of uncertainty over matters of taste and social appropriateness, an attractive and credible salesperson plays a vital role in establishing credibility. *Authenticity* is one reason for our continuing to buy diamonds when the naked eye cannot distinguish them from zircons.

6. *Intrinsic criteria*: The criterion that enters into most buying is intrinsic liking: how the product looks, feels, tastes, smells and sounds. Pleasing the senses is usually crucial. Buying purely on the basis of liking means the only objective is pleasure/enjoyment and nothing more. Anything that diminishes the prospect of the pleasure inhibits buying. Thus the new wave of 'functional foods' add nutritional attributes (like cholesterol-lowering margarine and so on) and so provide consumers with additional reasons to buy. Nonetheless, consumers appear unwilling to trade off taste for nutrition. But taste is not entirely subjective in that taste preferences are influenced by associations, in that preference for one brand of whiskey might be very much determined by those who endorse that brand. Intrinsic liking often rests on the images conjured up by emotive words, names and labels, though many would doubt that such associations could in themselves bring about an intensity of preference. Emotive ad words suggesting intrinsic criteria are 'enchanting'; 'juicy'; 'crisp'; 'sizzling'; 'gripping'; 'refreshing'; 'alluring'; 'sparkling'; 'elegant'; 'relaxing' and so on.

Csikszentmihalyi (1990) claims, contrary to current orthodoxy, that pleasure has a function beyond being indulged purely for its own sake, as it can be a reflex response built into the genes for the preservation of the species. He quotes the French anthropologist Roger Caillois on the pleasure of games:

- With competitive games, pleasure comes from meeting the challenge of an opponent; games of chance give pleasure by creating an illusion of controlling the future
- Games like riding the merry-go-round provide pleasure by transforming the way we perceive reality
- Games involving pretence and fantasy create the feeling of being more than we actually are.

These claims are intuitively reasonable, but surely these are not the only factors at work producing pleasure? Buying on the basis of intrinsic liking does not necessarily mean being driven by a desire for instant gratification. Consumers may postpone instant gratification to savor future possibilities of getting what they really want, like saving for that expensive dress. Intrinsic liking can be, within limits, molded through education. Thus we may look at a work of art without any pleasurable response until told about its associations, who made it and the criteria by which it should be judged. This is why the perfect counterfeit is not the same as the real thing. Knowing it is the real thing (authentic) makes all the difference.

Consumers are more likely to buy if they like the smell as smells connect directly with the emotional centers of the brain and immediately influence feelings and emotional memories. Examples in marketing are (Cook 1999):

- School books that smell of chocolates
- The smell of freshly mown grass in car ventilation systems
- The smell of lavender in dentists' surgeries
- The aroma of toast and fresh coffee exuding from an alarm clock
- Travel brochures smelling of suntan lotion
- Cigars that smell of herbaceous borders
- Airplane toilets that spray Chanel No. 5.

There are organizations like International Flavors & Fragrances in New Jersey that will design and manufacture the smells and tastes of crisps, grilled hamburger, pet food, toothpaste or just about any designer fragrance. It is big business.

The sense of touch is often neglected but also important. As Sheldon and Arens said in the 1930s:

> Every day the average person makes hundreds of judgments in which the sense of touch casts the deciding vote. Acceptance of a towel, hairbrush, underwear, stockings, hinge on how things feel in their hands...Designs should be executed with an appeal to the tactile senses.
>
> (Sheldon and Arens 1932)

Curiosity is the tendency to seek novel or complex stimuli. Intrinsic criteria include the *curiosity* appeal, as acting to satisfy curiosity can be an end in itself, just as we might seek to know things for the sake of knowing, though no doubt satisfying curiosity can on occasion provide knowledge that might contribute to survival. It is interesting to note how curious the general public is about the 'lives of the rich and famous'. In any case, seeking to satisfy curiosity can be exciting – and sometimes dangerous!

A stimulus is *novel* if it is new or different in an inviting way. Consumers have an appetite for novelty since, while the familiar reassures, it can be a bore. Novelty, though, can be too novel and complexity too complex in terms of the consumer's level of experience, education and willingness to persist in trying to comprehend. There is an optimal level of novelty and/or complexity for each individual at which point curiosity and the accompanying emotion are at a maximum. With the advent of the microchip, the provision of more features in, say, watches has become irresistible since little is added to cost but seemingly more in immediate appeal. Yet few of these additional features may be used but simply add to complexity, hindering operation.

Gronow (1987) quotes the German writers Mayntz and Nedelman to argue that consumers grow tired of continuous change and fall back on the 'tried and true', to feel 'at home' and oppose 'alien social forces' that demand constant change. This is true of many with 'old money', seen wearing old and unfashionable clothes. But then they can afford to buck the trend. Like many other fashion commentators, Gronow argues that fashion is a thoroughly esthetic phenomenon even if some fashion creations are ugly. The opposite of fashion is a uniform, and modern affluent societies reject uniformity, unless part of a shared expression of solidarity.

Esthetic appreciation has emotional overtones. In fact art has been defined as the expression of emotion though it is more correct to say that art has an emotional quality. The esthetic is all-pervasive in our lives and in products bought such as cars, clothes, furniture, the presentation of food as well as paintings, music, cinema, the countryside, birdsong and so on. Human appreciation of the esthetic influences all the choices consumers make in daily life in designing their environments and choosing what to buy. Fisher (1999) claims that *wonder* is the essential emotion of the esthetic experience. Fisher describes 'wonder' as the hospitality of the mind or soul to newness, with wonder allowing the mind to feel rejuvenated. 'Wonder' has some of the attributes of 'novelty' which is the key factor in drawing attention to any new product.

Consumers seek to turn their everyday lives into an esthetic enterprise when trying to achieve a coherent style in what they wear, and buy for the home. The coordinating principle for much durable goods purchasing is esthetic liking. What typically gives purchases coherence and links them together into a unitary whole is that they appeal to us esthetically. Like all intrinsic liking, esthetic pleasure is an end in itself. Esthetic judgments are based on a feeling of pleasure. Pleasure and perceptions of beauty may account for the unity in all esthetic experience.

MOODS AND EMOTIONAL SENTIMENTS

We return to the subject of 'mood' having already sketched the subject. We speak about the mood of the market or the mood of our customers all the time, as if the term was unproblematic. We have already discussed certain aspects of moods but the following on mood(s) is an extract on the subject from O'Shaughnessy and O'Shaughnessy (2003):

> Every conscious mental state has a characteristic that we refer to as mood. We are always in a mood that is pleasurable or non-pleasurable to some degree. It may be that bad moods reflect too little positive reinforcement in a person's life and too many punishments (Lewinsohn and Amenson 1978). In any case, moods are distinguished from emotions proper by not being tied to any specific object. As Goldie says, this distinction between moods and emotions is not entirely water-tight in that emotions proper need not be directed at objects that are very specific (we can be angry just at people generally), while there is always a sense of a mood having a general objective like the state of the world at large. Moods manifest themselves in positive or negative feelings, tied to health, personality or perceived quality of life and can relate to the emotions proper as the aftermath of an emotional incident such as failure to secure a loan. A mood on this basis is the mind's judgment on the recent past. In any case, it is simplistic to claim that moods are just emotions that are short-lived and felt less intensely. As Goldie says, an emotion can bubble up and down within a mood. Nor are moods, as we currently use the term, necessarily short-lived. On the contrary, an optimistic or pessimistic mood, say, can linger for a very long time, while emotions such as anger can be short-lived.
>
> What is important for marketing is that moods color outlooks and bias judgments in that a certain mood can depress or enhance confidence and mold responses to buying stimuli. There is evidence that both highly positive and highly negative moods are likely to encourage overindulgence. It seems, too, that ads that contribute to a positive mood are more easily recalled, while such ads also result in a more positive feeling towards the brand advertised. This is important since so many ads can show confrontational scenes that have a coarse realism that, while not inappropriate in a movie, can be disturbing in an ad.

Hence the importance of consumer confidence surveys since consumer confidence typically reflects national mood and affects buying. There is mood-congruence when thoughts and actions fall in line with mood. As Goleman (1998) says, there is a 'constant stream of feeling' which runs 'in perfect parallel to our stream of thought'. Mood congruence occurs because a positive mood evokes pleasant associations that lighten subsequent appraisals (thoughts) and actions, while a negative mood arouses pessimistic associations that influence future judgments and behavior. When consumers are in a good mood, they are more optimistic about buying, more confident in buying and much more willing to tolerate things like waiting in lines. On the other hand, being in a bad mood makes buying behavior less predictable. It is not surprising that efforts are made to put buyers in the 'right mood' by the use of music and friendly staff or, say, open bakeries in shopping malls that delight the passer-by with the smell of fresh bread.

Thayer (1996) views moods as a mixture of biological and psychological influences and, as such, a sort of clinical thermometer, reflecting all the internal and external events that influence us. For Thayer, the key components of mood are energy and tension in different combinations. A specific mixture of energy and tension, together with the thoughts they influence, produces moods. He discusses the four mood states:

1. Calm-energy, which he regards as the optimal mood of feeling good
2. Calm-tiredness, which he regards as feeling a little tired without any stress and so can be pleasant
3. Tense-energy, which involves a low level of anxiety suited to a fight or flight disposition
4. Tense-tiredness, which is a mixture of fatigue and anxiety which underlies the unpleasant feeling of depression.

People generally can 'feel down' or 'feel good' as a result of happenings in the world around them. This represents the national mood. People feel elated when the national football team wins an international match or depressed when their team has lost. An elated mood of calm-energy is an optimistic mood which is good for business. Consumers, as socially involved individuals, are deeply influenced by the prevailing social climate. Marketers recognize the phenomenon and talk about the national mood being, say, for or against conspicuous consumption, with displays of wealth no longer being considered socially appropriate behavior.

Moods do change though. Writing early in the nineteenth century, de Toqueville describes an American elite embarrassed by the ostentation of material display; in the 'gilded age' sixty years later, many were only too eager to embrace a materialistic vulgarity. The problem lies in anticipating changes in national mood since a change in mood affects everything from the buying of equities to the buying of houses and washing machines. Thayer would argue that we should be interested in national events that are likely to produce a move towards a tense-tiredness state or towards a calm-energy state since these are the polar extremes and so more likely to influence behavior. Novelists, sensitive to national moods, mark the long-term changes. For example, there is the long-term emotional journey from Charles Dickens's depiction of the death of little Nell to Oscar Wilde's cruel flippancy ('one would have to have a heart of stone not to laugh at the death of little Nell') which reflects the mood change from high Victorian sentimentality to the acerbic cynicism of the end of the century as shown by writers such as Thomas Hardy and artists such as Aubrey Beardsley.

Whenever the mind is not fully absorbed, consciousness is no longer focused and ordered. Under such conditions the mind falls into dwelling on the unpleasant with a negative mood developing. Csikszentmihalyi (2000) argues that humans have a need to keep consciousness in an ordered state and this experiential need to keep consciousness fully active is what influences a good deal of consumer behavior. Sometimes it does not matter what we are shopping for – the point is to shop for anything regardless because consuming is one way to respond to the void in consciousness when there is nothing else to do.

Mood influences buying behavior, if at all, in a way that is consistent with the mood; what we have called the *mood-congruence* effect. Mood, like other affective/emotional states, influences the selective retrieval of information from memory in a way that is reinforcing of the mood. But we do not necessarily go along with how we feel since other goals may intervene, just as I may not act this morning in line with my foul mood because I do not want to antagonize colleagues. Although no one has yet established the effect of mood on worker performance, a good mood of high energy and low tension is most obviously conducive to achievement. We have all heard of Japanese firms starting the day by creating that pleasant mood of solidarity with colleagues by bringing everyone together each morning for some collective activity.

Chapter 12

Social Psychology Continued: Lewin's Attitude Change Model, Strategies for Overcoming Resistance to Change, Motivation and Reversal Theory

LEWIN'S ATTITUDE CHANGE MODEL

Social psychology has particular relevance to marketing in offering insights and findings on emotion and persuasive strategies. Kurt Lewin is often regarded as the founder of social psychology. Kurt Lewin's (1968) model of attitude change is an approach to changing relevant perspectives ('getting people to see it our way'). Changing attitudes can be regarded as one element in persuasion. Lewin's attitude change model provides a framework for discussing the many influences on consumer behavior.

The Lewin model presupposes that 'rapport' has already been established among the parties involved. This cannot be assumed, so establishing rapport is added as a first step to Lewin's three steps. The resulting four steps for changing perspectives are: (i) establishing rapport; (ii) unfreezing; (iii) moving; (iv) refreezing. Each of these four steps is discussed below, together with other material that fits the stage.

Establish rapport

Establishing rapport as the first step is implicit recognition that, without small talk to create the right motivational climate, there will be no big talk later. In establishing rapport, we, for example, might:

- Seek common ground so as to bond through mutual interests. This can be anything at all by way of similarity with the buyer or consumer. It may have nothing to do with business: customers are just as interested in themselves, likely reference groups such as family or leisure activities.

- Mention in favorable terms something noticed about the customer's place of work or company reputation.
- Be supportive of the customer by voicing agreement or giving praise. This means listening to the customer to identify his or her concerns since what concerns the customer has emotional resonance.

Like all tactics of persuasion these are not certain to succeed; much depends on how skillfully the tactic is carried out. The shrewd customer sees through a pretence. On the other hand, just recognizing that what is being said or done is motivated by the desire to make a sale does not mean the 'salesperson' will be summarily dismissed. Customers can suspect the motive but still be pleased by the effort being made to make them feel comfortable. A salesperson who overdoes it, however, may be dismissed as ingratiating or lacking in judgment. But there is no reason why these things cannot be done genuinely.

The point in establishing rapport is to discover shared values and experiences as a basis for mutual trust. Where salesperson and customer share common values and possess a supportive relationship, rapport will have been established so that what the salesperson says in the introductory sales talk may simply serve as additional bonding. The problem arises when values and perspectives between salesperson and customer differ, as happens between subcultures and generations. One skill here lies in learning the language (the technical language if need be or the language of the subculture) of the customer to create a language for communication and understanding. There is a need in any case to show similarity by using phrasing and words of the target audience. (Many criticize this as polluting the language but these are not the target audience.)

We might remind ourselves of a claim made earlier that all persuasion is an *invitation* to *affiliation* and the customer actually buying can normally be viewed as his or her acceptance of that affiliation. This perspective directs our attention to inducing a friendly climate and ensuring the target audience is at home with the seller's behavior. It is a reminder that the customer needs to be wooed and not fooled.

Unfreezing the system

Establishing rapport is preliminary to 'unfreezing' in that it helps people relax. Unfreezing involves getting the customer to perceive a performance gap that can be filled by the firm's product. Another word for unfreezing is 'consciousness-raising' about the possibilities of what the salesperson has to offer. The prospect is viewed as having a latent want for the product, that is, a want that needs to be activated to show what the product can do for him or her. Just as a picture on film may be latent until the developer is applied, a want can be latent until awareness is created.

Consciousness-raising or activating a latent want involves highlighting what the product has to offer to meet the goals of the customer.

One useful tactic in unfreezing is *creative interrogation* where the salesperson plays back what the customer says to indicate understanding while at the same time questioning assumptions being made. Creative interrogation helps us disagree without being disagreeable. In this way, customers are more inclined to face up to discrepancies between expressed beliefs and actions taken. Understanding is demonstrated by restating the customer's viewpoint and, equally as important, showing an understanding of the customer's feelings. Feelings are inferred from the emotive language used as well as from accompanying body language. It is not a matter of saying 'I know how you feel' but naming the emotion likely to be felt: 'I know you must be anxious about the risks involved but...' Such recognition, concern and acknowledgment are seen as a mark of respect and a way of avoiding conflicts later. With creative interrogation, prospects are thrown back on to examining assumptions rather than being defensive. It is a way of changing a perspective toward accepting what the seller has to offer.

There are at least three types of direct appeals that can be used at the stage of unfreezing:

- Appeals based on product *benefits*
- Appeals based on the *problems* anticipated in adopting the product
- Appeals based on the *competitive* objective adopted.

Even if prospects do not buy at the time, putting across 'facts' tends to influence people in hindsight. This has come to be known as the *hindsight bias* whereby prospects underestimate the extent to which their knowledge has been augmented by some earlier discussion with a salesperson or others.

Appeals related to benefits. It is better to think of buyers not as buying a product per se, but as buying the benefits that emanate from the features possessed by the product/offering. Thus a consumer is not interested in a tube of toothpaste per se but in its benefits in terms of cleaning the teeth, whitening them, reducing cavities and so on. The focus must be on the benefits of most interest to the buyer which are unique to the seller. Every offering is a configuration of benefits, with customers seldom regarding the various benefits of equal importance. However, whatever the configuration of benefits, each benefit identified relates to a number of corresponding sales appeals, for example:

Benefit from purchase.	Appeals corresponding to benefit
Less labor needed per unit of output	(a) saving in labor cost
	(b) less dependent on labor
	(c) fewer labor turnover problems
	(d) saving in recruitment and training

One Continental Airlines advertisement positions itself as having the youngest jet fleet but carefully spells out in the same ad what this means in terms of benefits: flying the youngest jet fleet means more comfort, larger overhead bins, dependable service and an in-flight entertainment system that's standard on new Boeing aircraft. So, who would you rather fly with?

Appeals based on the problems anticipated in adopting the product. Customer appeals take account not only of product benefits but of the problems customers are likely to anticipate in buying the product (Lehman and O'Shaughnessy 1974).

Procedural problems occur in learning skills such as how to do whatever is needed; maintenance procedures, training others, sales service or learning how to sell the product. A buyer intent on minimizing the difficulties associated with adopting procedural-problem products will favor the supplier who is perceived as likely to reduce to a minimum the time and difficulty in learning. Hence sales appeals offering technical service, training and showing the ease with which the product can be operated and used are those that will be most appropriate.

If *performance* problems are anticipated, the buyer is likely to favor the supplier who can reduce doubts about whether the product will do the job. Reassurance or proof is sought. Sales appeals here stress free trial, sale or return, success in similar applications and the technical competence and flexibility of the supplier.

Finally, *political* problems associated with reaching agreement when the product affects several members of the family or several departments of the buying firm. Where the product is a political problem product, a buyer is likely to favor a supplier who possesses those attributes that must be good regardless of the application. Without such attributes, the product is a weak candidate when some participants to the buying decision seek to frustrate the purchase. Sales appeals here should stress the firm's reputation, known capability for service, delivery and flexibility.

These three categories of problem are not mutually exclusive and a particular product may involve all three types of problem whether performance, procedural or political.

Appeals based on the competitive objective. There can only be one of four selling objectives when it comes to selling a particular product to a particular customer: *retention, increase, convert* or *attract*. A *retention* (of current customers) objective may be stressed if increasing sales with these current customers is unlikely. The *increase* in sales is appropriate if there are further applications for which the customer might use the product, or sales per current customer are below expectations. A *convert* from rival sellers as an objective is appropriate if the product is an innovative substitute for rival products. Finally, *attract* new users as an objective is appropriate when a new set of prospective users is being sought or former objections to the use of the product have been overcome.

Not all ways of communicating with buyers are through speech. There are a number of different ways of communicating information to others, as shown in Table 12.1:

Table 12.1 Types of communication

	Verbal	**Non-verbal**
Non-verbal		Sign language; gestures
Vocal	Speech	Intonation

Body language plays a part in 'reading' behavior. People 'give off' as well as give information about themselves. We try to convey a certain impression of ourselves to others but the information we 'give off' may make it impossible to sustain that impression. The information we give off comes mainly from our non-verbal behavior such as the intonation (pitch and loudness, drawl and so on) of our voice and the gestures we make. Practically every aspect of our actions can be used to make inferences about us. Non-verbal behavior is typically used to infer personality, social status, liking and emotional state. Emotions often, too, express themselves non-verbally.

Non-verbal channels of communication. Leathers (1986) lists seven non-verbal channels that signal positive or negative messages:

- Facial expression, such as smiling, frowning, eyebrow raising or drooping, eye closure or widening, nose wrinkling, lip pursing, teeth baring, jaw dropping or forehead knitting
- Bodily communication, such as gestures, posture, good eye-contact and variation in speech rate as well as ways of walking
- Physical proximity to the other party (varies with the culture, subject matter and the relationship)
- Physical appearance, such as the right grooming and clothes
- Artifactual communication, such as whether the artifacts are worn by the persuader or part of the surroundings like flags and bunting
- Vocalic communication, such as voice loudness, pitch, vocal quality, articulation, intonation pattern and use of pauses
- Tactile communication in the use of touching since touch is one way to express empathy, warmth and reassurance.

This list sensitizes us to how much there is to consider in evaluating a specific selling performance while, in addition, assessing its coherence and relevance for the target audience. There are gender differences. Women respond (where socially appropriate) more positively to touch than do men, and women gaze at others more than do men. Women, too, are more uncomfortable than men when they cannot see the other person. (This has implications for telephone selling.)

Non-verbal behavior such as 'talking with one's hands' can be non-conscious behavior though some cultures do it more than others. The non-verbal can on occasion be more important than words in the interpretation of behavior, whether of a salesperson or people in an ad. The non-verbal may in fact be all that is necessary. Thus the Seri Indians of Mexico have speaking 'taboos' where fathers, sons and brothers never speak to each other once they are adult though they still manage to live and hunt together (Regal 1990).

Bolton (1986) points to the importance of vocal clues since the sound of the voice, the rate of speaking, frequency and length of pauses and so on can point to mood and current emotional state. He suggests the following correspondence between non-verbal behavior and emotion, though 'feelings' would be a better term than emotion since not all would be considered emotions (see Table 12.2).

Table 12.2   Non-verbal behavior and emotion

Non-verbal Behavior	Emotion
Monotone voice	Boredom
Slow speed, low pitch	Depression
High voice, emphatic pitch	Enthusiasm
Abrupt speech	Defensiveness
Terse speech, loud tone	Anger
High pitch, drawn-out speech	Disbelief
Hesitant speech	Nervousness
Fast talking, more intonation, high pitch	Confidence

Bolton points to the importance of eye contact as a sign that channels are open for communication, while sustained eye contact, within limits, is perceived as a sign of liking. Liking can be signaled by length of gaze and pupil size – though not without taking account of distance and level of illumination. Women indulge in more eye contact with people they like and less eye contact than do men with those they dislike. With respect to body posture, Bolton argues that arms and legs uncrossed suggests openness and interest, while a rigid body posture suggests being cold and aloof. We might add that context is all important here in interpretation since there are alternative hypotheses, for example arms and legs uncrossed can be influenced by the seat and the sitting position. Gestures in fact are never isolated signal boxes but convey meaning as part of a context.

Social *extroverts* gaze more in social situations, and typically choose brighter clothes and brighter colors. People who aspire to dominance tend to speak loudly, stand erect, are not inclined to smile and, while gazing less at the other party, can have long gazes which they break last (after the other party). Exhibiting dominance means standing one's ground, which is commonly accepted by others to avoid confrontation. Those who aspire to be high achievers tend to speak fast, put more intonation and high pitch in their voice while at the same time projecting more confidence. We should add to all of these 'other things remaining equal' since such behavior does not communicate completely on its own. No one should regard these claims as set in stone but all have intuitive appeal.

For salespeople who have to address, say, a buying committee and need to know the pivotal players, Bolton argues that those who are looked at most by the other members of the group are seen by them as the most powerful members of their group. Another indicator of status within a group is that people stand at more of a distance from those who are perceived to be of higher status, though Bolton acknowledges that this can also be a sign of dislike. The higher status party usually signals his or her desire to end a discussion by some non-verbal activity such as straightening papers on the desk, putting papers away, getting up, and stretching legs and so on.

The *structural approach* to the study of non-verbal behavior focuses on the whole of a person's gestures, claiming their meaning lies in the way they are combined. This contrasts with the *external variable approach* that relates particular gestures like pupil size to external factors such as the time spent looking at an advertisement. But no gesture or posture is, as already said, an isolated signal box. Just as we can be misled by the meaning of a word such as 'boot' when read in isolation (in that we may take it to mean an item of footwear; part of a car; an action to start the computer and so on), we can be equally misled about the meaning of some gesture unless we take the context into account.

The study of non-verbal behavior receives prominence in textbooks on salesmanship. There is often the assumption that, because it is non-conscious, it must have only one meaning or interpretation. This is not so as it would assume there is a *shared code* among people within the culture for correctly interpreting non-verbal behavior. But social scientists either deny the existence of such a code, or, more commonly, claim that the correct reading is always situational. Thus gaze can express intimacy or be used when people want to be either persuasive or deceptive. No single gesture can be regarded as unambiguous as to what it means. There is always some ambiguity in interpreting all behavior and this ambiguity is an inevitable part of social life.

Another aspect of salesmanship that is easily neglected is the overall tone of the salesman's selling. What is to be avoided is any peremptory, condescending or obsequious tone. This also applies to advertising and written communication. If service providers are to be emotionally in tune with customers they need to avoid communicating in a style that suggests the person addressed is of lesser worth. Over several years of examining correspondence with customers, the following criteria evolved with regard to what to avoid (O'Shaughnessy and O'Shaughnessy 2003).

- *Peremptory* style, whether verbal, written or through non-verbal communication, since it is perceived as showing a lack of respect that is likely to arouse anger in the person addressed. Consumers, like people in general, have a strong need for ego gratification and an emotional need to be seen as having status, power and being given respect. Humiliating someone, if done deliberately, is incompatible with showing respect. Unfortunately, it is more common to humiliate those incapable of retaliation who, through ignorance or poverty, are all too vulnerable to being demeaned.

- *Condescending or patronizing* style implies the person being addressed is less able and of lesser merit which is a blow to self-worth. Consumers, like people in general, have a strong emotional need for reassurance about personal worth. Patronizing, while seemingly being supportive, can be very undermining of the target audience.
- *Obsequious* style suggests ingratiating for a sale or approval – this inhibits an honest and open exchange of opinions which can be frustrating.

But it is not just the tone of a communication that can be off-putting but also the wording of the message in the need to avoid discursiveness, ambiguity and vagueness.

- *Discursiveness* in communicating, since 'long-windedness' frustrates the audience's desire for the communicator to come to the point
- *Ambiguity*, if what is being communicated can have several very different meanings which can be frustrating, given that few of us want to acknowledge ambiguity of meaning if the context suggests we should know which meaning is right
- *Vagueness*, if what is being communicated is not detailed enough or too abstract for clarity.

Courses on sales skills and interpreting non-verbal behavior are in danger of denying ambiguity if they assume that, regardless of context, there are fixed rules to be put across for ensuring success. Much, for example, depends on the initial expectations of the customer and seller since these must be complementary if frustration is not to result. Nonetheless, some attempt to develop skills in identifying and interpreting non-verbal behavior, as part of the set of interpersonal skills, is needed for selling. At the very least, it might help to do something about poor service: peremptory or condescending style or obsequiousness the other extreme.

Service and salespeople who do not like helping others, have a chip on their shoulder or believe themselves to be in a position of inferiority (and hence try to redress the balance by acting in a superior manner) think customers are just an irritant and describe them as such in their language to each other (for example, in one hospital study, patients were negatively labeled 'hits'). These people should not be employed in such work unless education, indoctrination and training are shown to be effective in changing attitudes. But salesmanship cannot be reduced to a set of predetermined rules since rules cannot cover the impact of personality (such as personal charm), speech and other personal characteristics, while it is the overall *coordinated performance* that has the ultimate impact. We could teach someone all that is known about persuasion, but such knowledge is no substitute for mastering the corresponding skills involved, and personality still makes a difference.

On the subject of the facial expressions accompanying the basic emotions, there is the claim for the universal portrayal of emotions regardless of culture. There is considerable interest in neuropsychosocial factors in emotion recognition in cognitive neuroscience and not just in social psychology. It was Darwin's *Expression of the Emotions in Man and Animals* (1898) that first paid attention to facial expression in arguing that facial expressions would be species-specific and not culture-specific as they are innate, not learnt. Darwin saw the expression of emotion as a way of communicating information to the receiver. Others have since argued that another function is to provide the sender with information about the emotion they are feeling.

Ekman and Friesen (1975) argued that universality would be found in the relationship between distinctive patterns of the facial muscles and particular emotions and that the facial expressions of the basic emotions of happiness, grief, disgust, fear, surprise and anger would have universal recognition. Their study compared faces judged by people in literate societies as illustrative of basic emotions, with people in preliterate societies who had had no opportunity to have known how those in literate societies interpreted facial expressions. They concluded 'universality in expression recognition' in that people in all cultures in the study agreed what emotion was being portrayed at above chance levels.

It was argued that this empirical criterion is the correct criterion to use in drawing conclusions about universality. Is this criterion water-tight as suggested? Because everyone recognizes a facial expression that is associated with, say, fear does not mean that such an expression is the one that is typically present when a person is in a state of fear. Widely recognized exemplars of fear in faces do not prove that that exemplar is the onw normally exhibited throughout all cultures. There are surely many facial expressions that signal fear. Even if these facial expressions are the same expressions that people *feign* when asked to feign an emotion (as has been shown) this does not confirm the thesis of the universality of emotion expressions – only the universality of feigned emotions. There are many universally agreed representations in cartoons, for example, that by convention stand for something else. They are usually exaggerated stereotypes of what they stand for. But one question that might be asked is: are these the expressions you find yourself or your friends making when in such emotional states or are they just a universal transparent code for such emotions? The defense to this argument would be that each of these emotions is associated with a certain neurophysiological profile which gives scientific corroboration to the universality claim.

Moving

Moving is the second stage of Lewin's model but the third stage in our list of revised steps. A buying situation is an approach/avoidance situation in that a customer may appreciate the benefits offered (the approach) but still be held back by objections to aspects of the offering (the avoidance). At the moving stage, the customer is aware by this stage of the product's potential but the customer's objections (avoidance factors) need to be overcome before buying. There are many uncertainties when buying a product for the first time. A tactic of persuasion is to make sure that the customer is aware that the salesperson has a thorough grasp of the objection by re-stating the objection as clearly as possible. After this, objections are dealt with in a way that demonstrates expertise and experience, together with case histories of satisfied customers that parallel the customer's own situation.

Persuasion can be reinforced by 'reference selling'. Reference selling means approaching a satisfied customer who agrees to talk to the prospective customer or at least recommend the product, preferably by showing success with the product in an application similar to the prospect's. (When marketers speak of satisfied customers, they refer to customers who have had their expectations, in respect to their want, met or exceeded. The satisfaction of a want or desire cannot be equated with the satisfaction of the whole person; satisfying a specific want is not the same as satisfying the person per se.)

In getting the prospect to move, the salesperson is inducing the customer to change an existing perspective. One way to make this process easier for the prospect is to overcome his or her objections. *Overcoming objections* moves the buyer towards buying, which is consistent with having no further objections to buying. It is consistent to buy if objections are removed. But even a disposition towards buying that manifests itself in an expressed intention to buy is not the same as saying 'I will buy' or 'I promise to buy'. An intention, as already claimed, is like going into gear while pressing the accelerator – exhibiting the 'will-to-buy'. The seller may have to adopt some way of triggering the sale by, say, a special offer, if the prospect is to move from intention to buying action. Salespeople need to be on the lookout for *intentional movements* and, whenever it seems opportune, try and close the sale, for example by summarizing benefits, getting successive agreement and then asking for the order and so on.

A good deal of time in salesmanship courses is spent on how to overcome objections. Is this attention to overcoming objections justified (Hawes et al. 1996)? Overcoming objections is always important as it:

- Equates with some initial stage of overcoming cognitive resistance to buying
- Is a way of reducing the likelihood of future regret and post-purchase dissonance

- Puts the emphasis where it should be, since potential losses are more emotionally painful than a corresponding gain (Kahneman and Tversy 1979).

There are always objections that need to be overcome. Even the door-to-door salesperson has to prepare to answer four common objections:

> 'I am not interested.'
> 'I've got no money.'
> 'I have one already.'
> 'I have no time to consider it at present.'

One superordinate goal of selling is usually to secure a customer and not just to secure a one-off sale. This means that customers should buy without reservations. From the customer's point of view, overcoming their objections is a way of reducing the perceived risk of buying. From the salesperson's point of view, customers who raise an objection are getting involved and giving guidance as to what for them are the crucial issues. Every objection successfully surmounted is a step towards selling success. A latent want can turn into a *passive* want if awakened, instead of into an active want, if objections remain as barriers to buying. The aim is to move from that passive want to buying intention, then arriving at the will-to-buy, and on to the act of buying itself. This sequence seems conceptually true though we still cannot guarantee it will occur.

The passive want is inhibited from turning into an active want by customer objections. Some ways of surmounting objections are:

- Boomerang: This is converting an objection into a reason for buying – 'You may say the car is small but that is what makes it so maneuverable'.
- Compensation: The objection is admitted but compensating benefits are demonstrated – 'Yes, you may feel the mileage is high for this car but the price is so low whereas cars today regard such a mileage as just breaking in'.
- Deny the objection if based on untrue facts: 'You may have heard that this make of car is not highly reliable but this is untrue as anyone who has bought this car will tell you and what our service department knows to be a fact'.
- Dispel the objection by demonstration: 'I know how you may feel about driving a bigger car but let's get in it and see if you still feel that way at the end of a test run'.
- Offer guarantee: 'This car comes with a seven-year or 60,000-mile warranty so you need not worry about things going wrong and it costing you plenty'.
- Answer a question with a broader question if a direct answer can be disadvantageous: (Customer) 'How loaded with features is the car?' (Salesperson) 'What features would you find useful?'

Another way to think about dealing with objections is to list the categories into which objections fall and anticipate answers:

Price: Price inhibits buying not because the price is beyond the customer (which would take him or her out of the market entirely) but because the price is more than the customer is prepared to pay. The problem lies in the relative weight attached to price versus benefits. Anything that minimizes the impact of price (like easy credit terms) or the importance attached to price (like getting the customer to treat price as an investment rather than a payment) alters the relative weight given to price. Price objections are probably the most common of all objections. The tactics to overcome this objection might be some combination of the following.

- Diminution of price, for example translate the total price into small units so a price of $50,000 for sound equipment that lasts twenty years becomes $2,500 per year, or $48 per week.
- Show value for money, for example by breaking price down to show the features additional to those offered by the competition so as to show price differences reflect differences in value. At the same time, stress the benefits that are unique to the seller and of central importance to the buyer. Choose positive language: not buying but owning; not a contract but an agreement; not a payment but an investment.
- Deny false beliefs about price such as that delivered cost is the most relevant cost but talk instead of life cycle costs which include operating costs, maintenance costs and down time.
- Draw attention to the potential costs of not buying, for example maintenance costs or poor service.
- Use the feel-felt-found sequence in your appeal, for example 'I know how you feel about price. I've had other customers who felt the same way. But what they found was ...'
- Favorable payment terms, so showing how the impact of price can be minimized by the supplier's financial arrangements.
- Get buyers to take small steps towards buying by, say, setting up calls to those customers with like application problems who found the extra price was worth it.

False beliefs: The price to the customer may seem high in relation to benefits (with the consequence that buying is inhibited) when, in fact, the evaluation of benefits rests on false beliefs. Thus there may still be many people wanting a home computer who do not buy because they believe that learning to use one would be much too difficult. False beliefs are a common problem for manufacturers. The various advertised 'torture' tests to which Timex watches were subjected (for example, a Timex watch attached to the outboard engine propeller of a speedboat) were designed to dispel false beliefs about cheap watches being unable to withstand tough treatment ('Timex takes a licking and keeps on ticking').

False beliefs often resist change as they are apt to be reinforced by the buyer's other beliefs. This means that individual false beliefs cannot usually be eradicated one by one as they are part of a set of mutually supporting beliefs. This can be a major problem in political marketing campaigns in that false beliefs about a candidate or his or her policies are integrated into a whole host of reaffirming beliefs. Thus the customer does not just believe timber-framed houses are not as good as brick houses but believes a whole host of propositions about housing such as durability of wooden structures, fire risks and so on. It is because the individual belief about a product, feature or attribute is part of a system of beliefs that an attack on the one belief may stimulate robust rebuttal based on these other beliefs. There is a need to think of taking on the relevant belief-system rather than the individual belief.

True beliefs: A customer may be held back from buying by true beliefs about the pros and cons of buying. Thus, in the early days of contact lenses many people who wanted their benefits were put off by the known discomfort they caused. Salespeople either had to get the consumer to perceive the discomfort as minor (difficult to do) or the manufacturer had to reduce the discomfort by developing a more comfortable product, which they did by creating soft lenses. Some beliefs that inhibit buying are neither true nor false at the time they are held but are simply beliefs about the future as, for example, when customers believe that products currently on the market are likely to be quickly superseded by something better and/or cheaper. Such beliefs are common in respect to new electronics products from smartphones to computers. But it should be stressed to the buyer that postponement of buying means not only postponement of consumption (instant gratification) but also the sacrifice of social rewards associated with being among the first to own the product.

Doubts about claims. The customer can want a product but be held back by doubts. Doubting a claim is different from disbelieving a claim. If I disbelieve the claim that product X will cure cancer, then I believe that product X will not cure cancer. However, if I doubt the claim I am simply saying I am uncertain as to whether to believe or not to believe the claim. Doubts about advertised claims abound, as exaggerated claims about products abound. Customers have learned from experience to discount claims about 'revolutionary' advances over competition. Such doubts impede the adoption of truly major innovations and so need to be anticipated and dispelled.

Social norms: A final inhibitor can be social norms. As purchases signal to the world something about the buyer's rank, values and preferred self-image, it follows that purchases should be socially endorsed. A customer may want something – even need something – but the purchase can be proscribed or at least discouraged by being a social no-no. Social factors inhibit sales of cosmetics to men. One firm trying to get around this employed at one time the macho, cigar-smoking Burt Reynolds in their advertisements, rejecting the label of cosmetics in favor of the phrase 'skin fitness and bath products'. By conjuring up the associations of 'skin fitness' and manliness, the firm hoped to change perceptions sufficiently to counter social inhibitions.

Even when a purchase is not going to be highly visible in the individual's social world, customers often act as if big (social) brother is watching them so fashion is even important in the bedroom. Appeals that violate social or group norms, rules or standards will find difficulty winning acceptance. On the other hand, when certain social norms are not an integral part of the relevant social group's way of life it is difficult to make them so. Thus the dress codes of Manhattan have little influence on retirement communities in Florida.

Where the sales situation is highly favorable, there is little need for lengthy product discussion. In any case, tentative *trial closes* need to be tried early in the sales interview as a test of how the sale is proceeding. Salespeople often hesitate to close a sale. The chief reason is fear of failure. It is for this reason that courses in salesmanship stress tactics for closing a sale. If the salesperson fails to get an order, he or she should at least get some commitment, such as a future appointment.

In any individual selling encounter, the salesperson, in adopting some tactic, needs to recognize whether the situation is one of converting a customer from a rival, increasing the level of business with that customer, attracting a new customer to the product or seeking to retain an existing customer. For any individual product and customer, these tactics are exhaustive and mutually exclusive. It is generally much easier to retain a current customer than seek to convert from rivals or attract new customers. Gillette, even though holding patents in respect to steel blades, were slow in responding to the steel blade introduced by Wilkinson Sword in the 1960s, yet when it entered the segment it still came to dominate it.

Refreezing

The refreezing stage in the Lewin model is the final stage and involves the post-sales reassurance about the wisdom of the purchase so as to overcome post-purchase doubts or dissonance. If this is achieved, we may have secured a customer and not just a one-off sale. Where social reality is concerned, the consumer can never be sure she has had, say, the best haircut, or the best dentist, until other 'experts' comment favorably.

THE LEWIN MODEL AND CIALDINI'S SIX MECHANISMS

The Lewin model just discussed can be shown to be consistent with Cialdini's six mechanisms. In Table 12.3, Cialdini's six mechanisms are related to Lewin's model of attitude change.

Social psychology has made the greatest contribution to the literature on persuasion. Not only is persuasion of major interest to marketing but how the consumer is influenced is one way to further our understanding of the consumer. Later in this chapter we have more to say about persuasion.

Table 12.3 Caldini's six mechanisms and Lewin's attitude change stages

Mechanism employed	Lewin's attitude change stages
Reciprocity	Establish rapport
Liking	Establish rapport
Consistency and commitment	Unfreezing
Reciprocity with contrast effect	Moving
Reciprocity	Moving
Scarcity	Moving
Close sale tactics	Refreezing

The major tool for persuasion is still advertising and the big development here has been in online advertising. *Online* advertising falls roughly into two camps. The first is search engine advertising, led by Google, where advertisers bid for keywords like 'laptop computers' so that when the surfer of the Web enters these words, up pop the ads alongside the search results. The second camp covers the display banners and videos which are becoming increasingly popular. Google increased its revenue by $16.5 billion in 2007 and $23.6 billion in 2009 mainly from the advertising on its site. In any case, placing ads in social media has had the great attraction of being able to measure the 'clicks' indicating interest in the product. Nike's three-minute commercial video 'Write the Future' involving the game of soccer was launched on Facebook. It was played and commented on more than nine million times by Facebook users. Even candy manufacturers are tending to use the Web more and more to reach the youth market. Kia Motors improved brand awareness among its target audience through using Google's YouTube, logging more than a million views online in just two months. It also, though, used television, with fun commercials employing human-sized hamsters that rap to a hip-hop group while driving Kia's Soul wagon. But Facebook is becoming the leader for those using Internet advertising: ads located to the right of the page.

The Internet has also given a lift to small businesses wishing to reach a widely scattered audience. But those who sell only on the Web still lose out to those retailers who use both the Web and brick-and-mortar outlets. What worries many critics is how the browsing history of users is tracked so that ads can be selected to fit that browsing history.

Other findings on persuasion: We have tried to accommodate ideas and findings on persuasion within the framework of Lewin's attitude change model. But more needs to be said. In looking at persuasion here we are in effect looking at consumer behavior evoked in interaction with a persuader. It must be said that just reasoning with someone, however logically compelling the argument, may be insufficient to induce a conversion. Otherwise books on persuasion could confine themselves to identifying illogicalities and flawed reasoning. Perhaps it is true what a colleague of mine once said about giving lectures to the public: 'Appeal to the prejudices, as reasoning will only make them feel uncomfortable'. It would sound less cynical if he had advised taking account of the existing perspectives and attitudes of the audience.

Persuasion is central to marketing, and social psychologists have done the most work on persuasion. In collaboration with Noah Goldstein and Steve Martin (2010), Cialdini wrote a book entitled *Yes! 50 Scientifically Proven Ways to be Persuasive* (Goldstein et al. 2010). No attempt was made in this book to explain behavior, as in Cialdini's earlier book, in terms of classical and operant conditioning. Instead there is recognition of how much work on persuasion has been done by social psychologists.

The book has been a bestseller, reflecting perhaps the persuasive power of the words *scientifically proven ways* which suggest persuasive tactics of scientific robustness. But there are no social laws of persuasion. What the authors mean is that the appeals or tactics discussed have been tested and received some corroboration. Typically, the results amount to showing that the percentage of people being influenced is higher (statistically significant) in the experimental group than in the control group or a past reference group.

A number of the tactics discussed in their book also appear in this book but there is utility in putting them together as the authors have done. What must be said is that there are always alternative explanations of findings and the extent to which findings can be generalized to other contexts or domains always remains a matter of judgment or further empirical investigation. There is a need to think about whether the strategies or tactics would be successful in the context or population of interest. Here is a synopsis of the fifty ways to persuade, though in fairness to the authors, readers are encouraged to read the whole book to ensure more depth of understanding.

1. The principle of social proof. When uncertain about what action to take, people look to others to decide what to do. For example, the sign that told guests at a hotel that the majority of guests recycled their towels at least once during their stay (social proof appeal) was more effective than a sign quoting an environmental protection message. The social proof appeal got a 26 percent increase in the recycling of towels. Social proof goes beyond showing an action to be socially appropriate since social proof demonstrates overt endorsement. The 'herd' instinct discussed in behavioral economics is linked to the notion of social validation.

2. Similarities with the target audience are factors in source attractiveness. Thus the celebrity or person in an ad might possess a background similar to that of the target audience and this contributes to their attractiveness: 'If others like me have gotten good results with this product, then it should be right for me too.' Attractiveness is an important factor in all interpersonal relationships but may be a weak one if the other person is just perceived as a likeable rogue; credibility also needs to be considered.

3. Giving publicity to the widespread nature of the behavior being condemned and which the authorities want to stop can actually increase its incidence because, in saying it is prevalent, you might be providing social proof for the 'normalness' of the behavior. Focusing attention on those who do engage in the desired behavior, and preferably being able to show they are the majority, is likely to be more effective.

4. There is a need to convey approval of those adhering to the positive behavior (such as recycling or voting).

5. There can be a problem in offering too many options. Thus in one experiment involving pension plans, when only two funds were offered, participation was roughly 75 percent, but the participation dropped to 60 percent when fifty-nine funds were offered. There have been recent studies (already discussed) that corroborate such results. All suggest that a firm may be offering such a large number of subcategories as to be hurting sales through information fatigue. This claim has been discussed elsewhere but, as the authors acknowledge, presenting many options can be helpful when customers are likely to know exactly what they want. BSkyB, the British satellite broadcaster, has 505 channels and this excludes the pay-to-view films; however, viewers do not surf through all these channels but seem to know what they want. Netflix in the US offers countless films from which to stream to one's television but uses 'recommendation' engines to predict from ratings of past choices what you are likely to enjoy. We might recall that in any large supermarket, there are numerous varieties of yogurt from which to choose. I suggest that few shoppers are confused or put off because of this.

6. Offering as a free gift something that is normally sold separately by the company can devalue the free gift and affect its sales when later sold independently. The advice is to remind customers of the value of the gift by inserting the actual price of the free gift. Any free feature of an offering (e.g. a free after-school club) should be promoted by saying what it would cost elsewhere (e.g. in a private school).

7. In deciding between just two brands, the less expensive is typically chosen, other things remaining equal, but if a third brand is offered that is more expensive than the existing two brands, consumer choice is apt to shift from the cheapest to the middle-price brand. The advice is that a seller can make the mid-range price more popular by offering a more expensive one first, as commonly occurs in the selling of houses.

8. In making an effective fear appeal, it is important to tell the target audience how to reduce or avoid the danger so they can do something about it; this typically does not happen often enough in the case of smoking when smokers are not given specific, feasible advice on how to stop.

9. The norm of reciprocity seems to be universal: people feel obliged to return a favor even if the favor is from someone they do not like. The *principle of reciprocity* lies behind gift-giving and free lunches to buyers. The practice of gift exchange has been one way throughout the

ages of creating group solidarity, though gifts on occasion can be a way of creating dependency and signaling superiority. From Aristotle to the Roman moralist Seneca, it was argued that human society was held together by the exchange of benefits. Births, baptisms, marriages, birthdays and funerals have all traditionally involved the exchange of gifts. If you do a favor for someone you create a social debt which the receiver feels obliged to reciprocate. Pharmaceutical houses are notorious for providing gifts to doctors in expectation of their products being favored. But if a gift always involves a reciprocal obligation, is it not just another example of the exchange relationship? This is a question much debated. To prevent corruption in the case of company purchasing officers, the rule should be 'zero tolerance' of receiving gifts so that buying is less influenced. 'Less influenced' since the salesperson through a pleasant personality and supportive behavior promotes the norm of reciprocity: we want to reward people we like. Natalie Davis (1999) even suggests that the European Reformation revolved around gifts in that it was about whether human beings could in fact reciprocate God's gifts and whether God could be obligated to reciprocate. Of course, not all giving occurs in the expectation of reciprocity as when people donate blood or bodily organs.

10. People pay attention when others introduce a personal touch in their communications. Thus the experiment in which a personal note on a Post-it, accompanying a survey asking respondents to complete it, had a 75 percent response rate as opposed to when the survey was sent out without the personal Post-it note, which got a 48 percent response rate. This is a more subtle application of the reciprocity rule in that 75 percent of the respondents felt the need to reciprocate for the personal note by complying with the request. The lesson is that the more personal you make a request, the more likely the compliance with that request. A personal note tells respondents their individuality is being recognized and acknowledged – just as saying 'Good morning' to someone acknowledges their presence.

11. Studies indicate that there are three factors that make a favor or a gift more attractive and so more likely to be reciprocated: (a) its perceived *significance*; (b) its *unexpectedness*; and (c) its being *personalized*. When the server at the restaurant gave two pieces of candy to everyone at the table as opposed to the usual one piece, it made the gift significant. The second factor is unexpectedness; the two candies were unexpected. The third factor is personalized as it seemed as if the server regarded these customers as rather special. The authors conclude that a restaurant that simply puts its candy at the exit misses an opportunity for the servers to give a token of appreciation (and get a better tip)!

12. In respect to cooperation, it is better to offer help in a way that is 'unconditional' with no 'strings attached'.

13. As time passes, the value of favors diminishes in the eyes of the receivers but increases for the giver. This is not, of course, entirely true.

Many of us, in later life, come for the first time to really appreciate favors going back to our youth and the help given by parents.

14. There is the 'foot-in-door technique' where getting people to agree to a small request paves the way for making a large request. This has already been discussed.

15. In one persuasive technique known as the 'labeling technique', a person is given a certain label (e.g. of a good Republican). If a request is made that is consistent with that label (e.g. vote Republican in the next election) subjects are more likely to act in the way the label suggests. Children in particular who are given positive labels like 'brave', 'clever', 'talented' will make an effort to live up to the label.

16. Simply asking a question can increase support for the questioner's position. This is why a questionnaire can be a persuasive tool. Thus asking voters to predict whether they would vote on election day and to provide a reason supportive of their prediction, led to a turnout 25 percent higher than the rate for those who were not asked. Hence when people publicly declare that they will act in some socially desirable way, they are motivated to act in a way consistent with their commitment. It is also better to present a request as a polite *question*, 'Will you please call if you have to cancel?', than simply to state requests: 'Please call if you have to cancel'. Similarly, it is better to ask people whether they would support some proposition and wait for an answer.

17. Commitments that are made actively, for example writing them down, yield more of a commitment and so have more staying power. Thus asking members of a team to write down a set of goals adds to their commitment. The doctor's clerical assistant usually writes on a card the date of the patient's next appointment. If the patient fills in the date of her next appointment herself, the appointment is more likely to be kept.

18. Being inconsistent (as argued earlier) can be emotionally disturbing, particularly for older people. In persuading older people, we need to avoid any suggestion that a change of mind indicates inconsistency on their part. Thus it can be pointed out that some previous decision was perfectly correct at the time with the information they then had but things have now changed.

19. Apparently Benjamin Franklin was right in saying he who once did you a kindness will be more ready to do you another. (Presumably, these requests should not happen too often!) It is as if we do not want to diminish the goodwill that currently exists.

20. If we ask little, as when we say 'even a penny will help', people are more likely to donate than if we simply ask: 'Would you be willing to help by giving a donation?'

21. A lower starting price in bidding can lead to a higher final price: (a) a lower starting price encourages participation; (b) the high number of bids projects a sort of social proof for new bidders; (c) early bidders justify time and effort already spent by continuing the bidding. A low price to start has more success when there is indeed the likelihood of

many bidders being involved, and least likely to be successful when there are few bidders.

22. Having someone else introduce you to an audience 'to blow your trumpet' has more credibility than doing it yourself. Hence, prepare a short biography of yourself for those who are to introduce you. It is also better to have a third party to handle negotiations (e.g. in contract negotiations) on your behalf.

23. The best informed are likely to be beaten to a correct solution by a body of people of relevant expertise. The lone decision-maker is usually outclassed by the wider knowledge and diverse perspectives of the group. This is not a recommendation for group decision-making but simply a recommendation about the process of idea generation.

24. Setting up someone for the role of devil's advocate (as a way of combating intellectual incest) is not as effective as an authentic dissenter since his or her views tend to be perceived as more 'principled'. This suggests there is no real substitute for developing a motivational climate where debate is vigorous and sharp while discouraging polarization.

25. Training should not focus purely on how good decisions are made but also on errors that are made which could have been avoided. This is common in sales training when showing what went wrong with a sale.

26. Arguing against one's own self-interest by exposing weaknesses can be successful in having consumers perceive you and your organization as being honest and worthy of trust ('We are No. 2, but we try harder' – Avis). This is preferably followed by the drawback having a benefit. (This relates to the 'Yes, but . . .' appeal in selling).

27. For two-sided persuasive appeals to be most effective, the negative part of the appeal must relate to the positive aspects that are conveyed. Thus in conveying the negative that the restaurant is very small, we add how cozy this makes it.

28. Instead of blaming others for failure, an organization that admits the cause was some internal failure is likely to be applauded by its audience for doing so. Admitting a failure can enhance reputational capital.

29. In selling we talk about similarity between seller and buyer as one basis for establishing rapport. It seems, however, that any similarity, such as name, school attended and so on can be helpful in persuading another person.

30. Strangely, people seem attracted to professions with names similar to their own (Prentice, the Dentist and so on). Names that are similar to the person addressed link to the attraction of things that remind them of themselves. Presenting a proposal? Name it after the individual whose business you seek.

31. Food servers who repeat word-for-word the order by the customer are likely to increase the size of their tip (by 70 percent in one study). In fact mirroring the other person in gestures, seating posture, clothes or whatever helps in bonding to the other person. Behavior *mirroring* in negotiations actually helped produce better results as it seemed to produce more trust.

32. Service people are asked to smile often but it seems those who give an authentic, as opposed to an artificial, smile generated more satisfaction from customers. An authentic smile can arise through self-generating positive feelings towards the customer.

33. Consumers are likely to show a much greater desire for a product that seems to be scarce. This is the *scarcity principle*. This is well exploited by sellers with announcements such as 'Last few'; 'Only one per customer'; 'Sale ends Thursday' and so on. It applies also to information. To suggest to someone that he is the only one you have told or the new 'Secret' magazine is sent only to a few selected people makes the information in the magazine seem more valuable.

34. In blind taste tests, Pepsi might have tested better than traditional Coke but this liking did not compensate in sales for the sense of losing traditional Coke. Blind taste tests, too, showed new Coke to be preferred but this verdict was helped by new Coke not being available (scarcity principle). The strong desire to retain traditional Coke shows the influence of the 'loss aversion' principle which states that people are more concerned with avoiding losses than with any compensating gains. It seems that stressing the idea of a potential loss unless some action is taken is better than just saying what can be gained. Instead of presenting your cost-reduction proposal as a saving, better to say what would be lost if this proposal is not adopted. But if there is always concern with avoiding losses, how come people continue to gamble? Could it be they do not imagine losing? It is easier to retain a customer than attract or convert new customers and that has something to do with being averse to losses since changing brands can appear risky.

35. Adding a reason for a request ('because...') can facilitate the acceptance of a request. Trying to jump the line for photocopying by just saying 'can I just do these few pages?' is not as effective as, for example, saying 'can I just do these few pages because I'm in a rush?' The hollowness of the reason does not seem to matter when there is little at stake, though more substantial reasons are required if there is more at stake.

36. In any promotion, asking respondents to name a number of reasons for choosing your product may not be as effective as asking them to provide just one reason. It is easier to think of just one reason than several and this ease of recall of a major reason can be decisive in making a final evaluation of your product. Other research by Ariely (2008) showed that merely imagining using your product can influence the buying decision – if it is easy to imagine doing so.

37. Consumers tend to be more attracted to easily pronounceable names than to those difficult to pronounce. A name that is easy to read and pronounce helps the name to be viewed positively and aids word-of-mouth recommendations. Similarly, handwriting that is easy to read is more persuasive. A persuasive message full of jargon and complex language is less persuasive and gives off a poorer view of the message source.

38. A rhyming message in an ad (e.g. 'Chef inspired, dog desired'; 'You have to be in it to win it'; 'If you can click a mouse, you can buy a house') can add to memorability which, together with easy name 'fluency', tends to result in the message being judged as more accurate. So liking and truthfulness can accompany a rhyme.

39. The quantity of information a consumer believes she has about something can be influenced by how much information she learns about something else. Thus after reading a persuasive communication on one fictitious store, subjects were asked to read a persuasive message for another fictitious store. If the initial message contained a large amount of information, the second message was judged to be less persuasive, but it was the opposite when the initial message included little information. The lesson is to make sure you discuss the merits of your product at length after spending only a short period discussing the rival product.

40. In considering some sort of rewards card, revitalizing and reframing the program offering a card that has been started but not completed, in contrast with a program that has yet to be started, leads to customers being more anxious to complete it. This claim seems to be related to the finding that there is always psychological pressure to finish some uncompleted plan, whether it is a course of study or the housework.

41. It seems that products with unexpected descriptions (e.g. Kermit green) and ambiguous two-category names (e.g. millennium orange) appear more desirable than other two-category names. The authors talk about such names creating a sense of mystery and intrigue, but an explanation that is more theoretically grounded is that they appeal to our curiosity and desire for novelty.

42. To avoid confusion of what ad goes with what brand (often ads of advertiser 'A' are attributed to advertiser 'B' of a rival brand), it is important to integrate the images, slogans and so on into the product packaging and in-store promotions.

    It is all too common for an advertisement using image association to be equally appropriate for the firm's rivals. This means the ad is not stressing any critical advantage. To avoid confusion there must be some way of uniquely attaching the ad associations with the brand being advertised.

43. When children had to look at themselves in a mirror as they took their allotted candy from the candy bowl, 'theft decreased from 33.7 percent to 8.9 percent'. The use of mirrors might similarly work in reducing theft in stores as will simply putting a picture of eyes looking down from above.

44. Being in an emotional state can be dysfunctional. In one experiment, sad buyers were willing to purchase an item for about 30 percent more than was the case with emotionally neutral buyers. Sad people seem less risk-averse. Negative emotions in general can impair decision-making. It is as well to avoid making important decisions

when in a negative mood in order to avoid making a mistake. But being optimistic (a joyous mood) can also lead to the consumer buying without enough deliberation, so both sadness and optimism can be dysfunctional for buying wisely.

45. When people are tired, it seems they are more gullible because of the corresponding decrease in mental energy. Distraction has a similar effect on people's susceptibility to persuasion. The two weaknesses most prevalent in cognitive ageing are: (a) being easily distracted; and (b) possessing a weakened information retrieval system, leading to slowness in thinking up options. Thus when driving, old people are more easily distracted and in an accident have more problems in thinking what to do.

46. A caffeinated drink like coffee taken by the target audience about ninety minutes before a presentation helps make the audience more receptive to a sound case.

47. The absence of voice inflection and physical gestures makes email more likely to result in miscommunication than will face-to-face communication.

48. Cultural differences do matter when it comes to persuasion. Collectivistic cultures like those typically in Asia, as opposed to individualistic 'Western' cultures, seem more susceptible to appeals that focus on benefits to a person's group members such as family. Thus one experiment showed that in persuading South Koreans, collectivistic rather than individual ads were more effective, while the reverse was true for the US.

49. In asking someone in Western societies for a 'favor', showing the favor fits what that person has done before helps but, in more collectivistic countries, it seems more effective to point out how doing the favor coheres with what the person's peer group has previously done: social proof is more important than past actions.

50. Individualistic cultures tend to put more stress on the information content of the communication, in contrast with collectivistic cultures where the relational function dominates. In collectivistic cultures there is a constant need in communication to further build up the relationship as opposed to, say, providing an overabundance of technical information about the product.

General selling tactics: It helps in understanding consumer behavior to appreciate the effectiveness of certain selling tactics. Selling tactics are important, though it is how these selling tactics are integrated into an overall coordinated performance that is really decisive. Some neat general selling tactics are those suggested by Larson (1995):

- Yes-yes technique where the seller seeks to get the prospect to respond 'yes' to each part of the sales appeal
- Don't ask 'if' but 'which?' so that you draw the prospect into making a choice, for example 'Which are you going to have?' (not: 'If you choose one...')

- Answer awkward questions with a question. For example, if the question is on price, the seller might say: 'Others might give you a price but would it not be better first to know what is being offered?'
- Get a partial commitment as evangelists do when they get their audiences to pray with them
- Ask for more than expected so prospects may at least concede something, for example by ordering a smaller amount than first requested
- Use the senses to open up a channel to the audience's memory, for example the seller shutting the door of the car so the prospect hears that solid 'thrunk'
- Get an IOU by putting the prospect under an obligation or a need to reciprocate in some way, such as by giving a little gift.

STRATEGIES FOR OVERCOMING RESISTANCE TO PERSUASION

In the discussion on behaviorism in Chapter 4, Cialdini's six techniques of persuasion via social conditioning were discussed. The chapter went on to describe other models of persuasion which mirrored the six techniques without any suggestion that these relied on the mechanism of conditioning. Most of these models were developed by social psychologists and so could have been commented on more appropriately at this stage. But it seemed useful to contrast these models with those of Cialdini and posit them as alternative yet supportive explanations. But the Cialdini principles did not cover the related problem of overcoming resistance to persuasion which has been left to this section.

Christie Aschwanden (2010), in her review of resistance to evidence-based medicine, quotes many examples where the evidence had very little impact in changing attitudes, beliefs or behavior. For example, among long-distance runners, the use of ibuprofen is extremely common to deal with the pain from running. However, the evidence shows there is absolutely no reason for runners to be using ibuprofen. But being confronted with the evidence did not change the practice of taking ibuprofen to kill the pain of running. The runners were convinced that ibuprofen reduced inflammation in the joints and muscles and allowed them to run with less pain. The runner's perspective (or mental model as the author calls it) of how things work, such as how ibuprofen works to reduce pain, was in conflict with the scientific claim being put forward: 'people process information through their existing beliefs, and it is hard to override these beliefs', so facts contradicting some set of firmly held beliefs are typically explained away.

If results of some study are supportive of what we believe to be so, they are accepted; if not supportive, people are apt to reject or 'nit-pick' the evidence. The author concludes that 'facts' alone are unlikely to change anyone's mind. In fact, as she points out, when people are presented with strong evidence in conflict with their beliefs, this stimulates them to re-examine the reasons they'd held these beliefs in the first place and this process of remembering helps reinforce their initial beliefs in spite of the contrary evidence. Typically, if we radically change our beliefs, new concepts have to be taken on board to replace old concepts. In other words, there is likely to be a radical change in perspective. If many consumers, in certain situations, can be so impervious to the hard evidence in making product choices, they are in the category of being resistant to change and not open to promotions that seek to appeal to reason.

Aschwanden points out that both persuader and audience need a shared vision (perspective) of what the problem is before persuasion can be effective. In moving from a perceived difficulty to diagnosing what the problem is, we all do so against a 'theoretical' background or perspective that points to where the solution might lie. Audiences may continue to draw on their own perspective which may be an impediment to any persuasive appeal tied to overcoming resistance to change. More usefully, Aschwanden claims that statistical analysis rarely persuades in contrast to the use of powerful anecdotes and metaphors: 'narratives form the backbone of medicine – they're the way people make sense of the evidence'. She quotes the metaphor used by one physician to counter the patient's family being upset at a surgery being postponed: 'His heart is shimmying like the front end of an old Chevy truck, and as long as it's shimmying, we can't do the surgery.' This satisfied the questioner. Aschwanden points out that any evidence-based message must feed the human need for comfort and provide a sense of empowerment. This is important. Explanations that offer hope always have an appeal since the opposite of hope is despair, which we all seek to avoid. Messages typically need to be framed in a positive light if they are to gain traction as this is part of being a message of hope.

People commonly follow a 'coherence theory of truth' in accepting that which already coheres with their belief system. This contrasts with the 'correspondence theory of truth', namely truth as corresponding to the facts. If we listen to debates on television, we are struck by how seldom people feel the need to quote empirical evidence but express as the truth that which coheres with their perspective. In offering advice, social scientists are typically obliged to resort to a coherence theory of truth rather than being able to quote direct empirical evidence in support of their advice.

Empirical evidence is, of course, not always required even in rational persuasion. Many of us might be persuaded by John Stuart Mill's essay *On Liberty* where the persuasive force lies not in the empirical evidence but with its ties to our values. If we had to justify most of what we say by quoting empirical evidence, there would be little we would be able to say. Doctors give opinions, as do consumer behavior specialists, based on what coheres with the things they have been taught or what experience would suggest. Specialists cannot wait for answers from research not yet undertaken. A good many of the statements in this book are based on the coherence theory in that they are justified as legitimate interpretations and/or inferences from what I believe to be valid. The coherence theory of truth can be used to explain difficulties in persuasion in that trying to overturn a particular belief is made difficult by its being part of a coherent set of beliefs, so there is a need to address the whole system (perspective) of beliefs.

Much less attention in psychology has been paid to overcoming resistance to persuasion than to enhancing the attractiveness and credibility of the persuasive message or its source. 'Resistance' is one of those words that can be treated as a product (outcome) in the form of a refusal to go along with the persuasive message, or as a motivational process wherein barriers and counter-arguments are developed to combat persuasive messages. Salespeople speak of 'overcoming objections' rather than overcoming resistance but the problem is the same since objections reflect one form of potential resistance.

Many social scientists working in persuasion leave the impression that persuasion is always achievable providing the 'right' persuasive techniques are skillfully used. This is not so. When the persuasive task involves changing perspectives, we may find that the subject's perspective is tied to his or her values or core self-interests or the values of the reference groups in her social milieu. These may be too fixed to bring about change. Paul Krugman, the economist, words it well, if not impartially, in talking about the problem of getting agreement over health care reform between Republicans and Democrats when they 'live in different worlds':

> How can the parties agree on policy when they have utterly different visions of how the economy works, when one party feels for the unemployed, while the other weeps over affluent victims of the 'death tax'?
>
> (Krugman 2010)

Sometimes we put a 'spin' on our position to suggest that our own position does not violate the other's values but may actually promote them. In other words, we try to show our own perspective is reconcilable with the subject's own. This is what 'spin' is all about.

In a book of readings, edited by Knowles and Linn (2004), the intention is to remedy the neglected area of overcoming resistance to change. This is an important topic since resistance to marketing persuasions is a characteristic of today's world. The readings in the book are written mainly by social psychologists. This is not surprising since, as one article says, 'the study of persuasion is at the core of social psychology, communication, rhetoric, advertising and public relations' (ch. 7, p. 117). Persuasion is basic to marketing and this is why social psychology should be of more interest in general to marketers.

Persuasion is all-pervasive in social life. It could in fact be argued that all social interactions involve trying to persuade or influence the other party to accept us, like us, agree with us, view us as someone of standing or with a more credible viewpoint. In social relations we want people to go along with us, affirm our views and act in our support, which is what makes persuasion all-pervasive. But how does persuasion relate to influence? *Influence* is more encompassing than persuasion, in that we commonly influence people, positively or negatively, without any attempt to persuade. To say someone is influential is to talk about their potential to influence events through their general command of resources, whether personal or otherwise, while to say someone is persuasive is to speak of their talent in getting people to go along with them.

Most of the actual experiments reported in what follows used student populations. Under experimental conditions, contexts can be fixed, which is not true in the real world. Nonetheless, our intuitive (folk psychology?) inclination would be to endorse the claim that behavior, as described in these studies, is likely to be similar in real life. What might, though, be stressed is that each persuasive tactic we adopt is not an isolated act but part of a persuasive performance. It is the whole performance geared to the target audience's perspective that counts so that an individual tactic's effect can be lost or swamped by other elements in the performance.

Every buying situation is an approach-avoidance situation in that there are approach-motives and avoidance-motives. Knowles and Linn (ch. 7) view 'approach-avoidance' as tied to two broad strategies that encompass persuasive tactics. 'Alpha' strategies persuade by increasing the approach forces, 'Omega' strategies persuade by decreasing the avoidance forces behind reluctance to change.

Knowles and Linn quote the seminal study by Dollard and Miller (1950), showing that, in an approach-avoidance situation, as we persuade someone to move closer to the position desired, the avoidance gradients rise more steeply than the approach gradients. This suggests the need for that final promotional push (for example, sales promotions as a trigger) if indecision is to be overcome. Knowles and Linn remind us that research on persuasion has focused largely on Alpha approaches that enhance the desirability of the approach factors by (as we have seen):

- Making messages more persuasive
- Adding incentives
- Increasing source credibility
- Emphasizing scarcity
- Engaging the norm of reciprocity
- Emphasizing consistency and commitment

...while neglecting avoidance factors.

Convincing someone to resist is more difficult than providing them with excuses to accept, and overcoming resistance is more difficult than inducing the 'neutral' buyer to buy. The consumer can want the product but still resist buying. Knowles and Linn refer to the work of McGuire (1964), at Yale, who first suggested an *inoculation strategy* where the motivation to resist is built up by providing those to be persuaded with 'weapons' of resistance. Targets of the persuasive message are taught to embark on 'attitude-bolstering'. This involves the selective recall of information that supports current attitudes or, alternatively, providing them with information that derogates the source of the persuasive message. Both of these are common tactics in marketing promotions.

Knowles and Lynn also reference the work of Brehm (1966) who talked of *cognitive reactance* as a source of resistance. A boomerang effect can occur if a persuasive message is perceived as a threat to a person's perceived freedom not to believe: cognitive reactance can occur when anything threatens freedom of choice. If the persuader is perceived as moving towards a position where the recipient feels his or her freedom of choice is being reduced, an uncomfortable state of reactance is said to occur which motivates an effort to resist and reassert one's freedom. Just as a young girl can be put off by a new boyfriend coming across 'too strong', those who try too hard in persuasion can come across as threatening freedom of choice. This is often forgotten when we are too anxious and impatient to persuade.

Knowles and Linn list the traditional Omega tactics of decreasing resistance:

- Sidestep the resistance. Thus we instruct salespeople to overcome the resistance of the buyer by redefining the sales interaction as a consultation, not a selling occasion. Such reframing is adopted to change perspectives.
- Depersonalize the interaction, for example just say that people might want to contribute to the charity as opposed to saying you should contribute to this charity.
- Minimize the request. This is the foot-in-the door technique mentioned earlier: requesting small incremental changes rather than one large change, since compliance with small requests facilitates compliance with larger requests later.
- Change the standard of comparison – introduce a comparison that makes the original offer seem more attractive. Any standard for comparison purposes becomes an 'anchor' or reference point by which the offer is judged. The door-in-the-face technique commonly operates this way. – the target's refusal of a large request (order) makes the acceptance of the smaller request more likely. A prominent display of the original price explains why a prominently promoted price reduction can be so effective. The original price constitutes an anchor point that influences expectations.
- Pushing choice into the future, since offers are more likely to be accepted if they require future action than if they require immediate action. Most professors have been 'trapped' this way by agreeing to some seemingly far-off date to lecture at some outside organization.
- Address the resistance by the offer of guarantees or, alternatively, by showing opposing messages being advocated.
- Address the resistance directly by playing on the self-esteem of the target, which may be done by casting the 'resister' in the role of expert. 'Well, you drive for a living, so you know what an advantage it is that this car has...'

- Distract resistance because any distraction reduces the opportunity for reflecting on the message. This is a common strategy in both advertising and personal selling. It is one tactic used on seniors since senior citizens are most easily distracted.
- Disrupt resistance by making vague or ambiguous statements since interpreting vague or ambiguous messages takes time.
- Consume resistance. This tactic refers to the Muraven and Baumeister's (2000) *ego-depletion theory* of self-control which implies that people will be less able to resist the second request than the first and so on. (Most parents facing the persistence of children will identify with this!) Resistance is quickly consumable and is a more slowly replenishable resource. This technique is seen on the Internet when an ad keeps appearing time and time again with some large promise such as fixing all your computer problems.
- Exploit resistance to promote change by: (a) saying publicly the opposite of what you privately believe and/or want (this can be risky); (b) paradoxical interventions – the insomniac advised to try and stay awake as this can provide the focus for the person's resistance to doing so; (c) acknowledging resistance, for example 'You are not going to believe this but I felt the way you do ...' which reduces defense.
- Offer other choices in that the need to resist may be satisfied in other ways.

In inducing resistance to persuasion one common approach is simply to forewarn the intended target. Quinn and Wood (ch. 1 in Knowles and Linn 2004) discuss findings on forewarnings. As might be expected, targets who are given a warning before the attempted persuasion are likely to be less subject to persuasion than those who are subject to the persuasive communication without any warning. However, warnings that additionally appeal to the target's self-image, as someone not easily influenced, can further block persuasive appeals. Forearming appeals can be framed to boost resistance in the interests of group solidarity and are often effective in countering persuasive appeals. This is particularly so if the appeal to solidarity is based on a hate figure or hated enemy. It is not surprising that political ads make this appeal employing the chief of the opposing party as the hate figure, using just about any slander when looking for something to stick.

Warnings are not always effective since, on occasion, they may result in the target's need to appear open-minded and more open to persuasion! The authors conclude by reminding us that there are multiple specific motives involved in resistance – and agreement – but claim that forewarnings are, in general, effective in generating resistance. The multiplicity of motives makes it difficult to identify which motive or motives are at work. Thus buying 'green' can be a way of proclaiming moral status rather than wanting to do the environmentally right thing.

Narratives are a common way of overcoming resistance, particularly in court trials. Whereas an anecdote is a short illustrative story, a narrative is a story that accounts for the sequence of events. Narratives, anecdotes and humor can be the foundation for any highly rated lecture or talk, together with ensuring an animated facial expression since this animates the talk. Narratives, found in slice-of-life advertising, have become important in social marketing, in efforts to include pro-social storylines in various television series, for example against teenage pregnancy, drug abuse and violence.

Cin, Zanna and Fong (ch. 9 in Knowles and Linn 2004), explicate the role of narratives in changing minds by the way they induce a change in perspective. Narratives can overcome resistance by increasing identification with the characters in the story which resonates with the emotions. The work of Green and Brock (2000) is quoted to support a claim that narratives are persuasive to the extent that they 'transport' their listeners or readers into the world portrayed by the narrative. As people are transported into the world of the narrative, prior perspectives can change, and changing perspectives are typically involved in serious cases of overcoming resistance to change. It is not surprising that changing perspectives is still likely to appeal to core values, reflecting core concerns which have an emotional base.

A very different approach to overcoming resistance is offered by Tormala and Petty (ch. 11 in Knowles and Linn 2004). Instead of viewing persuasion as an all or nothing affair, they recognize that persuasion can be a matter of degree. Thus people may ward off attacks but nonetheless find their attitudes changed in terms of the certainty with which they are held. Attitudes and behavior form an interacting system in that attitudes influence behavior and behavior can influence attitudes. The study by the authors suggests that resistance to a communication can decrease attitude certainty when the attack is perceived as weak, since there will be doubt as to whether a stronger attack would have been similarly resisted. What this suggests is that we might be able to successively undermine a position through a series of weak attacks as each attack successively corrodes attitude certainty. On the other hand, there will be an increase in attitude certainty when the target believes he or she has resisted the persuasive message when allied to the belief that that message was a strong one. The authors accept that these results may not be consistent with McGuire's inoculation theory since McGuire assumed that inoculation against persuasive attacks can be attained by exposure to an initial attack that is easily resisted.

Sherman et al. (ch. 9 in Knowles and Linn 2004) argue that one way to decrease resistance is to invite the intended target to engage in pre-factual thinking that stresses the probability of future *regret* if a certain action is taken. Political advertising exploits this fear of regret when arguing that it is better to stick with the devil you know than the one you don't know. There have been many studies on the subject of regret, with Bell (1982) showing that anticipated regret affects decisions currently being made. We act as if we calculate how much regret we will have if a decision turns out badly. The authors propose that cognitive reactance findings can be re-conceptualized in terms of the anticipation of the amounts of future regret for compliance versus reactance. To minimize future regret, people may exhibit reactive behavior rather than compliance.

Sherman et al. (in Knowles and Linn 2004) argue that techniques for overcoming resistance such as the scarcity principle ('this is the very last one'; 'offer ends today') as well as all fear appeals can be viewed as operating through a process similar to anticipated regret. Fear appeals are all-pervasive in politics (e.g. exploiting security concerns) and insurance selling ('it helps give you peace of mind') and are common elsewhere in the selling of medicines. It is the main appeal in selling gold, cashing in on the consumer's fear about the currency and ignoring the fact that the price of gold can fluctuate widely. Fear appeals are common elsewhere, for example when labels on electronic products warn the buyer that he or she should only buy the manufacturer's brand of battery. It seems humans are innately vigilant to potential threats, even if these threats have an exceedingly low probability of being realized, and this sensitivity to threats is what is exploited in fear appeals. A problem with fear appeals is whether the effect persists in that, unless reinforced, the fear may disappear within weeks.

Recent happenings tend to be recalled more easily ('the *availability heuristic*'), such as a recent murder, exaggerating the probability of the occurrence. This relates to the noted short-term memories of people; a factor exploited in politics where voters all too easily forget about their previous experience with an incumbent or party or forget happenings in the not-too-distant past. Of course, availability in memory need not be tied to recent happenings but be based on past emotional experiences. In any case, what we can say is that brand selection may simply be based on which brand comes more easily to mind.

In a study undertaken by Sherman et al., participants who explicitly focused on the alleged future regret were significantly more likely to comply with the persuasive message in contrast to participants not focused. Additionally, instead of being asked to directly take some action, participants were asked to predict what their future behavior would be in respect to some action. This occurred before presenting them with the full-blown request for some action. The compliance rate increased 38 percent: agreeing to take action at some future date seems risk-free as one need not resist any direct persuasive attempt. However, once that prediction is given, the likelihood of agreeing to the full-blown request is considerably increased. This technique is not uncommon in selling. Hence, seeking commitment to buy on some future date as opposed to this moment can give rise to much higher compliance rates.

Although *practical rationality* implies taking account of consequences, people (buyers) do not spontaneously think about the possibility of future regret so there is a need to remind them of this possibility. A question arises as to whether what people regret most will be what they anticipated they would regret most. The authors quote the work of Gilovich and Medvec (1995) showing people may mis-anticipate their future feelings and make decisions based on this mis-anticipation. This claim finds its place in considering post-purchase satisfaction. Consumers can often be told that their predictions of misgivings will turn out to be unfounded and some attempt made to induce more optimism. But disappointment is common. Thus I may long for a house on a golf course but regret the purchase since I had not anticipated (a) early morning lawn cutting; (b) golf balls breaking my windows; (c) golfers treading on my flower bed.

One general conclusion by Sherman et al. is that strategies or tactics that decrease resistance are likely to be more effective for near-time decisions (like voting in elections) than for distant decisions, whereas strategies or tactics that increase the attraction (approach) forces would be more effective for distant decisions than for near-time decisions. Sherman et al. remind us again of the importance of pre-factual thinking in imagining. Thus getting potential buyers to imagine how a product could enrich their lives ('What would it be like, REALLY like, to own that sports car with everyone admiring you?') is a common tactic in advertising. Can this be related to what we have called earlier the 'semantic autonomy' of words? In one study by Gregory, Cialdini and Carpenter (1982) participants were asked to imagine themselves subscribing to a cable television service and enjoying the benefits. The participants were later more likely to agree to have the cable service than those not asked to imagine having the cable television service.

Jacks and O'Brien (ch. 12 in Knowles and Linn 2004) test the relationship between self-affirmations and vulnerability to persuasion; that getting people to feel good about themselves decreases their resistance to persuasion. In fact just feeling good about oneself in an unrelated domain can make people more open to arguments. The authors claim self-affirmations can be an antidote to self-esteem damage. This is a truism in that getting people to feel better about themselves conceptually relates to boosting or repairing self-esteem. The authors call their approach the *self-concept approach* as it assumes that a major motivator of resistance to persuasion is the need to protect the self-concept from threat and change. For these authors, the self-concept is not so much the in-depth description one could give of oneself, but, more broadly, the set of self-conceptions, values and attitudes that provide people with a sense of control and predictability.

The notion of self-concept is pervasive in the consumer behavior literature, defined as the image one has of oneself arising possibly from one's perceptions of one's body, sense of competence, values and social roles as well as personality. There is the claim that consumers have a preference for products that cohere with that self-image, though whether this is any more explanatory than saying consumers prefer what appeals to their beliefs about what suits them is not very clear. It is the same with the notion of *extended self*, which refers to all the significant others in our lives as well as entities like professional and social networks. How does this differ in practice from the notion of various reference groups influencing what we buy?

To return to the thesis of the authors that even when self-affirmations are unrelated to the persuasive message, as well as when the self-affirmation is compatible with the persuasive message, self-affirmations undermine resistance to persuasion. The explanation is that self-affirmation has the power to weaken the personal threat of counter-attitudinal messages. One implication of their work, they claim, is that a way to increase the motivation to resist persuasion is to increase the perceived threat to self, and one way to decrease the motivation to resist persuasion is to lower the perceived threat to self. The authors do not work out the implications for fear appeals though certain fear appeals do increase threats to self.

Attempts to persuade are often accompanied by an effort to change the mood of the audience. Few doubt that putting people in a good mood, making them feel good about themselves and so on lowers their barriers to mind-change. But is reducing threats to self-concept sufficient as an explanation? Supportive interaction implies supporting the self-image of the other party, making the customer feel good about herself. Supportive interaction moves in the direction of increased liking and increased liking makes the customer more open to persuasion because the relationship becomes more trusting. Thus it is perhaps not just a matter of feeling good about oneself but feeling better about a more trusting relationship.

Somewhat related to the self-concept approach is the work of Brinol, Rucker, Tormala and Petty (ch. 5 in Knowles and Linn 2004) whose interest lies in relating individual characteristics to resistance to persuasion. One finding is that people's beliefs about their ability to resist have an effect on their actual resistance. When elaboration (the process whereby a particular memory is interpreted, elaborated and associated with other stimuli) is low, people who believe they are more resistant to persuasion show less attitude change than people who believe they are easily susceptible to persuasion. Would anyone have thought otherwise unless we believe that firm beliefs have no more influence than weakly held beliefs?

Haugtvedt et al. (ch. 14 in Knowles and Linn 2004) build on previous work on *priming*, defined as procedures for increasing the accessibility of something in memory. Exposing the consumer to certain visual factors that prime product attributes increases the likelihood that the consumer will interpret product information in terms of these previously activated attributes. The experiments suggest that priming affects elaboration of the message and that the attitudes based on this more reflective deliberation lead to subjects being less influenced by counter-persuasive messages. But is this really a matter needing empirical inquiry? Does not getting consumers to focus more on certain attributes imply more elaboration and that elaboration can make the consumer more knowledgeable to resist mind-change? Apart from calling the process 'priming', have we not always tried, by repeated exposures, to fix in the mind of the customer-target the distinctive attributes that favor our brand? Whether this is enough to ward off counter-attacks depends on what the competition is offering and doing. Repeated exposure to an ad makes it more familiar and with familiarity is apt to come more recognition and liking; brands, as with people, can just grow on you. Familiar things generally provide information anchors that help make life predictable and comfortable. We all hear about German propagandists in the Second World War claiming that the constant repetition of a lie will come to be believed. Politicians have taken it to heart since political ads do not seem squeamish about repeating a lie if it is to their party's advantage. But it all depends on whether the lie violates what is known through 'physical reality testing' or beliefs firmly held.

In referring to the *repeated exposure effect,* the question arises as to how this can be reconciled with 'wearout' where the impact and effectiveness of an ad declines at very high levels of repetition (Calder and Sternthral 1980). Whenever we hear something over and over again, its freshness diminishes and it becomes dull even if initially good entertainment. But what is put across in an ad when first introduced is not perceived as false just because of repetition. In fact repetition is likely to help support belief in the ad's message. It is almost a truism to say that the marginal impact and effectiveness of an ad will diminish with high levels of repetition; just as the pleasurable effect of a good joke or a fine song diminishes if we get too much of either within a short period. Repetition can deaden the emotions and the desire to listen. However, just as we continue to think well of the joke and the song, liking for the brand continues with further familiarity helping cement that liking by making the brand part of our life, even if at the same time we tire of the ad itself. But what about the 'finding' that television advertising returns no more than 32 cents to each dollar spent on it? Every such study needs to be treated with skepticism because the measurement of returns is always subject to controversy. Are we talking about immediate returns or returns over the long run which must necessarily be somewhat speculative? Some advertisers in repeat, reminder ads are now simply showing the opening part of a familiar ad, which reduces both costs and wearout effect.

Most of us at one time or another in writing essays have been told to grab the reader in the opening and closing paragraphs. This finds expression in psychology in the notion of *primacy* and *recency* effects. Both the first and last persuasive messages are more likely to be remembered but there is no firm evidence as to which to stress under what circumstances. A good way to think of the importance of primacy and recency effects is, as already mentioned, to take the example of some hotel at which you stayed and think about how your views of the hotel were influenced by both your reception and the smoothness and politeness of those facilitating your exit. Politeness is a necessary condition for facilitating social interaction and projecting attractiveness but is not sufficient. We might suspect that the polite interrogator of a criminal suspect is more effective than one who is always angrily threatening, but not always.

Haugtvedt et al. try to cash in on the notion that what is easily available in the mind is in the best position to be recalled, supported by linking this notion to the elaboration likelihood model of persuasion (ELM) of Petty and Cacioppo (1986). But are not consumers always 'primed' by their emotions and values to selectively attend to what resonates with them? This is the basis for selective perception. The extent to which this basic priming can be displaced by just ensuring something else is immediately available in memory is a matter for empirical investigation. Selective perception is also tied to expectations, that is, we are more likely to see what we expect to see. Perhaps this explains why the medieval papacy took so long to realize that the paper it used in its transactions all came from the Muslim world, stamped 'Allah is great' (Hinton 2005).

Fuegen and Brehm (ch. 3 in Knowles and Linn 2004) argue that it is the *affective* (emotive) component of attitude that is crucial in determining behavior. It would be better to speak of emotive attitudes being more influential with regard to behavior rather than talk of the affective component which suggests the view of attitude as resting on the tripartite model of attitude (cognition, affect and conation). This confuses a logical, conceptual order with a mental, evolutionary one. Although cognition, affect and conation can be separated at the conceptual level, and can be formed into a logical sequence, this does not mean they are separate processes in the mind.

Fuegen and Brehm in fact criticize the tripartite model for reasons other than those just given, namely that cognition may not determine *affect* in a monotonic manner or affect determine behavioral tendencies. The authors argue that instead of changing a person's attitude with facts and arguments, we should consider how to alter affective responses. Their studies reach the conclusion that the most effective way to reduce an individual's *affectively* based resistance to persuasion is to put forward a weak deterrent so as not to directly threaten cherished beliefs. Weak reasons, for not feeling the way one does, reduce resistance to attitude change in that weak reasons are perceived as offering little challenge to cherished attitudes.

Fuegen and Brehm acknowledge that their conclusions run counter to the Petty/Cacioppo elaboration likelihood model of persuasion which suggests that, if we wish to persuade, we should (as Fuegen and Brehm word it) 'employ messages from credible sources replete with facts and strong arguments'.

An article by Johnson et al. (ch. 11 in Knowles and Linn 2004) is another blow to the Petty/Cacioppo model. They argue that the persuasive impact of argument quality is much less about creating logical arguments than it is about suggesting good rather than bad valence (desirability) for the message recipient. Their findings suggest that argument quality may be a mere proxy for valence or the perception of positive consequences for the recipient. They claim that perception of veracity, good logical arguments, matter relatively little compared with perceptions of valence. Their studies support the conclusion that the perceived strength of arguments is strongly associated with perceived valence and not with the perceived likelihood of being true. Unlikely-and-good arguments were equally as persuasive as likely-and-good arguments: wishful thinking emerged, despite high elaboration likelihood. The research suggests that creating messages that suggest positive consequences for the recipient (positive valence) or creating a positive motivational stance that creates positive thinking about the message content are more important than making veridical assertions.

The authors draw on *Social Judgment-Involvement Theory*, which argues that a person's existing perspective or attitudes provide the interpretive base for an incoming message. Without giving it a label, this has been the claim made in this book. When a persuasive message or even an advertised price falls within or near a person's latitude of acceptance, there is an attitudinal shift towards the message so that the message is assimilated. On the other hand, if the persuasive message or price falls within the person's latitude of rejection, the message or advertised price is regarded as more distant from one's own attitude or perspective than it truly is, so no attitude change occurs and may in fact be resisted. This is consistent with the claim made earlier that source credibility is not some objective fact but a matter of perception, something ignored in the Petty/Cacioppo model. Even if we agree that source credibility is tied to that source's expertise and independence together with the source's similarity with the promoted brand image and audience, it is *perceptions* of expertise, independence and similarity that are involved. Given all these criticisms, it is surprising that the Petty/Cacioppo model is still presented as valid in much of the marketing literature.

Haugtvedt and Wegener (2002) show that attitudes, based on high and low levels of elaboration, change equally little when the attacking message is presented by a non-credible source – so credibility is crucial in persuasion. But how much credibility is necessary as opposed to being important since attractiveness may sometimes be enough – likeable rogues can also be persuasive. People make snap judgments about people based purely on their looks and non-verbal behavior. What is true is that if the other party likes you they are more willing to do something on your behalf.

The topic of credibility is important and has been given increased prominence with the undermining of advertising messages through their over use of 'puffery', spin, misrepresentation and, on occasion, outright deception. Credibility is a major factor if a product's claims are not observable, as with financial services and pharmaceutical products. It is common sense to suggest that independent evidence, sponsors with demonstrated expertise and the reputation of the firm are all factors that boost the credibility of an ad. But words can help deception to persist. Thus referring to a counterfeit watch as an 'authentic replica' helps the deception.

METAPHOR AND PERSUASION

What seems to be neglected in the above (but not elsewhere) is the importance of *metaphor* in changing perspectives or overcoming resistance to change as was the case with the metaphor of the mind being a computer. We often do change perspectives by putting a spin on things which means people see things differently. Metaphors, in affecting what we see, how we think and how we interpret, influence not only affect thinking but emotional reactions. It is when they are tied to physical experience rather than abstractions that they become so powerful. Metaphors, even when not completely transparent as to meaning, can induce new perspectives and ideas. As Klein (1998) says, metaphor structures our thinking and conditions our sympathies and emotional reactions. In structuring our thinking, metaphors may also mislead. This may be the case with talk about the mind 'encoding' and 'decoding' since such metaphors may in no way capture the processes at work. Metaphors are a favorite in comic ridicule of some ideology.

Every new technology saturates the language with a new wave of metaphors – 'hard-wired', 'software of the mind' and so on. The English language is full of metaphors drawn from the technologies of the twentieth century (such as 'switched on') and from major historical events such as the phrase 'over the top', a reference to the trench warfare of the First World War. In fact it has been persuasively argued that conscious thought itself is mainly figurative in being normally metaphoric, metonymic and ironic (Gibbs 1994). But most metaphors are dead metaphors, as when we say the 'mouth of the river' or the 'heart of the matter'. When interpreting what others say, we typically need to reflect on what lies beneath the metaphor. In adopting one perspective rather than another we may simply be showing adherence to one metaphor (an organization is a mechanism) rather than another (an organization is an organism). When we talk about reframing an argument it typically involves displacing an existing metaphor for another, for example when saying advertising is not an attempt to pull the wool over the eyes of the consumer but is simply trying to put its best foot forward. Both parties in a dispute may agree about the relevant 'facts' but interpret those facts through different conceptual lenses captured by metaphors.

We might remind ourselves of the experiment by Tversky and Kahneman (1981) discussed earlier where the framings of a situation so affected preferences. The framings revolved around the notions of 'gain' and 'loss'. We are more averse to losses than corresponding gains and this explains why the reframing worked. While this might be a definitive case of the effects of reframing, it suffers from the use of terms like probability, the implications of which in the context are not immediately grasped. The salesperson who describes cost as an investment rather than expenditure is an exemplar of reframing.

Nonetheless, Tversky and Kahneman's study on reframing led to the identification of many analogous examples in consumer behavior. Consumers may pay with a credit card even when there is a discount for paying with cash, yet reject paying the identical sum if it is described as including a surcharge for using a credit card. The consumer's disposition to avoid losses versus compensating gains reminds investment houses that preservation of capital is always a major objective in personal investment. This overweighting of losses versus gains applies generally to life. Thus a demotion is more traumatic because it is a humiliating loss of status and means more than would an equivalent promotion.

We might agree that the effective selling of a product or idea should be viewed as an offer of affiliation and its acceptance an act of affiliation. This means that overcoming resistance to change should proceed so as to generate feelings of affiliation between seller and buyer. This, as stated earlier, is the insightful claim made by Mayhew (1997).

MOTIVATION

Cognitive psychology has too little to say about motivation but other branches of psychology (including social psychology) do have. Motivation is discussed under social psychology because social psychologists have been most sensitive to the fact that emotion and motivation are related in that emotion can be said to energize motivation.

The study of motivation in psychology, as pointed out earlier, presupposes there are general things that can be said about the motives of people. But a common error is to assume that consumers have just one major motive (e.g. to enhance self-esteem) since several motives are usually at work or, alternatively, to assume that a person's motives remain the same at different times and in different cultures. They do not. We consider below two of the theories which have appeared in the marketing literature.

Maslow's hierarchy of needs: Abraham Maslow is perhaps the most noted name in the area of motivation, at least in marketing. It is difficult to pin down Maslow as he was influenced by Freudian psychology and anthropology as well as mainstream social psychology. He was the founder, with others, of humanistic psychology, which rejected the view of man as represented by behaviorism and Freudian psychology, though today humanistic psychology is no longer an active branch of psychology.

There is no generally accepted set of needs or motives. Maslow's so-called hierarchy of needs, dating back to the ancient Greeks, is a combination of 'needs' in the sense of absolute physiological needs and important social desires:

- Physiological needs such as desiring to satisfy hunger, thirst and the need for safety
- Social desires such as belongingness in desiring social support and interaction, self-esteem and self-actualization (Maslow 1954). Self-actualization is essentially the same as self-realization, a more popular term in the nineteenth century. Self-actualization moves in the direction of achieving an ideal self-image.

But the Maslow list is somewhat arbitrary, developed to attack the dehumanizing psychologies at the time, namely, behaviorism and psychoanalytic psychology, which were perceived as viewing humans in a very unfavorable light.

There have been considerable criticisms of Maslow's hierarchy, though these criticisms do not mean that the hierarchy is not suggestive in considering what can motivate the consumer. Typical criticisms:

- Maslow's categories are in practice non-operational in that the referential-meanings are often ambiguous.

- The operational meaning of 'being satisfied' is not very clear. Lower-level needs can still be highly motivating even when nominally satisfied since we can remember past privations and anticipate future needs.
- The hierarchy is presented as a process model, in which case we need to know the *mechanisms* leading from one stage to the next in the hierarchy. Maslow was later to suggest that one's stage in the hierarchy is related to a stage in life.
- Empirical support is lacking for any multilevel concept of motivation.
- Operational measures of self-actualization are missing because the operational meaning of self-actualization is vague.
- Human action is guided by beliefs (not just wants and needs) and beliefs can change the priority of the hierarchy (e.g. duty coming first). A motive can at best only give a general directional tendency.

McClelland's need categories: An equally popular motivation theory in the organization behavior literature is David McClelland's (1961) need categories of power, achievement and affiliation. McClelland began, not by examining the way a person acts but by finding out the way he or she thinks through applying projective techniques, specifically 'construction techniques' where the subject constructs a story around some vague picture. The basic assumption is that the more ambiguous the stimulus, the greater the scope for the respondent to project his or her basic motivations into the answer. After all, what concerns a person is apt to constantly occupy the mind and these concerns, being tied to the emotions, are likely to reveal a person's uppermost motivations. McClelland argues that the thought samples in such stories can be grouped to reflect three categories of motive:

- The need for power (n.Pow)
- The need for affiliation (n.Aff)
- The need to achieve (n.Ach).

The need for power is a concern for having a strong impact on others which McClelland regards as a needed characteristic of all leaders. Power over others always has its attraction. Its absence often leads to it being manufactured, for example when someone plays tricks on another or some isolated hacker seeks to influence behavior by hacking into another's computer and imagines its effect. More generally, some computer games are bought because they allow the user to fantasize about being all-powerful. When dealing with others, it often happens that the other person's behavior cannot be predicted, while that other person can predict your behavior. As a simple example, take the situation where you are trying to get a ticket in the subway. The ticket clerk exercises power by ignoring your presence, making his immediate accommodating behavior unknown, though he knows your behavior is to get a ticket. This gives him power over you. This happens in all sorts of service situations as we saw in the taking out of a mortgage in Chapter 3. There is a need to avoid the situation where the customer feels like a supplicant. It is a major problem for government bureaucracies manifested by the intense loathing by the public for big (read bureaucratic) government. Too many bureaucrats do adopt behavior that signals that they have power. If public loathing is to change, this behavior needs to change first.

A high affiliation need manifests itself in the need to seek friendships, intimacy and mutual understanding. A good deal of behavior falls under this category, just as the consumer may buy with an eye to seeking the approval of friends or aspirational groups. Finally, there is the achievement need which is the need to do something better than has been done before. This was of particular interest to McClelland as he saw it as basic to an entrepreneurial society. Many an athlete feels the need to buy the best equipment if his or her need for achievement is to be satisfied.

McClelland viewed his basic motivations as being learnt rather than something innate, which means people acquire the disposition to be power-hungry or affiliation- or achievement-oriented. But for many social scientists McClelland's classification of basic motives is somewhat simplistic, while it is often claimed that too much is being demanded of his methodology of using projective techniques. But for many others it has proved a pragmatic set of constructs.

REVERSAL THEORY: MOTIVATION AND EMOTION

A particularly interesting theory that is essentially a motivation theory is reversal theory, a branch of *structural phenomenology*. Phenomenology focuses on subjective experience, and is discussed in depth in the next chapter; but reversal theory seems to fit more comfortably in this chapter. Structural phenomenology accepts, as a given, that *subjective* experience does not consist of a 'blooming, buzzing mass' of unrelated items and events but forms a meaningful, coherent structure for thinking, feeling and doing. In structural phenomenology, the interest lies in the ways in which experience can be structured and how the structuring of that experience changes over time.

Reversal theory employs structural phenomenology in explicating the mental structures lying behind motivation and emotion (Apter 1989). It contrasts with mainstream cognitive psychology that focuses on *rational* processes and neglects emotion and motivation. Cognitive psychology typically studies rational (cognitive) decision processes, ignoring the fact that important decisions are often stressful, with the decision-maker anxious, worried, embarrassed or excited. There is also the danger in cognitive psychology of conflating a logical process with a psychologically (empirically) grounded process.

The basic assertion in reversal theory is that as our *arousal* increases it becomes either increasingly pleasant or increasingly unpleasant. When high arousal is pleasant there is *excitement*, and when high arousal is unpleasant there is *anxiety*, both excitement and anxiety being emotional states. Similarly, when low arousal is unpleasant there is *boredom*, and when low arousal is pleasant we have *relaxation*. Anxiety and boredom create emotional tension: in anxiety because the arousal is too high and in boredom because it is too low. In an anxiety-avoidance mental mode, we seek to avoid anxiety and experience relaxation. In an excitement-seeking mental mode, we seek excitement to avoid boredom.

The theory is called *reversal theory* because there is a frequent reversal or switching between the two modes – of either being motivated to seek the high emotional arousal of excitement or to avoid the high emotional arousal of anxiety. If bored, we seek excitement. If anxious, we seek relaxation. Harre (1997), in claiming that the physiological aspects of emotion need not be specific to the emotion, quotes reversal theory in support, since a central claim of reversal theory is that people who are highly aroused may switch immediately between the two modes.

Reversal theory speaks of anxiety-avoidance or excitement-seeking 'modes'; the word *mode* rather than 'state' is used as the word 'state' is reserved for particular *values* of the modes. The two modes of high arousal/excitement and high arousal/anxiety are mutually exclusive in that people can be either in one mode or the other but not both at the same time. They are also exhaustive in that people in high arousal are always in one or the other of the two modes. This accounts for the use of the term 'mode' rather than the term 'mood'; it emphasizes being obligated to be in one mode or the other (see Figure 12.1).

Reversal theory claims that not only are people motivated to reduce or increase arousal intensity (depending on their mode), but the motivation also has a directional tendency. The theory is not claiming that motives alone determine the precise action taken (since this generally depends

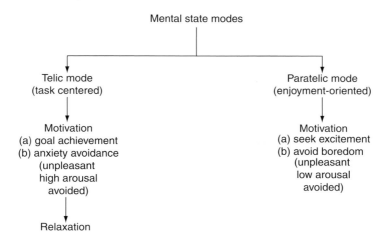

Figure 12.1   Reversal theory
Source: After Apter, 1989

also on beliefs) but simply that, at any one time, motivation must be concerned either with goal achievement or, alternatively, with just means and not ends. In a *telic mode* goal achievement is the primary motivation; consumers are task-oriented. But, in a *paratelic mode*, achieving the goal is secondary to the activity (means) itself; the consumer is motivated by enjoyment-seeking and being leisure-oriented. Thus in amateur sports, the goal of winning may be secondary to enjoying the game itself. In a telic mode, satisfaction is tied to making progress towards goal achievement, but in a paratelic mode the satisfaction comes from being involved with the activity itself because the satisfaction is intrinsic, not instrumental. The concept of paratelic mode can thus be related to the concept of *expressive behavior* discussed earlier in the book.

If in a telic mode, the focus is on goal achievement whereby means (activities) change as beliefs change as to the best means for goal achievement. In a paratelic mode, the focus is on means (activities) so that goals may change to ensure the continuation of the enjoyment. The telic mode is tied to a disposition to avoid the high arousal emotion of anxiety, while the paratelic mode is tied to a disposition to seek the high arousal of excitement.

Reversal theory claims that, while there will always be some felt anxiety or feelings of relaxation in the telic mode, this is never so in the paratelic mode. Similarly, there will always be some excitement or boredom occurring in the paratelic mode but never in the telic mode. This may sound counterintuitive in that we might expect both relaxation and anxiety to occur in the paratelic mode. But relaxation, as the opposite of anxiety, is always pleasant low arousal, not the unpleasant low arousal of boredom.

Why does anxiety not occur in a paratelic mode? The reason is because the paratelic mode provides protection against anxiety and consumers in a paratelic mode are less risk-averse and more open to buying. In a paratelic mode:

- There is the protection of feeling confident about dealing with any problems that come along
- Enjoying the activity is so absorbing that a person acts as if in a safety zone that is free of risk
- There is a sense of detachment from others even in threatening situations.

These three protections against anxiety are called *protection frames* as they (particularly the detachment frame) allow us to enjoy all emotions experienced when in the paratelic mode. This is reversal theory's explanation of our enjoyment of horror films where negative emotions are aroused.

We can relate the telic and paratelic modes to Thayer's (1996) work on moods. Moods are important in buying. When a consumer's spirits flag, the person holds back from buying. As reflected in consumer confidence measures, mood is a better indicator of downturns than the stock market. With an economic downturn, there is a sense of loss leading to less spending. In the summer of 1981, even though the economy was growing at 4 percent per annum, confidence measures suggested the subsequent dip (*The Economist*, 14 September 2002, p. 70). As already mentioned, Thayer argues that the central components of what we experience as moods are *energy* and *tension*. On this basis, as stated earlier in the book, he identifies four mood states arising from the two arousal continuums:

- *Calm-energy*. This is the optimal mood. It resembles the paratelic mode where there is an absence of anxiety. It is probably the mode we most admire in others when we view them as playing it 'cool'.
- *Calm-tiredness*. This mode also resembles a paratelic mode in that there is no stress, only a pleasant sense of calm-tiredness.
- *Tense-energy*. This goes with a telic mode. There is low-level anxiety, in preparation for a flight/fight response.
- *Tense-tiredness*. This also reflects a telic mode. Fatigue is mixed with nervousness, tension and anxiety, without relaxation. This is the mood that underlies depression with negative thoughts about oneself, leading to low self-esteem.

Apter (1989) argues that some people become locked into a telic or a paratelic mode. Those who get locked into a telic mode are constantly anxious about achievement. With a tense-energy mood in a telic mode there is a slight anxiety allied with energy. This mental state is probably common among high achievers. But a tense-tiredness mood in a telic mode is dysfunctional to both achievement and health. If we were permanently in a telic mode we would miss all the fun. On the other hand, while the paratelic mode embracing the mood of calm-energy makes us feel good, what we are doing must be *intrinsically* absorbing. In this mood consumers judge things more positively (as they do in an optimistic mood) and so are more susceptible to being persuaded. In a positive mood people reflect less and can be influenced as much by an invalid argument as by a valid one (Mackie and Worth 1989). The paratelic mode in a calm-tiredness mood is the mode to be in for a good night's sleep! To be locked completely into a paratelic mode results in a somewhat hedonistic lifestyle. A paratelic mode favors spending because there is less risk-aversion. Thus people spend more freely on holiday as they are more likely to be in a paratelic mode. On vacation we are most likely to break habits and experiment in trying out new products.

Because a product sampled on holiday can arouse emotional memories when recalled, this has given rise to *destination marketing*, whereby companies promote heavily in prime holiday areas. Beck's North America, the US division of the German brewery firm, has been one of the leaders in destination marketing in the belief that, if heavy promotion induces people to sample Beck's while on holiday, they will continue to buy when back home because they will associate Beck's with pleasant times. It might also be added that the consumer may have broken the habit of buying his old brand of beer so the new one is easier to accept. If a newspaper is more likely to be read in a telic mode (at breakfast or on the way to work) and an entertaining magazine in a paratelic mode (at weekends and so on), this is something advertisers need to keep in mind.

If being in one mode rather than the other is important to know in marketing, how can modes be changed? Whenever a change of mode is being induced, it changes the perceptions of ambiguous events: threatening when in a telic mode and pleasurably intriguing when in a paratelic mode. This is because the telic and paratelic modes can be regarded as distinct ways of interpreting experience. There is little 'tolerance for ambiguity' when in a telic mode because a person in a telic mode dislikes conflicting ways of interpreting the situation.

Reversal theory quotes three conditions that induce a switch from a telic to a paratelic mode and vice versa:

- The first condition is *satiation*, which builds up after a time to bring about a switch from one mode to another.
- The second condition giving rise to a reversal occurs when trying to act in one of the modes leads to *frustration*. Thus those in a telic mode who are unable to pursue their goal may just 'switch off' and fantasize or those in a paratelic mode who are frustrated in their excitement-seeking can be thrust into a telic mode. It would seem that many people suffering from goal frustrations are given relief by fantasizing, helped by advertising.
- The third condition is some *environmental happening* that inserts or removes one or more of the protective frames. 'When the going gets tough, the tough go shopping' – luxury shopping can be a highly pleasurable experience for those with a large disposable income as it is one way of changing from a telic to a paratelic mode. It might be added that luxury living is one way of combating loneliness, with luxury decried but never easily denied. Similarly, entering a place of entertainment can induce a paratelic mode, while any sudden loud noise or just entering one's place of work or one's office can induce a telic mode. This relates to another concept of reversal theory, namely the concept of 'cognitive synergy'.

Cognitive synergy is the experience of recognizing incompatible attributes in something. There are 'reversal synergies' and 'identity synergies'. In both cases synergistic effects are produced in that something appears to be X yet more than X. *Reversal synergy* occurs when the incompatible attributes follow each other as when, in the television advertisement, a man starts to walk up a wall and along the ceiling. *Identity* synergy occurs when some item, person or thing exhibits at one and the same time incompatible properties, as when, in an advertisement (already mentioned), a cheap, delicate-looking watch 'takes a licking and keeps on ticking'. Both synergies are (unknowingly?) commonly exploited in advertising for attention-getting by creating puzzlement. For those in a paratelic mode, synergies are enjoyed. For those in a telic mode, the synergies just irritate. This needs to be noted by advertisers who tend to assume their ads are going to be pleasant and attention-getting, regardless of mental state.

Not everyone switches easily from one mode to the other even when a change in conditions occurs. Switching is more difficult for some than for others so that one mode dominates. An operational measure of the degree to which one mode or the other dominates is provided by the *Telic Dominance Scale* mentioned by Apter (1989). Where the paratelic mode is dominant, people describe their experiences in an *evaluative* way, while those in a telic mode are more *factually* descriptive. Teenagers are much more likely to be paratelic-dominant, indulging in a wide variety of pursuits in a more spontaneous way, while those who are telic-dominant are more likely to be older married people, engaging in more planned activities as they seek to achieve their goals.

A company might usefully ask whether the buying of its product is conducted in a telic or paratelic mode. When in a telic mode consumers are just interested in efficiently conducting business and not in being entertained. When in a paratelic mode, consumers are seeking excitement, with boredom the chief sin. This is important to know. For example, consider the marketing of services. There are two types of pure services: (i) those such as banking and plumbing that are instrumental to utilitarian goals and (ii) those that are used, bought or consumed just for the enjoyment, such as a visit to Disneyland or the opera. Where the service is instrumental, customers are likely to shop in a telic mode, focused on efficiency and the satisfaction that comes from a feeling of progress being made towards achieving goals. What the customer wants to avoid are apprehensions, anxieties, fears, discourtesies and frustrations that might arise in the process of rendering the service. The customer wants the service provider to 'just get the job done' without fanfare. Any ambiguity is frustrating and distracting since the customer is just interested in goal achievement. Consumers are usually in a telic mode in a bank or pharmacy. What we term a business-like atmosphere is what is sought where the consumer perceives the service provider as reliable, customer-oriented, competent and responsive to special needs, with sales personnel perceived as courteous and accessible. When the service is to provide enjoyment (e.g. clubs), customer satisfaction/delight comes from the excitement and the avoidance of boredom. Whereas providing an exciting atmosphere in a bank would be out of keeping with that type of service, the atmosphere of any place of entertainment needs to be concerned with stimulating intrinsic liking and enjoyment.

While the essentials of good service are *customization* and *personalized execution*, there is a need to take account of whether customers are likely to be in a telic or paratelic mode. Many television 'instruction' programs, like programs on cooking, would benefit from knowing this. It can be very irritating to anyone watching the program who wants to learn to cook to find the instructor trying to be a comic.

Customization is realized to some extent by offering those options or features the consumer wants to buy. If it is 'bottom-up customization', the consumer is given a list of the options with corresponding prices and on that basis chooses what she wants. This does not lead to the same selection as occurs in 'top-down customization' where the consumer is given the price of a fully loaded car in terms of options and then deletes, one by one, the options he or she does not want. The top-down customization tends to result in more options being bought so that the price of the car is higher. This is not surprising, although it undermines the view of the consumer considering each attribute in isolation when that component or attribute is part of a system, in this case the car. We cannot consider an attribute in isolation when its meaning is tied to a whole. With bottom-up customization, the consumer is asked to visualize the functioning of the option in the whole car, while the top-down customization eliminates that need by showing the contribution of the option to the functioning of the whole system. There are, of course, other explanations in terms of the cognitive effort involved and the plausible claim that the initial price quoted becomes the 'anchor' price against which all other prices are compared. Those who undertake the bottom-up customization will be more sensitive to price.

CONCEPTUAL QUESTIONS COME BEFORE MATTERS OF TRUTH OR EMPIRICAL TESTING

A common complaint about research in the social sciences is that they often ignore the problem of ensuring concepts mean the same when used by different researchers. Conceptual questions come before matters of truth and empirical testing. It is all too common in marketing for definitions of conceptual variables to have little resemblance to the operational measures used to measure them in a study. The result is low reliabilities. Reliability is concerned with consistency. More formally, in statistics, the reliability of a result would be that part of the result that is due to permanent systematic effects which persist from sample to sample, as distinct from error effects which vary from one sample to another. Error effects are typically treated on the assumption that they are random without recognizing that many sources of error are in fact non-random, in which case they relate to the validity and not the reliability of the measures. Whereas reliability is concerned with consistency or agreement of data, validity is concerned with establishing that the measures do measure what they are supposed to measure so we can say the inferences made from the measures are justified. If the measures do not capture the concept, the results will not have validity. There is also the matter of alternative explanations of data; just confirming experimental data are consistent with hypotheses will not do. There can be rival hypotheses that fit the data equally well.

CASE: MY KEEPON

Toys 'R' Us is the toy retailer that obtained the exclusive rights to sell the new robot, My Keepon, in the US. The retailer is excited at the prospect of it being a great 'hit' in the Christmas sales of 2011. Developed as a therapeutic tool for autistic children in Japan by Hideki Kozima, a specialist in artificial intelligence and robotics at Miyagi University, the expectation was that a robot could establish an emotional bond with autistic children through supportive interaction with them. Autistic children tend to be overcome by social contact involving face-to-face interactions. It was suspected that by reducing the complexity of 'social' interaction by limiting communication to a few simple gestures on the part of a robot, autistic children could learn gradually to cope with normal human interaction. This led to the birth of My Keepon but only after considerable development costs. Dr Marek Michalowski in the US, a robotics expert with a background in psychology and computer science, went to Japan to work in Hideki Kozima's laboratory. He wrote software to enable My Keepon to dance and bob its head to music and swoon to slow dance routines. Michalowski made a video of My Keepon's performance which appeared on YouTube, generating nearly three million plays. It soon became apparent that My Keepon might also be marketed as a toy for children and Kozima and Michalowski approached the British toy maker WOW! Stuff to market the robot, promising that a percentage of sales would go towards autism research. The toy maker developed new software for the robot to enable it to better interact with people, while at the same time replacing the expensive custom-made parts with off-the-shelf components. It was at this stage that the robot was given the name My Keepon. The word 'kee' is an umbrella word for yellow, while 'pon' suggests bounce to give the name Keepon. My Keepon is like someone composed of two yellow tennis balls, one on top of the other, with the top ball being given two wide-open glass eyes and a button for a nose.

In clinical trials it was found that autistic children made more eye contact with the robot than with humans. The autistic children interacted with the robot in ways that are rare with people, for example touching and holding. There are two modes of operating for the new My Keepon. In the first mode the robot responds to touching like a pat on the head with a varied number of gestures such as wiggling, turning the head or even sneezing. If it is hit on the head six times it will bob up and down six times, emitting a range of beeps and other sounds. The second mode is the dance mode. My Keepon can dance, matching the rhythm and tempo of the music, but will vary its dance routine even if the music is the same. In fact the unexpectedness of My Keepon's responses is what gives the robot such novelty appeal. If neglected, it will cry for attention. It bobs, bows as it dances, while its microphone picks up any music, even tunes that are whis-tled or hummed, and takes the music's tempo and rhythm while adding a touch of randomness which provides the pleasure of not knowing what is coming next.

My Keepon is to be priced at around $50 and plans are under way to offer robotic enthusiasts the tools to program My Keepon to respond in even more creative ways. This idea, if implemented, would personalize the robot for the individual buyer.

Case questions

1. Why would it be argued that My Keepon, when in action, generates an emotional response in viewers? Include in your answer the notions of novelty, curiosity, surprise and anthropomorphism.
2. How might My Keepon facilitate supportive interaction among children?
3. How should Toys 'R' Us promote My Keepon in the store to indicate its novelty and distinguish it from similar toys?

DISCUSSION QUESTIONS ON CHAPTERS 11 AND 12 (SOCIAL PSYCHOLOGY)

1. Social psychology accepts that consumer behavior is influenced by both the presence of other people and by interacting with others. How does this modify the perspective of the individual decision-maker selecting goals, selecting options and choosing optimally?
2. Discuss the concept of cognitive dissonance. If known to be common among a target group of consumers, how might knowing this present an opportunity for changing attitudes?
3. If a consumer constantly talks about football or about his or her health, this indicates these are matters of concern to them. Show the relationship of these concerns to emotion and values.
4. It is argued that the concept of 'emotion' cannot be defined in terms of some essence that makes it unambiguously distinguishable, emotions nonetheless have a family resemblance in that they all exhibit a mix of several features. Take two emotions to illustrate this.
5. Discuss the notion of a consumer's 'high involvement' with a product and its relationship to a product having meaning for the consumer and the notion of an emotional bond with a product.
6. Can you think of buying situations where the 'reversal theory' has explanatory value?
7. 'Persuasion in selling is an offer of affiliation and successful persuasion leads to an acceptance of that offer.' Discuss.
8. In the text, a distinction is made between tactics for persuading a con-sumer to take some action and tactics for overcoming resistance to

change. Is this a meaningful distinction in that consumers will typically have some beliefs that have to be changed in all persuasive endeavors?

9. 'Advertising may activate emotion but the problem is still to channel that emotion in the direction of the brand advertised.' Discuss.

10. 'In a market of undifferentiated products, symbols can be decisive.' Explain.

Chapter 13

Sociology

SCOPE OF SOCIOLOGY

Sociology investigates society, social institutions, societal relationships and social interactions. There is thus an overlap between social psychology and sociology but the paradigms in sociology reflect more diversity of perspectives, each at one time or another having been viewed as the cutting edge of the discipline. The sociological categories below are the subject matter of this chapter. They are those of Jeffrey Alexander (1987) in his history of sociology since the end of the Second World War:

1. Structural-functionalism
2. Conflict theory
3. Exchange theory
4. Symbolic interactionism
5. Ethnomethodology
6. Cultural sociology.

Max Weber (1864–1920) and Emile Durkheim (1858–1917) were founding fathers of modern sociology. But, despite being contemporaries, they showed little recognition of each other's work. This was because their work came from different intellectual perspectives: Weber's views were grounded in the historical facts and situation, while Durkheim sought to develop 'pure types' as the building blocks for a theory of society, together with a rejection of any notion of sociology being built up from individual decision-making. These sorts of methodological differences run throughout sociology.

STRUCTURAL-FUNCTIONALISM

Functionalism's aspiration is to understand how a system like a society attains its ends through the contributions made by its components or subsystems. Functionalism in sociology studies the contribution to society of each of its subsystems (e.g. social groups, classes, institutions and so on) to explain their enduring presence. The perspective adopted by functionalism is that the existence and persistence of these subsystems is explainable by the contribution made by the subsystem to the *maintenance* of society.

Thus a functionalist study of marketing would focus on its contribution to society's prosperity and the success of corporations in a free market economy.

Structural-functionalism in sociology developed from functionalism in *social anthropology*. Social anthropology also conceptualizes society (or smaller units such as communities, social classes or business organizations) as a system; a system is defined as a set of interdependent parts that together form a unitary whole, with the purpose of achieving some objective. Social anthropology *explains* the components of society in terms of the contribution each makes to maintaining the whole system of society as a viable entity.

Structural-functionalism in sociology, as developed by Talcott Parsons (1951), imputes the existence and maintenance of the *social order* or *structure* in society to the *internalization* by members of society of the social norms of that society. Internalization implies the acceptance of such norms as one's own, while these social norms or societal norms are the socially approved means or standards of behavior to be followed in society in various walks of life. Societal norms influence and sometimes even determine consumer behavior. The consumer judges not only whether a product will fulfill some technical function, but whether it is socially appropriate or socially approved.

This section on Parsons' structural-functionalism provides a discussion of that influence and its limitations. Adherence to social norms facilitates social acceptance and, through that acceptance, generates a person's sense of personal worth. The social norms that guide action (such as buying action) Parsons viewed as having been internalized through both the *socialization process* by living in society and the *process of social control* (e.g. through social sanctions). Violation of *cultural* norms leads to feelings of *shame*, while violating the norms of one's social milieu results in feelings of *embarrassment*. Feelings of shame arise when, say, the consumer sees and accepts the connection between his or her actions (e.g. deshopping) and being perceived as violating cultural norms. Feelings of embarrassment are less intense than shame and arise when, say, the middle-class consumer believes others within her social milieu have seen her act (e.g. buying from a thrift shop) in a way that falls below the expectations of her peer group. To avoid embarrassment a person may show why what she did was perfectly normal, just as saying you did something for a dare can make the action acceptable. For someone to feel guilty, his or her actions must violate the law of the land or of God. We would accept that a consumer would feel guilty if he or she were caught stealing in the store.

People who are driven by the desire for social approval and acceptance are likely to have difficulty in acting decisively in the interests of the organization in case they suffer social condemnation or at least the disapproval of positive reference groups. Anticipating embarrassment and disapproval has prevented many an otherwise clever person from becoming an effective leader. Also, embarrassment at being seen to change one's mind has led to the non-adoption of worthwhile policies in a company when intellectual honesty often demands a change in beliefs.

Parsons imputed to society myriad social *roles* with each role having attached to it obligations or expected patterns of behavior. There could be *role conflict, role strain* and *role anomie*. To illustrate, a professional purchasing manager's role of 'advisor' can generate 'role conflict' with his or her role of 'policeman' in ensuring that commercial aspects of the purchase are given due weight. Similarly, there is 'role strain' whenever the purchasing manager is pulled in different directions by pressures from suppliers and users, and 'role anomie' when the purchasing manager is unclear about his or her exact role. It can be the same with the consumer. The perceived role of the consumer as ethical buyer can be in conflict with the role of efficient (cost-minimizing) buyer. The consumer can experience role strain when members of her family make competing demands in terms of items to buy. Finally, there can be role anomie when the consumer is unsure about whether her primary role in the family is one of gatekeeper, facilitator or advisor.

Parsons advocated an all-encompassing system of concepts for sociology as a basis for theory development, since concepts (as mechanisms or categories for classification) are the building blocks of theory. Robert Merton (1949), a prominent sociologist at Columbia, disagreed and argued that Parsons' attempt at developing an all-encompassing system of concepts would prove both futile and sterile: sterile in the sense that it would not have within it the seeds for its own development. Concepts arise as mechanisms for classification as a science advances. But concepts cannot just be created in an observational vacuum but emerge from experience as the need arises. Instead of seeking to develop a foundational overall system of abstract concepts, Merton suggested the need for theories of the *middle range* with concepts that can be given operational definition, that is, can be defined in observational terms to possess referential-meaning. It is easy to invent concepts of a highly abstract nature allegedly describing a mental or decision process or whatever which, though possessing sense-meaning, cannot be given any concrete referential-meaning.

Any concepts in theories of the middle range also need to possess conceptual clarity and this conceptual clarity must come before theory and quantification. Pinker (2007) claims that even the most abstract concepts are understood against a backdrop of concreteness. This is an echo of the claim that all abstract models, being a human creation, will to some extent reflect physical reality, while any descriptive model will to some extent be selective and so an abstraction. While this may be so, it is also true that the 'backdrop of concreteness' may be too blurred to establish what philosophers call a *rule-of-correspondence* between some abstract concept and the feature of physical reality that is of interest.

The most common criticism of Parsons is with regard to the prominence and significance he gives to the role of social norms in influencing behavior. Since the economist ignored social norms altogether, this was a needed counterbalance at the time. Bleicher (1982), an advocate of an interpretive (hermeneutic) social science, claims that under Parsons the spontaneity of individuals is all but obliterated, with the *intentionality* of action merely reflecting norms or society approved values and standards. But are people this constrained by social norms? Social norms operate roughly like rules in the game of chess; they may govern the overall game but are unlikely to predict the individual moves. Also, in conditions of high social and geographical mobility, people mix less with close friends and associates and are obliged to spend their time with casual acquaintances who are much less likely to frown on the violation of social norms. Social norms in Western societies act less and less as detailed constraints on the behavior of citizens though this is not true in much of the world.

In marketing we are more interested in the social norms of the subgroups to which our target consumers belong; subgroups whose norms may deviate a good deal from societal norms. Social but also subgroup norms are always something to consider. They may even suggest when customer demands are unreasonable, for example in demanding a level of service in a restaurant that does not cohere with the low prices charged.

A major criticism of Parsons' functional approach as applied to society is that it is ahistorical, too insensitive to the place of *symbolic structures* like the symbolism of the Supreme Court in American society and too concerned with how society maintains *equilibrium* or its balance in society rather than with how society *changes*. We cannot just be concerned with maintaining equilibrium in society if we have progress in mind.

While people may indeed be less influenced by societal norms, this does not mean they are not greatly influenced by *reference group norms*. If we look at buying, consumers as a whole may not seem to be conforming to some common set of societal norms. Yet their behavior does not reflect aberrant individualism but typically is *conformative* to the norms of some subculture or social group. Marketers may be paying less attention to identifying the norms of society but only in order to pursue, as a matter of some importance, an understanding of the norms of the groups their target audiences regard as positive (or negative?) reference groups.

CONFLICT THEORY

Conflict theory imputes to society the dynamism of constructive conflict in bringing about progress and change. Conflict theory arose in opposition to 'Parsonianism', caricatured as 'order theory' by critics. Coser (1956) critiques functionalism within a functionalist framework, pointing to the positive aspects of conflict for maintaining social systems: all conflict need not be destructive. There can be constructive conflict. In fact, whether in society or within a company or marketing department, managers ideally strive to create an organization where constructive conflict is vigorous and sharp but polarization and rancor are rare.

The bitterest attack on Parsonian functionalism was made by Rex (1961) (brought up amid the conflicts of South Africa) who asserted that the root metaphor for functionalism is the human *organism*, specifically physiology that does not undergo fundamental changes after maturity but maintains equilibrium or breaks down altogether. Parsons, he argues, assumes such high conformity to social norms that, as a matter of definition, it logically must lead to social stability. In other words, the claim of social stability becomes simply a conceptual truth. For Rex such conformity depends completely on a strong individual internalization of social values and norms. In contrast, Rex sees people's actions as self-serving and plays down the role of social norms in bringing about social stability. Instead Rex sees conflict as bringing about change, not social norms bringing about stability. In line with this way of thinking, conflict among rival firms for the consumer's dollar brings about innovation, not market stability. This is important since technical innovation is probably the major forcing variable in Western societies behind the growth in GDP (gross domestic product).

The basic difficulty for Rex involves explaining how order comes about when everyone is pursuing individual self-interest. (This is a problem for all such individualistic theories, a common concern at present in the US.) For Rex, order is imposed by those with the coercive power to enforce their will (shades of postmodernism here), though he also speaks of the possibility of a 'truce' whereby selfish motives are curbed in the interest of societal well-being as a whole. At the societal level there is this conflict between individual self-interest and the interests of society. Not everything a citizen wants to do is beneficial to society, for example using wrappings that go on to pollute the environment.

Individualism is the doctrine of the primacy of the individual over any social group or society. The strong version emphasizes individual self-reliance and the individual as the sole possessor of his talents and ability, owing nothing to society and owed nothing in return. Individualism emerged with the development of market societies in the eighteenth century, with individuals expected to take responsibility for their own lives and to undertake a broader range of economic and social choices. It deprecates big government and champions the role of the private sphere. Individualism has a natural attraction for marketers though its detractors see it as fostering greed and weakening societal bonds. There is always some sort of tension between individual desires and societal welfare.

The government is typically charged with developing and passing laws that bring about social order as it does in regulating various markets. The government in Western democracies is also the major buyer of goods of all types and this gives rise to debate as to the role of central government. Adam Smith in *The Wealth of Nations* noted three obligations of government: defense, administering justice and assuming public works which no one individual or private group would find it profitable to undertake. Milton Friedman, the economist, questioned the need for governments undertaking anything other than defense and administering justice, arguing that the market could supply all else except for the need to control the money *supply* to keep inflation down and secure economic stability (this claim is the core of the doctrine known as *monetarism*). We might ask ourselves whether Friedman is right. Despite the claims of neo-anarchists, government provision is needed when national coordination is a requisite on some topic like national security. What changed things in nineteenth-century Britain, from just insisting that the government should only be charged with national security, were the sanitary and public health issues brought on by factory and urban living during the industrial revolution. But a major motivating factor was the acceptance of the germ theory of disease popularized by Pasteur and Lister in the 1860s which meant everyone (the rich as well as the poor) was vulnerable unless there were regulations enforced by a central body. The *next* thing was the recognition of the need for everyone to be able to read and write to cope with the demands of newly emerging industries. A national policy was called for and national schools the result. With the arrival of the internal combustion engine there also arose the need for better roads, not just in London but throughout the country, while only the central government could coordinate the standardization needed with the coming of the railways. All other subsequent government services arose from this overall need to coordinate and enforce a national need on a national level. This includes the need to prevent the consumer from being 'ripped off' in one way or another. We have seen how easy it can be to mislead the consumer. Deceptive advertising has always presented a problem for governments because of the hypocrisy of enacting any laws against deception in advertising that does not include political advertising, the most deceptive advertising of all. Political advertising enjoys immunity from accountability for its assertions and this is what political advertisers have not been slow to exploit.

A basic issue in conflict theory is over the concept of 'conflict'. In society at large where there are permanent and clear conflicts of interest, the law usually comes into play. But elsewhere there is less clarity about the notion of conflict. Thus participants in group decision-making or a decision-making unit (DMU) will have differences arising from differential self-interest; differential perceptions of reality; differential information possessed and differential views about the consequences of proposed actions. There can be disagreement over consequences since knowledge as to likely consequences depends somewhat on experience and the experiences of participants can differ widely. If these differences lead to aggressive confrontation this is a *conflict situation*. But if all disagreement involving heated discussion is to be defined as conflict, some forms of conflict will be *constructive* and educational. What we try to do in marketing is to train people to manage the conflict which does arise on occasion in dealing with customers.

EXCHANGE THEORY

Exchange theory views social interactions, social structures and social order as exchange relationships which challenge any view that claims that internalized social norms alone are strong enough to direct action. As with functionalism, exchange theory had its origins in anthropology before being adopted by sociology. There are four major variations of exchange theory: (i) exchange behaviorism; (ii) exchange structuralism; (iii) Emerson's power exchange theory; (iv) Heath's exchange decision theory.

Exchange behaviorism: In its most influential form exchange behaviorism subscribes to *methodological individualism* by claiming it is *individuals* negotiating with others that determine social exchange results. Exchange behaviorism, associated with George C. Homans (1961), draws on a combination of operant conditioning and economic rationality. Exchange theories in exchange behaviorism take their perspective from behaviorism but go back to using the term 'reward' (not reinforcement) and substituting 'cost' for 'punishment' which brings then more in line with the cost–benefit approach of economics.

Homans agrees that functionalism puts too much faith in social norms as a basis for understanding behavior in society. But Homans's objection is that social norms change all the time and are never detailed enough to predict behavior. Social norms act as rules about how things should be done, but are apt to change through time (e.g. on wearing hats and ties), while there are many, many ways for action to be socially appropriate. He would tell marketing that societal or group norms are not sufficiently compelling to confidently predict action in a particular situation; that we need to look at actual behavior as a check.

Social interactions for Homans are a matter of offering rewards and applying sanctions (costs) so that a person's responses in interactions depend on his or her calculation of net profit or net benefits. This coheres with rational choice theory (RCT). The net profit from an exchange is reward minus cost. (A) in interaction with (B) tries to persuade (B) to give up something that is less costly to (B) than it is valuable to (A) in exchange for something more valuable to (B) than it is costly to (A). The exchange must be profitable to both parties. This is treated as a truism in negotiating with buyers and in consumers negotiating with service providers such as house painters.

What is missing from this cost–benefit perspective are the *intangible* rewards and costs, in that, for example, each party in negotiation will try to maintain 'face' and be equally concerned with maintaining (or on occasion saving) the 'face' of the other party. The rule to follow is to view the other person as always vulnerable to perceived slights or put-downs. This could be a rule for all our interactions with others since *humiliation* is particularly hurtful as it is perceived as a *loss* of status or self-esteem and the loss is felt more than what would be considered a corresponding gain. Humiliation is perhaps the single most hurtful of the self-assessment emotions and a whole nation can feel its sting in which case it can provide the motivation to seek redress in international affairs.

The desire to maximize material reward is seldom the sole motive. There are many motives at work and these can be both multiple and conflicting, as indeed can human values in that even liberty and equality can conflict. As Lepper and Greene (1978) show, the use of material rewards, at least in educational settings, can even diminish the intrinsic interest in the educational material itself. (It was for this reason that Ludwig Wittgenstein, the philosopher, recommended that those with an interest in philosophy should not study it for a degree as this took away the pleasure of doing philosophy.)

Homans (1950) openly subscribed to *methodological individualism* in arguing that social phenomena can only be explained by reference to the motivations of individuals, not groups. He was also a reductionist claiming sociology could be reduced to individual psychology, that is, sociological concepts are reducible to concepts describing individual behavior, though he does not deny that the group concepts have some utility. His book *The Human Group* (1950) caused a stir among fellow sociologists at the time of publication as Homans appeared to be preparing the ground for sociology to be absorbed by psychology.

If Parsons underplays self-interest and overplays the normative, Homans redresses the balance with his emphasis on 'calculable motives'. For Homans feelings and value inclinations are regarded as simply the result of profit anticipations. He underplays the role of emotions or feelings of emotion in assuming all action can be neatly expressed in a cost–benefit calculation. Which of these two is more right is an empirical question which no amount of surveys could conclusively answer. But we should disabuse ourselves of the ingenuous notion that costs and benefits can always be measured. Take the war in Iraq. The measurable cost in dollars is around one trillion but there is no money figure that can be put on the 100,000 Iraqi lives or the roughly 4,500 American lives that were lost, together with the lives of British soldiers and other nationalities and the cost of the injured. In addition, there is the heartache of the many people who had to flee their homes, with much of their country destroyed. And certainly no money figure can be put on the benefits which seem to be summed up by the phrase 'the world is a better place without Saddam Hussein while it prepares the way for democracy'. Many regard those who feel it 'was all worth it' as having a curious set of values that determine such trade-offs. When we have no common metric like money for expressing costs against benefits, values will be the final court of appeal.

Houston and Gasseheimer (1987) take critics of exchange behaviorism in marketing to task. They claim that, if there is to be any theory at all of market exchange, the all-rational, utility-maximizing consumer must necessarily be clearly alive and well. But the real issue lies not in whether consumers on occasion behave like economic man (they clearly do) but how much buying behavior can be satisfactorily explained by such a narrow view of human motivation. The economist's view of rationality opens Homans to the criticism leveled against all who draw on economic rationality, namely as to whether (except in a laboratory setting) people only calculate the individual cost to themselves versus the corresponding rewards. Mary Douglas (1986), the British anthropologist, predicts that any rational choice theory based purely on individual self-interest will fail to explain the behavior of individuals in groups (e.g. in industrial buying). Douglas is struck by the universality of 'self-sacrifice' despite the fact that opting out and being a 'free rider' is more enticing. In ignoring feelings, emotion, sentiment and sense of obligation, exchange behaviorism represents *egoistic hedonism*, namely that of a material reward-maximizing, cost-avoiding image of man.

While there is danger in adopting this one-dimensional perspective of man, motivated solely by self-interest, there is also the allied danger in assuming 'universal man' where people are motivated similarly by the same set of motives at all times and places. Consumer buying, if viewed overall, is not just a search for technical performance but also a search for status, prestige and personal integrity, which cannot readily be accommodated in exchange behaviorism. All of us seek *respect* but many of us are also vigorous in our efforts to achieve status. Companies today recognize this by giving fancy titles to subordinates, so that seemingly every MBA entering banking in New York is given the title of Vice-President.

Exchange structuralism: Exchange structuralism is the exchange theory of Peter M. Blau (1964). This version broadens the concept of rewards to embrace intangibles like social approval, esteem/respect and power over others. In fact Blau defines social exchange as embracing all behavior that is motivated by the expectation of some return or response from another. But this is still too limited a view of human motivation in that it excludes behavior motivated by duty or integrity since the intention is always to get something in return. However, in rejecting the concept of a completely economic man (basic to exchange behaviorism) Blau adopts a truer perspective of the consumer in that he claims:

- People rarely pursue one goal to the exclusion of all others. Consumers typically do have multiple and conflicting goals in buying.
- People are frequently inconsistent in their preferences.
- People rarely have complete information on alternatives.
- People never free themselves from social commitments that can constrain choices.

Emerson's power exchange theory: The exchange theories of both Homans and Blau leave themselves open to the charge of being tautologies. The tautology arises from the difficulty of defining and measuring the 'values' of participants in the exchange independently of their behavior. And values are always the final court of appeal when it comes to trade-offs. With Homans and Blau it is easy to say, when predictions prove false, that the measurement of 'values' was wrong so it becomes impossible to falsify their theories. Emerson (1976) sought to bypass this issue by viewing not the individual but the exchange *relationship* as the 'unit of analysis'. The individual agent's or actor's values are less central when the focus is on some ongoing relationship, though this is at the expense of seeking explanations at the individual level.

Emerson first distinguishes exchange theory in microeconomics from exchange theory in sociology. Exchange theory in microeconomics assumes transactions (i.e. individual paired exchanges where something concrete passes) are independent, one-off events. In contrast, Emerson regards sociological exchange theory as concerned with the ongoing relationship; social relationships that continue over time. Emerson agrees that people act in general to produce consequences which are beneficial to them. But any such actions are subject to satiation and diminishing marginal utility. This leads Emerson to argue that any ongoing relationship will result in a sense of interdependence which leads to less than rational (self-interested) motives coming into play, such as the norm of sharing, continuation of the group, altruism and so on. In other words, from repetitive exchanges emerge normative (rule/norm-governed) constraints on the use of one's power. The longer the relationship between, say, salespeople and their customers, the harder it is likely to be for either the buyer or the salesperson to be purely 'hardnosed'. This is because *supportive* interaction through time moves in the direction of increased liking. Each becomes a beneficiary of allegiance through supportive interactions, resulting in identification with the other's fortunes. This supports the notion of salespeople aiming at supportive interaction with buyers so that mutual sentiment develops which can facilitate being chosen first.

Like Homans, Emerson draws on the principles of operant conditioning. But he also wants to know how established relationships are affected by the use of power and the lack of balance in power among participants. If the exchange relationship shows a higher dependency of (B) on (A), then (A) has a power advantage over (B). The consequence is that (A) can elicit increasing costs on (B) within that exchange. This leads to the conclusion that, for bargaining to result in a fair deal for both sides, the power on each side should be roughly equal. This is true also for negotiations between management and unions. If unions have disproportionate power (as after the Second World War with the printing unions) they seek to dictate their terms. On the other hand, if management is disproportionately powerful, union action will be discounted. The same goes for countries. If two countries in negotiation are radically different in power, the more powerful is unlikely to strike a deal considered fair by impartial observers unless pressure is brought to bear on them from other countries. But every power advantage creates an unbalanced exchange which in turn gives rise to pressure for balance. Also, if one group has reason to believe its power will increase (e.g. through coalitions), it will focus on bringing about the expected increase rather than negotiation at the time. In any case, when conflict is acute it is inevitable that negotiations will not only be long drawn out but probably inconclusive, with a certain amount of vagueness in the settlement.

Whenever a supplier is a monopolist or quasi-monopolist, the supplier has a power advantage over the buyer. Thus, consider Microsoft's Windows. Logic suggests the following strategies are likely to be adopted by customer (B) to redress a power imbalance with monopolist (A):

- Pressure for decreasing the value to (B) of (A)'s offering, for example by looking for substitutes that can perform the same functions. Thus Linux (or more correctly the GNU) operating system, an open source software, has been adopted by many who hate the monopolist style of Microsoft and long to be free of its clutches.
- Pressure to increase the number of alternative sellers/suppliers that will supply (B), for example by looking to suppliers from other countries.
- Pressure to increase the value of the reinforcement provided by (B) to (A), for example paying on time or with cash.

Heath's exchange decision theory: This is the fourth and last of the exchange theories. Of particular interest to marketers is the addition of decision theory to exchange theory (Heath 1976). The focus in decision theory is on choosing from among many alternatives, whereas other exchange theories, linked as they are to conditioning, suggest the process of conditioning removes alternatives over time.

Heath claims that exchange theorists have typically adopted the 'rational choice model' that assumes consumers choose in conditions of certainty which means they can rank alternatives in order of preference and select the one that comes top of the list. He argues that such riskless choices are rare in practice. On these grounds Heath criticizes the compensatory (multiattribute) model because of its failure to take account of risk. This is true. Thus, while the perceived outcomes or consequences of purchasing one or other of two products may suggest identical utility, in practice the probability of actually achieving these outcomes will differ. This means there is a need to consider the probability of success.

Of particular importance to Heath are *consumer expectations* which are not just based on what is on offer but on past experiences or the experiences of contemporaries. This is why customer orientation should be viewed as matching/exceeding customer expectations, with the recognition that customer *expectations* will be based on:

- What is suggested by one's experience and that of others
- What competition is offering
- What has been promised and what costs (money and effort) are involved.

Heath believes that any theory of rational choice should take account of (i) the absence of complete information being available in order to distinguish between the truth of the consumer's actual beliefs and the rationality of what she does, given her beliefs; (ii) the likelihood of information only being collected to the extent needed to determine a brand preference and not to become an expert on the product itself; (iii) time pressures; and (iv) goals other than self-interest.

EXCHANGE THEORY IN MARKETING

Exchange theory attracts marketing academics since it offers the possibility of explaining and predicting the amount of (X) exchanged for (Y). At one time a basic claim was that the pivotal focus of marketing should be on the exchange relationship (Kotler and Levy 1969; Bagozzi 1975/1979; Hunt 1983) or the transaction (Kotler 1972). Whether or not there is a specific marketing exchange theory, Dwyer et al. (1987) claim marketing theory has persistently focused on exchange. If this is so, it is more in lip service than in research. The authors claim that research on the exchange relationship in buying has treated buyer–seller exchanges as discrete events (as the economist tends to do) not as ongoing relationships. In making out a case for the ongoing relationship, they are in fact simply repeating Emerson in moving away from a microeconomic viewpoint towards a sociological one. This is important as some exchanges are steeped in social nuances. Thus fundraisers in universities do not go around talking about what they are prepared to give to large donors. Association with the university is a given, but putting the donor's name on a building and so on has to be introduced with finesse as if it has been done simply to acknowledge the public standing of the donor. Canvassing with the caviar and soliciting with the salad is not confined to corporate salespeople.

One ongoing exchange relationship in marketing is *franchising* where franchisees invest in the franchiser's supplies and promotions, while franchisers undertake training and provide specialized know-how on running the business. There is inevitably going to be conflict over the authority and responsibility of the parties and over the fairness in the relationship.

The question arises as to whether day-to-day consumer shopping (choosing from a display and paying for it at a cash desk) captures the core meaning of exchange. Whether it does or not, day-to-day shopping should certainly modify our thinking on the nature of exchange.

If we were to sum up on exchange theory we might argue that, as so far developed, it shows the rationality of the overall act of exchange which is inadequate for the job of explaining the various buying actions carried out by the consumer.

SYMBOLIC INTERACTIONISM

Symbolic interactionism imputes to social interaction a process by which people in social interaction come to interpret and understand their situation. The study of social interaction is a major interest of sociologists though this interest has been shared with social psychologists addressing the question of how people interact with others and the world. People interact with others for (a) material, (b) emotional and (c) intellectual sustenance, constrained by the desire to preserve individuality, and not being at the mercy of others. The material that is exchanged may be tangible but much else is symbolic. All communication in social interaction carries not only a message but also a tone and all messages need to carry the right tone, avoiding anything sounding peremptory, condescending or obsequious. Tone is part of the *symbolism* in an interaction and there is a need to take account of it.

George Herbert Mead (1934), a pragmatist philosopher, sociologist and social psychologist, pioneered the study of interaction. For Mead, the 'self' is distinguished by its 'reflexivity', that is, it can be an object of itself. People can reflect on their own behavior and their own situation. A problem for Mead is how this 'self' is able to take on the different roles to guide its conduct. Mead introduced the concept of 'generalized other', which is the concept we possess of other people as social actors that arises through a process of abstracting from the common elements found in the attitudes and actions of others. In adopting the role of this 'generalized other' an individual internalizes many shared values and this lies behind the ability to engage in cooperative activities with others. This notion of generalized other and the role it might play in behavior has not been widely accepted though it seems to be a useful notion.

Mead accepted the behaviorist paradigm that reinforcement channels behavior, though he had a broader view than the behaviorist of what constitutes 'reinforcement'. While people choose whatever promises to provide the most gratification, Mead regarded *social adjustment* as being the most important gratification sought: people are primarily motivated to choose what most advances social adjustment. The consumer, like everyone else, wants to fit in to her social milieu, and consumer purchases, whether for personal use or presents for others, can facilitate that goal. Consumers are anxious to integrate or even to be assimilated into various social groups and this process involves achieving a level of social adjustment. The problem of social adjustment is a matter of getting the right balance between going along with the group and maintaining individuality. This is a theme exploited in advertising, promising group acceptance through use of the product or, alternatively, freedom to be oneself.

Most people talk of the need for *empathy* in understanding others, with empathy defined as 'feeling oneself into' or putting oneself in another's shoes, in contrast with *sympathy* which is 'feeling with'. This concept of empathy raises many problems, with a more recent view defining empathy as the ability to *simulate* the relevant situation of the other which, combined with some knowledge of their personality, helps to understand their present and likely actions. Empathy, as a process of simulating the context and thinking of the other, is probably the most defensible view to date.

There are at least four versions of symbolic interactionism: (i) symbolic meaning approach; (ii) collective behavior approach; (iii) self-theory approach; and (iv) the dramaturgical model.

The symbolic meaning approach: The approach is associated with Herbert Blumer (1969), a student of Mead's. Symbolic meaning is concerned with what some item, person, event or thing symbolizes, signifies, stands for or connotes for the individual. For Blumer, it is the symbolic meaning of things that *directs* people's (consumer) action. This goes beyond just saying that perceptions lie behind what action is taken since it is identifying the mechanism at work, namely what things symbolize is the motivator of action. Thus gifts can have a strong symbolism of friendship and receiving a gift from a friend makes the gift mean more than its market value. Gifts contribute to social bonding but also create social debts that people feel obligated to repay. Gift-giving carries risks of causing offense. Thus the gift may be perceived as inappropriate or inadequate. To what extent this occurs will depend on the existing relationship history between giver and receiver.

When we say 'meaning' directs behavior, we are saying in effect that it is *beliefs* about what something signifies (including symbolizes) for a person's *wants* that direct his or her actions. On this basis, 'meaning' in such a context is not something distinct from wants and beliefs but a convenient way of capturing in one construct the idea of wants and beliefs directing action. From Blumer's perspective, it is what a product 'stands for' or signifies or symbolizes in the mind of the consumer, as opposed to just the physical properties of the product, that is of interest in understanding consumer behavior.

'Symbolism' is a key concept for the whole of social science since various items, people or events can be sufficiently symbolic to activate emotional memories and responses so that, for example, viewers of a commercial can, on occasion, come to believe they have a special relationship with the characters in a slice-of-life advertisement and respond as strongly as if the relationship were genuine. As Humphrey (1983) says, there is the symbolism of characters performing under the viewer's own banner (e.g. like a flag) or there is symbolism that arouses sympathy with the character's situation emanating from actual experience or imagination.

Blumer's methodology is interpretive. For Blumer, *interpretation* is a process into which enters the symbolic meaning of things, molded by people's needs, particularly the need to act in a confident manner with others. Previously, we have defined 'meaning' in the sense of the significance of things for us. This significance can be in terms of what something symbolizes so the significance can be determined by the symbolism evoked. Whatever it is we are interpreting ('the text'), it has a symbolism which we take into account in our interpretations. Interpretations are a function of three interrelated elements: (a) experience, (b) perspective and (c) the needs/wants of those doing the interpretation so, that what things mean in social interaction depends on how these things relate to our experience, perspective and needs/wants. What things conjure up or symbolize for consumers influences buying behavior. Sidney Levy (1981), in marketing, illustrates this well:

> The idea of going out to eat at a restaurant interacts with the meanings of the various types of establishments to fit the sex and age grading, and family status dimensions... Lower class cafes and fancy restaurants

are adult in meaning, placed for adults at work away from home (truck stops, executive business lunches). At the heights, haute cuisine with its subtle sauces and other exotic efforts symbolizes an elite use of leisure, an extreme degree of refinement of the palate, and attendant sybaritic sensibilities. People eat dishes they never have at home and go beyond ordinary meats to expensive cuts and seafoods.

(Levy 1981: 58)

Although Blumer acknowledges authorities such as the legal system can initiate action to ensure compliance, they are for him more a framework within which actions are carried out, not determining of individual action itself. Social forces are constraints only, just like the rules of chess are constraints but do not determine individual moves. Bulmer in fact downplays the causal role of social forces that are so beloved by other sociologists. People interpret (give meaning to) a situation which then becomes the basis for action. If conflict theory and exchange theory ignore how individuals interpret the symbolic meaning of a situation, Blumer makes this process central to all interaction. People construct their own social world, and knowledge of a person's 'reality' emanates from understanding the process by which a person's reality is constructed.

To say that each individual constructs his or her own social world points to Blumer's individualistic stance; interpretations for Blumer are always personal. But more controversial than the view that interpretations are somewhat idiosyncratic is Blumer's view of symbolic meanings being completely created during the process of interaction. Thus Blumer would maintain that there is no way to understand group decision-making except as the decision unfolds or the outcome emerges in the process of interaction with others. This presupposes that participants do not bring to the process much in the way of firmly held beliefs and norms; that meanings arise through interpretations occurring during the process of interaction. Are interpretations so idiosyncratic and specific to situation? As Alexander (1987) points out, Blumer is obliged on occasion to acknowledge that people bring with them certain standard meanings which might correspond to what Parsons called social norms or values.

The *collective behavior approach* is the second version of interaction theory. This is a *holistic* approach that takes account of the influence of collective social factors. The approach builds up from case histories showing how change comes about as the processes of opinion formation and consensus creation get under way. Such an approach has application not only to research on strategy implementation issues but also to research on organizational buying, as suggested by a study by Pettigrew (1973). The use of case studies for building up theory and identifying causal structures is only recently being exploited. A summary of what has been happening can be found elsewhere (O'Shaughnessy 2009, ch. 6 on abduction).

Manfred Kuhn's (1964) *self-theory* is the third version of interaction theory. In sharp contrast to Blumer, whose perspective regards people as active in creating their own world to which they respond, Kuhn focuses on *social systems* as causal in molding an individual into taking the type of action he or she takes. This is another holistic (collectivist) approach which stresses collective causal explanations tied to the social forces at work.

Erving Goffman's (1959) *dramaturgical model of interaction* is the fourth approach. This model perhaps has had the most lasting impact in marketing. The dramaturgical model imputes the perspective of life viewed as a stage where each individual is an actor/player with an audience looking on. Consumers, like everybody else, seek to manage the impressions they make on real or even imagined audiences. *Impression-management* is an important motivator as we are motivated to project a favorable impression on others, with behavior influenced as if a real or hidden audience is observing what we do. We are also concerned with *saving face*, both our own and that of our audience. We stage a *performance* so people will form the impression of us we would like them to have.

The notion of consumers being concerned with impression-management and saving face has had wide appeal so that marketing commonly promotes products as being able to bring about the impressions consumers seek to project. *Expectations* are what guide players and Goffman speaks of three types of expectation as influencing behavior in any role we might play, whether the role of consumer, teacher, housewife or whatever:

- Expectations from the 'script' – that is, the norms attached to the position. Thus in the role of buyer, the consumer is expected to ask questions about any product being bought for the first time.
- Expectations from other players (demands of other people in the situation). In a DMU (decision-making unit), the other members of the group have expectations as to how they will be treated, their likely influence and about not being bullied into compliance.
- Expectations of some audience (real, hidden or imagined 'reference' groups). A consumer may talk about not buying a product because it did not meet the approval of a parent or significant other. Even if the other is long dead, the consumer can take account of the expectations of that other as well as some absent or imagined audience. In particular, buying behavior (e.g. running up credit) condemned by parents can be highly influential.

The extent to which a person's behavior is guided by his or her role depends on the extent to which these expectations are:

- Internalized in that the expectations are viewed as part of one's make-up
- The sanctions/rewards attached to conforming and
- The extent to which meeting expectations acts as a standard for ethical self-evaluation.

Everyone cares about interactions with others, not just with how they communicate with others, but with creating the 'right' impression. Consumers, like people generally, strive to influence the impression others have of them. Some behavior directed to this end has to be nuanced to create a positive impression. Appropriate behavior in any case is not always obvious. Thus speakers who mix criticism with sarcasm ('Yes, it is a hard life for all those Wall Street people having to manage all their millions') rather than speaking directly with anger ('Those on Wall Street are grossly overpaid') are likely to leave an impression of being less angry, more balanced and more in control (Winner and Gardner 1993). Whatever people say or do in interaction with others, there is never one conclusive interpretation, since people conceal beliefs and feelings for the purpose of manipulating perceptions. All of us are actors, concerned with impression-management. The problem is to make behavior consistent since any appearance of inconsistency generates doubts about the 'performance'. As in selling, consistency upholds credibility while at the same time not appearing to be trying too hard or not hard enough.

The Goffman dramaturgical model offers an insightful view of human nature but, for many people, Goffman presents a one-sided and depressing view of social life, made up of Machiavellian individuals using stealth and falseness to manipulate others. All *fronts* or appearances are simply invented for impression management. But Goffman does acknowledge there are 'standard fronts' attached to established social roles. These influence an actor's behavior, stemming from a desire to conform socially. It is these standard 'roles' that we generally use in advertising.

Certain norms or expectations attach to the 'roles' played by individuals within groups. Those sociologists who distinguish between role and status (relative rank) in a group define *role* as the behavior expected of a person with a given *status* in the group. Within the family there can be reciprocal or complementary roles as, say, between husband and wife. There can be an array of roles associated with a given position as occurs with the traditional housewife in her role of mother and household manager. There can be *role-conflict* if divergent role expectations occur as when, say, a mother sees a conflict between her role as mother of two children and her role as partner in a law firm. When responsibilities are ambiguous or unstable, a person suffers from such *role-ambiguity*. In any case, the roles people play within some group affects their decisions. This can be particularly so in organizational buying.

Goffman's dramaturgical model brings together at a minimum role playing and exchange theory: the role provides the script and exchange theory the rationale for following the script. The concept of role relates to the idea of *rule-governed* action in that the norms attached to a position act as rules, directing action. Decision-making that emanates from entrenched generalization is rule-governed decision-making. When the consumer acts on the basis of some entrenched generalization (in cases of doubt, buy the brand that is most familiar), the information on which the generalization is founded is less subject to recall. Thus acting on the generalization of buying the most familiar brand 'suppresses differences which a rule's justification would allow', for example price differences. Rule-governed decision-making is found in legal decision-making, though some laws are open-ended in that the law does not determine the decision process as when a law simply commands acting in the best interest of the child. That said, role theory and the concept of rule-governed action emanate from different traditions. We, as actors on the stage of life, practice impression management to improve the social terms of trade and reconcile cross-pressures (stemming from the social demands versus the conflicting demands of the private self), trying to convey the 'front' most likely to engender the cooperation of others.

More broadly, Goffman belongs to the broader interactionism tradition that combines symbolic interactionism, role theory (Park 1955) and exchange theory. This is because Goffman (1959) stresses in social life, in particular in considering how people develop a sense of themselves in social interaction. What something symbolizes is not something objectively and rationally linked with a physical thing in the world, as is the case with an icon, but relates to meanings in the mind. It is because of this symbolism that symbols are important in marketing. Thus diamonds are not just gems but symbols of luxury.

Goffman (1959) employs the term 'frame' as a metaphor for interpreting social life on the grounds that we act within some contextual frame. For Goffman, strict ritual, and the dread of being *embarrassed*, is what brings order to society, since embarrassment arises from breaking social norms operating in one's social milieu. This is what gives rise to impression-management: role-playing in society through managing the image one projects, which is something necessary in a society given over to status-seeking and saving face. Scheibe (2000) modifies Goffman in using the metaphor of the 'box' (frame with a third dimension) as more apt for signaling a context: change the box and you change the person, as occurs with faculty when transported from the classroom to a faculty meeting. This is because boxes transform perceptions.

There is an echo of Talcott Parsons in this talk of social norms though Goffman stresses fear of embarrassment, not socialization, as the enforcer. As said earlier, it is generally argued that societal norms are now less influential, superseded by conforming to the norms of the groups to which the individual belongs. Given the pervasiveness of political correctness in Western societies, there are obviously still, however, societal norms that can be compelling.

Goffman interprets social interaction through a perspective that sees the fear of embarrassment as dominant. William Miller (2004) goes further in stressing the distance between the self-understanding of one's performance in a role, and the private self, acting as a commentator on the performance in that role. *Fakery* is likely to accompany actions such as praising, apologizing, worshipping, making love, pursuing love interests and so on. We don't like to think about the pervasiveness of fakery as it so undermines what we would like to believe about our friends and others. But fakery is pervasive in social relations.

A person's role in a group influences behavior in that a person's behavior takes account of the role being played, while role expectations are influenced by the social norms attached to the position and by real or imagined reference groups. We might remind ourselves again that a *reference group* is any group that is used as a point of reference to influence one's behavior. There are negative and positive reference groups. There can be positive groups to which a consumer aspires (a higher status group), which may not be a group to which the consumer currently belongs, and this affects their buying. Thus there are voters supporting candidates whose policies do not promote the material interests of those voters as do the rival party's policies. That party being supported may be an *aspiration* group for the voter, being viewed as having more social status and possessing more traditional values.

ETHNOMETHODOLOGY

Ethnomethodology is founded on *phenomenological psychology*. Phenomenology historically is the study of appearances but Edmund Husserl (1859–1938), the most influential writer on phenomenology, came to define it as the science of the *subjective*. Those in market research who offer rich descriptions of what it is like for the consumer to reach a decision, use a product and so on are likely to be of a phenomenologist persuasion. Phenomenological psychology seeks to understand the meaning of social phenomena from the perspective of the individual since the reality of interest is what people perceive it to be. To give a phenomenological account of (y) is to say how (y) is *experienced* by some person or group. Phenomenology is always concerned with 'reality' as experienced.

Phenomenology, as part of social science, is concerned with understanding people's own *subjective interpretations* of their actions and incorporating them into a picture of the social world. Phenomenology is the subjective viewpoint focusing on how people view the world as opposed to what the objective facts suggest. Phenomenology links to ethnopsychology (Chapter 2) in that it relies on the acceptance of shared knowledge. Marketing is vitally concerned with the subjective and so has interest in phenomenology.

Phenomenology does not seek objective knowledge of the social world since it views the *social* world as a social creation, with the concepts used to describe it being socially constructed. Today, the term phenomenology is used to cover any method that explains action in terms of interpreting the meaning of that action from the point of view of the person taking the action. There is thus a phenomenological dimension to symbolic interactionism in that it takes some account of a person's subjective experience though phenomenology proper makes this its central concern, with consumer research focusing exclusively on consumer perceptions as being the reality of interest.

Phenomenology is considered part of Gestalt psychology which studies how wholes are perceived from different perspectives. Gestalt psychology shows, for instance, how objects that are close together tend to be grouped together in perception (the principle of proximity); the more symmetrical some closed area, the more it tends to be seen as a figure (the principle of symmetry) and so on. Gestalt psychology claims that the way parts are seen depends on the configuration of the whole. While the Gestalt principles do suggest how information might be organized in the mind, the Gestalt concept of organization has not become part of cognitive psychology which relies on more 'mechanistic' models to explain the same facts (Gardner 1985). Although it was common for a long time to regard Gestalt psychology as a spent force (Beloff 1973), Gestalt notions today are to be found in many diverse novel applications like the psychology of feeling.

Ethnomethodology implicitly draws on Schutz's phenomenology (see below) but does not subscribe to the view that the agent's own interpretation must be taken at face value but accepts, like Goffman, that social action may be staged to deceive an audience. In any case, ethnomethodology, though of a phenomenological nature, is concerned with the methods people employ in making sense of the situation in which they find themselves and how they sustain orderliness in their dealings with others. Such studies are carried out without feeling the need to study social norms or structural phenomena such as institutions. Ethnomethodology started as a critique of mainstream sociology that tends to accept social 'facts' as facts instead of recognizing that social facts emerge from social processes rather than some objective process. So-called facts can be just socially constructed or just be interpreted as facts.

Ethnomethodology studies the 'folk' methods (ethnomethodology) people employ to create a sense of social order. Interest centers, as in phenomenological psychology, on people's own words, not on the abstractions of social scientists. Ethnomethodologists ignore sociological constructs like social norms, structure, values and so on in favor of studying how people construct their own reality, and change their perceptions of reality. Ethnomethodologists are not interested in knowing specifically how social norms emerge but are interested in how people come to agree upon an impression that there are social norms to follow. Ethnomethodologists study how people create a sense of a common reality; how this sense of reality is constructed, reinforced or changed (Leiter 1980). In line with phenomenology, the reality of interest is that contained in people's accounts of reality ('what's out there'). It is this that links it to folk psychology.

In ignoring all the sensitizing concepts developed by social scientists, ethnomethodologists ignore what these sensitizing concepts have 'taught us to see', which means their interpretations of behavior will inevitably be impoverished. These sensitizing concepts constitute categories into which we can put individual observations, which is a step towards generalization of findings. On the other hand, this may be of little loss in terms of what ethnomethodologists are trying to do.

Indexicality is a key concept in ethnomethodology. It rests on the distinction between the agreed-upon meaning of a word as found in a dictionary and the specific *contextual* meaning. The indexicality of a word, phrase or sentence is that part of its meaning that is specific to the context in which it occurs: the indexicality of a word is unknowable without knowledge of that context. Ethnomethodology claims that all interactions are highly indexical and such indexicality is lost when social science attempts to establish universal generalizations. But this seems to assume no generalizations can cover the relevant range of contexts that are of interest. If contexts are unique, this may be true, but there will always come a stage where some further richness of description has to be sacrificed.

Garfinkel (1967), the originator of ethnomethodology, claims orthodox sociology (read Parsons) portrays action as completely determined by social norms. Garfinkel studied for his PhD at Harvard under Talcott Parsons and taught at the University of California, Los Angeles (UCLA). While many claim that to know the rules people live by suggests how their behavior might be predicted, Garfinkel recognized that the rules were context-bound and needed to be interpreted in the light of real-world circumstances. Not that rules were not important, but how they are interpreted and applied is a matter of negotiation at the time.

Like Blumer, ethnomethodologists accept that it is the meaning or the significance of things to the consumer that directs action, with such meaning resting completely on people's own interpretations, not fixed by social norms. But, as often pointed out, Parsons is simply claiming that interpretation of human action is *impossible* without a background of standards for guidance purposes and such standards he is calling 'norms'. We might remind ourselves that the word 'impossible' is used in two senses to mean (a) impossible physically, as in saying the consumer cannot make an omelet without breaking eggs; (b) impossible conceptually in thus saying that to 'interpret' *implies* standards for guidance purposes. Parsons meant the latter, since he did not conceive societal norms as outside causal forces but as conceptual tools used by the mind to create a sense of social structure – as do ethnomethodologists. Parsonian 'norms' are rules that guide rather than determine action. Garfinkel is not far different in seeing rules as procedures to be followed in going about everyday activities and showing how violating such rules can upset others as it fails to meet their expectations. (His most well-known illustration of this is asking his students on returning home to behave as if they are invited guests – and see the resulting puzzlement by parents.)

The ethnomethodologists' paradigm views people as interpreting cues, gestures, words and data to sustain their particular perspective of reality. That perspective of reality operates as a conceptual lens in viewing the world, so feedback from the world tends to reinforce that perspective. People's behavior is in general 'reflexive' and undertaken and carried out to support their beliefs even in the face of contrary evidence. This is not to suggest that people believe that black is white just because they want to do so but that evidence will be weighed and evaluated in an attempt to support systems of beliefs found to be comfortable. This is a strong position to take on the problem of changing beliefs as it makes the changing of beliefs so very difficult. But much will depend on the particular beliefs of interest since not all a person's beliefs will be held with the same tenacity. Yet it is a warning to marketers and the reason why 'wise' marketers are more likely to seek a change in perceptions to make the message fit beliefs rather than seek to undermine any well-established, comforting set of beliefs.

A constant criticism of ethnomethodology is its tendency to dismiss social and cultural norms, as if the meaning of action can be understood without reference to the broader cultural framework in which action takes place. There is also an objection to the claim that indexicality rules out social scientists from generalizing on the grounds that all meanings are specific to a situation. Collin (1985) makes the point that we get the impression in ethnomethodology that social action is never what it pretends to be but, following Goffman, is always something of an illusion. This may be because the unexpected is always of most interest. Nonetheless, it is much too limiting to ignore the role of social norms as ethnomethodologists do, while many contexts have a similarity that is sufficient to allow generalization.

CULTURAL (HERMENEUTIC) SOCIOLOGY

Cultural sociologists, like those advocating symbolic interactionism, ethnomethodology and phenomenology, and cultural anthropology, advocate an interpretive understanding of action. Cultural sociology is in fact frequently called hermeneutic to emphasize this interpretive methodology since all hermeneutic traditions accept the need for a subjective input into social science.

As an interpretive approach to understanding human behavior, cultural sociology makes the following claims:

- That understanding the actions of others such as consumers in society is made possible by a common culture or, at least, cultural overlap. This contrasts with conventional phenomenology which claims the ability to understand others derives from the ability to generalize from the individual experience, not the culture, as if culture does not come into it. Cultural sociology also contrasts with those versions of hermeneutics that confine themselves to subjective meanings, paying little or no attention to identifying general, underlying (cultural) systems of meaning.
- That human action is less a matter of rational calculation (as per the economist's rational choice theory) than *felt* expectations as to how the

action will be *experienced* in terms of its meaning or personal significance. Consumers commonly think in terms of 'what it would be like to possess that new car', rather than undertaking some rational calculation of a cost–benefit type. This is an important perspective and a view that finds expression in those academics in consumer behavior who focus on the experiential.

- That the meaning or personal significance of an action (like buying) reflects those interconnected meanings that form the individual's cultural or social milieu. In other words, the meaning or significance of an action to an individual is derived from his being part of some cultural or social milieu. This view 'seemingly' contrasts with Blumer's position which stresses the uniqueness of each individual's own world of meaning. 'Seemingly' since it could be argued that while at some level of detail there is uniqueness in an individual's own world of meaning, there is a common strain of meaning at a level that rises above the detail.
- There is general agreement with Ricoeur (1981), the postmodernist, and others who claim all actions can be treated as a 'text'. But this is only so because actions are a cultural product, guided by the cultural order.

Cultural sociology rests on the existence of intersubjective meanings of action based on cultural affinities. This arises from the commonality of concepts which consumers employ in the language. Alfred Schutz (1967), a major figure in the development of phenomenological sociology, claims that *all* human action is intelligible or rational within each person's mental representations (perspectives) of the world. In other words, people's actions are intelligible given their perspective or view of reality. The notion of action being completely irrational is alien to Schutz. All we need to do is to see things from the other's point of view. In order to understand a person's mental representations (perspective) of the world, we explore the *concepts* people use to describe and structure their environment.

Basic for Schutz is the distinction between the concepts of common sense and those of science. Common sense concepts, ideas and notions combine to form common sense knowledge or folk psychology. Schutz (following Husserl) views intersubjective knowledge as that identified in 'I know it, you know it, I know you know it and you know I know it' (Howarth-Williams 1977). This occurs because most of a person's knowledge is *socially mediated* through concepts. Schutz argues that people carry in their minds, as part of common sense knowledge, conceptions of appropriate social conduct in order to function effectively in society. On this basis, Schutz argues that explanations of a person's actions must be understandable to the subject herself and not just to the researcher. This is in line with Schutz's claim that social science theory should take account of, or be based on, people's own interpretations of their actions. This view is supportive of folk psychology. Whatever the limitations of focus groups and similar techniques designed to discover the consumer's views, the goal of getting the consumer's own understanding of things is important.

CASE: JIM BEAM

One heading in *Bloomberg Businessweek* was entitled 'Jim Beam's Gender-Bending Adventure' (17–23 October 2011, p. 32). This was a reference to the company's new strategy of marketing Jim Beam, a familiar brand of bourbon whiskey, also to women. This was not a repositioning strategy but an attempt to attract a new target group of customers or convert women from typically drinking wine on social occasions. Thus it was not like the repositioning strategy adopted for the Marlboro cigarette which aimed to shift its market from women to men through associating the cigarette with the tough Western cowboy. Women might continue to buy this mild smoke but they ceased to be the main target audience. Jim Beam, however, had no intention of neglecting to target men but wanted to convert a number of women wine drinkers to their whiskey. Until recently, Jim Beam belonged to Fortune Brands but is now financially separate from Fortune Brands.

Beam Inc. leads the spirits market in the US and currently produces several variations of Jim Beam Whiskey with promotion that focuses on associations with music and sport. The firm has already had success with female consumers. Jim Beam Red Stag, a black-cherry-flavored bourbon whiskey, has a consumer base that is 40 percent female. It might also be pointed out that Beam Inc. introduced a rose-flavored Courvoisier cognac which has half the alcohol content taken out. It is designed to be served cold so it is kept next to the wine in bars where women are more likely to see it. It has been a success.

As buyers, 76 percent of women are involved in spirit purchases so they are likely to be exposed to any variation of Jim Beam marketed to women.

Case questions

1. Given that Jim Beam whiskey has been promoted as the drink favored by the hard-living, macho-man, are we likely to have an image problem since this clashes with the image women may have of themselves?
2. Would choosing such a product (or at least one modified somewhat) help women socially adjust in mixed company? What do you think is the symbolic meaning for the woman choosing and drinking such a traditionally male-oriented bourbon whiskey?
3. Do you think that promoting such a product to women fits current societal trends?

DISCUSSION QUESTIONS ON CHAPTER 13 (SOCIOLOGY)

1. In the 1960s to 1970s exchange theory was commonly put forward as the key concept in marketing. Go through the various exchange theories and justify or reject this claim to be a key concept.
2. Discuss the concept of 'social adjustment' as a motivator and how it is or can be used in advertising.

3. Discuss the concept of 'symbolic meaning'. Make the case for asking about the symbolic meaning of your product to consumers.
4. As a consumer negotiating a deal, how might knowledge of Erving Goffman's dramaturgical model help?
5. If Alfred Schutz is right, all consumer actions are intelligible once we understand a consumer's perspective or point of view. Do you think this is a good rule to adopt in marketing research? If so, why?

Chapter 14

Cultural Anthropology

FACETS OF CULTURAL ANTHROPOLOGY

Herodotus, a Greek historian who lived in the fifth century BC, claimed that custom was 'the king of all things' and pointed out that if 'customs' were like goods in a marketplace, each person would choose their own above every other person's customs. In this Herodotus was recognizing the attraction of a culture to its people. To the Greeks other people were barbarians, from the Greek *barbaros*, as other peoples sounded like 'bar-bar-bar' in speech, though interestingly, unlike today, the word did not necessarily connote the barbarian as a savage heathen given to vandalism. This chapter focuses on the influence of culture on consumer behavior.

Anthropology has four sub-fields: physical, linguistic, archeological and cultural. This chapter focuses on *cultural* anthropology, which is of most interest to marketing since there is the possibility of revealing how cultures are alike and where they differ, and the implications for marketing.

Cultural anthropology's perspective imputes a socially constructed (man-made) and culturally learnt 'way of life' as influencing the behavior of the inhabitants of a country. This would include its values, its myths, its language, rituals, customs, laws, norms of behavior, dress and manners, together with the knowledge and artifacts created that belong to the entire society. People think and act drawing on a network of meanings of these things. They are embodied in perspectives that order the world and help interpret it. Within any culture there are subcultures based on, for example, ethnicity, age or social class, which are important to marketing as they may constitute distinct customer groups in terms of a specific product. This is not to suggest there is an anchored national culture that is not subject to change. There is always some *cultural drift* as values and social norms change, often through influences arising from another culture. A strong culture, though, and a well-integrated society make change less easy to bring about, since changing one part of the culture with the other parts unchanged sets up a resistance to undo the change. Thus a society may legislate against job discrimination but without much effect until it is recognized that change must occur simultaneously in the schools, in the families, the work environment and so on. This is not to minimize the importance of legislation since the law has a great effect on changing attitudes as it signals what is legitimate and ethical.

In every country there are advocates of *cultural monism,* demanding the assimilation of all minorities into the one dominant culture to minimize 'cultural conflict' through an aggressive program of 'cultural transmission' for passing along cultural values and norms. On the other hand, there are those who champion *cultural pluralism* on the grounds that cultural diversity fosters a cultural richness. Cultural monism would restrict freedom to choose, whereas cultural pluralism, under the banner of multiculturalism, is in danger of undermining the integration of minorities and with it the goal of *assimilation*, which can be helpful when there is a need to get the whole nation to pull together.

Knowledge of *cultural anthropology* is pivotal for those marketing to other cultures as well as in helping to understand one's own subcultures. *The Economist* (24 July 1999, p. 76) quotes a businessman, running a new Asian mobile phone business, as saying that the hardest part of his job was not language but culture since, for example, the dominant characteristic of Chinese businessmen is mistrust so it takes time to overcome suspicion. Of interest is a story relating back to the Opium Wars in the 1900s, of the puzzlement of the Chinese over the English playing tennis. One Chinese official was said to have asked a British consul why he did not pay someone to play tennis on his behalf (Lovell 2011).

The same *Economist* article says that Asian immigrants in the US and Canada have not sought to perpetuate a separate linguistic identity so they integrate themselves and their children into the new culture quickly. But customs still survive, like the cuisine, even if the language disappears. Pankaj Mishra comments in a tribute to the (recently deceased) Nirad Chaudhuri (*New York Review of Books*, 23 September 1999) that although Hindu xenophobia and jingoism are alive and flourishing, the dominant culture in India is a borrowing from the West, with its main emblems being not Pascal or Mozart but MTV and Coca-Cola!

Each culture tends to see its own culture as superior (after all it is *my* culture) so it is easy to make remarks about other cultures that are interpreted as offensive. The general rule is that only those belonging to that culture are forgiven for criticizing it. But this sense of pride in one's culture is also the reason why the adoption of aspects from another culture is not likely to destroy the culture of a nation, though some countries, by their legal restrictions, seem to think differently.

More than a superficial understanding of a foreign culture may be required for business expansion into that culture. The British firm of Marks & Spencer lost heavily in buying the famous American clothing firm of Brooks Brothers, while the UK's Midland Bank lost heavily in failing to understand the inner culture of Crocker National, a Californian bank with many hidden problems. The two UK supermarket giants, J. Sainsbury and Tesco, also failed in the US. Tesco, the market leader in the UK, opened a lot of small outlets called 'Fresh and Easy' on the West Coast of America.

It seems it underestimated the preference for frozen foods, established brands (Tesco pushed its own private label) and did not accept manufacturers' coupons. An article in the *Financial Times* (26 May 2006, p. 28) illustrates how some of the world's biggest firms lost their way in South Korea, a group that includes Wal-Mart, Carrefour, McDonald's, Coca-Cola, Google and Nokia, through insufficient acquaintance with South Korea's culture. It appears, for example, that Wal-Mart and Carrefour 'failed to adapt to local tastes', while their stores were a 'turn-off' for Korean consumers. The Western companies were 'resolute' in ignoring local ways in favor of their own way of doing things, believing they needed to do things differently to get attention. But this was a case where novelty did not have appeal. Many cultural practices are tied to cultural values which can be the final court of appeal in determining what will and what will not be accepted. When cultural values are firmly held, there is always the danger of *ethnocentrism* in believing one's own culture is distinctively more worthy than any other, which hinders the openness of a society to innovations from elsewhere.

Country of origin can be an important factor in a brand's image. Thus Germany is known for its fine engineering and this has helped enhance Mercedes and BMW as brand images, with a positive effect on sales throughout the world. This is something not considered by US manufacturers intent on lowering costs through offshore production. The unintended consequence can be to diminish America as a brand and, in the process, the distinctiveness of America itself. It has been difficult for South Korea to claim its cars are just as reliable as those from Japan and this has led to their being sold at a lower price than the equivalent Japanese cars. But this is changing. Before the Second World War, Japan was known for its exports of poor quality products which is certainly not true now.

There are always ongoing incremental changes in any culture. We might recall the OXO family disappearing from commercials, because in the era of TV dinners, the idea of two generations having dinner together lacked credibility. Zygmunt Bauman (1999) argues that today there is a pervasive sense of insecurity, uncertainty and danger. With both the nation and the family in disrepair, together with globalization and deregulation, people lose their social moral anchors and turn to a hedonistic lifestyle. This claim does not lack intuitive appeal but at base it is an empirical proposition that requires empirical support.

According to one left-leaning book of readings on globalization (Jameson and Miyochi 1999), globalization comes down to the global dominance of global capitalism. This, it is argued, has led to highlighting the weakness of national governments in their role of controlling capital and multinationals. The book draws attention to the transnational corporation, an evolving transnational capitalist class (which constitutes a global political elite) and the culture-ideology of consumerism or transnational popular culture. It is an interesting perspective but it is just one perspective that cannot be the whole story since it ignores the significance of the Islamic renaissance and the upsurge of Evangelical Protestantism, and even the role of the transnational intelligentsia. In respect to the Islamic revival, large numbers of Muslims 'consume' American cultural artifacts such as American fast food, clothing and music. An alternative perspective on globalization is that ably defended by Micklethwait and Wooldridge (2000) who promote globalization not on the grounds that it increases prosperity but because it increases individual liberty.

LaFeber (1999) claims that corporations like Nike, using the sports figure Michael Jordan as an accomplice, exploited the seductiveness of the US culture to 'influence the language, eating habits, clothes and television-watching of peoples around the world'. He sees this as generating resentment. While the spread of basketball via Jordan may have helped to produce a global era of 'Americanization', LaFeber claims that that very process has strengthened anti-Americanization globally. Whenever another country's cultural artifacts become an important pool from which consumers derive new experiences, there is resentment as there are losers, particularly among those who feel diminished at no longer being in the lead.

In Europe, France and the French government did everything possible to prevent (unsuccessfully) the importation of English words into the French language – and the importation of American culture and its products. But Hollywood illustrates the appetite throughout the world for American culture. As the most dominant country in the world, the US can expect resentment, as the British were resented when their influence spread throughout the world. Just being dominant in itself puts a country in a position where it is assumed it will feel superior to others. On the other hand, many in other countries seek to be like the US as if its power will rub off on them. When 'missionaries' from England went to India in the nineteenth century to set up private schools where teaching was to be in the native languages, they were quickly told by Indian parents that they wanted the instruction to be in English, 'the language of science'!

THE PERSPECTIVE OF CULTURAL ANTHROPOLOGY

Anthropology is the last of the social sciences to be reviewed for marketing insights. It is a latecomer in being a discipline on its own. The French grouped it under sociology and only awarded a degree in the subject in 1968.

The cultural anthropological perspective views behavior as being influenced, if not determined, by the shared cultural norms (standards), values, customs, rituals, myths, societal accumulated knowledge, arts, artifacts and beliefs. But how the word 'culture' is defined is often decisive as to what is studied by the anthropologist. As a consequence, all those adopting the cultural perspective do not investigate the same phenomena. This is because there are differences among researchers as to what *can be* studied. The *adaptationist* approach concentrates on material culture (artifacts) that can be seen, heard, smelt and touched. Under this approach, interest lies in artifacts used in everyday living and in society at large. On the other hand, the *ideationalist* approach views the core notion of culture as the shared beliefs, shared values, knowledge, meanings and ideas. These have to be discovered and inferred rather than objectively observed as is generally the case with artifacts. This ideationalist approach is the one most favored in consumer behavior.

Culturally shared values are the *superordinate* values whose preservation is seen as vital to society's way of life. They can be quoted as justifications for whatever actions are taken. Thus in American culture, claims are made for the values of meritocracy, equality of opportunity, egalitarianism, entrepreneurship, innovation, progress and so on. Such values are multiple and often in conflict. They are also incommensurable in that they cannot be measured on a common scale like money to measure their relative position in some hierarchy of values. Thus the value of achieving a more egalitarian society can conflict with the value of human advancement being based purely on merit, and trade-offs must be decided without any objective measuring tool.

The ideationalist approach also studies the underlying assumptions of a culture to identify the major beliefs and values that lie behind action. With regard to beliefs, over many years the great majority of Americans have endorsed such beliefs as: governments are inefficient and wasteful; the Federal government controls too much of our daily lives; government regulation of business does more harm than good; poor people have become too dependent on government handouts. There is, as a consequence, a general suspicion of government and politicians, who have to take such beliefs into consideration in their political campaigns.

What unites those studying culture is a rejection of a *positivist methodology* with its assumption that any putative science must employ the scientific methodology used by the natural sciences with its focus on quantification, experimentation and empirical verification. The response of cultural anthropologists has been that these methods have produced little useful knowledge, usually ending up with relatively trivial amounts of variance being explained. The same claim is made by some academics in marketing where interest purely in quantitative model building has led to top academics showing little or no interest in marketing management per se – and marketing managers have returned the compliment by showing little or no interest in what the model builders have to say. There are two complaints at present in respect to how quantitative methods are applied: (a) that confining research techniques to quantitative approaches has produced explanations that lack depth, being generally too simplistic for the marketing managers' purposes; and (b) that purely quantitative approaches are too often driven by *instrumentalism* where prediction is considered the main purpose of science, with only lip service paid to explanatory theory.

It is a pity if these attacks on mathematical model builders lead some marketing academics to a suspicion of all quantification, since mathematics draws out the implications of data which otherwise remain hidden, while numbers provide rankings and orders of magnitude among events – often of primary importance in policy decision-making. In any case, experimentation should not just be confined to scientific research but be part of a firm's bag of marketing tools. Instead of just believing that some strategy must be fully launched, there is often time to experiment with a pilot scheme to get some idea about desirability, feasibility and commercial viability.

One cultural anthropologist at the University of Chicago, Richard Shweder (2003), defines culture in terms of customary practices, values and community beliefs/ideas about what is true, efficient, good and beautiful. These elements of culture are said to lie behind social actions and social practices, with cultural anthropologists viewing cultural analysis as an interpretive study of behavior. The focus is on the *patterns* of behavior passed on from generation to generation and on the beliefs and doctrines that have significance in organizing and justifying a way of life.

Shweder distinguishes cultural psychology from cross-cultural psychology; a distinction seldom found in the marketing literature. *Cross-cultural psychology* concerns itself with boundary conditions for establishing boundaries for the application of generalizations that are presumptively interpreted as fundamental and universal. Cultural psychology, in contrast, provides a cultural account of behavior by establishing *within* a *culture* a correspondence between actual behaviors in the culture and the significant values, moral ideals and beliefs exhibited in the behaviors. As Shweder says, cultures are associated with a moral order even if various cultural moral judgments do not necessarily converge over time: one culture may be approving while another culture is damning of particular practices or doctrines.

The series of essays in Shweder's book (only a few co-authored with him) explicate his claim (given earlier but worth repeating) that:

> the knowable world is incomplete if seen from any one point of view, incoherent if seen from all points of view at once, and empty if seen from nowhere in particular.
>
> (Shweder 2003: 45)

This is a neat way of expressing Shweder's perspectivism anchored to a multiperspective approach; something endorsed in this book. But the quote is more than just 'neat', it incorporates the rationale and the logic of perspectivism.

Shweder provides a useful classification of 'camps' or schools in cultural anthropology:

1. *Identity politics* where anthropology is used to show how 'this is our custom' is used to enslave and exploit the vulnerable
2. *Skeptical postmodernism* which uses anthropology as an arena for deconstruction, viewing culture as a fiction and *ethnographic* 'findings' as largely constructed in the service of domination and exploitation

3. *Neo-positivism* which regards anthropology as a scientific inquiry that is value-neutral and non-moralizing (traditional positivists view culture in terms of what is observable, that is, what can be seen, heard, smelt and touched, and would eschew all mental constructs like beliefs and values)
4. *Romantic pluralism* that seeks to identify and describe cultural differences, avoiding and denying the concept of national stereotypes
5. The *cultural development view* where anthropological findings are used for explaining why 'Westernization' of cultures is required for economic growth. This is a position often advocated by marketing academics who see marketing and a free society as basic to economic development. This latter approach tends to equate globalization with Westernization, which, in turn, is equated with liberal democracy, free enterprise, private property, autonomy, individualism, equality and the protection of natural or universal rights, particularly property rights. The notion of 'natural rights' is, though, a difficult one in that logically for something to be a natural right, it would have to be present in everyone and be shown to arise without learning. It is better to speak of 'rights' when a right is an entitlement backed by law or the United Nations Declaration of Human Rights so that the entitlement carries with it some obligation on the part of others to enforce such rights.

Shweder endorses a pluralistic conception of culture to better understand the variations of human 'mentalities' across social groups. Shweder's cultural psychology assumes non-uniformity of mentalities across time and space. For him, psychology should be the study of multiple psychologies and not the study of a (mythical?) uniform psychology for all peoples of the world. People are not tokens of each other and neither are cultures. A cultural psychology should focus on population-based variations rather than seeking the holy grail of a cross-cultural psychology. This is an important claim (if valid) for social science generally and for marketing. But what is meant by the term 'distinctive mentalities' is left undefined by Shweder as if unproblematic and non-controversial. It is neither.

It was the French sociologist Levy-Bruhl who first promoted the notion of differences in mentalities together with the idea of there being a pre-logical mentality that was supposed to be a feature of primitive thought. Lévi-Strauss was to reject this claim (see later). The *mentalities approach* focuses on 'collectivities' not individuals; embraces the idea of unconscious assumptions and takes an interest in the structure of beliefs and their interrelations, as opposed to just focusing on beliefs taken in isolation. Lloyd (1990) attacks the validity and usefulness of this notion of distinct mentalities. He argues that the concept of mentalities merely identifies what has to be explained, without itself providing an explanation. As he says, collectivities do not think, only individuals do and no society or group consists of individuals with entirely uniform mental characteristics.

Shweder too rejects the notion of members of any community having uniform mental characteristics on the grounds that there are always many within-group differences. On the other hand, he accepts that there are wide differences between different national groups even as he rejects stereotyping and characterizing whole populations in terms of 'personality' tendencies, such as being 'achievement-oriented'. Lloyd, while recognizing that there are indeed important cultural differences between East and West, argues these relate more directly to differences in the weightings given to various concepts and categories and to differences in styles of interpersonal exchange than to some vague, unproven notion of different mentalities. But there are still differences in behavior. In entering the German market Wal-Mart forgot that the Germans prefer to bag their own groceries, while Germany is the home of the discounter so price could not be the competitive advantage.

Differences in the concepts that are employed in different languages can manifest themselves in important differences in style of reasoning and interpersonal exchange, and marketers have to be sensitive to these cultural differences. For example, sexual innuendoes, nudity and jokes at the expense of religion are common in European advertising but are taboo in the US and indeed in most other countries of the world. This could be interpreted as just a difference in weighting but it can make all the difference between acceptance and rejection. Also, market segments can vary. In 1978 Unilever (Hindustan Lever) discerned a segment for a face cream whose promise was a fairer skin in just six weeks – and better marriage prospects! They launched 'Fair & Lovely' to reinforce this colonial era prejudice (Jones 2010).

Nisbett (2004), in reviewing the literature, concludes there are major differences, enduring over the centuries, between the modes of thought of Asians and Westerners: characteristic thought processes of Asians and Westerners differ greatly. But Nisbett does not assert the differences are hard-wired. Cognitive differences (if they exist) are more likely the result of differences in cultural upbringing, rather than anything to do with nature. Asians born in the US or Europe do not seem to 'suffer' from their brains being wired differently from the rest of the population.

Nisbett claims that Asians see the world through a wide-angle lens, in contrast to Westerners who have more of a tunnel vision. Nisbett sees this as explaining the harmonious versus individualistic contrast between East and West. Westerners are categorized as preferring abstract universal principles in contrast to East Asians who seek practical rules for dealing with situations encountered. This can be questioned. Teaching executives around the world suggest that few people from East or West have a liking for abstract principles: anti-intellectualism is pervasive in the West but is it any better in the East among the population at large? Professors, at least at business schools, find that the majority of students (whether from East or West), like managers, favor *prescriptive rules* over any theory. Interestingly, when Clausewitz's book *On War* was first published in the nineteenth century, it was received with no more than posthumous respect, and not with the enthusiasm that was shown for the work of Antoine-Henri Jomini, a rival military writer. This was because Jomini's prescriptive rules on military strategy were much more congenial to military commanders, desperate for practical advice (Smith 2004). This is true also for executives who have no taste for abstraction.

Nisbett's claims are not based on any random samples from East and West populations, while college populations are often a questionable basis for generalizing to the population at large. The problem of obtaining representative samples is a major hurdle for all researchers. There is the further problem of extrapolating from the samples to yield warranted generalizations that have some stability. These are not problems encountered by natural scientists dealing with materials of uniform composition.

It is commonly argued that the interpretive disciplines are incapable of producing theories. Shweder (rightly) argues that this is necessarily true in the search for theories embracing explanatory law-like generalizations. Interpretive methods do not yield law-like generalizations, while timing and temporal differences in mental state can shape things dramatically. Shweder writes:

> universal generalizations are often bought at the price of describing the world of culture and mind at a level of abstraction so distanced from lived realities that they are devoid of sufficient content and meaning and have little predictive utility... I believe that some of the most reliable, useful and significant generalizations in the social and psychological sciences are those that are restricted in scope and are 'firmly wedded'... to historical, cultural and institutional circumstances. Rural Oriya Brahmans in India will react this way for these reasons under these circumstances, which is not the way middle-class Anglo-Americans will react, and for these reasons.
>
> (Shweder 2003: 300 and 308–9)

Earlier in the book we quote Kagan (2006) as saying much the same thing.

Shweder quotes Osgood's *semantic differential* to illustrate his case. This is misleading. The semantic differential was developed by Osgood for evaluating 'meaning' in the sense of meaning as the mediating variable between the input of the stimuli and the action taken. Factor analysis of the data emanating from applications of the scale revealed three dimensions: (i) evaluation (good–bad); (ii) potency (strong–weak); (iii) activity (fast–slow). Given these three dimensions, Shweder ridicules the scale on the grounds that it would classify God and ice cream as equivalent, because they are both judged to be good, strong and active! This wrongly assumes good, strong and active have all the same connotations or sense-meanings in the two cases of God and ice cream. In fact, the only common meaning is the positive overtones of 'good' and 'strong' and the negative overtones of the term 'bad'. Beyond this, the connotations are entirely different. In fact (to use the Wittgenstein metaphor) they belong to different language games. Wittgenstein, as pointed out earlier, employed the term 'language game' to highlight his assertion that speaking any language is part of some activity: a language game is made up of both the use of a word or sentence and the features of those activities in which examples of that use are embedded.

Shweder, like many in social science, advocates a the use of the term 'agency'. As an *agent*, the consumer freely acts according to his or her wants and beliefs. The agency concept avoids the hazards of 'dispositional' approaches (like viewing 'attitude' as a dispositional tendency to act in a certain way to some event, person or attribute) in which behavior is in danger of being interpreted as the by-product of mechanical forces pushing both from the inside (like personality traits) and from the outside (situational pressures). Agency comes with less theoretical baggage and fits admirably into the reason-giving explanation (see Chapter 2).

Shweder's final essay is a talk on the aims of education, a talk given as a faculty member at the University of Chicago. What is interesting about this talk is its attack on the widespread claim that culture explains why some nations are rich and some are poor. David Landes (1998), for example, sees culture as making the difference: that success or failure is ultimately determined from within, not imposed from without. While respectful of the research that went into Landes' book covering the economic history of the world, Shweder's own conclusion is that climate, natural resources and physical ecology probably have far more to do with the production of wealth than do cultural beliefs, religion or values; and those who get ahead first tend to stay ahead. This is more revealing of Shweder's sympathy with non-Western cultures than being a valid claim. It is true that Charles Murray (2003), in explaining human accomplishments, puts emphasis on environmental and circumstantial factors in explaining human achievements throughout the ages. However, cultural beliefs, religion and values are not the only elements of culture. If one of the artifacts of culture is government, good government must surely enter into the success of a nation. The factor most inhibiting economic progress in most of the world is corruption at all levels of government. *The Economist*, in a leader entitled 'Making it Smile', makes the following comment on Africa:

> Zimbabwe provides a dramatic illustration of how statist economic policies, corruptly enforced, swiftly impoverish. In the past five years Mugabe's contempt for property rights has made half the population dependent on food aid, while his cronies help themselves to other people's land and savings, and build helipads for their own mansions. But Zimbabwe's curse is also Africa's. The main reason the continent is so poor today is that Mugabe-style incompetent tyranny has been common since independence.

> (*The Economist*, 17 January 2004, p. 10)

In a society where there is little corruption, nepotism or support for government theft and where institutional policies reward risk-taking and innovation, that society is far more likely to prosper than its opposite.

A problem lies, though, in the short-term outlook of many CEOs who have more of an incentive to push up the value of stock options and to copy an innovation than reduce immediate profits for long-term gain. The stock market demands immediate results which, when allied to the short-term tenure of most CEOs, leads them to eschew investments with only long-term payoffs. It is for this reason that many governments have felt obliged to fund research in universities and elsewhere to make up for the dearth of real research on innovative products, particularly in pharmaceutical firms who should be at the forefront of innovation. It is hoped that such research includes consumers who can be a real source of novel ideas if they are asked what they *wished* was available as opposed to what they wanted.

The claim about religious beliefs influencing economic growth is by no means dead. An article in the *New York Times* by Felicia Lee (31 January 2004) quotes a study by Harvard economist Robert Barro and his wife Rachel McCleary who say:

> Our central perspective is that religion affects economic outcomes mainly by fostering religious beliefs that influence traits such as honesty, work, ethic, thrift and openness to strangers.

(Lee 2004: 17)

Their research based on six international surveys on religious beliefs and church attendance, showed that, within limits, religion and economic growth correlate. This work goes beyond Max Weber with his hotly contested claim for the Protestant ethic being tied to economic progress. Of course, the question is whether the correlation between religion and economic growth is not picking up other causal factors like the nation's laws and type of government. In any case, religious beliefs alone will not do it (or there would be no sinners among the religious) since there is also the matter of motivation.

Interpretations can differ even among those using the same basic disciplinary paradigm, as differing weighting of values can skew the basic perspective. A well-known example of differing interpretations as a result of differences in values is the case of two distinguished American anthropologists, Robert Redfield and Oscar Lewis, and their work in the Mexican village of Tepoztlan (Coleman and Watson 1992). Redfield's study was undertaken in the 1920s and concluded that the village was an idyllic place while, twenty years later, Lewis reached a very different conclusion, seeing the village as lacking harmony and full of suspicions and tension. The evidence would suggest, however, that it was not the village that had changed. The differences arose from differences in values, in that Redfield saw urban life as one of moral and social disintegration and the village of Tepoztlan as an attractive alternative to the horrors of the city. Lewis, on the other hand, saw the life of peasants as blighted by poverty and backwardness.

Kuper (1999) details a debate between the anthropologists Marshall Sahlins and Gananath Obeyesekere over the death of the famous English naval explorer, Captain Cook (1728–79), who was killed in Hawaii by the islanders. Obeyesekere attributes to Sahlins a perspective on native islanders that led Sahlins to view the natives as unreflecting slaves of custom, whereas a more mature perspective would recognize that humans everywhere take account of experience. It is only a sense of racial superiority that leads someone like Sahlins to believe that Cook's sailors appeared to the natives as gods. This is a good illustration of how the same historical 'facts' give rise in anthropology to different interpretations through differences in perspective.

'Sherlock Holmes' once asserted that it was a huge mistake to theorize in the absence of data, but a problem also arises from different theories being selective of different data and weighting data differently. Margaret Mead's *Coming of Age in Samoa* depicted an earthly paradise, with sexual joy without the guilt, but Derek Freeman, an ethnographer from New Zealand, who later studied Samoan society, came up with an entirely different picture of life in Samoa (Miller 2006). Margaret Mead, a cultural relativist at Columbia at the time, held values that were supportive of that sort of society with its free-love lifestyle and so on, but Derek Freeman was not of this persuasion.

CLAIMS OF CULTURAL (HERMENEUTIC) ANTHROPOLOGY

Hermeneutical social science covers interpretive psychology, cultural sociology and cultural anthropology. As in the case of symbolic interactionism, ethnomethodology and phenomenology, cultural anthropology rests on an interpretive understanding of action. Cultural anthropology is categorized as a hermeneutic discipline to emphasize this interpretive aspect.

All the hermeneutic social sciences accept the need for a subjective input in the interpretive process. Interpretation differs from deductive inference in that it involves conjecture to fill gaps in the evidence. While some interpretive social sciences represent themselves as seeking *scientific explanations*, this is often rejected by those advocating interpretive social science on the grounds that no laws are sought, while the purpose of interpretation is *understanding*, which does not carry the same logical force as do the laws in natural science. But to insist that there can only be an interpretive social science, while at the same time insisting there can be no scientific explanations in the social sciences, is to claim that explanation of a scientific nature is impossible in the social sciences. This runs against common usage of the term 'explanation' and is only likely to confuse.

Hermeneutics, as stated earlier in the book, is used today as an umbrella term to cover any interpretive approach to understanding. Cultural (hermeneutic) anthropology in marketing makes certain claims which stand repeating:

• That understanding consumer actions in any country is only made possible by a common culture or, at least, cultural overlap. This contrasts with conventional phenomenology which claims the ability to understand derives from the ability to generalize from the *individual* experiences, not from the culture itself. Cultural anthropology also contrasts with some versions of hermeneutics which confine themselves to the subjective meanings, paying little or no attention to identifying general, underlying (cultural) systems of meaning.

- That action is less a matter of rational calculation than *felt expectations* as to the meaning or significance of the action since people are motivated by the meaning or significance of things for them.
- That the meaning (significance) of an action (like the buying of a product or brand) mirrors somewhat the patterns of interconnected meanings constituting the individual's cultural or social milieu. This view contrasts with Blumer's relativist position which stresses the uniqueness of each individual's own world of meaning. This relativist position rules out any generalization of findings. Instead of understanding emanating from a common culture, the relativist suggests the need for empathy in order to interpret another's actions.

Cultural anthropology rests on there being intersubjective meanings of actions within society based on cultural affinities. While *society* is identified with the actual people themselves, culture goes further in embracing all the people's shared beliefs, values, knowledge, meanings and ideas. At least this is one view but, as has already been stated, there is an alternative definition of culture that focuses purely on what can be seen, heard, smelled or touched. But non-positivist cultural anthropologists like Geertz (1984) deny that culture can be defined in terms of observables as per the positivist tradition. For Geertz, there is the metaphor of every person being 'suspended' in *webs of meanings* that he himself has spun. These webs of meanings represent his culture so the analysis of culture should *not* be an experimental science in the search for universal laws but an interpretive activity in the search for the meaning (significance) of things. Geertz recommends that anthropologists seek explanations of culture 'connecting action to its sense rather than behavior to its determinants'. In other words, connecting action to its significance for the consumer rather than seeking the material causes of the behavior. This is done, not by using empathy (as Malinowski, an earlier anthropologist, had recommended) but through hermeneutics. Geertz in fact rejects the idea of any interpretation of human behavior being dependent on 'empathy'. For him the task is not to put oneself in another's shoes but to find out 'what they think they are up to'. To understand a culture we need to determine what the people take to be the point of what they are doing, search out and analyze their symbol systems, and not proceed as if the native point of view can be ignored.

In spite of Geertz, it is still common to claim that we need 'empathy' to successfully interpret the behavior of others. Traditionally, as stated earlier, empathy has been defined as 'feeling oneself into' (or 'putting oneself in another's shoes') in contrast to 'sympathy' which is 'feeling with'. It was Max Weber (1864–1920) who argued that understanding others stems from empathy or the ability to put ourselves in the shoes of another. But a more operational way of evoking empathy in ourselves is to *simulate* the situation of the other person. This is probably the best way of teaching employees how to empathize with customers. Employees need to be taught to empathize with their target customers or otherwise they are apt to make poor decisions in respect, say, to customer service (Patnaik 2009).

For Geertz (1995), culture is above all a system of symbols; not symbols at the very abstract level but the symbol systems like language that convey meaning in social situations. For him, the task of the anthropologist is to identify the symbol systems of a culture that give rise to the rules guiding behavior. If we could explain particular forms of human behavior as following rules, we could explain behavior in a way that differs fundamentally from explanations in the natural sciences. Rules, unlike scientific laws, can be broken and are not true or false but effective or ineffective. The content of a rule of action plays a part in making it happen, but in saying this we need to distinguish between those instances of behavior that are *guided* by a rule and those cases that can merely be *described* by a rule. If we are looking back we can usually describe some rule that is being followed but may not necessarily be able to predict what that rule would be.

If undirected by cultural rules and social norms, man's behavior would be chaotic since, unlike animals, human beings do not have any broad, comprehensive set of fixed, hard-wired, instinctive response patterns. What has characterized human evolution has been the increasing reliance on symbols (language, art, myth and ritual) for understanding the world, communication and self-control. Where cultural norms or standards are weak in bringing about conformity, it is the legal system that helps fill the gap. At the highest level, there are the cultural values of a society that implicitly are drawn on to help determine trade-offs in decision-making. However this is not to suggest cultural values cannot conflict. They do and this brings with it the problem of reconciliation.

Geertz views the mind as consisting of symbolic models, used to interpret the real world. These symbolic models are the source of conceptions of how things are to be understood and how things should be done. All conscious perception, to Geertz, involves identifying an object by instantaneously pairing it with something that is already part of the mind's symbolic models: culture, as a symbolic model, acts as a road map, transforming 'mere physical locations into places'. Symbolic models are what we have called 'perspectives' in this book, with the term 'symbolic' suggesting what structures the perspective. Geertz could be said to view a person's *perspective* on an issue as a *symbolic model* imputed to reality in order to interpret it. What Geertz says about the role of symbolic models could equally be said about the role of perspectives.

Geertz aims to grasp the subjects' point of view to determine what this group or that group takes to be the point of what they are doing. Geertz sets out to discover the significance and/or intentions lying behind the action by understanding relevant perspective(s). Intentions are generally easier to discern than motives and beliefs but they are not necessarily transparent. In fact the major problem in dealing with adversaries in international conflict is gauging intentions, not their abilities or resources.

Explanations in social science, for Geertz, do not result in 'laws' but in an 'unpacking of the conceptual world' in which the person lives. We understand concepts and what those concepts imply and the relationship between concepts such as that between desire and action, doubt and inaction, emotion and values and so on. The concepts that comprise a culture are basic to understanding that culture. (We might add that in learning any subject there is this need to focus on the sense-meaning and the referential-meaning of the subject's concepts.) This claim by Geertz is also made by Shutz, as discussed in Chapter 13, but also prominently in philosophy by Peter Winch.

Winch (1958), a student of Wittgenstein, directed attention to understanding a society through identifying the *concepts* of the culture, on the grounds that underlying these concepts are the rules being followed. For example, if a consumer says she buys brand X because it is 'familiar', the concept of *familiarity* suggests that the rule is, other things being equal, she buys the brand that is most familiar. Understand the concepts and we understand the rules lying behind the action. Prescriptive rules can be formulated as: If X, then do Y. The concept of meaning as used here is Wittgenstein's *meaning-in-use* which is not generally the 'meaning' sought and adopted in the social sciences. It is meaning in the sense of the significance of things to the individual which has been of most interest in social science. Thus, we want to know in marketing what is significant for the consumer because significance is tied to the consumer's concerns and people's concerns have an emotional resonance. But meaning-in-use of the concepts used by the consumer is still basic for understanding the consumer, which is another reason for listening to the consumer as she talks 'off the top of her head' to identify the concepts or categories employed (see Chapter 2).

Ethnography is that subdivision of anthropology devoted to the comparative study of individual cultures. If culture is read as a text, it is a text constructed by the ethnographer so there can be different 'readings' (interpretations). Geertz talks of seeking 'thick' description in 'reading' a culture as a text. Geertz's interpretive anthropology is founded on this concept of 'thick' description by which he means a description with *layers* of meaning from which to pick and choose, while drawing large conclusions from small, densely textured facts. It was the Oxford philosopher Gilbert Ryle (1949) who first made a distinction between thin and thick description but *not* with the same meaning as for Geertz. It is interesting to digress for a moment on Ryle as he was at one time such a dominant figure in ordinary language philosophy (known also as conceptual analysis or linguistic analysis).

Ryle argued that to describe behavior only in terms of *physical* movements is to describe that behavior thinly. In contrast, to describe the behavior in terms of the *actions* taken is to describe that behavior *thickly* since actions involve not just reference to physical movements but the intention lying behind the action and the social rules which give it meaning. Ryle's seminal and brilliant book, *The Concept of Mind,* was an attempt to dismiss the psycho-physical problem in claiming that arguments that question the relation between body and mind were improper questions in that the word 'mind' does not stand for a distinct organ but only one's ability and proneness to do certain things. Ryle's *logical* behaviorism led him to claim that hypotheses about hidden goings-on can do no more than allow us to observe behavior which we already in fact observe (p. 124).

Ryle provided intellectual support for the notion that all mental concepts like 'attitude' can be understood in terms of dispositional tendencies, such as an 'attitude' being a disposition to respond in a certain way to some person or thing. This view is known as 'logical behaviorism' in the philosophy of mind because mental states are simply *behavioral* dispositions, as opposed to being *internal* states. This is still an orthodox position to take. But critics point out that it is not clear how a disposition can be a forcing variable (cause) without taking into account mental states like wants and desires. If a consumer believes the Lexus car is the best car on the market, his or her attitude or disposition towards the Lexus is positive but whether this leads to buying the Lexus depends on whether the consumer wants the Lexus enough to buy it, and many other contextual factors are present. All this has led some philosophers to define mental states such as 'attitude' specifically in terms of their causal role: what activates that kind of mental state; what consequent behavior is likely to result and how does the mental state interact with other mental states such as other attitudes? This is the *functionalist approach* (see Chapter 13), which has considerable appeal but there are problems as to the feasibility of any research program based on the functionalist perspective.

Kuper (1990) attacks the notion that culture research demands 'thick description'. Whether the study of culture necessitates thick description depends on which aspects of culture are of interest. We need to ask: what is thick description best for? Kuper takes Geertz's example of a robbery in 1912 that included murder and retribution, involving a Jewish trader, a Berber sheik and a French colonial officer. Kuper argues, contrary to Geertz, that this case hides no cultural mysteries but makes perfect sense in non-cultural terms; that is, one needs no knowledge of cultural anthropology to analyze and understand the case. This is true of many studies in social science; stripped of jargon they are fully explainable in terms of folk psychology.

As we have said, Geertz views the mind as consisting of symbolic models. Symbolic models are one interpretation of the notion of consumers always drawing on some perspective in their inquiries or evaluations. If a perspective reflects a set of symbolic models, one of these symbolic models will be the person's language, which incorporates a web of meanings in the language's network of concepts and symbolic metaphors. The claim that people interpret or understand the world through symbolic models is said to contrast with the view that people simply make sense of experience (Blumer's view) or weigh up the objective material facts in order to choose the most rewarding action, as assumed by decision models. But is there a real difference between the symbolic model view of Geertz and making sense of experience? Surely 'making sense of experience' is against a background perspective or, in Geertz terminology, against a background of symbolic models? And are not decision models symbolic models? A symbolic model will be part of a perspective; a way of viewing reality, with the formal decision model having more structural clarity than the word symbolic model might in itself suggest.

In studying a culture, Geertz aims to determine what this group or that group takes to be the point of what they are doing. This focus on human *purposes* is one form of explanation, namely, the *goal-ascription* (*teleological*) mode of explanation. An explanation in terms of goals, objectives sought or functions performed is a form of explanation rejected by those regarding causal explanations as the only legitimate form of scientific explanation. Geertz passes over causal analysis since his goal is to understand the significance and/or intentions lying behind the action. This he does, not by employing empathy but through employing *hermeneutics*. For him, scientific (causal) explanation accounts for happenings from observations outside the happenings: anthropological understanding, in contrast, derives from trying to get inside the happenings. Thus he would have no interest in collecting information on the external factors that might have caused the consumer to buy product 'A', such as like the social pressure of an accompanying friend, but be concerned with what lies behind the choices as revealed by the concepts employed and the consumer's own self-understandings.

Geertz does not accept that the world's peoples are growing more and more alike; there is divergence rather than convergence of cultures. This is one opinion that might be borne in mind when talking of global marketing. It is a view endorsed in marketing by Russell Belk (1995), who rejects the notion of distinct cultures disappearing, pointing to the modifications cultures make in adopting foreign artifacts. Montaigne (1533–92), the father figure of skepticism, once said something to the effect that, if we were not alike, we could not be distinguished from the beasts but, if we were not different, we could not be distinguished from each other. While cultures overlap, they also differ and subcultures flourish – subcultures based on (say) racial and ethnic groups, social classes and geographic location.

Marketing is wise to identify subcultures and not be content with identifying cultural commonalities. Western cultures are rife with competing subcultures that seek, as Collins (1990) says, 'self-legitimation' of their cultural products; with marketers striving to persuade those who consume products that the subculture, and it alone, speaks the language of truth about life and how it should be lived. Collins reminds us that high culture (Culture with a capital 'C') has *not* been dominant since the eighteenth century, while low culture is better viewed as a rich plurality of beliefs/behavior systems. This is a view advertising has long accepted but it is a viewpoint for marketing generally.

Geertz (1973) adopts the metaphor of the *text* for interpreting all cultural social practices and, via the hermeneutic circle, aims to reveal the meaning in these practices. Though Geertz acknowledges that an ethnographer can neither put his or her language to one side nor see things exactly as those in the culture see things, he nevertheless seeks the point of any action from the 'native' point of view. But which native point of view? Even if there is a specific native point of view, unless an anthropologist is psychologically close to his subjects, there is a problem in trying to identify the native point of view: foreigners cannot at will just adopt the perceptions of the 'native'.

As we have seen, Geertz rejects causal explanation as the goal in cultural anthropology. For Geertz the search for meaning is the key focus. Interpretive, symbolic anthropology, linked to philosophy and the humanities is, for Geertz, the framework for the discipline. But many doubt whether the search for 'meaning' is sufficient for many purposes. As Hollis (1996) says,

> it offers no obvious way of accounting, still less of justifying an account of action ... to grasp the fuller meaning of an action, there is a need to know why it is done.

> (Hollis 1996: 265)

In other words, for a fuller meaning of the action, we need to know the causes and not only the meaning of the action for the individual. But much depends on what questions are being addressed, while in focusing on the meaning of the action the reasons for the action are likely to emerge.

Geertz borrows from the psychoanalyst Heinz Kohut the distinction between *experience-near* and *experience-distant* concepts. This is a useful distinction for marketing. An experience-near concept is a concept like 'desire' which is readily understood when applied either to oneself or to others, whereas an experience-distant concept is one like 'operant conditioning' which belongs to the vocabulary of specialists. The trick for Geertz is to comprehend the concepts that are experience-near and connect them in an insightful way to the experience-distant concepts that specialists use to describe the salient features of social life. This echoes what was said earlier about relating or translating the consumer's own everyday concepts into the *sensitizing* concepts developed in social science to provide more clarity, precision and generality. In other words, the problem lies in identifying the concepts the consumer uses and interpreting these in terms of the sensitizing concepts found in social science to supply greater depth.

If Geertz (1995) rejects the *verstehen* view of empathy (putting oneself in another's shoes), it is, as he says, because he cannot imagine himself as a Javanese rice peasant in order to see how and what the rice peasant thinks and feels. Geertz's hermeneutics does not focus on reliving the thoughts of the agent but on 'decoding' the point of the action. He describes himself as an ethnographer who moves from asking himself about lifestyle to asking what 'vehicles' (mainly concepts) embody that form of life (lifestyle).

If he is concerned with how a people within a culture define themselves (their self-identity), he analyzes the symbolic forms, words, images, institutions or behaviors because these are the means or vehicles by which people actually represent themselves to themselves and to one another (Geertz 1987). To repeat, Geertz conceptualizes the study of culture as following the methods of the humanities where the focus is not on the actions per se but people's own interpretations (understandings) of their actions. Geertz views social practices as a text and, via the method of the hermeneutic circle, hopes to reveal the meaning in these practices or the point of the action from the 'native's' point of view. This means listening to what the 'native' has to say (see Chapter 2).

Cases as texts can provide material for thick description, and thick descriptions of just a few texts (cases) may provide more understanding than an accumulation of individual social science statistical studies. But the question that might be asked of Geertz is: will seeking to capture the purely symbolic world make for a satisfactory anthropology even if such symbols signal underlying meanings?

GEERTZ'S IDEALISM VERSUS POSITIVISM AND REALISM

Geertz subscribes in his work to the philosophical perspective of *idealism*, not *realism*. Realism, contrary to some social scientists, does not equate with *positivism* though both realism and positivism entail *empiricism*, that is, the claim that what we know, we know only because the empirical evidence so far happens to point that way. But positivism endorses *methodological monism*: the notion that any discipline that aspires to be a science must follow the methodology of the natural sciences where interpretation does not loom large. This contrasts with *methodological pluralism* which accepts that there is no one best way or a coherent set of methods for establishing truth about the world. Realism does not necessarily endorse methodological monism.

There are several forms of realism but all involve claims about the actual existence of certain entities. 'Naive' realism or 'common sense' realism concedes to observation direct acquaintance with the physical world, that is, that we perceive reality not through sense-impressions but directly. But scientific realism is something different. There are two kinds of scientific realism (Hacking 1983):

- Realism about theories: realism asserts that theories are either true or false since truth is how the world is.
- Realism about unobservable theoretical entities: realism accepts the existence of many theoretical entities even though they are not observable.

There are those who are realists about theories but not about entities and vice versa. Thus, the British philosopher Bertrand Russell was anti-realist when it came to theoretical entities but was a realist about theories. There are some philosophers who believe in the existence of some theories or some theoretical entities and not others and so on.

Idealism, as claimed earlier, contrasts with realism in viewing reality as all in the mind; the contents of the mind are all that there is: all we have, or can be sure of, consists of ideas about what the world is like and this limits our claims to truth about the world. Those undertaking *qualitative* research may subscribe to either realism or idealism. Idealists undertaking qualitative research are *social constructionists*, claiming that all social life is socially constructed, rather than naturally given, and the social world is constantly being reinvented rather than being fixed in time. No one suggests that the currency system, the legal system and social institutions such as Congress or Parliament are other than social constructions. Controversy is sparked when the social constructionist claims that all social knowledge including scientific knowledge is a social construction, simply representations that are acted upon 'as if' true. To the scientist, scientific laws are discovered, not created, while their claims are corroborated through testing.

Social constructionism becomes a form of relativism in the debate between pro-science realists and the relativists in social constructionism. Relativism denies any absolutes exist so standards of truth and rationality are relative, with cultural relativism claiming that particular beliefs, values and practices only apply to one cultural setting. For many scientists relativism on this definition is unintelligible on the grounds that truth and rationality are objective matters and not culturally determined.

It was the postmodernist, relativist view that human values are pliant social constructions that led Isaiah Berlin (2006), an Oxford scholar in the history of ideas, to argue that there are universal human values (ultimate ideals), even if these values on occasion conflict. Thus Berlin talks of the universal value of 'negative liberty', defined as being able to express our thoughts without being interfered with by others. This he acknowledges could conflict with the value of maintaining security. The US Constitution guarantees *negative* liberty but has been less a guarantor than expected, with much negative liberty sacrificed since 9/11 in the interests of national 'security'.

Pro-science realists go along with the view that scientists transform our view of the world by scientific discoveries that simultaneously result in the development of scientific concepts to express those discoveries. In this narrow sense scientists construct their world but this in no way undermines the realists' concept of truth and objectivity. Realists accept a notion of truth as correspondence to reality (the correspondence theory of truth) while agreeing that we do not have direct access to reality in that access is mediated by concepts. There is no such thing as an unconceptualized world to study interrelationships among the entities in the world though different perspectives do break up the world differently. In any case, different perspectives of an event, action or attribute do not imply differing events, actions or properties. Realists are right in arguing, say, that brand 'A' is the same object even if 'A', as experienced, differs from one person to another. The fact that we construct our own representations of reality is not the same as creating that reality: the way we organize and describe the world through concepts should not be confused with creating reality itself.

Brown (2001), a philosopher, refers to the 'science wars' or 'war' over who rules (science or the literati). As he says, this is essentially concerned with epistemology (the nature of knowledge and its justification): What is evidence? What is objectivity? What is rationality? Natural scientists are characteristically realists and do not subscribe to any social construction-ist view of science. This latter claim, for those interested in this debate, is dispassionately and eloquently defended by Columbia University's Philip Kitcher (2001).

For Geertz, anthropology and idealism go together. Idealists reject the idea of there being laws of human behavior and deny there are unobserv-able realities like 'protons', electrons, attitudes, motives, beliefs and wants, regarding them all as simply useful fictions. Such 'useful fictions' have been part of science since the time of Isaac Newton with his talk of mass and force, while in social science all such fictions are viewed as social construc-tions, acting as tools for explanation and/or prediction. Idealists reject any notion of high rationality in human behavior, viewing people as motivated by ideas that can be irrational, even mystical. The economist's concept of rationality is 'high' rationality but only in the sense of seeking to select the best means of achieving a person's ends. It assumes rationality is the single-minded quest for whatever ends one desires without discussing the rationality of the ends themselves.

The Geertz approach is opposed to realism. As stated earlier, there are various forms of realism but all of them involve claims about the actual existence of things: with scientific realism generally asserting that scientific entities like the electron and/or scientific theories actually exist and there-fore must be either true or false because truth is how the world is. Judging something to be definitely either true or false is always emotionally satis-fying. This is why dogmatic assertions are so welcome to the faithful who hate the notion of there being some doubt about their beliefs. We want our beliefs to tell us how the world is: suspending judgment is emotionally unsatisfactory even if it is the correct stance to take, given the evidence. Searching for truth is elusive and most people simply use the pragmatic test of checking beliefs against experience in the real world. Beliefs provide expectations about happenings and life would be impossible if most of our expectations were not realized. But there are no universal law-like truths in social science because truth is always context-sensitive. We should regard idealism and realism generally as positions implicitly adopted by social sci-entists on pragmatic grounds: asking themselves which is most useful given their perspective.

CULTURE AND SYMBOLS

A culture holds certain symbols as central to its identity, for example the nation's flag or language. For cultural anthropologists, symbols act as psychological cement for holding a culture together. Claude Lévi-Strauss, the anthropologist, claimed that an analysis of such symbolism can reveal universal principles of thought. One problem here is that any symbolism is ambiguous, giving rise to arguments over its meaning. But this very ambiguity can on occasion make a particular symbol an effective means of uniting people, as all can interpret it their own way, as different people in the US interpret the significance of the flag.

Whether in political life or in the marketplace, where there is information overload or information fatigue, symbols of values may substitute for real knowledge and be decisive in generating support and purchase. This may be the case when a brand name substitutes for real knowledge about the product. Today there is certainly information fatigue when it comes to choosing in the marketplace, for example when it comes to choosing among electronic products. The many features of cell phones and smartphones push the consumer into relying on the advice of others. We have 'bounded rationality' and are happy to go through life on (as the military say) a need-to-know basis. Symbols economize on effort in necessitating little information search. But symbolic meanings do change. In previous generations, as already said, a tear in a trouser leg of one's jeans would indicate poverty and symbolize the wearer to be lower class. Today it may indicate youth and symbolize fashion. Whenever brands are undifferentiated, marketers fall back on building up associations of the brand with valued symbolic images, with the expectation that the aura of the images rubs off on the brand sufficient to trigger a sale.

To summarize so far: for Geertz, culture is a system of symbols; not the highly abstract symbol systems like mathematics but symbols (particularly natural languages) used to convey meaning in social situations. For him, the task of the anthropologist is to identify the symbol systems of a culture to give insight into the rules lying behind behavior. If undirected by such rules, man's behavior would be chaotic since, unlike animals, human beings do not have any broad, comprehensive set of fixed, instinctive response patterns. Humans are not hardwired in the way animals are. What has characterized evolution has been the increasing reliance on symbols (language, art, myth and ritual) for understanding the world, communication and self-control.

For Geertz, interpreting any culture amounts to interpreting its symbols, as happens in the humanities. Consumers, like people generally, live in a world of symbols and it is this symbolic world that activates behavior. This view, as we have already said, fits the philosophy of idealism, not realism. Idealism claims that reality is in some way mental; that the contents of the mind are all that there is in experience: whatever reality is out there is 'unknowable'; all we have consists of ideas about what the world is like.

It was George Berkeley (1685–1753) who argued that ideas alone exist and that experience simply supplies mental images. That the world outside is all mental is a view rejected by the natural sciences, though all accept that the 'furniture' of the world, such as government and money, is socially constructed. Something can be socially constructed but real like the currency, yet still not be a natural-type like trees and animals. Idealism asserts that there are different ways of looking at reality (i.e. different perspectives), none of which is more correct than the others. This relativism ignores the fact that some perspectives are more insightful than others, depending on the questions being addressed. If one accepts that various perspectives on reality can be equally valid, it is not surprising that Geertz does not offer, as Kuper points out, any criteria to allow us to separate good from bad interpretations of texts, even though he accepts that some ethnographic interpretations are more reliable than others. He seems to suggest that much depends on the sophistication of the cosmopolitan ethnographer. Nor does Geertz offer anything concrete on methods beyond hermeneutics and the application of some sort of in-depth clinical analysis of individual cases.

One insightful suggestion (not unique to Geertz) is that meanings are often revealed by means of *symbolic metaphors* and it is the ethnographer's job to identity the metaphors that give coherence and structure to any text of human behavior (Kuper 1999). Thus the symbolic metaphor that compulsory individual health insurance sends the nation down 'the slippery road to autocracy' captures the perspective of those opposing the Obama health legislation. But perhaps the symbolic metaphor of 'Big Brother', with its overtones of our actions being monitored and controlled by some government entity, conjures up the 'right' frightening scenario. The symbolic metaphor of consumers 'jumping on the bandwagon' signals dubious behavior without further explanation. But, beyond looking for symbolic metaphors by examining what the consumer says, there is no library of cultural symbolic metaphors to add to our understanding of consumer behavior – beyond looking at dictionaries of idioms for insight. Human actions, though, are texts that can possibly carry symbolic (metaphoric) messages to their 'readers'. We guess at their meaning(s), evaluate the guesses and draw tentative explanations. There are no laws or fixed generalizations as things change: we live in a fluid semiotic world.

Geertz, in studying a culture, aims to grasp the subject's point of view in order to determine what this group or that group takes to be the point of what they are doing. It is this focus on purpose which rules out the notion of cultural anthropology being like a natural science since the natural sciences do not adopt teleological (towards a predetermined end) explanations but causal ones, expressed as mathematical functions. Explanations in social science, for Geertz, do not issue in scientific 'laws' but an 'unpacking of the conceptual world' in which the person lives. As said earlier, he recommends that anthropologists seek explanations of culture 'connecting action to its sense rather than behavior to its determinants' through the medium of hermeneutics.

Geertz is sometimes viewed as a postmodernist since he expresses sympathy for postmodernist writers like Roland Barthes, Michael Foucault and Paul Ricoeur, but he is far from being a paid-up member. Geertz is eclectic in his interests, with an abiding interest in language which makes him an admirer of Oxford philosopher J.L. Austin in linguistic philosophy. On the other hand, he has no taste for the abstract, formalistic ethnographic work of the French anthropologist Lévi-Strauss, or for functionalism as developed in social anthropology. As to functionalism Geertz does not even try to discover the various functions served by a society's practices.

LÉVI-STRAUSS AND STRUCTURALISM

Structuralism sees an underlying order in everything and is one system for imputing a certain type of interpretation to cultural expressions, cultural norms and customs. Lévi-Strauss (1908–2009) originally used the word to describe linguists who took binary opposites like hot versus cold as the building blocks of language (Wilcken 2011). Lévi-Strauss is criticized for undertaking very little fieldwork but his interest lay not in studying how various cultures functioned but in how the mind dealt with the resources it had at its disposal to create culture by, say, logical oppositions or by the creation of myths. For him myths were the mind's way of bringing about a resolution of intractable problems emanating from an unacceptable reality.

Lévi-Strauss's structural anthropology is no longer in favor. The same goes for his mathematical diagrams designating cultural rules. Interestingly, as he set about to discern the unconscious logic of the mind, he recommended that anthropologists link up with neuroscientists to explain many of the mysterious patterns of behavior. He himself regarded all human thought as built up from binary opposites.

Lévi-Strauss is particularly noted for highlighting the incest taboo in all cultures. Without any nod to Freud, he viewed the taboo as nature's way of dividing women into prohibited and possible spouses, enabling communication between groups and intermarriage. Other anthropologists were to show that the incest taboo was by no means universal among cultures. Lévi-Strauss rejected the notion that there is a difference in the logic employed by primitive people, who he claimed were as logical in the same way as those in the so-called civilized societies. This claim ran contrary to the prevailing view which drew a strong distinction between civilized and primitive modes of thought. His perspective was influenced by Ferdinand de Saussure (1867–1913), the co-founder with Charles Sanders Peirce (1839–1914) of contemporary semiotics. Lévi-Strauss proposed that we view language as a self-contained system of *interrelationships*, namely, mainly binary opposites (e.g. belief versus doubt), rather than just a collection of words, each representing a 'real' object.

In anthropology, structuralism opposes any strong cultural relativity since it suggests that all human cultures are, in a final analysis, the expression of the underlying structures of the human mind: all thought processes of people in every culture are basically alike. Human thought works partly by constructing binary oppositions (analogous to the binary system of 0 or 1 on which computer programs are based). We are, for example, sensitive to contrasts in life, such as good versus evil, male versus female, purity versus impurity, chaos versus order. Different cultures divide the world up differently but all use oppositions. Meaning emerges from seeing a word and its opposite; 'evil' only makes sense against the concept of 'good'.

What distinguishes Lévi-Strauss is his search for universals in contrast to most anthropologists who look for differences, not commonalities. He is most associated with structuralism, accepting the linguistic model of 'binary oppositions', together with the notion of universal structures underlying all human action. His structuralism was a methodology that did not focus on the significance of individual elements of a culture but emphasized their interdependence. In his analysis of such cultural elements as myths, kinship and symbolism, he claimed their underlying structures were universal and to be understood in terms of binary opposition, such as male and female, left and right and so on.

Lévi-Strauss claims a structural unity lies behind all human myth-making. Myths, he claimed, were built up from binary oppositions as it is through these binary oppositions that people make sense of their world. The human mind is sensitive to binary contrasts in the human condition, like being healthy versus being ill. People reach an understanding of society through the contrast of one with the other. Lévi-Strauss sought to systematize all cultural phenomena on the basis of such binary oppositions; myths and so on were not studied on their own but studied with other cultural elements as part of a total system built up from these basic contrasts. One of his achievements was to challenge the perspective that primitive societies were temperamentally irrational and intellectually unimaginative. The tribes he studied in Brazil sought order, admired esthetic design and so on. But structuralism in anthropology has come under considerable criticism for its non-dynamic (static) nature and its neglect of the role of individuals in creating and changing cultures.

This concept of structuralism, so associated with Lévi-Strauss, differs somewhat from the *structural-functionalist* school originating with the British anthropologist A.R. Radcliffe-Brown (1881–1955) who claimed that every societal belief and custom had a specific function that served to maintain the structure (the ordered arrangement of its parts) of society. For Radcliffe-Brown, the job of the anthropologist was to investigate the ways in which beliefs and customs functioned to solve the problem of maintaining society. The focus was on society as a system (i.e. a set of interdependent parts that together form a unitary whole) and to examine the interconnections among the various parts. As we have seen, this approach was adopted by the American sociologist Talcott Parsons (1902–79) who dominated sociology in the immediate period following the Second World War.

POST-STRUCTURALISM, POSTMODERNISM AND ANTHROPOLOGY

Post-structuralism and postmodernism have influenced the study of anthropology in ways not always for the better. Structuralism and the semiotics (or semiology if we are to stick to Saussure's term) that inspired it claim that the signs and symbols in society represent a deep, meaningful reality. In contrast, post-structuralism claims that beyond signs (typically words or images) there are simply more signs with no underlying truths or certainties of meaning to be discovered by 'objective' observers. Post-structuralism emanates from 'deconstructionism' associated with the postmodernist Jacques Derrida, who disregards the socio-historical setting of texts and all attempts to discover intentional 'meaning'. Derrida (1991) argues that no single interpretation can claim to be the final one and demonstrates this by deconstructing the text in effect by showing its failure to be interpreted unambiguously. In deconstruction, the text at its literal level can be shown to be intensely metaphorical so that intentions are never fully transparent even to the author. The practice of deconstruction gives rise to alternative readings that are equally defensible. But Foucault (1981), also a postmodernist, argues that some interpretations are more fundamental than others so a choice can be made. Ricoeur (1981), another postmodernist, agrees, arguing that though a text may allow for several interpretations, the better ones emerge from a process of argumentation and debate. This is a position most would support.

With Derrida there is the 'death of the author'. Under the 'new criticism' movement this concept of the death of the author signals a reorientation in the interpretation of text from critical attention to the author's intentions, motives and purposes, to viewing texts as sites where reader interpretation seeks to wrest meaning from the signs themselves. Derrida distinguishes between 'differing', which argues it is only the oppositions between words that give them significance, and 'deferring', the notion that the resolution of an interpretation of meaning is endlessly put off by the interpreter in processing the many, many different aspects of the text.

The deconstructionist's notion of power lurking behind the choice of words has given rise to attempts, via 'political correctness', to purify the language. Sometimes this can be confusing. For instance, Inga Glendinnen (2003), in a generally excellent ethnographic study of the Australian Aborigines, refers to Aborigines as 'Australians' on the grounds that the word Aborigine is a colonial construct loaded with negative connotations. But is this not misleading since it ignores the fact that the dominant meanings or connotations of the word Australian, in isolation, are distinctly not Aborigine. Political correctness is a *symbolic strategy* in that it alters symbols in the hope that people will believe reality itself has been changed. A change in symbols or symbolic expressions can change perceptions, but not long term unless the underlying reality has also been affected or changed. We may call a refuse collector a 'sanitary engineer' and this does elevate the image initially but, without reality changing, the same initial connotations (sense-meaning) will return.

Deconstruction attacks hierarchies of authority of every kind whether we are thinking of the dominance of science in the intellectual hierarchy or social hierarchies, on the grounds that hierarchies of authority promote criteria such as 'certainty' and 'truth' purely for their own advantage. Those highly positioned in the hierarchy, such as the scientific community, are able to repress other elements that, as a consequence, become the 'unthought' or even the unthinkable. It is this repression of other elements that is disturbing. Derrida called this bias 'logocentrism'. Derrida argues that we are fortunate in being able to criticize this logocentrism, as whatever language is used it still carries traces of the repressed order. Derrida's deconstructionism involves a close analysis of the text to tease out the contradictions that shadow the text's seeming coherence. Deconstructionism is regarded as a core part of postmodernism, while Derrida and postmodernism are sometimes viewed (wrongly) as part of the *linguistic turn* in social science. Derrida denies this. He does not view his thinking as part of any linguistic turn but as a resistance to it.

Postmodernism, as a term coined by the American Marxist Fredric Jameson, expands on a whole collection of claims that enter into interpretations: (a) claiming all truth and value are relative; (b) that there are no invariant truths; no absolutes or universals when it comes to people; (c) that all knowledge is socially constructed even in the natural sciences; (d) rejection of the belief that science is built on a sound foundation of observable fact rather than simply being another cultural discourse guided by a self-serving ideology; (e) a rejection of all hierarchies of knowledge, with physics no longer being able to claim any special position at the top; (f) an interest in the local rather than the universal; (g) the migration from a focus on words to a stress on symbols or images (Lyon 1994). Such claims have come to form a perspective in investigations into cultures and in undertaking the study of literature generally.

Relativism and the social construction of reality are among the major characteristics of postmodernism, with objectivity regarded as a myth. Of course, a case could be made for the claim that complete objectivity even in science is a myth since all science is conducted through some perspective which has its own bias, but postmodernists would go further than this. The social construction of reality regards all things, collectively and socially, that are defined as real, as only becoming real in their consequences. The most sweeping version of the doctrine of social construction of reality claims that what is a 'fact' simply depends on what is generally agreed to be a 'fact'. Sometimes this is so but not often. Also, any move from the 'facts' to prescribing a course of action is simply a judgment call. Although some philosophers (following David Hume in the eighteenth century) argue that from an 'is' (the facts) one cannot derive an 'ought to' (ought to do), facts can be rather compelling as to what action to take, just as seeing we are out of food suggests going to the store.

We can view postmodernism as arising from the need to have guidance on interpretation beyond the superficialities of hermeneutics, even if it means postmodernism has to rely on what critics regard as outdated Marxist ideology, Freudian psychology and Derrida's deconstructionism.

Kuper (1999) claims the postmodernist movement has had a paralyzing effect on the discipline of cultural anthropology, making young ethnographers too nervous to voice strong opinions or even to go into the field at all. This is a frightening scenario. But it is not just the postmodernist aggressive dogma that can inhibit open discourse. At any one time, there is a tendency for orthodoxy to arise among journal editors and reviewers which, in spite of protests to the contrary, biases the review process through ignorance about alternative paradigms.

A card-carrying postmodernist anthropologist regards ethnographers as simply writing persuasive fiction since there are no privileged perspectives and no objective standards for judging the reliability of any interpretation. As with qualitative research, replication is not considered all that meaningful. Not that replication is common in any quantitative research. Both qualitative and quantitative research in social science 'replicate' (if at all) for reliability by alternative testing: in the case of quantitative research by testing the hypotheses in some different ways, while with qualitative research we reinterpret from a different angle or perspective and see if there is corroboration. Reliability is at risk when various interpreters make reference to the same concept since the concept may have different connotations for each interpreter: there is always a need to spell out and illustrate what the concept means in the context. We might add that it is still all too common for research articles to test their model or hypothesis on its own as opposed to a testing that eliminates rival hypotheses. Rival hypotheses may seem unlikely but confirming the *less likely* as in fact the *most likely* adds most to knowledge.

VALIDITY OF QUALITATIVE (INTERPRETIVE) RESEARCH VERSUS QUANTITATIVE

Those who reject interpretive approaches to social science debate the validity of its methodology for developing scientific theory. Others, who support alternative positions, may claim that there are often unconscious causes at work, or that objective external causes should be sought, or that functional analysis should be used to understand capacities for action and so on. This simply means there is a claim that other perspectives in social science offer additional windows into anthropology or ask different questions and their concerns need to be addressed. Where different explanations are really incompatible, we might follow the dictum found in the psychiatrist's diagnostic manual – choose the explanation 'not better explained by another diagnosis'.

The interest in qualitative (interpretive) research rests to some extent on the recognition that many qualitative aspects of human experience cannot be addressed by quantitative approaches, such as the appreciation of beautiful music, pleasures of social bonding and so on. However, this does not mean that quantitative techniques cannot play a role in quantifying the qualitative. But very, very few of the articles in the quantitative marketing journals, though they widely quote each other, have had much of an impact on marketing management.

ANTHROPOLOGY AND MARKETING

One well-known contribution of anthropology to marketing is that made by Mary Douglas whose views we noted earlier in the text (see Douglas and Isherwood 1979). Douglas claims that buying functions to:

1. Promote community with others
2. Make sense of what is happening in the world around: that consumer goods are bought to:

   • Transmit and receive information about the social scene
   • Help build bridges or erect social fences by, say, signaling to others the user's self-image, rank and values
   • Mark social events like marriage and births
   • Reduce chores to provide more time for social involvement
   • Give order to events through (say) newspapers, television, books and so on to make sense of the world around.

This is a useful classification for marketers thinking about the social functions performed by consumer products so we do not lose sight of the social aspect of buying. We might also be reminded that health care products and education are also as much consumer products as washing powder and cars.

McCracken (1988) applies anthropology more broadly to consumer behavior. McCracken contends that goods express and create a whole range of cultural meaning; that without consumer goods we would find certain acts of self-definition and collective definition (defining who and what we are) to be impossible. Goods, for example, help the consumer lay claim to status, to compete for status or to legitimize status.

McCracken speaks of the transfer of meaning (significance) from the culture to consumer goods and on to the consumer. In other words, what is meaningful or positively valued in the culture, sellers try to pass on to their products so that, in possessing the product, certain valued cultural associations rub off on to the consumer. McCracken asserts that whatever meaning is imputed to goods ultimately originates from the culture itself. This is a conceptual truth since culture includes language and all conceptual meanings are embedded in the language. All concepts like patriotism are cultural constructions that have a certain sense-meaning and referential-meaning within the language. We hence have the logical and conceptual sequence: Culture⇒Concepts⇒Categories in the language⇒Sense-meaning and Referential-meaning to products in the culture. Thus, as McCracken says, the sense-meaning or significance we give to goods and services originates in the culture.

With regard to the transfer of cultural meaning to products, McCracken focuses on advertising as the transfer vehicle. What advertisers try to do is to get the consumer to perceive the advertised brand through cultural categories like beauty, young love and so on that reflect the norms and values most favorable to a sale. McCracken recognizes there are other means of transferring meaning from a culture to goods and services (products). Thus fashion can make associations with the relevant persuasive cultural categories and can, on occasion, create new cultural meanings. McCracken does not join the chorus of those claiming the efficacy of advertising has been undermined by media clutter and consumer cynicism so advertising has lost all credibility with consumers too skeptical to believe its claims (Zyman and Brott 2002). Of course ads that do not catch the attention of the target audience will be ineffective but many of us, while deliberately avoiding some ads, are hooked on to those whose promise is meaningful to our wants. Just as few consumers will acknowledge they are influenced by brand name, few will acknowledge the influence of ads on their buying decision but research might suggest otherwise.

The final step is the transfer of cultural meaning from product to the individual consumer. McCracken sees four rituals involved in this transfer, namely 'exchange rituals', 'possession', 'grooming' and 'divestment':

Exchange rituals: McCracken focuses on the exchange of gifts, seeing the giver as being able, through gift-giving, to insinuate certain cultural meanings or symbolic messages into the lives of recipients. This may be so but it is not obvious that givers in general seek to project their own values. This is really an empirical question rather than a straight application of established anthropological theory. Many in giving think about what others would like, not about what symbolic meaning the giver (consciously or unconsciously) would wish to convey. Thus, if someone is known to enjoy smoking, is it not more likely we will bring them duty free cigarettes from abroad than a medical kit to reduce the addiction?

Possession ritual: In buying a product, the consumer establishes access to the meaning or meaningful properties of the product through the time he or she spends discussing, comparing, showing off, cleaning and even photographing the new possessions. In possessing the product the consumer learns more about what it has to offer over and above its obvious function. These ritual ways of getting acquainted induce bonding with the product. What McCracken does not discuss is how advertisers try to capture what access to those meaningful properties might do to enrich the lives of the target audience. On the other hand, it is because advertising can never substitute for the possession ritual that personal experience with the product is so important. It might be added that not all purchases fall into the 'product category' as discussed here. For example, most services do not fit the possession ritual as described.

Grooming ritual: There is a continual transfer and renewal of a product's meaning by repeating the act of consumption (e.g. the 'going out to dinner' ritual) or repeating some activity (e.g. cleaning the car).

Divestment ritual: In this ritual the consumer seeks to empty goods of their existing meaning so that 'contagion' does not take place. For example, McCracken claims that the (latent?) function of cleaning a newly purchased, previously owned, house is to erase the meanings (significant associations) with the previous owner. Similarly, when a person sells or gives away items of clothing he or she will clean them or otherwise feel strange, thinking of someone else wearing them. All this can be questioned. My thoughts in cleaning my newly purchased, pre-owned house (if I actually do this) are just to have it looking clean so my furniture looks its best, while washing my divested clothing is to avoid the sense of shame of giving someone dirty clothes: each of these alternative explanations being simply a matter of adhering to social norms.

McCracken explores the trickle down hypothesis in relation to the diffusion of fashion in clothing. In the original version of trickle down, influence is seen as flowing down from higher- to lower-status levels as subordinates imitate the fashion of their immediate social superiors. McCracken rightly points out that the name 'trickle down' is a misnomer in that the move comes from below as the subordinate social group 'hunts' the status of the next higher-level group, while the higher-level group seeks a hasty flight by further fashion differentiation. McCracken acknowledges the trickle down hypothesis has lost favor, being replaced by a trickle across model or by a multiflow hypothesis suggesting all flows can occur. But McCracken says the trickle down view helps us predict fashion change whereas the other views involve a major problem of identifying the influence source. He proposes a revised version of trickle down that would be truer than the old, yet preserves this feature of prediction. In his revised anthropological version, superordinate/superior status need not reflect social position but such things as gender, age, ethnicity and so on, while imitation need not be 'wholesale appropriation' but selective borrowing to an extent that still signals the type of status being sought but preserves those individual qualities the borrower-group seeks to preserve.

It is not clear how this revision differs from a multiflow viewpoint in that any type of borrowing from any group seeks to enhance 'status' as defined by McCracken. It could be argued that selective borrowing down the line has always been the case since complete copying is usually beyond the subordinate's means. It is also not even clear how the revised version would improve prediction of a fashion change, since the relevant reference ('status') groups would still be unknown as would the prediction of what will be selectively borrowed. McCracken does offer some guidance by saying we should concentrate on the 'end to which imitation is devoted'. Thus he argues that women adopt the clothing of male colleagues in the workplace to get accepted as competent and equal partners in the world of work. But unless we are to assume just this one motive/objective, this hint is not very helpful. Nonetheless, on this basis, McCracken predicts that men will react to the imitation by women by seeking differentiation to create once again an exclusive male clothing style. He quotes an article in *Esquire* talking about the development of the 'heroic' look that breaks with the conservative, understated symbolism of men's clothing. He argues that the emergence of this new style could have been foreseen from the moment women began to appropriate the 'authority' look.

Is McCracken really serious in saying we could have predicted the exact style? If so, there are fortunes to be made! The fact is that one swallow does not make a summer. If men's styles are changing in the direction of the heroic look, there has been plenty of time since his book was published (1988) for this to be demonstrated on the streets of New York or London. Certainly, there has been a trend towards informality affecting not just clothing but lifestyles as well. In the City of London, only the bowler hat is less visible which did differentiate men from women. Also, if we look around, with men adopting earrings, necklaces and using cosmetics, it is not at all apparent that men are seeking to distance and differentiate themselves from competing women! There is a *cultural determinism* about McCracken's claims that results in a confidence that is at variance with the general modesty of cultural anthropology when it comes to prediction.

Cultural determinism is the claim that human behavior is primarily determined by cultural factors rather than just being one contributory influence. Classical mechanics provides an exemplar of deterministic theory, while quantum mechanics is an exemplar of an indeterministic theory. Where the laws of classical physics apply we can predict the future by observing the past. In contrast, where quantum laws apply we can observe the past but cannot predict the future.

McCracken introduces an interesting concept for use in marketing, that of *displaced meaning*. McCracken claims that people's hopes and ideals remain alive through adopting the strategy of displaced meaning. The real (unpleasant) meanings of things are displaced by more comfortable meanings to avoid mental anguish. And this is important if we remember the opposite of hope is despair, something we all want to avoid. This strategy of displaced meaning reconciles hopes/ideals with harsh reality by what amounts to wishful thinking that the ideal will be a reality in the future (e.g. 'after we have socialism', 'after marriage', 'in heaven', 'after we have got rid of this government') or that the ideal is already a reality elsewhere (e.g. in another country). Perhaps this talk of needing 'to take our country back' by the Tea Party is a manifestation of displaced meaning. Wishful thinking combines fantasy beliefs with strong desires, enough to shut out anything that threatens the possibility of the ideal being realized.

McCracken offers a functional explanation of displaced meaning in claiming that it helps us cope with life and sustain hope in the face of impressive grounds for pessimism. Consumer goods, according to McCracken, can act as bridges to the hopes and ideals embedded in the displaced meaning. Such goods allow (say) people to have a link with the lifestyle of their dreams (e.g. native people buying something American in underprivileged parts of the world). However, when goods are chosen as a bridge they are goods that typically stretch the individual's purse so these are exceptional buys, bought in anticipation of eventually obtaining the whole dream package. For McCracken, the concept of displaced meaning offers a functional explanation for the willingness of consumers to make costly purchases. No doubt, if his book had been written today McCracken might have used the concept of displaced meaning to explain all the foolishness of those buying houses whose mortgages they could not afford. In any case, advertising does seek to exploit hopes and dreams, and the concept of displaced meaning may help refine its message.

One subtheme in the book lies in showing how cultural meanings change. For instance, 'newness' in earlier centuries was associated with 'commonness', while 'patina' (indicator of age that accumulates on the surface of valued objects) was a guarantee of standing: proof of a family's longevity and the duration of their genteel status. But the advent of fashion changed all that, since fashion required frequent replacement, investment in learning and more emphasis on individualism. Although the possession of the *symbols* of a pedigree background can add to a person's standing, McCracken may be giving these particular symbols too much weight since it is doubtful that more direct knowledge about the true, real gentry was not always at hand. If it were not, it would have been easy for the newly rich to buy heirlooms and so on in order to signal title to ancient status instead of just being spoken of (as they were) as the 'nouveau riche'.

Another topic in anthropology that is of interest to marketing is the coordinated nature of purchases. In speaking of lifestyle and consumption systems, marketers draw attention to the non-random nature of goods assembled in ownership. Goods in ownership exhibit some coherence to a lifestyle; they fit together. Douglas and Isherwood (1979) claim individual purchases are always coordinated with other purchases on the basis of what the purchaser wants to signal to the world. This belief that consumers maintain a certain consistency in their complement or assembly of goods, McCracken calls the Diderot effect (Diderot in the eighteenth century recorded an incident illustrating it). Certainly, where consumers have the resources to have discretion in their buying, they are likely to seek some coordinating theme. On the other hand, what the consumer may want to signal to the world is simply his or her good taste where the coordinating principle may be no more than personal liking. Nonetheless, the notion of a coordinating principle can be promoted by the seller to be accepted by consumers wanting to justify having some rationale in their assembly of purchases.

McCracken maintains that the concept of lifestyle has no explanatory base to allow its exploitation in respect to what is coordinated in a lifestyle. This is a strange assertion since, as a matter of fact, marketers do identify and classify lifestyles and so are obligated to have a basis for classifying into mutually exclusive categories of lifestyle. There are even formal systems for determining categories of lifestyle like VALS2. A product is part of a lifestyle so knowledge of that lifestyle can be helpful in both developing and positioning the product. The term 'lifestyle' points to a describable way of living that can act as an explanatory variable, for example in explaining why the Florida lifestyle induces informality in dress, golf cart communities and men in shorts.

McCracken claims that the 'unities' or coordination themes found in the consumer's assembly of goods reflect:

- The nature of meaning contained in the goods themselves. Thus the Rolex watch and the BMW car go together because they have a structural similarity in that they occupy the same relative position in their product categories. If McCracken is right and structural similarity can be a coordinating principle, it must be something that acts unconsciously as it is too subtle a notion to operate at the conscious level. There are many reasons why those owning a Rolex watch might also own a BMW car which have nothing to do with any desire to seek structural similarity or any belief that this should be the coordinating principle in buying. The coordinating principle may be nothing more than that both suggest status.
- The way in which meaning is given to things or enters into things. Thus the associations between Rolex and the BMW car could be the result of advertising, showing the Rolex owner driving a BMW car so that they become an accepted complementary twosome.
- The manner in which the meaning of goods is already built into the culture. Thus goods that go together tend to have the same symbolic properties. This is one reason why firms like Burberry, Ralph Lauren and so on can sell across so many product categories, because they all symbolize quality or status. McCracken focuses on this third reason, asserting that products travel in complements because they project the same symbolic properties. Like Douglas, McCracken argues that the things we buy affirm who we are and what we aspire to be, while acknowledging that the pattern of purchases can change as people seek new ideas, react to changed circumstances like marriage and so on, or experiment with new concepts of self.

What McCracken has to say about the principles underlying coordinated purchases has intuitive appeal, but the identification of symbolic properties is not unproblematic. Take the matter of sport. Why does it happen that those who prefer running also prefer canoeing and cross-country skiing, which seems to be the case? What symbolic properties unite them? If this commonality of preferences reflects a general preference for 'moving through nature in an autonomous and self-propelled way', would this reason emerge from seeking common symbolic properties?

McCracken takes to task those like Alison Lurie, a professor of English at Cornell and a novelist, who apply the metaphor of language to clothing without, he argues, seeing that the differences overwhelm the similarities. There is a failure to realize here that there are an infinite number of similarities and this means a judgment call as to which similarities are significant to contrast with differences. He further argues that the message read into what a person is wearing is much too stereotyped. It is true that we all do stereotype on the basis of clothing but also on the basis of haircut, way of talking, make-up and so on, so the stereotype on one basis may be counterbalanced on another as all may not cohere. McCracken goes on to maintain that when people dress in an unconventional manner, observers seem unable to read the message being conveyed, while clothing in any case does not convey emotion. But neither is completely true. Someone dressing unconventionally will project certain sense-meanings even if it is no more than being a rebel against convention, whereas a sexy dress can arouse emotions.

While all analogies and metaphors break down at some point, none of the points raised by McCracken destroys the utility of the metaphor of language applied to clothing. After all, much language interpretation is fairly standardized, too, while an inability to read mixtures of clothing is analogous to not knowing the relevant language. Alison Lurie (1983) does show in fact how clothing mixtures can be and are interpreted. Her book is one of the most insightful on clothing in the field... without having an anthropological background.

In a more recent book McCracken (2009), now at Massachusetts Institute of Technology, argues that companies in general fail to sense cultural currents, though there are exceptions like Steve Jobs and Martha Stewart. He makes a distinction between 'fast culture' and 'slow culture'. Companies are apt to follow fast culture whether it is the latest thing in smartphones or whatever. All too often they miss out by not studying slow culture, which constitutes the framework of the consumer's life. This recognition led P&G to move away from 'narrow focus groups', in investigating, say, why the consumer prefers one type of toothpaste over another, to trying to understand how people lived their lives and how the choice of toothpaste fitted in. (Is not McCracken here approving the utility of the concept of lifestyle previously rejected?) But focus groups are used to generate ideas and this function is not displaced by cultural studies as suggested. There is no 'one best way' of studying the consumer; each technique has its own role to play.

McCracken is right in pointing out the lack of cultural sensitivity when culture is defined to include the various subcultures within a market. But is he right to belittle fast culture which may in no way be ephemeral but merges through time into the slow culture? There is no way of asserting that fast culture will always be of less importance for study than slow culture. Everything depends on the questions to be addressed, as is the case with other competing perspectives.

LANGUAGE AND THOUGHT

Language is a major marker of a culture as it reflects much about that culture. One question in anthropology is that of *linguistic determinism*.

The so-called Whorfian hypothesis claims language determines how people think or how language determines thought: that one's native language determines what one is able to think. This would imply that those who speak languages totally different from our own would not be able to understand many of our most basic concepts. This would certainly justify the word 'alien' when it comes to very different cultures.

The Whorfian hypothesis is named after the American linguist Benjamin Lee Whorf (1897–1941), though it is not clear that Whorf advocated anything more than the claim that language influences thought. In any case, it is claimed that the facts do not back up the Whorf hypothesis, particularly the fact that we can learn concepts that are not native to our own language, and are not restricted to concepts embedded in our own language. Recently the whole notion of the relationship of language to thought has been re-investigated. In the more recent debate it is argued that the language we speak not only reflects or expresses our thinking but is apt to shape the thoughts we wish to express (Boroditsky 2010). While it is accepted now that language does not make it impossible for us to think certain thoughts that reflect concepts that are not part of our own language, it does oblige us to think about things in a certain way. Thus German and Latin languages oblige speakers to reveal gender so the grammar of the language prevents me from just saying 'I have been out with a friend' without giving the gender of that friend. Since all objects are split into male or female categories in these languages, this affects the attributes conjured up by products. Being obliged to refer to all products as a 'he' or 'she', it is not hard to give products a personality. When the Germans, though, call some product a 'he' and the Spanish call it a 'she', the speakers of the two languages think differently about the same products. Where the product is a 'he' like the word 'bridge' in Spanish, it is characterized with 'manly' properties such as strength, in contrast to the Germans for whom a bridge is a 'she' and thoughts about 'bridge' are in terms of slimness and elegance.

Since concepts are the basic mechanisms by which we break up the world into categories, this means language affects perspectives and very different languages provide different perspectives on reality (Prinz 2002). Thus different languages treat color concepts differently, with blue and green being distinct colors in English but merely shades of the same color in other languages. Observation may not be always theory-loaded but it is concept dependent. We see what we have been taught to see with the concepts we possess. Thus the concepts in our language do to some extent shape how we construct reality. It seems that if people learn another language, they inadvertently adopt a somewhat different perspective on the world. When a bilingual person moves from one language to another, they start to think differently. An extreme example are those 'geographic' languages where they talk of north, south, east and west but do not talk about something being to the left, right, front or back. This use of geographical coordinates instead of egocentric coordinates gives such speakers very different habits of mind (Deutscher 2010). It also indicates the extent of human abilities, not previously recognized.

Steven Pinker (2007) makes the point that demonstrating the validity of linguistic determinism would have to meet three conditions: (i) that speakers of one language would find it extremely difficult to think the way speakers of another language do; (ii) that the differences in language would affect actual reasoning to conclusions; (iii) that the difference in thought can be shown to be caused by a difference in language rather than merely being correlated with it for some reason such as the physical or cultural milieu. Applying such criteria would not be supportive of the notion of linguistic determinism.

Pinker rightly claims that language cannot be completely central for mental functioning because it has to be learnt, while it has been demonstrated that even pre-linguistic infants are sensitive to cause and effect, the notion of human agency and spatial relations. And when our language does not contain an appropriate concept demanded by the occasion, we make up for it by drawing on phrases and metaphors that help get over the problem. This is an important truth. Pinker agrees with others that unobtrusiveness is an entry requirement for the admission of a new word to the language. In this way the new word functions as a name and not additionally as a commentary.

CHANGING THE INTELLECTUAL ALLEGIANCE OF ANTHROPOLOGY TO THE HUMANITIES

Kuper (1999) asserts that, by and large, anthropologists are switching their intellectual allegiance from the social sciences to the humanities, and are likely to practice interpretation without reliance on any of the social sciences. If this means completely eschewing the other social sciences, it is an opportunity lost since the social sciences, as we have seen here, are full of insightful sensitizing concepts that would inform any interpretation. And Kuper accepts that appeals to cultural influences can only be a partial explanation of why people think and behave as they do. (This is one reason why this book advocates methodological pluralism.) But that partial explanation may serve the particular purpose we have in mind.

CONCLUSION

Perry (1984), in his *Intellectual Life in America: A History*, claims that the social sciences today are not a coherent movement but a set of alternative approaches to knowledge – with diminishing likelihood that any one approach could be used to disprove the other. These alternative approaches are reflected in the social science paradigms discussed in this book. They will not displace each other because they are either additional windows into a problem or they seek to answer different questions. Perry goes on to say that, while the individual scholar might feel his choice of paradigms was the best one, in actual fact, choice is often a matter of chance, like admiration for a great teacher, social rewards for one style of research and so on. This is very true. We adopt approaches we have been induced to practice and continue to do so if promoting that approach results in social visibility or eases publication in the best journals. Perry also notes the willingness of most social scientists to concentrate on some small patch of human experience and cultivate it without ever asking fundamental questions about either approaches or methodology. This is true because the reward system does not encourage revisionist drifts. Even if we talk about our work being on the 'cutting edge' of where things are going, it is usually the cutting edge within an accepted paradigm.

CASE: EXPERIENCES IN EXPANDING ABROAD – CARREFOUR S.A. VERSUS WAL-MART STORES

As home markets mature, firms turn to international expansion. Retail chains are no exception in seeking cross-border expansion though with uneven success. The latest is the exit of the electrical retail American giant Best Buy from the UK when just three years ago, it had plans to set up 200 stores throughout the country. The major error made by retailers crossing borders is in believing that there are few differences between the home market and the market across the border, whereas, with different cultures and climates, customer demands can vary widely. Luxury goods retailers, often tied to one manufacturer, seem to have fared best, with firms like Gucci, Ferragamo, Burberry, Hermes, Escada, Louis Vuitton, Tiffany's and Cartier having retail establishments in many different cities of the world. The challenge lies in knowing which regions go together in that, even in Switzerland, there are acknowledged to be at least three separate cultures. What has to be acknowledged is that cultural differences are not confined to the product itself since other parts of the offering can be equally decisive, while cultural preferences do not change easily.

We consider two companies in this case which have had contrasting success with expansion abroad.

Carrefour S.A. shares have dropped by over two-thirds since 2007. The investment of $5.5 billion in the company that year by a group of investors gave them a 9.8 percent stake in the company. That investment in 2011 was worth just $2 billion.

The Carrefour group was the first in Europe to open a hypermarket, defined as a large supermarket and department store under one roof. Its headquarters are in France but its retail outlets are in twenty-one countries throughout the world. Early on, Carrefour established itself in the UK, but today the old Carrefour stores are branches of the supermarket chain Asda. This exit also occurred in other countries, specifically Chile, Czech Republic (where it sold out to Tesco, the biggest UK grocery retailer), Hong Kong, South Korea (all thirty-two stores), Japan, Mexico (where it had twenty-nine hypermarkets), Portugal, Russia, Switzerland and the US.

The common explanation for this retreat was that Carrefour had expanded too rapidly, which stretched the company too thinly, while the markets became more competitive. In fact it expanded into twenty-four countries between 1994 and 2004. Its major success has been in China though there was one attempt to boycott the firm on the grounds that one of its major shareholders had donated to the Dalai Lama. Interestingly, in China in-store produce and fish departments were in line with the traditional Chinese street market supported by salespeople whose job it was to urge potential customers to stop and see what was on sale.

Wal-Mart found that when it expanded outside the US in the 1990s, its chief rival was Carrefour. By 2011, Wal-Mart's international sales of $109 billion were greater than the whole of Carrefour's sales, while Wal-Mart's operating margins have been between 6.2 percent and 7.5 percent as opposed to Carrefour's 4.6 percent to 5.5 percent. Wal-Mart, though, has not been universally successful since it has also had to exit from some international markets, specifically Germany. Wal-Mart followed a roll-out strategy in entering international markets, expanding cautiously from its first entry into Mexico.

With its strong competitive position in the US, it could afford to take its time, while Carrefour was faced in France with aging stores in locations that were no longer very convenient for its target group of consumers. Given the growth of zoning laws in France and other restrictions on finding new outlets, fast international expansion seemed the path to growth. Today (2011) Carrefour's turnabout strategy for fighting back is to invest $2.2 billion in a makeover for its 500 stores in Europe. Combined with lower prices and more private labels, these measures are expected to get Carrefour back on its feet.

Case Questions

1. If one contributory factor to Carrefour's poor performance internationally is that Carrefour expanded too rapidly, what might have happened? After all, time taken to expand is not a forcing variable and cannot in itself explain anything.
2. It has been claimed that Wal-Mart had an advantage in being an American firm with many consumers abroad buying into the American dream by buying American products. On the other hand, French luxury products have been immensely successful in sales abroad so would this not rub off on to other French products?
3. What would you have done to ensure cultural differences were identified and acted upon?

DISCUSSION QUESTIONS ON CHAPTER 14 (CULTURAL ANTHROPOLOGY)

1. What does Geertz mean when he says the cultural anthropologist is not seeking universal explanatory laws that govern a culture but is employed in 'unpacking the conceptual world of the people studied'? Peter Winch, philosopher, claims that if we wish to understand

a culture, we should study the concepts of that culture, since a culture's concepts are a guide to the rules of behavior. If a consumer in the English-speaking world talks of buying a brand because it is 'familiar', the concept of 'familiarity' suggests the rule of buying in this instance, for example the consumer buys the brand that is most familiar. What are your thoughts on all this?

2. If I talk about studying a culture's concepts, it is the meaning-in-use of those concepts, but when we speak of the meaning of a product, it is meaning in the sense of the significance of the product to us. Geertz argues that interpreting any culture is a matter of interpreting its symbols; that people live in a world of symbols and it is the meaning of such symbols that lies behind behavior. Cultural meanings are often revealed by the 'symbolic metaphors' used in a culture, so the ethnographer should identify such metaphors in order to give coherence and structure to any narrative of human behavior. Discuss.

3. Mary Douglas lists the various functions promoted by consumer buying. Is this list exhaustive and mutually exclusive? Compare it with the choice criteria used in Chapter 2.

4. McCracken says that without consumer goods, people would find certain acts of self-definition and collective definition impossible. Is this true or, if true, just a truism?

5. Show how the concept of displaced meaning can be applied to the Tea Party, the Occupy Wall Street movement in the US, and similar protests in London and elsewhere. In thus protesting against some major suppliers of services, these protesters inevitably have an image of better alternatives. Does not the concept of displaced meaning suggest they are bound to be disappointed?

6. 'Every language in the world embodies mini-perspectives since concepts do this.' Discuss.

Postscript

This book supports perspectivism and methodological pluralism. It claims the various perspectives or paradigms in the social sciences are often less in conflict than they are complementary in that they either offer additional windows through which to view the human condition or ask different questions about behavior. What has got in the way of appreciating this is the belief that rival paradigms make claims about the universality of their findings so there is no need for other approaches. But there are no universal laws in social science in that findings cannot be universally applied to all people at all times. There are always cases that are not covered because contexts (including the individuality of people) differ so widely. He or she may give a definite-sounding diagnosis of behavioral events, emanating from a certain perspective, but, if not just a best guess, it is not the only answer. This should be a liberating belief since it removes constraints on thinking, but applying a multiplicity of perspectives is not always regarded as a virtue since some social scientists still believe in one true reality or feel it necessary to achieve consensus. Thus Pfeffer (1993) in organization behavior argues that consensus is a necessary condition for scientific advance in that it provides an accepted and shared vocabulary for discussion, while fostering the discarding of concepts. But any organization that encourages differentiation provides positions for members with different perspectives to get a variety of viewpoints which act as a corrective to the one perspective.

Putting what has been said into a logic format offers an explication. Propositions that are *contraries* involve a universal affirmative proposition ('All S are T: e.g. 'all consumers weigh up the costs and benefits before buying') in opposition to a universal negative proposition ('No S are T: e.g. 'no consumers weigh up the costs and benefits before buying'). Contraries cannot both be true but both can be false. Propositions which are *sub-contraries* involve a particular affirmative proposition ('Some S are T: e.g. 'some consumers weigh up the costs and benefits before buying') in opposition to a particular negative proposition ('Some S are not T: e.g. 'some consumers do not weigh up the costs and benefits before buying'). With sub-contraries, both can be true but the falsity of one implies the truth of the other. Given this is so, seeking to displace a rival paradigm may rest on showing that it fails in its search for universality or, alternatively, on showing it is false. If there are no universals in social science of a non-trivial nature, it is inconsequential to show that findings emanating from a social science paradigm do not cover all cases. To displace a paradigm entirely, the focus would be on showing that the paradigm's claims are subsumed by some alternative rival paradigm of wider scope or showing that the paradigm is actually false, a much more difficult thing to do. If paradigm 'A' produces useful results, it will not be abandoned until another paradigm comes along that does more: explaining not only what paradigm 'A' explaining about behavior but explains other findings as well.

Fay (1996) points out that differences between paradigms can only be understood against a background of similarities; that competing paradigms in science must be about the same world and share a sufficient vocabulary and methods of inquiry for them to compete. Given that paradigms in social science do have a background of relevant similarities, social science paradigms cannot be incomparable. But they can be incommensurable in that we may be unable to translate rival paradigms into a common vocabulary. We should compare paradigms so as to choose which is best for our purposes, adopting a purely pragmatic approach rather than asking which paradigm can be proved to be true. But perhaps more commonly we might use knowledge of the paradigms discussed in this book as a source of sensitizing concepts and ideas that can be directly applied to the problem at hand.

Appendix

IMPUTATION IN ADVERTISING

We can illustrate imputation in advertising by looking at the same ad from various psychological viewpoints. Any ad can be interpreted for persuasive content by drawing on the various perspectives reviewed here. Take, for example, an ad that appeared in the UK for Linn Hi-Fi and quoted in an earlier book by the author but expanded on here. It is chosen for its shortness. The ad shows a head and shoulders photograph of a young, attractive girl, with the words:

SHE'S TERRIFIC IN BED. SHE'S WITTY, INTELLIGENT AND MAKES HER OWN PASTA. SHE DOESN'T HAVE A LINN HI-FI. BUT HER SISTER DOES AND SHE'S THE ONE I MARRIED.

ASSOCIATIONISM

The theoretical foundation for the effectiveness of *association* in influencing attitudes and choices is shown by (a) Gestalt psychology with its focus on the mind's search for structured wholes; (b) the halo effect whereby our evaluation of some outstanding trait associated with a person influences our evaluation of the whole person; and (c) the work of neuroscientists like Antonio Damasio who show why associations can be influential. But much depends on how well the following are exploited:

Association with social norms: This ad makes its impact by the violation of the social norms in choosing a marriage partner and in so doing dramatizes the Linn Hi-Fi.

Association with values: The appeal in the ad is to hedonistic values which is not inappropriate when selling an entertainment system.

Association with valued images: The image evoked on reading the ad is a sexual one, that of a very desirable female. It is this image that gets attention.

Association through projected solidarity with others: The ad seeks to bond with those who put great store on having the best hi-fi on the market.

Association with status and prestige: There is a strong suggestion in the ad of the Linn Hi-Fi conferring status and prestige, in that it is so good it could dissuade a man from what would be considered a more attractive choice of marriage partner.

Association with the mental modes of seeking excitement and experiencing relaxation: The ad's implicit promise is that the Linn Hi-Fi offers excitement.

Association with positive reinforcements: The target audiences are not those unfamiliar with a hi-fi. They have had past satisfactions with a hi-fi and so (hopefully) will respond to this ad, seeking positive reinforcement. It is assumed the target audience will give a highly positive evaluation of the ad, with the emotional dimensions of activation (sexual stimulation) and competence conveyed by the ad and the emotional reaction coming via classical conditioning.

COGNITIVE APPROACHES

Hierarchy of effects: The ad assumes the target audience is cognitively aware and comprehends the concept of a hi-fi. The ad is attempting to activate positive feelings for the Linn Hi-Fi, hoping it will lead on to the next conative stage of buying action.

The Elaboration Likelihood Model: The peripheral route is used since the focus is on affective cues. This is because the ad is meant to stimulate sufficient interest for the target audience to inquire further.

The Persuasive Communication Approach which covers:

Individual receiver of the communication: The ad gets attention by its 'sexy' imagery and claim. Its repetition rate is not known but if high this would help. The ad distracts by its imagery and humor to inhibit sober reflection on the claims being made. There is an emotional background in the imagery with its appeal to a sophisticated category of hi-fi buyer whose beliefs and values the ad reflects. Whatever the differences between the target audience's values and the ad's implicit values, the assimilation effect is likely to occur so the audience does not recognize differences in values. The ad implicitly anchors the claims for Linn Hi-Fi to the highest-quality level. This raises high expectations which Linn needs to fulfill. The ad induces self-persuasion by evoking positive feelings towards the product.

Source credibility and attractiveness: Interpreted in a literal way the ad does not have credibility in that the trade-offs would be absurd. But the assertiveness of the ad does evoke credibility for the Linn Hi-Fi. As to attractiveness, there is humor, her sexiness and surprise which are likely to be attractive to the target audience. But, in general, perceptions of credibility and attractiveness can be very idiosyncratic and this is a problem for those creating the ads.

THE PSYCHOANALYTIC APPROACH

Unconscious motives might be in terms of fantasizing about indulging in a hedonistic and sophisticated lifestyle. We can get a vicarious pleasure from fantasies generated by the lives of the rich and famous. 'Hidden' meaning is likely to revolve around who would be perceived as buying the brand. The ad conjures up a certain profile of the user (target audience) as male and between twenty-five and forty years old:

- Man-about-town
- Upper-middle class (the girl in the photograph seems of this class)
- Hedonist values
- Women are just a means to gratification.

(The Linn ad was considered tasteless by many and offensive to women. The ad was subsequently withdrawn.)

References

Adler, Mortimer, J. (1985) *Ten Philosophical Mistakes*. New York: Macmillan.

Akerlof, George and Shiller, Robert (2009) *Animal Spirits*: *How Human Psychology Drives the Economy, and Why It Matters for Global Capitalism*. Princeton, NJ: Princeton University Press.

Alexander, Jeffrey C. (1987) *Twenty Lectures*: *Sociological Theory since World War II*. New York: Columbia University Press.

Allais, P. M. (1953) 'The Behavior of Rational Man in Risk Situations', *Econometrica*, 21, 503–546.

Altran, Scott (2004) *In Gods We Trust*: *The Evolutionary Landscape of Religion*. Oxford: Oxford University Press.

Anderson, Alun (2011) 'Brain Work', *The Economist's the World in 2012*, p. 153.

Angell, Marcia (2011) 'The Illusions of Psychiatry', *New York Review of Books*, 14 July, pp. 20–22.

Angier, Natalie (2010) 'Abstract Thoughts? The Body Takes Them Literally', *New York Times*, 2 February, p. D2.

Anscombe, G. E. M. (1972) *Intention*. Oxford: Basil Blackwell.

Apter, Michael J. (1989) *Reversal Theory*. London: Routledge.

Ariely, Dan (2008) *Predictably Irrational: The Hidden Forces that Shape our Decisions*. New York: HarperCollins.

Arnold, M. B. (1960) *Emotion and Personality*, vol.1: *Psychological Aspects*. New York: Columbia University Press.

Aronson, Jerrold L., Harré, Rom and Way, Eileen Cornell (1994) *Realism Rescued*. London: Duckworth & Co.

Arrow, K. (1951) *Social Choice and Individual Values*. New York: Wiley.

Asch, S. E. (1952) *Social Psychology*. Englewood Cliffs, NJ: Prentice-Hall.

Aschwanden, Christie (2010) 'Evidence is Only Part of the Story', *Miller-McCune*, May/June, pp. 32–37.

Austen, Ian (2011) 'Proliferation of Choices Hurts Sales for RIM, Analysts Say', *New York Times*: *Business Day*, Saturday 17 December, p. B1.

Auyang, Sunny Y. (2001) *Mind in Everyday Life and Cognitive Science*. Cambridge, MA: The MIT Press.

Bagozzi, Richard (1975) 'Marketing as Exchange', *Journal of Marketing*, 39 (October) 32–9.

Bagozzi, Richard (1979) 'Toward A Formal Theory of Marketing Exchanges', in *Conceptual and Theoretical Developments in Marketing*, ed. O. C. Ferrell, S. W. Brown and C. W. Lamb. American Marketing Association.

Balda, R. P. and A. C. Kamil (1992) 'Long-term Spatial Memory in Clark's Nutcracker, Nucifraga Columbiana', *Animal Behavior*, 44, 761–769.

Baron, Jonathan (1988) *Thinking and Deciding*. Cambridge: Cambridge University Press.

Bass, Alan (2001) *Difference and Disavowal*. Cambridge: Cambridge University Press.

Baum, William M. (2007) 'Commentary on Foxall, "Intentional Behaviorism"', *Behavior and Philosophy*, 33, 57–60.

Belk, Russell W. (1995) 'Hyperreality and Globalization: Culture in the Age of Ronald McDonald', *Journal of International Consumer Marketing*, 8, 23–37.

Bell, David E. (1982) 'Regret in Decision-making Under Uncertainty', *Operations Research*, 30, 961–981.

Bell, David E. (1985) 'Disappointment in Decision-making Under Uncertainty', *Operations Research*, 33, 2–27.

Beloff, John (1973) *Psychological Sciences*. London: Crosby, Lockwood.

Bennett, M. R. and Hacker, P. M. S. (2003) *Philosophical Foundations of Neuroscience*. Oxford: Blackwell Publishing.

Berlin, Isaiah (2006) *Political Ideas in the Romantic Age: Their Rise and Influence on Modern Thought*, ed. Henry Hardy. Princeton: Princeton University Press.

Berner, Robert (2006) 'I Sold It Through The Grapevine', *Business Week*, 29 May, pp. 32–34.

Berry, Leonard L. and Mirabito, Ann M. (2006) 'Recapturing Marketing's Mission', in *Does Marketing Need Reform?*, ed. Jagdish N. Sheth and Rajendra S. Sisodia. Armonk, New York: M. E. Sharpe.

Birdwell, A. E. (1968) 'A Study of the Influence of Image Congruence on Consumer Choice', *Journal of Business*, 41 (January), 76–8.

Bittner, R. (2003) *Doing Things for Reasons*. Oxford: Oxford University Press.

Bizzi, Emilio (2007) 'Letter to The New York Times Magazine', *New York Times*, 25 March, section 6.

Blakeslee, Sandra (2004a) 'If You Have A "Buy Button" In Your Brain, What Pushes It?' *New York Times*, 19 October, p. 5.

Blakeslee, Sandra (2004b) 'Say the Right Name and They Light Up', *New York Times*, 7 December, p. 12.

Blau, Peter M. (1964) *Exchange and Power in Social Life*. New York: John Wiley & Sons.

Bleicher, Josef (1982) *The Hermeneutic Imagination*. London: Routledge and Kegan Paul.

Block, Ned (1980) 'Troubles with Functionalism', in *Readings in the Philosophy of Psychology, The Language of Thought Series*, ed. Ned Block. Cambridge, MA: Harvard University Press.

Blumer, Herbert (1969) *Symbolic Interactionism: Perspective and Method*. Englewood Cliffs, NJ: Prentice-Hall.

Bogart, Leo (2003) *Finding Out: Personal Adventures in Social Research – Discovering What People Think, Say, And Do*. Chicago: Ivan R. Dee.

Bogdan, Radu J. (2001) *Interpreting Minds*. Cambridge, MA: The MIT Press.

Bok, Derek (2010) *The Politics of Happiness: What Governments Can Learn from the New Research on Well-Being*. Princeton, NJ: Princeton University Press.

Bok, Sissela (2010) *Exploring Happiness from Aristotle to Brain Science*. New Haven, CT: Yale University Press.

Bolton, Robert (1986) *People Skills*. Englewood, NJ: Prentice-Hall.

Bolton, Ruth N. and Lemon, Katherine N. (1999) 'A Dynamic Model of Customers' Usage of Services', *Journal of Marketing Research*, 36, 171–187.

Boroditsky, Lera (2010) 'Lost in Translation', *Wall Street Journal*, 24 July.

Brandom, Robert B. (2009) *Reason* in *Philosophy*. Cambridge, MA: The Belknap Press of Harvard University.

Brehm, Jack (1966) *A Theory of Psychological Reactance*. New York: Academic Press.

Brett, Judith (2003) *Australian Liberals and the Moral Middle Class*. Cambridge: Cambridge University Press.

Brittan, Davis (1997) 'Spending More and Enjoying it Less', *Technology Review*, July, 4–7.

Brown, James Robert (2001) *Who Rules in Science*. Cambridge, MA: Harvard University Press.

Brown, Rex (2006) *Rational Choice: Decision Analysis for the Decider*. Hoboken, NJ: John Wiley & Sons.

Bruner, Jerome (1990) *Acts of Meaning*. Cambridge, MA: Harvard University Press.

Buller, David J. (2004) *Evolutionary Psychology and the Persistent Quest for Human Nature*. Cambridge, MA: The MIT Press.

BusinessWeek (2002) 'Not Entitled "Brand Loyalty" ', 25 November, p. 10.

Calder, B. and Sternthral, Brian (1980) 'Television Advertising Wearout: An Information Processing Viewpoint'. *Journal of Marketing Research*, 17, 173–86.

Calder, Lendol (1999) *Financing the American Dream: A Cultural History of Consumer Credit*. Princeton, NJ: Princeton University Press.

Campbell, Colin (1987) *The Romantic Ethic and the Spirit of Modern Consumerism*. Oxford: Blackwell.

Carey, Benedict (2007) 'Who's Minding the Mind?', *New York Times*, 31 July.

Carlat, Daniel (2011) *Unhinged: The Trouble with Psychiatry: A Doctor's Revelations about a Profession in Crisis*. New York: Free Press.

Carr, E. H. (1964) *What is History?* London: Penguin Books.

Carroll, Noel (1990) *The Philosophy of Horror*. New York & London: Routledge.

Carver, C. S. and Scheier, M. F. (1990) 'Origins and Functions of Positive and Negative Affect: A Control-process View', *Psychological Review*, 97, 19–35.

Cassidy, John (2009) *How Markets Fail*. New York: Farrar, Straus and Giroux.

Chalmers, David. J. (1996) *The Conscious Mind*. New York: Oxford University Press.

Cherniak, Christopher (1986) *Minimal Rationality*. Cambridge, MA: The MIT Press.

Chomsky, N. (1968) *Language and Mind*. San Diego: Harcourt, Brace and Jovanovich.

Christian, Brian (2011) *The Most Human Human: What Talking with Computers Teaches Us About What it Means to be Alive*. New York: Doubleday.

Churchland, P. M. (1989) A *Neurocomputational Perspective*. Cambridge, MA: The MIT Press.

Churchland, P. M. (1995) *The Engine of Reason, the Seat of the Soul*. Cambridge, MA: The MIT Press.

Cialdini, R. B. (1984) *Influence*. New York: William Morrow.

Clendinnen, Inga (2003) *Dancing with Strangers*. Melbourne: Text Publishing.

Cohan, William (2011) *Money and Power: How Goldman Sachs Came to Rule the World*. London: Allen Lane.

Cohen, Daniel (2003) *Our Modern Times*. Cambridge, MA: The MIT Press.

Cohen, Jonathan L. (1987) *The Dialogue of Reason*. Oxford: Oxford University Press.

Cohen, Josh (2005) *How to Read Freud*. London: Granta Books.

Cohen, Morris and Nagel, Ernest (1934) *An Introduction to Logic and Scientific Method*. New York: Harcourt.

Cole, Jonathan (1998) *About Face*. Cambridge, MA: The MIT Press.

Cole, Stephen (1972) *The Sociological Method*. Chicago: Rand McNally.

Coleman, Simon and Watson, Helen (1992) *An Introduction to Anthropology*. London: Tiger Books International.

Colley, Russell H. (1961) *Defining Advertising Goals for Measured Advertising Results*. New York: Association of National Advertisers.

Collin, Finn (1985) *Theory and Understanding*. Oxford: Basil Blackwell.

Collins, Jim (1990) *Uncommon Cultures: Popular Cultures and Post-Modernism*. London: Routledge.

Cook, Emma (1999) 'What's Getting Up Your Nose?', *The Independent on Sunday*, 16 May.

Coser, Lewis (1956) *The Functions of Social Conflict*. New York: Free Press.

Crews, Frederick (ed.) (1998) *Unauthorized Freud*. New York: Viking.

Crews, Frederick (2006) *Follies of the Wise*. Emeryville, CA: Shoemaker and Hoard.

Csikszentmihalyi, Mihaly (1990) *Flow: The Psychology of Optimal Experience*. New York: Harper and Row.

Csikszentmihalyi, Mihaly (2000) 'The Cost and Benefits of Consuming', *Journal of Consumer Research*, 27, 267–272.

Cunningham, Valentine (2002) *Reading after Theory*. Oxford: Blackwell.

Damasio, Antonio R. (1994) *Descartes' Error: Emotion, Reason and the Human Brain*. New York: A Grosset.

Damasio, Antonio (2010) *Self Comes to Mind*. New York: Pantheon Books.

Dancy, Jonathan (2000) *Practical Reality*. New York: Oxford University Press.

Dancy, Jonathan (2005) *Ethics without Principles*. Oxford: Clarendon Press.

Darwall, Stephen L. (1983) *Impartial Reason*. Ithaca, NY: Cornell University Press.

Davis, Natalie Zemon (1999) *The Gift in Sixteenth-Century France*. Madison: University of Wisconsin Press.

Davitz, Joel R. (1969) *The Language of Emotion*. New York: Academic Press.

Dennett, Daniel C. (1986) *Brainstorms: Philosophical Essays on Mind and Psychology*. Boston, MA: The MIT Press.

Dennett, Daniel C. (1989) *The Intentional Stance*. Cambridge, MA: The MIT Press.

Dennett, D. C. (1996) *Kinds of Minds*. New York: HarperCollins.

Derrida, J. (1991) *A Derrida Reader: Between the Blinds*, ed. P. Kamuf. Hemel Hempstead: Harvester Wheatsheaf.

De Sousa (1990) *The Rationality of Emotion*. Cambridge, MA: The MIT Press.

Deutscher, Guy (2010) 'You Are What You Speak', *New York Times Magazine*, 29 August, pp. 42–47.

Dittmar, Helga (1992) *The Social Psychology of Material Possessions*. New York: St. Martin's Press.

Dollard, J. and Miller, N. E. (1950) *Personality and Psychotherapy*. New York: McGraw-Hill.

Douglas, Mary (1986) *How Institutions Think*. Ithaca, NY: Syracuse.

Douglas, Mary (1996) *Thought Styles: Critical Essays in Good Taste*. New York: Sage.

Douglas, Mary and Isherwood, B. (1979) *The World of Goods*. New York: Basic Books.

Dretske, Fred (1988) *Explaining Behavior: Reason in a World of Causes*. Cambridge, MA: The MIT Press.

Duncker, K. (1945) 'On Problem Solving', *Psychological Monographs* 58, No. 270.

Dworkin, Ronald (2011) *Justice for Hedgehogs*. Cambridge, MA: Harvard University Press.

Dwyer, Robert, Schur, Paul H. and Sejo, Oh (1987) 'Developing Buyer-Seller Relationships', *Journal of Marketing*, 51, 11–27.

Dyson, Freeman (2011) 'The "Dramatic Picture" of Richard Feynman', *New York Review of Books*, 14 July, p. 39.

Eakin, Emily (2002) 'Penetrating the Mind by Metaphor', *New York Times*, Arts and Ideas section, 23 February.

Ekman, P. and Friesen, W. V. (1975) *Unmasking the Face: A Guide to Recognizing Emotions from Facial Expressions*. Englewood Cliffs, NJ: Prentice-Hall.

Elliott, Anthony (ed.) (1998) *Freud 2000*. Oxford: Polity.

Ellsberg, D. (1961) 'Risk Ambiguity and the Savage Axioms', *Quarterly Journal of Economics*, 75, 643–669.

Elster, Jon (1989a) *Solomonic Judgements: Limitations of Rationality*. Cambridge: Cambridge University Press.

Elster, Jon (1989b) *Nuts and Bolts for the Social Sciences*. Cambridge: Cambridge University Press.

Elster, Jon (1999a) *Strong Feelings: Emotion, Addiction and Human Behavior*. Cambridge, MA: The MIT Press.

Elster, Jon (1999b) *Alchemies of the Mind: Rationality and the Emotions*. Cambridge: Cambridge University Press.

Elton, G. R. (1969) *The Practice of History*. London: Fontana Library.

Emerson, Richard (1976) 'Social Exchange Theory', in *Annual Review of Sociology*, vol. 2, ed. Alex Inkelos and Neil J. Smelser. Palo Alto, CA: Annual Reviews.

Emmet, Dorothy (1985) *The Effectiveness of Causes*. Albany, NY: State University of New York Press.

Engel, Jonathan (2008) *American Therapy*. New York: Gotham Books.

Ericsson, K. A. and Simon, Herbert A. (1980) 'Verbal Reports as Data', *Psychological Review*, 87, 215–251.

Farley, John U. and Ring, Winston (1970) 'An Empirical Test of the Howard-Sheth Model of Consumer Buying Behavior', *Journal of Marketing Research*, 7, 427–435.

Fay, Brian (1996) *Contemporary Philosophy of Social Science*. Oxford: Blackwell Publishing.

Ferling, John (2003) *A Leap in the Dark: The Struggle to Create the American Republic*. New York: Oxford University Press.

Festinger, Leon (1957) *A Theory of Cognitive Dissonance*. Stanford, CA: Stanford University Press.

Fischer, David H. (1970) *Historians' Fallacies: Toward a Logic of Historical Thought*. New York: Harper & Row.

Fishbein, M. (1983) 'An Investigation of the Relationship between Belief about an Object and the Attitude towards the Object', *Human Relations*, 16, 233–40.

Fishbein, M. and Ajzen I. (1975) *Belief, Attitude, Intention, and Behavior*. Reading, MA: Addison-Wesley.

Fisher, Philip (1999) *Wonder, the Rainbow, and the Aesthetics of Rare Experiences*. Boston, MA: Harvard University Press.

Flanagan, Owen (1996) *Self-expressions: Mind, Morals and the Meaning of Life*. New York: Oxford University Press.

Fletcher, Winston (2003) 'Sigmund Fells Trendy Straw Men', *The Times*, Higher Educational Supplement, 11 July, p. 15.

Flyvbjerg, Bent (2003) *Making Social Science Matter*. Cambridge: Cambridge University Press.

Fodor, J. (1975) *The Language of Thought*. Cambridge, MA: The MIT Press.

Fodor, Jerry A. (1981) *Representations: Philosophical Essays on the Foundations of Cognitive Science*. Cambridge, MA: The MIT Press.

Fodor, Jerry A. (1987) *Psychosemantics: The Problem of Meaning in the Philosophy of Mind*. Cambridge, MA: The MIT Press.

Fodor, J. A. (1998) *In Critical Condition*. Cambridge, MA: The MIT Press.

Fodor, Jerry (2004) 'You Can't Argue with a Novel', *London Review of Books*, 4 March, pp. 30–31.

Fodor, Jerry (2011) 'Fire the Press Secretary', *London Review of Books*, 28 April, pp. 24–25.

Foucault, Michel (1981) *Power/Knowledge*, ed. Colin Gordon. New York: Pantheon.

Foxall, Gordon (1990) *Consumer Psychology in Behavioral Perspective*. London: Routledge.

Foxall, Gordon R. (2007) *Intentional Behaviorism, Behavior and Philosophy*, 33, 1–55.

Foxall, Gordon (2009) *Interpreting Consumer Choice: A Behavioral Perspective Model*. London: Routledge.

Frank, Robert H. (1988) *Passions within Reasons*. New York: W. W. Norton.

Friedman, Milton (1962) *Capitalism and Freedom*. Chicago: The University of Chicago Press.

Friedman, Richard A. (2006) 'What's the Ultimate? Scan a Male Brain', *New York Times*, 25 October, p. 10.

Frijda, N. H., Kuipers, P. and ter Schure, E. (1989) 'Relations Among Emotion, Appraisal, and Emotional Action Readiness', *Journal of Personality and Social Psychology*, 57, 212–228.

Gadamer, H. G. ([1960] 1975) *Truth and Method*. London: Continuum.

Gardenfors, Peter (2000) *Conceptual Spaces: The Geometry of Thought*. Cambridge, MA: The MIT Press.

Gardial, Sarah Fisher, Clemons, D. Scott, Woodruff, Robert B., Schumann, David W. and Burns, Mary Jane (1994) 'Comparing Consumers' Recall of Prepurchase and Postpurchase Product Evaluation Experiences', *Journal of Consumer Research*, 20, 548–60.

Gardner, Howard (1985) *The Mind's New Science: A History of the Cognitive Revolution*. New York: Basic Books.

Gardner, Howard (2004) *Changing Minds*. Cambridge, MA: The Harvard Business School Press.

Garfinkel, Harold (1967) *Studies in Ethnomethodology*. Englewood Cliffs, NJ: Prentice-Hall.

Gassaniga, Michael S. (2008) *Human*. New York: Ecco and HarperCollins.

Geertz, Clifford (1973) *Interpretation of Cultures*. New York: Basic Books.

Geertz, Clifford (1984) *Local Knowledge: Further Essays in Interpretive Anthropology*. New York: Basic Books.

Geertz, Clifford (1987) 'From the Native's Point of View: On the Nature of Anthropological Understanding', in *Interpreting Politics*, ed. Michael T. Gibbons. New York: New York University Press, pp. 133–147.

Geertz, Clifford (1995) *After the Fact*. Cambridge, MA: Harvard University Press.

Gibbs, R. W. (1994) *The Poetics of the Mind: Figurative Thought, Language, and Understanding*. Cambridge: Cambridge University Press.

Gilbert, D. (1993) 'The Assent of Man: Mental Representation and the Control of Belief', in *Handbook of Mental Control*, ed. D. M. Wegner and J. W. Pennebaker. Englewood Cliffs, NJ: Prentice-Hall.

Gilovich, Thomas (1991) *How We Know What Isn't So*. New York: Free Press.

Gilovich, T. and Medvec, V. H. (1995) 'The Experience of Regret: What, When and Why', *Psychological Review*, 102, 379–395.

Gintis, Herbert, Bowles, Samuel, Boyd, Robert and Fehr, Ernst (eds.) (2005) *Moral Sentiments and Material Interests: The Foundations of Cooperation in Economic Life*. Cambridge, MA: The MIT Press.

Giroux, Henry (2000) *The Mouse that Roared*. New York: Rowman & Littlefield.

Givvs, Raymond W. (1994) *The Poetics of Mind*. New York: Cambridge University Press.

Glimcher, Paul W. (2003) *Decisions, Uncertainty, and the Brain: The Science of Neuroeconomics*. Cambridge, MA: The MIT Press.

Goffman, E. (1959) *The Presentation of Self in Everyday Life*. Garden City, NY: Doubleday Anchor.

Goffman, E. (1971) *The Presentation of Self in Everyday Life*. Harmondsworth: Penguin.

Goldie, Peter (2000) *The Emotions: A Philosophical Exploration*. Oxford: Oxford University Press.

Goldman, A. L. (1970) *A Theory of Human Action*. Englewood Cliffs, NJ: Prentice-Hall.

Goldman, Alvin (1995) 'Interpretations Psychologized', in *Folk-Psychology*, ed. Martin Davies and Tony Stone. Oxford: Blackwell, pp. 74–100.

Goldstein, Noah, J., Martin, Steve and Cialdini, Robert B. (2010) *Yes! 50 Scientifically Proven Ways to be Persuasive*. New York: Free Press.

Goleman, Daniel (1995) *Emotional Intelligence*. New York: Bantam Books.

Goleman, Daniel (1998) *Working with Emotional Intelligence*. New York: Bantam Books.

Goodman, Nelson (1969) 'Seven Strictures on Similarity', in *Problems and Projects*, ed. Nelson Goodman. Indianapolis: Bobbs-Merrill.

Gordon, R. M. (1987) *The Structure of Emotions*. Cambridge: Cambridge University Press.

Gosling, J. C. B. (1969) *Pleasure and Desire: The Case for Hedonism Reviewed*. Oxford: Clarendon Press.

Grayling, A. C. (2003) 'From Rome to the Renaissance, We Always Needed to be Afraid', *The Times*, 10 May, p. 2.

Green, M. C. and Brock, T. C. (2000) 'The Role of Transportation in the Pervasiveness of Public Narratives', *Journal of Personality and Social Psychology*, 79, 701–721.

Green, Paul E. (1990) 'Conjoint Analysis in Marketing: New Developments with Implications for Research and Practice', *Journal of Marketing*, 54 (October), 3–19 .

Greenwald, A. G., Draine, S. C. and Abrams, R. L. (1996) 'Three Cognitive Markers in Unconscious Semantic Activation', *Science*, 273, 1699–1702.

Greenwald, A. G., Leippe, M. R., Pratkanis, A. R. and Baumgardner, M. H. (1986) 'Under What Conditions Does Theory Obstruct Research Progress?', *Psychological Review*, 93, 216–229.

Gregory, W. L., Cialdini, R. B. and Carpenter, K. M. (1982) 'Self-relevant Scenarios as Mediators of Likelihood Estimates and Compliance: Does Imagining Make it So?', *Journal of Personality and Social Psychology*, 43, 89–99.

Griffiths, Paul E. (1997) *What Emotions Really Are*. Chicago: The University of Chicago Press.

Gronow, Jukka (1997) *The Sociology of Taste*. London: Routledge.

Gross, Jane (2004) 'A Dream Life Freud Would Have Envied', *New York Times*, Sunday Styles, section 9, pp. 1–2.

Guiso, Luigi, Sapienza, Paola and Zingales, Luigi (2005) 'Cultural Biases in Economic Exchange', NBER Working Papers 11005, *National Bureau of Economic Research, Inc.*

Gul, Fauk and Pesendorfe, Wolfgang (2005) 'The Case for Mindless Economics', in *The Foundations of Positive and Normative Economics: A Handbook*, ed. Andrew Caplin and Andrew Schotter. New York: New York University Press.

Habermas, Jurgen (1981) *The Theory of Communicative Action*, vol. 1. Boston: Beacon Press.

Hacking, Ian (1983) *Representing and Intervening*. Cambridge: Cambridge University Press.

Hacking, Ian (1995) *Rewriting the Soul: Multiple Personality and the Sciences of Memory*. Princeton, NJ: Princeton University Press.

Handy, Rollo and Harwood, E. C. (1973) *A Current Appraisal of the Behavioral Sciences*. Great Barrington, MA: Behavioral Research Council.

Hare, R. M. (1979) 'Contrasting Methods of Environmental Planning', in *Ethics and Problems of the 21st Century*, ed. K. E. Goodpaster and K. M. Sayre. Indiana: University of Notre Dame Press.

Harlow, H. F. (1953) 'Mice, Monkeys, Men and Motives', *Psychological Review*, 60, 23–32.

Harman, Gilbert (1986) *Change of View*. Cambridge, MA: The MIT Press.

Harré, Rom (1995) 'Discursive Psychology', in *Rethinking Psychology*, ed. Jonathan Smith, Rom Harré and Luk Van Langenhove. London: Sage Publications.

Harré, Rom (1997) 'Social Life as Rule-governed Patterns of Joint Action', in *The Message of Social Psychology*, ed. Craig McGarty and S. Alexander Haslam. Oxford: Blackwell.

Harré, R. and Secord, P. F. (1973) *The Explanation of Social Behavior*. Totowa, NJ: Littlefield, Adams & Co.

Harris, Sam (2011) *The Moral Landscape: How Science Can Determine Human Values*. New York: Free Press.

Haugtvdt, C. P. and Wegener, D. T. (2002) *Raw Data*. Columbus: Ohio State University Press.

Hawes, John, M., Strong, James T. and Winick, Bernard S. (1996) 'Do Closing Techniques Diminish Prospect Trust?', *Industrial Marketing Management*, 25, 349–360.

Heath, Anthony (1976) *Rational Choice and Social Exchange*. Cambridge: Cambridge University Press.

Hebb, D. O. (1955) 'Drives and the C.N.S (Conceptual Nervous System)', *Psychological Review*, 62, 243–54.

Heidegger, Martin (1962) *Being and Time*. Trans. John Macquarrie and Edward Robinson. Oxford: Blackwell.

Heider, Fritz (1958) *The Psychology of Interpersonal Relations*. New York: John Wiley & Sons.

Henderson, David (1999) 'Misguided Virtue: False Notions of Corporate Social Responsibility', Hobart paper 142, *Institute of Economic Affairs*.

Herbert, Wray (2010) *On Second Thought*. New York: Crown Publishers.

Hill, Dan (2003) *Body of Truth*. Hoboken, NJ: John Wiley & Sons.

Hinton, David (2005) *Gold and Gilt, Pots and Pins: Possessions and People in Medieval Britain*. Oxford: Oxford University Press.

Hirschman, Elizabeth C. and Holbrook, Morris B. (1982) 'Hedonic Consumption: Emerging Concepts, Methods and Propositions', *Journal* of *Marketing*, 46, 92–101.

Ho, Teck H., Lim, Noah and Camerer, Colin F. (2006) 'Modeling the Psychology of Consumer and Firm Behavior with Behavioral Economics', *Journal of Marketing Research*, 43, 307–331.

Hoch, Stephen J. and Deighton, John (1989) 'Managing What Consumers Learn from Experience', *Journal of Marketing*, 53 (April), 1–20 .

Hodge, Robert and Kress, Gunther (1988) *Social Semiotics*. Ithaca, NY: Cornell University Press.

Holbrook, M. B. (1988) 'Steps Towards a Psychoanalytic Interpretation of Consumption: A Meta-Meta-Analysis of Some Issues Raised by the Consumer Behavior Odyssey', in *Advances in Consumer Research*, ed. M. I. Houston. Provo, UT: Association for Consumer Research.

Holbrook, Morris B. (2003) 'Review in "New Books in Review" ', *Journal of Marketing Research*, 40, 298–501.

Holbrook, Morris (2008) 'Consumers Just Wanna Have Fantasies, Feelings and Fun', in *Consumer Behavior*, ed. Banwari Mittal et al. Cincinnati: Open Mentis.

Hollis, Martin (1996) *Reason in Action: Essays in the Philosophy of Social Science*. Cambridge: Cambridge University Press.

Homans, George C. (1950) *The Human Group*. NY: Harcourt Brace Javanovich.

Horgan, John (1999) *The Undiscovered Mind: How the Brain Defies Explanation*. London: Weidenfeld & Nicolson.

Houston, Franklin and Gasseheimer, Jude B. (1987) 'Marketing and Exchange', *Journal of Marketing*, 51, 3–18.

Howard, John A. and Sheth, Jagdish N. (1968) *The Theory of Buyer Behavior*. New York: Wiley.

Howarth-Williams, Martin (1977) *R. D. Laing: His Work and Its Relevance for Sociology*. London: Routledge & Kegan Paul.

Hughes, Christopher (2004) *Kripke: Names, Necessity and Identity*. Oxford: Oxford University Press.

Humphrey, Nicholas (1983) *Consciousness Regained*. Oxford: Oxford University Press.

Hunt, Shelby D. (1983) 'General Theories and the Fundamental Explanada of Marketing', *Journal of Marketing*, 47, 9–17.

James, Oliver (2009) *Contented Dementia – a 24 Hour Wraparound Care for Lifelong Wellbeing*. London: Vermilion.

Jameson, Fredric and Miyochi, Masao (1999) *The Cultures of Globalization*. Durham, NC: Duke University Press.

Janis, Irving L. (1982) *Groupthink: Psychological Studies of Policy Decisions and Fiascoes*. New York: Houghton Mifflin.

Janis, I. L. and Mann, L. (1977) *Decision-making: A Psychological Analysis of Conflict, Choice and Commitment*. New York: Free Press.

Johnson, D. M. and Erneling, C. E. (eds.) (1997) *The Future of the Cognitive Revolution*. New York: Oxford University Press.

Jones, Geoffrey (2010) *Beauty Imagined: A History of the Global Beauty Industry*. Oxford: Oxford University Press.

Jung, C. G. (2009) *The Red Book*, ed. Sonu Shamdasani. New York: W. W. Norton & Company.

Kagan, Jerome (1989) *Unstable Ideas: Temperament, Cognition and Self*. Cambridge, MA: Harvard University Press.

Kagan, Jerome (1999) *Three Seductive Ideas*. Cambridge, MA: Harvard University Press.

Kagan, Jerome (2006) *An Argument for Mind*. New Haven, CT: Yale University Press.

Kahl, Lynn R., Beatty, Sharon E. and Homer, Pamela (1986) 'Alternative Measurement Approaches to Consumer Values: The List of Values (LOV) and Values and Lifestyle', *Journal of Consumer Research*, 13, 405–409.

Kahneman, Daniel (2011) *Thinking, Fast and Slow*. New York: Farrar, Straus and Giroux.

Kahneman, Daniel and Tversky, Amos (1979) 'Prospect Theory: An Analysis of Decision under Risk', *Econometrica*, 47, 263–291.

Kahneman, D. and Tversky A. (1982) 'The Simulation Heuristic', in *Judgment and Uncertainty*, ed. D. Kahneman, P. Slovic and A. Tversky. Cambridge: Cambridge University Press.

Kahneman, D. and Tversky, A (1984) 'Choices, Values and Frames', *American Psychologist*, 39, 341–350.

Kaletsky, Anatole (2009) 'Three Cheers for the Death of Old Economics', *The Times* (London), 29 October, p. 19.

Katz, Daniel (1960) 'The Functional Approach to the Study of Attitudes', *Public Opinion Quarterly*, 24, 163–204.

Kelly, George A. (1963) *A Theory of Personality*. New York: W. W. Norton.

Kirsch, Irving (2011) *The Emperor's New Drugs: Exploding the Antidepressant Myth*. New York: Basic Books.

Kirsh, David (1983) 'The Role of Philosophy in the Human Sciences', in *The Need for Interpretation*, ed. Sollace Mitchell and Michael Rosen. London: The Athlone Press.

Kitcher, Philip (2001) *Science, Truth, and Democracy*. New York: Oxford University Press.

Klein, G. A. (1993) 'A Recognition-Primed Decision Model of Rapid Decision-Making', in *Decision-Making in Action: Models and Methods*, ed. G. A. Klein, J. Orasanu, R. Calderwood and G. E. Zsambok. Norwood NJ: Ablex.

Klein, G. A (1998) *Sources of Power: How People Make Decisions*. Cambridge, MA: The MIT Press.

Knowles, Eric S. and Linn, Jay A. (eds.) (2004) *Resistance and Persuasion*. Mahwah, NJ: Lawrence Erlbaum.

Kosslyn, Stephen Michael (1980) *Image and Mind*. Cambridge, MA: Harvard University Press.

Kotler, Philip (1972) 'A Generic Concept of Marketing', *Journal of* Marketing, 36 (April), 46–54.

Kotler, Philip and Levy, Sydney J. (1969) 'Broadening the Concept of Marketing', *Journal of Marketing*, 33 (January), 10–18.

Kotulak, Ronald (1996) *Inside the Brain: Revolutionary Discoveries on How the Mind Works*. Kansas City, MO: Andrews & McMeel.

Krausz, Michael (1993) *Rightness and Reasons: Interpretation in Cultural Practices*. Ithaca, NY: Cornell University Press.

Krugman, Herbert E. (1965) 'The Impact of Television Advertising: Learning without Involvement', *Public Opinion Quarterly*, 29 (Fall), 349–56.

Krugman, Paul (2009) 'How Did Economists Get it So Wrong', *New York Times Magazine*, 6 September, pp. 36–43.

Krugman, Paul (2010) 'Senator Bunning's Universe', *New York Times* OP.ED, 5 March, p. A21.

Kuhn, Deanna (1991) *The Skills of Argument*. Cambridge: Cambridge University Press.

Kuhn, James W. (2005) 'Business Managers and the Ethics of Competitive Markets' (Draft, unpublished article).

Kuhn, M. (1964) 'Major Trends in Symbolic Interaction Theory in the Past Twenty Five Years', *Sociological Quarterly*, 5, 61–84.

Kuhn, Thomas, S. (1962) *The Structure of Scientific Revolutions*. Chicago: The University of Chicago Press.

Kuhn, Thomas S. (1977) *The Essential Tension*. Chicago: The University of Chicago Press.

Kuhn, Thomas S. (1977) 'Second Thought on Paradigms', in *The Structure of Scientific Theories*, ed. F. Suppe. Urbana: University of Illinois Press.

Kuper, Adam (1999) *Culture: The Anthropologist's Account*. MA: Harvard University Press, preface, pp. x–xi.

Kyburg, Henry E. (1983) *Epistemology and Inference*. Minneapolis: University of Minnesota Press.

La Berge, D. (1975) 'Acquisition of Automatic Processing in Perceptual and Associative Learning', in *Attention and Performance*, vol. 5, ed. P. M. A. Rabbitt and S. Dormic. London: Academic Press.

LaFeber, Walter (1999) *Michael Jordan and the New Global Capitalism*. New York: W. W. Norton & Company.

Lakoff, G. (1996) *Moral Politics: What Conservatives Know that Liberals Don't*. Chicago: The University of Chicago Press.

Landes, David S. (1998) *The Wealth and Poverty of Nations: Why Some Are Rich and Some Are Poor*. New York: W. W. Norton.

Larson, C. U. (1995) *Persuasion*. Belmont: Wadsworth.

Lazarsfeld, P. F. (1970) *Main Trends in Sociology*. New York: Harper Torchbooks.

Lazarus, R. S. (1991) *Emotion and Adaptation*. New York: Oxford University Press.

Lazarus, R. S. (1994) 'Meaning and Emotional Development', in *The Nature of Emotion*, ed. P. Ekman and R. J. Davidson. New York: Oxford University Press.

Lear, Jonathan (1988) *Open Minded*. Cambridge, MA: Harvard University Press.

Leathers, D. (1986) *Successful Nonverbal Communication: Principles and Applications*. New York: Macmillan.

Le Bon, Gustave (2002) *The Crowd: A Study of the Popular Mind*. New York: Dover Publications.

LeDoux, Joseph (1998) *The Emotional Brain*. New York: Simon & Schuster.

Lehmann, Donald (1999) 'Consumer Behavior and Y2X', *Journal of Marketing*, 63, 14–18.

Lehman, Donald R. and O'Shaughnessy, John (1974) 'Difference in Attribute Importance for Different Industrial Products,' *Journal of Marketing*, 38 (April), 36–42.

Lehrer, Jonah (2009) *How We Decide*. New York: Houghton Mifflin Harcourt.

Leiter, Kenneth (1980) *A Primer on Ethnomethodology*. New York: Oxford University Press.

Lepper, M. R. and Greene, D. (eds.) (1978) *The Hidden Costs of Reward*. Hillsdale, NJ: Erlbaum.

Levenson, R.W., Ekman P. and Friesen, W. V. (1990) 'Voluntary Facial Expression Generates Emotion-Specific Nervous System Activity', *Psycho-physiology,* 27, 363–384.

Levi, Isaac (1985) 'Illusions about Uncertainty', *British Journal of Philosophy of Science*, 36, 331–340.

Levy, Sidney J. (1981) 'Interpreting Consumer Mythology: A Structural Approach to Consumer Behavior', *Journal of Marketing*, 44, Summer, 49–61.

Levitt, Theodore (1960) 'Marketing Myopia', *Harvard Business Review*, 38 (July–August).

Levy, Sydney J. (1999) ' "Motivation Research" in Brands, Consumers, Symbols and Research', in *Sydney Levy on Marketing*, ed. Dennis W. Rook. Thousand Oaks, CA: Sage.

Lewin, Kurt (1968) 'Group Decision and Social Change', in *Readings in Social Psychology*, ed. Eleanor E. Maccoby, T. M. Newcomb and E. L. Hartley. New York: Holt, Rinehart and Winston.

Lewinsohn, P. M. and Amenson, C. S. (1978) 'Some Relations between Pleasant and Unpleasant Mood-Related Events and Depression', *Journal of Abnormal Psychology*, 87, 644–654.

Lewis, Anthony (1999) 'Big Brother Pounces', *New York Times* OP.ED, 7 December.

Lewis, David (1973) 'Causation', *Journal of Philosophy*, 70, 556–567.

Leymore, V. L. (1975) *The Hidden Myth*. New York: Basic Books.

Libet, B. (1993) 'Unconscious Cerebral Initiative and the Role of Conscious Will in Voluntary Action', in *Neurophysiology of Consciousness*. Boston: Birkhauser, 269–306.

Lipton, Peter (1991) *Inference to the Best Explanation*. London: Routledge.

Llewellyn, Karl (1960) *The Common Law Tradition: Deciding Appeals*. Boston: Little, Brown.

Llewellyn-Jones, Rosie (2007) *The Great Uprising in India 1857–58*. London: Boydell.

Lloyd, G. E. R. (1990) *Demystifying Mentalities*. Cambridge: Cambridge University Press.

Loewenstein, George and Ubel, Peter (2010) 'Economics Behaving Badly', *New York Times* OP.ED, 15 July, p. A.27.

Lovell, Julia (2011) *The Opium War, Dreams and the Making of China*. London: Picador.

Luce, Mary, Frances, Bettman, James R. and Payne, John W. (2001) *Emotional Decisions: Tradeoff Difficulty and Coping in Consumer Choice*. Chicago: University of Chicago Press.

Luce, R. D. (1959) *Individual Choice Behavior*. New York: Wiley.

Lurie, Alison (1983) *The Language of Clothes*. New York: Vintage.

Lyon, David (1994) *Postmodernity*. Buckingham: Open University Press.

Lyons, W. (1980) *Emotion*. London: Cambridge University Press.

Lyons, William (2001) *Matters of the Mind*. Edinburgh: Edinburgh University Press.

McClelland, D. C. (1961) *The Achieving Society*. New York: Von Nostrand.

MacCorquodale, Kenneth and Meehl, Paul E. (1948) 'Hypothetical Constructs and Intervening Variables', *Psychological Review*, 55, 95–107.

McCracken, Grant (1988) *Culture and Consumption*. Bloomington: Indiana University Press.

McCracken, Grant (2009) *Chief Culture Officer*. New York: Basic Books.

McGaugh, James (2003) *Memory and Emotion*. New York: Columbia University Press.

McGinn, Colin (1982) *The Character of Mind*. New York: Oxford University Press.

McGuire, W. J. (1964) 'Inducing Resistance to Persuasion: Some Contemporary Approaches', in *Advances in Experimental Psychology*, ed. L. Berkowitz. New York: Academic Press, vol.1, pp. 191–229.

McGuire, William J. (2000) *Constructing Social Psychology: Creative and Critical Processes*. New York: Cambridge University Press.

McHugh, Paul (2007) 'Diagnosis: Diffident', *The Wall Street Journal*, W8, November 3–4.

MacInnis, C., Moorman, C. and Jaworski, B. (1991) 'Enhancing and Measuring Consumer Motivation, Opportunity and Ability to Process Brand Information from Brands', *Journal of Marketing*, 55, 32–53.

MacInnis, Deborah J. (2004) 'Where Have All the Papers Gone? Reflections on the Decline of Conceptual Articles', *ACR News*, 4, Spring, 1–3.

MacIntyre, Alasdair (1981) *After Virtue: A Study in Moral Theory*. Notre Dame, IN: University of Notre Dame Press.

Mackie, Diane and Worth, Leila (1989) 'Processing Deficits and the Mediation of Positive Affect on Persuasion', *Journal of Personality and Social Psychology*, 57, 27–40.

McMahon, Darrin, M. (2005) *Happiness: A History*. New York: Atlantic Monthly Press.

Manstead, Anthony and Edwards, Roselyne (1992) 'Communicative Aspects of Children's Emotional Competence', in *International Review of Studies of Emotion*, ed. K. T. Strong. New York: Wiley.

Marder, Eric (1987) *The Laws of Choice: Predicting Customer Behavior*. New York: Free Press.

Margolis, Joseph (1980) *Art and Philosophy*. Atlantic Highlands, NJ: Humanities Press.

Maslow, A. H. (1954) *Motivation and Personality*. New York: Harper & Row.

Mathews, Gerald, Zeidner, Moshe and Roberts, Richard D. (2002) *Emotional Intelligence: Science and Myth*. Cambridge, MA: The MIT Press.

Mayhew, Leon H. (1997) *The New Public*. Cambridge: Cambridge University Press.

Mead, George Herbert (1934) *Mind, Self and Society*, ed. Charles W. Morris, Chicago: The University of Chicago Press.

Medin, D. L. (1989) 'Concepts and Conceptual Structure', *American Psychologist*, 44, 1469–1481.

Mele, A. (1992) *Springs of Action*. New York: Oxford University Press.

Merton, Robert K. (1949) *Social Theory and Social Structure*. Glencoe, IL: Free Press.

Micklethwait, John and Wooldridge, Adrian (2000) *A Future Perfect*. London: Heinemann.

Miller, John J. (2006) 'Myth Mongering', *National Review*, 28, 42–43.

Miller, William Ian (2004) *Faking It*. Cambridge: Cambridge University Press.

Millikan, Ruth Garrett (2004) *Varieties of Meaning*. Cambridge, MA: The MIT Press.

Montgomery, H. (1984) 'Decision Rules and the Search for Dominance Structure: Towards a Process Model of Decision-making', in *Analyzing and Aiding Decision Processes*, ed. P. C. Humphreys, O. Svenson and A. Vari. Amsterdam: North-Holland.

Moore, R. Laurence (1994) *Selling God*. New York: Oxford University Press.

Muraven, M. R. and Baumeister, R. F. (2000) 'Self-Regulation and the Depletion of Limited Resources: Does Self-Control Resemble a Muscle?', *Psychological Bulletin*, 126, 247–259.

Murphy, Gregory L. (2002) *The Big Book of Concepts*. Cambridge, MA: The MIT Press.

Murphy G. L. and Medin D. (1985) 'The Role of Theories in Conceptual Coherence', *Psychological Review*, 92(1), 289–316.

Murray, Charles (2003) *Human Accomplishment*. New York: HarperCollins.

Nagel, T. (1979) *Moral Questions*. Cambridge: Cambridge University Press.

Nisbett, Richard E. (2004) *The Geography of Thought: How Asians and Westerners Think Differently – and Why*. New York: Free Press.

Norman, D. A. and Shallice, T. (1986) 'Attention to Action: Willed and Automatic Control of Behavior', in *Consciousness and Self-Regulation: Advances in Research and Theory*, vol. 4, ed. R. J. Davidson, G. E. Schwartz and D. Shapiro. New York: Plenum Press.

Novemsky, Nathan and Kahneman, Daniel (2005a) 'The Boundaries of Loss Aversion', *Journal Of Marketing Research*, 42, 119–128.

Novemsky, Nathan and Kahneman, Daniel (2005b) 'How Do Intentions Affect Loss Aversion?', *Journal Of Marketing Research*, 42, 139–140.

Novitz , David (1987) *Knowledge, Fiction and Imagination*. Philadelphia: Temple University Press.

Nozick, Robert (1975) *Anarchy, State and Utopia*. New York: Basic Books.

Nozick, Robert (1993) *The Nature of Rationality*. Princeton, NJ: Princeton University Press.

Nussbaum, Martha C, (2001) *Upheavals of Thought: The Intelligence of Emotions*. New York: Cambridge University Press.

Nye, Mary Jo (2011) *Michael Polanyi and His Generation: Origins of the Social Construction of Science*. Chicago: University of Chicago Press.

O'Brien, Geoffrey (2001) 'All the Luck in the World', *New York Review of Books*, 8 March, 15–20.

Orasanu, J. and Salas, E. (1993) 'Team Decision-making in Complex Environments', in *Decision-making in Action: Models and Methods*, ed. G. A. Klein, J. Orasanu, R. Calderwood and G. E. Zsambok. Norwood, NJ: Ablex.

Ortony, A. and Taylor, T. J. (1990) 'What's Basic about Basic Emotions?', *Psychological Review*, 97, 315–331.

Ortony, Andrew, Clore, Gerald L. and Collins, Allan (1988) *The Cognitive Structure of Emotions*. Cambridge: Cambridge University Press.

O'Shaughnessy, Brian (1980) *The Will: A Dual Aspect Theory 2*. Cambridge: Cambridge University Press.

O'Shaughnessy, John (1986) *Why People Buy*. New York: Oxford University Press.

O'Shaughnessy, John (1995) *Competitive Marketing*. London: Routledge.

O'Shaughnessy, John (2009*) Interpretation in Social Life, Social Science and Marketing*. London & New York: Routledge.

O'Shaughnessy, John and Holbrook, Morris B. (1988) 'Understanding Consumer Behaviour: The Linguistic Turn in Marketing Research', *Journal of the Market Research Society*, 30, 197–223.

O'Shaughnessy, John and O'Shaughnessy, N. J. (2003) *The Marketing Power of Emotion*. New York: Oxford University Press.

O'Shaughnessy, John and O'Shaughnessy, N. J. (2004) *Persuasion in Advertising*. London and New York: Routledge.

Palmer, R. E. (1969) *Hermeneutics: Interpretation Theory in Schleiermacher, Dilthey, Heidegger and Gadamer*. Evanston, IL: Northwestern University Press.

Park, Denise C. and Gutchess, Angela Hall (1999) 'Cognitive Aging and Everyday Life', in *Cognitive Aging*, ed. Denise Park and Norbert Schwarz. New York: Psychology Press.

Park, Robert E. (1955) *Society*. New York: Free Press.

Parkinson, Brian (1995) *Ideas and Realities of Emotion*. London and New York: Routledge.

Parsons, Talcott (1951) *The Social System*. New York: Free Press.

Patnaik, Dev (2009) *Wired to Care: How Companies Prosper When they Create Widespread Empathy*. Upper Saddle River, NJ: F. T. Press.

Peck, Abe (2010) 'The Third Way to Media Success', *Miller-McCune*, November/December, pp. 38–45.

Penman, Danny (2008) 'Can We Really Transplant a Human Soul?', *Daily Mail*, London, 9 April, p. 14.

Pennington, N. and Hastie, R. (1993) 'A Theory of Explanation-based Decision-making', in *Models and Methods*, ed. C. Klein, et al. Norwood, NJ: Abex.

Perry, Lewis (1984) *Intellectual Life in America: A History*. Chicago: University of Chicago Press.

Peters, R. S. (1960) *The Concept of Motivation*. London: Routledge & Kegan Paul.

Pettigrew, A. M. (1973) *The Politics of Organizational Decision-making*. London: Tavistock.

Petty, Richard E. and Cacioppo, John T. (1979) 'Issue Involvement Can Increase or Decrease Persuasion by Enhancing Message Relevant Cognitive Responses', *Journal of Personality and Social Psychology*, 37, 1915–26.

Petty, Richard and Cacioppo, John (1986) *Communication and Persuasion: Central and Peripheral Routes to Attitude Change*. New York: Springer-Verlag.

Pfeffer, Jeffrey (1993) 'Barriers to the Advance of Organizational Science: Paradigm Development as a Dependent Variable', *Academy of Management Review*, 18, 599–620.

Pfeffer, Jeffrey (2010) *Power*. New York: Harper Business.

Pfeifer, Rolf and Bongard, Josh (2005) *How the Body Shapes the Way We Think*. Cambridge, MA: The MIT Press.

Pigou, A. C. (1929) *Industrial Fluctuations*. London: Macmillan.

Pillar, Paul. R. (2011) *Intelligence and US Foreign Policy: Iraq, 9/11 and Misguided Reform*. New York: Columbia University Press.

Pinker, Steven (1994) *The Language Instinct*. New York: William Morrow.

Pinker, Steven (2002) *The Blank Slate: The Modern Denial of Human Nature*. New York: Viking Press.

Pinker, Steven (2007) *The Stuff of Thought*. New York: Penguin Books.

Pinker, Steven (2011) *The Better Angels of our Nature*. New York: Viking Press.

Plutchik, Robert (1980) *Emotion: Psychoevolutionary Synthesis*. New York: Harper and Row.

Polanyi, Michael (1958/1962) *Personal Knowledge*. Chicago: The University of Chicago Press.

Polya, G. (1957) *How to Solve It: A New Aspect of Mathematical Method*. New York: Doubleday Anchor.

Pratkanis, A. R. and Aronson, A. (1991) *The Age of Propaganda*. New York: Freeman Press.

Prinz, Jesse J. (2002) *Furnishing the Mind: Concepts and Their Perceptual Basis*. Cambridge, MA: The MIT Press.

Putnam, Hilary (1975) 'Minds and Machines', in *Mind, Language and Reality Philosophical Papers*, ed. Hilary Putnam. Cambridge: Cambridge University Press.

Quine, W. V. (1951) 'Two Dogmas of Empiricism', *Philosophical Review*, 60, 20–43.

Quine, W. V. (1953) *From a Logical Point of View*. Cambridge, MA: Harvard University Press.

Quine, W. V. (1987) *Quiddities*. Cambridge, MA: Belknap Press.

Radner, D. (1996) *Animal Consciousness*. Amherst, NY: Prometheus Books.

Raphael, D. D. and Macfie, A. L. (1984) *The Theory of Moral Sentiments*. Indianapolis, IN: Liberty Fund.

Rapoport, A. (1953) *Operational Philosophy*. New York: Wiley.

Rawls, J. (1972) *A Theory of Justice*. Oxford: Oxford University Press.

Ray, Michael L. (1982) *Advertising and Communication Management*. Englewood Cliffs, NJ: Prentice-Hall.

Reber, Arthur S., Allen, Rhiannon and Reber, Emily S. (2009) *The Penguin Dictionary of Psychology*. London: Penguin Books.

Regal, Philip, J. (1990) *The Anatomy of Judgment*. Minneapolis: University of Minnesota Press.

Rex, John (1961) *Key Problems in Sociological Theory*. London: Routledge & Kegan Paul.

Ricoeur, P. (1981) *Hermeneutics and the Human Sciences: Essays on Language, Action and Interpretation*, ed. and trans. J. B. Thompson. Cambridge: Cambridge University Press.

Ringen, Stein (2003) *The Norwegian Study of Power and Democracy*. Available at http://www.sv.uio.no/mutr/english/index.html.

Robinson, Daniel N. (1985) *Philosophy of Psychology*. New York: Columbia University Press.

Rockwell, W. Tweed (2005) *Neither Brain Nor Ghost*. Cambridge, MA: The MIT Press.

Rokeach, Milton (1973) *The Nature of Human Values*. New York: Free Press.

Rose, Hilary and Rose, Steven (eds.) (2000) *Alas Poor Darwin: Arguments Against Evolutionary Psychology*. London: Harmony Books.

Rose, Hilary and Rose, Steven (2011) 'Never Mind the Bollocks', *London Review of Books*, 28 April, pp. 17–18.

Rumbaugh, Duane M. and Washburn, David A. (2003) *Intelligence of Apes and other Rational Beings*. New Haven, CT: Yale University Press.

Ryan, Alan (2003) 'The Way to Reason', *New York Review of Books*, 4 December, pp. 43–45.

Rycroft, Charles (1995) *A Critical Dictionary of Psychoanalysis*. London: Penguin.

Ryerson, James (2004) 'Sidewalk Socrates', *New York Times Magazine*, 26 December, p. 35.

Ryle, Gilbert (1949) *The Concept of Mind*. London: Hutchinson & Co.

Saad, Gad (2011) *The Consuming Instinct*. Amherst, NY: Prometheus.

Saadi, Sommer (2011) 'Consumer Research Tool MRI Scans', *Bloomberg Businessweek*, 15–28 August, p. 108.

Samuel, Lawrence R. (2011) *Freud on Madison Avenue*. Pennsylvania: University of Pennsylvania Press.

Savage, L. J. (1954) *The Foundations of Statistics*. New York: Wiley.

Scheibe, Karl E. (2000) *The Drama of Everyday Life*. Cambridge, MA: Harvard University Press.

Schiffer, Frederic (1998) *Of Two Minds: The Revolutionary Science of Dual-Brain Psychology*. New York: Free Press.

Schreibman, Laura (2006) *The Science and Fiction of Autism*. Cambridge, MA: Harvard University Press.

Schutz, Alfred (1967) *The Phenomenology of the Social World,* trans. George Walsh and F. Lehnert. Evanston: Northwestern University Press.

Schwanenflugel, P. J. (1991) 'Why are Abstract Concepts Hard to Understand?', in *The Pschology of Word Meanings*, ed. P. J. Schwanenflugel. Hilldale, NJ: Lawrence Erlbaum.

Scriven, Michael (1992) 'Evaluation and Critical Thinking: Logic's Last Frontier', in *Critical Reasoning in Contemporary Culture*, ed. Richard A. Talaska. Albany, NY: State University of New York.

Searle, John (1981) 'Minds, Brains and Programs', in *The Mind's I: Fantasies and Reflections on Self and Soul*, ed. Douglas R. Hofstrader and Daniel Dennett. Brighton, Sussex: Harvester Press.

Searle, John (1992) *The Rediscovery of Mind*. Cambridge, MA: The MIT Press.

Searle, J. R. and Freeman, W. (1998) 'Do We Understand Consciousness?', *Journal of Consciousness Studies*, 5, 718–733.

Sehon, Scott (2005) *Teleological Realism*. Cambridge, MA: The MIT Press.

Seligman, Adam B. (1997) *The Problem of Trust*. Princeton, NJ: Princeton University Press.

Sen, Amartya (2003) *Rationality and Freedom*. Cambridge, MA: Belknap Press of Harvard University Press.

Sen, Amartya (2010) *The Idea of Justice*. Boston, MA: Belknap Press of Harvard University Press.

Shapiro, Lawrence A. (2004) *The Mind Incarnate*. Boston, MA: The MIT Press.

Sheldon, Roy and Arens, Egmont (1932), quoted in Stuart Ewen (1988), *All Consuming Images*, New York: Basic Books.

Shweder, Richard A. (2003) *Why Do Men Barbecue? Recipes for Cultural Psychology*. Cambridge, MA: Harvard University Press.

Simon, H. A. (1957) *Administrative Behavior*. New York: Macmillan.

Simon, Herbert A. (1957) *Models of Man: Social and Rational*. New York: John Wiley & Sons.

Sims, Andrew (1995) *Symptoms in the Mind: An Introduction to Descriptive Psychopathology*. London: W.B. Saunders.

Singer, P. (1979) *Practical Ethics*. Cambridge: Cambridge University Press.

Sinha, R., Lovallo, W. R. and Parsons, O. A. (1992) 'Cardiovascular Differentiation of Emotions', *Psychosomatic Medicine*, 54, 422–435.

Smith, Hugh (2004) *On Clausewitz*. London: Palgrave Macmillan.

Story, Louise (2006) 'What We Talk About When We Talk About Brands', *New York Times*, 24 November, p. C7.

Strawson, Galen (2009) *Selves: An Essay in Revisionist Metaphysics*. Oxford: Oxford University Press.

Surowiecki, James (2004) *The Wisdom of Crowds: Why the Many are Smarter than the Few*. Boston: Little, Brown.

Szymanski, David M. and Henard, David H. (2001) 'Customer Satisfaction: A Meta-Analysis of the Empirical Evidence', *Journal of the Academy of Marketing Science*, 29, 16–35.

Tadajewski, Mark (2006) 'Remembering Motivation Research: Toward an Alternative Genealogy of Interpretive Consumer Research', *Marketing Theory*, 6, 429–466.

Tajfel, H. (1981) *Human Groups and Social Categories*. Cambridge: Cambridge University Press.

Taper, Mark L. and Lele, Subhash R. (eds.) (2004) *The Nature of Scientific Evidence*. Chicago: The University of Chicago Press, preface.

Tax, Stephen S., Brown, Stephen W. and Chandrashekaran, Murali (1998) 'Customer Evaluations of Service Complaint Experiences', *Journal of Marketing*, 62, 60–77.

Taylor, Charles (1983) 'The Significance of Significance: The Case of Cognitive Psychology', in *The Need for Interpretation*, ed. Sollace Mitchell and Michael Rosen. London: The Athlone Press.

Taylor, Gabriele (1985) *Pride, Shame and Guilt: Emotions of Self-Assessment*. Oxford: Oxford University Press.

Thagard, Paul (2000) *Coherence in Thought and Action*. Cambridge, MA: The MIT Press.

Thaler, Richard. H. (1985) 'Mental Accounting and Consumer Choice', *Marketing Science*, 4, 199–214.

Thayer, Robert E. (1996) *The Origin of Everyday Moods: Managing Energy, Tension, and Stress*. New York: Oxford University Press.

Thompson, Clive (2003) 'There's a Sucker Born in Every Medial Prefrontal Cortex', *New York Times Magazine*, 26 October, pp. 54–57.

Toulmin, Stephen (1964) *The Uses of Argument*. Cambridge: Cambridge University Press.

Toulmin, Stephen (2001) *Return to Reason*. Cambridge, MA: Harvard University Press.

Tugend, Alina (2010) 'Too Many Choices: A Problem That Can Paralyze', *New York Times: Business*, 27, p. B5.

Tversky, A. (1969) 'Intransitivity of Preferences', *Psychological Review*, 79, 281–299.

Tversky, A. (1972) 'Elimination by Aspects', *Psychological Review*, 76, 31–48.

Tversky, Amos (1977) 'Features of Similarity', *Psychological Review*, 84, 327–352.

Tversky, A. and Kahneman, D. (1973) 'Availability: A Heuristic for Judging Frequency and Probability', *Cognitive Psychology*, 5, 207–232.

Tversky, A and Kahneman, D. (1981) 'The Framing of Decisions and the Psychology of Choice', *Science*, 211, 453–458.

Tversky, A. and Kahneman, D. (1983) 'Extensional versus Intuitive Reasoning: The Conjunction Fallacy in Probability Judgment', *Psychological Review*, 90, 293–315.

Underhill, Paco (1999) *Why We Buy: The Science of Shopping*. London: Orion Business Books.

Unger, R. M. (1984) *Passion: An Essay on Personality*. New York: Free Press.

Useem, Jerry (2003) 'This Man Can Read Your Mind', *Fortune*, 20 January, p. 48.

Vargo, S. L. and Lusch, R. (2004) 'Evolving to a New Dominant Logic for Marketing', *Journal of Marketing*, 68, 1–17.

Velleman, J. David (1989) *Practical Reflection*. Princeton, NJ: Princeton, University Press.

Velleman, J. David (2000) *The Possibility of Practical Reason*, vol. 39. New York: Oxford University Press.

Von Neumann, J. and Morgenstern, O. (1947) *Theory of Games and Economic Behavior*. Princeton, NJ: Princeton University Press.

Von Wright, G. H. (1971) *Explanation and Understanding*. Ithaca, NY: Cornell University Press.

Von Wright, G. H. (1983) *Practical Reason*. Oxford: Basil Blackwell.

Vroom, Victor (1964) 'Some Psychologial Aspects of Organizational Control', in *New Perspectives in Organizational Control*, ed. W. W. Cooper, H. J. Leavitt and M. W. Shelly. New York: John Wiley.

Vyse, Stuart A. (1997) *Believing in Magic: The Psychology of Superstition*. New York: Oxford University Press.

Wade, Nicholas (2006) *Before the Dawn: Recovering the Lost History of Our Ancestors*. New York: Penguin.

Wapshott, Nicholas (2011) *Keynes Hayek: The Clash that Defined Modern Economics*. New York: W. W. Norton.

Watson, P. C. and Johnson-Laird, P. N. (1972) *The Psychology of Reason: Structure and Content*. Cambridge, MA: Harvard University Press.

Webster, Frederic E. (1992) 'The Changing Role of Marketing in the Corporation', *Journal of Marketing*, 56, 1–17.

Weiss, Gary (2006) *The Rampant Greed and Dishonesty that Imperil your Investments*. New York: Portfolio.

Wiggins, D. (1978) 'Deliberation and Practical Reason', in *Practical Reasoning*, ed. Joseph Raz. London: Oxford University Press.

Wilcken, Patrick (2011) *Claude Levi-Strauss: The Poet in the Laboratory*. London: Bloomsbury.

Wilcocks, Robert (2001) *Mousetraps and the Moon*. Lexington: Lexington University Press.

Wilson, Timothy D. (2002) *Strangers to Ourselves: Discovering the Adaptive Unconscious*. Cambridge, MA: The Belknap Press of Harvard University Press.

Winch, Peter (1958) *The Idea of a Social Science and its Relation to Philosophy*. London: Routledge & Kegan Paul.

Wines, Michael (2011) 'Picking the Pitch-Perfect Brand Name in China', *New York Times*, 12 November, p. A4.

Winner, E. and Gardner, H. (1993) 'Metaphor and Irony: Two Levels of Understanding', in *Metaphor and Thought*, ed. A. Ortony. New York: Cambridge University Press.

Wittgenstein, Ludwig (1953) *Philosophical Investigations*, ed. G. E. M. Anscombe and Rush Rhees, trans G. E. M. Anscombe. Oxford: Basil Blackwell.

Wolf, K. (ed.) (1950) *The Sociology of George Simmel*. Chicago, IL: Free Press.

Wollheim, Richard (1999) *On the Emotions*. New Haven, CT: Yale University Press.

Woodward, Joan (1965) *Industrial Organisation*. Oxford: Oxford University Press.

Wootton, David (2006) *Bad Medicine: Doctors Doing Harm since Hippocrates*. Oxford: Oxford University Press.

Wright, Robert (1994) *The Moral Animal*. New York: Pantheon Books.

Wright, Robert (2009) *The Evolution of God*. Boston: Little Brown.

Young, Lawrence (ed.) (1997) *Rational Choice Theory and Religion*. London: Routledge.

Zaltman, Gerald (2002) *How Customers Think: Essential Insights into the Mind of the Market*. Cambridge, MA: Harvard Business School Press.

Zaltman, Gerald, LeMasters, Karen and Heffring, Michael (1982) *Theory Construction in Marketing: Some Thoughts on Thinking*. New York: Wiley.

Zimmer, Carl (2005) 'A Career Spent Learning How the Mind Emerges from the Brain', *New York Times*, 10 May, p. D3.

Zyman, Sergio and Brott, Armin (2002) *The End of Advertising As We Know It*. New York: Wiley.

Index